WELFARE, INCENTIVES, AND TAXATION

Welfare, Incentives, and Taxation

JAMES A. MIRRLEES

OXFORD
UNIVERSITY PRESS

OXFORD

UNIVERSITY PRESS

Great Clarendon Street, Oxford OX2 6DP

Oxford University Press is a department of the University of Oxford.
It furthers the University's objective of excellence in research, scholarship,
and education by publishing worldwide in

Oxford New York

Auckland Cape Town Dar es Salaam Hong Kong Karachi
Kuala Lumpur Madrid Melbourne Mexico City Nairobi
New Delhi Shanghai Taipei Toronto

With offices in

Argentina Austria Brazil Chile Czech Republic France Greece
Guatemala Hungary Italy Japan Poland Portugal Singapore
South Korea Switzerland Thailand Turkey Ukraine Vietnam

Oxford is a registered trade mark of Oxford University Press
in the UK and in certain other countries

Published in the United States
by Oxford University Press Inc., New York

British Library Cataloguing in Publication Data

Data available

Library of Congress Cataloging in Publication Data

Data available

Typeset by Newgen Imaging Systems (P) Ltd., Chennai, India
Printed in Great Britain
on acid-free paper by
Biddles Ltd., King's Lynn, Norfolk

ISBN 0–19–829521–9   978–0–19–829521–1
ISBN 0–19–926181–4 (Pbk.)   978–0–19–926181–9 (Pbk.)

1 3 5 7 9 10 8 6 4 2

Preface

The papers collected in this volume are, with one or two exceptions, about welfare economics. Some economists believe that welfare economics can be briefly stated: competitive markets should be allowed to operate without interference, and the role of government is to maintain the rule of law and attempt to eliminate the exercise of monopoly. These papers embody a different view. They assume that governments should do good, and try to work out how, specifically, they should do it. Markets play a role, but so do taxes, of many kinds. The aim is always to induce people to do what they should do, in their own interest, and the interests of others. If we were all perfectly competent at making decisions and carrying them out, there would be no need to analyse mathematically how much a person should save, how much devote to medical insurance, how many children to have. If we were ideally virtuous, there would be no need to study what people should pay in taxes to finance subsidies to the poor, the employment of a police force, and provision of an urban infrastructure, or to find ways of reducing the environmental damage we do.

It would be satisfactory if welfare economics told us, simply, that free trade is best. Then there would be no need to establish a good empirical model, and specify a widely agreed quantitative measure of welfare, in order to provide a recommendation. Sometimes such general principles do arise. The fifth paper discusses a proposition that optimal scales of production are achieved if production takes place in towns each producing a single commodity (with economies of scale). Firms exercise monopoly power (in labour markets), and yet, in these circumstances, the exercise is benign. Sadly, the conclusions that can be drawn in welfare economics are seldom so general and qualitative. We cannot provide a straightforward numerical answer to the question how much a person, or a country, should save. But only a precise numerical answer is worth having. At least, we need to understand what facts and values determine that answer, and how. Fortunately it is an interesting problem. Governments are still thinking about the determination of pensions and pension contributions. Regrettably, they frequently decide to make life easier for successor governments by determining the contributions and not the pensions.

Economists (and most others) have long recognized that the marginal tax rate on labour income should not be a 100 per cent., because taxing away all income increments eliminates the incentive to supply labour. That is an interesting point, but not very. The really interesting question is how high income-tax rates should be. Again, it is a quantitative question. A qualitative remark is really of no value: indeed deploying the simple argument has been pernicious: in a strange way it is used to justify claims that fifty per cent. tax rates must be too high, or even that twenty-five per cent. is as high as it should go. Clearly precise analysis is required. The sixth paper in the volume provides such an analysis, inevitably for a very simple model. There is more (including rigorous proofs) in the eleventh paper, and the tenth, twelfth and thirteenth papers pursue the exploration further. The fourteenth paper tries to apply the ideas more directly to real policy issues.

This simple model was intended to be realistic. In economics, realism is hard to assess or achieve. It means that the most important features of economic reality are represented in approximately accurate quantitative proportions. But it is a treacherous judgment to decide what are the important features. The model in the optimal income tax paper has no time dimension, and in particular consumers have no uncertainty about their futures. People in the model differ in only one aspect: the hourly wage rate. Now that is an important feature of economic reality. The fact that people are different, to a substantial degree, is an essential element in any economic model (but a feature that has very often been missing in the models economists use). Certainly it is a key feature if we are to study income taxation. I decided that the time dimension was not nearly as important. People's lifetime labour supply was collapsed into a single variable; and their lifetime consumption, of all goods, at all times, was similarly reduced to one variable. Then the observed inequality of wage-income in one country at one time was taken as a realistic figure for inequality of lifetime wage-rates in the model. What else could one do? The results do not constitute recommendations to any particular country. They indicate the sorts of results one would get for a more realistic model.

It is hard to establish a realistic economic model with a sufficiently rich set of variables. It is even quite hard to determine realistic values of the parameters describing preferences for the simple model used in the paper. The New Jersey income-tax experiments showed that for the people in the experiment, making relatively short-term labour-supply decisions, the elasticity of substitution between labour and consumption was fairly low, and varied considerably in the population (a feature not easily captured in the simple model). Economists working with real-business-cycle models claim that the elasticity is very high, for the models to mimic real economic history. I am sure the experiments came closer to the truth, although it is true that they do not tell us about higher wage individuals. It is a pity that I did not explore the connections between labour-supply preferences and optimal tax rates in that paper. Good work has been done since, by Tuomala and others. The tax rates found in my paper were relatively low, and in many cases decreased with income in the upper income range. The later calculations, with what I believe are more realistic specifications, gave much higher rates.

The paper provided a method for calculating solutions to principal/agent problems of a particular kind. These are problems where one wants to find the optimal budget constraint, or contract that the principal would wish to impose on agents, each of whom knows perfectly his own preferences and the outcome of actions. The principal cannot observe the characteristics of individual agents: the budget constraint must therefore be the same for all. It is this asymmetric information that gives the problem its particular character. The challenge is to identify the optimum, which means providing sufficient conditions for optimality. In all principal/agent problems, one cannot be satisfied with necessary conditions. That is what standard mathematical techniques provide, but it is of no use to present a solution that might be the optimum: we need to be able to prove that it is, and for that sufficient conditions are required. It is satisfactory that in the income-tax problem, one can, under economically reasonable assumptions, find such conditions, and compute optima. Unfortunately, when one goes to more general settings, which could be more realistic, for example models with more than one unobservable characteristic, it is even less straightforward to obtain sufficient conditions.

Since that paper was published, a number of new results have been found, and are still being found. I describe four. The first, and most notorious, is the proposition that the marginal tax rate on the highest income (if there is one) should be zero. My paper only considered models with an unbounded distribution of wage rates, and therefore did not have such a result. I believe that was the right strategy. The zero-rate proposition should be expressed by saying that the marginal tax rate on the highest income that might occur should be zero. In any particular year (or lifetime in a country), the actual highest income will generally be much lower than the highest possible. The zero rate is therefore practically irrelevant. Nor is it a good approximation to tax rates within, say, ten per cent. of the highest possible: Tuomala's calculations show that. The fourth result I am going to discuss will throw further light on that.

The second result is one that is satisfyingly general. Atkinson and Stiglitz found that in a multi-commodity model, where preferences among consumption goods are the same for everyone, so that the unobservable difference between people is their preferences between labour and consumption in general, the optimum can be achieved without any taxes on consumption goods: a tax on labour income is sufficient. This is indeed very general. It applies when unobservable characteristics are multi-dimensional, and in more general situations, the same principle shows which subgroups of commodities should be taxed at the same rate. The assumption of separable preferences for consumption goods is surely not realistic, but it turns out that the same principle can be applied to models in which labour supply and commodity preference interact. It can be shown that commodities should be taxed more highly when they are substitutes for labour (in a certain, natural, sense). This makes a case, say, for subsidizing education and medicine, and taxing luxury food and alcoholic drink. But a feature I want to highlight is that the optimal commodity taxes should usually depend not on the amount of the commodity bought, but on income too. For different informational reasons, that is often not feasible. If it is, consider how complicated optimal tax systems can be.

The third result is one I have not yet published. It bears on the interesting and important question how low-income earners should be subsidized. The model is the same one as in the Exploration paper. There is one unusual assumption: it is postulated that utility is an increasing function of labour, up to a point, and decreasing beyond that point. Otherwises to labour/consumption preferences are general, as is the form of welfare judgments. The result is easily stated. It is that the marginal tax rate for a range of low incomes should be 100 per cent. The result holds when the distribution of wage rates (i.e. of individual productivity) is not be too thin at the lowest incomes. All income-distribution densities that have been used in practice satisfy this assumption. Many actual tax systems have this feature, of subsidies that happen to decrease by the same amount as earnings rise; but economists have generally claimed that is a dreadful mistake. Results in principal/agent theory are often quite surprising.

The final result, which I have noticed only recently, concerns the relationship between labour-supply elasticities and optimal tax rates. It seems to be thought, at least by supply-side economists, that a high elasticity of substitution between labour and consumption would justify and require low income-tax rates. Do not believe it. Consider a population of people for whom consumption and labour are perfectly substitutable, with an upper bound on labour supply (in efficiency units). Notice that labour and consumption cannot be close substitutes over the whole range of feasible labour supply. Maximize total utility, where individual utility is a concave function of consumption minus labour. Then it can be shown that the optimal budget constraint has consumption a concave function of labour earnings, and generally, including realistic wage-distributions, the marginal tax rate approaches 100 per cent. as income rises.

The reason for this result can be readily understood. Indifference curves, in consumption-labour space, are straight lines (between zero labour and the upper bound). For incentive compatibility, the budget constraint is the lower envelope of a selection of these straight lines, one for each type of consumer. It is therefore concave, as stated. Since the indifference curves are flatter for higher-wage people, the slope of the consumption-earnings graph becomes flatter at higher incomes, converging to zero. The techniques of the Exploration paper make a rigorous solution of the model possible.

This result helps to show how misleading is the theorem that the marginal tax rate should be zero at the top, when there is an upper bound to possible incomes. In this extreme model, there would be a corner in the consumption-earnings schedule at the highest income level. The result also shows that the impression gained from calculations in the Explorations paper, and Tuomala's book, that marginal tax rates should decrease with rising income (except possibly at lower incomes), though it may be right for realistic models, is certainly not a general truth.

Some of the papers in the volume are about principal/agent models in which the agent is uncertain about the consequence of his or her actions. Different techniques are required for the solution of these moral hazard problems. The second paper, which covers a number of different topics rather rapidly, showed that apparently well-posed problems of this kind could fail to have a solution. Typically it occurs when there is some way of approximating to the first-best, which could be attained if there were no moral hazard constraint. It had been shown before that in moral hazard models, it might be possible to approximate the first best by repeating the interaction between principal and agent a large number of times, and using accumulating evidence. The example in my paper induces nearly first-best behaviour on the part of the agent, without any repetition of the interaction. It is done by imposing very large penalties with very low probability, on unusually bad outcomes. Clearly that is not an appropriate contract in practice, but the possibility of this situation arising in what can appear to be a realistic and relevant, though oversimplified, model is disturbing. There is some brief discussion of what is wrong in the first paper in the volume.

One can study an analogue of the optimum-income-tax model where consumers do not know their own types, their wage rates: people make labour supply decisions, such as choice of occupation, but at that stage do not know what they will be paid. Some of that is realistic: the assumption in the income-tax model that consumers were perfectly certain about the impact of effort on net earnings is not satisfactory. Varian considered such a model. With the usual assumptions about consumers utility functions, and a log-normal distribution of wage rates, exactly the extreme-penalty problem arises: the lowest incomes should be taxed, and other incomes redistributed so as to equate marginal utilities.

One is forced therefore to introduce consumer uncertainty into the income-tax problem in a more sophisticated way. It can be assumed that some labour-supply decisions have uncertain consequences, but others (such as when to retire, or how much overtime to do) have perfectly known effects. Even then, the problem of extreme-punishment solutions may not go away, for it is then optimal to offer agents a set of alternative tax schedules to choose from (before working), and, according to the mathematics, it can be nearly optimal for all these alternative tax schedules to take the extreme-penalty form. That forces yet further complexity in the model, perhaps with types described by several variables, rather that simply variations in skill.

As the development of models proceeds along these lines, the analysis comes up with more complicated solutions. It is not inconceivable that people can be offered choices of contracts—it may happen in negotiation of the terms of employment in senior business positions. Such choices could therefore form part of the tax system. But it is hard to believe that it is truly optimal to do so, particularly because of the costs of taking decisions, and the costs of making mistaken choices. None of the papers in this volume make that next step, of studying models in which decisions can be mistaken. It is going to be even harder to establish realistic models of that kind.

The papers in part V, those concerned with optimum growth, also face issues of identifying solutions to apparently well-posed problems where solutions may not exist, or may not be easily found. For example, in working on the paper on optimum saving with economies of scale, with Avinash Dixit and Nicholas Stern, it turned out that what we first believed was the optimum was not. It was a tricky business to obtain sufficient conditions that would solve the problem: I think the theorems are interesting, though special. Once we get away from the simplest optimization problems, without time, and without incentive compatibility, the pursuit of the elusive solution often requires special techniques, and is much more interesting. Unfortunately it is always much harder to do comparative statics, to elucidate the impact of changing model specification on the optimum.

These papers do not help very much towards a general theory of principal/agent problems that would allow us to identify the boundaries between models with different kinds of optima. For example, as is shown in paper 17 on the theory of moral hazard, it may well be optimal to place the agent in a position of indifference among a set of possible decisions, while requiring that only one of the set is actually chosen. That outcome can be approximated by setting up incentives slightly different from the formal optimum, so that the agent has a unique best choice. In such a case, first-order conditions for the agent s problem do not adequately described the constraint on the principal. Peter Diamond and I found, when studying a model of pensions, that it could be optimal to make the agent indifferent over almost the full range of possible decisions (in this case the retirement age). The main theorem in paper 17, giving sufficient (but highly restrictive) conditions for a moral hazard problem to be nicely behaved, in the sense that the agent s first-order conditions provide a valid incentive-compatibility constraint, gave me a lot of trouble, so that the paper was only published after (quite long after) a correct proof was given by Rogerson.

It would be nice to identify exactly what features of a model lead to such solutions, and more generally to have very general principles about the form of solution to be sought in each model. But perhaps it will always be necessary to exercise care in the particular case, and not trust mechanical procedures. A general theory may not be possible.

REFERENCES

Diamond, P. A. and Mirrlees, J. A. (1977). 'A model of social insurance with retirement.' *Journal of Public Economics*, vol. 10, pp. 295–336.

Rogerson, W. (1985). 'The first order approach to principal-agent problems.' *Econometrica*, vol. 53, pp. 1357–1368.

Tuomala, M. (1990). *Optimal Income Tax and Redistribution*, Oxford: Clarendon Press.

Varian, H. R. (1980). 'Redistributive taxation as social insurance.' *Journal of Public Economics*, vol. 14, pp. 49–68.

James A. Mirrlees
August 2005

Contents

Part I Welfare Economics

1. Information and Incentives: The Economics of Carrots and Sticks   3

2. Notes on Welfare Economics, Information, and Uncertainty   23

3. The Desirability of Natural Resource Depletion
   with John A. Kay   39

4. The Economic Uses of Utilitarianism   69

5. Welfare Economics and Economies of Scale   100

Part II Tax Theory

6. An Exploration in the Theory of Optimum Income Taxation   131

7. On Producer Taxation   174

8. The Optimum Town   183

9. Population Policy and the Taxation of Family Size   205

10. Optimal Tax Theory: A Synthesis   229

11. The Theory of Optimal Taxation   259

12. Migration and Optimal Income Taxes   309

13. Taxing Uncertain Incomes   330

Part III Public Expenditure

14. Arguments for Public Expenditure   345

15. Optimal Taxation and Government Finance   366

Contents

Part IV Contract Theory

16. The Optimal Structure of Incentives and Authority
    within an Organization   387

17. The Theory of Moral Hazard and
    Unobservable Behaviour: Part I   420

Part V Growth Theory

18. The Dynamic Nonsubstitution Theorem   445

19. Agreeable Plans
    with Peter J. Hammond   458

20. Fairly Good Plans
    with N. H. Stern   481

21. Optimum Saving with Economies of Scale
    with Avinash Dixit and Nicholas Stern   500

Part VI Development Economics

22. A Pure Theory of Underdeveloped Economies   533

23. Project Appraisal and Planning Twenty Years On: Appendix
    with Ian Little   554

Index   559

PART I

WELFARE ECONOMICS

1

Information and Incentives: The Economics of Carrots and Sticks

1. THE INVISIBLE HAND

In a lecture that will deal chiefly with ignorance, it may seem natural to begin with Adam Smith's most famous contribution to economics, his vision of independent selfish beings who by living and working together in the economic system somehow do what is best for one another. First, in *The Theory of Moral Sentiments*, he said

> The rich only select from the heap what is precious and agreeable. They consume little more than the poor, and in spite of their natural selfishness and rapacity . . . they divide with the poor the produce of all their improvements. They are led by an invisible hand to make nearly the same distribution of the necessaries of life which would have been made, had the earth been divided into equal portions among all its inhabitants. (IV.i.10)

This is far from the later conception of an economic equilibrium that is 'optimal' in Pareto's sense. Indeed as quoted, Smith's early claim is not very plausible. It does set the major themes: the working of the economy as a system, and the good or otherwise, for everyone, that can flow from it. Later in the *Wealth of Nations*, he argued correctly that individual profit-maximization implies maximization of what we would call national income, and goes on to say that,

> by directing that industry in such a manner as its produce may be of the greatest value, [every individual] intends only his own gain, and he is in this, as in many other cases, led by an invisible hand to promote an end which was no part of his intention. (IV, Chapter II)

This says nothing about possible advantage to the poor, indeed nothing about the distribution of gains at all.

As taught to generations of economists, there are two parts to the doctrine of the invisible hand. The first is that an economic equilibrium is Pareto-optimal: it is an allocation of commodities and activities to people with the property that no other allocation could make everyone better off. It is a good allocation in

This article, a transcript of the Nobel Prize Lecture, 9 December 1996 (© the Nobel foundation 1996), was published in the *Economic Journal*, Vol. 107 (1997), pp. 1311–29, Blackwell Publishing Ltd.

rather a weak sense, but better for everyone than a lot of other possible allocations. The economic equilibrium has to be perfectly competitive. The second
part says that any Pareto-optimal allocation can be an economic equilibrium.
For that to be, the initial distribution of assets among people has to be set right.
It may be required that the earth is indeed divided into equal portions among its
inhabitants for the desired allocation to emerge. This second proposition, at
least in its standard form, makes assumptions about the nature of technological
possibilities such that a perfectly competitive equilibrium can occur. Essentially
economies of scale have to be excluded, or production levels in such industries
determined in some other way, for example by some kind of planning. That is
an interesting issue, but will be ignored here.[1]

These propositions were the essential content of welfare economics as I
learned it in the 1950s. Ian Little (1950) and particularly Jan Graaff (1957)
brought out the many serious difficulties in the theory, particularly if it were to
be taken as a basis for economic advice and policy and ideology. The theory
underlay much of what economists thought they could tell the world and its
rulers. It was the basis for free trade arguments, for urging the control of monopoly, for methods of cost–benefit analysis, and the justification of marginal-cost
pricing by publicly owned firms. It was also used to support the extension of
free markets and private ownership of property, and to recommend the use of
price systems even in planned economies.

Yet the defects of the theory seemed serious. Many economic transactions
take place between individual agents or firms, with significant monopoly on at
least one side of the market. Taking a later view, that seems to be because of
search costs and switching costs and uncertainty about the fulfilment of contracts in the future (as in credit markets). These have no place in the competitive
model of the economy. One might possibly be able to claim that these deviations from the assumptions are small, within the margins of error that economics can aspire too; though for myself I do not think they are.

The other major defect is the need to have a particular distribution of assets
to people before one can claim that the resulting equilibrium is good. That
requirement, when properly understood, was plainly impossible to fulfil.

What is the nature of this difficulty? It had, I think, become quite clear by the
1950s. It was clear in William Vickrey's writings, for example.[2] If we are to
have a good equilibrium, we shall have to imagine a good government that does
what is needed, namely to create a distribution of assets to people such that the
desired allocation is indeed an equilibrium. It can be done. In one exceedingly
simple model, which perhaps many economists had in mind, people are all the
same, and each person obtains utility from a single consumption good, of

---

[1] There are ways of extending the proposition, discussed in Mirrlees (1995), and work referred
to therein.

[2] The problem is discussed, somewhat elliptically, in Vickrey (1945), and that paper puts
forward essentially the model of redistributive taxation discussed later in this chapter.

which a fixed amount is available. Then it is easy for the government to do it. Assuming diminishing marginal utility of consumption, and comparability of individual utilities, an equal distribution of assets is what we require. No information, other than a census, is required for that. People might have some doubts about the measurability, perhaps even about the meaningfulness, of utility; but at least, in a rough and ready way, there was a strong case for thinking that transfer from richer to poorer was an improvement. Carrying that to the logical extreme, the riches of the earth should be equally distributed.

It was not a popular policy, in part for good reasons. Obviously, if a perfectly equalising policy were carried out, the ordinary incentive to work would be eliminated. 'From each according to his abilities, to each according to his needs' (Karl Marx, *Criticism of the Gotha Programme*) is not thought to be feasible, even if desirable. Nothing in the simple model allowed for that.

2. TAXATION

What exactly was the problem? In general, and in reality, the redistribution of assets required by the first welfare theorem needed information the government could not obtain. This ideal government had to know what wealth people already had, and what they were capable of doing, before it could work out how much to give and take. If people knew it needed that information, they could in one way or another dissemble, and would if it benefited them to do so. The information requirements of the second welfare theorem cannot be fulfilled. Transfers to or from a person that depend on the characteristics of that person, not his behaviour, are known as lump-sum transfers. Desirable lump-sum transfers are, in effect, impossible, because they require information that is not available. The attempt to implement them would be expected to destroy the value of the information on which they would have to be based.

Following that line of thought, in the mid-1960s, Peter Diamond and I were convinced that one should think about economic welfare and economic policy in the context of public finance. At first we studied a general economic model in which the government was not able to use lump-sum transfers at all.[3] Clearly that was going too far, and we went on to allow that the government could use uniform lump-sum taxes or, more plausibly, subsidies. Otherwise it had to use taxes, taxes that from the point of view of the pure welfare theorems are regarded as distorting. This was a model in which all consumers and producers were price-takers, but they did not necessarily face the same prices, because tax rates could make the two parties to a transaction face different effective prices. It was a conventional model, in having competitive behaviour of private agents; but it was a distorted economy, and the distortion could be optimal. That was what we wanted to study.

---

[3] The theory we developed was eventually published in two papers, Diamond and Mirrlees (1971).

There was a significant earlier literature on distorting taxes. The theory had been started by Frank Ramsey (1927), at the request of A. C. Pigou. He considered an economy of identical consumers and assumed that revenue had to be raised entirely through commodity taxes. M. Boiteux (1956) in France had later, but independently, developed the isomorphic theory of pricing by a public utility with a zero-profit constraint, in an economy where, paradoxically, perfect lump-sum transfers were supposed to be happening. And Serge-Christophe Kolm (1971) also developed a systematic general theory.

What is interesting for the story I have to tell now is the form of the theory we developed, rather than its content and implications. It was the theory of a government whose actions were a function only of what it could observe. No observations about the nature of individual consumers were assumed to be available, only observations of their behaviour. The leading example of that is a commodity tax, which provides revenue proportional to the quantity of the commodity consumers choose to buy. Policy choice takes account of consumer responses to tax changes, namely changes in amounts purchased. A uniform lump-sum subsidy requires no information at all, and is therefore allowed. All these policy instruments are, as we say now, incentive-compatible: the government takes full account of people's self-interested response to the tax system.

There is one respect in which information about consumer characteristics is needed, the distribution of these characteristics within the population. The government somehow knows this distribution. In principle it could obtain it by asking people, or putting them through various tests. Since the information is used only in aggregate form, an individual has nothing to lose (or gain) by telling the government the truth. Only if individual tax liability were affected by these revelations would incentive-compatibility be violated. We supposed that the government would obtain and use an econometric model of consumers, in which the distribution of consumer types—their intensity of taste for different commodities, their labour supply characteristics—would be estimated from the behaviour of a sample of consumers. Calculations of optimal taxes and of desirable directions of tax change have been done on in that way. One should allow explicitly for uncertainties about the distribution of characteristics in the population, with the budget-balancing issues it raises, but we did not trouble about what is a relatively minor complication.

This then was a model with asymmetric information, where, at the time when government policy is determined, individual consumers know more about their tastes and abilities than the government does. Since all kinds of policy parameter could be mentioned in the model, it was quite general. That generality was not fully exploited.

3. INCOME TAXATION

It is interesting to be more specific, and study a particular economic model that has some of the most salient features of real economies. One such model pictures the economy as timeless, with people enjoying a single consumption good, and supplying labour. As mentioned above, William Vickrey had stated the optimum tax problem for such a model, though he was not able to solve it. In such a model, redistributive taxation can be described simply as an income tax, which has the effect of determining each individual's consumption as a function of that individual's labour income.

The point about income taxation is that tax can be a highly complicated function of income: tax need not be proportional to income, and in the real world seldom is. In the real economy, income actually consists of several elements. It is often easy to distinguish between labour income and income from capital, conceptually at least. (In practice, particularly with the self-employed, the distinction might be hard to enforce; and net income from capital, including housing, can itself be hard to measure.) In what follows, I shall assume we are dealing with labour income. Labour income can be taxed nonlinearly. So can a number of other commodities, such as telephone calls, electricity, and the like. Fully nonlinear taxation is, like linear taxation, incentive compatible: the calculation of tax is still based on the publicly observable behaviour of the consumer. The presumption is that nonlinearity will be advantageous, because more general than linear taxation.

In practical terms, one could not tell in advance how advantageous nonlinearities might be. Most countries had and have large differences in marginal labour-income tax rates, and in most cases the income-tax law specifies marginal tax rates that increase with income. There are also other elements in the social insurance and tax arrangements of countries that are very like a form of income taxation, e.g. unemployment insurance, or low-income support arrangements. In many cases, these have the effect of creating quite high marginal tax rates on low incomes: benefits are reduced as income increases, sometimes almost one-for-one. The typical real tax system, therefore, has high marginal tax rates for low incomes and for high incomes, and low marginal tax rates in the intermediate range. It is tempting to think of most taxes, other than taxes on capital income, as amounting to a tax on labour income: that would be right if different consumer goods were taxed at the same rate. At any rate, one can approximate real tax systems quite closely in these terms.

The next step in thinking about an optimum income-tax system was, paradoxically, to move back from thinking explicitly about tax rates, and instead to think about allocations of real commodities and labour. It proved to be advantageous to go back to thinking about optimality as in the general welfare economics from which all this work had begun, but now to have a new kind of constraint, incentive compatibility, in addition to the constraint that the allocation should be feasible. The idea of incentive-compatible transfers by the government had been captured by thinking in terms of tax rates. But it is really a more fundamental idea. The question to ask was: what allocations are possible if policy has to be incentive-compatible? It seemed best to think about this in a special model, but in fact the answer turned out to be quite simple in a fairly general model.

The special model was one that had long seemed natural to me, in which individual consumers can choose how much labour to supply. Each consumer's situation is described by two variables, consumption and labour supply. Each consumer's type is defined by a single parameter, productivity, or, equivalently, that person's wage rate. There is a given distribution of wage rates in the economy, known to the government. These are real, the actual productivity of the different individuals. The government can observe the total product of each individual, that is the product of the wage rate and the amount worked, but is unable to observe either of these alone. That observability assumption is a bit extreme, and I shall come back to it. But there are certainly severe limits on what the government can observe, and this particular assumption corresponds to what tax systems almost invariably do: they relate only to total income, not to wage rates.

The government was also supposed to have an aim, a measure of welfare that it wishes to maximise, a sum of individual utilities, consistent with individual preferences for consumption and work. That does not matter for the first step in the analysis, which is to find a way of describing the real allocations that are possible for the government, that is to say the real distributions of consumption and work in the population that are incentive-compatible. These are the allocations that are possible with some labour-income tax system, but I wanted to describe what allocations were possible without reference to taxes, and that was the essential step to having a computable model of general taxes.

I have said the answer was simple. It is shown in Fig. 1.1. For each consumer, call the product of wage and labour, income. Incentive compatibility required that each consumer would choose from a set of available consumption/income

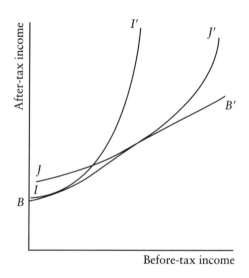

Figure 1.1. *Incentive-compatibility*

pairs. That set is defined by the allocation of consumption and income among consumers. A curve, labelled BB' in the diagram, describes that allocation, showing consumption at different income levels. Each consumer chooses from that curve: each has an indifference curve tangential to the allocation curve, such as II' and JJ' in the figure. To be more precise, what I have called a curve might, technically, not be: it could well have corners. Still, it followed from this simple argument that the curve must be a lower envelope to a collection of individual indifference curves, one for each type of consumer. As a consequence, utility increased as the wage increased, at a rate equal to the derivative of utility with respect to the wage, holding consumption and income constant. And also income was an increasing function of the consumer's wage rate. These two facts together fully characterized the set of incentive-compatible consumption/income allocations.

One key assumption was needed to justify that conclusion. It had to be assumed that people with higher wage rates always found it easier to produce more income (by working) than those with smaller. That is more restrictive than it sounds, and is much more than a definition of increasing wage, but seems an entirely reasonable and plausible assumption. In the figure, the assumption means that different people's indifference curves cross one another once only. The condition is known as the single-crossing property (or sometimes the Spence–Mirrlees condition).[4] With that assumption, one had a full characterization of incentive-compatible allocations.

Furthermore, and crucially, the original optimal-income-tax problem could now be converted into something very like a standard control-theory problem, with utility as the state variable, income the control variable. The envelope condition just described was essentially equivalent to a statement that the rate at which utility increased in the population, with respect to the wage rate, was equal to the partial derivative of the individual's utility with respect to the wage rate, just a known function of that individual's consumption, income, and wage. To tell a little more of the truth, one has to generalize all this somewhat, for utility may not always be smooth function of the wage. Consequently, the full mathematical justification of all this is quite complex. Computation of results was not trivial either, because in fact one had to check whether there were ranges of consumers all of whom would make the same income; but it could be done.[5]

An exciting feature of this analysis, and one that came as a complete surprise, was its validity. That puts the issue too starkly. Let us rather say that the use of fully nonlinear taxation does solve one problem that has troubled tax theorists. In the optimal commodity tax analysis that Peter Diamond and I had done, we

---

[4] Michael Spence (1973) used the condition for models of markets with asymmetric information.

[5] All of this is set out in Mirrlees (1971), while the full mathematical justification (in a Nuffield College, Oxford discussion paper) appeared in print only in Mirrlees (1986).

had obtained first-order conditions for optimal taxes, and explored various interpretations and implications; but these conditions were necessary conditions for optimality, not sufficient conditions. In any particular model, computation of optimal taxes should require much more than solving the first-order conditions, unless by good fortune there were a unique solution. That problem need not afflict simple welfare economics with perfect lump-sum transfers. In the income-tax problem, relatively simple conditions, easily checked for the particular model I was using, implied that the solution of the equations did give an optimum: the conditions were sufficient as well as necessary. When the computations were done, one knew one had the right answer, not just an answer that might be right.

Solution of the model in any particular case shows how consumption should be related to income. From that one can talk about income tax rates, interpreting the difference between income and consumption as tax. Remember that in the model the allocation would be achieved with just that tax. The income tax in the model corresponds to the sum of the real-world labour-incomes taxes and taxes on consumption, such as value-added tax.

Computation of the model was done for particular cases. There are three key assumptions: the distribution of wages, the nature of individual preferences between consumption and work, and the extent to which it is supposed desirable to transfer from the better off to the less well off, i.e. the way that the welfare function incorporates individual preferences. In the 1971 paper, the simplest reasonable assumption was made about consumption/work preferences, namely unit elasticity of substitution between consumption and leisure. At least for male workers, work since then suggests that elasticity is considerably too high. Later work[6] shows that marginal rates of tax should as a consequence be greater than they were in these first calculations. The distribution of labour incomes is not all that easy to observe. In any case, intertemporal aspects are important in the real world and completely absent in the model. Both lognormal distributions and distributions with Pareto tails were tried, and gave distinctly different results, particularly at upper incomes. Different welfare specifications had much more effect at low incomes than high, and there are good theoretical grounds for that. A required level of public expenditure (on defence, police, etc.—not welfare spending, which is part of the optimal tax system) was also postulated.

The kinds of results obtained are illustrated in Figs 1.2 and 1.3, giving calculations by Matti Tuomala. The two parameters, β and ϵ, describe the degree of egalitarianism assumed, and the elasticity of substitution between consumption and labour-supply. $\epsilon = 1$ corresponds to the cases calculated in the 1971 paper, $\epsilon = 0.5$ is probably a more realistic value.

Several things were striking about the results. In many cases, marginal tax rates were highest in the middle of the range of incomes, and fell towards higher

[6] Tuomala (1990).

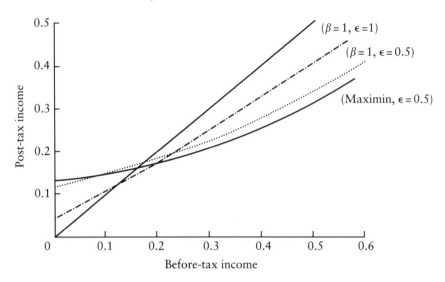

Figure 1.2. *Optimal income-tax schedules β = 1 means welfare is the sum of utilities.*
ε is the consumer elasticity of substitution between consumption and labour
Source: Tuomala (1984).

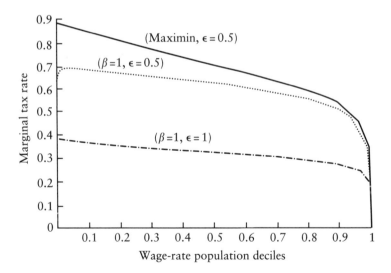

Figure 1.3. *Marginal tax rates*
Source: Tuomala (1984).

incomes and lower. This was the opposite of actual tax systems. It was a feature that at that time seemed quite robust, though later computations and results suggest that marginal tax rates can be quite high at the lowest incomes. (With a very highly egalitarian form of welfare judgement, the marginal tax rate appears to fall all the way up the income range.) Another result, not numerically very striking, but on consideration important, was that it is optimal to have a positive amount of unemployment. People who chose to earn no income at all are paid a subsidy, since we did not wish them to starve, and those with very low productivity therefore found pay insufficient to justify working.

One can get some insight into the problem and the results by thinking about an extreme case where inequality of incomes is rather low. The limiting case is where everyone has the same income. Then there is no incentive-compatibility problem. It is optimal to raise the funds required for pure public expenditure by a lump-sum tax. The marginal tax rate is zero. Now let there be a little inequality, with wages ranging all the way from zero to some high level, but a small variance. For people in the middle of the wage range (who are most of the population) taxes should be very similar to what they were in the equal-wages case, i.e. a low marginal tax rate, and an average tax rate big enough to pay for public expenditure. But that cannot apply to people on the lowest incomes, because they could not have paid that lump-sum tax—it would have meant negative consumption. The consumption income schedule must therefore be curved at the lower end, always remaining below the indifference curve of an average wage-earner. One cannot see from this argument quite how low the gradient of the consumption/income schedule should be at the lower end, but it will surely be a lot lower than at the average income, which is to say that the marginal tax rate will be much higher at the lower end than in the middle.

As the wage distribution gets more unequal, the optimal consumption/income schedule changes in shape in quite a complicated way. Another possible reason for high marginal tax rates in the lower range can come into play. If people in fact like to do some work, it may not be so important to provide labour incentives to people with low wage rates. That can mean tax rates at or close to 100 per cent can be optimal at the bottom of the income range. In higher ranges, recent work of Peter Diamond, as yet unpublished, shows that the inverted U-shape of the consumption/income schedule is quite common, with marginal tax rates rising at the mode of the distribution, but eventually falling.

There have been further qualitative results of interest for this model and its generalizations. The best known is that of Phelps (1973) and Sadka (1976) that the optimal marginal tax rate for the highest-wage person (if there is one) is zero. In my own paper, all wage distributions were unbounded above. The Phelps–Sadka result really says that the highest income that could possibly happen should be subject to a zero marginal tax rate. There is considerable uncertainty about the actual highest income: it is very unlikely to be close to the level at which the marginal tax would be zero.

There is an important general result due to Atkinson and Stiglitz (1976), who found nice general conditions for a model with many consumption goods to have the property that the optimum can be obtained using only a labour-income tax. This turns on separability of consumption goods in preferences from labour and consumer characteristics. If these conditions hold for intertemporal preferences, it follows that one should not have a tax on capital income: that is the case where a uniform expenditure tax is optimal. There is a closely related result of Christiansen (1981) that, when there is a public good grouped with the private consumption goods, separately from labour and wage, the Samuelson public good rule, that the sum of marginal rates of substitution should equal the marginal rate of transformation, holds. These results require the possibility of arbitrary nonlinear taxation of labour income, which is perfectly reasonable. It is interesting that the general model of incentive-compatible systems gives results so much neater than those obtainable when only linear taxation is allowed.

Finally, it is worth remarking that the model is more general than it looks, for income in the model is visible income, and consumption is what the consumer is seen to be paid, net. Tax evasion can perfectly well be accommodated in the structure, with the consumption variable being apparent after-tax income, and income what is reported to the tax authority. What is missing then is other kinds of inspection and assessment. But that could be used even without deliberate tax evasion. In some countries, the possibility that evasion varies with the level of taxes is believed to be more important than variations in labour supply.

4. ASYMMETRIC INFORMATION

The tax model we have been considering is only one situation in which there is asymmetric information between a principal (here the government) and an agent or agents (the consumers). The individual consumer knows more about his or her own capabilities than the government. The government can think of itself as dealing with a representative consumer, but not knowing that consumer's type. Many economic relationships are of the principal–agent type, particularly employer–employee relationships. The kind of analysis I outlined applies when the agent's performance is observable and measurable but the agent knows more than the principal, for example about the relationship between unobservable effort and performance. Adam Smith knew there was a problem (although he does not explicitly mention the uncertainties that make shirking possible):

It is the interest of every man to live as much at his ease as he can; and if his emoluments are to be precisely the same, whether he does, or does not perform some very laborious duty, it is certainly his interest, at least as interest is vulgarly understood, either to neglect it altogether, or, if he is subject to some authority which will not suffer him to do this, to perform it in as careless and slovenly a manner as that authority will permit (*Wealth of Nations*, V.i.f.7).

It might be thought that he is too neglectful of monetary incentive systems, but it is important to be reminded that authority could be a good description of the relationship. An optimal payment system, with asymmetric information, could well have an authoritarian character, if it showed pay rising rapidly with performance over some range, low at lower incomes, and not rising much further at higher. That would come close to the principal saying: Do this, or else. It is an interesting feature of the schedules found to be optimal in the income-tax problem that consumption never rises more rapidly than income (equivalently, the marginal tax rate is never negative). Most probably, so harsh a relationship is never optimal in realistic cases of asymmetric information.[7]

The employment relationship raises many interesting new possibilities, such as relating pay to other people's performance. That is not worth doing if the two people are quite unrelated, in that their abilities are uncorrelated. When they are correlated, and the agents cannot or do not combine together, there is indeed scope for having pay depend to some extent on relative performance.

We probably do not expect to have our government introduce taxes that depend on our neighbour's (or distant competitor's) income as well as our own. But such possibilities have played an interesting role in the further development of mechanism design beyond the simple model of asymmetric information described above. Agents can be asked to choose among much more complex sets of messages than we would use to describe their simple performance or income. Maskin (1985) introduced the idea of asking people to place themselves in the overall wage distribution, while faced with incentives that punish severely any inconsistency in the answers. By that device he was able, in a sense, to implement a first-best optimum. That theory appeared terribly demanding of information among agents, but Piketty (1993) has developed more plausible ways of getting the first best within the same general set of ideas. The simple model of incentive compatibility by no means exhausts the possible incentive mechanisms in situations of asymmetric information.

Among the other fields of application for asymmetric information are the control of firms by regulators, and pricing by utilities. In a very interesting line of development, first Baron and Myerson (1982), and then Laffont and Tirole (1993) have shown how one can analyse regulation by treating the firm as an agent who knows its cost structure, and the regulator as a principal who is uncertain about the firm's costs. The firm's outputs and the prices it charges for them are related by market demand, and they are public information. One way of thinking about regulation is to have an output-variable tax. This can be analysed using the methods I have described.

Similarly, utilities face consumers with varied preferences, and can relate price to quantity used in complex ways. As with the regulatory model, there are multiple products, and one should consider the simultaneous pricing of consumption at different times. This gets really hard when consumers' tastes vary in a multi-dimensional way. The simple techniques I have described are much less effective in such multi-dimensional problems, but Wilson (1993) and Armstrong (1996) have made significant progress in solving problems of this type.

---

[7] Some of this is explored in Mirrlees (1976).

In all of these areas of application, the time dimension is potentially important. Going back to the taxation problem, it can be seen that some new and awkward problems arise. We can think of taxing each generation, or cohort, in the way appropriate to them. Each will contribute to the common pool, but we can clearly identify the year of birth, and use that as a tax base. Theoretically, therefore, we should consider having a different tax system for each cohort. Governments do not do that, and I will come back to why and whether we would like them to.

It is to be presumed that each individual's ability is quite strongly correlated with future ability. For simplicity, consider a model where everyone's wage remains the same throughout the working life. Some particular incentive-compatible tax system applies to first-year income. People decide how hard to work, what to work at: some get high incomes, some low. If the theory already developed applies, people with higher wages will choose to earn higher incomes. Next year, the government knows what incomes they earned last year, and can therefore deduce their wage rates. Now it can tax on the basis of the wage rate rather than income, that is to say on the basic characteristic of the consumer. There is no longer any need to worry about incentives, not at least in the present period. Tax can be made independent of income actually earned, and related simply to the wage (observed on the basis of performance in the previous period). On the margin, incentives are optimal. In effect, the wage-related taxes implement lump-sum taxes, and would be expected to be high for high-wage people, low, indeed negative, for low-wage people. Indeed, it turns out that in reasonable models, low-wage people will be better off than high-wage ones.

If that is going to happen in the second year, people in the first year will probably decide they would rather not earn enough to be labelled high-wage. They could well all choose the same income, say zero. The second-year government cannot work out wages after all, and everything collapses. The hoped-for optimum described is not an equilibrium. There is an equilibrium with no-one doing anything, but it is extremely unsatisfactory. The trouble is that in the second year it will be rational for the government to act as described. It is the anticipation of that rational behaviour by government that causes the trouble. What we have is a particularly bad case of intertemporal inconsistency. If the government can commit itself in advance to the tax system that will apply to the cohort in all future years, we can get back to the 'second-best' equilibrium already described as an optimal tax system. Probably it can do rather better than that. The puzzle is that governments do not, to any significant extent, commit themselves to future tax rates, and indeed cannot easily do so; and yet the problem described does not arise. By accepting a convention that people born at different times are all subject to the same tax system, the government may be taken to provide such a guarantee, at the cost of giving up a desirable basis for tax discrimination.

Perhaps one should not mention it out loud. Like the man who starts thinking about how he manages to walk, we may get ourselves in a lot of trouble by thinking. We have the same problem that Kydland and Prescott (1977) identified in macroeconomic policy. In microeconomic policy, we do not take it seriously. There is trouble lurking here, perhaps in the area of capital taxation.

5. MORAL HAZARD

In some degree, individual economic agents are also uncertain about their tastes and abilities when they take decisions. The extreme case, where the agent is no better informed than the principal, is well known in insurance as moral hazard. If the agent's behaviour is unobservable, it is usually not possible to deduce the individual's action from performance when the connection between action and performance is uncertain. There are many relationships where this better describes the situation than does the asymmetric information model. Medical care has been regarded as a prime example in the economics literature,[8] perhaps surprisingly. Sharecropping with farmers paying for the use of land with a share of profits or income seems a good example, and so are many cases of accident insurance. Usually, of course, there are elements of each. I shall come to that at the end of the lecture.

It is interesting to examine the consumption/income model as though it were a moral-hazard model.[9] Suppose then that effective labour supply decisions are taken early in life, decisions how hard to work in school or career choices. The consequences are uncertain. In the pure moral-hazard model, everyone is identical at the point of decision. The government has to devise a tax schedule that will induce people to work or try hard at that early stage, presumably making rewards increase with income, so that these prospects will encourage early effort. It might (in simple cases it would) have wanted everyone to have the same income, but then there would be no incentive to try hard initially.

Problems of this kind are usually analysed with the assumption that people try to maximize their expected utility. There are some good reasons for thinking that may be a mistake. At least, the consequences of alternative theories of decisions under uncertainty for these situations should be explored. But I shall go on with the conventional theory.

Some particular level of effort is optimal. Incentives will have to be set up so that people will do it. If this is a nicely behaved problem, and in simple cases it is, we have to arrange that the marginal effect of effort on the expected utility of consumption takes some particular value. At the same time, the government is constrained by the total consumption that is going to be available when people do that amount of effort. Subject to these two constraints, it wants to maximize

---

[8] See Arrow (1963), who has something to say about asymmetric information too, and Pauly (1968).

[9] Such a model has been examined by Varian (1980), but my discussion will be primarily a translation to the present context of part of Mirrlees (1974).

expected utility. To get incentives right, some consumption levels will be low, presumably at lower income levels. At lower income levels, more effort will reduce the probability of that outcome. Reducing consumption improves incentives, though it lowers expected utility.

It follows that consumption should be lowered most at income levels where the incentive improvement is greatest, relative to the utility loss, i.e. where the elasticity of output probability with respect to effort is great. A fairly simple idea then: reduce consumption at observed output levels where effort has a large proportional effect on the probability of that level.

There is a striking feature of the lognormal distribution of incomes for this model. If that is the nature of uncertainty about the effect of effort on income, the elasticity of probability with respect to effort tends to infinity as income goes to zero. Therefore, in the model, the government can achieve a very satisfactory outcome, almost as though the incentive constraint could be ignored, and it does that by instituting very low consumption at very low incomes. How much it can achieve that way depends on how low utility goes as consumption gets very small.

This is very peculiar, and of course unacceptable. In this particular model, one reason why it is unacceptable is that people can in fact change their labour supply 'at the last minute'. Another is that it assumes people can calculate intelligently about events of very small probability, which is surely not always the case. Finally, the assumption that all kinds of effort to avoid very low-income outcomes automatically increases the probability of high-income outcomes is not realistic.

Yet the analysis is trying to tell us something, something rather paradoxical. It is saying that incentives by means of punishments, which is how we might describe very low consumption when there is a very poor outcome, are most appropriate, if at all, in principal–agent situations with moral hazard. These are cases where the agent does not know the consequences of actions. More precisely, punishment may be appropriate where actions have very uncertain consequences, spread over all possible outcomes. In the opposite case, where the agent knows very well the consequences of actions, punishment is not appropriate. It just might be best to have draconian punishments for serious car accidents, but not for deliberate crime. On the whole, I do not persuade myself that solution is correct, but much remains to be done to reformulate the model so as to remove the most extreme features of the solution of what is apparently the most straightforward and natural case.

There is one feature of these solutions that is persuasive. In cases such as employment relationships, where it is not possible to impose any very great punishment on the agent, dismissal will happen in a range of bad outcomes, and then rewards may rise rather rapidly over a range of outcomes. In such cases, one is getting a result not unlike a relationship of authority, where an order is given, and expected to be obeyed. Such a solution is illustrated in Fig. 1.4.

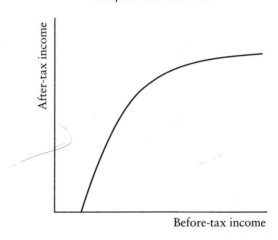

Figure 1.4. *Optimum pay schedule under moral hazard*

Often one gets perfectly reasonable payment schedules in such problems, with payment, or rather the marginal utility of payment, related to the elasticity of probability with respect to effort. This gives some impression of the shape of the payment schedule, but exact computations are somewhat troublesome. The method of solution indicated does not always work, however. There are cases, and they are not at all special, where one cannot well describe the moral hazard constraint, that is the constraint that incentives induce the desired level of effort, as a first-order condition the agent's choice must satisfy.[10] Sometimes the agent should be made indifferent among two or more alternatives, and induced to choose just one. For example, in a model of optimal retirement, studied by Peter Diamond and me (1977), it is a main feature of the optimum pension system that the agent, who is subject to the random onset of disability, is made indifferent as to the date of retirement, although only one particular retirement date is the right one. A very slight perturbation of the optimum schedule can induce the agent to choose that right retirement age for sure.

It is not always very easy to tell in advance what models can properly be solved by using the agent's first-order condition as a constraint. A set of sufficient conditions I had conjectured was shown to be valid by Rogerson (1985). Surely more general conditions can be found. We have not come close to identifying the boundaries between the different cases. It is striking that in the asymmetric-information model the method of taking as the incentive-compatibility constraint essentially the first-order (calculus) conditions for choice by the agent or agents works so well, at least in the sense that a simple, manageable, and understandable condition is enough to justify it. When moral hazard is present, a different approach is needed.

[10] Mirrlees (1975).

These complications make it particularly hard to give any general rules as to what we would want or expect payment schedules to look like when the relationship between principal and agent involves moral hazard. The sharply rising middle section of the payment curve that I have referred to is by no means universal. Yet simple sharing rules are surprisingly difficult to generate with plausible examples. It is all the more striking that Holmström and Milgrom (1987) have found an example with continuous action over time where incentives are linear.

6. IMPERFECT INFORMATION IN GENERAL

Although one should always seek simplicity, it is necessary to consider what happens when there is asymmetric information, with the principal knowing less about the relationship between input and output than the agent who chooses input, but the agent also being in some ignorance. As the theory of these relationships was developed in the 1970s, it was found that new forms of contract arose. For concreteness, let us talk about the consumption/income model again. Each consumer knows something about the effect of his labour on his income. It is different for different people, and no-one knows it for sure. When this is the case, there is a natural two-period structure. First, the consumer chooses what to do; then, in the next period, the outcome becomes known.

In these circumstances it is almost always worthwhile for the principal to offer a choice of payment schedules to consumers, a choice that is to be exercised before income is generated, indeed before the consumer knows what income he will get as a result of his labour decisions. There is one schedule designed, perhaps one should say destined, for each type of consumer. Each consumer chooses the one that suits best. Unfortunately, the only examples that are fairly easy to work out are those where each agent's actions have a full range of possible effects, and consequently it is optimal to have a punishment schedule for each type of consumer. Maybe that is some kind of approximation to the optimal set of contracts between principal and agent, but the model is not very believable. A better model, with consumers making a succession of labour supply decisions, needs to be worked out. It is unlikely that governments will adopt such complex tax systems, or other principals impose such incentive systems on their agents, but we ought to get some sense of what the systems would look like, and by how much such possibilities might improve outcomes, both for principals and agents.

The sense that the degree of complexity implied by optimal design of incentive systems is unacceptable and unusable becomes even clearer if we make another step towards realism, and allow that consumers take a series of labour supply decisions over time: education, career choice, early efforts to achieve promotion, job search, practice and exercise, hours of work, years of work. There is some uncertainty about the consequences at each stage, sometimes great, sometimes quite small. The formal structure of the model implies that agents should be offered not just choices among schedules, but choices among sets of schedules, among which choices will later be made. Pay or tax systems of that complexity are not conceivable. Why not? You could say that humans are not intelligent enough to take decisions of the complexity required. More reasonably, it would be very costly to calculate the decisions, and it is undesirable to impose these decision costs on people. Part, perhaps a substantial part, of that cost is the cost that results from making mistakes. Mistakes are not part of the standard economic models.

Simplicity of contracts and systems is a slippery concept indeed. To recognize the desirability of simplicity is not at all to conclude that simplest is best. There may well be many equally good ways of being simple. In the area of incentive systems, it is nice linear contracts that seem to be simple. For example, it is, and has long been, tempting to conclude that a constant marginal tax rate, the same for all incomes, would do perfectly well. Some at least of the calculations that I and others have done for the asymmetric-information problem suggest that there would not be a great cost in adopting such a system, as compared with an optimal one. At least it might do just as well as any of the tax systems we have in our various countries. It has the appeal of neatness and elegance. The simplicity of so simple a tax system is not, I think, a great advantage over the slightly greater complexity of varying tax rates. The question is whether it would be much worse than an optimal tax system, and that deserves to be estimated.

But there are kinds of complexity that should still be studied. One particular example is the possibility of relating taxation to wage rates, rather than only to income. I have touched on that obliquely several times already. It is not at all as easy to study as it may seem. The earlier discussion was couched in terms of wage rates, because they are concrete and readily understandable. Formally, the definition I was using was the ratio of income to a measure of the effort an individual is making. If effort were hours of work, it would be the wage rate in the usual sense. Often effort cannot be measured that way. Using the conventionally measured wage rate, income divided by hours, as an element of the tax base would not, I suppose, add much to the use of income. It is therefore unlikely that there is much advantage in so extending the tax system. What is really wanted is taxation in relation to occupation, to the type of job, perhaps, as well as income. I do not at all know what such a optimal tax system would look like. It would be interesting to find out.

Another interesting set of questions concerns taxation at the upper end of the income scale, where the relationship between pay and productivity is often far from simple. Two examples come to mind, both in need of serious analysis. The first is managers whose pay comes from contracts arising from principal–agent relationships within the firm. Because the contract of each manager will not in each year equate pay to productivity, does that mean marginal tax rates should be adjusted appropriately? The problem is made the more interesting because the form of the contract between firm and manager is influenced by the form of taxation.

The second example is that of rewards from innovation, invention, creation, and competition. I might say, the question is how to treat prizes. The best singer may not be much better than the second-best, and may be primarily motivated by the wish to sing better than the second-best, or just to sing well. What does that tell us about desirable incentive contracts, and, then, about taxation at these levels? We may expect that marginal tax rates should be rather higher if high incomes are indeed generated through competitions of this kind.

Whenever one looks at a principal–agent situation, one can think of many ways in which incentives might be created. In recent years, the theory and practice of what is variously called the design of economic mechanisms, or contract theory, or principal–agent problems, has gone well beyond the situations discussed in this lecture. The account given here has been one-sided, for the principal always set the terms of the contract, and the agent took the actions. It is true that many economic relationships are one-sided, in just that way. Many others are not, and involve cooperative arrangements or bargains between people in similar situations. It is not so much the asymmetry of information that is special about principal–agent relationships, but the asymmetry of responsibilities, with the principal moving first, the agent following. That makes the problems easier, and so we have made some progress. Now we can better appreciate that anonymous market relationships are only a part of economic reality, perhaps not even the largest part. Most economic problems and possibilities involve instead relationships between and among individual agents, whether taxes, contracts and bargains, fights and thefts, learning and search. It is a world still only imperfectly explored.

REFERENCES

Armstrong, C. M. (1996). 'Multiproduct nonlinear pricing.' *Econometrica*, vol. 64, pp. 51–76.

Arrow, K. J. (1963). 'Uncertainty and the welfare economics of medical care.' *American Economic Review*, vol. 53, pp. 941–69.

Atkinson, A. B. and Stiglitz, J. E. (1976). 'The design of tax structure: direct versus indirect taxation.' *Journal of Public Economics*, vol. 6, pp. 55–75.

Baron, D. and Myerson, R. (1982). 'Regulating a monopolist with unknown costs.' *Econometrica*, vol. 50, pp. 911–30.

Boiteux, M. (1956). 'Sur la gestion edes monoples publics astreints à l'équilibre budgétaire.' *Econometrica*, vol. 24, pp. 22–40.

Christiansen, V. (1981). 'Evaluation of public projects under optimal taxation.' *Review of Economic Studies*, vol. 48, pp. 447–57.

Diamond, P. A. and Mirrlees, J. A. (1971). 'Optimal taxation and public production.' I and II, *American Economic Review*, vol. 61, pp. 8–27 and 261–78.

——and——(1977). 'A model of social insurance with retirement.' *Journal of Public Economics*, vol. 10, pp. 295–336.

Graaff, J. de V. (1957). *Theoretical Welfare Economics*, Cambridge: Cambridge University Press.

Holmström, B. and Milgrom, P. R. (1987). 'Aggregation and linearity in the provision of intertemporal incentives.' *Econometrica*, vol. 55, 303–28.

Kolm, S.-C. (1971). *La Théorie des contraintes de valeur et ses applications*, Paris: C.N.R.S. Dunod.

Kydland, F. E. and Prescott, E. C. (1977). 'Rules rather than discretion: the inconsistency of optimal plans.' *Journal of Political Economy*, vol. 85(3), pp. 473–92.

Laffont, J-J. and Tirole, J. (1993). *A Theory of Incentives in Procurement and Regulation*. Cambridge, MA: MIT Press.

Little, I. M. D. (1950). *A Critique of Welfare Economics*. Oxford: Clarendon Press.

Maskin, E. (1985). 'The theory of implementation in Nash equilibria.' In *Social Goals and Social Organization* (ed. L. Hurwicz, D. Schmeidler and H. Sonnenschein). Cambridge: Cambridge University Press.

Mirrlees, J. A. (1971). 'An exploration in the theory of optimum income taxation.' *Review of Economic Studies*, vol. 38, pp. 175–208.

——(1974). 'Notes on welfare economics, information and uncertainty.' In *Essays in Equilibrium Behavior* (ed. M. Balch, D. McFadden and S. Wu). Amsterdam: North-Holland.

——(1975). 'The theory of moral hazard and unobservable behaviour.' Mimeo, Nuffield College, Oxford. To appear in *Review of Economic Studies*.

——(1976). 'The optimal structure of incentives and authority within an organization.' *Bell Journal of Economics*, vol. 7, pp. 105–31.

——(1986). 'The theory of optimal taxation.' In *Handbook of Mathematical Economics*, vol. III (ed. K. J. Arrow and M. D. Intriligator). Amsterdam: North-Holland.

——(1995). 'Welfare economics and economies of scale.' *Japanese Economic Review*, vol. 46, pp. 38–62.

Pauly, M. (1968). 'The economics of moral hazard: Comment.' *American Economic Review*, vol. 58, pp. 531–6.

Phelps, E. S. (1973). 'The taxation of wage income for economic justice.' *Quarterly Journal of Economics*, vol. 87, pp. 331–54.

Piketty, T. (1993). 'Implementation of first-best allocations via generalized tax schedules.' *Journal of Economic Theory*, vol. 61, pp. 23–41.

Ramsey, F. P. (1927). 'A contribution to the theory of taxation.' *Economic Journal, vol. 37, pp. 47–61.*

Rogerson, W. (1985). 'The first order approach to principal-agent problems.' *Econometrica*, vol. 53, pp. 1357–68.

Sadka, E. (1976). 'On income distribution, incentive effects and optimal income taxation.' *Review of Economic Studies*, vol. 43, pp. 261–8.

Spence, M. (1973). 'Job market signalling.' *Quarterly Journal of Economics*, vol. 87, pp. 355–74.

Tuomala, M. (1990). *Optimal Income Tax and Redistribution*. Oxford: Clarendon Press.

Varian, H. R. (1980). 'Redistributive taxation as social insurance.' *Journal of Public Economics*, vol. 14, pp. 49–68.

Vickrey, W. S. (1945). 'Measuring marginal utility by reactions to risk.' *Econometrica*, vol. 13, pp. 319–33.

Wilson, R. (1993). *Nonlinear Pricing*. Oxford: Oxford University Press.

2

Notes on Welfare Economics, Information, and Uncertainty

1. INTRODUCTION

These notes, although not entirely tentative, are less systematic than I would wish. Their purpose is to show how, in a world with imperfect and unreliable information, the Arrow–Debreu framework for welfare economics is unsatisfactory, and that models akin to those now used in the theory of public finance may be more appropriate. I shall not discuss all the reasons that urge one to extend or avoid the standard models. In particular, as Arrow and others have pointed out, the production of information—as in medical care, invention, or, presumably, the educational system—requires special treatment; but I shall not say much about it.

What I am going to consider is the information a government might have about consumers, or consumers about government. I shall be thinking of welfare economics as a mode of discussing alternative government policies, and also as part of the discussion about alternative systems of government. The policies a government can adopt, and the policies it should adopt, depend upon information about consumers, what they *do* and what they *are*. Thus, the fundamental theorem of welfare economics invites governments to distribute to households quantities of resources that are a function of what the households are (not what they choose to do), in the hope that the right competitive equilibrium will establish itself. In the Arrow–Debreu theory, this distribution of resources is carried out in advance of knowing the state of the world, but with complete information about the characteristics of the households. A great many insurance and futures markets are required if the optimum is to be a competitive equilibrium, but I shall not concern myself directly with that well-known difficulty. I shall ask what should be done—for reasons to be explained—(1) if the distribution depends on the state of nature, and (2) if information about the characteristics of households is imperfect. I shall also include some remarks on preferences regarding uncertainty.

This chapter was originally published in M. S. Balch, D. L. McFadden, and S. Y. Wu (eds.), *Essays on Economic Behavior under Uncertainty* (Amsterdam: North-Holland, 1974). Reproduced by kind permission of the editors.

2. REDISTRIBUTION AND RISK-TAKING

The Arrow–Debreu formulation of welfare economics accepts each household's beliefs—possibly expressible by means of subjective probabilities—in the same way that it accepts the household's tastes. If a man believes strongly but wrongly that the end of the world is at hand, he will be given his wealth now and allowed to spend it all at once. He will then starve, in circumstances he believed would not occur, but an Arrow–Debreu welfare function does not care. We should like to be able to discuss policies for a government that does care about such outcomes and is, in some respects, better informed about possible states of nature than some of the households for which it claims responsibility. Among these policies would be income distributions that are a function of the state of nature.[1]

Another reason for studying such distribution is the impossibility of identifying all states of nature 'objectively'—this is the phenomenon of moral hazard, well recognized in the literature. A farmer cannot perfectly in sure his crop against adverse circumstances, for the degree of adversity can, in practice, be assessed perfectly only by looking at the size of the crop, and that is affected by actions under the farmer's control. If perfect insurance were possible, distribution by government could (apart from the difficulties just mentioned) without disadvantage be independent of the state of nature. Since perfect insurance is not possible, the government presumably ought to relate distribution to the actual outcome of the harvest, as a proxy for the state of nature.

In this case, we clearly have what has come to be called a 'second-best' problem—that is, a problem that will not have for solution the straightforward competitive equilibrium familiar in simpler problems. The term 'second-best' may be a bit misleading since, in such a case as that of the risk-taking farmer—or the assistant professor—the first-best is an even more unattainable theoretical construction than the 'second-best'.

The first case, of 'Allais optimality', seems to have an easy formal solution, at least in the extreme case where household's probability beliefs are irrelevant, and policies are discussed in terms of a welfare function which has as arguments each household's utility in each state of nature (for example expected welfare, with the government's probabilities, or yours or mine). As usual, one wants to have shadow prices for each commodity in each state of nature. Producers should maximize profits (interpreting the shadow prices conditional upon the state of nature); and households should work out their plans separately for each state of nature, in the light of these prices and the government's plans for distribution of wealth, which are conditional upon the state of nature. Formally, if x_s^h is the vector of h's consumption in state of nature s, $u_s^h = u^h(x_s^h)$ is h's utility,[2] we want to maximize

$$W(u.) = W(u_1^1, u_2^1, \ldots, u_1^2, u_2^2, \ldots) \qquad \text{(monotonically increasing)},$$

---

[1] This distinction between *ex ante* and *ex post* optimality is fairly well known. See [2].
[2] The utility function itself could vary with the state of nature s.

with the competitive equilibrium conditions satisfied for each assigned budget b_s^h. Then, aggregate excess demands $\sum_h x_s^h$ in the various states of nature being feasible together, the production plan $(y_1, y_2 \ldots)$ (equal to aggregate excess demands in the various states of nature) maximizes $\sum p_s \cdot y_s$, and each x_s^h maximizes u_s^h subject to $p_s \cdot x_s^h$ being no greater than b_s^h where p_s is the competitive price vector for state s. This is a standard argument.

The problem associated with 'Allais optimality' is that consumers must not trade insurance: it must be impossible to trade a quantity of a commodity contingent upon a different state. If there were perfect contingent markets between consumers, it would not in general be desirable to allow producers to trade in these same markets: one would want to see commodity taxes imposed, for example. The Arrow–Debreu equilibrium would not be optimal. We shall come upon this need to prohibit markets again.

When the moral-hazard aspect of the economy is brought in, even this rather unstable competitive result is not optimal. I have no interesting general results as yet, but the following special example seems to capture the essence of the matter.[3]

Consider an economy of independent peasant farmers, producing corn on their own farms with their own labour, enterprise, and attention. The probability density of corn output y when there has been labour input z is $f(y, z)$. The government relates the farmer's consumption x to his output through a function

$$x = c(y), \tag{1}$$

which represents redistribution of output between farmers. The farmers, identical to one another, and each interested only in himself, choose z to maximize expected utility

$$\int u(x, y, z) f(y, z) \, \mathrm{d}y, \tag{2}$$

subject to (1). Let us take u to be a concave increasing function of x, and a decreasing function of y and z. I shall also assume that u tends to $-\infty$ when x tends to zero, so that farmers would give first priority to avoiding zero consumption. The government accepts (2) as its own welfare function, so that all the farmers should find its policies appealing. Everything has to take place under the aggregate production constraint which, on the assumption of a very large number of farmers, insensitive to small variations in consumption and with stochastically independent production possibilities, can be taken to be

$$\int y f(y, z) \, \mathrm{d}y - \int c(y) f(y, z) \, \mathrm{d}y = 0. \tag{3}$$

---

[3] I first came across problems of this kind in connection with population policy. That analysis is given in [5].

There is no harm in assuming everything is suitably differentiable and that the requisite Lagrange multipliers exist. I use the multiplier r for the constraint (3), and a multiplier s for the constraint

$$\int u_z f \, dy + \int u f_z \, dy = 0, \tag{4}$$

which arises from utility maximization by the farmers. Notice that we have a second-order condition from that maximization,

$$A \equiv \int u_{zz} f \, dy + 2 \int u_z f_z \, dy + \int u f_{zz} \, dy \leq 0. \tag{5}$$

The first-order conditions for the government's maximization are that, for each y,

$$u_x f - rf + s u_x f_z + s u_{xz} f = 0, \tag{6}$$

from variations of c, and

$$r \int (y - c(y)) f_z \, dy + sA = 0, \tag{7}$$

from variation of z. Notice that this last condition is simplified by use of (4). It is more illuminating to write (6) in the form

$$(r - s u_{xz})/u_x = 1 + s(f_z/f). \tag{8}$$

A 'first-best' optimization would of course have made u_x the same for all y. It is to be expected that if, as in the application I have in mind here, larger z is to be encouraged, c will be so chosen that u_x diminishes as y increases. To show this, it is convenient first to impose the convention that

$$\int y f(y, z) \, dy = z \tag{9}$$

for all z, and natural to suppose that

f_z/f is an increasing function of y, negative for small y
and positive for large y. $\tag{10}$

I must also assume that $u_{xz} = 0$.

It follows from (10) that r must be positive, since u_x always is, and the right-hand side of (8) sometimes is, positive. We have to show that s is positive. Write $h(y) = f_z/f$, with the optimum z. Then (8), which now reads $r/u_x = 1 + sh(y)$, tells us that x is a function of $sh(y)$ and y, $x = g(sh(y), y)$, where the derivatives of g are

$$g_1 = -\frac{1}{r}\frac{u_x^2}{u_{xx}} \quad \text{and} \quad g_2 = -\frac{u_{xy}}{u_{xx}}. \tag{11}$$

Assuming that u is concave, $g_1 > 0$. with this notation, we can write (7) in the form

$$r = -sA + r \int g(sh(y), y)h(y)f \, dy. \tag{12}$$

Here we have used the fact that $\int yf_z dy = 1$, which follows from by differentiation.

Suppose that

$$u_{xy} \le 0. \tag{13}$$

I shall show that this assumption implies that s is positive. If we had $s \le 0$, $g(sh(y), y)$ would be a non-increasing function of y, by (10), (11) and (13), and, y_1 being such that $h(y_1) = 0$,

$$\int g(sh(y), y)h(y)f \, dy = \int [g(sh(y), y) - g(0, y_1)]h(y)f \, dy \le 0.$$

The first step is implied by $\int hf dy = \int f_z dy = 0$, since $\int f dy = 1$; and the second is implied by (10). Also, we know from (6) that $A \le 0$. Therefore, under assumption (13), the right-hand side of (12) is non-positive if s is non-positive: but that is impossible, since $r > 0$. I have proved, then, that when x and y are weakly complementary, in the sense that (13) holds, and x and z are independent, $s > 0$; and, by (8), u_x is a decreasing function of y. In the special case $u_{xy} = 0$ (which might hold, for example, because the farmer does not care about output itself, and needs no labor to gather it in) we can further conclude that x is an increasing function of y.[4]

The assumptions used to obtain these results are rather strongly sufficient, but it will be clear from the analysis that the 'perverse' case, where x decreases with y, is not entirely impossible.

It can be seen from formula (8) that the government's optimal policy c is not generally linear, or even particularly simple. To extend the argument, one would expect, administrative and political reasons apart, to recommend quite complicated allocation rules for medical care, police protection, car insurance, and educational expenditures. One curious feature of rule (8) is highlighted by

---

[4] One might also think that in the optimum one would have $c'(y) < 1$; or at least that $y - c(y)$ would change sign only once, from negative to positive, as y increased. I have not found any nice assumptions that I can prove imply these results; and I suspect that they cannot easily be guaranteed.

its response to the apparently sensible assumption that agricultural output is distributed lognormally:

$$f(y, z) = \frac{C}{y} \exp\left[-\left(\log \frac{y}{z} + 1/2\sigma^2 \right)^2 \middle/ (2\sigma^2) \right] \tag{14}$$

(C is a constant). Equation (14) implies that

$$f_z/f = \left(\log \frac{y}{z} + 1/2\sigma^2 \right) \middle/ (\sigma^2 z). \tag{15}$$

According to (15), f_z/f tends to $-\infty$ when y tends to 0. But that is, by (8), inconsistent with any value of s other than 0. Yet $s = 0$ does not give an optimal policy. This is obvious because (depending on the utility function) a rule for distributing the available output that leaves everyone with the same u_x may leave no incentive for the farmers to produce anything! From a technical point of view, for this apparently well-set problem, no optimum exists.

The fact is, in this case, that one does better the more one penalizes those farmers who turn out to have very low output. The point can be made rigorously by considering what happens if all farmers whose output is less than a small number η receive consumption ϵ (another small number), while the others receive what they would receive in the *first-best* optimum—call it $c^*(y)$. This will be possible if it is possible at the same time to induce farmers to adopt the first-best optimum level of z—call it z^*. For that we require

$$\int_0^\eta u(\epsilon, y, z^*) f_z(y, z^*) \, dy + \int_\eta^\infty u(c^*(y), y, z^*) f_z(y, z^*) \, dy$$
$$+ \int_0^\eta u_z(\epsilon, y, z^*) f(y, z^*) \, dy + \int_\eta^\infty u_z(c^*(y), y, z^*) f(y, z^*) \, dy = 0.$$

Recollect that u_z is independent of x, so that the third and fourth terms can be written, together, as $\int_0^\infty u_z(y, z^*) f(y, z^*) dy$. Thus we have to choose ϵ and η so that

$$\int_0^\eta \{u(c^*(y), y, z^*) - u(\epsilon, y, z^*)\} f_z(y, z^*) \, dy$$
$$= \int_0^\infty \{u(c^*(y), y, z^*) f_z(y, z^*) + u_z(y, z^*) f(y, z^*)\} \, dy.$$

The right-hand side of this equation is equal to

$$r^* \int_0^\infty \{c^*(y) - y\} f_z(y, z^*) dy,$$

where $r^* = u_x(c^*(y), y, z^*)$, by first-best optimality; and this expression will normally be negative, since

$$\int_0^\infty (c^* - y) f_z \, dy = \int_0^\infty (c^* - y) h(y) f \, dy < 0 \qquad \text{if } c^{*\prime}(y) < 1$$

by assumption (10), and this is ensured by the weak assumption that $u_{xy} \leq -u_{xx}$.

Thus, for any $\eta > 0$, we can choose ϵ so as to get z^* chosen. Yet, given any number M, we can choose η so small that $f_z < -Mf(y < \eta)$, so that

$$\int_0^\eta u(c^*(y), y, z^*) f(y, z^*) \, dy - \int_0^\eta u(\epsilon, y, z^*) f(y, z^*) \, dy$$

$$< -\frac{1}{M} \int_0^\eta \{u(c^*(y), y, z^*) - u(\epsilon, y, z^*)\} f_z(y, z^*) \, dy$$

$$= -\frac{1}{M} \int_0^\infty \{u(c^*(y), y, z^*) f_z(y, z^*) + u_z(y, z^*) f(y, z^*)\} \, dy \to 0 \text{ as } M \to \infty.$$

In this way, we can approximate as closely as we wish to the first-best optimum, by imposing penalties (presumably of great severity) on a small proportion of the population.

Although these farmers suffer severely, there are so few of them that their sufferings are outweighed by the encouragement their fate, or rather the prospect of it, gives to farmers taking production decisions. It seems that models of this kind can in certain cases provide some justification for extreme punishment of negligibly small groups.

The problem has been presented as one of government policy, but with the coincidence between private and government ends postulated, the solution may instead be interpreted as a prediction of the kind of insurance system that would arise in the society considered. It is interesting and important to consider further solutions in which the government adopts criteria different from those of the farmers *ex ante*, on utilitarian or egalitarian grounds; but I do not consider this further in the present notes.

3. THE CHARACTERIZATION OF HOUSEHOLDS

We may think of the standard problem of welfare economics in the following form. A household of type h has utility function $u(x, h)$ in terms of its trades x with the rest of the economy (i.e. excess demands). Production constrains $y = \sum_h x(h)$ to lie in the production set Y. $W(u)$ is to be maximized. The 'fundamental theorem' asserts that the optimum is a competitive equilibrium if there is a suitable distribution of budgets defined by a function $b(h)$. The point I want to emphasize, obvious though it is, is that the consumers are then supposed to choose what trade they will do rationally in terms of their own self-interest, but are supposed to reveal the necessary information about themselves, symbolized by the variable h, without regard to their own self-interest. The usual notation obscures this. The following example, which has some correspondence with reality, may highlight the difficulty.[5]

Consider an economy with one consumer good, produced with labour. A household of type n provides labour of quantity ny when it works for time y. Every household has utility function $u(x, y)$ in terms of consumption x and labour time y. The welfare function is completely separable in terms of individual consumption, so that the utility function can be chosen to ensure that the welfare function is $W = \int u(x(n), y(n)) f(n) dn$, f being the density function giving the distribution of ability n. Welfare is quasi-concave in individuals' consumption, since u is concave. The optimum policy allocates consumption and time as functions of n in such a way that $\int x(n) f(n) dn$ is producible with labor input $\int ny(n) f(n) dn$. Denote the optimum by $x^*(n), y^*(n)$.

Proposition. $u^*(n) = u(x^*(n), y^*(n))$ *is a* decreasing *function of n if (and only if) labour time is a strictly normal commodity.*

Recollect that to say time is a strictly normal commodity for the consumer means, by definition, that an increase in non-labour income would, in a market economy, lead the consumer to reduce his labour supply. It is a very plausible assumption.

The proof of the proposition, which is routine, is given in the appendix. The point of the proposition is that one would naturally assume that individuals have some control over the information they convey to government about their abilities; it is presumably easier to pretend to less ability than one has than it is to pretend to more. In any case, there is no incentive to provide the information that the government must have if it is to bring the optimum about: on the contrary, there is an incentive for any individual not to provide the information. The model has some unrealistic features which serve to overstate the difficulties; but it is plausible that a government which attempted to realize the optimum of basic welfare economics would fail because of these difficulties.

In order to capture this feature of welfare economics, I propose to reformulate the basic problem in the form of two-level maximization, with households maximizing under a government-imposed constraint, and the government choosing the constraint in order to maximize welfare. Let us then interpret the vector x not only as trades but, more generally, as behavior. Thus, if some kinds of work can be observed directly, as amount of time or energy spent as well as through productive effects, both aspects could appear in the list x. Denote by k those aspects of individuals that are publicly known, independently of behavior (age, sex, place of birth, ...), and by h those aspects which, although they affect behavior through the consumer's choices, are not 'visible', at least to government. The individual will choose x so as to maximize $U(x, h, k)$, but will be

---

[5] It generalizes a special case mentioned in [4].

constrained, first by his consumption set $X(h, k)$, and secondly by the constraints imposed by government and the markets of the economy, $A(k)$.

Proof. $x(h, k)$ maximizes $U(x, h, k)$ subject to $x \in X(h, k) \cap A(k)$.   (16)

The production constraint is that

$$\Sigma x(h, k) \in Y. \tag{17}$$

(Some of the components of Σx, corresponding to non-trade behavior, are redundant.) Write $u(\cdot)$ for the function of h and k defined by $u(h, k) = U(x(h, k), h, k)$. Then the government seeks to maximize $W(u(\cdot))$, subject to the constraints (16) and (17), by choice of $A(\cdot)$.

The government is supposed to know the nature of the population, the number of people for each h and k. Specifically, it is most interesting to suppose h and k continuously distributed with density function $f(h, k)$; so that the production constraint should be written

$$\int x(h, k) f(h, k) \, dh \, dk \in Y. \tag{17'}$$

The government's maximand would depend both upon the utility outcome $u(\cdot)$ and upon the distribution $f(\cdot)$. For example, it might take the completely separable form—which is the easiest to handle—

$$W = \int u(h, k) f(h, k) \, dh \, dk.$$

Two objections to this formulation of welfare economics will so readily occur to the reader that I must answer them now. The first is that the government's knowledge of $f(\cdot)$ is hard to reconcile with its ignorance of any particular man's h. To this I answer that $f(\cdot)$ embodies *statistical* information, as opposed to personal information, which could be collected under the secrecy normal for census and sample. There is no incentive to hide information that will be used in this non-personal way. Of course the information obtained by census or sample may be quite poor—but $f(\cdot)$ represents the government's beliefs, even if they are inaccurate. The only correspondence between $f(\cdot)$ and reality that is required for application of the theory is that, in the outcome, markets clear: if they did not, the government would have to change its beliefs. Finally, I note that it will, in general, be possible to deduce the distribution of h and k from observation of the distribution excess demands x, as they actually appear (given the model of consumers expressed by $U(x, h, k)$).

The second objection, to which the problem as posed is open, is that it is too hard to answer usefully. This objection can be answered only by a complicated analysis, for which this is not the place. A special case has been analyzed in Mirrlees, and in unpublished work; and I can derive necessary conditions for

optimality in reasonably simple form. The power of the theory is illustrated by
a result quoted below. In some cases, this problem may have a simple solution.

Example

Consider the special case to which the above proposition applies. Denote labor
supply by z. Then behavior is (x, y, z) and is constrained by $z \leq ny$. This assumes
unproductive work is possible. The government does not know n. In terms of
the model, maximization can be achieved (subject to the usual convexity
assumptions, etc.) by distributing income according to observed ability z/y in
such a way that everyone receives the same utility; specifically, by assigning the
same income to everyone, whatever his z/y. But this assumes that, by some
means or other, individuals are induced to make z as large as possible, for given
y, when it matters to them not at all. Otherwise, when this inducement is
absent, there is, strictly speaking, no optimum; the government can always do
better by making the utility distribution more equal. With that proviso, we
have an example in which the optimum, though not the first-best optimum, is a
competitive equilibrium.

Generally speaking, with u depending on h, the optimum for the above
problem is not a competitive equilibrium (which would have A described by
$p \cdot x \leq b(h', k)$, where h' is an estimate of h deduced from x by means of the
consumption set $X(\cdot, k)$, and p are the correct producer prices), because A can
be nonlinear. (I have discussed the above example, with y invisible, in [4])
One really general result is the desirability of production efficiency ([3]). Under
very general assumptions, optimum production for the above problem lies
on the frontier of the production set; thus decentralization of production
decisions may be possible. The argument in support of this conclusion is simple:
if production were in the interior of the production set, a sufficiently small
subsidy (an equal lump-sum payment to everyone) would make everyone better
off and, presumably, change aggregate demands by an amount small enough to
leave them in the production set.

Some points

Uncertainty. The model as it stands allows for misleading information, but
not for imperfect information. In general, we expect the government to have
imperfect information about consumer behavior and about the consumer
characteristics labelled k. Suppose first that all consumer characteristics are
visible, so that the variable h does not appear in the formulation. The government observes k'. k and k' have a joint probability density function $f(k, k')$.
(This expresses the imperfect information about k that observation of k' provides.) The government imposes on consumers a budget constraint of the form
$x \in A(k')$, but the individual knows k and therefore maximizes $U(x, k)$ subject
to $x \in X(k) \cap A(k')$.

The point I want to make is that this problem has essentially the same features as the problem set in (16) and (17) above. The optimum is not (in general) a competitive equilibrium, except on the production side. The optimum budget constraint will be nonlinear. To see this, consider what the optimum must be. Optimum production y^* is equal to $\int y^*_{k'} f(k, k') dk$, where $y^*_{k'}$ is the aggregate production made available to all consumers who appear to have characteristic k'. Consider one particular value of k'. Then, given the optimal allocations to everyone else, $A(k')$ must have been chosen so as to solve a problem of the form of (16) and (17) with $y^*_{k'}$ given.

A special case may make the point clearer. Consider the example discussed before, with the additional assumption that the government, unable to observe y, makes inaccurate observations n of n'. The joint density function for n and n' is $f(n, n')$. The government wants to maximize

$$\int u(x(n,n'), y(n,n'))f(n,n')\,\mathrm{d}n\,\mathrm{d}n', \tag{18}$$

where the budget constraint may be taken to have the form, for an (n, n')-man, $x \le c(ny, n')$. since ny is his supply of labour, and n' is information the government possesses about him. Then for each (or, I suppose, for almost all) n', the government should choose the optimum income tax schedule (leading to the constraining consumption function) given the part of production allocated to those who are labelled n', to maximize $\int ufdn$. Naturally, in income tax theory, the optimum schedule is related to the shadow prices of the commodities—in this example to the marginal productivity of labor—and these must be the same for all n'. But that does not ensure that the various budget constraints have a similar form, for the form of the optimum depends upon the distribution of skills in the population, i.e. on $f(\cdot, n')$ for each n', and also on the production made available to the class in question.

Thus imperfect information leads to essentially the same economic considerations as misinformation. By the same argument, a satisfactory theory for the problem of (16) and (17) could be very easily extended to the case of imperfect information.

Rationing versus the price system.   The particular form of the general welfare economics problem stated above in which the budget constraint is linear in x (i.e. A is a convex cone) has been studied in [3] (where the variable k is not considered explicitly). There it is stated that when optimum commodity taxes prevail—i.e. when A is optimal subject to being linear— it may actually be desirable to introduce rationing for some commodities, thus replacing the market. Rationing should be understood in this context as a constraint imposing maximum levels of 'trade', which are functions only of k, while leaving the rest of the budget constraint unaffected by the amounts of the rationed commodities actually traded. (There may be a problem of ensuring that the ration quantity allows a consumption plan in the consumption set. For instance, in the special example we have been discussing, it is not possible to impose a ration on z if all abilities down to zero are represented.) Many social services have the characteristics of rationing.

It is an interesting question how far rationing schemes are desirable. The problem is not susceptible to general theorems, but is a question of what is plausible, given what we know of the real world. Some of the main reasons for rationing are omitted from the welfare economics problem we are considering. Within the context of the model, it is easy to see that universal rationing is generally far from optimal. Universal rationing means that every consumer supplies the same and receives the same from the market. In the case of a convex aggregate production set, almost everyone will be better off if he faces a budget constraint set $(1/H)Y$, where H is the number of consumers, and the resulting demands are feasible. In general, this will not be the optimal A, but it is better, and usually far better, than the rationing proposal. It seems likely that one can similarly construct a fairly liberal constraint set that is better than rationing of a single commodity, but I do not yet see how to do it.

In this context, it should be noted that some kinds of 'rationing' may be obtained by social arrangements not accessible to government. Many aspects of behavior, above all care and efficiency at work, are not directly visible to government but, to some extent, visible to other individuals. Social norms may make behavior in these respects more nearly uniform, and perhaps socially more useful, than it would otherwise be. Uniform behavior by work groups might be regarded as regrettable in a world with perfect distribution, but may actually be desirable, though an infringement of individual preferences, in a world of imperfect information.

Uniform prices versus progression and discrimination. At the opposite extreme to rationing, we may consider tax systems with uniform nondiscriminatory consumer prices. If the optimum had this character, no undesirable trading among households would take place. In general, there is no reason why uniform prices should be optimal: it is then desirable that trading among households be prevented if possible, since it would change the constraint set actually operating. (Of course, it might change the constraint set differently for different groups, and in that case it *might* be desirable.) I suggest two interesting questions: first, when is a policy of uniform subsidies supplemented by commodity taxes approximately optimal? Second, when will uniform commodity taxes be part of the optimal system?

In connection with the second question, the following particular case may be of interest. (I believe Stiglitz has obtained results of the same kind.) Generalize the particular example above to many consumer goods, assuming that the typical household has utility function

$$u(v(x), z/h), \tag{19}$$

where x is now a vector of consumer goods. We may take it that the optimal budget constraint, defining A, will have the form $b(x) \leq z$.

I can prove that in fact the optimum can be obtained by a budget constraint of the form

$$\beta(p \cdot x) \leq z, \tag{20}$$

where p is the vector of producer prices (in terms of which the optimum aggregate $\int x(h) f(h) dh$ maximizes profits within the production set). In effect, this enables the economy to provide the desired levels of v at minimum cost. The optimum is achieved by having a tax, generally nonlinear, on labor income, and no taxes on other commodities. Considerable generalization of this result is possible.

4. THE CONSUMER'S INFORMATION

It may be conjectured that it would usually be desirable, in terms of the problem presented in the previous section, that consumers be as well informed as possible about their own characteristics, measured by the variables h. To take the extreme case, if no-one knew anything to differentiate himself from anyone else, we should have the 'rationing' solution, and we have seen that that can be improved upon. But this is surely misleading. It seems that many people get satisfaction from beliefs about their relative intelligence, strength, beauty, charm or quality of judgment. The requirements of the economy apart, it might be a pity if their information on these subjects were very accurate. Perhaps some of us are better for a precise knowledge of our failings and abilities, but a meritocracy in which everyone knew his ability beyond doubt is not, I think, an attractive prospect.

Therefore, even if it were possible accurately to ascertain each person's abilities and other characteristics, it would not, I suggest, be desirable to do so— although it may well be desirable to obtain statistical information of this type from small samples. If a man believes he receives a low labour income because he chooses not to work very hard, rather than because he lacks the required abilities, there is a case for leaving things that way, rather than attempting to assess his abilities, and subsidize him accordingly. This is a reason for welcoming uncertainty and for going beyond the Arrow–Debreu version of welfare economics under uncertainty.

Appendix

The proposition on p. 30 is to be proved. In the optimum, we must have, for shadow prices p, q independent of n,

$$u_x = p, \qquad u_y = -qn.$$

Differentiating with respect to n, we obtain

$$u_{xx}x' + u_{xy}y' = 0, \qquad u_{xy}x' + u_{yy}y' = -q,$$

where primes denote derivatives with respect to n. Therefore

$$\frac{du}{dn} = u_x x' + u_y y' = \frac{(u_x u_{xy} - u_y u_{xx})q}{u_{xx}u_{yy} - u_{xy}^2}$$

which has the same sign as $u_{xx} - (u_x/u_y)u_{xy}$. This last expression is negative if and only if y is a normal commodity.

REFERENCES

[1] Arrow, K. J. *Essays in the Theory of Risk-Bearing*. North-Holland: Amsterdam (1971).

[2] Diamond, P. A. 'Cardinal welfare, individualistic ethics and interpersonal comparisons of utility: comment'. *Journal of Public Economics* (October 1967).

[3] Diamond, P. A. and Mirrlees, J. A. 'Optimum taxation and public production'. *American Economic Review* (March and June 1971).

[4] Mirrlees, J. A. 'An exploration in the theory of income taxation'. *Review of Economic Studies* (April 1971).

[5] Mirrlees, J. A. Population policy and the taxation of family size'. *Journal of Public Economics*, 1 (1972), 169–198.

COMMENTS

Peter Diamond

Economists have not yet learned to incorporate an interesting theory of information into general models of resource allocation. I suspect that the difficulty arises from the basically dynamic nature of the former and the essentially static nature of most of the latter. Given this situation, Professor Mirrlees has followed the standard approach of treating information (or policy tools) as either costlessly available or totally unusable. This approach permits progress (to which he has made major contributions) in the understanding of resource allocation where the fundamental welfare theorem of first-best economics is not applicable. Since the problems at hand are so difficult—mathematically complicated, and not amenable to the intuitions we have developed so far—it seems good research strategy to proceed on this basis without attempting to incorporate information modelling into these problems too (and conversely to examine information in models where resource allocation questions are very simple).

Unfortunately, the models used in these notes are mathematically very complicated. But the difficulty lies with the problems not the author since the model he has used to start this paper is the simplest possible of general models—one can't consider resource allocation without a choice variable; one can't have uncertainty without a random variable; and one can't have public policy without an observable variable (which can't coincide with either of the other two variables if the problem is not to vanish). Add the assumption that everyone is identical to the three-good model and we have the simplest possible situation, short of going to specific functional forms. In this setup, the model focuses on the desirability in general of nonlinear policy tools to deal with the moral hazard problem—the problem arising from individual maximization given the alternatives made available by public policy which result in individuals facing shadow prices which differ from social shadow prices. (This is the same problem as the deadweight burden of taxation—if individuals determined demand by prices which ignored taxes, the excise tax world would coincide with the lump sum tax world.)

Moral hazard comes in three forms. Individuals may falsify reports (reports nonexistent accidents or incorrect damage estimates). For my division of types, this represents an attempt to alter distributions but not a resource-using decision. Resource allocation decisions can be distinguished as occurring before or after the outcome of the random event is known. The most familiar example of the latter arises in medical care where people presumably purchase excessive services, once sick, since they bear only a fraction or none of the costs. An example of the former, which is the focus of Mirrlees's analysis, would be fire insurance, where insufficient protection is taken *ex ante* to limit either the probability or extent of damage of fire. Presumably the natures of the information difficulties in the two cases are different (although possibly not significantly so) in that everyone is making (socially) poor resource allocation decisions in the second case, but only those who have accidents (are sick) are doing so in the first. If one were to try to improve decisions within the framework of the information structure, one might try subsidizing fire extinguishers (or fertilizers) in the first case. Taxing medical care, however, would defeat the purpose of the insurance with the second case.

The second conventional insurance problem is adverse selection. Because of an inability to distinguish among individuals for whom the cost of service varies, the insurer charges a uniform price—an average cost price rather than a marginal cost price. When individuals know more about themselves than the company does, good risks don't buy insurance (or buy little) while bad risks buy (or buy much). (Mirrlees also mentions the reverse case, where individuals know less about their true accident probabilities than the government or the insurance company.) In terms of trading commodities of uncertain quality, the problem has been nicely characterized by George Akerlof as a 'market for lemons' (*Quarterly Journal of Economics*, 84 1970, 488–500). Mirrlees approaches this problem by means of a double index of observed and unobserved traits. Since he is considering social policy, individuals are not allowed to opt out, although the inefficiency from average cost pricing remains present, but less starkly so than in the Akerlof case. (Again, the problem has an analogue in tax theory in consideration of taxes to correct externalities where the same tax is levied on everyone although different people give rise to different degrees of externality (for example, fast versus slow drivers). As with the Akerlof example, this can take the extreme form of making it impossible to have any corrective value in taxation.)

Since Mirrlees is focusing on a single activity or single decisions, he does not mention the problem which has been called 'externalization by transfer' by Guido Calabresi (*The Costs of Accidents*, Yale, 1970). Here many activities get lumped together in a single insurance policy for administrative reasons. Thus, the price to the individual does not vary with his choice of activities. (A similar problem arises with prices that depend on the choice of activity (like car owning) but not the level of activity (miles driven). Thus, summarizing these three problems the shadow prices may be wrong for an individual choosing his level of activity because of the needs of insurance, the grouping of the individual with others, or of the activity with others.)

The information problem is further complicated by the passage of time and the presence of many individuals who may have relevant information. Since the past is given, taxing it will not alter past behavior. However, present behavior will be altered when it is anticipated or feared that future taxation will depend on (then) past behavior. This relationship does not seriously allow the past to be a base for lump-sum taxation, but the complexities of time and individual rigidities also may not be well caught in a static equilibrium model which has instantaneous response to tax policy. Mirrlees mentions social arrangements which may take advantage of different sources of knowledge. An additional example he does not cite is private law suits serving as a deterrent to externality generating behavior, which is frequently dubbed a 'private attorney general'. This indicates a role for social policy to encourage good social use of private information.

The problems of welfare economics in the presence of complexities of information and uncertainty are great. These arise both in the difficulty in analyzing individual models and in the absence, so far, of an overall framework in which to locate different models. Mirrlees' notes are very valuable as approaches to dealing with a number of these problems. The next instalment is eagerly awaited.

3

The Desirability of Natural Resource Depletion

With John A. Kay

ADVICE TO THE READER

This chapter was written for a conference on natural resources, and we were asked to talk about the *Club of Rome* model, which we had been examining. Having formed a poor opinion of that model, we decided to devote only an initial section to it, and that is written in a polemical style. Those who have had much to do with the world dynamics debate will understand why we thought it necessary to express ourselves in terms more vigorous than we would usually think proper. Economists are advised that the real content of the chapter is in Sections 2 and 3, and accordingly recommended to start reading at Section 2.

Section 2 contains some numerical calculations which are intended to shed light on the way in which economies do in fact use exhaustible resources, which we see as a necessary preliminary to any consideration of the extent to which these resources are substitutable for other factors of production. Section 3 discusses the reasons for thinking resource depletion may be taking place at a non-optimal rate, and develops some theoretical arguments which are new and can give some striking indications of the direction and extent of non-optimality. The more technical analysis is contained in an appendix.

The authors would like to acknowledge Alan Chambers's assistance with computing and the compilation of data, and comments by J. Flemming, G. Heal, R. Lecomber and P. Simmons.

1. RESOURCES AND WORLD DYNAMICS

We were initially invited to talk to this conference on the resource aspects of the global models developed by J. W. Forrester, D. L. Meadows, and others,[1] and

This chapter, co-authored by John A. Kay and James A. Mirrlees, was originally published in D. W. Pearce with J. Rose (eds.), *The Economics of Natural Resource Depletion* (London and Basingstoke: Macmillan, 1975). Reproduced with permission of Palgrave Macmillan.

[1] J. Forrester, *World Dynamics* (Wright-Allen Press, Cambridge, Mass., 1971); D. H. Meadows, D. L. Meadows, J. Randers and W. Behrens III, *The Limits to Growth* (Earth Island, London, 1972); D. L. Meadows and associates, *World III* (to be published 1974). *The Limits to Growth* does not

since there is still some interest in their work the first section of the paper is devoted to it. The topic need not detain us for long. We agree with the opinion of those who are competent to judge, that the models are worthless. The most detailed economic appraisal known to us is that of Nordhaus.[2] While he deals mainly with the original model of Forrester, his strictures apply equally to the Meadows work, which turns out on examination to be no significant advance on Forrester's model.[3] Nordhaus concludes that 'The work marks a significant retrogression in scientific technique, treatment of data, and humility', while two control engineers[4] have concluded that

World Dynamics is essentially trivial. It may be worse. Whether civilization is restrained or not, one supposes that there will always be gullible people. If education, science and technology should serve the purpose of gulling them, it is shameful.

Even the team at the Sussex Science Policy Research Unit, though disposed to see some value in the kind of modelling done by Meadows and his group, gave a 'largely negative...judgement', tempered by the kindly suggestion that *The Limits to Growth* was 'a stimulus for an extremely fundamental debate'.[5] When research is congratulated on the importance of its subject, beware!

Nevertheless, we make only modest apologies for devoting yet more space to these models. Many people are reluctant to accept that a product so superbly marketed can be totally without merit; and the work continues to receive the acclaim of those too credulous or too busy to subject it to critical scrutiny. A journalist, Antony Lewis, has proclaimed *The Limits to Growth* as 'likely to be one of the most significant documents of our age', and a former US cabinet member, Elliot Richardson, has called it 'too thorough, too thoughtful, too significant, to ignore'. Economists are not, after all, very good at predicting the balance of payments, while the successes of physics are all around us. It is, therefore, understandable, if unfortunate, that scientists give more credence to engineers who claim to be able to predict the future of the world economy than we would to economists who claimed to be able to land men on the moon.

specify the model used, though there are numerous hints. *World III*, most of which we have seen in typescript, is a revised version of the unpublished technical report that explained the model for *The Limits to Growth*. That technical report formed the basis of the critique done by a team at the Sussex Science Policy Research unit—H. S. D. Cole, C. Freeman, M. Jahoda, K. L. R. Pavitt *et al.*, *Thinking About the Future* (Chatto & Windus, for Sussex University Press, 1973).

[2] W. D. Nordhaus, 'World Dynamics: Measurement without Data', *Economic Journal* (Dec 1973), and Cowles Foundation Discussion Paper CF-20510 (1972).

[3] The team have looked at much more emprical data than Forrester did, and some parts of the model have been made much more complicated (by disaggregating the population by age groups, for example). However, as we shall substantiate below in the case of one sector, the changes do not lead to sensible models in most cases, and the use made of empirical data is both primitive and, quite often, perverse. The work does seem to exemplify two serious faults in the practice of simulating modelling: the tendency to take any old model that happens to be available as a starting point, and the fallacy that any increase in complexity is an increase in realism.

[4] D. Graham and D. C. Herrick, 'World Dynamics', *I.E.E.E. Transactions on Automatic Control* (Aug 1973).   [5] D. Graham and D. C. Herrick, 'World Dynamics', p. 13.

In consequence, much work is in progress developing the Forrester–Meadows models, or conducted in similar style. We understand that a group of scientists in the Department of the Environment are engaged in a project of this kind, which is presumably intended to influence British government policy. Other groups at Sussex, in Argentina, Japan, Switzerland and the United States are engaged in similar exercises. We ought, therefore, to look closely at the resource sector of the Meadows model. We will not learn much from it about resources, but we may learn something about models.

In order to understand the Meadows model, we have simplified the equations of *World III* (a somewhat revised version of the model on which *The Limits to Growth* was based), by translating them out of the Dynamo compiler language in which they are formulated, using continuous time and conventional notation, and eliminating redundant variables. In the case of the resources sector of the model, the procedure yields three equations:

$$\dot{r} = -Nf(Y/N) \tag{1}$$

$$Y = \frac{1}{3} K\{1 - g(r)\} \tag{2}$$

$$\dot{K} = sY - \delta K \tag{3}$$

where r is the stock of resources remaining; N is the population; Y is the industrial output (gross); K is the capital stock; and f and g are numerically specified functions, as are the parameters s (savings ratio) and δ (depreciation).[6]

This is more or less a Harrod–Domar growth model with a resource constraint. One might object to the assumption that *gross* saving will be a fixed proportion of *gross* income, but since the capital–output ratio has been assumed constant it makes little difference in the model as it stands. The empirical inadequacy of a model with a constant capital–output ratio is well known to economists, and presumably obvious to most other people. We return to the assumptions about resources.

The resource constraint is peculiar in form. As r falls—resource shortage increases—an increasing *fraction* of capital has to be devoted to resource extraction. It would be more reasonable to assume an increasing absolute amount (related also to the volume of resources being extracted). We can easily derive a function for the cost of resource extraction from the model, by dividing the loss of industrial output because of resource-exploitation costs by the volume of resources being extracted:

$$\text{Extraction costs per unit} = \frac{Kg(r)}{Nf[K\{1 - g(r)\}/(3N)]}.$$

[6] The numerical specification of the *World III* model is
$$s = 0.33, \quad \delta = 0.0714, \quad r(0) = 1.$$
The functions f and g are given by Figures 9A and B.

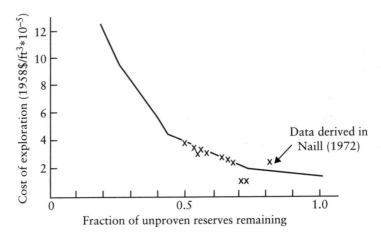

Figure 3.1. *Cost of exploration for US natural gas versus fraction of*
unproven reserves remaining

Source: Data derived in Naill (1972), from cost and discovery data in API, 1967, and
AGA, 1944–63.

It is plausible that the cost of resource extraction should depend on the volume
of resources remaining; it is less plausible that the costs should depend on K and
N in this particular way. But consider the quantitative dependence of extraction costs on r. If we set K and N equal to their initial values, we find that the
cost of resource extraction rises twenty times by the time 90 per cent of known
reserves are exhausted. That is hard to believe, and it is a good deal greater than
is suggested even by the extrapolations presented by the Meadows team. Possibly their formulation in fractional terms misled them.

Since the relationship between resource exhaustion and extraction costs is
crucial in inducing the 'crises' of *World III*, it is interesting to examine the
empirical evidence used in support of it. This evidence is cited in the technical
report. There is a relationship derived by Naill (a member of the Meadows team)
and reproduced from that report, in Fig. 3.1. The crosses apparently represent
observations, and the curve shown has been fitted to them. Comment would be
superfluous. Another source of data—on the costs of oil exploration in the
United States—is at first sight more convincing. This is shown in Fig. 3.2. The
data has been computed on a set of rather speculative assumptions described in
the *World III* technical report.

It is a little surprising to find that data on exploration costs should be used to
predict the fraction of capital allocated to obtaining mineral resources, since for
most minerals exploration costs are small relative to development and production costs. This is rather serious, since development costs for US oil, which
are a good deal larger in absolute magnitude, show something more like a
declining trend over the period. Moreover, the rising trend in exploration costs
is based on data for the United States which excludes Alaska, the area in which

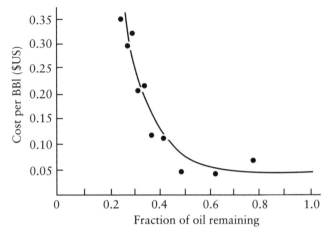

Figure 3.2. *Exploration cost of domestic oil as a function of remaining oil*
Source: Data derived from C.R.A.M., 1969, p. 186.

most recent exploration and discovery has occurred. The authors of *The Limits to Growth* were presumably unaware of the research which has been undertaken on finding and development costs by M. A. Adelman[7] which does not support the relationship they used.

The final source of evidence for the *The Limits to Growth* relationship is taken from a diagram prepared by Barnett and Morse,[8] and reproduced in the technical report (Fig. 3.3). This diagram appears in a chapter entitled 'Ambiguous Indicators of Resource Scarcity', and is presented in the context of a discussion which concludes 'the extractive labour and the extractive capital percentages are not significant as indicators of increasing scarcity'. The work of Barnett and Morse represents the best empirical study of the relationship sought by the Meadows team known to us. In other parts of the book, they set up and test the 'strong hypothesis' that economic scarcity of natural resources, as measured by the trend of real cost of extractive output, will increase over time in a growing economy; and the 'weak hypothesis', that the unit cost of extractive output rises relative to that of non-extractive output. They find that in the case of minerals, empirical evidence from the United States contradicts both hypotheses.

We would not wish to argue that, because increasing scarcity has not manifested itself in the past, it will not do so in the future. As Adelman puts it, 'The history of every mineral industry is a constant struggle between increasing

---

[7] M. A. Adelman, 'Trends in the Cost of Finding and Developing Oil and Gas Reserves in the United States, 1946–66', in *Essays in Petroleum Economics*, ed. S. Gardner and S. Hanke (Colorado School of Mines, 1967), and *The World Petroleum Market* (Johns Hopkins Press, Baltimore, 1972).

[8] H. J. Barnett and C. Morse, *Scarcity and Growth* (Johns Hopkins Press, Baltimore, 1963).

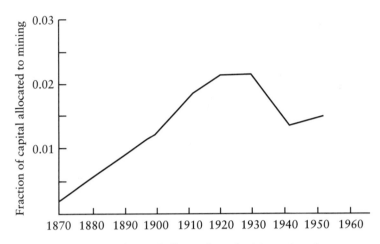

Figure 3.3. *Fraction of capital allocated to obtaining mineral resources, US, 1870–1950*

Source: Data derived from H. J. Barnett and C. Morse, *Scarcity and Growth* (Baltimore, 1963, Johns Hopkins Press), p. 220.

costs . . . and the growth of knowledge',[9] and we would not speculate on how that struggle will develop. What we do wish to argue is the more limited and more serious charge that there is no valid empirical basis provided for the relationship used in *World III*, and that the attempt to give one rests on a selective use of evidence.

The other important empirical input to the model is the quantity of available resources. This is set at 250 times current consumption. The explanation of this choice is given as follows:

Theoretically, the level of available nonrenewable resources NR should reflect a crustal quantity, or the absolute geological availability of the resources. Such a large number might reflect the optimistic belief that 'free' energy will enable the world economy to satisfy its resource needs from basic rock. However, such an assumption must also include an estimate of the cost of this process in terms of necessary labour and capital, or the amount of unusable solid waste and pollution produced. A more realistic range for the aggregate reserve index is probably between 50 and 500 years, based on available estimates of proven and unproven reserves. The current model uses 250 years as an order-of-magnitude estimate of the 1970 aggregate reserve life index of world resources.[10]

This vagueness is understandable, but it is not very impressive as empirical substantiation.

The behaviour of the model is obvious. Combining equations (2) and (3) yields

$$\dot{K} = \left(\frac{1}{3}s - \delta\right)K - \frac{1}{3}sKg(r).$$

[9] Gardner and Hanke, *Essays*, p. 57.   [10] *World III*, typescript, pp. v–34.

Since $s > 3\delta$, and $g(r)$ is initially small, $\dot{K} > 0$, so that K and Y increase. This implies that $\dot{r}$ is positive and increasing, and as a result $g(r)$ rises, reducing the growth rate and then the absolute level of Y. In due course, this leads to $\dot{K} < 0$, so that finally output declines both on account of decreasing K and on account of increasing $g(r)$. The solution is easily quantified too. If in the next seventy-five years population were to grow by 2 per cent per annum on average, and output per head had not by the end of the period fallen again to below its present level, a simple calculation shows that K will be declining at the end of the seventy-five years. A more careful calculation would show that it will then be falling quite rapidly, and Y will be falling very rapidly. With a 1 per cent population growth rate, the same can be said with seventy-five years replaced by 100 years. It is easy to see, therefore, that 'catastrophe within 100 years' is implied by the model, provided population projections are at all realistic. This only takes a few minutes to check. The extensive computer calculations reported in *The Limits to Growth* and *World III* can hardly be said to give the conclusions greater weight.

Having found just what substance there is in the technical report, which is a revised version of the unpublished basis for *The Limits to Growth*, it is as well to recall the claims made by the authors of that work:

Ours is a formal, written model of the world. It constitutes a preliminary attempt to improve our mental models of long-term, global problems by combining the large amount of information that is already in human minds with the new information-processing tools that mankind's increasing knowledge has produced—the scientific method, systems analysis, and the modern computer . . . . We believe that it is the most useful model now available for dealing with problems far out in the space–time graph. To our knowledge it is the only formal model in existence that is truly global in scope, that has a time horizon longer than thirty years, and that includes important variables such as population, food production and pollution, not as independent entities, but as dynamically interacting elements, as they are in the real world . . . . We feel that the advantages listed above make this model unique among all mathematical and mental world models available to us today.[11]

The sponsors of the project further asserted that 'the report presents in straightforward form the alternatives confronting not one nation or people but all nations and all peoples, thereby compelling a reader to raise his sights to the dimensions of the world problematique'.

Yet, on examination, we find that the most important parts of the model are naive in conception, amateurish in construction, and make negligible—and warped—use of empirical data. The verdict of Graham and Herrick, which we cited above—'essentially trivival'—is precisely right. The notion that this model might seriously be used for forecasting long-term trends in resource utilization is absurd. (We should add that the resources sector of the Meadows model is not the worst part: the pollution sector is even slighter; the agricultural sector

---

[11] *World III*, pp. 21–2.

so complex that we have been unable to make serious assessment of its realism; the 'capital', i.e. production, sector is the worst of all.)[12]

As an exercise in this kind of model building, we have explored the effect on the Meadows model of making the minimum modifications required to give it some plausibility. We wanted to modify the production function so as to allow for the possibility of economy in resource use. We therefore chose a CES production function in resources and capital, which allows us, by choice of the elasticity of substitution to take different views on the extent to which capital may be substituted for resources. We altered the savings assumption slightly, so that net investment was set proportional to net output. Finally, we imposed increasing economy in resource use by setting the price of the resource to rise at a constant annual rate with producers equating the price of the resource with its marginal product. The model is thus

$$Y^\alpha = aK^\alpha + br^\alpha, \tag{4}$$

$$\dot{K} = sY, \tag{5}$$

$$\frac{\mathrm{d}}{\mathrm{d}t}\left(\frac{\partial Y}{\partial r}\right) = c\frac{\partial Y}{\partial r}. \tag{6}$$

We further took $s = 0.11$, $a = 3^{-\alpha}$, $b = 0.02$, $K_0 = 3$ and $r_0 = 1$, values which seem fairly plausible and similar to those implied by the *The Limits to Growth* model. We computed the behaviour of the model for a number of different values of α. An interesting problem arose on a number of computer runs. If the elasticity of substitution between capital and resources is less than one ($\alpha < 0$), then the CES assumption implies that resources are essential, in the sense that production without net resource use is impossible. It is also true that $\partial Y/\partial r$, the marginal product of the resource, is bounded above. Suppose the output of our economy were metal pans. Then it is impossible to produce a pan without using *some* metal; and, while one can make thinner and thinner pans, there is a limit to this process also. Thus, it eventually becomes impossible to effect the economies in resource use which our model demands. We have, therefore, assumed, following the spirit of *The Limits to Growth*, that our economy is such that, when resource economy conflicts too much with growth, it is resource economy which is abandoned. We told our computer not to allow the growth rate to fall below 2 per cent per annum: if this were going to happen, it was instructed to abandon economy and use whatever resources were necessary to allow growth at 2 per cent to continue.

By choosing different values of c and α within the range which we thought to be plausible, we obtained a wide range of different scenarios. We could come

[12] The equations of the model (which cannot be immediately extracted from *World III*), with discussion of the methodology of modelling, and further comment on some of the assumptions are given in our paper, 'Simulation Modelling for World Problems', mimeo (Nuffield College, 1974).

near to the *The Limits of Growth* model by assuming very low possibilities of substitution and slight incentives to resource economy, such as $\alpha = -10$ and $c = 0.01$. On these assumptions, output grows over the next 250 years by a factor of 8,677. This miracle of compound interest is accompanied by a 7,000-fold growth in resource use, and requires a total resource input equal to around 200,000 times current annual consumption. Perhaps that is too much. Let us impose resource economy by making the resource price rise at 10 per cent per annum. Then output in the year 2223 will be a relatively manageable 236 times its present level. This involves a cumulative resource use of 8,000 years' current consumption.

These figures, though high, do not sound so ridiculous. What would happen if the possibilities for substitution were greater? $\alpha = -1$ means that the elasticity of substitution between the factors is 1/2. A 1 per cent annual rise in resource prices now means that output will grow 6,205 times over 250 years, resource use 1,814 times, and total resource use is 62,000 times the present level. But a faster rise in resource prices now involves a substantial substitution of capital for resources. With a 10 per cent rate of increase, growth is clipped back to a factor of 218. But this is accompanied by a less than tenfold growth in resource use, which is made possible by an initial supply of resources only 500 times current use. If the elasticity of substitution is higher still, the problem of resources becomes negligible. With $\alpha = 0.1$, so that the elasticity of substitution is slightly greater than one, a 3 per cent rise in resource prices would allow output to grow 40,000 times with an eightfold growth in resource use.

No doubt most people find these figures quite absurd. How can output possibly grow by a factor of 200, far less 40,000? Yet they should not dismiss such numbers too readily. It is almost certainly a conservative estimate that the output of the British economy has grown by 500 times in the past 250 years. It is fair to ask what such a statement actually means; nevertheless, this is what the 2–3 per cent growth rate which the economy has actually experienced over the period implies. For the United States, where population has grown a thousand-fold as well, the figure of 40,000 is probably on the low side. The resources required for this growth have been found. True, there have been worries from time to time:

By the sixteenth century, the enclosures and the demands of industry for fuel had brought about a shortage of timber trees that seemed likely to hamper shipbuilding and so to threaten national security. Among the causes of this dearth, the voracity of the ironworks was regarded as the chief, and it was urged that the industry should be closely regulated, if not entirely suppressed.... When a commission was appointed to enquire into the ironworks of the Weald, it was asserted that the shortage of wood was so great that soon Calais, Boulogne, Rye, Hastings, Dover, and other towns on both sides of the Channel would be without fuel, and that the fishermen would not be able to dry their clothes or warm their bodies when they came in from the sea.[13]

[13] T. S. Ashton, *Iron and Steel in the Industrial Revolution* (Manchester University Press, 1951), p. 9.

The models may demonstrate that many things can happen; but we do not intend that they should be taken very seriously. From what we know of the economic system, and the availability of resources, we believe they are more plausible than the models of the Meadows team. But as forecasts of the future, these models are as bad as theirs. No rational person could possibly believe that any such model will tell him what output will be in the year 2223. Do they serve any other purpose? It is hard to think of one. They do show that the future is very uncertain; and that the extent to which economic growth is constrained by resource shortages depends on the availability of resources and the ease with which other factors can be substituted for them. They alert us to what all this might mean quantitatively; but, in fact, we did not need computer simulations to tell us. At most, the models demonstrate that anyone who predicts the future for 150 years and claims that 'the basic behaviour modes we have already observed in this model appear to be so fundamental and general that we do not expect our broad conclusions to be substantially altered' is mistaken. We should not need a computer to tell us that, either.

Should one conclude that modelling in the social sciences is a waste of time? We think, on the contrary, that mathematical models are an indispensable tool for the economist. But what is wrong with the Forrester–Meadows work is not just that it is badly done. Like alchemists and astrologers, they set themselves the wrong task, developing useless models for illegitimate ends. No doubt we can expect the next few years to produce the world-dynamic equivalent of alchemists who are careful to emphasize that they have not produced gold yet and astrologers who claim to do no more than delineate the outlines of character: such work, more restrained and careful, will have as little value as that of Forrester and Meadows, though its adverse consequences will probably be less severe. There are numerous reasons why we should not aim at vast, complicated, global simulation models. Perhaps the most important one in the case of exhaustible resources is that forecasting models whose time horizon extends beyond a decade or so are worthless. If one can abandon the naive view that science is quantitative forecasting, one can think of using models in a flexible, piecemeal way to get insight into relatively limited, but specific, aspects of social systems. To this end, it is often a help to formulate questions of policy, and then to concentrate on what seem to be essentials. It appears that a model that is 'global' in scope is a nuisance, rather than an advantage: the need for computer simulation, which arises only for a model too complex to be understood, should be regarded provisionally as a sign of an ill-formulated model. In later sections we indicate how models might be applied to resources with better effect.

2. WHERE DO RESOURCES GO?

In our view, some knowledge of where non-renewable resources do in fact go is an essential preliminary to any serious discussion of resource depletion. Naive assumptions of linear relationships between resource use and output, or about the inexorability of exponential growth of all economic time series, serve only to disguise the wide diversity of actual experience. Over the two decades from 1950 to 1969, British industrial production grew by around 80 per cent and GDP by about 70 per cent. Iron and steel production grew roughly in step, at about the lower of these figures. Aluminium usage almost doubled, while copper consumption increased by around 30 per cent. Our consumption of zinc and lead rose only slightly, while tin consumption fell. Phosphates were used less, but potash more.

We have constructed an index of aggregate use of non-renewable resources. This index is based on ten materials—iron, copper, aluminium, lead, zinc, tin, nickel, magnesium, phosphate, and potash. We weighted quantity relatives by estimated values of resources used derived from consumption data and world prices of the materials involved. We also derived a 'total' resource index by adding in three 'power' resources—coal, oil and natural gas—on similar principles. Table 3.1 sets out these indices for the United Kingdom, the United States, and Germany. This shows that aggregate resource use has indeed increased with output and industrial production, though rather more slowly than in either two of the other three countries. In Germany the reverse is true for the period as a whole, but the base of 1950 is in this case low and somewhat unrepresentative, and since, say, 1955 the pattern conforms to that observed in the other two. This is, of course, in the context of a much more rapid rate of growth. The apparent year-to-year fluctuations should not be taken too seriously, since our 'consumption' series normally reflects deliveries rather than actual consumption. Stock building by consumers, therefore, appears as a change in use.

Table 3.2 presents calculations of a similar nature in a cross-section comparison of resource use in ten different countries in 1969. This demonstrates substantial variations in per capita consumption of particular resources, and smaller but still significant variations in total use measured either per head or per dollar of output. The United States appears at the top of the list for per capita usage, but near to the bottom in terms of the resource intensity of its output (Table 3.3). This latter competition is comfortably won by Japan. These differences may be exaggerated, since the conversion of these 1969 outputs at the then prevailing exchange rates may be thought to underestimate the value of Japanese output relative to that of the United States, but this factor is unlikely to be sufficient to account for a difference of almost 100 per cent.

Perhaps the most interesting feature of these calculations is that the differences they reveal are likely to be less surprising to the layman than to the economist. The tourist knows that Holland and Denmark are largely agricultural, that Italy is backward, and has heard that Japan is one extensive assembly line. The economist, on the other hand, knows that the differences between developed countries in the fraction of output accounted for by

Table 3.1. *Resource use, 1950–1969*

Year	United Kingdom				United States				Germany			
	Non-power	Total	Ind. prod'n	GDP	Non-power	Total	Ind. prod'n	GDP	Non-power	Total	Ind. prod'n	GDP
1950	100	100	100	100	100	100	100	100	100	100	100	100
1951	102	103	106	103	104	104	109	108	108	112	119	110
1952	102	103	102	103	99	103	113	111	129	127	128	120
1953	97	101	107	108	116	112	124	116	134	131	138	130
1954	110	110	115	112	98	102	115	114	162	149	157	140
1955	120	117	122	116	120	117	131	123	201	178	183	156
1956	119	118	122	118	120	120	135	125	204	184	196	167
1957	121	118	123	120	118	120	136	127	210	188	206	176
1958	119	118	122	120	102	109	125	126	212	188	213	182
1959	119	119	130	125	114	117	143	134	239	209	130	195
1960	134	131	139	131	111	117	148	137	283	243	257	229
1961	128	128	139	136	114	119	148	140	282	247	273	242
1962	124	128	141	137	122	125	160	149	277	248	285	252
1963	130	134	146	142	136	135	169	155	276	254	294	261
1964	149	147	158	150	154	146	179	163	329	295	317	278
1965	150	149	163	154	165	154	194	174	322	295	335	294
1966	143	144	166	157	177	163	212	185	300	279	340	302
1967	134	138	166	161	166	161	214	190	293	275	335	301
1968	141	145	176	166	159	161	224	199	351	338	273	323
1969	144	149	182	167	165	167	234	205	406	382	423	348

Sources: Annual Abstract of Statistics, Metallgesellschaft—*Metal Statistics*; US Department of Interior—*Minerals Yearbook*; Iron and Steel Board—*Iron and Steel Annual Statistics*; National Accounts of OECD countries; UN *Annual Bulleting of Statistics*.

Table 3.2. *Resource consumption* per capita, *UK* = 100 (1969)

	Iron	Copper	Aluminium	Lead	Zinc
United States	156	105	261	84	117
United Kingdom	100	100	100	100	100
Germany	143	111	151	104	126
France	103	87	104	80	91
Italy	82	59	69	55	60
Netherlands	91	41	59	76	51
Sweden	164	123	145	138	91
Denmark	103	14	20	81	47
Canada	115	148	150	64	106
Japan	139	96	115	38	113
	Tin	Nickel	Magnesium	Phosphates	Potash
United States	81	108	299	252	197
United Kingdom	100	100	100	100	100
Germany	67	103	608	168	197
France	60	108	74	388	276
Italy	36	52	37	109	38
Netherlands	107	8	22	99	111
Sweden	14	344	62	214	180
Denmark	52	3	—	311	423
Canada	67	107	100	222	125
Japan	72	113	55	84	78

Sources: OECD, *Statistics of Energy*; British Steel Corporation, *Statistical Handbook*; *Metal Statistics*; National Accounts of OECD Countries; *UN Annual Bulletin of Statistics*.

Table 3.3. *Non-power resource consumption*[a]

	Resources per capita	GDP per capita	Resources per $ of GDP
United States	158	238	66
United Kingdom	100	100	100
Germany	134	137	98
France	100	133	75
Italy	74	79	94
Netherlands	77	112	69
Sweden	156	181	86
Denmark	77	146	53
Canada	121	169	72
Japan	125	84	149

[a]Estimated by authors.

manufacturing industry are very small; that Italy, Holland, and Denmark are by no means the least industrialized among them; and that Japan still has a very extensive agricultural sector.

This suggests that resource use may be largely attributable to a small number of conspicuous industries. We have attempted to ascertain which products are the principal users of particular resources. The main problem here is that the main user of aluminium, say, is the aluminium fabrication industry. It is therefore necessary to trace resources through successive processes until they reach the product in which they are finally incorporated; and conversely to hold the car industry responsible for all the steel in cars, whether they are used directly in body pressing or indirectly in manufacturing the headlamps. Input–output analysis allows this in cases where there is a well-identified resource extraction or processing sector. The UK matrices are insufficiently disaggregated for this to be attempted, but in the US tables we could identify eight suitably defined sectors, which enable us to make estimates of the ultimate disposition of resources for aluminium, chemical and fertilizer minerals, coal, copper, lead, petroleum and natural gas, steel, and zinc.

The results of this are reproduced in Table 3.4, which lists the industries which are principal users of each of these resources. It may require emphasis that all of these are final uses. This means, for example, that the item 'fertilizers' includes only fertilizers sold directly to consumers; fertilizers sold to producers are

Table 3.4. *Principal uses of resources (% of total resource use attributable to direct or indirect use by these industries)*

	%		%
Aluminium		*Chemical and fertilizer minerals*	
Construction	26.9	Food manufacture	14.9
Motor vehicles	11.2	Construction	13.5
Industrial machinery	7.5	Industrial chemicals	10.0
Aircraft	6.1	Wholesale and retail trade	3.2
Food manufacture	5.1	Motor vehicles	3.1
Ordnance and accessories	4.8	Clothing	2.9
Other transport equipment	4.6	Fertilizers	2.7
Communication equipment	2.8	Cleaning preparations	2.3
Wholesale and retail trade	2.0	Petroleum refining	1.9
Refrigeration equipment	0.9	Industrial machinery	1.7
Metal household furniture	0.8	Drugs	1.0
		Cigarettes, cigars, etc.	0.9
Total of these	72.6	Total of these	58.0
Coal		*Copper*	
Electric utilities	17.4	Construction	29.5
Construction	14.2	Industrial machinery	9.0
Motor vehicles	6.5	Motor vehicles	8.2
Food manufacture	5.7	Communication equipment	3.9
Wholesale and retail trade	4.9	Electrical apparatus	3.1
Industrial machinery	3.8	Aircraft	3.0
Clothing	1.4	Ordnance and accessories	2.1

Table 3.4. (*Contd*)

	%		%
Petroleum refining	0.9	Refrigeration machinery	1.7
Industrial chemicals	0.8	Food manufacture	1.5
Hospitals	0.7	Wholesale and retail trade	1.5
		Pipes, valves and fittings	0.9
		Shipbuilding and repairs	0.8
Total of these	56.2	Total of these	65.2
Lead		*Petroleum and natural gas*	
Construction	17.6	Refined petroleum products	43.5
Storage batteries	15.1	Construction	9.7
Motor vehicles	11.0	Gas utilities	9.1
Industrial machinery	9.5	Wholesale and retail trade	6.6
Food manufacture	4.8	Food manufacture	6.1
Ordnance and accessories	4.5	Motor vehicles	2.1
Industrial chemicals	4.3	Industrial machinery	2.0
Aircraft	3.9	Toilet preparations	1.7
Wholesale and retail trade	3.3	Electric utilities	1.3
Communication equipment	2.3	Industrial chemicals	1.0
Jewellery	1.5	Air transport	0.9
Clothing	1.3	Clothing	0.8
Petroleum refining	1.2	Motor freight transport	0.8
Shipbuilding and repairs	1.2	Passenger transport	0.7
		Repair services (non-auto)	0.7
Total of these	81.2	Total of these	87.1
	%		%
Steel		*Zinc*	
Construction	30.0	Construction	25.6
Motor vehicles	19.6	Motor vehicles	19.5
Industrial machinery	10.7	Industrial machinery	10.2
Food manufacture	5.6	Aircraft	4.1
Other transport equipment	4.0	Domestic appliances	3.8
Domestic appliances	2.3	Ordnance and accessories	2.4
Aircraft	2.2	Wholesale and retail trade	2.3
Wholesale and retail trade	1.6	Storage batteries	1.9
Fabricated plate works	1.3	Industrial chemicals	1.7
Shipbuilding and repair	1.0	Miscellaneous hardware	1.2
Communication equipment	0.9		
Total of these	79.3	Total of these	72.7

attributed to the product whose manufacture they assist. Similarly, the refined petroleum products, which it is not surprising to discover are the principal users of the outputs of petroleum refineries, comprise, in the main, petrol and domestic fuel oil; the oil which heats a food factory appears under food manufacture. It is not possible to pursue the logic of this approach as far as would be ideal because capital goods represent a final use in empirical input–output tables. Refrigeration equipment, therefore, appears as such, and is not and cannot be allocated to whatever it refrigerates.

The pattern which emerges most clearly from these data is that the construction and motor vehicle industries are much the most voracious users of resources. Together they absorb 50 per cent of steel output, 45 per cent of zinc, about 40 per cent of lead, 38 per cent each of copper and aluminium. By contrast, a number of apparently important uses are quantitatively rather small. Thus, the main oil-using products are things which burn it rather than things made from it, and cars use much more aluminium than aircraft. (Aircraft use rather a lot of lead too. This may be a mistake. If a lot of lead is used in making the kinds of things which are used in making aircraft, our approach will suggest that aircraft are relatively lead-intensive, even if special things for aircraft are relatively lead-free. Our conclusions are vulnerable to errors of this kind.)

In Table 3.5 we consider which are the most resource-intensive products; those products in which the proportion of the total value of output accounted for by direct and indirect use of the resource is greatest. Such a list tends, of course, to be dominated by intermediate goods. Steel tubes are particularly dependent on steel. We have, therefore, excluded all products for which more than 95 per cent of total domestic sales are made to other producers. The six

Table 3.5. *Resource-intensive industries (% of total value of product accounted for by direct and indirect use of the resource)*

	%		%
Aluminium		*Chemical and fertilizer minerals*	
Metal foil	28.4	Fertilizers	11.6
Electrical industrial goods	7.0	Industrial chemicals	3.4
Sheet metal work	6.3	Agricultural chemicals	2.7
Tanks and components	5.7	Plastics	1.5
Trucks and trailers	4.9	Misc. chemical products	1.0
Trailer coaches	4.1	Paints	0.9
Coal		*Copper*	
Federal electric utilities	17.6	Small arms and ammunition	7.7
State and local utilities	6.9	Pipes, valves and fittings	6.5
Metal barrels, drums, pails	1.5	Transformers	3.7
Fabricated plate works	1.3	Motors and generators	3.3
Railroad and street cars	1.3	Welding apparatus	2.8
Sheet metal work	1.2	Switchgear	2.4
Lead		*Petroleum and natural gas*	
Storage batteries	24.5	Refined petroleum products	53.0
Small arms and ammunition	8.4	Gas utilities	27.8
Paints	1.4	Industrial chemicals	6.2
Printing trade machinery	1.2	Air transport	5.2
Metal foil	1.1	Agricultural chemicals	5.0
Industrial chemicals	1.1	Paints	4.2

Table 3.5. *(Contd)*

	%		%
Steel		*Zinc*	
Fabricated plate works	39.8	Miscellaneous hardware	2.6
Railroad and street cars	35.7	Storage batteries	2.2
Sheet metal work	34.1	Small arms and ammunition	1.0
Safes and vaults	34.0	Household laundry equipment	0.7
Metal stampings	29.8	Commercial laundry equipment	0.6
Fabricated metal goods	25.9	Electric housewares	0.5

products which then remain at the top of the list are given in the table. These are the goods on which resource scarcities would exert the greatest pressure; here the incentives for both producers and consumers to find substitutes would be greatest.

These figures are presented in an endeavour to increase the information available to those discussing resource depletion, rather than in support of any particular line of argument. But we suggest that anyone who examines them is likely to obtain a sense of perspective which some apocalyptic writing on the subject appears to lack. When we know that lead mostly goes into car batteries, we realize that if we want to conserve lead it is a good deal easier and more effective to design a car that does not need a lead–acid accumulator than to halt economic growth.

The diversity of experience, both by country and by resource, also suggests that a rather microeconomic approach to the economic theory of exhaustible resources may be the most useful. In the remaining sections of the paper, we pursue an analysis on these lines, using a simple model as our point of reference, but trying not to let it completely dominate the discussion.

3. SOME ECONOMICS OF RESOURCE DEPLETION

The chief question at issue is, we think, whether there is, in the world economic system as it works now, a significant bias towards using resources too rapidly. This question leads on to others about the quantitative extent of any bias, and the measures that might be adopted by nations, independently or in consort, to counteract the bias. One should also consider whether there may be other undesirable aspects of the current system, but we shall concentrate on the simple issue of bias. If we are to discuss it, we must have a model of the system as it works now, and there is no question that prices play an important role in that system.

The basic economic principles of exhaustible resources, and the way in which the price system may be thought to deal with them, was worked out many years ago by Hotelling.[14] More recently, many economists have looked at the issues

[14] H. Hotelling, 'The Economics of Exhaustible Resources', *Journal of Political Economy*, xxxix (1931).

in more detail, using the techniques of control theory, particularly Heal and Dasgupta, Koopmans, Stiglitz, and Dixit.[15] We shall say what we can without going into the more difficult control theory problems.

Consider the owner of a stock of resources, of total amount R, and suppose that he believes the price for this resource at time t will be p_t. He has to incur exploitation costs $c(x, t)$ at time t if he is then extracting resources at the rate x. Assuming that he wants to maximize the discounted sum of his profits, his rate of interest being i, he will relate the marginal cost of extraction at t to the price at t by the equation

$$p_t = c_x(x_t, t) + Qe^{it}. \tag{7}$$

The first term on the right is the marginal cost of extracting the resource. The second term is the imputed cost of drawing on his stock of the resource: this cost obviously rises at a rate equal to the rate of interest because he has the option (at the margin) of lending at interest i instead of keeping the resource in stock. Q is, then, defined as the value, to the owner, of a unit of the resource (not yet extracted) at time 0. Its level is such that he plans to just exhaust his stock. (One modification is required in equation (7): if p_t is too low, the owner will not plan to extract any of the resource at t, and it is permissible in that case that $p_t \leqslant Qe^{it}$. For example, he may plan to exhaust his stock at some date T, because after that the term Qe^{it} is so large that it exceeds the difference between the price obtainable and the marginal cost of extraction.) Equation (7) by no means captures all the important aspects of resource exploitation: in general, extraction costs depend upon the stock remaining, for example. This extension is discussed in the technical appendix. But the form of the relationship is quite general, and the case described is sufficiently rich for us to hang a number of arguments upon it.

Notice that p_t is the price the owner expects to get for his resource: since future markets do not exist for any substantial time ahead, we should not think of the p_t as market-clearing prices in the future. For example, if purchasers of the resource are also price-takers, and if short-run equilibrium is reached fairly rapidly, the actual price—let us denote it by P_t—will be a determinate function of the amount of the resource offered for sale:

$$P_t = f(\Sigma x_t, t), \tag{8}$$

where Σx_t means the total offered for sale by all owners of this particular resource and p_t is the resource-owner's estimate of P_t. Presumably p_t will

[15] The paper by Dixit is as yet unpublished. P. S. Dasgupta and G. Heal, 'The Optimal Depletion of Exhaustible Resources', *Review of Economic Studies* (1974); J. Stiglitz, 'Growth with Exhaustible Resources', *Review of Economic Studies* (1974); T. C. Koopmans, 'Some Observations on "Optimal" Economic Growth and Exhaustible Resources', in *Economic Structure and Development*, ed. H. C. Bos (North-Holland, Amsterdam, 1973).

depend upon the behaviour of P_τ at times τ in the past, and also on other evidence of future demand and supply of the resource.

One circumstance in which resource–owners might be expected to predict prices rather well is when Q is, for most of them, very small, and the market is, therefore, pretty much like a rather competitive market for a non-exhaustible commodity. This is a more likely case than one might have thought: it can arise, roughly speaking, when current consumption of the resource is small relative to total stocks of the resource. A numerical example will bring this out. Let c_x be a constant, taken to be 1 for convenience, and suppose the demand schedule is constant, with price elasticity ϵ: $f(x) = x^{-1/\epsilon}$. Assuming that price expectations are correct, we may as well pretend there is only one resource-owner, with quantity R. Then

$$x_t = (I + Qe^{it})^{-\epsilon} \tag{9}$$

and Q is determined so that $\int x_t\, dt = R$. Thus, if $\epsilon = 1$

$$R = \int_0^\infty \frac{dt}{1 + Qe^{it}}$$

$$= \frac{1}{i}\log\frac{1 + Q}{Q}$$

so that $Q = 1/(e^{iR} - 1)$
if $\epsilon = \frac{1}{2}$

$$R = \int_0^\infty \frac{dt}{\sqrt{(1 + Qe^{it})}}$$

$$= \frac{2}{i}\log\frac{1 + \sqrt{(1 + Q)}}{\sqrt{Q}}$$

so that $Q = 4e^{iR}/(e^{iR} - 1)^2$
Using these formulae we obtain the following table:

iR	Q	
	$\epsilon = 1$	$\epsilon = \frac{1}{2}$
1	0.58	3.68
2	0.16	0.72
4	0.02	0.08
6	0.00	0.01

Thus, when iR is greater than 6, Q is less than 1 per cent of the marginal cost of extraction, and may as well be neglected for practical purposes. The rate at which the resource is depleted is pretty much what it would be if there were no property rights in the resource. If, to take a figure not quite at random, $R = 250$ (i.e. resource stocks are 250 times current consumption of the resource), and the (real) interest rate is 5 per cent, $iR = 12.5$: in that case, it will be 130 years before iR falls as low as 6. The equilibrium price will remain close to the marginal extraction cost until remaining stocks are less than forty times current annual consumption.

The results of this calculation would not be quite so striking if we allowed for increasing demand; but then, for many resources, 250 years' stock is a very low figure to assume, and unity a low estimate for the long-run price elasticity. The point we want to make is simply that when extraction (and transportation etc.) costs are borne in mind there is no reason to expect resource prices to be more uncertain than other prices.

This is important, because if prices are correctly predicted we may conclude that resources are being exploited at an optimal rate. The structure of this argument is familiar to economists, but we give a brief outline of it here.

Resource conservation is an investment in the future. It requires us to give up present consumption for the sake of future benefits. In this it resembles other forms of investment which are undertaken in the economy: in education or in plant and machinery. Now efficiency requires that the returns on all these forms of investment should be the same. Otherwise we could increase consumption both now and in the future by expanding one type of investment and contracting the others. A competitive firm will be led to make exactly the same sort of calculation. It will compare the returns from resource conservation and other investment opportunities, and adjust the volume of each it undertakes so that the returns from each are the same. If not, it could increase its profits by devoting more of its funds to the higher yielding investment. Thus, the calculation which a firm will make in deciding how rapidly to exploit exhaustible resources will be the same as the one society would make if it were choosing an optimal depletion rate on the firm's behalf.

Of course, this argument when carefully specified depends on a number of strong and implausible assumptions. But it is useful to describe the assumptions under which actual and optimal depletion rates would be the same, since this provides a basis for assessing the ways in which actual and optimal depletion rates will in reality diverge. We must now consider a number of possible reasons for such bias.

Neglect of future generations

It is sometimes suggested that leaving resource exploitation to the mercies of the market neglects the interests of our children and grandchildren, or of countries that have not yet become industrialized. But this is a mistake. If prices are correctly predicted, the demands of our children, grandchildren, etc., are being taken into account by resource–owners, who are saving up resources to sell to them when the time comes. True, there may be a general bias in the economy to consume now and leave too little to our children or our future selves. If so it would be reflected in high rates of interest, which will lead to somewhat more rapid depletion of resources.

Many conservationists might take the view that this did describe their position: that the rate of interest was too high as a result of society's 'defective telescopic faculty' (as Pigou described it). But if this is so, it implies that we are undertaking too little investment of all kinds. And this, in turn, carries the implication that the present rate of economic growth is too low, and that we should increase the investment ratio in an attempt to raise it. It is our impression that rather few of those who worry about excessively rapid resource depletion would accept that conclusion, but, if not, they must find some other basis for their intuition. Similarly, we think that the use of natural resources now to benefit Englishmen instead of in a hundred years' time to benefit Indians is of a piece with the other ways in which all factors of production are unequally applied to the good of Englishmen and Indians, and we believe that restraint in using resources would actually be a very expensive way of shifting the balance.

Incorrect price predictions

There is no guarantee that resource–owners will correctly predict resource prices. If owners are on average over-estimating future prices p_t (as compared with the equilibrium prices P_t), they will supply less than the equilibrium amount now, while planning to supply more in the future. This will raise prices currently. So long as price anticipations are governed by past as well as present prices in a positive way—and the assumption of interpolative expectations in the long run is reasonable—higher current prices will mean that a slower rate of increase of prices in the long run is expected. Then supplies will increase somewhat, bringing current prices closer to equilibrium prices: demand responses tend to bring about a rate of increase of the market price which is less than the rate of increase of the equilibrium price, which is itself less than the long-run rate of price increase expected by resource owners. This gap between experience and expectation should narrow in time, bringing supplies and prices closer to their equilibrium levels. This heuristic argument, which suggests that the system has stabilizing tendencies which could be accelerated by speculation, demand and resource–stock forecasting, etc., is, being non-mathematical, inconclusive.

In fact, we seem to observe that the price of resources which are very far from exhaustion are often much higher than the marginal cost of extraction and transportation. At least, recent substantial rises in raw material prices were apparently not related to cost increases. Since the extent to which resource owners want to deliver currently depends on their price expectations, and these cannot be very firmly based, there is scope for very great divergence of actual prices from equilibrium prices. If our initial argument suggests there are forces for convergence towards equilibrium, it does not suggest that the adjustment of actual towards equilibrium prices would be particularly rapid. For example, it is surely possible for over-supply to persist for many years before the drying up of major sources gives prices the upward push needed to bring about revision of expectations.

The question that has to be considered is whether there is any reason to expect a particular bias, either upwards or downwards, in the formation of expectations. While no very general answer seems possible, our basic equation (7) does provide an important pointer. As we have seen, the second term, Qe^{it}, will not be important when the total stock of the resource is still large; that is to say, the equilibrium price will not be much greater than the marginal cost of extraction. It does not seem likely that an actual price *below* the extraction cost could persist for long. Therefore, if there is a bias, it must be in the upward direction, keeping the price higher than it should be, and thus bringing about under-exploitation of the resource.

We can see this by returning to equation (9), and asking what would happen if resource–owners believed the resource would be worthless in future, so that they dumped it on the market until price fell to the level of extraction costs. In that case, price would remain constant at 1, so that over the next 150 years total resource use would be 150 times current consumption. If they had anticipated the whole spectrum of future prices correctly, so that the optimum path was followed, cumulative resource use over this period would be 149.87 times current consumption at $\epsilon = 1$, and 149.73 times current consumption at $\epsilon = \frac{1}{2}$. In other words, if there is more than 100 years' supply of the resource remaining, the maximum extent of possible bias towards over-depletion is negligible.

At a later stage, however, one might expect a tendency for the price to be too low. For when the term Qe^{it} becomes important, the equilibrium price, having previously been constant or perhaps falling, should begin to rise, and the rise would accelerate until the price is eventually growing at a rate approaching i (if the resource has not already ceased to be used). It is plausible that people will tend to underestimate distant prices if in fact the rate of price rise is going to accelerate. In that case, there will be a bias towards over-exploitation, which might be significant in the period when the second term in equation (7) begins to be significant. Probably this argument does not deserve too much weight, since as a matter of fact expectations of the kind we are discussing tend to be revised discontinuously, and there may well be over-reaction when it is realized that resource–rent elements in costs are beginning to be important. On balance, we think that incorrect price expectations are more likely to cause under-exploitation of resources than over-exploitation.

Risk aversion

For the sake of clarity, we have not mentioned explicitly the uncertainty about future prices, resource supplies, etc., which tend to dominate discussions of resource depletion. One effect of this uncertainty is that the resource-owner is more uncertain about the price he can expect to obtain for his resource in the future than about the price he can expect to obtain now (periods of unusual current confusion apart). If he is risk-averse, he will tend to discount future prices (as he sees them) somewhat, and deliver more of the resources now than he would have done if he had known for certain that future prices would be what he expects. Since the socially important benefits of the resource will be widely distributed, not being especially large for any one person, it may be argued that the private owner's risk aversion implies an undesirable bias towards present depletion.

For example, if half the profits of the resource-owner are paid to government, as a result of taxation, the owner and the government receive the same amounts. The government may have no reason to be risk-averse in regard to what, from its point of view, are small risks; while the owner, if for some reason he has failed to diversify his own portfolio and share the risks of his resource ownership with others, may act in a very risk-averse manner. This argument assumes fixed taxation, and that the income of the resource owner himself is not of significant social value. There are, also, important cases where a country, much of whose national wealth is in a particular natural resource, may be more risk-averse than the owner. Economists have perhaps been too ready to assume that in general, and without regard to the particular ways in which costs and benefits are distributed, privately motivated decisions will be too risk-averse. In the present case, a good deal of work requires to be done—allowing, as John Flemming has been doing, for the effects of risk aversion on exploration as well as on depletion—before one can be sure even of the direction in which uncertainty biases depletion, far less its quantitative importance.

In this connection, we note that it may not pay even risk-averse owners to explore for new reserves to the extent that would be socially desirable, because the information about reserves is actually valuable to others besides themselves. As with most production of information, there are external economies, and, therefore, there is a presumption that too little is invested in research.

Ownership uncertainty

Another way in which uncertainty is important is when the owner is uncertain about the future security of his rights to the resource, or the profits from it. If the resource–owner believes there is a significant risk that the resource will be taken from him with imperfect compensation—say by government expropriation—he has an incentive to deplete his stocks sooner rather than later. Oddly enough, private owners appear to have better prospects of compensation than public owners: a deposed sheikh has no further rights to the oil still in the ground; nor can a government defeated at the polls expect to gain credit or patronage from as yet unexploited reserves. But, although political instability could in this way lead to over-exploitation, the case of oil suggests that transfer of ownership to the resource's own nation can be expected to eliminate any bias to exploit the resource too rapidly.

Monopoly

Many resource–owners appear to earn very considerable profits even when the world stock of the resource is many hundred times current consumption. Our earlier analysis suggests that this is strong evidence of monopoly, which may, of course, be exercised by implicit collusion, or by local government taxes.

Ignoring uncertainty for the moment, a profit-maximizing monopolist would wish to choose his rates of sale x_t so that

$$f(x_t) + x_t f'(x_t) = c_x(x_t) + Q'e^{it}, \tag{10}$$

Q' being at such a level that $\int_0^\infty x_t dt = R$. Initially, when $Q'e^{it}$ is small, x_t will, of course, be smaller under monopoly. More generally, we can show that, when f and c are independent of t, and the elasticity of demand is constant, x_t is smaller at any given stock of resource than it would be if there were no monopoly. This is proved in section 3 of the technical appendix. When the elasticity of demand is not constant, one can construct counter-examples, but under-depletion may be regarded as the general rule. Thus, under monopoly, probably, in cases where a natural resource has, or a group of resources subject to explicit or implicit collusion have, a rather inelastic demand, there is a strong bias towards under-exploitation of the resource, as compared at any rate with the competitive outcome.

The distribution of benefits

In a competitive economy without government intervention, part of the benefits from the resource accrues to the owner; in monetary terms, using our previous notation, the present value is QR. It seems that in the case of most natural resources, this gain goes either to relatively few very rich individuals, or to governments. If we are talking about possible economic policy, it would be very odd to regard the gains accruing to a rich oil-well owner in the same way as gains accruing to an average user of petrol or heating oil. The natural approximation is to regard the gains to a private owner as having no social value. Gains to government revenue might be regarded as having a high or low value depending upon the nation or government in question: how should one regard Malaysia, Chile, and the United States from this point of view? But take the case where the resource is privately owned within our country. Then the government should be advised to tax away the whole of the QR that accrues to the owner. In practical terms, this means imposing a tax on purchases of the resource which is, at time t, just equal to Qe^{-it}. If the government does that, the rate of production and consumption of the resource will be just the same as before intervention, but the rents accrue to government, not to the owner of the resource. The peculiarity of the tax is that it rises quite rapidly towards the end of the life of the resource.

In fact, since exploitation costs are different for different resource–owners, taxation of resource rents faces the same practical difficulties as taxation of land rents. Instead, the government might use a profit tax, taking almost all the profits accruing to the resource–owner after payment of extraction costs. The interesting point is that the rate of depletion should not be affected by the government intervention. We may put the conclusion this way: if we attach no weight to rents accruing to resource–owners, it will be possible to increase welfare by altering depletion rates in either direction; but the tax which leads to the greatest increase in welfare will leave depletion rates unchanged. In this sense, the chief income-distributional argument leads to no presumption of bias.

In the common situation where the resource is subject to some degree of monopoly, and the profits accrue abroad so that profit taxation is not a practical possibility, buyers can only get together and threaten to cut demand, for example by taxation, and they are very likely to have to carry out the threat. In this sense, one might want to see a further reduction in the rate of resource depletion, even though it is already less than optimal, when regarded from a different point of view. But, just as in the competitive case, it is possible that the taxation measures of buyers will not, if properly judged, change rates of depletion, but will simply transfer some of the profits (those arising from ownership of the resource rather than the opportunity to restrict supply) to the buyers' governments.

Taxation

Tax treatment of resource-extractive industries is typically rather complicated, but its effect on the rate of resource depletion may be substantial. The simplest case is that in which resource-owners are subject to a profits tax on receipts less operating expenditures like other producers. In that case the tax will not affect the rate of depletion if it is expected to be applied at a constant rate over time. But a profits tax will, of course, reduce the rate of return a firm obtains from its other investments, and hence lead it to invest too much in conservation relative to other forms of productive investment. Since rates of profits tax are usually high, this effect may be substantial.

The tax, while not affecting the time profile of receipts, will reduce its size, and this will have a disincentive effect on exploration and development expenditure. Thus the existence of a profits tax may lead to a strong bias towards insufficiently rapid resource depletion: less of the resource will be discovered, less of what is discovered will be developed, and what is developed will be produced too slowly. The complexities of actual tax structure, which involve special tax treatment of development expenditures and of resource-related profits, and divergences from our simplified profits tax on other activities (such as free depreciation) will modify and may mitigate this general bias.

We should note also that the governments of producing or consuming countries often impose revenue-raising taxes on the use of exhaustible resources.

The effect of this is essentially equivalent to increasing the degree of monopoly in resource extraction, and as we argue above this will tend to lead to insufficiently rapid depletion.

4. ECONOMIC POLICY

The most important point in the previous section, which is demonstrated more generally in the technical appendix, is that the price of a resource ought to be little more than the marginal cost of extracting and transporting it, unless the resource is rather close to exhaustion. Thus, the analysis of economists who have concentrated on the case of zero extraction costs, though technically important, is quantitatively misleading.[16] We can best summarize the significance of our proposition, and the rest of our arguments, by outlining the policies that appear to be implied by them.

(*a*) The general trend of the argument is that resource depletion often takes place too slowly because of monopoly power exerted by resource-owners. Because of demand inelasticity, it is quite likely that the losses arising from monopoly are very large, although it must be remembered that they are sustained chiefly by the industrialized countries, and those who make considerable use of resource-intensive products. The usual measures against monopoly, including negotiation with the governments of countries within which the monopoly profits accrue, are presumably desirable.

(*b*) In many cases it is desirable to impose taxes on exhaustible resources, not because they are being depleted too rapidly, but as a means of taxing pure profits generated by the resource. These policies, if properly carried out, would not change the rates of depletion.

(*c*) Since most of the value of resource stocks is in the last few decades of their life, these taxes on resource use do not become significant until only a few decades of resource life remain (at then current rates of depletion). There is no particular argument in favour of taxing the use of natural resources as such when hundreds of years of reserves exist. (This is not to say there may not be other reasons for imposing commodity taxes on sales of exhaustible resources and commodities made from them, reasons of the same kind which lead one to favour taxes on jewellery, cars, and cigarettes.)

(*d*) If monopoly power is expected to grow, or taxation is expected to become more difficult (for example, because of its magnitude), there may be a case for government stockpiling of exhaustible resources; but we have not yet explored this possibility.

---

[16] We note also that the case of monopoly gives a misleading impression when extraction costs are ignored, because in that case the constant-elasticity demand function implies that a monopolist depletes at the same rate as a competitive industry. This follows because the effect of monopoly is identical to the effect of a proportional tax on sales, which is simply a profits tax when extraction costs are zero.

(e) Since there may be reasons for inadequate amounts to be spent on research into resources reserves (or methods of exploiting them), there is a case for governmental and intergovernmental subsidy of surveys and research in this area.

(f) Since it is difficult for participants in resource markets to predict resource prices correctly, governments and intergovernmental agencies can contribute to optimal resource use by gathering the information—about existing proved and probable reserves, demand, including substitution possibilities, development of substitute sources, etc.—and developing econometric models to predict resource prices.

Our analysis may have seemed sketchy to those who are prepared to be impressed by the vast apparatus deployed by devotees of world dynamics, and unaware of the iceberg of economic analysis which lies behind the kind of work we have done. We are uncomfortably aware that to many scientists such arguments will look rather casual, and yet will actually be incomprehensible. We would challenge defenders of the large simulation and forecasting models to consider whether they really do understand the arguments we have put forward, and how the work of the modellers has been or could be an answer to them. For ourselves, we find no reason to prefer the kind of work done by the global dynamicists to the more staid analysis undertaken by economists. We confess to having provided no forecasts of the very long-run effects of natural resource depletion. Such forecasts would have very little basis, and, therefore, would be subject to enormous errors. They are neither a necessary nor a sufficient basis for policy recommendations. An approach that begins from policy questions shows what kind of data and evidence are most needed, and where further research is likely to be most fruitful.

Economists are well aware that the world's store of exhaustible resources is limited. But in the light of the arguments presented here, we wish to suggest that there is a real danger that the world's resources are being used too slowly. No doubt some materials are being used prodigally: but in general we believe that the interests of future generations will be better served if we leave them production equipment rather than minerals in the ground. In the currently topical case of oil, the arguments that the world is using too little rather than too much seem irresistible.

Technical Appendix

1. It will be useful to derive the theories of optimal and equilibrium depletion of a resource, for the case where future costs and prices are known with certainty. We consider optimality first.

A rather general way of formulating the problem is to assume that the society wishes to maximize total utility, summed over time, where utility at any time depends both upon the rate of use of the resource x and the total stock remaining R:

$$\max W = \int v(x_t, R_t, t)\, dt. \tag{11}$$

The case of a fixed stock, the extraction costs of which are independent of the amount remaining, is a limiting, but unrealistic, case of equation (11).[17] A special case is where utility is a function of consumption $u(z_t)$, where

$$z_t = f(k_t, x_t, t) - \dot{k}_t - c(x_t, R_t),$$

in which k is the capital, f is the output, and c is the cost of extracting the resource; capital accumulation is chosen optimally, k_t is a fixed function of t, and the maximand can be written in the form of equation (11). More generally, it is natural to write (11) in the form

$$\max W = \int v(x_t, c(x_t, R_t), t)\, dt \tag{12}$$

(with $v_x > 0$, $v_c < 0$, $c_x > 0$, $c_R < 0$, $c_{RR} > 0$), and to note that c, being measured in terms of a conventional numeraire (the consumption good in the special case just mentioned)

$$i_t = -\frac{dv_c}{dt}\frac{1}{v_c}, \tag{13}$$

is the rate of interest, which will be the rate of time preference or social discount rate in the optimum.

Turning to the maximization of equation (12), we could simply apply Euler's equation (since $x = -\dot{R}$), but we prefer to use the integral for R,

$$R_t = R_0 - \int_0^t x_\tau\, d\tau, \tag{14}$$

and deduce that a variation of the depletion rates gives

$$
\begin{aligned}
W &= \int_0^\infty \left[(v_x + v_c c_x)\delta x_t - v_c c_R \int_0^t \delta x_\tau\, d\tau \right] dt \\
&= \int_0^\infty \left[v_x + v_c c_x - \int_t^\infty v_c c_R\, d\tau \right] \delta x_t\, dt.
\end{aligned}
\tag{15}
$$

Thus, at the optimum, since $\delta W \leqslant 0$ for any feasible variation,

$$v_x + v_c c_x \leq \int_t^\infty v_c c_R\, d\tau \tag{16}$$

with equality if $x_t > 0$. Using (13), we can write this as

$$\frac{v_x}{-v_c} = c_x - \int_t^\infty \exp\left(-\int_t^\tau i_\theta d\theta\right) c_R\, d\tau \tag{17}$$

so long as the optimal $x_t > 0$. When the left-hand side is smaller than the right, x_t must be zero. (Recollect that $v_c < 0$.)

The term on the left-hand side of (17) is the marginal rate of substitution between use of the resource at t and the numeraire at t; c_x is marginal cost; and the integral is the

---

[17] The limiting case has $v_R = 0$ for $R > 0$, $v = -\infty$ for $R < 0$.

generalization to the present problem of the term Qe^{it} that appeared in the text. Consumption of the resource will fall to zero when (17) is satisfied for $x = 0$. In general, this might happen more than once, depending on how v depends on t. For simplicity, let us concentrate on the case where, once x falls to zero, the resource is never used again. Exploitation of the resource stops when

$$\frac{v_x(0, c(0, R), t)}{-v_c(0, c(0, R), t)} = c_x(0, R) - c_R(0, R) \int_t^\infty \exp\left(-\int_t^\tau i_\theta d\theta\right) d\tau$$

$$= c_x(0, R) - c_R(0, R) 1/i \tag{18}$$

in the case of a constant rate of interest i. At this point, one would expect $-c_R(0, R)$ to be large, and the marginal rate of substitution of the resource for the numeraire to greatly exceed the marginal cost. But consider the situation when stocks are still considerable—or, to be more precise, when $-c_R$ is small. If $-c_R$ will be small for a period sufficiently long for $\exp(-\int_t^\tau i_\theta d\theta)$ to have become small, the integral in (17) will be small, and the exhaustibility of the resource is, therefore, approximately irrelevant until significantly large $-c_R$ is in sight. This is the general proposition illustrated for the limiting case by the examples in the text.

It should be noted that there are now resources for which $-c_R$ is already quite significant and likely to become large. In such cases, we have from (17) an approximate condition for optimality:

$$\frac{v_x}{-v_c} = c_x + \frac{-c_R}{i}, \tag{19}$$

where $-c_R$ is an average value of the effect of resource depletion on costs in the medium future, and i is a long-term rate of interest. Perhaps one can get the best impression of the last term in (19) if one writes it in the form

$$\frac{c}{iR} \cdot \frac{-Rc_R}{c} = \frac{\text{annual extraction costs}}{\text{imported interest on resource stock}}$$

$$\times \text{ elasticity of costs with respect to resource stock.} \tag{20}$$

2. Turning to equilibrium, it is not necessary for us to rework the analysis, but only to reinterpret what has already been done. In competitive equilibrium, producers are supposed to maximize total discounted profits at given prices. Thus, the owner of a resource will want to maximize

$$\int_0^\infty \exp\left(-\int_0^t i_\theta \, d\theta\right) \{p_t x_t - c(x_t, R_t)\} \, dt, \tag{21}$$

which is an expression of the same mathematical form as (12); i_t is now interpreted as the market interest rate, and p_t is the price obtainable for the resource at t. Notice that the analogue of (13) holds. Applying our previous analysis, we have as our condition for equilibrium

$$p_t = c_x - \int_t^\infty \exp\left(-\int_t^\tau i\theta d\theta\right) c_R \, dt, \tag{22}$$

which is effectively the same relationship as (17).

In fact—and this is no more than basic welfare economics tells us—the equilibrium will be the optimum if actual prices p_t are equal to the social marginal rates of substitution $v_x/(-v_c)$, and market interest rates are equal to social rates of time preference.

3. Next, we look at the case of a monopolistic resource-owner who manipulates prices for his own long-run advantage. The general case appears to be somewhat complicated. We restrict ourselves here to the special case mentioned in the text, where there is a time-independent demand function

$$pt = f(x_t), \qquad f' < 0 \tag{23}$$

and the monopolist takes it that his marginal revenue is a constant fraction λ (< 1) of the price. (He would be right if f were a constant elasticity function.) Furthermore, there is a constant rate of interest, and the stock of resource is assumed limited although extraction costs are independent of R. Thus, equilibrium is given by

$$\left. \begin{aligned} \lambda f(x_t) &= c_x(x_t) + Q e^{it} \qquad \text{for } x_t > 0 \\ \int_0^\infty x_t \, dt &= R_0 \end{aligned} \right\} \tag{24}$$

We can use these equations to obtain a relationship determining x_0 as a function of R_0,

$$\begin{aligned} iR_0 = i \int_0^\infty x_t dt &= \int x_t d[\log \{\lambda f(x_t) - c_x(x_t)\}] \\ &= -x_0 \log (\lambda f(x_0) - c_x(x_0)) + \int_0^{x_0} \log \{\lambda f(x) - c_x(x)\} \, dx \end{aligned} \tag{25}$$

on integrating by parts, and assuming that x_t becomes, or tends to, zero eventually.

Equation (25) shows us how x_0 depends on λ for given R_0. Differentiating, we obtain

$$x_0 \frac{\lambda f'(x_0) - c_{xx}(x_0)}{\lambda f(x_0) - c_x(x_0)} \frac{\partial x_0}{\partial \lambda} = - \int_0^{x_0} \left\{ \frac{f(x)}{\lambda f(x) - c_x(x)} - \frac{f(x_0)}{\lambda f(x_0) - c_x(x_0)} \right\} dx.$$

With our assumptions that $f' < 0$ and $c_{xx} > 0$, the coefficient of $\partial x_0/\partial \lambda$ is positive, and $f/(\lambda f - c_x) = (\lambda - c_x/f)^{-1}$ is an increasing function of x, so that the integral on the right is negative. Thus,

$$\partial x_0/\partial \lambda > 0. \tag{26}$$

This means that *an increase in the degree of monopoly*, i.e. a reduction in λ, *reduces x_0, the rate of resource depletion.*

Note particularly that this means monopoly reduces the rate of resource depletion, given the level of resources. It does not mean that the monopolist will plan a future rate of sale that is always less than would have been planned by a competitive industry. But our proposition is the interesting one, since it says what reduced monopoly power, or reduced taxation, should bring about, whenever it should be achieved.

4

The Economic Uses of Utilitarianism

Some economists, when evaluating alternative economic policies, are utilitarians. At any rate they look at something they call the total utility of the outcome. This paper is intended to argue in favour of this procedure.[1] It may be as well first to exemplify it.

An interesting question is how much income ought to be redistributed from those with high wages and salaries to those with low wages. To answer it, one can set up a model in which each individual's utility is a numerical function of his net income, after taxes and subsidies, and of the quantity of labour he supplies. Each individual, supposedly knowing how his income depends on the labour he supplies, decides how much to supply by computing what will maximize his utility. All these labour supply decisions taken together determine the output of the economy. A redistributive system, consisting of taxes and subsidies, is feasible provided that the output of the economy is sufficient to provide for public and private expenditures, private expenditures being determined by private net incomes. The object of the exercise is to find which feasible redistributive system yields the greatest total utility.

This is not the place to defend the simplifications of such an economic analysis, far less to discuss how it might be improved. Even within the model outlined, assumptions as to the kinds of taxes and subsidies that are possible have a substantial effect on the results. I shall want to return to this aspect later, by way of illustration. The first issue is whether it is possible to specify numerical utility functions, in order to carry out such an analysis of redistributive policies.

This chapter was originally published in Amartya Sen and Bernard Williams (eds.), *Utilitarianism and Beyond* (Cambridge: Cambridge University Press, 1982). A public lecture with the same title was given at University College, London, in February 1977. The main arguments were the same, but it is doubtful whether there are any common sentences. Nevertheless I am grateful for that invitation and the opportunity it provided to attempt to articulate an economist's defence of utilitarian methods, as used in much contemporary welfare economics. I should like to acknowledge valuable discussions on these questions with J. R. Broome, P. A. Diamond, and A. K. Sen, and their comments on the first draft of this paper. Comments by P. S. Dasgupta and Q. R. D. Skinner were also useful.

[1] There have been so many papers presenting versions of utilitarianism, or defending it against criticism (many of which I have read only cursorily or not at all), that it is hard to defend writing another. But there are differences of emphasis from the major statement by Vickrey (1960), and more substantial differences from Harsanyi (1953, 1955, and later books), both of whom discuss these matters from the point of view of economic problems. Taking that point of view, I found that I wanted to deal with a number of matters not discussed by Hare (1976) and Smart (1973) in their statements.

The utility functions are partly tied down by the assumption that individuals' labour supplies are determined by utility maximization. Observations on labour supply behaviour can therefore provide some check on the correctness of the utility functions; but only to a limited extent. Many distinct utility functions predict the same behaviour. When choosing a particular specification, do economists believe they are talking about quantities of pleasure less pain? If so, they show remarkably little interest in devising methods of actually measuring pleasure and pain. Edgeworth's ingenious suggestion that an absolute unit of utility is provided by the smallest perceptible change for the better has not found much favour.[2] I shall want to return to the question why this is not an acceptable measure of utility—as I think it is not—despite being the only one that seems to provide an objective basis for interpersonally comparable measurement.

Sen, in a recent discussion of utilitarianism (1979*b*), says, that he will take 'utility ... to stand for a person's conception of his own well-being', a formulation which, though adopted specifically to emphasize its factual character, might be accepted by many economists as an adequate definition. But on one count it is not acceptable; and on another it may not be, if its meaning is made more precise. In the first place a person's *own* conception of his well-being should not always determine, other things being equal, the outcome for him. In the economic analysis sketched above, it was assumed that it should: that assumption might be wrong. People sometimes have mistaken conceptions of their well-being. At least the conception must somehow be purified of obvious errors of foresight or memory. More, one ought to be willing to entertain the possibility that some experiences are not usually correctly valued by the individual: that, in certain respects, people do not know what is good for them. For example, it has been claimed that many give too little weight to future experiences. Provided that the modification of measured well-being thus contemplated is empirically based, it is surely convenient to let the term 'utility' describe the well-being rather than the conception of it. Sen would, I think, regard this as too elastic a definition of 'utility', and prefers to make the same kind of point by saying that non-utility information about outcomes is sometimes relevant; though he would go further and allow 'non-utility information' that is not simply empirical evidence as to what is in fact a person's well-being. At any rate, I would use 'utility' in a wider sense, and think that other economists sometimes do too.[3]

Sen is right to emphasize the factual nature of utility. Yet his definition does not help one understand how it might be numerically measured. This is the

---

[2] Edgeworth (1881) was very clear that one must provide an operational definition of utility. Sen (1970*a*, ch. 7) gives references, and adds to the stock of negative opinions. Ng (1975) has analysed the possibilities further in an interesting way.

[3] Sen (1970*a*, p. 98, 16) has remarked on the way that economists customarily extend the meaning of 'utility', as compared to the classical utilitarians. Indeed, most economists recognize that the psychological theory on which utilitarianism was first based is incorrect. The term 'utility' is still used to suggest that, in many ways, it can be used as Bentham used it.

second count on which the definition may not be acceptable. It is precisely the difficulty utilitarians have in explaining how their method for evaluating outcomes could be effected in specific instances, so as to yield definite conclusions, that makes many people sceptical of the method. As far as I can see, there is one and only one way in which measurability of utility can be achieved. A person who conceives of himself in two alternative states can have preferences regarding different combinations of outcomes for himself in these states. He can arbitrarily fix two very similar outcomes A and B in state 1 as the standards of comparison, A being assigned zero utility and B unit utility. The utility difference between outcomes P and Q in state 2 is taken to be unity if he is indifferent between the combinations (A, Q) and (B, P). In this way the relative utility of all outcomes in state 2 can be calibrated, to within the standard of accuracy given by the degree of similarity of A and B. To calibrate utility in state 1, the same procedure is used, with particular P and Q in state 2 as the standard outcomes.

This must be what economic utilitarians have usually had in mind. Ways of calibrating utility that are equivalent to it are to be found in the writings of Irving Fisher, Paul Samuelson, William Vickrey, and John Harsanyi, among many others.[4] For the method to be satisfactory, it is necessary:

(1) to identify situations in which individuals express preferences among outcomes for alternative selves; and to show that the observer should always deduce essentially[5] the same utility function if he applies the method with different standard outcomes, or to different situations in which there is choice on behalf of alternative selves;
(2) to show how the utility function obtained allows interpersonal comparability; and
(3) to explain why this way of measuring utility leads to a way of evaluating alternative economic outcomes that has moral force.

In what follows, I endeavour to deal with these issues. Then I discuss some implications, and deal sketchily with some possible objections. The paper concludes with a summary.

1. ALTERNATIVE SELVES

What a person plans to do can be described as the totality of what he plans to do at particular times, and under particular circumstances. He could be a rational economic man, whose choices always conform to an underlying preference ordering, without it being logically possible to assign numerical utilities to his actions and experiences in particular time-periods and circumstances. For it to be possible to introduce numerical measurement of utility in the way just

---

[4] Fisher (1927), Samuelson (1937), Vickrey (1945), Harsanyi (1953).
[5] i.e. apart from addition of a constant of multiplication by a positive constant, transformations that evidently do not matter.

mentioned, it is necessary that his preferences regarding what he will be doing at one particular time in one particular set of circumstances be independent of what he may be planning for all other times and circumstances. For someone whose preferences display this degree of what economists have come to call separability, his choices can be represented as maximizing some function of the utilities generated in the various periods and eventualities of his life. Symbolically, he can be said to maximize $W(\ldots, u(c_s, s), \ldots)$, where c_s represents his 'consumption'—i.e. all he does—in state s, and s is a short period of time in one particular possible development of his life.

It is unlikely that many people have preferences conforming to this model. Everything that has to do with life as a connected whole—such as habit, memory, preparation for future action, anticipation, achievement and failure— seems to have been ignored. But one can imagine inviting the person to consider what he would choose for one state if there were to be no consequential effects of outcomes in other states, e.g. if consumption in that state would be neither foreseen nor remembered. He could even be invited to consider choices among alternative memories, backgrounds, and prospects, as well as the more obvious choices among consumer goods and work activities. In this way one can hope to assign utility to the consumption of alternative selves in different states. It remains an empirical issue whether persons performing these thought-experiments have separable preferences. It appears plausible that they should, for what is happening in one state is, by the terms of the experiment, irrelevant to experience in other states. The possibility of doing the thought experiment shows what utility is. It involves insisting that what is good for me can be analysed into experiences in different states, experiences in a larger context certainly, but experiences that are tied to time and circumstance.

Standard utilitarianism requires something more, for in that method it is required that individual preferences can be represented as a sum of utilities, not just as a function of utilities. This is the case if the individual's preferences about consumption in any two states, taken together, are independent of what he may be planning for other states. Thus one requires a stronger formulation of the principle that what is going to happen at another time, or under different circumstances, should be ignored, except in so far as memory, anticipation, and so on are affected. This is an empirical claim, but one that is not, or, at any rate, not entirely, a claim about the behaviour of people in the ordinary business of life. It is a claim about the preferences that they would have if they had clearly understood the artificial choices that would have to be put to them, and had honestly observed and appreciated the consequences of these choices for themselves. We might insist that, for example, experiences that will have been forgotten ought to have no influence on preferences for activities at yet later times, even when early plans are being made. Better for utilitarianism if we can claim that in fact they would have no influence. The evidence in favour of that view is primarily that it seems so unreasonable that such forgettable experiences should have relevance to choices about later times.

The argument I have put is that utility must be given meaning, if at all, in terms of individuals' preferences. It is often said that the utilitarian view sees people as though they conformed to the model of rational economic man. Certainly people often do not conform to that model. They do many things that they would not if they had carefully, coolly, and in full knowledge of the facts, considered what to do, and been able to do what they had decided to do. Experiences determine behaviour, as well as considered choices. But we can ask what people would do if they could succeed in conforming to the simple rational-choice model and use that as a standard for judging what is best for them, individually.

Many of the difficulties about memory, anticipation, and so on, which can make the model of rational man seeking to maximize the sum of his utilities over time seem implausible, are avoided if instead one considers choice under uncertainty, where the individual is asked to choose the lives he would follow under different circumstances. This way of deducing utility has been the subject of many contributions.[6] It is, after all, natural to assign probabilities to possible worlds, and consumers do sometimes enter into well-considered insurance contracts. In many situations, actual decisions under uncertainty appear not to conform well to the utility model, even when there is no obvious doubt about the relevant probabilities.[7] This is hardly surprising, for skill at taking decisions under uncertainty is rare and requires training. The merit of considering choices among probabilistic lotteries for alternative selves, only one of whom will actually occur, is that what is planned for some alternatives would plausibly have no effect on considered preferences regarding what happens to the other alternative selves. Such emotions as regret have to be discounted. Nevertheless, it should be possible to perform the thought-experiments required to calculate utility.

While choices among alternative uncertain outcomes can define and measure utility for alternative lives taken as wholes, it would be more useful for many purposes if one could assign utility to subperiods of lives, as my earlier discussion suggested one could. If one can deduce utility from consideration of altern- atives for one set of circumstances only, it would be a pity if choices among lotteries did not maximize the mathematical expectation of the lifetime sum of utilities. Again there is no logical necessity that they should. An independence property analogous to that mentioned above is required.[8] Specifically, prefer- ences with respect to outcomes in two possible states of nature at one time should be independent of what is planned for all other states of nature, and all other times in these states of nature; and, similarly, preferences with respect to outcomes at two times in one state of nature should be independent of all other plans. As far as I can judge, it does not seriously violate observation of carefully

---

[6] Vickrey (1945), Harsanyi (1953, 1955). The method has been criticized by Pattanaik (1968) and Sen (1970a, Chapter 9).   [7] Kahneman and Tversky (1979).
[8] Gorman (1968).

considered consumer decisions in real-life situations to assume this independence property. As in the previous case, it seems reasonable, and therefore is probably true, that what is irrelevant would not be allowed to influence rational choice. It surely might become difficult to maintain the assumptions in the face of an accumulation of certain kinds of evidence. If so, we should bear in mind the possibility that a weaker kind of independence might hold for rational preferences. In that case, it would still be possible to define utility, and show how it could be measured; but it would be best for individuals to maximize not the sum of utilities, but some other function of utility levels. A reconstruction of utilitarianism would then be required and possible.

The deduction of utility from individual behaviour presupposes that, at some level, man has immutable preferences. It is sometimes said that this assumption is contrary to fact. Many of the tastes expressed by consumers are, it seems, easily influenced: does advertisement change tastes, or change the consumer's knowledge of his own tastes, one way or the other, and how in any case can we hope to decide that? Do we not often find, when important issues are at stake, that it is very hard to be sure what our preferences are? If all taste is whim, these are not the data on which to base large moral judgements. These issues deserve extended treatment, but one can surely hope to conclude that most people do have firm preferences for many possible choices, and also that they do not have firm or certain preferences for many choices that a utilitarian would like them to be able to make. Utilitarianism will sometimes be usable, but not always: I shall develop this claim in a later section. It should be emphasized that uncertainty about one's tastes, and consequent openness to suggestion, whether from advertisers or music critics, is not evidence that firm preferences are absent. One does not know what visiting the Taj Mahal is going to be like: but, when one is there, uncertainty about tastes is much diminished.

Yet it is not right to let utility rest entirely on individual tastes. Though the meaning of utility, and the calibration of the utility function, is, in principle, derived from individual preferences, it must be possible to allow for convictions about what is good for one that, though unshakable, are nevertheless mistaken. In formulating my preferences, I may be unable to free myself from the conventional view that more money would always make me better off; yet there may be good evidence that, beyond a point, more money leads similar individuals into alcoholism, excessive self-concern, and other phenomena that I would, if I understood them, dislike. Such facts should influence the utility function. It must be legitimate, in principle, to advance arguments in favour of modifying the utility function that exactly represents my existing tastes. It cannot be wrong in principle to try to get someone to do what would be better for him even though he does not recognize it: but there must be some basis for saying that, with full understanding, he would come to accept the rightness of the altered utility function, or, rather, of the underlying preferences. Those who jump to the defence of consumer sovereignty at any mention of attempts to supplant individual tastes must be asked to wait for a later section in which policy procedures will be discussed. At the present stage of the argument, only the evaluation of outcomes is under consideration. There may well be arguments in favour of *procedures* that respect individual preferences even if there are none in favour of moral evaluations that completely respect them.

Having seen how utility can be defined, we can see why the proposal to measure utility in units of minimum perceptible improvement is not acceptable. On many occasions, a just perceptible improvement in musical performance means much more to me than a just perceptible quantity of drink; there is no reason to regard this as an ill-informed or unconsidered preference. There is no plausible connection between intensity of preference and the number of perceptible steps, even for one individual considered in isolation.

2. INTERPERSONAL COMPARISONS

Having constructed utility for an individual, we can proceed to apply it to evaluating outcomes in a society of identical individuals.[9] Such a society exists only as a theoretical model. It is often said to be of little importance: 'Any genuine attempt at evaluating social welfare must take into account the differences in preference patterns of individuals' (Pattanaik 1968). I believe that this view is seriously misleading if it is thought to imply that the model society of identical individuals is irrelevant to our moral judgements on social policy. In this section, I shall argue that there are at least three reasons why the simplest case of social choice is important.

In the first place, we can make the model correspond to the real world much more closely than is initially apparent. This can be done by extending the concept of identity, which is I suppose fairly straightforward in the present context, to that of isomorphy. It will be shown that it is possible to regard individuals who are, by reason of age, skills, sex, strength, or culture, apparently very different, as nevertheless identical for the purposes of social judgement. This effective identity is achieved by setting up an isomorphism between the different individuals, relating like experience to like experience. In this way, it is possible to apply the utilitarian methodology in a disciplined way to such issues as that of income distribution alluded to at the beginning of the chapter.

The second, and somewhat less important, use of the simple model is as an approximation to more complex worlds, in which individuals, though not identical, or even isomorphic, are rather similar. What judgements one would make for the more complex world should be similar to the judgements that are correct for the simpler world.

The third reason why the simple model is useful is that it provides a test for other moral theories. If it were agreed that utilitarianism tells us which outcomes to prefer in the simple world of identical individuals, then any acceptable

---

[9] Vickrey (1960) highlighted this case, but even he moves on quickly to worry about non-identical (and non-isomorphic) individuals.

moral theory must come to the same conclusions in this special case. I claim that this use of the model leads to the rejection of the standard alternatives to utilitarianism.

The argument of utilitarianism in a society of identical individuals runs as follows.[10] For any one of the individuals, the sum of his utilities describes his considered preferences regarding the lives of his alternative selves. Therefore in choosing among outcomes for himself alone, i.e. with outcomes the same for everyone else, he ought to choose the pattern of outcomes with greatest total utility. With individuals identical, there is no reason for treating a fully described outcome for one of his own selves any differently from that outcome for the self of another individual in corresponding circumstances. Roughly speaking, the totality of all individuals can be regarded as a single individual. Therefore total social utility, the sum of the total utilities of the separate individuals, is the right way to evaluate alternative patterns of outcomes for the whole society. That should be the view of any individual in the society, and therefore also of any outside observer.

None of the three steps of this argument is a logically necessary implication. The first step, from preferences to individual values, has been challenged by Sen,[11] who suggests one might, for example, decide it is right to have greater equality of utilities in one's own life than maximizing the sum of utilities implies. I understand that, for Sen, utility is defined in a different way from the one I have used, though I remain unconvinced that there is a different way of doing it. If Sen's form of argument were applied to the first step in the social argument as I have presented it, I should want to object when 'moral intuition' presents itself as a hair-shirt morality in conflict with the individual's preferences: that intuition is not moral, and should be resisted. There is more to be said about equality, and I return to it below.

The second step in the argument is an expression of impartiality and universalizability, which I take to have enormous weight in matters of morality. Certainly there are circumstances in which loyalty to one's own self, or to one's family, should be given special weight, even in the absence of explicit or implicit contracts and promises (which anyone would agree sometimes have utility). But that seems to me to have to do with the right way for an individual to behave, taking account of the influence of behaviour on future experience, understanding, and behaviour. Thus, we are in the realm of procedures rather than the evaluation of outcomes. In the evaluation of the outcomes of public policy, loyalty, and other kinds of partiality should be excluded.[12]

---

[10] A related approach is taken by Parfit (1973).

[11] Sen (1979b, pp. 470–1), commenting on Parfit's argument.

[12] Hare (1976, ch. 1) argues against Williams (1973) that pursuing one's own projects (almost) regardless can hardly count as moral behaviour. The same must be true of any restriction on the group whose ends are to count. Where the Williams case has force is in the suggestion that acting as a utilitarian is inconsistent with what is best for one as an individual, not just because effects on others must be counted, but because this kind of selflessness is inconsistent with the pursuit or

The final step in the argument treats moral principles as though they were proposals put forward for assent or rejection, and appears to suggest that rejection would nullify them, perhaps even rejection by one person. We are accustomed to think that when Tom says *A* is right and Dick says *B* is wrong, then they are disagreeing. One reason why that is a valuable way to think is that it encourages Tom and Dick to explore their evidence and arguments and the sources of their 'disagreement'. But if these values were otherwise recognized, it is hard to see why it should be advantageous to insist that the logic of values follow the same rules as the logic of fact or deduction. Some degree of acceptance of the usage 'good in Tom's opinion' rather than 'good' understood absolutely seems reasonable, even desirable. In this spirit, when moral judgements are agreed (after 'serious consideration') matters should be concluded in that sense. That is why I find the final step persuasive.

We must now extend the argument to cover models of societies consisting of isomorphic individuals. Two individuals are isomorphic if they are described in formally identical terms by means of changes in the variables that describe their situations. The simplest example of isomorphy, which is indisputably acceptable, is that of individuals who are identical except for being born at different times or (perhaps) in different places. More disputable examples are:

(1) A strong man might be regarded as identical to a weak man, except that the same subjective effort by the former exerts twice the force.

(2) A child may be regarded as an adult for whom a unit consumption of ice-cream means twice as much and a unit consumption of quiet conversation half as much as for a 'normal' adult; and so on for all aspects of consumption. This isomorphy is commonly used in econometric analysis of consumer behaviour, and is important for the construction and interpretation of 'family equivalence scales'.[13]

(3) A person receiving a high annual labour income may be related isomorphically to another person receiving half of his earned income by supposing that they are identical except that the first takes half as much time to earn a pound sterling as does the second. In the models of redistribution, briefly described at the outset, a plausible, though still very approximate, correspondence between the model and reality is obtained in this way.

The idea of picturing a complex reality, where individuals are, by common agreement, not at all similar to one another in many important respects, by

achievement of certain high ends. A possible example is artistic creation. More generally, it is unlikely that having everyone constantly attempt to add to social utility is an arrangement calculated to maximize social utility. But I want government ministers to try to maximize utility, even if their personal sense of achievement is gravely compromised, their crazy industrial dreams unfulfilled: the ministers' utility deserves no significant weight in our assessments of utility in comparison to the millions who may suffer. To this extent, the morality of economic policy is simpler than that of personal life or culture.

[13] Deaton and Muellbauer (1980, ch. 8).

mapping it to a formal model in which individuals are, by suitable change of variables, isomorphic to one another, has proved to be rather powerful in recent economics. The technique has limitations. One cannot claim that every important question of economic policy can be handled by such a model—only that many can. When they can, utilitarianism provides a method for evaluating policies.

The possibility of setting up an isomorphism between individuals does not automatically make their utility functions comparable. The very fact that there is some identifiable way in which they differ, so that one is seen to be rich, another poor, allows us the mathematical possibility of relating the utility functions in all kinds of ways. Some simple formalism is needed to bring this out. Suppose that, for everyone, utility is a function of disposable income, labour earnings, and labour efficiency; and that we want to use the isomorphism that treats labour earnings divided by labour efficiency as meaning the same thing for different people. Then we write the utility function as[14]

$$u\left(x, \frac{z}{n}\right), \quad x = \text{disposable income}$$
$$z = \text{labour earnings}$$
$$n = \text{labour efficiency}.$$

But why should one not write

$$nu\left(x, \frac{z}{n}\right)$$

instead? The two individuals still have the same preferences in regard to x and z/n, so there is no economic–empirical way in which we can distinguish the two procedures. I have no doubt that the first is much the more plausible procedure. This means that I think there is some warrant for the belief that the iso-morphism relates similar experiences; that when two persons, rich and poor, have the same z/n, the same x means the same to both, in terms of subjective feelings. The particular example may suggest that this is an easier matter to settle than it usually is. Some economists seem to have made a particular choice of utility correspondence by inadvertence rather than after due consideration of the possible alternatives. That does not mean that there is no evidence to allow intelligent choice: it is an empirical matter, to which the kinds of evidence economists usually use is not relevant.

The conception of an economic model as an imperfect picture of the real society suggests also how utilitarianism could say something about societies of non-isomorphic individuals. In two economies that are fairly similar (say, one a simplified version of the other), the way we evaluate outcomes should be fairly similar too. More precisely, the method of evaluation should be a continuous

---

[14] For the sake of the illustration, let us take u to be always positive.

function of the collection of individuals that constitute the society.[15] Therefore one should not strongly disapprove of a method of evaluation applied to a simplified but apparently rather similar society in which individuals are isomorphic.

There are ways in which utilitarianism can be extended to societies of non-isomorphic individuals. So long as individuals can accurately imagine themselves being other individuals, each individual has a basis for his values in preferences by the method already described. A normal white adult may not be very good at imagining himself a child, a genius, or a black, if he is not one already. That does not affect the principle. The difficulty is to decide what should be done about the different utility functions that different, though careful and prudent, individuals would presumably discover in their preferences. This will be discussed further below. The point I want to make here is that, whatever general method of evaluation is proposed to deal with societies of non-isomorphic individuals, it must be consistent with utilitarianism when society consists of isomorphic individuals. Plainly, this is not true of a maximin criterion, or of the more sophisticated, less precise version of this criterion advanced by Rawls.

It is interesting to note that a theory of the maximin type runs into difficulties that appear to be more severe than those of utilitarianism. The trouble is that it is sometimes not possible to use preferences about outcomes for alternative selves who are different, such as man and child, clever and stupid, or whole and handicapped, to determine whether, with specific outcomes, one or other of the two selves has greater utility. Relative marginal utilities can be deduced from preferences, but not relative absolute utilities. I can reveal how much I think money would help me if I had no arms, but not how much I would pay to avoid losing them—unless I can affect the probability. Claims about which self is better off cannot therefore be checked, however imperfectly, by market behaviour revealing preference; and indeed, the meaning of such claims must be in doubt. I think such a claim involves an implicit belief that there is an isomorphism of some kind between the individuals.

3. EQUALITY

As is quite well known, utilitarianism implies that, in general, a society of isomorphic, though not completely identical, individuals should *not* have equal utility. Thus, the equal treatment implicit in the utilitarian procedure does not guarantee equal outcomes, or even equally valued outcomes. An example will show what is involved. Consider a society of two individuals, Tom and Dick, who have the same utility as a function of income, and of hours worked. Incomes are spent on output, which comes from the labour of these two. One

[15] At this level, continuity is an ambiguous notion, and anyway one has something much more demanding, but less precise, in mind: that one can roughly tell whether the likeness of two economies is great enough for the utility costs of following the optimal policies for one in the other to be small enough to justify terminating the analysis.

hour of Tom's labour produces twice as much as an hour of Dick's. Utility obeys the law of diminishing marginal utility—more income makes extra income less valuable, and less work makes extra leisure less valuable. It is also reasonable— because apparently realistic—to assume that more income would make them more eager to substitute leisure for income.[16] Utilitarianism says that, in the ideal state of this society, Tom and Dick are called upon to work such amounts, and, given such income, that producing an extra unit of output would reduce either one's utility by the same amount.

A fairly easy piece of economic theory shows that (i) Tom, the more productive, should work more than Dick; but that (ii) Tom's income should be less than Dick's; and indeed that (iii) Tom's utility should be less than Dick's.[17] The principle is, of course, 'From each according to his ability, to each according to his need'; and it turns out that utilitarianism can recommend that this redistribution should be extremely radical. The wrong reaction is to reject utilitarianism as failing to conform with our moral intuitions. I, for one, had no prior intuitions about this simple economic problem, moral or otherwise. Anyway, appeal to prior moral opinions or beliefs is inappropriate. If utilitarianism is to be a valuable moral theory, one had better be surprised sometimes by its conclusions. Instinctive rejection of the conclusions of a utilitarian argument can be a good reason to check the argument, particularly for omitted considerations, not a reason for rejection.

A more interesting response to the example, which is intended, after all, to represent an important feature of human society, is to point out that, under a utilitarian government, Tom, if he acts selfishly—as well he might, however he votes—will pretend to be no more productive than Dick. That should not be hard for him. Therefore the proposed allocation, subject to the constraint that Tom should not be worse off than Dick—so as to ensure that he has no incentive to dissemble his productivity—is one that provides each with the same utility (though Tom still works more than Dick). This is the way in which utilitarianism is most likely to recommend equality: as the weakest way of not destroying incentives. Where incentives must be positively preserved—as when the government can identify Tom and Dick only by the amounts they choose to produce, so that the one who works more (Tom) must not want to work less and be content with Dick's income—then inequality can go the other way, with the more productive having more utility.

The example emphasizes that utilitarianism can lead to all kinds of inequality. It can even recommend inequality between individuals who are similar in all respects—truly identical, not just isomorphic. It is theoretically possible that randomizing the income tax would increase total utility.[18] This is a sophisticated version of the simple idea that two castaways in a rowing boat with one

---

[16] The technical, and precise, statement of these assumptions is that utility is a concave function of income and leisure, and that leisure is not an inferior good.

[17] This is proved in Mirrlees (1974, p. 258).   [18] Weiss (1976).

oar may be wise to allocate most food to the oarsman, even if they both like rowing.

It is the case that many people are affected by inequality, and have tastes about it. Therefore inequality in the society affects their utility, in some ways increasing it, but mostly, I suppose, decreasing it. We have, to my knowledge, no estimates of the magnitude of these effects. Indeed, hardly any economist has addressed the question of formulating the kind or kinds of inequality people care about. The indexes of inequality developed by statisticians and economists have been carefully and thoughtfully examined by statisticians and economists, but not checked for relevance. None of them corresponds well to the fairly well substantiated, though not formally precise, notion of relative deprivation.[19] One reason for not finding out how much people care about which kinds of inequality is the conceptual difficulty of determining the influence of external facts on utility. Probably one can do little better than ask oneself and others how much they would pay for changes in inequality. Another reason for not attempting an empirical analysis of the influence of inequality on utility is the difficulty of distinguishing values from preferences. Inequality can affect the morally insensitive, by inducing envy, pride, or discomfort at adjusting to the behaviour of the rich or the poor. But these are feelings that have some tendency to melt away under the close self-scrutiny required. On the other hand, many have an aversion to inequality which is the outcome of moral considerations, and this aversion might be increased by self-scrutiny. Is this an aspect of preferences, or a matter of values not relevant to the estimation of utility? All of this emphasizes the practical difficulty of estimating the effect of inequality on utility: it does not imply that inequality should be allowed for separately and additionally.

Inequality, like torture and slavery, attracts strong moral and political feelings. Expressed values about it form a test of moral soundness within systems of intellectual, social, and political commitment. So someone might be apprehensive about committing himself to a moral calculus that cannot be guaranteed to come up with conclusions that fit. Commitments to concrete policies may be necessary for influence and action. But in considering methods of policy evaluation, nothing should be taken for granted, everything subjected to critical analysis. Inequality would in any case have to be analysed, because it is quite unclear, in advance, what it is, i.e. how it is supposed to be measured. This makes clear, what I suppose is in any case an evident requirement, the need to derive badness of inequality from something else—if not its unpleasantness, or the utility-increasing effects of redistribution, or its bad incentive effects, then what?

Lest it be suspected that these considerations do not fully deal with inequalities, I readily agree that there are other ways, besides the direct effect on individual utilities, in which inequality comes into a satisfactory analysis of economic policies. The processes of public and private decision-taking are

[19] Runciman (1966).

affected by the inequalities in society. Thus, the connections between the levers of economic policy and the outcomes whose utility is to be measured vary with the degrees and kinds of inequalities. The kind of thing I have in mind is that special tax allowances designed to encourage the movement of resources to where they are needed in the medium term may provide interested parties with resources to resist desirable later removal of these tax allowances. As everyone knows, inequality can be associated with concentration of power to pursue narrow interests.

One would surely not capture considerations of this kind by combining utilities in a social maximand that tries to make them equal, as with the maximin welfare function. There are many less extreme ways of giving weight to the equality of utilities.[20] They have no rationale, because they are not directed at any of the identifiable flaws in simple utilitarianism: that it neglects the unpleasantness of inequality, and its effects on the distribution of power. In any case, these external effects of inequality may be quite small. Most of us, most of the time, are totally forgetful of inequality and our places in it. It will, and should, require some empirical arguments and evidence to change the models that economists are inclined to treat currently as standard.

None of this discussion is intended to argue that people's utility is likely to display a low degree of aversion to inequality in the distribution of goods. Despite what was said at the outset about utilitarianism implying the desirability of inequality, the optimal degree of inequality in utilities may be rather small. That depends on the form of utility functions that describe preferences among alternative selves. If people would be very reluctant to plan different levels of well-being for themselves in different states of nature, e.g. depending on the wage or family responsibilities they would then have, it follows that the sum of utilities will, as a criterion, display considerable aversion to inequalities of incomes, or indeed of utilities. I think that people behave in ways that make them seem not very averse to large variations in their fates, e.g. by gambling, for excitement, or not having enough of the right kinds of insurance, because they are in these areas ill-informed, not very rational, and anyway rightly sceptical about the terms insurance companies offer. Their coolly considered preferences would be much more inequality-averse, and not only for the reason—irrelevant to social utility—that adjustment to new standards of living is costly.

4. UNLIKE INDIVIDUALS

It would be good if utilitarianism (or anything else) could provide us with a compelling method of evaluating outcomes for a society in which people have (substantially) different utility functions. But it is hard to conceive how

[20] Sen (1979*b*) describes one class of such methods, namely replacing the sum of utilities by the sum of a concave function of utilities, as 'Mirrleesian'. I wish he had not. At the time I used it, I had no intention of avoiding the addition of utilities, but rather of looking at the effect on optimal policies of having a more inequality-averse utility function.

individuals, who have, after careful, critical, well-informed study, discovered in themselves essentially different assessments of utility, could have their moral opinions aggregated by a morally compelling social decision function. There is no way of deducing what is absolutely good from what Tom thinks good and Dick thinks good. A social decision function could be a device for cutting the argument short, because it is agreed to be too costly to go on postponing a decision in the hope of reaching agreement by further consideration of arguments and facts. The criteria for an aggregation device to be good for that purpose are quite different from the criteria for a good method of combining individual tastes into evaluations of social welfare.

It seems likely that discussion and further consideration among people who have abandoned entrenched positions, or at least among open-minded utilitarians, will tend to reduce divergence among their evaluations of social outcomes. I do not rely on the well-known socio-biological methods of achieving agreement through Johnson's principle that 'No two men can be half an hour together, but one shall acquire an evident superiority over the other.' We might rather imagine discussion about utilities taking the following form:

Tom: I have been thinking very seriously about my pension and savings, and about my car insurance and investments, and I find that the square root of consumption[21] accurately represents my utility now and in the future, so long as I am healthy. Of course, you, Dick, are a rather different kind of person from me, not sleeping so long and enjoying giving parties and all that. I've thought about what I would feel being you, and I must say, I think you get more out of the things money can buy than I do, even if you don't get much pleasure from long walks in the country. Allowing for that, I can see your utility is the square root of consumption multiplied by 1.2.

Dick: It's nice of you to allow me that extra twenty per cent, but I don't think you realize how boring I often find these bigger parties are. If I could agree with the square root of consumption, I would say that ten per cent was ample allowance for my monetary needs. But I find my utility is proportional to the cube root of consumption, and it does not seem to me that being you would make any difference to that. It would just mean that I spent a bit less time on enjoying the things money can buy. My enjoyment of extra consumption in the week really does fall off faster than your square-root function suggests, and I must say I would not coolly take quite as many risks with my investments as that utility function implies.

Tom: Well, it seems people aren't as like one another as I thought, and I do see, now you draw my attention to it, that a big dip in your consumption affects you relatively more than it would me. You've persuaded me that the cube root is right for your utility function. And now I realize why we were disagreeing about ten or twenty per cent. It wasn't conventional politeness: after all, we *are* Utilitarians. It was just that I had last year's consumption in mind, before we got our rises. Now that we both get £10,000 a year, I suggest that we measure our consumption in pennies, thus making us both millionaires,

---

[21] On almost any reasonable view, the utility functions discussed by Tom and Dick are far from sufficiently inequality-averse. The square root and cube root were chosen for their relative euphony—compared to 'minus the reciprocal of the square of consumption', say.

and allow us to take the square root of consumption for my utility, and eleven times the cube root of consumption for yours.[22]

Dick: Fine, but now what about Harry? He claims his utility function reaches its maximum at £5,000 a year, and that he can see we aren't any better off for being richer than that either. I know he means it, and behaves accordingly, but it's absurd...

Thus, reasonable men may tend towards agreement; but they need not— Harry will be a problem. Apparently disagreement can be about facts, or about the way the facts are experienced. When there is disagreement, quick compromise seems to be the right answer, because there is no right answer.

5. OPEN JUDGEMENTS

The utilitarian method does not answer all questions. Is there any reason to think we are in a better position to decide how much to spend on kidney machines than we are to decide how long this universe will last? That one does not know the answer to many moral questions is a reason for developing systematic procedures. But even after attempted analysis, not knowing may be the correct answer. Two examples of this are the treatment of handicapped people, and the question of optimum population.

In his lectures on inequality (1973), Sen has directed particular attention to the allocation of resources between whole and handicapped individuals. If nothing will improve the well-being of the handicapped individual, e.g. because he is permanently in coma, the utilitarian finds it easy to say that no further resources should be transferred to that person. By continuity, he must be prepared to contemplate providing the handicapped individual with rather few resources if his capability of enjoyment is very low—say because he is conscious for only a minute a day. That is how I would allocate resources to myself in such a state, if I could control the allocation, and consequently I take the same view about others. Most cases of handicap are, however, unclear. It is difficult to get inside the other person's skin when the other person's situation is very different from one's own. There are no good tests of whether one's beliefs as to what it is like are correct. It would not be unreasonable to refuse to make a judgement. Then one should not mind what is done about the handicapped person. Maybe others know what is right, and even if one thinks they do not, having no basis for an opinion, one cannot object to whatever they decide to do. The best hope for comparison is partial isomorphism: in some situations people are alike, but some people have good information for appreciating modulations into states of handicap.

Consideration of extreme proposals—half the national product to the blind, nothing for the deaf—strongly suggests that total ignorance is not a sustainable position about handicap. Rather, uncertainty about the nature of the experiences should be expressed by means of probabilities, and the mathematical expectation

---

[22] Martin Gardner addicts will want to work out what rise they got.

of utilities used as the measure of utility. But the example helps to show what moral ignorance implies.

In the case of variations in population size,[23] moral ignorance may appear to be almost irresistibly the correct position. To get preference information relevant to comparing states of the society with different numbers, the individual has to perform a thought experiment in which the number of alternative selves varies, and to decide which of the two positions he prefers. I suppose this is the purified question of choice about length of life. Can one consider this question without the corruption of thinking about it as one's own life, rather than variation in the number of experiences? The value of a year of human life has been discussed,[24] and estimated, and used in cost–benefit analysis by the Road Research Laboratory. If one can decide about that without—as in practice one does—getting it confused with the impact on family, etc., then one has a utilitarian basis for evaluating alternative population sizes.

It seems to me a reasonable position that one cannot decide whether one would like another year of life, nor therefore whether more or fewer people in the world is desirable. It is not reasonable to take this position totally. Another year of bliss is good: a year during which one is torturing others is certainly bad. Correspondingly, more people at a high standard of living is good, and more people at very low standards of living is bad. Specifically, one might argue that the population of the world is now too large, without claiming that no one should have a child until it has come right and without wishing to claim that one knew what the optimum size of the world population is. But even in so difficult a case as this, extensive research on the value of human life might make so open an opinion on the question difficult to sustain.

6. PROCEDURES AND OUTCOMES

There are many reasons why a utilitarian should not, in practice, insist that the utility functions he has come to believe in must govern economic policy, even if he has the power to do so. I (like others) may have made random errors in estimating utility functions, neglecting evidence, or even simply calculating wrongly. I may have a tendency to be biased in favour of, or even against, people like myself. It might be costly, in my view, to have my evaluation prevail. In order to gain influence for my evaluations (which, allowing for the first two points, are nevertheless my view of what is right), it may be necessary to agree to some degree of influence for the considered valuations, or even the tastes, passions, and whims, of others. All of these are reasons for taking account

---

[23] I am referring to variations in the population of a closed society, e.g. the whole world. Migration from one country to another poses no special problems for evaluating outcomes, just for getting people to accept right policies.

[24] See Jones-Lee (1976). This approach, which assumes expected utility maximization, has been criticized by Broome (1978*b*) on the ground, unacceptable to a utilitarian, that it is in principle impossible to compare the value of a life with the value of (mere) commodities.

of the views of others; and they are reasons why the external observer should adopt evaluations influenced by the evaluations of all individuals. The first two reasons, at least, are also, be it noted, reasons why evaluations of outcomes for a particular society should be influenced, perhaps rather strongly, by the assessments of those who do not belong to it, e.g. those who lived a long time ago. On the basis of all these considerations, I conclude that a utilitarian should not be much in favour of dictatorship, even benign dictatorship; but that he should favour methods of compromise among alternative evaluations, in which the weight accorded to particular evaluations is related to the quality of the arguments on which they are based. Intuitions, beliefs in rights, and responses to polls and questionnaires should count only to the extent that political necessity warrants—which may be considerable.

This line of argument goes some way to meet the claim that, to paraphrase Diamond (1967*a*), 'Utilitarianism is concerned only to evaluate outcomes, whereas in considering, e.g. the determination of economic policies, we should also be concerned about the process of choice.' This claim has often been advanced, but the example Diamond provides is a particularly cogent one. It compares a policy which always leaves Tom with a low utility and Dick with a high to one in which Tom and Dick experience an equivalent lottery. It must be agreed that a utility-maximizing government may not be the best kind to try to have, because it would not in fact be a utility-maximizing government, but would respond to pressures, have quirks, thoughtless tastes, loyalties to particular interests, etc., just as governments always have had. It may be better to have a constitution-constrained government, in part controlled also by conventions that it should consult all concerned groups on issues, and not discriminate against particular groups, or between people who are in certain superficial respects alike. One way of making it hard for officials to be corrupt, or partial, is to insist that large classes of people be treated the same. This conflicts with crude utilitarianism. In Diamond's example, the government might or might not plan to give different people different positions in the income distribution in different states of nature. If I happen never to get a good job from the government, I shall probably suspect it of bias. If I *knew* it was utilitarian, I would not, and would have no grounds for objection to always being the less fortunate one.

A rather different claim, that utilitarianism (or indeed a larger class of doctrines) is inconsistent with the proper respect of individual liberty, is Sen's liberalism argument[25] that utilitarianism conflicts with rights to free choice by the individual over matters that are his own prerogative. Sen's argument rests on a moral intuition that in some kinds of situation Tom's pleasure from Tom's consumption should count for more than Dick's pleasure from Tom's consumption. I try not to suffer from moral intuitions, but I can think of

---

[25] This is expounded in detail in Sen (1970*a*, ch. 6*), and the discussion in Sen (1979*b*) is particularly illuminating.

reasons why we should give less weight to evidence that Dick's utility is affected by Tom's consumption than to evidence that Tom's utility is so affected, e.g. that it is cheap for Dick to pretend; and of reasons why publicly known decision procedures should give less weight to Dick's negative feelings about Tom's consumption, e.g. that these are feelings it is possible, and desirable, to discourage. Note that it is possible for some, perhaps any, of us to stop being upset by someone doing something we believe to be wrong. This in no way weakens the force of our disapproval. There is no virtue, very much the contrary, in being miserable about wrong things happening; unless we need that as motivation to act to diminish wrong. Stopping Lewd reading his book because his reading it will make Prude unhappy seems undesirable because Prude could just decide not to be unhappy. If that is not the case, and Prude is incapable of not feeling sick at the reading, and it cannot be kept from him, then Prude is as much a consumer of the reading as Lewd, and non-reading is better. This argument is a utilitarian one, provided that I am allowed the rather elastic sense of utility that makes utilitarianism an acceptable doctrine. It provides some strong reasons for ignoring some external effects. Indeed, a utilitarian should be prepared to agree that liberties are extremely important, as protection against the personal and other biases that affect policy and its contact with individuals.

Utilitarianism does not give an instant answer to the question what kind of constitution, bill of rights, or government is optimal. It is first a way of providing optimal answers to questions from an ideal government. On the question of optimal government, some work remains to be done.

7. SUMMARY

Utility is a way in which the considered preferences of an individual, regarding allocation to his alternative selves, can be described. For the purposes of evaluating outcomes for the individual, it may have to be somewhat modified, so that it need not exactly coincide with his preferences.

In a society of isomorphic individuals, i.e. individuals who are the same with respect to some way of comparing their experiences, the outcomes of economic (or social) policies ought to be evaluated by adding their individual utilities, because everyone ought to agree to have every other individual treated as one of his alternative selves.

Any acceptable method of moral evaluation should agree with utilitarianism at least in the case of a society consisting of isomorphic individuals.

Economic models with isomorphic individuals can provide quite useful pictures approximating the real world. Using such a model, the sum of utilities is a reasonable maximand to use for choosing economic policies to be applied to the real world.

Utilitarianism can be extended to societies with non-isomorphic individuals, but in these cases it is likely to be necessary that some conventional method of compromise among different utility functions be used.

In extreme cases, it may be that there are no grounds for moral choice at all, so that, in such a case as that of population size, there are no grounds for objecting to one size or another, within a wide range.

Utilitarianism should not attempt to answer all questions simply by maximizing utility and assuming governments and individuals will meekly play their allotted roles. Using total utility as a criterion, one can go on to examine questions about the optimal information to use in determining economic policies, and the optimal system of economic government by individuals behaving realistically.

It might even be suggested that one could study the optimal economic advice to give, this being in general not the advice that would, if adopted, maximize utility. But that I would resist, believing that economists, like real people, cannot be trusted to give advice unless it is subject to the checks of publishable analysis.

BIBLIOGRAPHY

Allais, M., 1947, *Economie et Interêt*, Paris: Imprimerie Nationale.

Allingham, M., 1975, 'Towards an Ability Tax', *Journal of Public Economics*, 4, pp. 361–76.

Anscombe, F. J. and Aumann, R. J., 1963, 'A Definition of Subjective Probability', *Annals of Mathematical Statistics*, 34, pp. 199–205.

Anscombe, G. E. M., 1958, 'Modern Moral Philosophy', *Philosophy*, 33, pp. 1–19.

Archibald, G. C., 1959, 'Welfare Economics, Ethics and Essentialism', *Economica*, 26, pp. 316–27.

Arrow, K. J., 1950, 'A Difficulty in the Concept of Social Welfare', *Journal of Political Economy*, 58, pp. 328–46.

—— 1951, *Social Choice and Individual Values*, John Wiley and Yale University Press. 2nd edition, 1963.

—— 1953, 'Le rôle des valeurs boursières pour la repartition la meilleure des risques', *Econometrie*, 11, pp. 41–8. Translated as Arrow 1964.

—— 1963, See Arrow 1951.

—— 1964, 'The Rôle of Securities in the Optimal Allocation of Risk-Bearing', *Review of Economic Studies*, 31, pp. 91–6.

—— 1971, *Essays in the Theory of Risk Bearing*, Amsterdam: North-Holland Publishing Co.

—— 1973, 'Some Ordinalist-Utilitarian Notes on Rawls' Theory of Justice', *Journal of Philosophy*, 70, no. 9, pp. 245–63.

—— 1974, *The Limits of Organization*, New York: W. W. Norton and Company.

—— 1977, 'Extended Sympathy and the Possibility of Social Choice', *American Economic Review*, Supplementary issue of the Proceedings, pp. 219–25.

—— 1978a, 'Extended Sympathy and the Possibility of Social Choice', *Philosophia*, 7, Sec. 2, pp. 223–37. This is a longer version of Arrow 1977.

—— 1978b, 'Nozick's Entitlement Theory of Justice', *Philosophia*, 7, pp. 265–9.

Asch, S., 1956, 'Studies of Independence and Conformity. I. A Minority of One Against a Unanimous Majority', *Psychological Monographs: General and Applied*, 70, no. 9.

d'Aspremont, C. and Gevers, L., 1977, 'Equity and the Informational Basis of Collective Choice', *Review of Economic Studies*, 44, pp. 199–209.

Atkinson, A. B., 1974, 'Smoking and the Economics of Government Intervention' in *The Economics of Health and Medical Care*, edited by M. Perlman pp. 428–41, ch. 21, London: Macmillan.

Barry, B., 1973, *The Liberal Theory of Justice*, Oxford: Oxford University Press.

—— 1979, 'And Who Is My Neighbor?', *The Yale Law Journal*, 88, pp. 629–35.

Basu, K., 1979, *Revealed Preference of Government*, Cambridge: Cambridge University Press.

Bentham, Jeremy, 1843, *The Works of Jeremy Bentham*, edited by John Bowring, vol. 8, *Chrestomathia*, Edinburgh: William Tait.

—— 1948, *An Introduction to the Principle of Morals and Legislation*, Oxford: Blackwell.

Bergson, A., 1938, 'A Reformulation of Certain Aspects of Welfare Economics', *Quarterly Journal of Economics*, 52, pp. 310–34.

Berlin, Isaiah, 1969, *Four Essays on Liberty*, Oxford: Oxford University Press.

Bernholz, P., 1974, 'Is a Paretian Liberal Really Impossible?', *Public Choice*, 20, pp. 99–107.

Boudon, R., 1977, *Effets Pervers et Ordre Social*, Paris: Presses Universitaires de France.

Bowles, Samuel and Gintis, Herbert, 1977, *Schooling in Capitalist America*, New York: Basic Books.

Brandt, R. B., 1955, 'The Definition of An "Ideal Observer" Theory in Ethics', *Philosophy and Phenomenological Research*, 15, pp. 407–13; 422–3. This paper constitutes a discussion of R. Firth's essay in vol. 12 of the same journal (see Firth 1952). Also included is a reply by Firth, and some further comments by Brandt.

—— 1959, *Ethical Theory*, Englewood Cliffs, N.J.: Prentice-Hall Inc.

—— 1963, 'Towards a Credible Form of Utilitarianism', *Morality and the Language of Conduct*, edited by H.-N. Castaneda and G. Nakhnikian. Detroit.

—— 1979, *A Theory of the Good and the Right*, Oxford: Oxford University Press.

Broome, J. A., 1978a, 'Choice and Value in Economics', *Oxford Economic Papers*, 30, pp. 313–33.

—— 1978b, 'Trying to Value a Life', *Journal of Public Economics, 9, pp. 91–100*.

Buchanan, Allen, 1975, 'Revisability and Rational Choice', *Canadian Journal of Philosophy*, 3, pp. 395–408.

Buchanan, J. M., 1976, 'The Justice of Natural Liberty', *Journal of Legal Studies*, 5, pp. 1–16.

Buchanan, J. M. and Tullock, G., 1962, *The Calculus of Consent*, Ann Arbor, University of Michigan Press.

Burston, W. H. (ed.), 1969, *James Mill on Education*, Cambridge: Cambridge University Press.

Calabresi, G. and Bobbitt, P., 1978, *Tragic Choices*, New York: Norton.

Cohen, G. A., 1977, 'Robert Nozick and Wilt Chamberlain: How Patterns Preserve Liberty', *Erkenntnis*, 11, pp. 5–23.

Cyert, R. M. and DeGroot, M. H., 1975, 'Adaptive Utility', in *Adaptive Economic Models*, edited by R. H. Day and T. Groves, New York: Academic Press.

Daniels, Norman, 1979, 'Wide Reflective Equilibrium and Theory Acceptance in Ethics', *Journal of Philosophy*, 76, pp. 256–82.

Dasgupta, P., 1980, 'Decentralization and Rights', *Economica*, 47, no. 186, pp. 107–24.

Dasgupta, P. and Hammond, P., 1980, 'Fully Progressive Taxation', *Journal of Public Economics*, 13, pp. 141–54.

Dasgupta, P., Hammond, P. and Maskin, E., 1979, 'The Implementation of Social Choice Rules: Some General Results on Incentive Compatability', *Review of Economic Studies*, 46, no. 2, pp. 185–216.

—— 1980, 'A Note on Imperfect Information and Optimal Pollution Control', *Review of Economic Studies*, 47, pp. 857–60.

Deaton, A. S. and Muellbauer, J., 1980, *Economics and Consumer Behaviour*, Cambridge: Cambridge University Press.

Debreu, G., 1959, *Theory of Value*, New York: John Wiley.

Deschamps R. and Gevers, L., 1978, 'Leximin and Utilitarian Rules: A Joint Characterisation', *Journal of Economic Theory*, 17, pp. 143–63.

Dewey, John, 1943, *The School and Society*, Chicago: University of Chicago Press.

—— 1946, *The Problems of Men*, New York: Philosophical Library.

Diamond, P. A., 1967a, 'Cardinal Welfare, Individualistic Ethics, and Interpersonal Comparisons of Utility: A Comment', *Journal of Political Economy*, 75, pp. 765–6.

—— 1967b, 'The Role of a Stock Market in a General Equilibrium Model with Technological Uncertainty', *American Economic Review*, 57, pp. 759–76.

Dixit, A. and Norman, V., 1978, 'Advertising and Welfare', *Bell Journal of Economics*, 9, pp. 1–17.

Donagan, Alan, 1977, *The Theory of Morality*, Chicago: University of Chicago Press.

Drèze, J. H., 1962, 'L'utilité sociale d'une vie humaine', *Revue Française de Recherche Operationelle*, pp. 93–118.

—— 1970, 'Market Allocation Under Uncertainty', *European Economic Review*, 2, pp. 133–65.

—— 1974, 'Axiomatic Theories of Choice, Cardinal Utility and Subjective Probability: A Review', in *Allocation under Uncertainty: Equilibrium and Optimality*, edited by J. H. Drèze, London: Macmillan, ch. 1, pp. 3–23.

Duncan, Otis Dudley, 1967, 'Discrimination Against Negroes', *Annals of the American Academy of Political and Social Science*, 371, pp. 85–103.

Durkheim, Émile, 1956, *Education and Sociology*, translated by Sherwood Fox, New York: The Free Press.

Dworkin, Ronald, 1977, *Taking Rights Seriously*, Cambridge, Mass.: also London: Duckworth, 1977, A new impression (corrected) with an appendix came out in 1978, Duckworth.

—— 1978, 'Liberalism', in *Public and Private Morality*, edited by Stuart Hampshire, Cambridge: Cambridge University Press.

—— 1981, 'What is Equality? Part One: Equality and Welfare', *Journal of Philosophy*.

Edgeworth, F. Y., 1881, *Mathematical Psychics—An Essay on the Application of Mathematics to the Moral Sciences*, London: Kegan Paul.

Elster, J., 1976, 'A Note on Hysteresis in the Social Sciences', *Synthèse*, 33, pp. 371–91.

—— 1978a, *Logic and Society*, London: Wiley.

—— 1978b, 'Exploring Exploitation', *Journal of Peace Research*, 15, pp. 3–17.

—— 1978c, 'The Labour Theory of Value', *Marxist Perspectives*, 1, no. 3, pp. 70–101.

—— 1979, *Ulysses and the Sirens*, Cambridge: Cambridge University Press.

—— 1980, 'Un historien devant l'irrationel; Lecture de Paul Veyne', *Social Science Information*, 19, pp. 773–803.

—— (forthcoming), 'Belief, Bias and Ideology', in *Rationality and Relativism*, edited by M. Hollis and S. Lukes, Oxford: Blackwell.

Engels, F., 1975, *The Condition of the Working Class in England*, in Marx and Engels, *Collected Works*, vol. 4, London: Lawrence and Wishart.

Erickson, Donald A., 1969, 'Showdown at an Amish Schoolhouse: A Description and Analysis of the Iowa Controversy', in *Public Controls for Nonpublic Schools*, edited by Donald A. Erickson, Chicago: The University of Chicago Press, pp. 15–59.

Farber, L., 1976, *Lying, Despair, Jealousy, Envy, Sex, Suicide, Drugs and the Good Life*, New York: Basic Books.

Farrell, M. J., 1976, 'Liberalism in the Theory of Social Choice', *Review of Economic Studies*, 43, pp. 3–10.

Festinger, L., 1957, *A Theory of Cognitive Dissonance*, Stanford: Stanford University Press.

—— 1964, *Conflict, Decision and Dissonance*, Stanford: Stanford University Press.

Firth, Roderick, 1952, 'Ethical Absolutism and the Ideal Observer', *Philosophy and Phenomenological Research*, 12, pp. 317–45. See also vol. 15 (pp. 414–21) of this journal for Firth's reply to R. B. Brandt's subsequent discussion of this paper (Brandt 1955).

Fishburn, P. C., 1973, *The Theory of Social Choice*, Princeton: University Press.

Fisher, I., 1927, 'A Statistical Method for Measuring Marginal Utility', in *Economic Essays in Honor of J. B. Clark*, New York.

Frankel, C., 1958, *The Case for Modern Man*, Boston: Beacon Press.

Frankfurt, Harry, 1971, 'Freedom of the Will and the Concept of a Person', *Journal of Philosophy*, 67, no. 1, pp. 5–20.

Fried, Charles, 1978, *Right and Wrong*, Cambridge, Mass.: Harvard University Press.

Friedman, M., 1953, 'Choice, Chance and the Personal Distribution of Income', *Journal of Political Economy*, 61, pp. 277–99.

—— 1962, *Capitalism and Freedom*, Chicago: University of Chicago Press.

Friedman, M. and Savage, L. J., 1948, 'The Utility Analysis of Choices Involving Risk', *Journal of Political Economy*, 56, pp. 279–304.

Friedman, M. and Savage L. J., 1952, 'The Expected Utility Hypothesis and Measurement of Utility', *Journal of Political Economy*, 60, pp. 463–74.

Gärdenfors, P., 1978, 'Rights, Games and Social Choice' (mimeo.).

Gaertner W., and Krüger, L., 1981, 'Self-supporting Preferences and Individual Rights: The Possibility of Paretian Liberalism', *Economica*, 48, pp. 17–28.

Gibbard, A., 1974, 'A Pareto Consistent Libertarian Claim', *Journal of Economic Theory*, 7, pp. 399–410.

—— 1979, 'Disparate Goods and Rawls' Difference Principle: A Social Choice Theoretic Treatment', *Theory and Decision*, 11, pp. 267–88.

Goldman, A., 1972, 'Toward a Theory of Social Power', *Philosophical Studies*, 23, pp. 221–68.

Goodman, Nelson, 1973, *Fact, Fiction, and Forecast*, 3rd edition, Indianapolis: Hackett.

Gorman, W. M., 1968, 'The Structure of Utility Functions', *Review of Economic Studies*, 35, pp. 367–90.

Gottinger, H. W. and Leinfellner, W. (eds.), 1978, *Decision Theory and Social Ethics: Issues in Social Choice*, Dordrecht: Reidel.

Graaff, J. de V., 1957, *Theoretical Welfare Economics*, Cambridge: Cambridge University Press.

Gutmann, Amy, 1980, 'Children, Paternalism and Education; A Liberal Argument', *Philosophy and Public Affairs*, 9, no. 4, pp. 338–58.

Hahn, F. and Hollis, M.(eds.), 1979, *Philosophy and Economic Theory*, Oxford: Oxford University Press. There is a substantial Introduction by the editors.

Hammond, P. J., 1976a, 'Changing Tastes and Coherent Dynamic Choice', *Review of Economic Studies*, 43, pp. 159–73.

——1976b, 'Equity, Arrow's Conditions and Rawls' Difference Principle', *Econometrica* 44, pp. 793–800. Reprinted in Hahn and Hollis 1979.

——1980, 'Some Uncomfortable Options in Welfare Economics Under Uncertainty', Stanford University mimeo.

——1981a, 'Liberalism, Independent Rights and the Pareto Principle', in *Logic, Methodology and the Philosophy of Science*, edited by L. J. Cohen, J. T'os, H. Pfeiffer and K.-P. Podewski, Amsterdam: North-Holland, vol. VI, chapter 45, pp. 221–34.

——1981b, 'Ex-Post Optimality as a Consistent Objective for Collective Choice Under Uncertainty', Economics Technical Report, Institute for Mathematical Studies in the Social Sciences, Stanford University.

——1981c, 'Consistent Dynamic Choice Under Uncertainty and Bayesian Rationality', Economics Technical Report, Institute for Mathematical Studies in the Social Sciences, Stanford University.

——1981d, 'On Welfare Economics with Incomplete Information and the Social Value of Public Information', Economics Technical Report, Institute for Mathematical Studies in the Social Sciences, Stanford University.

Hare, R. M., 1952, *The Language of Morals*, Oxford: Oxford University Press.

——1963, *Freedom and Reason*, Oxford: Oxford University Press.

——1971, *Practical Inferences*, London: Macmillan.

——1972a, *Applications of Moral Philosophy*, London: Macmillan.

——1972b, 'Rules of War and Moral Reasoning', *Philosophy and Public Affairs*, 1, pp. 166–81.

——1972c, *Essays on the Moral Concepts*, London: Macmillan.

——1972d, *Essays on Philosophical Method*, London: Macmillan.

——1972/3, 'Principles', *Proceedings of the Aristotelian Society*, 73 pp. 1–18.

——1973a, 'Language and Moral Education', in *New Essays in the Philosophy of Education*, edited by G. Langford and D. J. O'Connor, London: Routledge & Kegan Paul.

——1973b, 'Critical Study—Rawls' Theory of Justice', *Philosophical Quarterly*, 23, pp. 144–55; 241–52.

——1974, 'Some Confusions about Subjectivity', Lindley Lecture, University of Kansas.

——1975a, 'Abortion and the Golden Rule', *Philosophy and Public Affairs*, 4, pp. 201–22.

——1975b, 'Contrasting Methods of Environmental Planning', in *Nature and Conduct*, edited by R. S. Peters, London: Macmillan, pp. 281–97.

——1976, 'Political Obligation', in *Social Ends and Political Means*, edited by T. Honderich, London: Routledge & Kegan Paul, pp. 1–12.

Harrod, R. F., 1936, 'Utilitarianism Revised', *Mind*, 45, pp. 137–56.

Harsanyi, John C., 1953, 'Cardinal Utility in Welfare Economics and in the Theory of Risk-Taking', *Journal of Political Economy*, 61, pp. 434–5. Reprinted in Harsanyi 1976.

—— 1955, 'Cardinal Welfare, Individualistic Ethics, and Interpersonal Comparisons of Utility', *Journal of Political Economy*, 63, pp. 309–21. Reprinted in Harsanyi 1976.

—— 1958, 'Ethics in Terms of Hypothetical Imperatives', *Mind*, 67, pp. 305–16. Reprinted in Harsanyi 1976.

—— 1967/8, 'Games with Incomplete Information Played by "Bayesian" Players', *Management Science*, 14, pp. 159–82; 320–34; 486–502.

—— 1975a, 'Can the Maximin Principle Serve as a Basis for Morality? A Critique of John Rawls' Theory', *American Political Science Review*, 69, pp. 594–606. Reprinted in Harsanyi 1976.

—— 1975b, 'The Tracing Procedure: A Bayesian Approach to Defining a Solution for n-Person Noncooperative Games', *International Journal of Game Theory*, 4, pp. 61–94.

—— 1975c, 'Nonlinear Social Welfare Functions: Do Welfare Economists Have a Special Exemption From Bayesian Rationality?', *Theory and Decision*, 6, pp. 311–32. Reprinted in Harsanyi 1976.

—— 1976, *Essays in Ethics, Social Behaviour, and Scientific Explanation*, Dordrecht: Reidel.

—— 1977, 'Rule Utilitarianism and Decision Theory', *Erkenntnis*, 11, pp. 25–53.

Hart, H. L. A., 1979, 'Between Utility and Rights', 79 *Columbia Law Review*, pp. 828–46.

Haslett, D. W., 1974, *Moral Rightness*, The Hague: Martinus Nijhoff.

Hayek, F. von, 1945, 'The Use of Knowledge in Society', *American Economic Review*, 35, pp. 519–30.

—— 1948, *Individualism and Economic Order*, Indiana: Gateway Edition.

—— 1960, *The Constitution of Liberty*, London: Routledge & Kegan Paul.

—— 1976, *The Mirage of Social Justice: Law, Legislation Liberty*, vol. 2, London: Routledge & Kegan Paul.

Hirschman, A. O., 1982, *Shifting Involvements*, Princeton: Princeton University Press, chapter 4.

Hirst, P. H., 1972, 'Liberal Education and the Nature of Knowledge', in *Education and the Development of Reason*, edited by R. F. Dearden, P. H. Hirst and R. S. Peters, London: Routledge & Kegan Paul, pp. 391–414.

Hostetler, J. A. and Huntington G. E., 1971, *Children in Amish Society: Socialisation and Community Education*, New York: Holt, Rinehart and Winston.

Hurwicz, L., 1972, 'On Informationally Decentralized Systems', in *Decision and Organization*, edited by C. B. McGuire and R. Radner, Amsterdam: North-Holland, ch. 14, pp. 297–336. Also in *Studies in Resource Allocation Processes*, pp. 425–59, edited by K. J. Arrow and L. Hurwicz, Cambridge: Cambridge University Press, 1977.

—— 1973, 'The Design of Mechanisms for Resource Allocation', *American Economic Review* (Papers and Proceedings), 63, pp. 1–30.

Hyman, Herbert H. and Wright, Charles R. 1979, *Education's Lasting Influence on Values*, Chicago: University of Chicago Press.

Hyman, Herbert H., Wright, Charles R. and Reed, John Shelton, 1975, *The Enduring Effect of Education*, Chicago: The University of Chicago Press.

Jeffery, R. C., 1965, *The Logic of Decision*, New York: McGraw-Hill.

—— 1974, 'Preference among Preferences', *Journal of Philosophy*, 71, pp. 377–91.

Jencks, Christopher (with M. Smith; H. Acland; M.–J. Bane; D. Cohen; H. Gintis; B. Heyns; S. Michelson), 1972 *Inequality: A Reassessment of the Effect of Family and Schooling in America*, New York: Basic Books. Also published London: Allen Lane, 1973; Peregrine Books, 1975.

Jennings, M. Kent, 1980, 'Comment on Richard Merelman's "Democratic Politics and the Culture of American Education"', *American Political Science Review*, 74, pp. 333–8.

Jones-Lee, M. W., 1974, 'The Value of Changes in the Probability of Death or Injury', *Journal of Political Economy*, 82, pp. 835–49.

—— 1976, *The Value of Life: An Economic Analysis*, London: Martin Robertson. Also published Chicago: University of Chicago Press.

—— 1980, 'Human Capital, Risk Aversion, and the Value of Life', in *Contemporary Economic Analysis*, edited by D. A. Currie and W. Peters, London: Croom-Helm. vol. 2, ch. 10, pp. 285–321.

Kahneman, D. and Tversky, A., 1979, 'Prospect Theory: An Analysis of Decision Under Risk', *Econometrica*, 47, pp. 263–91.

Kanbur, S. M., 1979, 'Of Risk Taking and the Personal Distribution of Income', *Journal of Political Economy*, 87, pp. 769–97.

Kant, Immanuel, 1785, *Grundlegung zur Metaphysik der Sitten*, translated by H. J. Paton as *The Moral Law*, London: Hutchinson, 1948.

—— 1803, *Pädogogik*, translated as *On Education*, Ann Arbor, Michigan, 1960.

Kelly, J. S., 1978, *Arrow Impossibility Theorems*, New York: Academic Press.

Kenny, A., 1965/6, 'Happiness', *Proceedings of the Aristotelian Society*, N.S. 66, pp. 93–102.

Kolm, S. C., 1969, 'The Optimum Production of Social Justice', in *Public Economics*, edited by J. Margolis and H. Guitton, London: Macmillan.

—— 1972, *Justice et Equité*, Paris: Editions du centre national de la recherche scientifique.

—— 1979, 'La philosophie bouddhiste et les "hommes economiques"', *Social Science Information*, 18, pp. 489–588.

Koopmans, T. C., 1957, *Three Essays on the State of Economic Science*, New York: McGraw-Hill.

Körner, S., 1976, *Experience and Conduct*, Cambridge: Cambridge University Press.

Laffont, J. J. (ed.), 1979, *Aggregation and Revelation of Preferences*, Amsterdam: North-Holland Publishing Co.

Laffont, J. J. and Maskin, E., 1981, 'The Theory of Incentives: An Overview', mimeo., University of Cambridge.

Leibniz, G. W. F., 1875–90, *Die Philosophische Schriften*, 7 vols, edited by C. I. Gerhardt, Berlin; Weidmannsche Buchhandlung.

Lerner, A. P., 1944, *The Economics of Control*, London and New York: Macmillan.

—— 1972, 'The Economics and Politics of Consumer Sovereignty', *American Economic Review* (Papers and Proceedings), 62, pp. 258–66.

Levi, I., 1974, 'On Indeterminate Probabilities', *Journal of Philosophy*, 71, pp. 391–418.

—— 1980, *The Enterprise of Knowledge*, Cambridge, Mass.: MIT Press.

Lewis, C. I., 1946, *An Analysis of Knowledge and Valuation*, La Salle, Ill.: The Open Court Publishing Company.

Little, I. M. D., 1950, *A Critique of Welfare Economics*, Oxford: Oxford University Press.

Lukes, S., 1974, *Power. A Radical View*, London: Macmillan.

Lyons, David, 1965, *Forms and Limits of Utilitarianism*, Oxford: Oxford University Press.

Mackie, J. L., 1977, *Ethics: Inventing Right and Wrong*, Harmondsworth: Pelican.

—— 1978, 'Can there be a Right-based Moral Theory?', *Midwest Studies in Philosophy*, 3.

Malinvaud, E., 1972, *Microeconomic Theory*, Amsterdam: North-Holland.

Marschak, J. and Radner, R., 1972, *Economic Theory of Teams*, New Haven: Yale University Press.

Mas-Colell, A., 1978, 'An Axiomatic Approach to the Efficiency of Non-cooperative Equilibrium in Economics with a Continuum of Traders', IMSSS Technical Report No. 274, Stanford University.

Maskin, E., 1978, 'A Theorem on Utilitarianism', *Review of Economic Studies*, 45, pp. 93–6.

—— 1980, 'On First-Best Taxation', in *Limits of Redistribution*, edited by W. R. C. Lecomber.

—— 1981, 'Randomization in the Principal-Agent Problem', mimeo, Cambridge University.

Meade, J. E., 1964, *Efficiency, Equality and the Ownership of Property*, London: George Allen & Unwin.

Merton, R. K., 1957, *Social Theory and Social Structure*, Glencoe, Ill.: Free Press.

Mill, John Stuart, 1950, *Philosophy of Scientific Method*, a selection of Mill's writings, edited by E. Nagel, New York: Hafner.

—— 1962, *Utilitarianism* (1861), London: Collins.

—— 1974, *On Liberty* (1859), Harmondsworth: Pelican Classics.

Mirrlees, J. A., 1971, 'An Exploration in the Theory of Optimum Income Taxation', *Review of Economic Studies*, 38, pp. 175–208.

—— 1974, 'Notes on Welfare Economics, Information and Uncertainty', in *Essays on Economic Behaviour under Uncertainty*, edited by M. S. Balch, D. McFadden and S. Y. Wu, Amsterdam: North-Holland.

—— 1981, 'The Theory of Optimal Taxation', in *Handbook of Mathematical Economics*, edited by K. J. Arrow and M. Intriligator, Amsterdam: North-Holland.

Mishan, E. J., 1971, 'Evaluation of Life and Limb: A Theoretical Approach', *Journal of Political Economy*, 79, pp. 687–705.

Moore, G. E., 1903, *Principia Ethica*, Cambridge: Cambridge University Press.

Mueller, D. C., 1979, *Public Choice*, Cambridge: Cambridge University Press.

Myerson, R., 1980, 'Optimal Coordination Mechanisms in Principal-Agent Problems', mimeo, Kellog Graduate School of Management, Northwestern University.

Nagel, Thomas, 1979, *Mortal Questions*, Cambridge: Cambridge University Press.

Nell, Onora [Onora O'Neill], 1975, *Acting on Principle: an essay on Kantian ethics*, New York: Columbia.

Nelson, Leonard, 1917–32, *Vorlesungen über die Grundlagen der Ethik*, 3 vols, Leipzig: Veit.

Ng, Y.-K., 1975, 'Bentham or Bergson? Finite Sensibility, Utility Functions, and Social Welfare Functions', *Revue of Economic Studies*, 42, pp. 545–69.

Nozick, R., 1974, *Anarchy, State and Utopia*, New York: Basic Books; Oxford.

Nozick, R., 1978, *Strategy and Group Choice*, Amsterdam: North-Holland.

Parfit, D., 1973, 'Later Selves and Moral Principles', in *Philosophy and Personal Relations*, edited by A. Montefiore, London: Routledge & Kegan Paul.

—— 1976, 'On Doing the Best for Our Children', in *Ethics and Population*, edited by M. Bayles, Cambridge, Mass.: Schenkman Publishing Company Inc., pp. 100–15.

Pattanaik, P. K., 1968, 'Risk, Impersonality and the Social Welfare Function', *Journal of Political Economy*, 76, pp. 1152–69. Also appears in *Economic Justice*, edited by E. Phelps, London: Penguin, 1973.

—— 1971, *Voting and Collective Choice*, Cambridge: Cambridge University Press.

—— 1978, Strategy and Group Choice, Amsterdam: North-Holland.

Phelps, E. S., 1973, 'Taxation of Wage Income for Economic Justice', *Quarterly Journal of Economics*, 87, pp. 332–54.

Piaget, Jean, 1962, *The Moral Judgement of the Child*, New York: Collier.

Plott, C. R., 1976, 'Axiomatic Social Choice Theory: an Overview and Interpretation', *American Journal of Political Science*, 20, pp. 511–96.

Postman, Neil, 1979, *Teaching as a Conserving Activity*, New York.

Radner, R., 1979, 'Rational Expectations Equilibrium: Generic Existence and the Information Revealed by Prices', *Econometrica*, 47, pp. 655–78.

Radner, R. and Marschak, J., 1954, 'Note on Some Proposed Decision Criteria', in *Decision Processes*, New York: Wiley, pp. 61–8.

Ramsey, F. P., 1926, 'Truth and Probability', in *The Foundations of Mathematics and Other Logical Essays*, edited by R. Braithwaite, London: Kegan Paul, 1931, pp. 156–98.

Rawls, John, 1955, 'Two Concepts of Rules', *Philosophical Review*, 64, pp. 3–32.

—— 1957, 'Justice as Fairness', *Journal of Philosophy*, 54, pp. 653–62.

—— 1958, 'Justice as Fairness', *Philosophical Review*, 67, pp. 164–94.

—— 1971, *A Theory of Justice*, Cambridge, Mass.: Harvard University Press. Also published by Oxford University Press, 1972.

—— 1974–5, 'The Independence of Moral Theory', *Proceedings and Addresses of the American Philosophical Association 47*.

—— 1975, 'A Kantian Conception of Equality', *The Cambridge Review*, 96, no. 2225 (February), pp. 94–9.

—— 1980, 'Kantian Constructivism in Moral Theory', *The Journal of Philosophy*, 77, no. 9, pp. 515–72.

Richards, D. A. J., 1971, *A Theory of Reasons for Action*, Oxford: Oxford University Press.

Roberts, K. W. S., 1980a, 'Price Independent Welfare Prescriptions', *Journal of Public Economics*, 13, pp. 277–97.

—— 1980b, 'Interpersonal Comparability and Social Choice Theory', *Review of Economic Studies*, 47.

Ross, Sir W. D., 1930, *The Right and the Good*, Oxford: Oxford University Press.

—— 1939, *Foundations of Ethics*, Oxford: Oxford University Press.

Rowley, C. K. and Peacock, A. T., 1975, *Welfare Economics: a Liberal Restatement*, London: Martin Robertson.

Runciman, W. G., 1966, *Relative Deprivation and Social Justice*, London: Routledge & Kegan Paul.

Russell, Bertrand, 1955, *John Stuart Mill*, Oxford: Oxford University Press.

Samuelson, P. A., 1937, 'A Note on Measurement of Utility', *Review of Economic Studies*, 4, pp. 155–61.

—— 1938, 'A Note on the Pure Theory of Consumers' Behaviour', *Economica*, N.S. 5, pp. 61–71. See also the addendum on pp. 353–4 of same volume.

Savage, L. J., 1954, *The Foundations of Statistics*, New York: John Wiley. 2nd revised edition—Dover, 1972.

Scanlon, T. M., 1975, 'Preference and Urgency', *Journal of Philosophy*, 72, pp. 665–9.

Schelling, T. S., 1978, 'Economics, or the Art of Self-Management', *American Economic Review*, 68, Papers and Proceedings, pp. 290–4.

Schick, F., 1969, 'Arrow's Proof and the Logic of Preference', *Journal of Philosophy*, 66, pp. 127–44.

—— 1980. 'Welfare, Rights and Fairness', in *Science, Belief and Behavior: Essays in honour of R. B. Braithwaite*, pp. 203–16, edited by D. H. Mellor, Cambridge: Cambridge University Press.

Sen, A. K., 1970a, *Collective Choice and Social Welfare*, San Francisco: Holden Day. Also London: Oliver and Boyd, 1970.

—— 1970b, 'The Impossibility of a Paretian Liberal', *Journal of Political Economy*, 78, pp. 152–7.

—— 1973, *On Economic Inequality*, Oxford: Oxford University Press.

—— 1974, 'Choice, Orderings and Morality', in *Practical Reason*, edited by S. Körner, Oxford: Blackwell.

—— 1975, *Employment, Technology and Development*, Oxford: Oxford University Press.

—— 1976, 'Liberty, Unanimity and Rights', *Economica*, 43, pp. 217–46.

—— 1977a, 'On Weights and Measures: Informational Constraints in Social Welfare Analysis', *Econometrica*, 45, pp. 1539–72.

—— 1977b, 'Rational Fools: a Critique of the Behavioural Foundations of Economic Theory', *Philosophy and Public Affairs*, 6, pp. 317–44.

—— 1979a, 'Personal Utilities and Public Judgements: Or What's Wrong with Welfare Economics', *Economic Journal*, 89, pp. 537–58.

—— 1979b, 'Utilitarianism and Welfarism', *Journal of Philosophy*, 76, no. 9, pp. 463–89.

—— 1979c, 'Informational Analysis of Moral Principles', in *Rational Action: Studies in Philosophy and the Social Sciences*, edited by R. Harrison, Cambridge: Cambridge University Press, pp. 115–32.

—— 1980, 'Equality of What?', in *Tanner Lectures on Human Values*, I, edited by S. McMurrin, Cambridge: Cambridge University Press.

—— 1981, 'Plural Utility', *Proceedings of the Aristotelian Society*, 81.

—— 1982, 'Rights and Agency', *Philosophy and Public Affairs*, 11.

Sharp, Lynda, 'Forms and Criticisms of Utilitarianism', thesis, deposited in the Bodleian Library at Oxford.

Sidgwick, Henry, 1962, *Methods of Ethics*, 7th edition (reissue), London: Macmillan.

Simon, H., 1957, *Models of Man*, New York: John Wiley & Sons.

—— 1960, *The New Science of Management Decision*, New York: Harper & Brothers.

Singer, Marcus George, 1961, *Generalization in Ethics*, New York: Knopf.

Singer, Peter, 1972, 'Famine, Affluence and Morality', *Philosophy and Public Affairs*, 1, pp. 229–43.

Singer, Peter, 1974, 'Sidgwick and Reflective Equilibrium', *The Monist*, 58, pp. 490–517.

Smart, J. J. C. and B. A. O. Williams, 1973, *Utilitarianism: For and Against*, Cambridge: Cambridge University Press.

—— 1961, *An Outline of a System of Utilitarian Ethics*, Melbourne: Melbourne University Press. Also in Smart and Williams 1973.

Smith, Adam, 1976, *Theory of Moral Sentiments*, Clifton, N.J.: Kelley.

Starr, R. M., 1973, 'Optimal Production and Allocation Under Uncertainty', *Quarterly Journal of Economics*, 87, pp. 81–95.

Stiglitz, J. E., 1976, 'Utilitarianism and Horizontal Equity: the Case for Random Taxation', IMSSS Technical Report No. 214, Stanford University.

Stouffer, S. (with E. A. Suchman, L. C. De Vinney, S. Star and R. M. Williams Jr), 1949, *The American Soldier*, Princeton: Princeton University Press.

Strasnick, S., 1976, 'Social Choice Theory and the Derivation of Rawls' Difference Principle', *Journal of Philosophy*, 73, pp. 85–99.

—— 1978, 'Extended Sympathy Comparisons and the Basis of Social Choice Theory', *Theory and Decision*, 10, pp. 311–28.

Strotz, R. H., 1956, 'Myopia and Inconsistency in Dynamic Utility Maximization', *Review of Economic Studies*, 23, pp. 165–80.

Suppes, Patrick, 1966, 'Formal Models of Grading Principles', *Synthèse*, 16, pp. 284–306.

Suzumura, K., 1978, 'On the Consistency of Libertarian Claims', *Review of Economic Studies*, 45, pp. 329–42.

Taylor, Charles, 1977, 'What is Human Agency?', in *The Self: Psychological and Philosophical Issues*, edited by T. Mischel, Oxford: Blackwell.

Thomson, Judith J., 1976, 'Self-defence and Rights', *The Lindley Lecture*, University of Kansas.

Tinbergen, Jan, 1957, 'Welfare Economics and Income Distribution', *American Economic Review*, Papers and Proceedings, 47 (May), pp. 490–503.

Varian, H. R., 1974, 'Equity, Envy and Efficiency', *Journal of Economic Theory*, 9, pp. 63–91.

Veyne, P., 1976, *Le Pain et le Cirque*, Paris: Seuil.

Vickrey, W. S., 1945, 'Measuring Marginal Utility by Reactions to Risk', *Econometrica*, 13, pp. 319–33.

—— 1960, 'Utility, Strategy, and Social Decision Rules', *Quarterly Journal of Economics*, 74, pp. 507–35.

Von Neumann, J. and Morgenstern, O., 1944, *Theory of Games and Economic Behaviour*, Princeton: Princeton University Press; 3rd edition—1953.

Von Weiszäcker, C. C., 1971, 'Notes on Endogenous Change of Taste', *Journal of Economic Theory*, 3, pp. 345–72.

Warnock, G. J., 1971, *The Object of Morality*, London: Methuen & Co.

Watzlawick, P., 1978, *The Language of Change*, New York: Basic Books.

Weiss, L., 1976, 'The Desirability of Cheating Incentives and Randomness in the Optimal Income Tax', *Journal of Political Economy*, 84, pp. 1343–52.

Weitzman, M., 1978, 'Optimal Rewards for Economic Regulation', *American Economic Review*, 68, pp. 683–91.

Williams, B. A. O., 1972, *Morality: An Introduction to Ethics*, New York: Harper & Row. Also published: Harmondsworth: Pelican Books, 1973; Cambridge: Cambridge University Press, 1976.

—— 1973, 'A Critique of Utilitarianism', in Smart and Williams 1973.

—— 1976a, 'Persons, Character and Morality', in *The Identities of Persons*, edited by A. Rorty, Berkeley: University of California Press, pp. 197–216. Reprinted in Williams 1981.

—— 1976b, 'Utilitarianism and Moral Self-Indulgence', in *Contemporary British Philosophy*, Series 4, edited by H. D. Lewis, London: Allen & Unwin, pp. 306–21. Reprinted in Williams 1981.

—— 1978, *Descartes—The Project of Pure Enquiry*, Harmondsworth: Pelican.

—— 1981, *Moral Luck*, Cambridge: Cambridge University Press.

Wollheim, R., 1973, 'John Stuart Mill and the Limits of State Action', *Social Research*, 40, pp. 1–30.

5

Welfare Economics and Economies of Scale

1. INTRODUCTION

The 'fundamental' theorems of welfare economics say that a competitive equilibrium is Pareto-efficient and that a welfare optimum can be implemented as a competitive equilibrium. The second theorem assumes there are no economies of scale in production—to be precise, that the aggregate production set is convex.[1] The first theorem does not assume that, but all the standard theorems about when a competitive equilibrium exists assume that there are no economies of scale.

In this paper, it will be shown that, in reasonably general circumstances, a welfare optimum can be implemented as an equilibrium, when there are economies of scale in production. There are well-known necessary conditions for a welfare optimum, roughly that for producers who produce positive quantities marginal cost should be equal to price (and corresponding statements about inputs).[2] Brown and Heal (1983) have discussed marginal-cost-pricing equilibria. These are not equilibria that could exist without effective direction by a central planner and obedience by individual agents: they are not incentive-compatible for producers interested in profits, or almost anything else. Also, they are not unique, and it seems difficult to extend the necessary conditions to a set of sufficient conditions for optimality.

Arrow pointed out that, generally, when there are economies of scale, it is optimal for producers with identical technologies to do different things; and

This article first appeared in the *Japanese Economic Review*, Vol. 46 (1995), pp. 38–62 and is reproduced by kind permission of Blackwell Publishing Ltd. Suggestions and comments from participants in seminars at Yale, Harvard/MIT, Brown, the Australian National University, and the Tokyo Centre for Economic Research Summer Conference in Economic Theory are gratefully acknowledged, and particularly comments from Richard Arnott, Bill Brainard, Peter Diamond, Drew Fudenberg, John Geanakoplos, Cecilia García Peñalosa, Koichi Hamada, J. V. Henderson, Barry Nalebuff, Herb Scarf, and T. N. Srinivasan.

[1] Textbook statements of the theorem usually assume also that consumers have convex preferences. When there is a continuum of different consumers, convexity of preferences is not required. Other conditions are required as well, of course.

[2] A more precise and general statement for an economy where consumers have strictly convex preferences is that, at an optimum, aggregate supplies equal aggregate demands at current prices p, and no producer has a profit-increasing direction. A profit-increasing direction from production plan y in production set $Y \subset R^n$ is given by a smooth function $z: [0, 1]Y$ such that $z(0) = y$, $p \cdot z'(0) > 0$.

that therefore it is not possible to have a function relating optimal producer response to a central message. As a consequence, no general decentralized implementation seems possible. The models considered in this paper are by no means general. They do have realistic features. In them, economies of scale are sufficiently important for competitive equilibria not to exist. It is found that the optimum can be implemented as a monopolistic equilibrium. In that equilibrium, the Arrow problem is resolved by producers being indifferent between a number of alternatives (as is also true in the standard model when there are constant returns), with equilibrium forcing a particular distribution of choices.

When there are economies of scale in production, we expect, broadly, three kinds of consequence. Limits of managerial competence may be important, so that the actual scale of production is determined by a combination of technological possibilities and increasingly incomplete exploitation of these possibilities as scale increases beyond some point. Secondly, production units will be lumpy, investment being done from time to time in large amounts.[3] There is a trade-off between economies of scale and increased futurity as larger facilities take longer to create. Thirdly, production units will be geographically concentrated, with a trade-off between economies of scale and increased transport costs. It is this third aspect that the paper addresses. Managerial competence will be ignored, as will intertemporal allocation, except for some concluding comments.

The transport costs that play the major role in the paper are those of workers, who on average cost more to transport between residence and workplace the more are employed in a production unit. This makes the utility of workers a function of total employment in production within a town.

This geographical concentration of production is a major concern of urban economics, and the theory of local public goods also in effect deals with geographical concentration. Fujita (1989, ch. 5, sec. 7) analyses the one-good model, where technology provides economies of scale, at least up to some scale, and identical consumers have preferences depending on consumption, residential space occupied, and distance from the place of work. He shows that an equilibrium in which employers set wages and maximize the sum of profits and land rents is an optimum, and remarks that it can also be shown that an optimum is such an equilibrium. These results are generalized in Sections 2 and 3 below, with some modifications, avoiding the assumption (implicit in Fujita) that all towns have the same size, and the assumption that all consumers have the same utility. In later sections, I extend the theorems to many commodities, and to heterogeneous consumers.

Fujita seems to have been the first in the urban economics literature to see that one cannot rely on first-order conditions when discussing optimality for a model with economies of scale. Scotchmer (1985) had earlier noted a similar

---

[3] Weitzman (1972) and Dixit *et al.* (1975) address intertemporal allocation with economies of scale in simple models.

argument for a model of local public goods, with 'utility-taking' welfare maximization in each locality. Henderson (1985, 1988) developed and discussed necessary conditions for optimality in an urban economics model with production, but with an unusual specification of production possibilities that effectively excludes economies of scale. He implements optimal city size by a kind of competitive equilibrium.

The theorems to be discussed show the equivalence of optimality and a free-entry monopolistic equilibrium of Chamberlin type, where the monopoly is exercised in the labour market. There is a considerable literature on the corresponding equilibrium where monopoly is exercised in product markets, there being transport costs for goods, and a geographically dispersed population of consumers distributed among producers. Mills and Lav (1964) pointed out that in this model a Chamberlinian equilibrium is not optimal, because in equilibrium price is not equal to marginal cost, a necessary condition for optimality.[4] In the somewhat different model of Dixit and Stiglitz (1977), not a locational model, equilibrium and optimality coincide only in a special case. It is striking that product-market and factor-market monopolistic equilibrium have such different properties. That is because, in the models to be analysed, consumers are assumed to have no mobility costs in the long run (from employment to employment), only in the short run (from residence to workplace).

Rather than state and prove the most general theorem I can provide, the paper first illustrates the general idea in a very simple case, with one good, identical consumers, in-town congestion, fixed labour supply per consumer, and no transport costs. In this and all other cases studied, the population is taken to be very large relative to the number of production units that it will be optimal to have, so that the number of workers in any one unit may be thought of as continuously variable; and that number is supposed also to be very large, so that the number of production units can be treated as varying continuously when the number of workers in each is varied continuously. This simple case allows us to identify a particular restriction on the kind of economies of scale, which allows us to deduce that an allocation is optimal if and only if it is a monopolistic equilibrium with free entry.

Land use (as in Fujita's analysis) and variable labour supply are then introduced separately, in Sections 3 and 4. The central sections of the paper study a many-commodity model, first with identical consumers, then with heterogeneous consumers. In all of these models, the optimum has one producer per town, since goods can be moved costlessly between towns. The final section discusses economies in which there are transport costs for commodities, and it may therefore be optimal for several commodities to be produced in each geographical unit. In all cases, the same general equivalence of optimality and free-entry

---

[4] Curiously enough, there is a literature that claims to refute this, e.g. Benson (1984). The argument in Benson seems to me to be mistaken: in the model used, the price paid by consumers should be marginal cost plus transport cost for optimality, and that does not hold in equilibrium.

monopolistic equilibrium of town-owners holds. The assumption that all land and production in a town has one owner becomes very strained: the implications of relaxing it are discussed in the last section.

Throughout the paper, it is assumed that a government can redistribute income by lump-sum transfers. Until Section 6, when consumers are heterogeneous, that is not a problem, since such redistribution is incentive-compatible: either it is not required, or is done at random within the population. The second-best optimum, with consumer budget constraints required to be the same for all, to ensure incentive compatibility, is not discussed. Since the novel features of the implementation of the optimum involve producers, it might be thought that similar results would hold for second-best optima, but I am not sure that is true: the issue is one for further work.

2. A SIMPLE CASE

An economy has one produced good and labour. The available technology is described by a production function $f(n)$ giving output from a single production unit as a function of the number of workers n employed in that unit. It is assumed that

A1: $f(0) = 0$.
A2: $f(n)$ is an increasing function of n.
A3: $f(n)/n$ is a concave function of n where it is increasing.

Assumption A3 allows a substantial but limited degree of increasing returns. It is automatically satisfied when f is concave, for then f/n is nonincreasing. It will be interesting to consider later the consequences of weakening the assumption so that it is required to hold only asymptotically, i.e. when we assume that f/n is concave or nonincreasing for large n. Define per capita output

$$\rho(n) = \frac{f(n)}{n}.$$

Consumers in the economy are identical. They have preferences described by a utility function $u(x, n)$, where x is consumption of the produced good and n is the number of people employed in the production unit where this consumer is working. The idea is that the workers for a production unit all live in the same town, each unit being in a different town. It is assumed that

B1: u is an increasing function of x.
B2: u is a decreasing function of n.
B3: u is a concave function of x, n.

It is not necessary for what follows that u be a decreasing function of n except for large enough n, since evidently it is optimal to expand the scale of production until u is decreasing in n. The reasons for this congestion cost will be addressed explicitly in the next section, when land use and worker transport costs are introduced explicitly.

It will be convenient to define the equation of the consumer's indifference curves (the conditional expenditure function in this one-good model):

$$x = c(n, v) \quad \text{when } v = u(x, n).$$

Assumptions B1–B3 imply that c is increasing and convex in n, v.

There are supposed to be large numbers of consumers. An allocation in the economy is taken to be a distribution of the population into towns (i.e. production units) of sizes n with per capita consumption x. Since it is optimal to have equal consumption within a town, we can avoid notational complications by confining attention to allocations that have equal x within each town. We then say that an allocation is feasible if the mean of $\rho(n) - x$, within the whole economy, is zero. By defining feasibility this way, we implicitly assume an infinite population. The feasibility requirement says that total production in the economy equals total consumption.

An optimal allocation is a feasible allocation that maximizes mean utility among feasible allocations. This restricts the results to utilitarian welfare functions; but they generalize easily to general individualistic welfare functions. When individuals are identical, it might be thought this would not matter, but we shall see that it is not generally true that the utilitarian optimum for the identical-consumer case allocates the same outcome to everyone. It might be optimal to have more than one kind of town, with different utility for consumers in the different kinds of town.

A free-entry monopolistic equilibrium is an allocation in which all producers employ $\hat{n}$ workers,

$$\hat{n} \max f(n) - c(n, \hat{v})n,$$

$$f(\hat{n}) - c(\hat{n}, \hat{v})\hat{n} = 0. \tag{1}$$

Producers have to pay a wage $c(n, \hat{v})$ to attract workers who can obtain utility $\hat{v}$ elsewhere. The first condition says they maximize profit subject to the need to attract workers. The second says that profit is zero, since otherwise there would be entry or exit. This is a monopolistic equilibrium as introduced by Chamberlain, except that the monopoly is in the factor, not the product market.

Theorem 1. *Assume A1–A3, B1–B3. An allocation is optimal if and only if it is a free-entry monopolistic equilibrium.*

Proof. Fig. 5.1 illustrates. The optimum maximizes the mean of utility v subject to the constraint that the mean of

$$d(n, v) = \rho(n) - c(n, v)$$

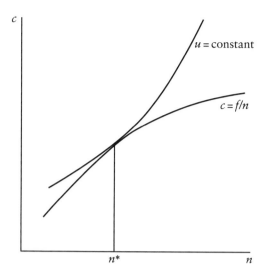

Figure 5.1.

in the economy is zero. Since d is a decreasing function of v, n maximizes d in each town at the optimum. Define

$$\gamma(v) = \max_n d(n, v).$$

This is also a decreasing function of v. At an optimum, the mean of v is maximized subject to the mean of $\gamma(v)$ being zero. Now γ is a concave function, since d is concave in both arguments, by assumptions A3 and B3. Therefore it is optimal to have v the same in all towns; and v must satisfy $\gamma(v) = 0$.

Thus an allocation is optimal if and only if v is constant; n maximizes d, given v; and $d(n, v) = 0$. Equivalently, $nd = 0$ at the optimum, and $nd \leqslant 0$ for all other n. These conditions are the same as (1). ☐

It is interesting to consider what the optimum is when assumption A3 does not hold.[5] Now government intervention in the form of lump-sum transfers may be required to implement the optimum as an equilibrium. When A3 does not hold, $\gamma = \max_n d$ need not be a concave function of v. The largest value of the mean of v will be obtained by concavifying γ and setting the concavified function equal to zero. This procedure never requires more than two values of v (see Fig. 5.2.)

The optimum may therefore involve two utility levels, v_1 and v_2, with corresponding employment levels n_1 and n_2. For this to be achieved as an equilibrium, there will need to be lump-sum transfers between consumers: the

---

[5] Fujita (1988) assumes implicitly that all towns are the same size at the optimum: that is not justified unless A3 is assumed.

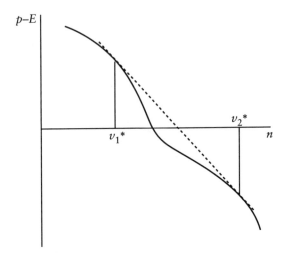

Figure 5.2.

population is divided into two groups, those who are to work in towns with utility level v_1, and the others. Members of these groups receive lump-sum income b_i. The wage paid to someone receiving b_i to ensure utility v is

$$w_i = c(n, v) - b_i.$$

If we set

$$b_i = c(n_i, v_i) - \rho(n_i),$$

we have an equilibrium in which both kinds of producer make zero profits; each is maximizing profit subject to being able to attract labour from other producers of the same kind; and no consumers working for one kind of producer would prefer to work for the other kind. This last 'incentive compatibility' condition follows because, when $i \neq j$,

$$
\begin{aligned}
b_i + w_j &= c(n_i, v_i) - \rho(n_i) + w_j \\
&\leqslant c(n_j, v_i) - \rho(n_j) + w_j, \text{ by profit maximization} \\
&= c(n_j, v_i), \text{ since profit is zero.}
\end{aligned}
$$

Thus, the optimum is a free-entry monopolistic equilibrium, in which firms of two different sizes occur, induced by consumer inequality created by lump-sum transfers. This is an example where a utilitarian (or almost any individualistic welfare function) implies that inequality of utilities is desirable in a population of identical people.[6]

---

[6] This kind of optimum was noted in a superficially different context in Mirrlees (1972).

If one imposes a requirement that everyone have the same utility, or uses a Rawlsian welfare function, the situation is a little simpler. There may be two kinds of firm, choosing employment levels n_1 and n_2, both of which maximize $\rho(n) - c(n, v)$, and the resulting maximum has to be zero in both cases (since the mean is). There is no need for redistributive action by a government.

3. LAND USE

Rather than have consumer utility depend directly on the number of people employed in the town, let us now have utility depend on distance from the place of work and land area occupied. The need to occupy land means that people have to move some (varying) distance to work, at a cost, which is implicit in the utility function. Specifically, preferences are described by a utility function in terms of consumption x, land area occupied a, and distance from work r. Each individual has a unique location and occupies contiguous land: a is a density. Utility is written as $u(x, a, r)$.

In a town, $N(r)$ denotes the number of people living within distance r of the workplace. We shall make assumptions that ensure N is a differentiable function of r in any equilibrium or optimum. We then write $n(r) = N'(r)$. In an optimum or an equilibrium, everyone at a particular distance r from the town centre occupies the same land area $a(r)$: we confine attention to such allocations. The area occupied by anyone at distance r from the centre is inversely proportional to the population density $n(r)$ at that distance. It is therefore convenient to define area by $a = 1/n(r)$. (In a circular town, it would be more conventional to have instead $a = 2\pi r/n(r)$. The validity of the assumptions to be made is not affected by dropping this factor proportional to r.)

We assume

C1: u is a continuously differentiable function.
C2: u is an increasing function of x.
C3: u is an increasing function of a.
C4: u is a concave function of x and a.

Assumption C1 is made for convenience, to ensure that the optimal allocation within a town is described by functions continuous in r. Notice that u is not assumed monotonic or concave in r.

In a town, where a production unit operates, mean utility of the population is

$$\frac{1}{N(R)} \int_0^R u(x, a(r), r)n(r)\, dr, \tag{2}$$

where R is the radius of the town. Note that $a(r)n(r) = 1$. An allocation in the economy is feasible if the mean in the economy of production less consumption,

$$f(N(R)) - \int_0^R xn\, dr, \tag{3}$$

is zero. Again, we express preferences by the indifference curves, with

$$x = c(a, r, v). \tag{4}$$

By C1–C3, c is a decreasing function of a and an increasing function of v. By C4, c is a convex function of a, v.

I want to characterize the optimal allocation in this economy. This is done in two stages. First we find the minimum cost of achieving a given mean utility level in a town of given size. Then we consider what town sizes will maximize mean utility in the economy subject to mean production equalling mean consumption. It is somewhat easier to do this under the constraint that everyone have the same utility; or, to put it another way, for a Rawlsian welfare function, maximizing minimum utility in the economy. That is done first, and then the utilitarian optimum is characterized in the same way. In both cases, there is equivalence between optimality and free-entry monopolistic equilibrium. In the utilitarian case, lump-sum transfers are required: a natural decentralized rule for the re-distributive branch of government is provided.

Consumer equilibrium in this economy requires that each consumer in a town choose x, a, and r to maximize utility subject to the budget constraint

$$x + q(r)a = w + b,$$

where $q(r)$ is the price of land at distance r from the town centre, w is the wage rate per person, and b is lump-sum income received by the consumer. The consumer must also obtain utility at least as great as is available to him in any other town. Rewriting the budget constraint, we see that v is maximized subject to

$$[w + b - c(a, r, v)]\frac{1}{a} = q(r).$$

Since c is increasing in v, this is equivalent to saying that, for each r, $a(r)$ maximize $[w + b - c(a, r, v)]/a$; and that r maximizes the difference between this and $q(r)$. If there are no lump-sum transfers, $b = 0$, and v is the same for everyone. For each position to be occupied, we require

$$q(r) = \frac{\max}{a} \frac{1}{a}[w - c(a, r, v)], \quad r \leqslant R.$$

If there are lump-sum transfers, consumers with different b will choose different r, and v will vary with r.

In the first case, everyone has to have the same utility: we seek to characterize and implement the allocation that maximizes utility v^* subject to feasibility, and every consumer obtaining utility v^*. Assume that an optimum exists. This could be ensured by assuming, for example, that there is a number T such that every consumer must have $r < T$, with T not too small, lest no feasible allocation exist.

It will be useful to define a function that gives the minimum per-worker cost (in terms of consumption good) of employing a number of people in a town, each with a given utility level:

$$k(N, v) = \min\left\{ \frac{1}{N} \int_0^R c(a, r, v)n \ dr \middle| \int n \ dr = N, \ a(r)n(r) = 1 \text{ for } 0 \leqslant r \leqslant R \right\}.$$

The radius of the town, R, as well as the land allocation described by a and n, is chosen to minimize cost.

Lemma 1. *If N people live in a town, all with utility v, and are in consumer equilibrium with mean consumption x, then $x = k(N, v)$. Conversely, there is a consumer equilibrium with N people in the town having utility u and mean consumption $k(N, v)$.*

Proof. Denote the equilibrium land allocation by $a^*(r)$, with $a^*(r)n^*(r) = 1$. For all r, $0 \leqslant r \leqslant R$,

$$a = a^*(r), \quad s = r \text{ minimize } c(a, s, v) + q(s)a.$$

The minimum is independent of r: call it μ. Then

$$c(a^*(r), r, v) + q(r)a^*(r) = \mu \leqslant c(a, r, v) + q(r)a, \quad \text{for all } a.$$

It follows, since $\int n^*(r)dr = N$, and $a^*(r)n^*(r) = 1$, that

$$\int c(a^*(r), r, v)n^*(r) \ dr + \int q(r) \ dr = \mu N;$$

i.e.

$$Nx = \mu N - \int q(r) \ dr.$$

We also have, from the inequality on the right, that, for any alternative land allocation to the same number of people,

$$\int c(a(r), r, v)n(r) \ dr + \int q(r) \ dr \geq \mu N.$$

Thus,

$$Nx \leq \int c(a(r), r, v)n(r) \ dr, \quad \text{whenever} \int n \ dr = N \quad \text{and} \quad an = 1.$$

This proves that $x = k(n, v)$, as was to be shown.

To prove the converse, let $a^*(r)$ be the cost-minimizing land allocation corresponding to $k(N, v)$. We have to show that it is a consumer equilibrium with some land-rent function $q(r)$. Define

$$q(r) = -c_a(a^*(r), r, v).$$

This implies that $a^*(r)$ minimizes $c(a, r, v) + q(r)a$.

We have to show that, for $0 \leqslant r \leqslant R$,

$$a = a^*(r), \qquad s = r \text{ minimize } c(a, s, v) + q(s)a.$$

From the definition of k, there must be a constant μ such that

$$\frac{\partial}{\partial a}\left(\frac{c}{a}\right) = \mu \frac{\partial}{\partial a}\left(\frac{1}{a}\right),$$

at $a = a^*(r)$, $0 \leqslant r \leqslant R$. This reduces to $c - ac_a = \mu$. Therefore, using the definition $q = -c_a$, we have

$$c(a^*(r), r, v) + q(r)a^*(r) = \mu \leqslant c(a, r, v) + q(r)a,$$

for any a. Furthermore, since the right-hand inequality holds for any r, we have shown that the consumers are also in locational equilibrium, as was required. $\square$

The equal-utility optimum is obtained by finding the maximum v for which the mean over all towns of $f(N)/N - k(N, v)$ is zero. This is very similar to the situation in the previous section. Notice that k is mean consumption in a town, which is equal to the wage, less land rent paid by the consumer. $f(N) - k(N, v)N$ equals the output of the producer less the wage, plus land rents. The optimum is now realized by an equilibrium in which the producer owns all the land in the town, and allows for changes in income from land that result from changes in the number employed. This condition has been noted as a necessary condition for a town to be of optimal size, and is called the 'Henry George theorem' (Stiglitz 1977).

Theorem 2. *An allocation is an equal-utility optimum if and only if it is a free-entry factory-town, monopolistic equilibrium, where each producer owns all land in his town, and there are no lump-sum transfers.*

Proof. The optimum has town sizes chosen so that v is maximum subject to the mean over all towns of $F(N)/N - k(N, v)$ being zero. This mean is a decreasing function of v. Therefore each N must maximize $F/N - k(N, v^*)$, where v^* is the maximum v. The maximum must therefore be zero; and N maximizes $F - k(N, v^*)N$, this maximum also being zero. The allocation is therefore a free-entry, factory-town, monopolistic equilibrium.

Conversely, such an equilibrium selects N to maximize $F/N - k(N, v)$, and the maximum is zero. A larger value of v would therefore have $F/N < k(N, v)$ for all N, and is therefore not feasible. Thus the equilibrium is an optimum. $\square$

Notice that there is no need for the optimum to involve more than one town size, and in general all towns must be the same size.

Now consider a utilitarian optimum, where total utility is to be maximized, and there is no constraint that everyone have the same utility. In general, there will be unequal utilities within a town. With the addition of lump-sum transfers, we get essentially the same result as Theorem 2. The argument follows the same lines as the previous one, with additional complications to allow for utility being a function of r.

Define a minimum mean cost function, this time in terms of the number of people in the town, and their mean utility:

$$K(N, V) = \min\left\{\frac{1}{N}\int_0^R c(a, r, v)n \; dr \;\middle|\; \int n \; dr = N, \; \int vn \; dr = NV, \; an = 1\right\}.$$

Lemma 2. *If N people live in a town, in consumer equilibrium with mean consumption x, and there are lump-sum transfers with mean zero such that mean utility V is maximized, then $x = K(N, V)$. Conversely, there is a consumer equilibrium with N people, and mean-utility maximizing lump-sum redistribution, where mean consumption is $K(N, V)$.*

Proof. The equilibrium has

$$a = a^*(r), \qquad s = r \text{ minimize } c(a, s, v^*(r)) + q(s)a,$$

where $v^*(r)$ is the equilibrium utility of someone living at distance r from the town centre. Redistribution by lump-sum transfers implies that $c_v(a^*(r), r, v^*(r)) = \lambda$, a constant independent of r. Therefore, since c is convex in a, v,

$$a = a^*(r); \qquad s = r, \quad v = v^*(r) \text{ minimize } c(a, s, v) + q(s)a - \lambda v.$$

Since this has to be true for all r, $0 \leqslant r \leqslant R$, the minimum must be a constant, which we call μ.

We then have for an arbitrary allocation,

$$c(a(r), r, v(r))n(r) - \lambda v(r)n(r) - \mu n(r) \geqslant -q(r),$$

while at the equilibrium allocation we have equality here. Integrating over $[0, R]$, we find that, for an allocation with given N and V,

$$\int c(a(r), r, v(r))n(r) \; dr \geq \lambda NV + \mu N - \int q(r) \; dr,$$

and this right-hand side is equal to aggregate consumption in the equilibrium. It follows that mean consumption in the equilibrium is equal to $K(N, V)$, as was to be shown.

The converse is proved in a way exactly similar to the proof of Lemma 1, using first-order conditions for the minimum in the definition of $K(N, V)$. These imply, as before, that the cost-minimizing allocation has $c + q(r)a^*(r) = \lambda v^*(r) + \mu$, for constants λ and μ; and from that we deduce that location is chosen optimally by consumers.

Theorem 3. *An allocation is an optimum if and only if it is a free-entry, factory-town, monopolistic equilibrium with lump-sum transfers used to maximize the sum of individual utilities.*

Proof. The optimum maximizes the mean of V in the population, subject to the mean of $f(N)/N - K(N, V)$ being zero. Since K is an increasing function of V, in a town with mean utility V, N should maximize $f/N - K(N, V)$. Define

$$\Phi(V) = \max_N \left[\frac{f(N)}{N} - K(N, V) \right].$$

Φ is a decreasing function of V. The optimum is given by a convex combination of points on the graph of Φ with the mean of Φ equal to zero. Therefore we either have a single value of V for all towns, in which case the optimum is a free-entry, factory-town, monopolistic equilibrium, with lump-sum transfers only within towns; or the optimum has two values, V_1 and V_2, with Φ_V the same for both types of town. Lump-sum transfers are made between two groups of consumers, who work in the two types of town: the lump-sum payment to workers in a town is $-\Phi(V_i)$. Allowing for these transfers, all producers make zero profit, while N_i maximizes $f/N - K(N, V_i)$. Thus, again we have a free-entry, factory-town, monopolistic equilibrium.

Such an equilibrium, with utility-maximizing lump-sum transfers, has each producer maximize $f - [K(N, V_i) - b_i]N$, where b_i is the lump-sum transfer to consumers in group i. The transfers are set so that K_V is the same in all towns. Feasibility requires that the population mean of $f/N - K$ be zero. The conditions for an optimum are therefore satisfied.   □

Having established that land-use and personal transportation can be used to justify the dependence of utility on town size, and implementation results obtained, I revert to the congestion model, with utility simply a function of numbers employed, for the rest of the paper.

4. VARIABLE LABOUR SUPPLY

Let utility depend not only on consumption and the number employed in the town, but also on the amount of labour the consumer supplies: $u = u(x, n, y)$. Output in a firm employing n people, each of whom does labour y, is $f(n, y)$. We could define a free-entry, monopolistic equilibrium with a wage $w(n)$ that is the price for labour, and have the firm choose n to maximize $f - wn$ while the worker chooses y to maximize $u(wy, n, y)$. But that would not be optimal.

In the optimum, v is to be maximized, subject to

$$f(n, y) = c(n, y, v)n,$$

where c is again the consumption required to provide utility v when there are n workers and individual labour is y. Following the same line of argument as before, at the optimum we should have

$$n^*, y^* \ \max \ f(n, y) - c(n, y, v^*)$$

and the maximum should be zero. Thus, the optimum is implemented by a monopolistic equilibrium in which the firm chooses both n and y, allowing for the utility v^* that workers must receive. And such an equilibrium is an optimum.

When utility is quasi-concave in x, y, this equilibrium is equivalent to an equilibrium in which there is a two-part wage schedule

$$W(y) = \alpha + \beta y,$$

where α and β are chosen by the firm, and y is then chosen by the worker.

The use of a two-part wage recalls the use of two-part tariffs for public utilities; but there the two-part tariff is a way of combining a balanced budget for the utility with efficient pricing, whereas here the two-part wage is the producer's profit-maximizing choice.

5. MANY COMMODITIES AND IDENTICAL CONSUMERS

In the previous sections, the optimality properties of free-entry monopolistic equilibrium have been demonstrated in a very special model. The major question is whether similar results hold for an economy with many commodities and heterogeneous consumers. In the next section, it will be shown that the equivalence result still holds under quite general assumptions, always assuming zero commodity-transportation costs. The present section provides an introduction to the more general Theorem 5 by proving, for a multi-commodity economy of identical consumers, equivalence between the Rawlsian optimum and a free-entry monopolistic equilibrium without lump-sum transfers.

Let there be m commodities. Output of commodity i in a plant employing n workers and using commodity inputs z is $f_i(n, z)$. There are no costs for transporting commodities. Consequently, in an optimum or an equilibrium, each commodity will be produced in a separate town. Denote by n_i the number of workers in a town producing commodity i. Define the restricted per-worker profit functions

$$\rho_i(p, n) = \max_z \left[\frac{p_i f_i(n, z)}{n} - p \cdot z \right].$$

Producer i's demand for input of commodity j, the maximizer in this definition (which is uniquely defined by assumption D2, below), is denoted by $z_j^i(p, n)$.

Consumers are identical, with preferences described by a utility function $u(x, n)$, where x is a vector of consumption levels. The consumption vector of a worker in a town producing commodity i will be denoted x^i. The consumer's restricted expenditure function, the minimum cost of commodities to provide utility v to a consumer in a town of size n, is $E(p, n, v)$, where p is the vector of commodity prices. A consumer's compensated demand for commodity i (uniquely defined, by assumption D1 below) is denoted by $x_i(p, n, v)$.

Assume:

D1: $u(x, n)$ is defined for all nonnegative x, n, and is an increasing, concave function of x.

D2: For each i, $f_i(n, z)$ is defined for all nonnegative n, z. For each n, f_i is an increasing, concave function of z.

D3: u is concave in n.

D4: $f_i(n, z)/n$ is concave where increasing in n.

As in Section 2, it is simpler to state and prove the equivalence theorem under the concavity assumptions D3 and D4. They will be relaxed subsequently. D3 implies that E is a convex function of n. D4 implies that ρ is a concave function of n.

The following way of expressing feasibility will be convenient. Define the unit simplex

$$S = \left\{ p \mid \sum_i p_i = 1, p_i \geqslant 0 \right\}.$$

Lemma 3. *In this multi-commodity economy, given employment levels n_i and proportions m_i of the population working in towns producing commodities i, there is a feasible allocation in which consumers in towns of type i get utility v_i if and only if*

$$\min_{p \in S} \sum_i m_i [\rho_i(p, n_i) - E(p, n_i, v_i)] \geqslant 0. \tag{5}$$

Proof. Assume feasibility, with consumption levels x^i and production-input levels z^i. Then, since total production is sufficient to supply consumption, and production inputs,

$$\sum_j m_j \left(x_i^j + \frac{z_i^j}{n_j} \right) = m_i \frac{f_i(n_i, z^i)}{n_i}, \qquad i = 1, \ldots, m. \tag{6}$$

By the definitions of ρ and E, we have, for all p, and all i,

$$\rho_i(p, n_i) \geqslant \frac{p_i f_i(n_i, z^i) - p \cdot z^i}{n^i} \tag{7}$$

and

$$E(p, n_i, v_i) \leqslant p \cdot x^i. \tag{8}$$

Using (7) and (8), we deduce from (6)

$$\sum_i m_i[\rho_i(p, n_i) - E(p, n_i, v_i)] \geqslant 0 \tag{9}$$

for all p. That implies (5).

Now assume (5). To deduce feasibility, we use the following property of concave functions:

Lemma 4. *Let* $g_1, g_2, \ldots, g_m$ *be concave functions on a set* X. *Let* $z \in X$. *Then, if*

$$\sum_{i=1}^{m}[g_i(x) - g_i(z)] \leqslant y \cdot (x - z), \quad x \in X, \tag{10}$$

there exist $y^1, y^2, \ldots, y^m$ *such that* $\sum_{i=1}^{m} y^i = y$, *and for* $i = 1, \ldots, m$,

$$g_i(x) - g_i(z) \leqslant y^i \cdot (x - z), \quad x \in X.$$

The lemma is proved in the appendix.

The lemma can be applied to (5), in the form (9), with $y = 0$, $z = 0$, since $-\rho_i$ and E are concave functions of p, and by homogeneity (9) holds for all $p \geqslant 0$. It implies that there exist x^i and y^i (corresponding to the y^i in the lemma, divided by m_i) such that

$$\sum_i m_i x^i - \sum_i m_i y^i = 0 \tag{10a}$$

and for all i, and all $p \geqslant 0$,

$$\rho_i(p, n_i) \geqslant p \cdot y^i, \tag{11}$$

and

$$E(p, n_i, v_i) \leqslant p \cdot x^i. \tag{12}$$

Inequality (11) implies that y^i is a feasible production vector, i.e. that

$$y_i^i \leqslant \frac{f_i(n_i, z^i)}{n_i},$$

where z^i is the vector of components of $-n_i y^i$ other than the ith. To prove this, take p to be prices at which inputs z^i would be chosen, so that $\rho_i = [p_i f_i(n_i, z^i) - p \cdot z^i]/n_i$: (11) now implies that $p_i f_i(n_i, z^i)/n_i \geqslant p_i y_i^i$, as was to be shown.

In a similar way, it can be shown that (12) implies that $u(x^i) = v_i$. Then (10) says that the allocation defined by the x^i and y^i is feasible. $\qquad\square$

Assume that everyone is to get the same utility. Subject to that requirement, the optimum is an allocation that maximizes v subject to

$$u(x^i, n_i) = v, \quad i = 1, \dots, I$$

and feasibility. Write $n^* = (n_1^*, \dots, n_m^*), v^* = (v_1^*, \dots, v_m^*)$ for the optimal employment levels and population proportions. Lemma 3 implies that the optimum is characterized by

$$n^*, v^* \max v \text{ subject to } \min_{p \in S} \sum_i m_i[\rho_i(p, n_i) - E(p, n_i, v)] = 0, \quad m \in S$$

The second constraint, that v be in the unit simplex, is because v are the proportions of the population in the different types of town. We write equality here now because v is being maximized, and the left-hand side of (5) is a decreasing function of v. Indeed we can write v^* for the maximized level of utility, and characterize the optimum by

$$m^* \in S, n^* \max \min_{p \in S} \sum_i m_i[\rho_i(p, n_i) - E(p, n_i, v^*)] \tag{13}$$

$$\min_{p \in S} \sum_i m_i^*[\rho_i(p, n_i^*) - E(p, n_i^*, v^*)] = 0. \tag{14}$$

A free-entry, monopolistic equilibrium (with no lump-sum transfers) is defined by producer profit-maximization,

$$n = n_i \max \rho_i(p, n) - E(p, n, v), \quad i = 1, \dots, I, \tag{15}$$

zero profits,

$$\rho_i(p, n_i) - E(p, n_i, v) = 0, \quad i = 1, \dots, I, \tag{16}$$

and market clearing. Here the wage in a town employing n is $w(n) = E(p, n, v)$, since that is what has to be paid to attract a consumer to reside and work in that town. The compensated demands are equal to demands at prices p, employment levels n_i, and incomes $w(n_i)$.

Theorem 4. *In a multi-commodity economy without transport costs, where assumptions D1–D4 hold, an allocation is equal-utility optimal if and only if it is a free-entry, monopolistic equilibrium without lump-sum transfers.*

Proof. Consider first the optimum, denoted by asterisks. To show it is an equilibrium, we need the following

Lemma 5. *Let $G(x, y)$ be a concave function of x for each y, and a convex function of y for each x. Then, if*

$$x^* \max \min_y G(x, y),$$

there exists y* such that

$$x^* \text{ max } G(x, y^*) \text{ and } y^* \text{ min } G(x^*, y).$$

(The lemma is proved in the appendix.)

The optimum satisfies (13). By Lemma 5, with $x = (m_1, \ldots_1, n_1, \ldots)$ and $y = p$, there exists p^* such that

$$n^*, m^* \text{ max } \sum_i m_i[\rho_i(p^*, n_i) - E(p^*, n_i, v^*)] \text{ subject to } m \in S \qquad (17)$$

and the maximum here is zero. Maximization by m^* in (17) implies that $\rho(p^*, n_i^*) - E(p^*, n_i^*, v^*)$ has the same value for all i with $m_i^* > 0$. Since the maximum is zero, that value must be zero. Where $m_i^* = 0$, $\rho - E \leqslant 0$. (17) implies that, for each i with $m_i^* > 0, n_i^*$ maximizes $\rho - E$. It must also be true that $m_i - E \leqslant 0$ if $m_i^* = 0$, for otherwise it would be possible to make the maximand positive. Therefore (15) and (16) both hold. To prove market clearing, we use Lemma 4. That lemma implies that there exist x^{*i} and y^{*i} such that

$$\sum_i m_i^*(x^{*i} - y^*i) = 0, \qquad (18)$$

$$p^* \text{ min } \rho_i(p, n_i^*) - p \cdot y^{*i}, \qquad i = 1, \ldots, m, \qquad (19)$$

$$p^* \text{ min } p \cdot x^{*i} - E(p, n_i^*, v^*), \qquad i = 1, \ldots, m. \qquad (20)$$

The minima in (19) and (20) are zero, since the minimands are homogeneous of degree 1 in p. By arguments used in the proof of Lemma 3, (19) implies that y^{*i} is a profit-maximizing production plan for a producer of commodity i, and (20) implies that x^{*i} is a utility-maximizing consumption plan for a consumer with income $E(p^*, n_i^*, v^*)$. Equation (18) says that markets clear. We have shown that an optimum is an equilibrium.

Now consider an equilibrium allocation. Equations (18), (19), and (20) hold. Multiplying (19) and (20) by m_i^* and adding, and using (18), we have

$$p^* \text{ min } \sum_i m_i^*[\rho(p, n_i^*) - E(p, n_i^*, v^*)],$$

and the minimum, being a sum of zeros, is zero. Therefore (14) holds. Equilibrium conditions (15) and (16) imply that n^* and v^* maximize $\Sigma[\rho - E]$. Therefore (13) holds. This proves that the allocation is an optimum. □

Assumptions D3 and D4 were made so that we could assume there was one size of town for each commodity. The discussion in Section 2 applies here as well: if these assumptions do not hold, there may be two town sizes for the production of some commodities, each maximizing $\rho - E$. The optimum can still be implemented as a free-entry monopolistic equilibrium, but in general lump-sum transfers will be required, for we can only say that the mean of $\rho - E$

over the two types of town must be zero. The level of $\rho - E$ in a town defines the lump-sum payment to be made to a number of workers equal to the number required in towns of that type. The lump-sum transfer will be positive for people who work in the larger of the two towns, negative for those in the smaller.

It is, no doubt, a striking feature of this more general form of the theorem that lump-sum transfers may be required (and in general are required) to ensure equal utilities. As Section 3 will have suggested, a utilitarian optimum does not in general have equal utilities. The marginal utilities may be the same in two towns even though utilities are not, because it will be optimal to have different numbers producing different commodities, since economies of scale are stronger for some commodities than for others. Rather than develop the theory of the utilitarian optimum in detail for the multi-commodity economy with identical consumers, we shall go on immediately to formulate a model in which consumers need not be identical.

6. MANY COMMODITIES AND HETEROGENEOUS CONSUMERS

In keeping with the assumption of a large population, assume a continuum of consumers, described by one parameter. In fact, the parameter could be multi-dimensional, and the arguments to be developed below would still go through. The essential assumption is that the types of consumer are sufficiently varied that each type of consumer will, optimally, work in only one type of town. In some sense the number of (industrial) commodities is assumed to be much less than the number of consumer-types.

A consumer of type α has preferences described by an expenditure function

$$E(p, n, v, \alpha).$$

The distribution of consumers is described by a density function $g(\alpha)$. An optimum is an allocation that maximizes

$$\int v(\alpha)g(\alpha)\,d\alpha.$$

It will be assumed that consumers of type α work in towns of size $n(\alpha)$, where goods of type $i(\alpha)$ are made. Any one commodity will be made in a continuum of different towns, with workers of different types in each one. The wage rate may vary from town to town, and the lump-sum transfer received may vary as well. If a worker were to move to another town, he would continue to receive the same lump-sum income, but his wage would change to that of the town to which he moved. In an equilibrium, no worker should wish to be in a different town.

In other respects, the model is the same as that of the previous section.

We define a free-entry, monopolistic equilibrium as follows. Lump-sum transfers are given. The lump-sum payment to a consumer of type α is $b(\alpha)$. Equilibrium prices are p^*. Consumers of type α have utility $v(\alpha)$. The wage in a town where n workers of type α are employed is

$$w(n, \alpha) = E(p^*, n, v(\alpha), \alpha) - b(\alpha). \tag{20a}$$

Producers employing workers of type α produce a particular commodity $i(\alpha)$ and employ $n(\alpha)$ people. They maximize profit, and by free entry that profit is zero:

$$i = i(\alpha), n = n(\alpha) \ \max \ \rho_i(p^*, n) - w(n, \alpha) \tag{21}$$

$$\rho_{i(\alpha)}(p^*, n(\alpha)) - w(n(\alpha), \alpha) = 0. \tag{22}$$

We also require market clearing. By the same arguments as in the previous section, that is equivalent to

$$\min_p \ \int [\rho_{i(\alpha)}(p, n(\alpha)) - E(p, n(\alpha), v(\alpha), \alpha)]g(\alpha)\, d\alpha = 0, \tag{23}$$

with the equilibrium prices p^* minimizing the integral.

It is an implication of these equilibrium conditions that no worker would wish to seek employment in a town other than the one in which he is employed; or, what comes to the same thing, that the wage paid by each producer is the smallest wage necessary to persuade workers to take that employment. If a worker of type α, receiving lump-sum income $b(\alpha)$, were to work for a producer who is using workers of type β, he would need to be paid $w(n(\beta), \alpha)$ if he were to get utility $v(\alpha)$. By (21) and (22),

$$w(n(\beta), \alpha) \geqslant \rho_{i(\beta)}(p^*, n(\beta)),$$

since an α-producer cannot increase profit by producing a different commodity and employing a different number of people. The right-hand side of this inequality is equal to $w(n(\beta), \beta)$, by (22). Therefore

$$w(n(\beta), \alpha) \geqslant w(n(\beta), \beta),$$

meaning that the wage the worker would receive would not provide greater utility than $u(\alpha)$. The wage in any n-town is $\min_\alpha w(n, \alpha)$.

Another implication of the equilibrium conditions is that there is a balanced budget for lump-sum transfers,

$$\int b(\alpha)g(\alpha)\, d\alpha = 0, \tag{24}$$

which follows from (23) on substituting $w(n(\alpha), \alpha)$ for ρ and $w(n(\alpha), \alpha) + b(\alpha)$ for E.

We now define equilibrium behaviour for a utility-maximizing government, in a natural way. Lump-sum transfers maximize mean utility, given prices and firm sizes:

$$v(.) \ \max \ \int vg(\alpha) \, d\alpha \text{ subject to}$$

$$\int E(p, n(\alpha), v(\alpha), \alpha)g(\alpha) \, d\alpha = \text{constant}. \tag{25}$$

Then, since E is convex in v, there is a constant λ such that, for each α,

$$v(\alpha) \ \max \ \lambda v - E_v(p, n(\alpha), v, \alpha). \tag{26}$$

When redistribution is done in this way, we say there are utility-maximizing transfers. Note that the redistributing government simply looks at consumers and decides what transfers should be made among them: it is in equilibrium when it does not want to change the system of lump-sum transfers. It does not calculate how transfers would affect the whole allocation.

Theorem 5. *For a multi-commodity economy with heterogeneous consumers, an allocation is optimal if and only if it is a free-entry monopolistic equilibrium with utility-maximizing transfers.*

Proof. Let n^*, v^*, i^* describe an optimal allocation. To prove that the allocation is an equilibrium, we use the same method as in the proof of Theorem 4. The optimum is characterized by

$$n^*, v^*, i^* \ max \ \int v(\alpha)g(\alpha) \, d\alpha \tag{27}$$

$$\text{subject to} \min_{p} \ \int [\rho_{i(\alpha)}(p, n(\alpha)) - E(p, n(\alpha), v(\alpha), \alpha)]g(\alpha) \, d\alpha = 0.$$

By the same argument as before, there is a minimizing p^* such that

$$n^*, i^* \ \max \ \int [\rho_{i(\alpha)}(p^*, n(\alpha)) - E(p^*, n(\alpha), v^*(\alpha), \alpha)]g(\alpha) \, d\alpha.$$

Therefore, for each α,

$$n^*(\alpha), i^*(\alpha) \ \max \ \rho_{i(\alpha)}(p^*, n(\alpha)) - E(p^*, n(\alpha), v^*(\alpha), \alpha). \tag{28}$$

Now define $b(\alpha)$ as the negative of the maximum in (28). Conditions (21), ..., (23) for a free-entry, monopolistic equilibrium are satisfied. Furthermore, v^* satisfies (25), with n^*. Thus, lump-sum transfers are utility-maximizing.

For the converse, let n^*, v^*, i^* describe an equilibrium with utility-maximizing transfers. Thus (26) holds. Let n, v, i describe an alternative feasible allocation. They satisfy

$$\int [\rho_{i(\alpha)}(p, n(\alpha)) - E(p, n(\alpha), v(\alpha), \alpha)]g(\alpha) \, d\alpha \geqslant 0 \tag{29}$$

for any prices p.

Since ρ_i is concave in n and E is convex in (n, v), utility-maximizing transfers along with profit-maximization imply that

$$i^*(\alpha), n^*(\alpha), v^*(\alpha) \ \max \ \rho_i(p, n) - E(p, n, v, \alpha) + \lambda v \tag{30}$$

for some positive constant λ. Integrating, we have

$$\int [\rho_i(p, n) - E(p, n, v, \alpha) + \lambda v] g(\alpha) \, d\alpha$$

$$\leqslant \int [\rho_{i^*}(p, n^*) - E(p, n^*, v^*, \alpha) + \lambda v^*] g(\alpha) \, d\alpha$$

$$= -\int b(\alpha) g(\alpha) \, d\alpha + \lambda \int v^*(\alpha) g(\alpha) \, d\alpha.$$

Using (25) and (30), this implies

$$\lambda \int v(\alpha) g(\alpha) \, d\alpha \leqslant \lambda \int v^*(\alpha) g(\alpha) \, d\alpha. \tag{31}$$

Therefore total utility is maximized at the equilibrium.

If ρ_i is not concave, then as in the discussion in Section 2, ρ_i should be concavified with respect to n, and for each α there may be up to two values of n^* maximizing

$$\rho_i(p, n) - \min_v \ [E(p, n, v, \alpha) - \lambda v]. \tag{32}$$

This may require additional lump-sum transfers among people of the same type. With that modification, the theorem is valid. □

7. MULTI-COMMODITY TOWNS

In reality, towns contain many firms, producing different commodities. And it is surely also optimal for there to be multiple production plants in towns, since there are transport costs for commodities.[7]

Beckman and Koopmans (1957) showed for a general integer allocation program that the presence of transport costs implied that the optimum could not be obtained as a market equilibrium.[8] It may therefore be expected that transport costs will make decentralized implementation of an optimum difficult or impossible. There are indeed difficulties. But for the technologies being considered in this paper, I believe they are of a rather different kind from those brought out in the Beckman–Koopmans analysis.

[7] Another possible reason for multiple production units is the natural advantages of particular locations. I take that to be relatively unimportant compared with transport costs.

[8] This is in a model where, in the absence of transport costs, the optimum is a competitive equilibrium.

The general model with transport costs seems to be complicated to handle. I therefore take the opposite extreme to the zero-transport-cost model studied in the previous sections, that of infinite transport costs between towns. Then all towns will be self-sufficient, producing all commodities that their citizens choose to consume. That is true both for the optimum, and for any equilibrium allocation one may consider.

For simplicity, continue with the same technology as in the previous two sections, except for the requirement of self-sufficiency, and assume, as in Section 5, that consumers are identical. Since there is no transportation of goods between towns, all towns will be identical. The population is divided into these identical towns, with equal numbers of inhabitants. Let n_i be the number of people employed in the production of commodity i in a single town. The population of the town is $\sum_i n_i$.

Consider the uniform-utility optimum. The feasibility condition of Lemma 3 in Section 5 now becomes

$$\min_p \left[\sum_i n_i \rho_i(p, n_i) - E\left(p, \sum_i n_i, v\right) \right] \geq 0.$$

The optimum is characterized by

$$n^* \ \max \ \min_p \left[\sum_i n_i \rho_i(p, n_i) - E\left(p, \sum_i n_i, v^*\right) \right] \tag{33}$$

$$\min_p \left[\sum_i n_i^* \rho_i(p, n_i^*) - E\left(p, \sum_i n_i^*, v^*\right) \right] = 0. \tag{34}$$

It is now easy to define the equilibrium that implements the optimum:

Theorem 6. *An allocation n^* is optimal if and only if there are prices p^* such that:*

$$n^* \ \max \ \sum_i n_i \rho_i(p^*, n_i) - E\left(p^*, \sum_i n_i, v^*\right),$$

$$\sum_i n_i^* \rho_i(p^*, n_i^*) - E\left(p^*, \sum_i n_i^*, v^*\right) = 0$$

and markets clear.

Proof. The argument is essentially the same as that of Theorem 4 in Section 5. If an allocation is optimal, (33) and (34) hold. Then p^* exists by Lemma 4, and the previous arguments show that all three conditions stated in the theorem hold.

Now consider an allocation satisfying the conditions of the theorem. Another feasible allocation with uniform utility v has employment levels n that satisfy

$$\sum_i n_i \rho_i(p^*, n_i) - E\left(p^*, \sum_i n_i, v^*\right) \geq 0. \tag{35}$$

As before, this follows from multiplying the market-clearing equations by the corresponding prices p_i^* and using the definitions of the profit function and expenditure function. The first two conditions in the theorem imply that

$$\sum_i n_i \rho_i(p^*, n_i) - E\left(p^*, \sum_i n_i, v^*\right) \leq 0.$$

Comparing this with (35), we deduce that $v^* \geq v$, which is to say that the allocation specified is optimal. □

Theorem 6 can be interpreted as saying that optimal allocations and free-entry, monopolistic equilibria are equivalent when all production in each town is owned by one producer. The assumption that producers are price-takers in commodity markets is here much less reasonable than in models with zero commodity transport costs. Implementation of the optimum now requires effective control of monopoly in product markets (but not in factor markets). This regulation has to be achieved without introducing competition by increasing the number of firms.

It is reasonable to consider equilibrium for this model when the production facility for each commodity is owned by a different person. When there are several owners of production, one cannot expect that an equilibrium will be optimal. The characterization of the optimum above makes it clear that there is an externality between producers. If n_i is chosen by producer i, and the different producers act independently, each would neglect the effect of a change in his own employment on the wages paid by other employers. But matters are more awkward than that. In general, it turns out, no reasonable equilibrium, with price-taking in product markets, exists. Indeed, it seems that allowing for monopoly power in product markets does not help. When an equilibrium does exist, towns are larger than is optimal.

Free entry is not exactly the right assumption now, but the concept of contestability has been proposed with the same consequence when there are no sunk costs (Baumol *et al.* 1982). Since the models here studied are timeless, that is a not unreasonable assumption. Assume then that, in equilibrium, profit in the production of each commodity is zero. Otherwise, one must suppose, another producer will set up a competing production facility, displacing the existing one. It should also be the case in equilibrium that n_i^* maximizes profit per worker,

$$\rho_i(p, n_i) - n_i E(p, n_i + n_{-i}^*, v^*),$$

where n_{-i} is total employment by firms producing commodities other than i. Also, supply must equal demand for each commodity within the town. There are then three equilibrium conditions for each commodity, but only two variables (p_i and n_i^*) for each commodity, along with the single variable v^*. These equilibrium conditions overdetermine the system.

Here is an explicit, robust example of a model in which there is no equilibrium. Each commodity is produced with a fixed cost and a constant marginal cost, using labour alone:

$$f_i(n) = \begin{cases} \gamma_i(n - v_i) & n \geqslant v_i \\ 0 & n < v_i \end{cases}$$

Assume that the expenditure function is

$$E(p, N, v) = \prod_i p_i^{\beta_i}(v + N), \qquad \sum_i \beta_i = 1,$$

where $N = \sum_i n_i$. With these assumptions, there must be positive production of every commodity. Zero profit and market-clearing for commodity i imply that

$$n_i = \beta_i N.$$

The profit-maximization condition with the other conditions requires that

$$v = N - \frac{\beta_i N(\beta_i N - v_i)}{v_i}, \qquad i = 1, \dots, m. \tag{36}$$

When there are more than two commodities, in general there are no values of v and N that satisfy (36); thus, an equilibrium does not exist.

One case where an equilibrium exists is the very special case where the economy is perfectly symmetrical as between commodities. In that case, n_i and p_i are the same for all i. We may as well set all prices equal to unity. Prices will then be omitted from the argument lists for ρ and E. Equilibrium $\hat{n}$ and $\hat{v}$ are determined by the conditions for profit maximization and zero profit:

$$\hat{n} \text{ max } \rho(n) - E(n + (m - 1)\hat{n}, \hat{v}) \tag{37}$$

$$\rho(\hat{n}) = E(m\hat{n}, \hat{v}). \tag{38}$$

Market-clearing is satisfied automatically. In the symmetric case, the optimum is given by

$$n^* \text{ max } \rho(n) - E(mn, v^*) \tag{39}$$

along with (38) for n^*, v^*. Assume E is an increasing function of n. Then, if $n^* \geqslant \hat{n}$,

$$\rho(n^*) \leqslant E(n^* + (m-1)\hat{n}, \hat{v})$$
$$\leqslant E(mn^*, \hat{v})$$
$$< E(mn^*, v^*), \quad \text{since } v^* > \hat{v}$$
$$= \rho(n^*), \quad \text{by (38) for the optimum.}$$

Since this is impossible, we have:

Theorem 7. *In a fully symmetric multi-commodity model with infinite commodity transport costs, town employment in a free-entry monopolistic equilibrium is greater than the optimal level.*

The reason is the external diseconomy between producers that was pointed out above. Inspection of conditions (37)–(39) suggests that the difference between $\hat{n}$ and n^* would be quite large. The distortion can be corrected by a suitable tax on the employment of labour.

Appendix: **Proofs of Lemmas 4 and 5**

Lemma 4. *Let $g_1, g_2, \ldots, g_m$ be concave functions on a set X. Let $z \in X$. Then, if*

$$\sum_{i=1}^{m} [g_i(x) - g_i(z)] \leqslant y \cdot (x - z), \qquad x \in X, \tag{10}$$

there exist $y^1, y^2, \ldots, y^m$ such that $\sum_{i=1}^{m} y^i = y$, and for $i = 1 \ldots, m$,

$$g_i(x) - g_i(z) \leqslant y^i \cdot (x - z), \qquad x \in X,$$

Proof. The result is trivially true if $m = 1$. Assume true for $m - 1 \geqslant 1$.

We can write (10) as

$$\sum_{i=1}^{m-1} [g_i(x) - g_i(z)] \leqslant y \cdot (x - z) - [g_m(x) - g_m(z)], \qquad x \in X.$$

The left-hand side is a concave function of x, the right-hand side a convex function. Therefore, by the separation theorem for convex sets, there is a hyperplane separating the graphs of the left-hand-side function and the right-hand-side function. It cannot be vertical. Thus, there exists t such that

$$\sum_{i=1}^{m-1} [g_i(x) - g_i(z)] \leqslant t \cdot (x - z) \leqslant y \cdot (x - z) - [g_m(x) - g_m(z)], \qquad x \in X.$$

The induction hypothesis applied to the first inequality establishes the existence of $y^1, \ldots, y^{m-1}$ summing to t. Defining $y^m = y - t$, the lemma is proved by induction. $\qquad\square$

Lemma 5. *Let $G(x, y)$ be a concave function of x for each y, and a convex function of y for each x. Then, if*

$$x^* \text{ max } \min_y G(x, y)$$

there exists y^* such that

$$x^* \text{ max } G(x, y^*) \text{ and } y^* \text{ min } G(x^*, y).$$

This is true by the 'envelope theorem' when G is differentiable and there is a unique minimizing y for each x. We need the result with weaker assumptions.

Proof. It is a standard result that, for such a function G,

$$\max_x \ \min_y \ G = \min_y \ \max_x \ G$$

when either side exists. The hypothesis says that the left-hand side exists. Let y^* minimize $\max_x G$. Then

$$G(x^*, y^*) \geqslant \min_y \ G(x^*, y) = \max_x \ G(x, y^*) \geqslant G(x^*, y^*).$$

Hence the inequalities here are actually equalities, and the conclusion of the lemma follows. □

REFERENCES

Arnott, R. (1979) 'Optimal City Size in a Spatial Economy', *Journal of Urban Economics*, Vol. 6, pp. 65–89.

Baumol, W. J., J. C. Panzar, and R. D. Willig (1982) *Contestable Markets and the Theory of Industry Structure*. San Diego: Harcourt Brace Jovanovich.

Beckmann, M. J. and T. C. Koopmans (1957) 'Assignment Problems and the Location of Economic Activities'. *Econometrica*, Vol. 25, pp. 53–76.

Benson, B. L. (1984) 'Spatial Competition with Free Entry, Chamberlinian Tangencies, and Social Efficiency'. *Journal of Urban Economics*, Vol. 15, pp. 270–86.

Bewley, T. (1981) 'A Critique of Tiebout's Theory of Local Public Expenditure'. *Econometrica*, Vol. 49, pp. 713–40.

Brown, D. and G. M. Heal (1983) 'Marginal vs. Average Cost Pricing in the Presence of a Public Monopoly'. *American Economic Review*, Vol. 73, pp. 189–93.

Dixit, A. K. and J. E. Stiglitz (1977) 'Monopolistic Competition and Product Diversity'. *American Economic Review*, pp. 297–308.

Dixit, A. K., J. A. Mirrlees, and N. H. Stern (1975) 'Optimal Saving with Economies of Scale'. *Review of Economic Studies*, Vol. 42, pp. 303–25.

Fujita, M. (1989) *Urban Economic Theory: Land Use and City Size*, Cambridge: Cambridge University Press.

Henderson, J. V. (1985) *Economic Theory and Cities*, London: Academic Press.

——(1988) *Urban Development, Theory, Fact, and Illusion*, Oxford: Oxford University Press.

Mills, E. and R. Lav (1964) 'A Model of Market Area with Free Entry'. *Journal of Political Economy*, Vol. 72, pp. 278–88.

Mirrlees, J. A. (1972) 'The Optimum Town'. *Swedish* [now *Scandinavian*] *Journal of Economics*, Vol. 74, pp. 114–35.

Scotchmer, S. (1985) 'Profit Maximizing Clubs'. *Journal of Public Economics*, Vol. 27, pp. 25–45.

Stiglitz, J. E. (1977) 'The Theory of Local Public Goods'. In M. Feldstein and R. Inman (eds.), *The Economics of Public Services*, London: Macmillan.

Weitzman, M. L. (1970) 'Optimum Growth with Scale Economies in the Creation of Overhead Capital'. *Review of Economic Studies*, Vol. 37, pp. 555–70.

PART II

TAX THEORY

6

An Exploration in the Theory of Optimum Income Taxation

1. INTRODUCTION

One would suppose that, in any economic system where equality is valued, progressive income taxation would be an important instrument of policy. Even in a highly socialist economy, where all who work are employed by the State, the shadow price of highly skilled labour should surely be considerably greater than the disposable income actually available to the labourer. In Western Europe and America, tax rates on both high and low incomes are widely and lengthily discussed:[1] but there is virtually no relevant economic theory to appeal to, despite the importance of the tax.

Redistributive progressive taxation is usually related to a man's income (or, rather, his estimated income). One might obtain information about a man's income-earning potential from his apparent IQ, the number of his degrees, his address, age, or colour: but the natural, and one would suppose the most reliable, indicator of his income-earning potential is his income. As a result of using men's economic performance as evidence of their economic potentialities, complete equality of social marginal utilities of income ceases to be desirable, for the tax system that would bring about that result would completely discourage unpleasant work. The questions therefore arise what principles should govern an optimum income tax, what such a tax schedule would look like, and what degree of inequality would remain once it was established.

The problem seems to be a rather difficult one even in the simplest cases. In this paper, I make the following simplifying assumptions.

(1) Intertemporal problems are ignored. It is usual to levy income tax upon each year's income, with only limited possibilities of transferring one

This paper was first published in the *Review of Economic Studies*, April (1971), pp. 175–208. Work on this paper and its continuation was begun during a stimulating and pleasurable visit to the Department of Economics, MIT. The influence of Peter Diamond is particularly great, and his comments have been very useful. Earlier versions were presented at the Cowles Foundation, to the Economic Study Society, at the London School of Economics, and to CORE. I am grateful to the members of these seminars and to A. B. Atkinson for valuable comments. I am also greatly indebted to P. G. Hare and J. R. Broome for the computations.

[1] Discussions on (usually) orthodox lines, including many important points neglected in the present paper, can be found in Vickrey (1947), Blum and Klaven (1953), Musgrave (1959), [chs. 5; 7, 8], and [Sharp (1969), chs. 11 and 12]. Diamond (1968), is close in spirit to what is attempted here.

year's income to another for tax purposes. In an optimum system, one would no doubt wish to relate tax payments to the whole life pattern of income,[2] and to initial wealth; and in scheduling payments one would wish to pay attention to imperfect personal capital markets and imperfect foresight. The economy discussed below is timeless. Thus, the effects of taxation on saving are ignored. One might perhaps regard the theory presented as a theory of 'earned income' taxation (i.e. non-property income).

(2) Differences in tastes, in family size and composition, and in voluntary transfers are ignored. These raise rather different kinds of problems, and it is natural to assume them away.

(3) Individuals are supposed to determine the quantity and kind of labour they provide by rational calculation, corresponding to the maximization of a utility function, and social welfare is supposed to be a function of individual utility levels. It is also supposed that the quantity of labour a man offers may be varied within wide limits without affecting the price paid for it. The first assumption may well be seriously unrealistic, especially at higher income levels, where it does sometimes appear that there is consumption satiation and that work is done for reasons barely connected with the income it provides to the 'labourer'.

(4) Migration is supposed to be impossible. Since the threat of migration is a major influence on the degree of progression in actual tax systems, at any rate outside the United States, this is another assumption one would rather not make.[3]

(5) The State is supposed to have perfect information about the individuals in the economy, their utilities, and, consequently, their actions. In practice, this is certainly not the case for certain kinds of income from self-employment, in particular work done for the worker himself and his family; and in some countries, the extent of uncertainty about incomes is very great. Yet it seems doubtful whether the neglect of this uncertainty is a simplification of much significance.

(6) Various formal simplifications are made to render the mathematics more manageable: there is supposed to be one kind of labour (in a special sense to be explained below); there is one consumer good; welfare is separable in terms of the different individuals of the economy, and symmetric—i.e. it can be expressed as the sum of the utilities of individuals when the individual utility function (the same for all) is suitably chosen.

(7) The costs of administering the optimum tax schedule are assumed to be negligible.

---

[2] Cf. [Vickrey, ch. 6].

[3] The relation of optimum tax schedules to propensities to migrate is discussed in another paper under preparation.

In Sections 2–5, the more general properties of the optimum income tax schedule, and the rules governing it, are discussed. The treatment is not rigorous. Nevertheless a reader who wants to avoid mathematical details can omit the last page or two of Section 3, and will probably want to glance through Section 4 rather rapidly. In Section 6 I begin the discussion of special cases. The mathematical arguments in Sections 6–8 are frequently complicated. If the reader goes straight to Section 9, where numerical results are presented and discussed, he should not find the omission of the previous sections any handicap. He may, nevertheless, find it interesting to look at the results and conjectures presented at the beginning of Section 7, and at the diagrams for the two cases discussed in Section 8.

Rigorous proofs of the main theorems will be given in a subsequent paper, Mirrlees (1970), contained in Chapter 11 of this Volume.

2. MODEL AND PROBLEM

Individuals have identical preferences. We shall suppose that consumption and working time enter the individual's utility function. When consumption is x and the time worked y, utility is

$$u(x, y).$$

x and y both have to be non-negative, and there is an upper limit to y, which is taken to be 1. In fact, it is assumed that: u is a strictly concave, continuously differentiable, function (strictly) increasing in x, (strictly) decreasing in y, defined for $x > 0$ and $0 \leq y < 1$. u tends to $-\infty$ as x tends to 0 from above or y tends to 1 from below.

The usefulness of a man's time, from the point of view of production, is assumed to vary from person to person. To each individual corresponds a number n such that the quantity of labour provided, per unit of his time, is n. If he works for time y, he provides a quantity of labour ny. There is a known distribution of skills, measured by the parameter n, in the population. The number of persons with labour parameter n or less is $F(n)$. It will be assumed that F is differentiable, so that there is a density function for ability, $f(n) = F'(n)$. Call an individual whose ability-parameter is n an n-man.

The consumption choice of an n-man is denoted by (x_n, y_n). Write $z_n = ny_n$ for the labour he provides. Then the total labour available for use in production in the economy is

$$Z = \int_0^\infty z_n f(n)\mathrm{d}n, \tag{1}$$

and the aggregate demand for consumer goods is

$$X = \int_0^\infty x_n f(n)\mathrm{d}n. \tag{2}$$

In order to avoid the possibility of infinite labour supply, I assume that

$$\int_0^\infty nf(n)\,dn < \infty. \tag{3}$$

Each individual makes his choice of (x_n, y_n) in the light of his budget constraint. Using an income tax, the government can arrange that a man who supplies a quantity of labour z can consume no more than $c(z)$ after tax: the government can choose the function c arbitrarily. It makes sense to impose the restriction on the government's choice of c, that c be upper semi-continuous, for then all individuals have available to them consumption choices that maximize their utility, subject to the budget constraint:[4]

$$(x_n, y_n) \text{ maximizes } u(x, y) \text{ subject to } x \le c(ny). \tag{4}$$

Notice that (x_n, y_n) may not be uniquely determined for every n.[5] I write:

$$u_n = u(x_n, y_n). \tag{5}$$

Proposition 1. *There exists a number $n_0 \ge 0$ such that*

$$\begin{aligned} y_n &= 0 && (n \le n_0), \\ y_n &> 0 && (n > n_0). \end{aligned} \tag{6}$$

Proof. If $m < n$, and $y_m > 0$, $u[c(my_m), y_m] < u[c(n \cdot (m/n)\, y_m), (m/n)y_m] \le u_n$. Consequently, $y_m = 0$ if $y_n = 0$, since then $y_m = 0$ gives the utility u_n to n-man. Thus,

$$n_0 = \inf[n \mid y_n > 0]$$

has the desired properties.

---

[4] To say that c is upper semi-continuous means that

$$\limsup c(z_i) = c(z) \text{ when } \lim_{i \to \infty} z_i = z.$$

If
$$u_n = \sup\,\{u(x,y) \mid x \le c(ny)\}, \text{ and } u(x_i, y_i) \to u_n, \; x_i \le c(ny_i)$$
we can suppose that $x_i \to x$ and $y_i \to y$ (since $\{y_i\}$ and therefore $\{x_i\}$ is bounded). By the upper semi-continuity of c,

$$x \le \limsup c(ny_i) = c(ny);$$

and by the continuity of u, $u(x, y) = \lim u(x_i, y_i) = u_n$. Therefore the supremum is attained.

[5] In other words, we have a *correspondence*, providing a set of utility maximizing choices for n-men. It arises when the consumption function c coincides with the indifference curve for part of its length. It is convenient nevertheless to use the notation of the text, despite its suggestion that we are dealing with a function.

Proposition 2. *Any function[6]of* n, (x_n, y_n), *that satisfies* (4) *for some upper semi-continuous function* c *also satisfies* (4) *for some non-decreasing, right-continuous function* c'.

Proof. Define $c'(z) = \sup_{z' \leq z} c(z')$. If $x'_n \leq c'(ny'_n)$, then, for any $\epsilon > 0$, there exists $y''_n \leq y'_n$ such that $x'_n - \epsilon \leq c(ny''_n)$. Thus, $u(x'_n - \epsilon, y''_n) \leq u_n$, which implies, since u is a decreasing function in y, that $u(x'_n - \epsilon, y'_n) \leq u_n$. Letting $\epsilon \to 0$, $u(x'_n, y'_n) \leq u_n$. It follows that (x_n, y_n) maximizes u subject to $x \leq c'(ny)$.

c' is clearly a non-decreasing function of z. To prove that it is right-continuous, take a decreasing sequence $z^i \to z$. $c'(z^i)$ is a non-increasing sequence, and therefore tends to a limit, which is not less than $c'(z)$. If it is equal to $c'(z)$, there is no more to prove. Suppose it is greater. Then for some $\epsilon > 0$ each $c'(z^i) > c'(z) + \epsilon$. Therefore, there exists a sequence $(\bar{z}^i)$ such that $\bar{z}^i \leq z^i$ and $c'(z^i) \geq c(\bar{z}^i) > c'(z) + \epsilon$. The second inequality implies that $\bar{z}^i > z$. Thus $\bar{z}^i \to z$. Yet $\limsup c(\bar{z}^i) > c(z)$, which contradicts upper semi-continuity. Thus, in fact, c is right-continuous.

This proposition says that the marginal tax rate may as well be not greater than 100 per cent. We shall consider later whether it should be positive.

The government chooses the function c so as to maximize a welfare function

$$W = \int_0^\infty G(u_n) f(n) \mathrm{d}n. \tag{7}$$

I use the function G here, rather than writing u_n alone, because I shall later want to devote special attention to the case $u_{xy} = 0$ (when u can be written as the sum of a function depending only on x and a function depending only on y). In maximizing welfare, the government is constrained by production possibilities: it must be possible to produce the consumption demands, X, arising from its choice of c, with labour input no greater than Z. The production constraint is written

$$X \leq H(Z). \tag{8}$$

We have not yet fully specified the possibilities available to the government, since, if (x_n, y_n) is not uniquely defined, it is not clear whether the government or the consumer is allowed to choose the particular utility-maximizing point. Perhaps it is reasonable to suppose that the government can choose, and that the necessity for market-clearing will make its choices actual. But it will turn out that the issue is of no significance when we make the following assumption, as we shall:

(A) y_n is uniquely defined for all n except for a set of measure 0.

Thus, the class of functions c from which the government chooses is further restricted by the requirement that the function lead to choices satisfying (A). It

---

[6] It is easy to see that the result is true for a correspondence also.

will appear in due course that (A) is satisfied for *all* functions c in the particular cases we shall be most concerned with.

3. NECESSARY CONDITIONS FOR THE OPTIMUM

On the assumption that an optimum for our problem exists, we shall now obtain conditions that it must satisfy. The mathematical argument will not be rigorous. To do the analysis properly, one must attend to a number of rather tricky points. Since these technical details tend to obscure the main lines of the argument, rigorous proofs will be presented separately, in the continuation of this paper. The nature of these neglected difficulties will be discussed briefly in the next section.

The key to a reasonably neat solution of the problem is to find a convenient expression of the condition that each man maximizes his utility subject to the imposed 'consumption function' c. If we suppose that c is differentiable, the derivative of $u[c(ny), y]$ with respect to y must be zero. Denoting the derivative of u with respect to its first and second arguments by u_1 and u_2, respectively, we have

$$u_1 n c'(ny) + u_2 = 0. \tag{9}$$

Recollect that u_n is the utility of n-man. Then a straightforward calculation, using the first-order condition (9), yields

$$\frac{du_n}{dn} = u_1 y c' = -\frac{y u_2}{n}. \tag{10}$$

(The expressions on the right are, of course, alternative expressions for the *partial* derivative of u with respect to n, evaluated at the maximum. The case where n enters u in a more general manner can be analysed by using this more general equation. We shall return to this point later.)

Our problem is to maximize w subject to the constraint of the production function, $X \leq H(Z)$, the differential equation (10), and the definition $u_n = u(x_n, y_n)$. Those who are familiar with the Pontriyagin Maximum Principle will see that this is a form of problem fairly suitable for treatment by it. Shadow prices p and w have to be introduced for X and Z. Then we would like to maximize

$$W - pX + wZ = \int [G(u_n) - p x_n + w y_n n] f(n) \, dn \tag{11}$$

subject to (10). u_n is to be regarded as the state variable, y_n (say) as the control variable, while x_n is determined as a function of u_n and y_n from the equation $u_n = u(x_n, y_n)$. The Hamiltonian is

$$M = [G(u_n) - p x_n + w y_n n] f(n) - \phi_n \frac{y_n u_2}{n},$$

where ϕ_n is a function of n satisfying the differential equation

$$
\begin{aligned}
\frac{\mathrm{d}\phi}{\mathrm{d}n} &= -\frac{\partial M}{\partial u} \\
&= -\left[G'(u_n) - \frac{p}{u_1}\right]f(n) + \phi\frac{y_n u_{12}}{n u_1}
\end{aligned}
\tag{12}
$$

y_n should then be chosen so as to maximize M:

$$
\left[wn + \frac{p u_2}{u_1}\right]f(n) + \phi_n\frac{\psi_y}{n} = 0,
\tag{13}
$$

where the function $\psi(u, y)$ is defined by

$$
\psi(u, y) = -y u_2(x, y), \qquad u = u(x, y),
\tag{14}
$$

and ψ_y is its partial derivative with respect to y. (Notice, at the same time, that $\psi_u = -y u_{12}/u_1$.)

Equation (12) can now be integrated to obtain an expression for ϕ_n; which, when substituted in (13), provides us with an equation to be satisfied by the optimum we seek. Before going on to use this equation, however, we shall derive it in a different way, by a more explicit use of the methods of the calculus of variations. The use of the Maximum Principle has a number of serious disadvantages. It does not show us how to obtain certain important supplementary conditions on the optimum. The analysis provides no hint as to how it could be made rigorous. It does not provide any insight into the kind of maximization that is going on. When we have done a more explicit variational analysis, we shall be able to see better where the logical holes are, and to understand why things come out the way they do.

For this purpose, I prefer to write (10) in integrated form:

$$
\begin{aligned}
u_n &= -\int_0^n y_m u_2(x_m, y_m)\frac{\mathrm{d}m}{m} + u(c(0), 0), \\
&= \int_0^n \psi(u_m, y_m)\frac{\mathrm{d}m}{m} + u_0,
\end{aligned}
\tag{15}
$$

using the notation ψ introduced above, and denoting the utility allowed to a man who does no work by u_0. Suppose first that ψ is independent of u (corresponding to the special case $u_{12} = 0$). If we consider a variation from the optimum which changes the functions u_n and y_n by 'small' variations δu_n and δy_n, we deduce from (15) that these variations must be related by

$$
\delta u_n = \int_0^n \psi_y \delta y_m\frac{\mathrm{d}m}{m} + \delta u_0.
\tag{16}
$$

This variation will bring about changes in W, X, and Z. As before, introduce shadow prices (in terms of welfare) for X and Z. Then the variation must leave (11) stationary:

$$
\begin{aligned}
0 = \delta &\int [G(u_n) - px_n + wy_n n] f(n) dn \\
= &\int \left[G'(u_n) \delta u_n - p \left(\frac{1}{u_1} \delta u_n - \frac{u_2}{u_1} \delta y_n \right) + w \delta y_n n \right] f(n) dn,
\end{aligned}
\tag{17}
$$

where the variation in x is calculated as follows:

$$
\delta u_n = \delta u(x_n, y_n) = u_1 \delta x_n + u_2 \delta y_n.
\tag{18}
$$

It remains to substitute (16) in (17), yielding

$$
\begin{aligned}
0 = &\int_0^\infty \left\{ \left[G'(u_n) - \frac{p}{u_1} \right] \left[\int_0^n \psi_y \delta y_m \frac{dm}{m} + \delta u_0 \right] + \left[wn + p \frac{u_2}{u_1} \right] \delta y_n \right\} f(n) dn \\
= &\int_0^\infty \left\{ \int_n^\infty \left[G'(u_m) - \frac{p}{u_1} \right] f(m) dm \cdot \frac{\psi_y}{n} + \left(wn + p \frac{u_2}{u_1} \right) f(n) \right\} \delta y_n dn \\
&+ \int_0^\infty \left[G'(u_n) - \frac{p}{u_1} \right] f(n) dn \cdot \delta u_0.
\end{aligned}
\tag{19}
$$

The second equation is obtained by inverting the order of integration in the double integral.[7] Equation (19) is to be satisfied for all possible variations of the function y_n, and the number u_0. Since u_0 can be either increased or decreased at the optimum (if, as is to be expected in general, some people will do no work at the optimum),

$$
\int_0^\infty \left[G'(u_n) - \frac{p}{u_1} \right] f(n) dn = 0
\tag{20}
$$

at the optimum.

---

[7] The double integral is

$$
\int_0^\infty \left[G'(u_n) - \frac{p}{u_1} \right] f(n) \int_0^n \psi_y \delta y_m \frac{dm}{m} \cdot dn.
$$

The region over which the integration takes place is defined by $0 \le m \le n$. Thus, when the order of integration is inverted, n ranges between m and ∞ for given m. The integral can therefore be written

$$
\int_0^\infty \int_m^\infty \left[G' - \frac{p}{u_1} \right] f(n) dn \cdot \psi_y \delta y_m \frac{dm}{m},
$$

which is seen to justify (19) on permuting the symbols m and n.

If all variations in y_n were possible—and this is a question we shall take up shortly—we could also claim that the expression within braces ought to be zero:

$$\left(wn + p\frac{u_2}{u_1}\right)f(n) = \frac{\psi_y}{n}\int_n^\infty\left[\frac{p}{u_1} - G'(u_m)\right]f(m)\,\mathrm{d}m. \tag{21}$$

It should be noticed that this equation will be valid only for $n \geq n_0$: it does not apply to n for which $y_n = 0$ (except n_0) because, there, not all variations of the function y_n are possible, since y_n cannot be negative.

Finally, we know that the marginal product of labour should be equal to the shadow wage:

$$pH'(Z) = w. \tag{22}$$

Equations (20) and (21) have been worked out under the special assumption that ψ is independent of u. In the more general case, we have to replace (16) by

$$\delta u_n = \int_0^n T_{mn}\psi_y\delta y_m\frac{\mathrm{d}m}{m} + T_{0n}\delta u_0, \tag{23}$$

where

$$T_{mn} = \exp\int_m^n \psi_u\frac{\mathrm{d}m'}{m'}. \tag{24}$$

To show this, we can go back to the differential equation (10). Applying the variation, we obtain from it

$$\frac{\mathrm{d}}{\mathrm{d}n}\delta u_n = \frac{1}{n}\psi_u\delta u_n + \frac{1}{n}\psi_y\delta y_n. \tag{25}$$

This is a first-order linear equation, and can therefore be solved by the standard method to give the solution (23).

Having replaced (16) by (23), we can now go through the rest of the calculation as before. We find that (20) is generalized into

$$\int_0^\infty [G'(u_n) - p/u_1]T_{0n}f(n)\,\mathrm{d}n = 0, \tag{26}$$

while (21) becomes

$$(wn + pu_2/u_1)f(n) = \frac{\psi_y}{n}\int_n^\infty [p/u_1 - G'(u_m)]T_{nm}f(m)\,\mathrm{d}m. \tag{27}$$

Notice that we have T_{nm} here, although it was T_{mn} that appeared in (23).

If these equations are correct, the two integral equations, (15) and (27), may be thought of as determining the two functions u_n and y_n, given the three parameters u_0, w, and p. The values of these parameters are fixed by the three equations (26), (22), and (8). We have enough relations to determine the optimum tax schedule, since the function c can be determined once we know u_n and y_n.

4. NECESSARY CONDITIONS: A COMPLETE STATEMENT

The argument used to derive these conditions for the optimum tax schedule had a number of weak points. It is indeed unlikely that the relationships derived above hold in general. Among the weak points of the argument, notice that

  (i) the existence of the shadow prices p and w was assumed without proof;
  (ii) the optimum tax schedule, and the resulting functions x_n, y_n, and u_n, were assumed to be differentiable;
  (iii) the application of the variation was quite heuristic; and
  (iv) no justification was provided for assuming that the function y_n could be varied arbitrarily (for $n > n_0$).

I shall not comment on (i) and (iii), which, though important, are technical matters: they can be justified. (ii) is not satisfied in general: there was no reason to suppose that it would be. When (ii) is not satisfied, the first-order condition, (9), for maximization of utility ceases to be meaningful. Finally, (iv) is never justified. The function y_n is derived from the imposition of the consumption function c, and we have no *a priori* information about it. We must expect that some conceivable functions y_n can never arise from the imposition of a consumption function. The class of possible y-functions is no doubt quite complicated in certain cases. Fortunately, it is possible to specify that class quite simply in the realistic cases, and it is then possible to use the variational argument rigorously.

Problem (ii) is dealt with in the rigorous analysis by depending on equation (15) instead of the differential first-order condition (9). It is a remarkable fact that this condition holds if and only if the various functions arise from utility maximization under an imposed consumption function, even when that function is not differentiable. For proof, the reader is referred to Mirrlees (1970).

To deal with problem (iv), we have to restrict the class of utility functions considered. We assume that

(B) $V(x, y) = -y u_2 / u_1$ is an increasing function of y for each $x > 0$ (and bounded in $0 \leq x \leq \bar{x}, 0 \leq y \leq \bar{y}$ for any $\bar{x} < \infty$ and $\bar{y} < 1$).

It will be noticed that this is an assumption about preferences, not just about the form of the utility function used to represent preferences. The second part of the assumption is readily acceptable. The first and main part of the assumption holds if and only if, for a given level of consumption x, a 1 per cent increase in the amount of work done requires a larger increase in consumption to maintain the same utility level, the greater is the amount of work being done. It is equivalent to assuming that (in the absence of taxation) the consumer's demand for goods is an increasing function of the real wage rate (at any given non-wage income.[8] Few individuals appear to have preferences violating (B), and intuitively it is rather plausible. We shall later use the fact that (B) holds if preferences can be represented by an additive utility function. (It will be noticed that, as $y \to 1$, $V \to +\infty$, so that the assumption must hold for some ranges of y.) If the assumption does not hold, the theory of optimum taxation is more complicated.

The point of the assumption is indicated in the following theorem.

Theorem 1. *Under Assumption (B), $z_n = ny_n$ maximizes utility for every n under some consumption function c if and only if*

(i) z_n *is a non-decreasing function defined for $n > 0$;*
(ii) $0 \leq z_n < n$ *for all $n > 0$.*

For a rigorous proof of this theorem, the reader is referred to (Mirrlees (unpublished)). For a heuristic justification, suppose that z_n is differentiable, and that c is twice differentiable. The first-order condition, (9), can be written

$$\frac{\partial}{\partial z} u(c(z), z/n) = \frac{u_1}{z}[zc'(z) - V(c(z), z/n)] = 0. \tag{28}$$

Furthermore, we have the second-order condition, that the derivative is non-increasing at z_n. Since it is zero there, this is also true when we drop the positive

---

[8] This equivalence is fairly obvious from an indifference curve diagram. For a formal proof that (B) implies that consumption is an increasing function of the wage rate, let w be the wage rate, and m non-labour income (both measured in terms of goods). (B) states that wy, regarded as a function of x and y, is an increasing function of y. Write x and y as functions of w and m, putting $x = x(w, m)$, $y = y(w, m)$ and $x' = x(w', m)$, $y' = y(w', m)$ where $w' > w$. I shall show that $x' > x$. To do this, choose w'' and m'' such that $x'' = x(w'', m'') = x$, and

$$y'' = y(w'', m'') = \frac{w}{w'} y.$$

Since $x'' - w' y' = m$, (x', y') is preferred to (x'', y''); and therefore

$$x' - x > w''(y' - y'')$$
$$= \frac{w''}{w'}(w'y' - w'y'') = \frac{w''}{w'}(w'y' - wy)$$
$$= \frac{w''}{w'}(x' - x),$$

since $x' - w'y' = m = x - wy$. This implies, with our assumption $w'' < w'$, that $x' > x$. The converse proposition can be proved by reversing the steps.

factor u_1/z. In other words,

$$\frac{\partial}{\partial z}[zc'(z) - V(c(z), z/n)] \leqq 0, \qquad \text{at } z = z_n. \tag{29}$$

Now differentiate the equation $z_n c'(z_n) - V(c(z_n)z_n/n) = 0$ with respect to n:

$$\frac{\partial}{\partial z}[zc' - V]\Big|_{z=z_n}\frac{dz_n}{dn} = -V_y(c(z_n), z_n/n)z/n^2. \tag{30}$$

It follows from (29) and Assumption (B) that

$$\frac{dz_n}{dn} > 0 \tag{31}$$

unless $z_n = 0$. In fact z_n is strictly increasing when $n > n_0$ and c is differentiable; a corner in c causes z_n to be constant for a range of values of n. (An indifference curve diagram makes this clear.) Condition (ii) of the theorem clearly has to be satisfied by the utility-maximizing choice.

To prove that a suitable consumption function exists for a given z-function satisfying the two conditions, one defines c by the first-order condition (28). Equation (30) then shows (nearly) that the second-order condition for a maximum is satisfied. This does not yet prove global maximization of utility, but that also is true.

It should be noticed that, as a corollary of Theorem 1, condition (A) holds when condition (B) holds, for z_n is shown to be non-decreasing even if it is a correspondence. It therefore takes a single value for all but a countable set of values of n. *A fortiori*, condition (A) is satisfied in this case.

Theorem 1 at once implies that z_n and therefore also x_n are non-decreasing functions when the optimum tax schedule is imposed. Furthermore, it shows us quite straightforwardly what changes in the function y_n we are allowed to contemplate when applying the variational argument that allowable small changes should make only a second-order difference to the maximand. The rigorous argument is still complicated, in part because one has to allow for the possibility that z_n is constant over some intervals, and discontinuous at some values of n. The full statement of the result, which is proved in (Mirrlees (1970)), is as follows:

Theorem 2. *If preferences satisfy Assumption (B) and (u_n, x_n, y_n) arise from optimum income taxation, then*

(i) $z_n = ny_n$ is a non-decreasing function of n;

(ii) $u_n = u_0 - \int_0^n [y_m u_2(x_m, y_m)/m]dm \quad (n \geqq 0);$ $\tag{32}$

(iii) *at all points of increase of z_n (i.e. where $z_n > z_{n'}$ for all $n' < n$, or $z_n < z_{n'}$ for all $n' > n$)*

$$A_n \equiv [w + u_2^{(n)}/nu_1^{(n)}]f(n) - \frac{\psi_y}{n^2}\int_n^\infty \left[\frac{1}{u_1^{(m)}} - \lambda G'(u_m)\right]T_{nm}f(m)\,dm$$

$$= 0, \tag{33}$$

where superscripts (n), etc., indicate that the function is evaluated at n-man (etc.)'s utility-maximizing choice, and

$$\psi_y = -u_2^{(n)} - y_n u_{22}^{(n)} + y_n u_2^{(n)} u_{12}^{(n)} / u_1^{(n)}, \tag{34}$$

$$T_{nm} = \exp\left[-\int_n^m y_{m'} u_{12}(x_{m'}, y_{m'})/u_1(x_{m'}, y_{m'}) \cdot dm'\right]; \tag{35}$$

(iv) *If $n \in [n_1, n_2]$, where z is constant on $[n_1, n_2]$, and $[n_1, n_2]$ is a maximal interval of constancy for z,*

$$\int_{n1}^n A_m dm \geqq 0, \qquad \int_n^{n2} A_m dm \leqq 0; \tag{36}$$

(v) *If z is discontinuous at n, $\bar{y}_n$ is defined to be $\lim_{m \to n-} y_m$, $\bar{x}_n$ is defined by*

$$u(\bar{x}_n, \bar{y}_n) = u_n = u(x_n, y_n),$$

and $\bar{u}_1$, etc., denote $\bar{u}_1$ evaluated at $\bar{x}_n, \bar{y}_n$, while u_1, etc., denote evaluation at x_n, y_n,

$$\frac{(wy_n - x_n/n) - (w\bar{y}_n - \bar{x}_n/n)}{\bar{y}_n \bar{u}_2 - y_n u_2} = \frac{w + u_2/nu_1}{\psi_y} = \frac{w + \bar{u}_2/n\bar{u}_1}{\bar{\psi}_y} \tag{37}$$

If ψ_y is a non-decreasing function of y for constant u, z_n is continuous for all n.

(vi) $$\int_0^\infty \left[\frac{1}{u_1} - \lambda G'(u_m)\right] T_{0m} f(m) dm = 0, \tag{38}$$

(vii) $X = H(Z),$ $\tag{39}$

$w = H'(Z).$ $\tag{40}$

It will be noticed that in this statement w is the commodity shadow wage rate (w/p in the earlier notation), while λ ($1/p$ in the previous notation) is the inverse of the marginal social utility of commodities (national income). The second part of (v) should be particularly noted, since we are quite likely to be willing to assume that ψ_y is a non-decreasing function of y, and it is a great advantage not to have to worry about possible discontinuities in z_n. It does not seem possible, unfortunately, to delimit a class of cases in which one can be sure that $[0, n_0]$

will be the only interval of constancy for z. It should be mentioned that, when ψ_y is not non-decreasing, and (37) may possibly apply, the conditions of Theorem 1 may define more than one candidate for optimality, and then only direct comparison of the welfare generated by the alternative paths so defined will solve the problem.

5. INTERPRETATION

If n is not in an interval of constancy for z, and $c(\cdot)$ is therefore a differentiable function at z_n, the first-order condition (9) applies. It can be written

$$-u_2/nu_1 = c'(z). \tag{41}$$

If we denote the marginal tax rate, $[d/d(wz)][wz - c(z)]$, by θ, we have

$$
\begin{aligned}
w\theta &= \frac{d}{dz}[wz - c(z)] = w + \frac{u_2}{nu_1} \\
&= \frac{\psi_y}{n^2 f(n)} \int_n^\infty \frac{1 - \lambda G' u_1}{u_1} T_{nm} f(m)\, dm,
\end{aligned}
\tag{42}
$$

by (33). Equation (42) suggests the considerations that should influence the magnitude of the marginal tax rate. First, it can tell us something about the sign of θ: we already know that θ will not be greater than 1, but we were not previously able to say anything about its sign. Of course, we expect that it will not usually be negative. Using (42) and the conditions in Theorem 1, we can establish this rigorously.

Note first that $1 - \lambda G' u_1$ is a non-decreasing function of n, since x_n is a non-decreasing function of n, and $(\delta/\delta x)G = G' u_1$ a decreasing function of x. If $1 - \lambda G' u_1$ were always positive or always negative, (38) could not be satisfied. Therefore

$$\int_n^\infty \frac{1}{u_1}(1 - \lambda G' u_1) T_{nm} f(m)\, dm$$

is increasing in n for n less than some $\bar{n}$; but in any case is positive for $n > \bar{n}$. (Here we use the properties $u_1 > 0$, $T_{mn} > 0$.) Since the integral is zero when $n = 0$, it is non-negative for all n. Consequently the marginal tax rate is non-negative at all points of increase of z. If n is not a point of increase of z, c is not differentiable at z_n. It is easily seen that, if $[n_1, n_2]$ is a maximal interval of constancy of z, $-u_2/nu_1$ is equal to the left derivative of c at n_1, and the right derivative at n_2. Thus, both the 'right' and 'left' marginal tax rates are non-negative in this case. Summarizing:

Proposition 3.[9] *If Assumption (B) is satisfied, $wz - c(z)$ (the 'tax function') is a non-decreasing function for all z that actually occur (and may therefore be taken to be a non-decreasing function for all z).*

Having established that the integral in (42) is non-negative for all n, we can see that the marginal tax rate will be greater if there are relatively few n-men than otherwise; or if the utility-value of work, $-yu_y$, is more sensitive to work done (utility being held constant); or if n is closer to $\bar{n}$, the value of n at which $1 = \lambda G' u_1$ (and the integral is therefore a maximum). If f is a single-peaked distribution, the first consideration suggests that marginal tax rates should be greatest for the richest and the poorest; but the last consideration tells the other way.

In any case, it is important to note than n_0, the largest n for which $y_n = 0$, may be quite large: if the number who do not work in the optimum regime is large, the marginal tax rate may not be high at zero income. Explicitly, we can rewrite (38) in the form

$$\left[\frac{1}{u_1(x_0, 0)} - \lambda G'(u_0)\right] F(n_0) + \int_{n_0}^{\infty} \left[\frac{1}{u_1} - \lambda G'\right] T_{n_0 m} f(m) \mathrm{d}m = 0, \qquad (43)$$

which, when combined with (33) (for $n = n_0$), gives

$$w + \frac{u_2(x_0, 0)}{n_0 u_1(x_0, 0)} = \psi_y(u_0, 0) \frac{F(n_0)}{n_0^2 f(n_0)} \left[\lambda G'(u_0) - \frac{1}{u_1(x_0, 0)}\right]. \qquad (44)$$

Unfortunately, one cannot get much information from these 'local' conditions, at least for small n. For any detail, and in particular for numerical results, one must examine the whole system of equations. It is easier to do that for particular examples of the general problem, and that is what we shall do in succeeding sections. It may be noted, however, that (44) does provide us with *some* information about n_0 and x_0. For example, it is clear that n_0 can be zero only if F/nf tends to 0 as n tends to 0; indeed, since the left-hand side of (44) is bounded, $n_0 = 0$ only if $x_0 = 0$, and therefore $1/u_1 = 0$. It follows that $n_0 = 0$ only if $F/(n^2 f)$ is bounded as $n \to 0$, which means that F tends to zero faster than $\exp(-1/n)$. This excludes the cases usually considered by economists. We may conclude at this stage that it will be optimal, in the most interesting cases, to encourage some of the population to be idle.

A number of conclusions have been obtained, but they are fairly weak: the marginal tax rate lies between zero and one; in a large class of cases, consumption and labour supply vary continuously with the skill of the individual;

---

[9] The analysis and result can be generalized to the utility function $u(x, z, n)$ where the parameter n can indicate variations in tastes as well as skill. The extension is fairly routine and will not be discussed here.

there will usually be a group of people who ought to work only if they enjoy it. The main feature of the results is that the optimum tax schedule depends upon the distribution of skills within the population, and the labour-consumption preferences of the population, in such a complicated way that it is not possible to say in general whether marginal tax rates should be higher for high-income, low-income, or intermediate-income groups. The two integral equations that characterize the optimum tax schedule are, however, of a reasonably manageable form. One expects to be able to calculate the schedule in particular cases without great difficulty. In the next sections of the paper, I shall show how this can be done in certain special cases, and obtain further properties of the optimum tax in these cases.

6. ADDITIVE UTILITY

An interesting case arises when, for all x and y,

$$u_{12} = 0. \tag{45}$$

Thus u_1 depends only on x, and u_2 only on y.

Proposition 4. *If (45) is satisfied, $V(x, y)$ is an increasing function of y, bounded for small x and y.*
    Proof. $V = -yu_2(y)/u_1(x)$, and $V_2 = (-u_2 - yu_{22})/u_1 > 0$. Boundedness is obvious.

Corollary. *Under (45), Theorem 1 applies.*

In particular, we know, from statement (v) of that theorem that y_n is continuous provided that ψ_y is non-decreasing. In the present case, this condition is equivalent to the requirement that

$$-yu_2(y) \text{ is convex.} \tag{46}$$

There is no reason why this assumption should hold in general, but it is easily checked for any particular case. We shall now restrict attention to cases for which (46) holds.[10]
    If we restrict attention also to cases where z is strictly increasing when $n > n_0$, the optimum situation will be a solution of

$$\left. \begin{aligned} \left(w + \frac{u_2}{nu_1}\right)n^2 f(n) &= \psi_y \int_n^\infty \left(\frac{1}{u_1} - \lambda G'\right)f(m)\mathrm{d}m, \qquad (47) \\[2ex] u_n &= u_0 - \int_0^n y_m u_2 \frac{\mathrm{d}m}{m}. \qquad (48) \end{aligned} \right\}$$

---

[10] In Mirrlees (1970) a theorem is proved which states that the conditions of Theorem 2 are in fact *sufficient* (as well as necessary) for an optimum in the special case now being considered.

We shall further assume that f is continuously differentiable. Since x_n, y_n are continuous in this case, it follows that u_n and $(w + u_2/nu_1)/\psi_y$ are differentiable functions of n. Write

$$v = \frac{w + u_2/nu_1}{\psi_y}. \tag{49}$$

u and v are continuously differentiable functions of x and y. Since $\partial u/\partial x > 0$, $\partial u/\partial y < 0$, and, as can easily be seen, $\partial v/\partial x < 0$, $\partial v/\partial y < 0$, the Jacobian $\partial(u, v)/\partial(x, y)$ is always negative. Consequently x and y can be expressed as continuously differentiable functions of u and v, and are therefore themselves differentiable functions of n.

We can now write (47) and (48) as differential equations:

$$\frac{dv}{dn} = -\frac{v}{n}\left(2 + \frac{nf'}{f}\right) - \frac{1}{n^2 u_1} + \frac{\lambda G'}{n^2}, \tag{50}$$

$$\frac{du}{dn} = -\frac{yu_2}{n}, \tag{51}$$

which, as we have just shown, can be thought of as equations in u and v. The particular solution we seek, and the particular value of λ, are defined by the boundary conditions, (39), (40),

$$v_{n_0} = \frac{F(n_0)}{n_0^2 f(n_0)}\left[\lambda G'(u_{n_0}) - \frac{1}{u_1(x_{n_0})}\right], \tag{52}$$

which is the form (38) takes here, and

$$v_n n^2 f(n) \to 0 \quad (n \to \infty), \tag{53}$$

which is apparent from (47). Provided that z_n is strictly increasing for $n \geq n_0$, a solution that satisfies all those conditions will, by Theorem 2 of Mirrlees (1970), provide the optimum.

Equations (39) and (40), the production function and the marginal productivity equation, may be ignored in the calculations. Corresponding to the particular values of w and λ used in the calculation, one obtains values for X and Z. Thus, we know the optimum tax schedule when the marginal product is w and the average product is X/Z. In this way one could obtain a range of tax schedules corresponding to different average products and marginal products—which is what one wants. Of course, it is desirable to choose λ so that the average product will be related to the marginal product, w, in a reasonable way. This should not present any great difficulty.

To determine the sign of $dz_n/dn = y_n + n(dy_n/dn)$, we calculate, from (49),

$$\psi_y \frac{dv}{dn} = \left(\frac{u_{22}}{nu_1} - v\psi_{yy}\right)\frac{dy}{dn} - \frac{u_2}{n^2 u_1} - \frac{u_2 u_{11}}{nu_1^2}\frac{dx}{dn}$$

$$= \left(\frac{u_{22}}{nu_1} - v\psi_{yy}\right)\frac{dy}{dn} - \frac{u_2}{n^2 u_1} + \frac{u_2^2 u_{11}}{nu_1^3}\frac{dy}{dn} - \frac{u_2 u_{11}}{nu_1^3}\frac{du}{dn}$$

$$= \frac{1}{n}\left(\frac{u_{22}}{nu_1} - v\psi_{yy} + \frac{u_2^2 u_{11}}{nu_1^3}\right)\frac{dz}{dn} - \frac{y_n}{n}\left(\frac{u_{22}}{nu_1} - v\psi_{yy}\right) - \frac{u_2}{n^2 u_1}, \qquad (54)$$

substituting from (51). Therefore, using (50),

$$\left[\frac{u_{22}}{nu_1} - v\psi_{yy} + \frac{u_2^2 u_{11}}{nu_1^3}\right]\frac{dz}{dn} = \frac{yu_{22}}{nu_1} - yv\psi_{yy} + \frac{u_2}{nu_1} - \left(2 + \frac{nf'}{f}\right)v\psi_y$$

$$- \frac{\psi_y}{nu_1} + \frac{\lambda\psi_y G'}{n}$$

$$= -\psi_y\left\{\left(2 + \frac{nf'}{f} + \frac{yv\psi_{yy}}{\psi_y}\right)v + \frac{2}{nu_1} - \frac{\lambda G'}{n}\right\}.$$

$$(55)$$

We may therefore check the assumption $dz/dn \geqq 0$ by examining the solution to see whether

$$\left(2 + \frac{nf'}{f} + \frac{yv\psi_{yy}}{\psi_y}\right)v + \frac{2}{nu_1} - \frac{\lambda G'}{n} \geqq 0. \qquad (56)$$

Equation (56) is equivalent to $dz/dn \geqq 0$ because the expression in square brackets in (55) is negative, term by term.

In computation, one can proceed as follows:

(1) A value of λ is chosen. To get the right order of magnitude, one can calculate $\int_0^\infty u_1^{-1} f dn / \int_0^\infty G' f dn$ (cf. (38)) for some particular feasible, and *a priori* plausible, allocation of consumption and labour.

(2) A trial value of $n_0 > 0$ is chosen. (It should be borne in mind that the inequality $v_{n0} \geqq 0$ may, with (52), restrict the range of possible n_0.)

(3) Bearing in mind that $y_{n0} = 0$, the values of v_{n0} and u_{n0} are obtained from (49) and (52).

(4) The solution of (50) and (51) is calculated for increasing n until either (56) fails to be satisfied, or it becomes apparent that (53) will not be satisfied (see step (6) below).

(5) If (56) fails to be satisfied, z_n is kept constant, u_n (and v_n) being calculated from (49) until (56) is satisfied again, when z_n is allowed to increase and the solution pursued as in (Mirrlees(1970)).

(6) The attempted solution should be stopped if u_n or x_n begins to decrease, or v_n or y_n falls to zero, or x_n, y_n cannot be calculated (e.g. because u_n exceeds the upper bound of u, if there is one). Other stopping rules can be given for particular examples, depending on the structure of the solutions of the equations.

(7) A range of trial values of n_0 must be used to find the one that most nearly provides a solution satisfying (53). Efficient rules for iteration might be obtained in particular cases.

7. FEATURES OF SOLUTIONS

Solutions may, for all I know, be very diverse in their characteristics; but examination of the equations suggests a number of comments. First, we note that v_n will always lie between 0 and $1/\psi_y(0)$, since

$$0 \leqq \frac{1 + u_2/nu_1}{\psi_y} \leqq \frac{1 + u_2/nu_1}{\psi_y(0)} < \frac{1}{\psi_y(0)}. \tag{57}$$

We are therefore led to expect that v tends to a limit as $n \to \infty$. (It might cycle for certain forms of f, of a kind one would perhaps be unlikely to use.) y is also bounded, by 0 and 1, and is therefore likely to tend to a limit. One is then led to certain conjectures about the limits, which ought to hold for sufficiently regular f and u.

Let

$$-\frac{nf'}{f} \to \gamma + 2 \leqq \infty. \tag{58}$$

(Since $\int_0^\infty nf \, dn < \infty$, $\gamma \geqq 0$: otherwise $n^2 f$ is increasing for large n, therefore bounded below.) Further, suppose

$$u_1 \sim \alpha x^{-\mu} \quad (\mu > 0) \tag{59}$$

as $x \to \infty$. Then there appear to be three cases; in each of which one expects the following results to hold:

(i) $\mu < 1$. As $n \to \infty$,

$$y_n \to 1 \tag{60}$$

and

$$v_n \to 0. \tag{61}$$

The marginal tax rate,

$$\theta \to 1. \tag{62}$$

(ii) $\mu = 1$. As $n \to \infty$,

$$y_n \to \bar{y}, \tag{63}$$

where $\bar{y}$ is defined (uniquely) by

$$\bar{y}u_2(\bar{y}) = -\alpha, \tag{64}$$

and

$$v_n \to [-(1+\gamma)u_2(\bar{y}) - \bar{y}u_{22}(\bar{y})]^{-1}. \tag{65}$$

Furthermore,

$$\theta \to \frac{1+v}{1+v+\gamma}, \tag{66}$$

where

$$v = \frac{\bar{y}u_{22}(\bar{y})}{u_2(y)}. \tag{67}$$

(iii) $\mu > 1$. As $n \to \infty$,

$$y_n \to 0, \tag{68}$$

and

$$v_n \to [-(1+\gamma)u_2(0)]^{-1}. \tag{69}$$

$$\theta \to \frac{1}{1+\gamma}. \tag{70}$$

(It may be noted that, in a natural sense, (66) holds for all cases.)

Before indicating the reasons for these conjectures, a few words of interpretation may be in place. On the whole, the distribution of income from employment appears to be of Paretian form at the upper tail:[11] (58) holds with γ between 1 and 2, roughly speaking. It is not improbable, however, that marginal productivity per working year is distributed differently from actual incomes: the lognormal distribution is the most plausible simple distribution. For this, $\gamma = \infty$, and

$$-\frac{nf'}{f} \sim \frac{\log n}{\sigma^2} \tag{71}$$

for large n (σ^2 is the variance of the distribution of logarithm of incomes).

---

[11] See the general assessment by Lydall (1968).

The realism of alternative assumptions about utility may be assessed by calculating the response of the consumer to a linear budget constraint, $x = wy + a$. It is easy to see that utility maximization requires (since $u_{12} \equiv 0$)

$$-\frac{u_1(x)}{u_2(y)} = \frac{1}{w}, \qquad x = wy + a. \tag{72}$$

If $u_1 = \alpha x^{-\mu}$, we have to solve

$$\alpha w = -(a + wy)^\mu u_2(y). \tag{73}$$

(If $\alpha w \leq -a^\mu u_2(0)$, $y = 0$.) Clearly, the solution has the following properties:

$$\left. \begin{array}{l} y \to 1 \text{ as } w \to \infty \text{ if } \mu < 1 \\ y \to 0 \text{ as } w \to \infty \text{ if } \mu > 1 \end{array} \right\} \tag{74}$$

(cf. (61) and (68)). Also,

$$\left. \begin{array}{ll} x \sim a + w & (\mu < 1), \\ x \sim \left(\dfrac{aw}{u_2(0)} \right)^{1/\mu} & (\mu > 1) \end{array} \right\}. \tag{75}$$

These asymptotic properties suggest that the case $\mu = 1$ is particularly interesting.

When $\mu = 1$, since, by (73)

$$\frac{a}{w} = -\frac{\alpha}{u_2} - y,$$

$$-yu_2 \to \alpha \text{ as } w \to \infty;$$

i.e.,

$$y \to \bar{y}, \tag{76}$$

where $\bar{y}$ is defined by (64) (cf. (63)). If in addition,

$$u_2(y) = -(1 - y)^{-\delta} \qquad (\delta > 0), \tag{77}$$

we have

$$\bar{y}(1 - \bar{y})^{-\delta} = \alpha,$$

$$\bar{y}(1 - \bar{y})^{-1} = v.$$

The choice of α may be influenced by considering that $y = 0$ when $w/a \leq 1/\alpha$. It is interesting to note that, if $\alpha = 2$, $\delta = 1$, $\gamma = 2$, $\bar{y} = 2/3$, and $v = 2$, and if our conjectures are correct, then

$\theta \to 60\%.$

This case is perhaps not completely unrealistic; but it should be remembered that the homogeneous form for u means that the decision not to work depends only on the *ratio* of earned to unearned income, which is not a very realistic assumption.

It will be noticed that, in this case, the asymptotic marginal tax rate is very sensitive to the value of μ (in the neighbourhood of 1).

The reasons for the conjectures (60)–(70) (in fact, I can provide a proof of (iii) and will do so below) are as follows. One expects that, as $n \to \infty$, the relevant solution of the differential equations will tend towards a singularity of the equations: not only will y and v tend to limits, but $n(dy/dn)$ and $n(dv/dn)$ will tend to zero. Denote the postulated limit of y_n by $\bar{y}$. Consider first the case $u_1 = \alpha x^{-\mu} (\mu < 1)$.

In this case utility is unbounded. I shall show that $\bar{y} = 1$. If not, u_2 and ψ_y tend to finite limits, and, from (51), we have

$$nu_1 \frac{dx}{dn} = -u_2\left(y + n\frac{dy}{dn}\right) \to -\bar{y}u_2(\bar{y}). \tag{78}$$

Therefore, since

$$u_1\frac{dx}{dn} = \alpha\frac{d}{dn}\left[\frac{1}{1-\mu}x^{1-\mu}\right],$$

$$\frac{\alpha}{1-\mu}x^{1-\mu} = -\bar{y}u_2(\bar{y})\log n[1 + o(1)]. \tag{79}$$

This implies that

$$nu_1 = 0[n(\log n) - \frac{\mu}{1-\mu} \tag{80}$$

$$\to \infty. \tag{81}$$

Therefore

$$\frac{1}{n^2 f(n)}\int_n^\infty \left[\frac{1}{u_1} - \lambda\right]f(m)dm = \frac{1}{\psi_y}\left[1 + \frac{u_2}{nu_1}\right] \to \frac{1}{\psi_y(\bar{y})} > 0, \tag{82}$$

which is readily seen to be inconsistent with (80) if the distribution is either Paretian or lognormal.

We must therefore expect that $\bar{y} = 1$. Suppose now that $1 + u_2/nu_1$, the marginal tax rate, tends to a limit $\bar{t} < 1$. Then

$$\frac{dx}{dn} = -\frac{u_2}{nu_1}\left(y + n\frac{dy}{dn}\right) \to 1 + \bar{t}, \tag{83}$$

and consequently

$$\frac{x}{n} \to 1 - \bar{t}. \tag{84}$$

This implies that

$$\frac{1}{u_1} = \frac{1}{\alpha}(1 - \bar{t})^{\mu} n^{\mu}[1 + o(1)], \tag{85}$$

from which we can deduce the behaviour of

$$I = \frac{u_1}{nf} \int_n^{\infty} \left(\frac{1}{u_1} - \lambda\right) f(m) \mathrm{d}m \tag{86}$$

as $n \to \infty$. In the Paretian case, $f \sim n^{-2-\gamma}$, it is easily seen that

$$I \to (2 + \gamma - \mu)^{-1} > 0. \tag{87}$$

Since $1 - \bar{t} = \lim (\psi_y/u_2)(u_2/nu_1)I$, and $\psi_y/u_2 = -1 - (\mathrm{d}/\mathrm{d}y) \log |u_2|$ tends to $-\infty$ as $y \to 1$ (if it tends to a limit at all), we must have $u_2/nu_1 \to 0$, which is inconsistent with the assumption $\bar{t} \leq 1$. In the lognormal case, one obtains

$$1 - \bar{t} = \lim \frac{\psi_y}{u_2} \frac{u_2}{nu_1} \frac{\text{constant}}{\log n}. \tag{88}$$

If $(\psi_y/u_2)(1/\log n)$ tended to a finite limit, since

$$\log |u_2| \sim \log(1 - \bar{t}) + \log(nu_1) \sim (1 - \mu) \log n,$$

$(1/\log |u_2|) (\mathrm{d}/\mathrm{d}y) \log |u_2|$ would tend to a finite limit as $y \to 1$; which is clearly impossible. Thus, in the lognormal case too, we expect that $\bar{t} = 1$. This explains the conjectures in the case $\mu < 1$.

If $\mu = 1$,

$$\alpha \frac{\mathrm{d}(\log x)}{\mathrm{d}(\log n)} = nu_1 \frac{\mathrm{d}x}{\mathrm{d}n} = -u_2\left(y + n\frac{\mathrm{d}y}{\mathrm{d}n}\right), \tag{89}$$

which therefore cannot tend to ∞, since in that case $u_1^{-1} = x/\alpha > n^M$ eventually for any finite M, so that $(1/n^2 f(n)) \int_n^{\infty} (1/u_1) f(m) \mathrm{d}m$ becomes unbounded as $n \to \infty$.

We can expect, therefore, that $y \to \bar{y} < 1$ and

$$\alpha \frac{\log x}{\log n} \to -\bar{y}u_2(\bar{y}). \tag{90}$$

It is easily seen that the only plausible value of $\bar{y}$ has $\log x/\log n \to 1$, i.e.

$$\bar{y}u_2(\bar{y}) = -\alpha. \tag{91}$$

Then, if $1 + u_2/nu_1 \to \bar{t}$, we shall have

$$n\alpha x^{-1} \to \frac{-u_2(\bar{y})}{1 - \bar{t}},$$

and

$$\frac{\psi_y}{n^2 f(n)} \int \left(\frac{1}{u_1} - \lambda\right) f(m) dm \to \frac{(1 - \bar{t})\psi_y(\bar{y})}{-u_2(\bar{y})} \frac{1}{\gamma};$$

which suggests that

$$\bar{t} = (1 - \bar{t}) \frac{\psi_y(\bar{y})}{-u_2(\bar{y})} \frac{1}{\gamma} \tag{92}$$
$$= (1 - \bar{t})(1 + v)/\gamma,$$

in the notation (57). This is equivalent to (56). In particular, we expect that $\bar{t} = 0$ in the lognormal case.

When $\mu > 1$, the utility function is bounded above, and a more general and rigorous treatment is easy. u_n is an increasing function, and being now bounded tends to a finite $\bar{u}$. We shall write

$$u(x, y) = \chi(x) + \rho(y). \tag{93}$$

Since x is an increasing function, $\chi(x)$ also tends to a finite limit $\bar{\chi}$. Thus, $\rho(y)$ tends to a limit, and so does y. The limit of y must be zero, since otherwise (32) implies $u \to \infty$, which is now impossible.

Now

$$v + \frac{1}{nu_1} = \frac{1}{\psi_y} + \left(1 + \frac{u_2}{\psi_y}\right) \frac{1}{nu_1} \tag{94}$$
$$\to \frac{1}{-u_2(0)}$$

in this case (since $1/nu_1$, being $\leq 1/-u_2$, is bounded). Therefore (50) becomes

$$n \frac{dv}{dn} = (\gamma + 1 + 0(1))v + \frac{1}{u_2(0)} + 0(1) \tag{95}$$

in the Paretian case. From (95) one deduces, by the usual method of solving a first-order linear differential equation, that

$$v \to \frac{1}{-u_2(0)(\gamma + 1)}, \tag{96}$$

from which it follows at once that the marginal tax rate tends to $(\gamma + 1)^{-1}$. It is easily checked that in the lognormal case the marginal tax rate tends to zero.

In the next section, a particular case is examined in detail, and provides confirmation for some of our conjectures.

8. AN EXAMPLE

Case I

Let us, by way of illustration, analyse the following case:

$$
\left.
\begin{aligned}
u &= \alpha \log x + \log(1-y) \\
G(u) &= -\tfrac{1}{\beta} e^{-\beta u} \quad (\beta \geq 0)^{1} \\
f(n) &= \tfrac{1}{n} \exp\left[-\tfrac{(\log n + 1)^2}{2}\right]
\end{aligned}
\right\}. \tag{97}
$$

(The last assumes a lognormal distribution of skills: the average of n is $1/\sqrt{e} = 0.607\ldots$).
We put $w = 1$. With these assumptions, (50) and (51) become

$$
\frac{dv}{dn} = v \frac{\log n}{n} - \frac{x}{\alpha n^2} + \frac{\lambda}{n^2} e^{-\beta u},
$$

$$
\frac{du}{dn} = \frac{y}{n(1-y)},
$$

where

$$
v = \left[1 + \frac{u_2}{nu_1}\right] \Big/ \psi_y = \frac{1 - (x/\alpha n(1-y))}{1/(1-y)^2} = (1-y)\left(1 - y - \frac{x}{\alpha n}\right)
$$

and

$$
e^u = x^\alpha (1-y).
$$

For simplicity, we consider the case $\beta = 0$ first, and put

$$
s = 1 - y,
$$
$$
t = \log n.
$$

The equations become, since $u = \alpha \log(\alpha n) + \alpha \log(s - v/s) + \log s$,

$$
\frac{dv}{dt} = v\left(t + \frac{1}{s}\right) - s + \lambda e^{-t}, \tag{98}
$$

$$
\frac{ds}{dt} = \frac{[1 - \alpha - (1+\alpha)s](s^2 - v) + \alpha s(vt + \lambda e^{-t})}{(1+\alpha)s^2 - (1-\alpha)v}. \tag{99}
$$

---

[12] In the case of $\beta = 0$, we define $G = u$.

Solutions of these equations are depicted in Fig. 6.1. We now establish their properties. We remember that, in the optimum solution, $0 < v < s^2$ (for the marginal tax rate, v/s^2, is between 0 and 1). Using this fact, we can deduce from the first equation that

$$v \to 0 \qquad (t \to \infty).$$

Suppose that, for some $t, vt \geqq 1$. Then

$$\frac{d}{dt}v \geqq vt + \frac{v - s^2}{s} > vt - 1 \geqq 0,$$

since $v > 0$, and $s \leqq 1$. Therefore v is increasing at an increasing rate, contradicting $v < s^2 \leqq 1$. This shows that, in fact,

$$0 < v < 1/t. \tag{100}$$

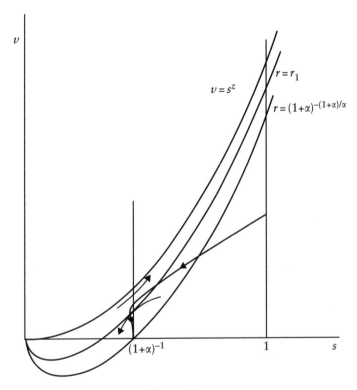

Figure 6.1.

The two equations together imply that

$$\frac{d}{dt}[s^{(1-\alpha)/\alpha}(s^2 - v)] = \frac{1 - (1+\alpha)s}{s}s^{(1-\alpha)/\alpha}(s^2 - v), \tag{101}$$

as one may see if one multiplies the first by αs, and the second by $[(1+\alpha)s^2 - (1-\alpha)v]$, and subtracts. Write

$$r = s^{(1-\alpha)/\alpha}(s^2 - v). \tag{102}$$

so that

$$\alpha\frac{dr}{dt} = \frac{1 - (1+\alpha)s}{s}r. \tag{103}$$

When $s < 1/(1+\alpha)$, r increases; when $s > 1/(1+\alpha)$, r decreases. For this reason s cannot tend to a limit other than $1/(1+\alpha)$: we shall show more, that $s \to 1/(1+\alpha)$ (cf. Fig. 1).

Since $v \to 0$, given $\epsilon > 0$, there exists t_0 such that $0 < v_t < \epsilon$ for all $t \geq t_0$. Then

$$s^{(1+\alpha)/\alpha} - \epsilon s^{(1-\alpha)/\alpha} < r < s^{(1+\alpha)/\alpha} \ (t \geq t_0). \tag{104}$$

If $r_t > (1+\alpha)^{-(1+\alpha)/\alpha}$, the right-hand inequality implies that

$$s_t > \frac{1}{1+\alpha}. \tag{105}$$

Therefore r is decreasing. If

$$r_t < (1+\alpha)^{-(1+\alpha)/\alpha} - \epsilon \max[1, (1+\alpha)^{-(1-\alpha)/\alpha}], \tag{106}$$

we obtain from the left-hand inequality (104)

$$s_t^{(1+\alpha)/\alpha} < (1+\alpha)^{-(1+\alpha)/\alpha} - \epsilon\{\max[1, (1+\alpha)^{-(1-\alpha)/\alpha}] - s_t^{(1-\alpha)/\alpha}\}$$
$$\leq (1+\alpha)^{-(1-\alpha)/\alpha} \tag{107}$$

if either $\alpha \leq 1$ (in which case $\{\dots\} \geq 0$ since $s \leq 1$), or $\alpha > 1$ and $s_t \geq 1/(1+\alpha)$. Thus, in fact

$$s_t < \frac{1}{1+\alpha}, \tag{108}$$

and, by (98), r_t is increasing. Combining these two results, we deduce that

$$r_t \to (1+\alpha)^{-(1+\alpha)/\alpha},$$

which in turn implies, since $v > 0$, that

$$s_t \rightarrow \frac{1}{1+\alpha}. \tag{109}$$

Our demonstration that v and s tend to limits 0 and $1/(1+\alpha)$, respectively, confirms the conjectures for the special case. It is readily checked that exactly the same arguments apply to the case $\beta > 0$. As we have noted previously, the marginal tax rate is v/s^2. Thus, as $t \rightarrow \infty$

$$\theta \rightarrow 0. \tag{110}$$

It is a striking result; but we should note at once that 0 is a poor approximation to v/s^2 even for large t. This becomes apparent when we demonstrate that $vt \rightarrow 1/(1+\alpha)$.

Suppose the contrary, that $|vt - 1/(1+\alpha)| > \epsilon > 0$ for an unbounded set of values of t. If $vt > 1/(1+\alpha) + \epsilon$, and t is large enough to imply that $s_t < 1/(1+\alpha) + \frac{1}{2}\epsilon$, then

$$\frac{dv}{dt} > \frac{1}{2}\epsilon. \tag{111}$$

Thus, vt continues greater than $1/(1+\alpha) + \epsilon$, and $\frac{dv}{dt} > \frac{1}{2}\epsilon$ for all larger t: but this implies that $v \rightarrow \infty$, which we have already shown to be false. If on the other hand $vt < 1/(1+\alpha) - \epsilon$, and t is greater than $2/\epsilon$, and is large enough to imply

$$v_t < \frac{1+\alpha}{4}, \qquad \lambda t e^{-t} < \frac{1+\alpha}{4}, \qquad s_t > \frac{1}{1+\alpha} - \frac{1}{2}\epsilon,$$

then

$$\begin{aligned}
\frac{d}{dt}(vt) &= v + t(vt - s) + \frac{vt}{s} + \lambda t e^{-t} \\
&< \frac{1+\alpha}{2} + \frac{1/(1+\alpha) - \epsilon}{1/(1+\alpha) - \frac{1}{2}\epsilon} - \frac{1}{2}\epsilon t \\
&< 1 - \frac{3}{2} = -\frac{1}{2}.
\end{aligned} \tag{112}$$

This implies that vt becomes negative, which is impossible. Therefore $|vt - 1/(1+\alpha)| < \epsilon$ for all large enough t:

$$vt \rightarrow \frac{1}{1+\alpha}. \tag{113}$$

Thus,

$$\theta = v/s^2 \sim \frac{1+\alpha}{t}. \tag{114}$$

Only 1 per cent of our population have $t \geq 1.7$ (one in a thousand have $t \geq 2.4$). Since one might want to have α as low as 1, the above approximation is clearly rather bad even at $t = 2$.[13,14] How bad will become apparent in the next section.

Case II

It is also of interest to examine the case of a skill distribution with Paretian tail:

$$\frac{nf'}{f} \to \gamma + 2, \qquad \gamma > 0. \tag{115}$$

The equations for the optimum become (with $\beta = 0$),

$$\frac{dv}{dt} = v\gamma(t) + \frac{v}{s} - s + \lambda e^{-t}, \tag{116}$$

$$\frac{ds}{dt} = \frac{[1 - \alpha - (1+\alpha)s](s^2 - v) + \alpha s(v\gamma(t) + \lambda e^{-t})}{(1+\alpha)s^2 - (1-\alpha)v}; \tag{117}$$

and, exactly as before, one has the equation

$$\frac{dr}{dt} = \frac{1 - (1+\alpha)s}{s} r \tag{118}$$

where $r = s^{(1+\alpha)/\alpha}(s^2 - v)$. The situation is portrayed in Fig. 6.2. The broken curves have equations

$$s^{(1-\alpha)/\alpha}(s^2 - v) = r_i \qquad (i = 1, 2, 3) \tag{119}$$

with $0 < r_1 < r_2 < r_3$. It will be noted that such a curve, with equation

$$v_1 = s^2 - rs^{(1-\alpha)/\alpha} \qquad (r \text{ constant}), \tag{120}$$

---

[13] In this example, $\sigma^2 = 1$; that is, the standard deviation of $\log n$ is 1. This is done merely for convenience in manipulations. A precisely similar theory holds for a general lognormal distribution.

It can be shown, by continuing the methods of the text, that $vt \sim 1/(1+\alpha) - 1/t$ while $s = 1/(1+\alpha) + 0 \ (1/t^2)$. The fact that the optimum path is tangential to the vertical at $(s, v) = (1/(1+\alpha), 0)$ implies that $s < 1/(1+\alpha)$, for large t, since otherwise r would be decreasing, and that, as can be seen from the diagram, is inconsistent with $dv/ds \to \infty$. Thus we have the situation portrayed in Fig. 6.1.

[14] The case $\beta > 0$ can be treated in a precisely similar way, to obtain the same qualitative results.

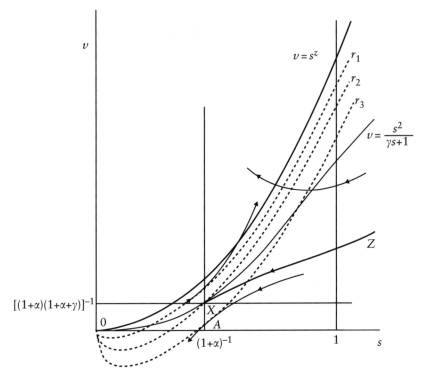

Figure 6.2.

always cuts from below the curve

$$v_2 = \frac{s^2}{\gamma s + 1} + p \qquad (p \text{ constant}) \tag{121}$$

that passes through the same point. This follows from the calculation

$$\frac{dv_1}{ds} - \frac{dv_2}{ds} = \frac{d}{ds}\left(\frac{\gamma s^3}{\gamma s + 1} - rs^{(1-\alpha)/\alpha}\right) > 0. \tag{122}$$

This remark will prove very useful; but first we want to establish that, for large t, the sign of dv/dt is nearly the same as the sign of $v - s^2/(\gamma s + 1)$.

Let ϵ' be a positive number, and let t_1 be so large that $|v\gamma(t) + \lambda e^{-t} - v\gamma| > \epsilon'$ when $t \geq t_1$. Since $s = 1$ at $t_0 = \log n_0$, $s < 1/(1+\alpha)$ at t only if $s = 1/(1+\alpha)$ for some previous t_1; if (for the given t) t_1 is the greatest such, we have from (118)

$$r_t > r_{t_1} = (1+\alpha)^{-(1-\alpha)/\alpha}\left(\frac{1}{(1+\alpha)^2} - v_{t_1}\right)$$

$$\geqq (1-\alpha)^{-(1-\alpha)/\alpha}\inf\left\{\frac{1}{(1+\alpha)^2} - v_t\,\middle|\,s_t = \frac{1}{1+\alpha},\ \frac{dv_t}{dt} < 0\right\}$$

$$= \Delta > 0, \tag{123}$$

since as $t \to \infty$, $0 > dv/dt$ implies

$$v_t < \frac{s_t^2}{\gamma s_t + 1} + 0(1) \tag{124}$$

$$< s_t^2 - \gamma s_t^3 + 0(1).$$

Therefore s_t is positively bounded below, say

$$s_t \geqq \Delta' > 0. \tag{125}$$

Hence, when $t \geqq t_1$,

$$\frac{dv}{dt} = v\gamma(t) + \frac{v}{s} - s + \lambda e^{-t}$$

$$> \left(v - \frac{s^2}{\gamma s + 1}\right)\left(\gamma + \frac{1}{s}\right) - \epsilon' \tag{126}$$

$$> \epsilon',$$

if

$$v > \frac{s^2}{\gamma s + 1} + \frac{2\epsilon'}{\gamma + 1/\Delta'}. \tag{127}$$

Similarly, we can show that

$$\frac{dv}{dt} < -\epsilon' \tag{128}$$

if

$$v < \frac{s^2}{\gamma s + 1} - \frac{2\epsilon'}{\gamma + 1/\Delta'}. \tag{129}$$

Now write $\epsilon = \epsilon'/(\gamma + 1/\Delta')$. It is clear that if, for some $t \geqq t_1$,

$$v > \frac{s^2}{\gamma s + 1} + \epsilon \quad \text{and} \quad s \geqq \frac{1}{1+\alpha},$$

then $dv/dt > 0$ and also $dr/dt < 0$. Therefore, by the properties of the two sets of curves (cf. Fig. 6.3), $v - s^2/(\gamma s + 1)$ is increasing. Thus, for all subsequent t,

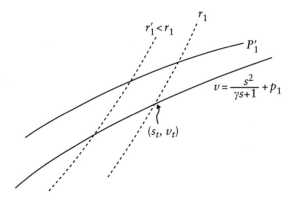

Figure 6.3.

$dv/dt > \epsilon'$, and $v \to \infty$. Such a path cannot be optimum. Consequently on the optimum path, if $t \geqq t_1$,

$$\text{either } s < \frac{1}{1+\alpha} \quad \text{or} \quad v \leqq \frac{s^2}{\gamma s + 1} + \epsilon. \tag{130}$$

Similarly, for $t \geqq t_1$,

$$\text{either } s > \frac{1}{1+\alpha} \quad \text{or} \quad v \geqq \frac{s^2}{\gamma s + 1} - \epsilon. \tag{131}$$

Suppose that at t_1, $s > 1/(1+\alpha)$. (An exactly similar argument applies if $s < 1/(1+\alpha)$.) Then r is decreasing, and continues to do so until

$$r = r' = (1+\alpha)^{-(1-\alpha)/\alpha} \left(\frac{1}{(1+\alpha)^2} \frac{\gamma}{(1+\alpha+\gamma)} + \epsilon \right).$$

Only then can s become less than $1/(1+\alpha)$ (cf. Fig. 6.4). Once $s < 1/(1+\alpha)$, r increases again. Therefore at no time is

$$r < r'' = (1+\alpha)^{-(1-\alpha)/\alpha} \left(\frac{\gamma}{(1+\alpha)^2(1+\alpha+\gamma)} - \epsilon \right).$$

Nor can we have $r > r'$ at any later time. Thus we have found t_2 such that, when $t \geqq t_2$, (s_t, v_t) lies in the curvilinear parallelogram $LMPQ$ in Fig. 6.4, which contains X, and can be made as small as we please by suitable choice of ϵ'. Therefore as $t \to \infty$,

$$s_t \to \frac{1}{1+\alpha}, \quad v_t \to \frac{1}{(1+\alpha)(1+\alpha+\gamma)}. \tag{132}$$

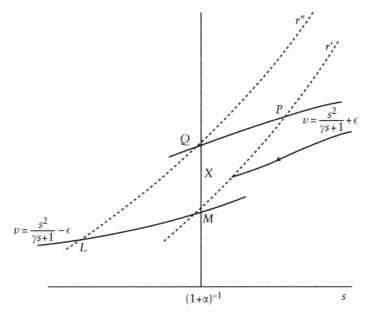

Figure 6.4.

The optimum path is indicated by XZ in Fig. 6.2. On it, the marginal tax rate,

$$\theta = \frac{v_t}{s_t^2} \to \frac{1+\alpha}{1+\alpha+\gamma};$$

(133)

which confirms our conjecture in this special case.[15,16]

It should be noted that we have not shown, in either of these cases, that s diminishes (nor even that $z = ny = e^t(1 - s)$ increases) all along the path: the possibility that z is constant for some range of n, in the optimum regime, remains in both the examples we have discussed. Calculation of specific cases is required to settle this issue. Such calculation is not difficult with the information about the solution that we now have.

9. A NUMERICAL ILLUSTRATION

The computations whose results are presented in the tables below were carried out for the first case examined above, with $\alpha = 1$, but with a more

---

[15] The case $\beta > 0$ can be treated in a precisely similar way, to obtain the same qualitative results.

[16] It is possible to calculate optimum tax schedules explicitly for a uniform (rectangular) distribution of skills; but since that distribution is of no great interest in the present context, the analysis is omitted.

realistic value for σ^2. Computations have also been carried out for the case $\sigma^2 = 1$, and these provide an interesting contrast to the main set of calculations. In all cases, we take $w = 1$; and for computational convenience, the average of $\log n$ is -1. This means that the average marginal product of a full day's work is $e^{\frac{1}{2}\sigma^2 - 1}$, but it amounts only to a choice of units for the consumption good. The results show, for particular values of the average product of labour, X/Z, what is the optimum tax schedule, and what is the distribution of consumption and labour in the population.

For purposes of comparison, one naturally wants to know what would have been the optimum position if it had been possible to use lump-sum taxation (or, equivalently, direction of labour). Let us consider this first for the case $\beta = 0$. We shall assume a linear production function

$$X = Z + a \tag{134}$$

(which one thinks of as applying only over a certain range of values of Z, including all those that are to be considered). In the full optimum, we maximize

$$\int [\log x + \log(1 - y)] f(n) \mathrm{d}n \tag{135}$$

subject to

$$\int x f(n) \mathrm{d}n = \int n y f(n) \mathrm{d}n + a.$$

It is clear that x will be the same for everyone:

$$x = x^0, \tag{136}$$

and that y_n must maximize

$$\log(1 - y) + ny/x^0, \tag{137}$$

for otherwise we could improve matters by changing y_n (for a set of n of positive measure, of course) and changing the constant x correspondingly. Maximization of (137) yields

$$y_n^0 = [1 - x^0/n]_+, \tag{138}$$

where the notation $[\ldots]_+$ means max $(0, \ldots)$.

It is worth noticing that, in the full optimum, only men for whom $n > x^0$ actually work, and an interesting curiosity that, with the particular welfare function specified in (135), utility will be less for more highly skilled individuals. This is, as we have seen, impossible under the income tax. The value of x^0 is determined by the production constraint:

$$x^0 = \int_{x^0}^{\infty} (n - x^0) f(n) \, \mathrm{d}n + a, \tag{139}$$

where, for convenience, we have taken $\int_0^\infty f(n)\mathrm{d}n = 1$. In the case of the special lognormal distribution used here, it can be shown that this equation reduces to

$$2x^0 - x^0 F(x^0) - e^{\frac{1}{2}\sigma^2 - 1}[1 - F(e^{-\sigma^2}x^0)] = a. \tag{140}$$

Solution of this equation gives the consumption level in the full optimum, and also the skill-level below which no work is required of a man, namely that at which a full day's labour would provide a wage equal to the consumption level.

When $\beta > 0$, a similar theory holds. In that case, $x > x^0$ for men with $n > x^0$, but it is still the case that such men are made to have a lower utility level than their less skilled neighbours. The equation corresponding to (140) is a little more complicated and will not be reproduced. For $n > x^0$, consumption and labour are

$$
\begin{aligned}
x_n &= (x^0)^{(1+\beta)/(1+2\beta)} n^{\beta/(1+2\beta)}, \\
y_n &= 1 - (x^0/n)^{(1+\beta)/(1+2\beta)}.
\end{aligned} \tag{141}
$$

In the tables, certain features of the optimal regime under income taxation are given, along with x^0 for the full optimum for the same linear production function. In Tables 6.1–6.12 the lognormal distribution has parameters

Table 6.1. (*Case 1*) $\alpha = 1$, $\beta = 0$, $\sigma = 0.39$, *mean* $n = 0.40$, $X/Z = 0.93$. *Full optimum for* $X = Z - 0.013$: $x^0 = 0.19$, $F(x^0) = 0.045$. *Partial optimum* (*income-tax*): $x_0 = 0.03$, $n_0 = 0.04$, $F(n_0) = 0.000$.

$F(n)$	x	y	$x(1-y)$	z	Full optimum x
0	0.03	0	0.03	0	0.19
0.10	0.10	0.42	0.05	0.09	0.19
0.50	0.16	0.45	0.08	0.17	0.19
0.90	0.25	0.48	0.13	0.29	0.19
0.99	0.38	0.49	0.19	0.45	0.19
Population average	0.17			0.18	0.19

Table 6.2. (*Case 1*) $\alpha = 1$, $\beta = 0$, $\sigma = 0.39$, *mean* $n = 0.40$, $X/Z = 0.93$. *Full optimum for* $X = Z - 0.013$: $x^0 = 0.19$, $F(x^0) = 0.045$. *Partial optimum* (*income-tax*): $x_0 = 0.03$, $n_0 = 0.04$, $F(n_0) = 0.000$.

z	x	Average tax rate (%)	Marginal tax rate (%)
0	0.03	—	23
0.05	0.07	−34	26
0.10	0.10	−5	24
0.20	0.18	9	21
0.30	0.26	13	19
0.40	0.34	14	18
0.50	0.43	15	16

Tax Theory

Table 6.3. (*Case 2*) $\alpha = 1$, $\beta = 0$, $\sigma = 0.39$, *mean* $n = 0.40$, $X/Z = 1.10$.
Full optimum for $X = Z + 0.017$: $x^0 = 0.21$, $F(x^0) = 0.075$.
Partial optimum (*income-tax*): $x_0 = 0.05$, $n_0 = 0.06$, $F(n_0) = 0.000$.

$F(n)$	x	y	$x(1-y)$	z	Full optimum x
0	0.05	0	0.05	0	0.21
0.10	0.11	0.36	0.07	0.08	0.21
0.50	0.17	0.42	0.10	0.15	0.21
0.90	0.27	0.45	0.15	0.28	0.21
0.99	0.40	0.47	0.21	0.43	0.21
Population average	0.18	—	—	0.17	0.21

Table 6.4. (*Case 2*) $\alpha = 1$, $\beta = 0$, $\sigma = 0.39$, mean $n = 0.40$, $X/Z = 1.10$.
Full optimum for $X = Z + 0.017$: $x^0 = 0.21$, $F(x^0) = 0.075$.
Partial optimum (*income-tax*): $x_0 = 0.05$, $n_0 = 0.06$, $F(n_0) = 0.000$.

z	x	Average tax rate (%)	Marginal tax rate (%)
0	0.05	—	—
0.05	0.09	−80	21
0.10	0.13	−30	20
0.20	0.21	−5	19
0.30	0.29	3	17
0.40	0.37	6	16
0.50	0.46	8	15

Table 6.5. (*Case 3*) $\alpha = 1$, $\beta = 1$, $\sigma = 0.39$, mean $n = 0.40$, $X/Z = 1.20$.
Full optimum for $X = Z + 0.030$: $x^0 = 0.16$, $F(x^0) = 0.016$.
Partial optimum (*income-tax*): $x_0 = 0.07$, $n_0 = 0.09$, $F(n_0) = 0.000$.

$F(n)$	x	y	$x(1-y)$	z	Full optimum x
0	0.07	0	0.07	0	0.16
0.10	0.12	0.28	0.08	0.07	0.18
0.50	0.17	0.37	0.11	0.14	0.21
0.90	0.26	0.43	0.15	0.26	0.25
0.99	0.39	0.46	0.21	0.42	0.29
Population average	0.18	—	—	0.15	0.21

Table 6.6. (*Case 3*) $\alpha = 1$, $\beta = 1$, $\sigma = 0.39$, *mean* $n = 0.40$, $X/Z = 1.20$.
Full optimum for $X = Z + 0.030$: $x^0 = 0.16$, $F(x^0) = 0.016$.
Partial optimum (*income-tax*): $x_0 = 0.07$, $n_0 = 0.09$, $F(n_0) = 0.000$.

z	x	Average tax rate (%)	Marginal tax rate (%)
0	0.07	—	23
0.05	0.11	−113	28
0.10	0.14	−42	27
0.20	0.22	−8	25
0.30	0.29	2	23
0.40	0.37	7	21
0.50	0.45	10	19

Table 6.7. (*Case 4*) $\alpha = 1$, $\beta = 1$, $\sigma = 0.39$, *mean* $n = 0.40$, $X/Z = 0.98$.
Full optimum for $X = Z - 0.003$: $x^0 = 0.14$, $F(x^0) = 0.007$.
Partial optimum (income-tax): $x_0 = 0.05$, $n_0 = 0.07$, $F(n_0) = 0.000$.

$F(n)$	x	y	$x(1-y)$	z	Full optimum x
0	0.05	0	0.05	0	0.14
0.10	0.10	0.33	0.07	0.08	0.17
0.50	0.15	0.41	0.09	0.15	0.20
0.90	0.24	0.46	0.13	0.28	0.23
0.99	0.37	0.48	0.19	0.44	0.26
Population average	0.16	—	—	0.17	0.19

Table 6.8. (*Case 4*) $\alpha = 1$, $\beta = 1$, $\sigma = 0.39$, *mean* $n = 0.40$, $X/Z = 0.98$.
Full optimum for $X = Z - 0.003$: $x^0 = 0.14$, $F(x^0) = 0.007$.
Partial optimum (*income-tax*): $x_0 = 0.05$, $n_0 = 0.07$, $F(n_0) = 0.000$.

z	x	Average tax rate (%)	Marginal tax rate (%)
0	0.05	—	30
0.05	0.08	−66	34
0.10	0.12	−34	32
0.20	0.19	7	28
0.30	0.26	13	25
0.40	0.34	16	22
0.50	0.41	17	20

Table 6.9. *(Case 5)* $\alpha = 1$, $\beta = 1$, $\sigma = 0.39$, *mean* $n = 0.40$, $X/Z = 0.88$.
Full optimum for $X = Z - 0.021$; $x^0 = 0.13$, $F(x^0) = 0.004$.
Partial optimum (income-tax): $x_0 = 0.04$, $n_0 = 0.06$, $F(n_0) = 0.000$.

$F(n)$	x	y	$x(1-y)$	z	Full optimum x
0	0.04	0	0.04	0	0.13
0.10	0.09	0.36	0.06	0.08	0.15
0.50	0.14	0.43	0.08	0.16	0.18
0.90	0.23	0.48	0.12	0.29	0.22
0.99	0.36	0.50	0.18	0.45	0.25
Population average	0.15	—	—	0.17	0.19

Table 6.10. *(Case 5)* $\alpha = 1$, $\beta = 1$, $\sigma = 0.39$, *mean* $n = 0.40$, $X/Z = 0.88$.
Full optimum for $X = Z - 0.021$; $x^0 = 0.13$, $F(x^0) = 0.004$.
Partial optimum (income-tax): $x_0 = 0.04$, $n_0 = 0.06$, $F(n_0) = 0.000$.

z	x	Average tax rate (%)	Marginal tax rate (%)
0	0.04	—	35
0.05	0.07	−43	39
0.10	0.10	−3	36
0.20	0.17	15	31
0.30	0.24	20	27
0.40	0.31	22	24
0.50	0.39	21	21

Table 6.11. *(Case 6)* $\alpha = 1$, $\beta = 1$, $\sigma = 1$, *mean* $n = 0.61$, $X/Z = 0.93$.
Full optimum for $X = Z - 0.013$; $x^0 = 0.25$, $F(x^0) = 0.35$.
Partial optimum (income-tax): $x_0 = 0.10$, $n_0 = 0.20$, $F(n_0) = 0.27$.

$F(n)$	x	y	$x(1-y)$	z	Full optimum x
0	0.10	0	0.10	0	0.25
0.10	0.10	0	0.10	0	0.25
0.50	0.14	0.15	0.11	0.06	0.28
0.90	0.32	0.41	0.19	0.54	0.44
0.99	0.90	0.49	0.46	1.84	0.62
Population average	0.18	—	—	0.20	0.32

Table 6.12. *(Case 6)* $\alpha = 1$, $\beta = 1$, $\sigma = 1$, *mean* $n = 0.61$, $X/Z = 0.93$. *Full optimum for* $X = Z - 0.013$; $x^0 = 0.25$, $F(x^0) = 0.35$. *Partial optimum (income-tax):* $x_0 = 0.10$, $n_0 = 0.20$, $F(n_0) = 0.27$.

z	x	Average tax rate (%)	Marginal tax rate (%)
0	0.10	—	50
0.10	0.15	-50	58
0.25	0.20	20	60
0.50	0.30	40	59
1.00	0.52	48	57
1.50	0.73	51	54
2.00	0.97	51	52
3.00	1.47	51	49

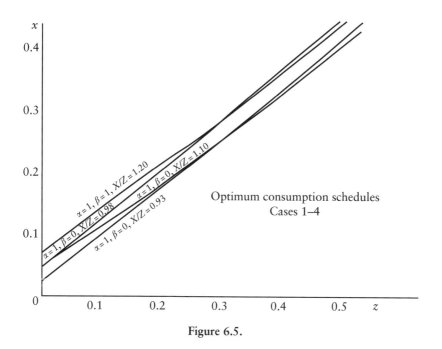

Figure 6.5.

$\sigma = 0.39$. This figure is derived from Lydall's figures for the distribution of income from employment for various countries (Lydall, p. 153). It is intended to represent a realistic distribution of skills within the population. In each case, x_0, n_0, and the values of x, y and $x(1 - y)$ (which measures utility) at the 10, 50, 90, and 99 per cent points of the skill distribution are given. In separate tables, the average and marginal tax rates are given for a representative range of values of z. Graphs of the optimal consumption schedule $(x = c(z))$ are given in Figs. 6.1 and 6.2. In Fig. 6.2, the distributions of x_n and z_n are displayed in case 5.

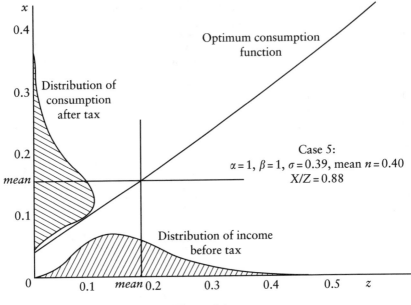

Figure 6.6.

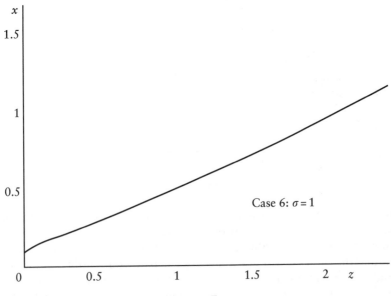

Figure 6.7.

It will be noticed at once that, under the optimum regime, practically the whole population chooses to work in each of these cases: this contrasts, in some cases, with the full optimum, where sometimes a substantial proportion of the population is allowed to be idle. In most cases, a significant number work for less than a third of the time. It is also somewhat surprising that tax rates are so low. This means, in effect, that the income tax is not as effective a weapon for redistributing income, under the assumptions we have made, as one might have expected. It is not surprising that tax rates are higher when $\beta = 1$. When objectives are more egalitarian, more output is sacrificed for the sake of the poorer groups. Nevertheless, the difference between the optimum when only an income tax is available, and the full optimum, is rather large.

The examples have been chosen for X/Z fairly large: this corresponds to economies in which the requirements of government expenditure are largely met from the profits of public production, or taxation of private profits and commodity transactions. Tax rates are, as one might expect, fairly sensitive to changes in X/Z (i.e. to the production possibilities in the economy, and the extent to which income taxation is used to finance government expenditure as well as for 'redistribution'). Tax rates are mildly sensitive to the choice of β. (When $\alpha = \frac{1}{2}$, the main features are unchanged.)

Perhaps the most striking feature of the results is the closeness to linearity of the tax schedules. Since a linear tax schedule, which may be regarded as a proportional income tax in association with a poll subsidy, is particularly easy to administer, it cannot be said that the neglect of administrative costs in the analysis is of any importance, except that considerations of administration might well lead an optimizing government to choose a perfectly linear tax schedule. The optimum tax schedule is certainly not exactly linear, however, and we have not explored the welfare loss that would arise from restriction to linear schedules: nevertheless, one may conjecture that the loss would be quite small. It is interesting, though, that in the cases for which we have calculated optimum schedules, the maximum marginal tax rate occurs at a rather low income level, and falls steadily thereafter.

This conclusion would not necessarily hold if the distribution of skills in the population had a substantially greater variance. The sixth case presented has $\sigma = 1$. So great a dispersion of known labouring ability does not seem to be at all realistic at present, but it is just conceivable if a great deal more were known to employers about the abilities of individual members of the population. The optimum is in almost all respects very different. Tax rates are high: a large proportion of the population is allowed to abstain from productive labour. The results seem to say that, in an economy where there is more intrinsic inequality in economic skill, the income tax is a more important weapon of public control than it is in an economy where the dispersion of innate skills is less. The reason is, presumably, that the labour-discouraging effects of the tax are more important, relative to the redistributive benefits, in the latter case.

10. CONCLUSIONS

The examples discussed confirm, as one would expect, that the shape of the optimum earned-income tax schedule is rather sensitive to the distribution of skills within the population, and to the income–leisure preferences postulated. Neither is easy to estimate for real economies. The simple consumption–leisure utility function is a heroic abstraction from a much more complicated situation, so that it is quite hard to guess what a satisfactory method of estimating it would be. Many objections to using observed income distributions as a means of estimating the distribution of skills will spring to mind. Yet the assumptions used in the numerical illustrations seem to fit observation fairly well, and are not in themselves implausible. It is not probable that work decisions are entirely, or even, in the long run, mainly, determined by social convention, psychological need, or the imperatives of cooperative behaviour; an analysis of the kind presented is therefore likely to be relevant to the construction and reform of actual income taxes.

Being aware that many of the arguments used to argue in favour of low marginal tax rates for the rich are, at best, premissed on the odd assumption that any means of raising the national income is good, even if it diverts part of that income from poor to rich, I must confess that I had expected the rigorous analysis of income taxation in the utilitarian manner to provide an argument for high tax rates. It has not done so. I had also expected to be able to show that there was no great need to strive for low marginal tax rates on low incomes when constructing negative-income-tax proposals. This feeling has been to some extent confirmed. But my expectation that the minimum consumption level would be rather high has not been confirmed. Instead, virtually everyone is brought into the workforce. Since this conclusion is based on the analysis of an economy in which a man who chooses to work can work, I should not wish to see it applied in real economies. So long as there are periods when employment offered is less than the labour force available, one would perhaps wish to see the minimum income level assured to those who are not working set at such a level that the number who choose not to work is as great as the excess of the labour force over the employment available. A rigorous analysis of this situation has still to be attempted. The results above do at least suggest that we should allow the least skilled to work for a substantially shorter period than the highly skilled.

I would also hesitate to apply the conclusions regarding individuals of high skill: for many of them, their work is, up to a point, quite attractive, and the supply of their labour may be rather inelastic (apart from the possibilities of migration). There is scope for further theoretical work on this problem too. I conclude, for the present, that:

(1) An approximately linear income-tax schedule, with all the administrative advantages it would bring, is desirable (unless the supply of highly

skilled labour is much more inelastic than our utility function assumed); and in particular (optimal!) negative income-tax proposals are strongly supported.[17]

(2) The income-tax is a much less effective tool for reducing inequalities than has often been thought.

(3) Therefore it would be good to devise taxes complementary to the income tax, designed to avoid the difficulties that tax is faced with. In the model we have been studying, this could be achieved by introducing a tax schedule that depends upon time worked (y) as well as upon labour-income (z): with such a schedule, one can obtain the full optimum, since one can, in effect, construct a different z-schedule for each n.[18] Such a tax would not be fully practicable, but we have other means of estimating a man's skill-level—such as the notorious IQ test: high values of skill indexes may be sought after so much for prestige that they would not often be misrepresented. With any such method of taxation, the risks of evasion are, of course, quite great: but if it is true, as our results suggest, that the income tax is not a very satisfactory alternative, this objection must be weighed against the great desirability of finding some effective method of offsetting the unmerited favours that some of us receive from our genes and family advantages.

REFERENCES

Blum, W. J. and Kalven, H. Jr. *The Uneasy Case for Progressive Taxation* (University of Chicago Press, 1953).

Diamond, P. A. 'Negative Income Taxes and the Poverty Problem—a Review Article', *National Tax Journal* (September 1968).

Lydall, H. F. *The Structure of Earnings* (Oxford, 1968).

Mirrlees, J. A. 'Characterization of the Optimum Income Tax' (Mineo, Nuffield College, 1970[19]).

Musgrave, R. A. *The Theory of Public Finance* (McGraw-Hill, 1959).

Shoup, C. S. *Public Finance* (Weidenfeld & Nicolson, 1969).

Vickrey, W. *Agenda for Progressive Taxation* (Ronald Press, NY, 1947).

---

[17] The essential point of these proposals is that the marginal tax rate (as represented by rules for deductions from social security benefits) should be significantly less than 100%. Proposals of this kind have sometimes been put forward in terms that suggest—quite wrongly of course—that any plausible-sounding negative income-tax proposal is better than a system in which all earnings are deducted from social security benefits. It was a major intention of the present study to provide methods for estimating desirable tax rates at the lowest income levels, and a surprise that these tax rates are the most difficult to determine, in a sense. They cannot be determined without at the same time determining the whole optimum income-tax schedule. To put things another way, no such proposal can be valid out of the context of the rest of the income-tax schedule.

[18] I am indebted to Frank Hahn for pointing this out. It would seem to be true that lump-sum taxation is possible in any formal model where uncertainty is not introduced explicitly.

[19] Revised and contained in Chapter 11 of the Present Volume.

7

On Producer Taxation

1. Dasgupta and Stiglitz have recently discussed the optimum taxation of profits accruing to firms under diminishing returns to scale, and the implications for optimum commodity taxation and public production. Their main theorem asserts that, when the rents of different producers can be taxed at different rates, production efficiency is desirable. In the analysis of commodity taxation and public production by Diamond and myself, it was assumed that constant returns prevailed in the private sector, and we had supposed that productive efficiency would not usually be desirable when this assumption was violated. It may therefore be interesting to see how the new result can be obtained by the methods of our paper. In this way, I hope that it may be easier to understand the reason for their result. It also appears that one, possibly important, modification must be made in it. The final theorem has a quite unusual form.

2. The theorem does require that 100 per cent profit taxation is used, if desirable. But 100 per cent profit taxation removes all incentives to do one thing rather than another. Having discussed the conditions for production efficiency, I therefore go on to consider a model in which there is reason to provide profit incentives to producers, because the supply of entrepreneurial and managerial activities is influenced by the rewards from undertaking them. In this model, aggregate production efficiency is not in general desirable, so that the prices faced by private producers should be different from the shadow prices used in the public sector. But the rules governing optimum taxes, of both households and private producers, are relatively simple. It appears, therefore, that it is possible to have a good theory of commodity taxation even when the simple theory of firm behaviour implicit in the assumption of constant returns is substantially weakened.

3. For convenience, I recall the essential argument of the Diamond–Mirrlees paper. Consumers (with diverse tastes and given budgets) face consumer prices q. Aggregate demands are $x(q)$; the indirect social valuation function is $V(q)$. Let the private production set be F, the public production set be G. By commodity taxation alone, one cannot do better than to maximize (by choice of q^*)

$$V(q) \text{ subject to } x(q) \in F + G. \tag{1}$$

This article first appeared in the *Review of Economic Studies*, Vol. 39 (1972), pp. 105–11. Some of the work for the paper was done while the author was visiting MIT.

So long as some small price change can increase welfare (e.g. the reduction of the price of some commodity consumed by everyone, or the reduction of an optimum poll tax if one is being levied), that small price change must move $x(q)$ out of the set $F + G$. Hence $x(q^*)$, the optimum production vector, is on the frontier of the production set.

If there is free disposal, and F and G are convex, a price vector, $p \geq 0$, exists such that $x^* = x(q)$ maximizes py for y in $F + G$. Suppose that $y^* + z^*$, with y^* in F and z^* in G, is the optimum production vector. Then y^* maximizes py for y in F. Therefore private producers would not mind choosing y^*. It follows that the optimum is such that both private and public production maximizes the value for production in terms of producer prices p: aggregate productive efficiency is desirable.

It has been assumed in this analysis that consumer welfare is unaffected by producer prices. This is the case if there are constant returns to scale in private production, or if all the profits of private production accrue to government. If private producers earn pure profits, which they distribute to consumers, the assumption is violated.

4. Consider therefore an economy with m producers, who have production sets $Y_1, Y_2, \ldots, Y_m$. These sets are convex: we are interested in the case where they are not cones. I shall suppose that each set contains the origin and allows free disposal. Define, for each producer, a profit function,

$$r_j(p) = \max \; [py \mid y \in Y_j]. \tag{2}$$

These profits are distributed to consumers (each consumer getting a fixed proportion of each producer's profits, let us say). Thus, the social valuation must be written

$$V(q,r) = V(q, r_1, r_2, \ldots, r_m). \tag{3}$$

Aggregate demands, x, also depend on r now.

Assume, at this state of the argument, that the State can make different producers operate under different prices. The State can also impose proportional profit taxes: we may as well suppose that this is achieved by varying the *level* of prices imposed upon the firm. Thus, the policy problem is to maximize

$$V(q,r) \text{ subject to } x(q,r) = y_1 + y_2 + \cdots + y_m + z,$$

$$\text{where } y_j \text{ maximizes } p_j y \text{ for } y \text{ in } Y_j, \text{ and } z \text{ is in } G. \tag{4}$$

We can think of achieving the maximization by choice of z, q, and the p_j ($j = 1, \ldots, m$); but we may also be interested in the choice of the y_j.

Consider the less constrained problem, to maximize

$$V(q,r) \text{ subject to } x(q,r) \in Y_1 + Y_2 + \cdots + Y_m + G, \tag{5}$$

by choice of q and r. This is a problem of the same kind as (1). The solution to it, $x(q^*, r^*)$, is productively efficient, as we have seen. Consequently it can be achieved by setting prices $a_j p$ to producer j, where p is the vector of producer prices corresponding to the optimum production, and the a_j are scalars, which may vary from producer to producer if we want. We now have the solution of problem (4), *if* we can choose these a_j in such a way that

$$r_j^* = a_j p \cdot y_j^* \qquad (j = 1, \ldots, m), \tag{6}$$

where y^* is production of firm j in the solution to (5). If this is possible, we have shown that the solution to (4) is actually the solution to (5), and therefore efficient.

We shall only fail on our attempt to satisfy (6) if for some j, $r_j^* > 0$ and $p y_j^* = 0$. This is likely to happen if we want some producer to abstain from production. We therefore proceed as follows. Denote by double asterisks the solution to (4). Distinguish the three classes of producers:

J_1: producers for whom $p_j^{**} = 0$; i.e., a 100 per cent profit tax is imposed on them;
J_2: producers for whom $p_j^{**} y_j^{**} = r_j^* > 0$;
J_3: the remaining producers.

(Any producer who has constant returns to scale could be included in class J_1, since his profit is bound to be zero.)

Now solve problem (5), *given $r_j = 0$ and $y_j = y_j^{**}$ for j in J_3, and also $r_j = r_j^{**}$* for the other producers. Since the problem is still of the form (1), productive efficiency *for the set* $\sum_{J_1 \cup J_2} Y_j + G$ is implied. The optimum is therefore achieved if all producers not in J_3 maximize the value of production in terms of the same producer prices p (which also guide public production). Varying profit taxes $1 - a_j$ are then levied: for producers in J_1, $a_j = 0$.

The argument suggests, however, that we may want some producers not to produce, even although they would wish to produce if faced with prices p. Thus, we have a rather odd situation in which aggregate production efficiency is desirable for a class of producers, namely those who are to produce at all, but that some have to be prohibited from producing.

5. The following example, which is illustrated in Fig. 7.1, shows that inefficiency can be desirable. There is one consumer and two private producers. The only commodities are labour and a consumption good. The government has a quantity of the consumption good, which it would wish to dispose of through the tax-and-subsidy system. The amount of the commodity that the government has is OA. The production frontier of one producer is AX; the production frontier of the other is AYZ. Clearly, it is never efficient to have the second producer produce, since the productivity of labour is always higher for the first. But the first producer produces under constant returns to scale, and can therefore generate no profits in equilibrium. Thus, if only the first producer produces, the government's commodity stock can

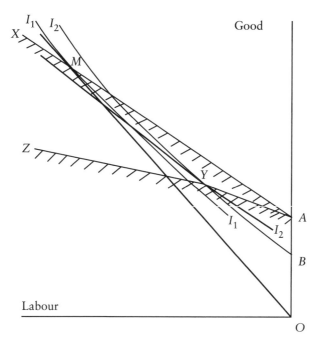

Figure 7.1.

be distributed only through a subsidy to the commodity price. The best that can be done is to get the consumer on to indifference curve $I_1 I_1$. The budget line is then OM, and the consumer chooses the point M. If a lower consumer price were charged for the good, consumer demands would be infeasible.

However, if the first producer is prevented from operating, and the second producer produces at Y, facing producer prices that generate a positive profit OB, the consumer can be faced with budget line BY. He will then be on indifference curve $I_2 I_2$, and therefore better off then at point M. In this case, therefore, it will be better for the government to adopt policies that lead to productive inefficiency.

This example assumes, for the sake of diagrammatic exposition, that there is only one consumer. When there are many consumers, and the government desires to make lump-sum transfers between them, if that were possible, it is plausible that inefficient production in diminishing-returns production owned by more deserving households should be encouraged so as to make the desirable transfer possible.

6. It is a special feature of the examples that, in one of the sectors, constant returns rule up to a certain scale of production, but not beyond. If this is not the case, and all producers either operate under constant returns or obtain positive profit for any non-zero production under non-zero prices, optimum

production cannot be inefficient, if it exists.[1] For the proof, I introduce the notation

$$Y_j^f = [y \in Y_j \mid y' >> y \text{ implies } y' \notin Y_j] \tag{7}$$

for the production frontier of producer j. By imposing suitable producer prices on the jth firm, he can be rendered willing to choose any point of Y_j^f. Thus,

$$V(q^{**}, r^{**}) = \max \left[V(q, r^{**}) \mid x(q, r^{**}) \in \sum_j Y_j^f + G, \ y_j \neq 0 \ (j \in J_2) \right]$$

(where y_j is the production choice in Y_j^f required to generate $x(q, r^{**})$, and non-zero restrictions are imposed for reasons already discussed)

$$= \max \left[V(q, r^{**}) \mid x(q, r^{**}) \in \sum Y_j^f + G \right],$$

since x and V are continuous functions, and V therefore attains the same maximum on the closure of a set as on the set itself. Now this last maximum is equal to

$$\max \left[V(q, r^{**}) \mid x(q, r^{**}) \in \sum Y_j + G \right],$$

since this maximum, being a case of problem (1), is achieved in $\sum Y_j^f + G$, and indeed in the frontier of $\sum Y_j + G$. Thus, $x(g^{**}, r^{**})$ is the production plan maximizing welfare in the case where all production is under the control of the government, and is therefore efficient. In this case, the fact that producers are in the private sector does not reduce the welfare attainable, despite the existence of pure profits.

But the assumption that an optimum exists is excessively strong in this case. Indeed, we know that, given the transfers r^{**}, the production policy that would be chosen by a government in complete control of production might have $y_j = 0$ for some j such that $r_j^{**} > 0$. If that is the case, clearly the maximum V for the problem with private production is not attained.

To provide an example, we can consider an economy with two producers, one operating under constant returns to scale, the other under diminishing returns. Suppose, furthermore, as in the previous example, that the second producer is unambiguously less efficient than the first. Nevertheless, there may be some advantage in allowing the second producer to produce; for if he does, he will earn positive economic rent, and this enables the government to arrange lump-sum transfers to those who have shares in his rents. In principle this can be done whatever scale the second producer operates at. Since he is inefficient, the less he produces, the better; but he must produce something. Thus, we can always improve on any particular production plan, either

---

[1] This assumption, which is not, I suppose, particularly realistic, is satisfied if all production functions are differentiable, as is assumed in Dasgupta (1972).

by reducing production by the second producer, or by having him produce if he were not already doing so. No optimum exists. We can get as close as we please to maximum welfare, however: in order to do so, we have to allow inefficiency.

To conclude, we have seen that productive inefficiency can be desirable when there are diminishing returns, even when a different profit tax is imposed on each producer. But this inefficiency arises only under rather exceptional circumstances, where the existence of an economic rent to an inefficient producer provides an opportunity for lump-sum subsidies that are not otherwise available. In general, once the optimum levels of these profit-associated transfers are fixed, productive efficiency is desirable for the usual reasons.

7. If we are to have production efficiency, we must assume that the profits of each producer are subjected to an optimal profits tax, possibly 100 per cent. When that assumption is removed, production efficiency is not desirable; but optimal taxation can still be characterized quite simply.

Let us now introduce into the model deliberate choice of managerial and entrepreneurial activity by the household. The necessity of providing some incentive if these activities are to be undertaken excludes the possibility of 100 per cent profit taxation from the optimal solution. Naturally, aggregate production efficiency is not in general desirable, but the first-order conditions for optimal taxation have a reasonably simple form. We could discuss the case where each producer (or each of several classes of producer) is taxed at a different rate; but, for simplicity, I suppose that the profit-tax rate is uniform, and all commodity taxes paid by producers are uniform. The prices faced by producers, net of commodity and profit taxes, and p, consumer prices q, and shadow prices (i.e. prices net of consumer or producer taxes) s. Each firm is controlled by a single producer. (The difficulties that arise when we consider joint control of enterprises will be alluded to later.) The production set controlled by household h is $Y^h(m_h)$, and depends upon the supply of managerial effort of that household, represented by the variable m_h.

With these assumptions, household h chooses m_h, x^h, and y^h so as to maximize

$$u(x, m) \text{ subject to } qx \leqq py \text{ and } y \in Y^h(m). \tag{8}$$

It is convenient, and perhaps not very unsatisfactory in the present context, to suppose that the profit-maximizing choice of production plan, $y^h(p, m_h)$, is uniquely defined for each p and m_h. We see from (8) that x^h, and y^h will both be functions of both q and p. Thus, our problem takes the form:

$$\max \ V(q, p) \text{ subject to } \sum_h [x^h(q, p) - y^h(q, p)] \in Z, \tag{9}$$

where Z is the public production set (possibly consisting only of 0).

Let s be shadow prices for public production at the optimum. Then it can be shown[2]—as one expects—that, at the optimum, the derivatives of the Lagrangean

$$L(q,p) = V(q,p) - \lambda s \sum_h (x^h - y^h) \tag{10}$$

vanish (except possibly for zero prices). Consumer taxes are $q - s$; producers are taxes on their transactions at specific rates $s - p$. Since net tax revenue,

$$T = (q - s) \sum x^h + (s - p) \sum y^h = \sum (qx^h - py^h) - s \sum (x^h - y^h)$$
$$= -s \sum (x^h - y^h),$$

then by the budget constraints we can write (10) in the form

$$L(q,p) = V(q,p) + \lambda T(q,p,s), \tag{11}$$

where the dependence of T on the three kinds of price is shown explicitly.

Now it is easily checked—and possible—that

$$V_q = -\sum_h \beta_h x^h, \qquad V_p = \sum_h \beta_h y^h, \tag{12}$$

where β_h is the marginal social utility of household h's income. Using (12), and supposing that the optimal prices are all positive, we obtain the optimal tax rules on equating the derivatives of L to zero:

$$\left. \begin{array}{l} \sum \beta_h x^h = \lambda T_q \\[2mm] -\sum \beta_h y^h = \lambda T_p \end{array} \right\}. \tag{13}$$

In words, consumer taxes should be set at such a level that marginal increments in tax revenue are proportional to 'value-weighted' consumer demands, and producer taxes should be set at such a level that marginal increments in tax revenue are proportional to the net demand of producers, weighted by their 'social worth' as consumers. The first set of rules are identical in form to those in Diamond and Mirrlees (1971) for the case of zero profits. The second set

---

[2] One can see this intuitively, at least when the relative shadow prices corresponding to optimum production are unique and can therefore be interpreted as marginal rates of transformation. If small changes are made in two prices in such a way that $s[\Sigma x - \Sigma y]$ remains constant, the change in public production required will be possible, or as nearly possible as makes no difference. Thus, the resulting change in V must not be positive. So long as optimum prices are positive, the same price changes can be made with opposite sign. Therefore in fact the change in V must be zero. It follows that the derivatives of V should be proportional to the derivatives of $s[\Sigma x - \Sigma y]$.

It will be seen that this argument, though plausible, is by no means watertight. A valid argument on these lines can be constructed, with some difficulty, provided one assumes that tax revenue is not a local maximum at the optimum; i.e. there are possible changes in prices that would increase tax revenue if the demands could actually be satisfied. This is done in Diamond and Mirrlees (1971).

of rules implicitly sets the gain in revenue from increasing a producer tax off against the loss in revenue from discouraging the taxed production. Because of the effect of 'distributed' profits, it is now optimal to tax trade between the public and private production sectors. But the first-order conditions governing producer taxation are not unduly cumbersome or unnatural.

8. It may be noted that the rules (13) also hold if profits of private production are distributed according to conventional rules (fixed shares, for example), and have no effect on managerial or entrepreneurial behavior. In that case, the first-order conditions for producer taxation take a particularly simple form. If household h receives a proportion y_{hj} of the profits from producer j, it can be shown that

$$\sum_{h,j}(1 + \beta_h - T_I^h)\gamma_{hj}y^j = \sum_i (s_i - p_i)\frac{\partial \bar{y}}{\partial p_i}, \tag{14}$$

where T_I^h is the derivative of household h's net tax payments with respect to income, and $\bar{y} = \sum y^j$. Since the case is not particularly interesting, I shall not pause to prove (14); but merely note that, when profits of all producers are shared in the same proportion among households, (14) asserts that

$$\frac{\sum_i(s_i - p_i)(\partial y_k/\partial p_i)}{y_k} \quad \text{is independent of } k. \tag{15}$$

This expression is approximately the proportionate change in production of commodity k resulting from imposition of the optimal producer taxes, at least when these taxes are small.

9. The chief moral of the analysis in the latter part of this paper is that the general principles of commodity taxation remain unchanged when pure profits, and the taxation, optimal or otherwise, of pure profits, are introduced into the model; and, furthermore, analogous principles apply to the determination of optimum taxes on producers (which are not in general zero). The methods can even be extended further, to cases in which 'conventional' profit margins in different sectors create pure profit incomes made possible by monopoly situations: this extension is straightforward, and will be left to the reader.

But a major difficulty remains, which is, I suppose, a major difficulty for the construction of a satisfactory general equilibrium theory, in that cooperative activity by managers appears to have productive advantages. If fixed conventional rules allocate the profits within the team, an analogous theory to the above is easily constructed; but such rules appear to operate only in the short run. In effect, the profits and profit allocation associated with any set of consumer and producer prices must be, from the authorities' point of view, uncertain. Subject to that, the general principles expressed in (14) presumably apply.

It appears, then, that productive efficiency is desirable under more general assumptions than those in Diamond and Mirrlees (1971), but that in plausible models, and in particular those that provide some reason within the system for the maximization of profits, production efficiency is not desirable. However, tax rules of the same general kind as those developed in [2] apply, to the determination of both consumer and producer taxes. (And the notions of consumer and producer taxes seem to provide the appropriate language for expressing the tax rules even when there is no public production without managerial incentives.) In suitable cases, where profit allocations are conventional, and have negligible effect on managerial activity, and differences in household 'portfolios' are not systematically related to the social marginal utility of income or the propensity to pay taxes, producer taxes should be imposed in such a way as to bring about approximately the same percentage change in the net production of all commodities (cf. (15)). Thus, in such a case, Ramsey's principle [3] applies to private production (but not, since there are many consumers, to household consumption).

REFERENCES

Dasgupta, P. S. and Stiglitz, J. 'On Optimal Taxation and Public Production', *Review of Economic Studies* (January 1972).

Diamond, P. A. and Mirrlees, J. A. 'Optimal Taxation and Public Production', *American Economic Review* (March and June 1971).

Ramsey, F. P. 'A Contribution to the Theory of Taxation', *Economic Journal*, 37 (1927), 47–61.

8

The Optimum Town

1. INTRODUCTION

Our customary economic models are not exactly suited to the analysis of land use and transportation. I shall propose a rather simple model, by means of which we can discuss such matters as the optimal taxation of land, and the optimal pricing of transportation. The simplest answer to the optimal use of land, which is suggested, if not exactly proved, by general welfare economics, is the competitive pricing of land, associated with a suitable distribution of the revenues arising from land rents. This solution includes, for example, charges to road-users for the land they use when travelling. I shall show that this answer is, under the assumptions we would expect to have to make, satisfactory; but I shall want to draw particular attention to the implications of this solution for the distribution of incomes.

The main purpose of the paper is, however, a different one. We need convenient models, which could be used to discuss the many second-best problems that arise in this area: the model presented here may be useful for such further developments. Furthermore, it enables us to discuss environmental externalities, which arise, to a not inconsiderable extent, from the population density in a person's neighbourhood. These externalities invalidate the simple solution just mentioned. It will be shown that the authorities can, in principle, correct for them by introducing commuter subsidies (or taxes). The general introduction of housing estates provides an alternative institutional solution to the problem.

Finally, conditions will be derived for the optimum size of town, in the simplified world modelled in the paper. The conditions derived are quite simple, and seem to provide interesting suggestions for the discussion of urban growth in the real world. The analysis in the final section provides an example of welfare economics carried out for an economy with decreasing costs in production.

This paper was first published in the *Swedish Journal of Economics*, vol. 74 (1972), pp. 114–35; Blackwell Publishing Ltd. is one of a series of papers dealing, in a rather theoretical manner, with the determination of optimal taxes. The first version of the paper was written while the author was visiting MIT. He would like to thank the Department of Economics for their hospitality. He is grateful for comments by R. M. Solow, L. Gevers, W. M. Gorman and a number of those who heard earlier presentations at the Barcelona meeting of the Econometric Society and in Oxford.

The model analysed in the paper is intended to be as simple as is consistent with an interesting analysis of the problems. It incorporates two basic indivisibilities that seem to be important in geographical economics. Employment is concentrated, while residence is—or may be—relatively dispersed. At the same time, all the land that a man lives on is concentrated in a single location. It is assumed that the entire population of a town works in one place (each member working a fixed working day), and that individuals are identical, with preferences regarding consumption of goods, distance from work, area occupied by residence, and population density in the immediate neighbourhood. This last variable—which represents environmental externalities—is not introduced until Section 7. The concentration of the labour force is presumably a consequence of economies of scale in manufacturing; but the population of the town will be considered variable only in Section 9.

2. THE CONDITIONS FOR OPTIMALITY

Assuming that social preferences respect individual preferences, and assuming complete separability with respect to individuals,[1] we may pose the welfare problem as that of maximizing

$$\int u(c, a, r) \, rf(r) \, dr. \tag{1}$$

The utility function u represents the individual's preferences regarding $c =$ his consumption, $r =$ his distance from work, $a =$ the area occupied by his residence.

We also have the notation, $f(r) =$ population density at distance r from the centre.

In writing total welfare in the form of an integral with respect to r, we are implicitly assuming that c and a are functions of r. It would be possible to consider allocations in which people at distance r have a variety of consumption levels and dwelling sizes. But it is easily verified that this cannot happen, either in the optimum or in a competitive equilibrium, if we make the following assumption, which will be maintained throughout the paper:

For each r, u is a concave, increasing function of c and a.   (2)

We also assume that

For all c and a, u is a decreasing function of r.   (3)

---

[1] More precisely, it is assumed that social preferences regarding the preferences of any subset of the whole population can be defined independently of what is proposed for the rest. Certain unimportant regularity conditions are also implicit in the representation (1). All functions introduced will be assumed differentiable if convenient.

One might want to suppose that u increases with r for small r, but this adds nothing of interest to the analysis.

Granted the above definitions, we notice that, wherever all land is occupied,

$$a(r)f(r) = 1,\tag{4}$$

provided that transportation between dwelling place and work uses no land. (This last assumption will be relaxed in Section 6.) If N = the population of the town (divided, for convenience, by 2π) and Y = total production of the one commodity, we have the constraints in our welfare problem,

$$\int rf(r)\,\mathrm{d}r = N,\tag{5}$$

$$\int c(r)\,rf(r)\,\mathrm{d}r = Y.\tag{6}$$

In writing the production constraint in the form (6), we are supposing that c is the absorption of goods by the individual: some of this may be used for transportation, and the rest for his consumption. Thus, transport costs are implicitly included in the form of the utility function through its dependence on r. For that to be possible, constant returns in transportation (at any place) must be assumed.

If a finite amount of land is available to the town, the integrals in (1), (5), and (6) must have limits 0 and $\bar{r}$, where $\bar{r}$ is a fixed number. If an unlimited plane is available, we can put $\bar{r} = \infty$. Not all the plane need be occupied, of course. In fact, we would want to assume that individuals cannot live further than a certain distance from work. For the present, assume there is no constraint on area.

We want to consider the optimum allocation of space and goods. Necessary conditions for optimality can be derived heuristically as follows. Maximum welfare (1), subject to the constraints (5) and (6), can be written as a function of Y and N,

$$W(Y,N) = \max \int u(c(r), a(r), r)\, rf(r)\,\mathrm{d}r.\tag{7}$$

Suppose we have the optimal allocation. Then the effect of adding a unit of consumption to the town should be the same regardless of the particular individual to whom the increase is given; that is,

$$W_Y = u_c(c(r), a(r), r) \qquad \text{if } f(r) > 0.\tag{8}$$

(Subscripts denote derivatives with respect to the indicated variable.) Similarly, the effect of adding an extra man to the town should be the same—in terms of welfare—regardless of the place in which space is found for him. Suppose we put him at distance r. Then we give him consumption $c(r)$, at someone's expense, and we reduce the area given to people at distance r by

$a(r)$, in aggregate. Thus,

$$W_N = u(c(r), a(r), r) - c(r)u_c - a(r)u_a, \tag{9}$$

provided that, at r, $f(r) > 0$. Equations (8) and (9) in effect characterize the optimal allocation, for W_Y and W_N are constants, independent of r, whose values can be determined by using the constraints (5) and (6). We define

$$\lambda = W_Y, \qquad \mu = W_N.$$

This argument has neglected the two possibilities $a(r) = 0$ and $f(r) = 0$. The first corresponds to a maximum-density housing development, the second to unoccupied land. It is clear that we can want $a = 0$ only at $r = 0$, for when population density is already infinite, a further increase in population does not matter, and everyone prefers smaller r for given a. Similarly, we can want $f = 0$ only on the periphery of the town, for anyone would move to a vacant space nearer the centre of town. A complete statement of the conditions, which are in fact sufficient for optimality, is as follows:

Suppose there exist functions $c(\cdot)$ and $a(\cdot)$, both non-negative, and defined for $0 \leqslant r < r_1$, and a non-negative number n_0, and numbers λ and μ, such that

$$u_c = \lambda \tag{10}$$

when $c = c(r)$, $a = a(r)$, $0 \leqslant r < r_1$;

$$u = au_a + \lambda c + \mu \tag{11}$$

when $c = c(r)$, $a = a(r)$, $0 < r < r_1$;

$$u(c(0), 0, 0) \leqslant \lambda c(0) + \mu \tag{12}$$

with equality if $n_0 > 0$;

$$u(c, \infty, r) \leqslant \lambda c + \mu \tag{13}$$

for all $c > 0$ and $r > r_1$;

$$n_0 + \int_0^{r_1} \frac{r\,dr}{a(r)} = N; \tag{14}$$

and

$$n_0 c(0) + \int_0^{r_1} c(r) \frac{r\,dr}{a(r)} = Y. \tag{15}$$

Then the allocation defined by $c(\cdot)$, $a(\cdot)$ and n_0 (the number of people concentrated at $r = 0$) is optimal.

The proof of this proposition is entirely standard in form. Consider some alternative allocation, and indicate it by attaching primes to the variables. Assume, as one safely may, that $a' = 0$ only at $r = 0$, if at all. I claim that

$$n_0[u(c(0), 0, 0) - \lambda c(0) - \mu] \geq n_0'[u(c'(0), 0, 0) - \lambda c'(0) - \mu]; \tag{16}$$

$$\frac{u - \lambda c - \mu}{a} \geq \frac{u' - \lambda c' - \mu}{a'}, \qquad \text{when } 0 < r < r_1; \tag{17}$$

$$0 \geq \frac{u' - \lambda c' - \mu}{a'}, \qquad \text{when } r > r_1. \tag{18}$$

Inequality (16) is proved by using (12) to show that the left-hand side is actually equal to zero, and (10) to show that

$$u(c'(0), 0, 0) - \lambda c'(0) \leq u(c(0), 0, 0) - \lambda c(0) \leq \mu, \quad \text{by (12).}$$

Inequality (17) follows from (10) and (11) and the concavity of u: by concavity,

$$u' \leq u + u_c(c' - c) + u_a(a' - a) = \mu + \lambda c' + u_a a', \qquad \text{by (11) and (10).}$$

Dividing by a' (which is positive since $r > 0$), we obtain (17), since $u_a = (u - \lambda c - \mu)/a$, by (11). To derive (18), we use (13) and the assumption that u is increasing in a:

$$u' \leq u(c'(r), \infty, r) - \lambda c'(r) + \mu.$$

Having proved (16), (17), and (18), we put them together to prove the desired result. (17) is integrated between 0 and r_1, and (18) from r_1 to ∞. The results are added together and to (16), giving

$$n_0 u(c(0), 0, 0) + \int u \frac{r \, dr}{a(r)} - \lambda Y - \mu N \geq n_0' u(c'(0), 0, 0)$$

$$+ \int u' \frac{r \, dr}{a(r)} - \lambda Y' - \mu N' \tag{19}$$

Since the alternative allocation fits the given constraints, we have $Y = Y'$ and $N = N'$; (19) therefore shows that the allocation satisfying (10)–(15) gives at least as much welfare as any alternative feasible allocation. This proves the stated proposition. □

The earlier discussion should have convinced the reader that the stated conditions are also necessary for an optimum. The extra complication of a finite population concentrated at the centre can be excluded by assuming that

$$u(c, a, r) \to -\infty \qquad \text{as } a \to 0 \tag{20}$$

It is then impossible that (12) should be satisfied with equality, and n_0 must consequently be zero. Assumption (20) is not unrealistic, but there may be advantages in the vivid picture of infinitely dense housing becoming optimal when the population of the town becomes large: for this reason it may be more interesting not to assume (20). In the present paper, the possibility $n_0 > 0$ will not be further considered.

3. THE DISTRIBUTION OF POPULATION

From (10) and (11) we can derive further information about the distribution of population in the town under the optimum regime. Differentiating (11) with respect to r, we obtain

$$u_r + u_c \frac{dc}{dr} + u_a \frac{da}{dr} = u_a \frac{da}{dr} + a \frac{d}{dr} u_a + \lambda \frac{dc}{dr},$$

which simplifies, using (10), to give

$$\frac{d}{dr} u_a = u_r/a. \tag{21}$$

We also have, from (10),

$$\frac{d}{dr} u_c = 0. \tag{22}$$

Putting (21) and (22) together, and eliminating dc/dr, we get, after some manipulation,

$$\frac{da}{dr} = \frac{-u_{cc}}{u_{aa}u_{cc} - u_{ac}^2} (u_{ar} - u_r/a). \tag{23}$$

By the concavity of u, the first factor here is necessarily non-negative. Therefore the sign of da/dr is the sign of $u_{ar} - u_r/a$. It is clearly possible that a should decrease with r, at least for certain ranges. But the following (excessively strong) sufficient condition for a to be an increasing function is rather plausible, and one may therefore take it that, normally, a does increase with r. We have

$$\frac{u_{ar}}{u_r} < \frac{u_{ar}}{u_r} - \frac{u_{aa}}{u_a} = \frac{\partial}{\partial a} \log |u_r/u_a|. \tag{24}$$

Thus, $u_{ar} \leqslant u_r/a$ so long as the marginal rate of substitution of work-proximity for dwelling-space increases, if at all, by less than one per cent when area increases by one per cent, distance being constant.

It will be noticed that the sign of (23) is affected by the interpersonal comparison of marginal utilities that is adopted. A more egalitarian choice of welfare function could affect the result. This is not true of the strong sufficient condition just derived.

4. COMPETITIVE REALIZATION

There is more to say about the appearance of the optimal allocation itself, but further results are most conveniently derived after we have at our disposal the theorem proved in this section, that the optimum is a competitive equilibrium, for the right income distribution. For the model we are discussing, this result is not readily derived from the corresponding theorem for a conventional economy, where preferences do not refer to location. In any case, we have a continuum of commodities and a continuum of consumers, and nonconvexity in the consumption set (since consumers cannot live in two places at once). The general theorems that may be available for such cases are difficult to prove. It is best therefore to ignore them and concentrate on the special case.

If there is a competitive equilibrium in our model, it will be characterized by a distribution of incomes—denoted by m for a particular individual—and a rent function p, such that the price for land at distance r from the centre is $p(r)$. An individual with income m will maximize, by choice of c, s, and r,

$$u(c, a, r) \quad \text{subject to} \quad c + p(r)a \leqslant m. \tag{25}$$

The distribution of incomes, described by a density function g ($g(m)\mathrm{d}m$ of the consumers have incomes between m and $m + \mathrm{d}m$), must be such that the demand for and supply of land are equal at all r. That is, the integral of g over all m for which the chosen r is less than or equal to r' must be equal to $\pi r'^2$. The average level of incomes will be so chosen that the demand for consumer goods just equals what is available.

Differentiation of (25) shows that the consumer will satisfy

$$u_a = u_c p(r), \; u_r = u_c a p'(r). \tag{26}$$

We must expect, therefore, that, if the optimum is to have a competitive realization, the rent function is defined by

$$p(r) = u_a^* / u_c^*, \tag{27}$$

where here and afterwards asterisks denote evaluation at the optimum. It is readily verified, by using (10) and (11), and differentiating with respect to r, that (27) implies the second equation in (26). We need more than that, however: it is not sufficient that the consumer satisfies the first-order conditions for utility maximization. If the consumer is given a particular income, he must be as content to live where the welfare maximizer wishes him to as anywhere else. We have to prove that, if a person is given income

$$m = c^*(r) + a^*(r)p(r) \tag{28}$$

(so that we want him to be willing to live distance r from the centre), no alternative consumption plan (c, a, s) that satisfies his budget constraint,

$$c + ap(s) \leqslant c^*(r) + a^*(r)p(r), \tag{29}$$

gives him greater utility. When we have proved that, we have established that the optimum has a competitive realization: for (27) tells us what rents must be, and we can then deduce the required distribution of incomes from (28).

The proof of the desired proposition goes as follows.

$$u(c, a, s) \leqslant u(c^*(s), a^*(s), s) + u_c^*(s)[c - c^*(s)] + u_a^*(s)[a - a^*(s)],$$

by concavity, where $u_c^*(s)$ and $u_a^*(s)$ denote evaluation of the partial derivatives at $(c^*(s), a^*(s), s)$,

$$
\begin{aligned}
&= \mu + \lambda c + u_a^*(s)a, &&\text{by (10) and (11)} \\
&= \mu + \lambda c + \lambda p(s)a, &&\text{by (27)} \\
&\leqslant \mu + \lambda c^*(r) + \lambda p(r)a^*(r), &&\text{by (29)} \\
&= u(c^*(r), a^*(r), r), &&\text{by (27) and (11).}
\end{aligned}
\tag{30}
$$

This proves the result we want, and establishes the possibility of competitive realization. We shall return to this issue later when externalities are introduced.

5. THE OPTIMAL DISTRIBUTION OF WELFARE

The most interesting feature of the optimal allocation, which our assumption of identical consumers was intended to highlight, is the distribution of utility. In the optimal allocation, utility is a function of r: it is constant only in special cases.[2] We can see this in the following way. We know that there exists a land rent function p and a distribution of incomes such that the optimum is a competitive equilibrium. If utility is independent of r, everyone must have the same income, since a person with a higher income can always obtain higher utility for himself. Let the income level be m. An individual chooses a and r so as to maximize

$$u(m - ap(r), a, r).$$

In order that the population spread itself out over the area of the town, the maximum with respect to a for fixed r must be independent of r. Therefore, if we define a function $v(c, x, r) = u(c, x/p(r), r)$, we have

$$\max_x \ v(m - x, x, r) \text{ is independent of } r.$$

One case where (31) holds is that in which v does not depend on r explicitly, i.e.

$$u = v(c, az(r)) \tag{31}$$

---

[2] Professor Gorman pointed some of these special cases out to me.

for some function z. It is readily verified that this utility function implies uniform utility at the optimum. Equations (10) and (11) now take the form

$$v_c = \lambda, \qquad v - cv_c - azv_2 = \mu, \tag{32}$$

where v_2 denotes the derivative of v with respect to az. Inspecting (32), we see that we have two equations in two variables, c and az, which are therefore determined independently of r. It is now clear from (31) that u is independent of r in this case.

There are, however, other cases that lead to uniform utility. For example, preferences homothetic in c and a will do it:

$$u(c, a, r) \quad \text{homogeneous in } c \text{ and } a \tag{31'}$$

This is readily verified directly, as is the case of the following utility function:

$$u = e^{kc} w(a, r). \tag{31''}$$

I do not know whether the three cases (31), (31'), (31'') exhaust all the possibilities: it seems unlikely.

It is easily seen, however, that utility will not usually be uniform. Suppose that preferences were such that, for any particular pattern of rents, an increase in income would make people want to move inwards. (If utility were as in (31), an increase in income would have no effect on the choice of location.) Then, in the optimum, utility must be a decreasing function of r. For the optimum is a competitive equilibrium, and consumers will have to be given a higher income to induce them to live nearer the centre. I am inclined to regard this as the plausible case.

One can examine the plausibility of these assumptions by considering a special case of the general utility function. Let

$$u = v(c - tr) + w(a, r). \tag{33}$$

In this form, the enjoyment of consumption is separated from the enjoyment of space and location, but some part of the absorption of goods must be used to meet transport costs (at a constant rate t per mile distance from work). From (33), an easy calculation gives us the formula

$$\frac{du}{dr} = \frac{w_r^2}{aw_{aa}} \left[\frac{\partial}{\partial a} \left(\frac{aw_a}{w_r} \right) - \frac{w_a}{w_r^2} v't \right]. \tag{34}$$

It is clear from (34) that utility is more likely to be an increasing function of r the greater are transport costs: this is plausible, since the price of moving outwards has increased. One might expect, on the other hand, that the first term in square brackets, $(\partial/\partial a)(aw_a/w_r)$, would be positive. It is positive if, when consumption is fixed and transport costs are zero, a uniform proportional increase in rents moves a man outwards. (This may be verified directly; but it follows from the consideration that, when t is zero and c is fixed, a proportional increase in rents is the same as a reduction in income for a man with utility function w.)

This brief discussion suggests that, to some extent, the shape of the outcome depends on the balance between transport costs and 'natural preference'. If, as is realistic, transport costs are greatest near the centre of the town, utility might be an increasing function of r near the centre, but a decreasing function beyond a point. It is interesting to consider that in this case, under the competitive realization, many people have to be indifferent between each of two different locations, which are fairly widely separated. It is curious that, nevertheless, competitive realization is possible.

The particular direction in which u changes is not quite as important as the more basic implication that utilities should not be equal. In this model individuals are identical in tastes and initial endowment of skills and abilities. Yet it is not, except in special cases, optimal for them to be treated equally. I sometimes think it is obvious that this should be so: people cannot, when their locations have to be related to a single central point, be treated indentically, and there is no reason, from the purely utilitarian standpoint, why different treatment should lead to the same utilities. Thus, the technological desirability of geographically concentrated production activity is, in itself, and apart from all considerations of diverse tastes and skills, a reason for advocating some inequality of incomes. The question how great an inequality of incomes might plausibly be justified in this way remains to be examined.

One may feel that inequality is not necessary for optimality in our model, since no harm is done by frequently changing the treatment of individuals while keeping the overall distribution of incomes constant. After all, it does not matter who receives a high income, only that some people should receive relatively high incomes. But there is no consideration in the model to show that such a constant permutation of incomes would yield an improvement in social welfare. If, therefore, there is any cost—as there surely is—to changing a man's place in the world, the 'optimum with equality' that is obtained by changing the positions of individuals within the income distribution is actually inferior to the more straightforward solution. It should also be noted that, if a more general social welfare function were considered, which gives some positive value to equality as such and for itself—which the completely separable form used in this paper does not—the same general conclusion would follow: that complete equality is not, in general, optimal.

Finally, it is interesting to notice that the tax system required to obtain the optimum in this model is both lump-sum and, from any point of view, feasible. The usual reasons for thinking the optimal lump-sum transfers are not possible do not apply in the present case, for nothing a man does, or is thought to be capable of doing, affects his income. The inequality of incomes is entirely unrelated to personal characteristics or behaviour. This may not seem very appealing. But it seems to me that the reasons leading to the conclusion have some force, and arise from real considerations.

6. TRANSPORT COSTS

We have already seen that the model as it stands allows us to incorporate transport costs that have to be met by the expenditure of goods. One may as easily incorporate the costs of time used through the direct dependence of u on r. But we have excluded the possibility that transport needs space.[3] It is interesting to derive the conditions for optimality in the more general case, and to show formally that optimality is achieved by charging road users the rent for the land they cross in travelling between home and work. For simplicity, let us restrict attention to the case where the width of road required is proportional to the number of people using it. This constant-returns-to-scale assumption excludes the possibility of congested movement. That more general case can be analysed in an entirely similar way.

Let one person require a road of width k to transport him between his residence and the centre, so that, if

$$2\pi N(r) = \text{the number of people living at least distance } r \text{ from the}$$
$$\text{centre of the town,} \tag{35}$$

a proportion $kN(r)/r$ of the circle with radius r must be used for road. We have to assume that there is an inner disc (surrounding the place of work) where no one lives, of radius $r_1 = kN$. All of the boundary of this disc is used for roads. Let

$$f(r) = \text{the population density at distance } r \text{ on land not}$$
$$\text{occupied by roads.} \tag{36}$$

Then

$$-N'(r) = [r - kN(r)]f(r). \tag{37}$$

We want to maximize

$$-\int u(c(r), a(r), r)N'(r)\, dr, \tag{38}$$

subject to (37), with $N(r_1) = N$ and $N(\infty) = 0$, and the production constraint

$$-\int c(r)N'(r)\, dr = Y. \tag{39}$$

Notice that $a(r)f(r) = 1$.

---

[3] Solow and Vickrey (1971) discussed this problem for the 'long linear city', but under rather different assumptions about the relationship of land use to travel requirements.

Incorporating an undetermined multiplier λ for the constraint (39), we have to choose the functions c and N so as to make the integral

$$\int \left[u\left(c, -\frac{r - kN}{N'}, r\right) - \lambda c \right] N' \, dr \tag{40}$$

stationary. By variation of c, we see that, as before,

$$u_c = \lambda, \tag{41}$$

while the Euler–Lagrange equation obtained by varying the function N is

$$\frac{d}{dr}(u - \lambda c - au_a) = ku_a. \tag{42}$$

Equation (42) generalizes our earlier condition (11). It is easily seen that, in the case of variable transport costs, k is to be interpreted as the marginal road-width requirement for an extra traveller: it would then be a function of N.

Competitive realization for this case will be achieved by subjecting the consumer with income m to the budget constraint

$$c + p(r)a + \int_{r_1}^r kp(s) \, ds \leqslant m, \tag{43}$$

where $p(r) = u_a^* / u_c^*$. The argument used to prove that one can find an income distribution such that, with this rent function, the optimum is a competitive equilibrium goes through with only routine modifications to the calculation given in Section 4. It turns out, as should be expected, that one may allow k to depend on r and N without affecting the argument. Thus, the presence of, for example, decreasing costs in the provision of roads does not prevent competitive realization of the optimum.

7. ENVIRONMENTAL EXTERNALITIES

It seems to me that the local population density, and the features of the environment that are derived from it, are as important to many people as the area of land they occupy. But this is a true externality, since a man can influence the local density only by moving to another place. In this section and the next I discuss the measures that might be taken by a government to correct for the loss of welfare sustained by any competitive equilibrium on this account.

Let the typical individual have utility function

$$u(c, a, r, f). \tag{44}$$

We now have the population density appearing explicitly: people will not be able to choose f independently of r—it is the result of other people's choices. For simplicity, let us revert to the assumption that transportation does not use space. Then for all r

$$af = 1. \tag{45}$$

Formally, the optimization problem is the same as before, with a utility function $\bar{u}(c,a,r)=u(c,a,r,\ 1/a)$. The only difference, and it might be not unimportant, is that we may be unwilling to assume that $\bar{u}$ is a concave function of c and a. I shall only assume that

u is concave in c and a for given r and f. $\qquad(46)$

However, even without the assumption that $\bar{u}$ is concave in c and a, the same first-order conditions for maximization hold. Assuming that $\bar{u}\to-\infty$ as $a\to0$, we can ignore the possibility that some of the population is concentrated at the centre. Then if $a<\infty$ (i.e. if anyone is present at r from the centre), the first-order conditions take the form

$$u_c = \lambda, \qquad(47)$$

$$u - cu_c - au_a + fu_f = \mu. \qquad(48)$$

We also have a second-order condition for maximization with respect to the area function $a(\cdot)$,

$$\frac{\partial^2\bar{u}}{\partial a^2}\leqslant 0 \qquad(49)$$

The proof that (47), (48), and (49) are necessary conditions for maximization is straightforward. (47) derives from the consideration that goods should be distributed so as to maximize the sum of utilities; (47) and (49) can be proved by considering the effect of changing the population by one, where the man is added to or removed from the part of the population living at distance r from the centre.

An example will illustrate how these conditions can be used to derive the optimal distribution of population in a particular case. Let

$$u = \log c - r + fe^{-f}. \qquad(50)$$

In this example, it may prove desirable to concentrate some population at the centre: it is quite interesting to see how this arises. Clearly, c is constant: we can omit 'log c' in (50). So long as $f>0$ and $r>0$, (48) and (49) apply:

$$\begin{aligned} -r+(2-f)fe^{-f} &= \mu \\ f^2 - 4f + 2 &\leqslant 0. \end{aligned} \qquad(51)$$

The last condition implies that $f>0$ only in the interval

$$2 - \sqrt{2} < f < 2 + \sqrt{2}. \qquad(52)$$

Within this interval, (51) defines f uniquely as a decreasing function of r (for fixed μ) (see Fig. 8.1). Reference to condition (12), which applies to the point where population may be concentrated, shows that $\mu\geqslant 0$. This in turn implies, by (51), that $f\leqslant 2$. Since f is a decreasing function of μ, the population that can be accommodated by our solution is a decreasing function of μ. When $\mu = 0$, the population is, if none is concentrated at the centre,

$$\int f \, dr = - \int_{2-\sqrt{2}}^{2} r \, df = \int_{2-\sqrt{2}}^{2} (2-f)fe^{-f} \, df = 0.65\ldots = N_0, \text{ say} \quad (53)$$

If total population is less than N_0, none of it is concentrated at the centre, since the only possible solution then has $\mu > 0$. If $N > N_0$, the concentration at $r = 0$ is $N - N_0$.

Summarizing, part of the population may be concentrated at the centre; the rest is distributed within a finite disc where the population density, given by (51), diminishes with increasing r until $f = 2 - \sqrt{2}$. Beyond that, there is no one.

Can the optimum be realized? I shall discuss two methods by which it might be achieved. The first and most obvious is to introduce a commuter subsidy or tax. In other words, the income a man receives to spend on goods and land is to have two components: a 'random' component, as was required in the absence of the externality, and a component that is related to the distance of his dwelling from the centre. If the commuter subsidy is $q(r)$, a man with income m will be seeking to maximize

$$u(c, a, r, f(r)) \quad \text{subject to} \quad c + p(r)a \leqslant m + q(r). \quad (54)$$

I shall show that it is possible to choose the functions p and q in such a way that a man who chooses to live at r will also choose as his consumption and dwelling area the levels $c^*(r)$ and $a^*(r)$ that correspond to the optimum allocation. For a suitable distribution of incomes, we then have a competitive realization of the optimum.

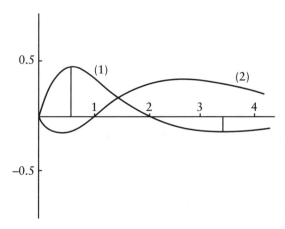

Figure 8.1. (1): $r + \mu = (2-f)fe^{-f}$; (2): $w - \mu = (f-1)fe^{-f}$

We shall, of course, want to set $p(r)$ equal to the marginal rate of substitution of goods for land,

$$p(r) = u_a^*/u_c^*. \tag{55}$$

The maximization of (54) with respect to r implies that

$$u_r + u_f f'(r) = u_c[ap'(r) - q'(r)].$$

If this is to hold at the optimum, with p defined by (55), we have

$$u_c^* q'(r) = a\frac{\mathrm{d}}{\mathrm{d}r}u_a^* - u_r^* - u_f^* f'(r), \tag{56}$$

using (47). If we differentiate (48) with respect to r, bearing (47) in mind, we obtain

$$u_r^* - a^*(r)|\frac{\mathrm{d}}{\mathrm{d}r}u_a^* + 2f'(r)u_f^* + f(r)\frac{\mathrm{d}}{\mathrm{d}r}u_f^* = 0. \tag{57}$$

Combining (56) and (57),

$$u_c^* q'(r) = f'(r)u_f^* + f(r)\frac{\mathrm{d}}{\mathrm{d}r}u_f^* = \frac{\mathrm{d}}{\mathrm{d}r}(fu_f^*). \tag{58}$$

Thus, it seems that we ought to set

$$q(r) = f^*(r)u_f^*/u_c^*. \tag{59}$$

I claim that, with these definitions of p and q, global maximization by the consumer is consistent with the optimum. The proof follows the same lines as that in Section 4, and therefore will be set out in less detail. We have, for an alternative consumption plan (c, a, s) satisfying the budget constraint specified in (54),

$$u(c, a, s, f(s)) \leqslant u(c^*(s), a^*(s), s, f(s))$$
$$+ [c - c^*(s)]u_c^*(s) + [a - a^*(s)]u_a^*(s),$$

by concavity of u with respect to c and a, and this expression

$$= -f^*(s)u_f^*(s) + \mu + \lambda c + \lambda p(s)a, \text{ by (48)}$$
$$= \mu + \lambda[c + p(s)a - q(s)], \text{ by (59)} \tag{60}$$
$$\leqslant \mu + \lambda m, \text{ by the budget constraint.}$$

If then m has been set at such a level as to make the choice of r and its associated optimum $c^*(r)$ and $a^*(r)$ possible, i.e. $m = c^*(r) + p(r)a^*(r) - q(r)$, we see from (60), (47), and (48) that

$$u(c, a, s, f(s)) \leqslant u(c^*(r), a^*(r), r, f^*(r)),$$

as claimed.

This proves that the introduction of a suitable commuter subsidy system into the competitive economy can completely correct the distortion arising from environmental externalities, provided these can be represented by dependence of u on population density.

It is not very easy to guess whether this subsidy would generally be positive or negative (i.e. a tax). So long as population density is unpleasant on the margin, the expression in (59) is of course negative. But the interesting quantity is the rate at which q changes with r, since that is the subsidy paid for living further away. The addition of a constant to q is in fact irrelevant, since it can be compensated for by a change in the income distribution:

$$\lambda q'(r) = f'(r) u_f + f(r) \frac{d}{dr} u_f. \tag{61}$$

To calculate this, one must calculate $c'(r)$ and $a'(r)$ from the first-order conditions. The result is too complicated to interpret readily. But it is quite interesting to look at the very special case of utility function,

$$u = v_1(c - tr) + v_2(r) + w(a, f). \tag{62}$$

In this case, some calculation shows that

$$\lambda q'(r) = (w_f + f w_{ff} - a w_{af}) f'(r) = \frac{(w_f + f w_{ff} - a w_{af})(v_2' - t\lambda)}{a^3 w_{aa} - 2a w_{af} + f w_{ff} - 2w_f}. \tag{63}$$

The denominator here is nonpositive, by the second-order condition (49), and the second factor in the numerator is negative. Thus, the sign of q' is the sign of $w_f + f w_{ff} - a w_{af}$. This *could* take either sign: it is not possible to deduce *a priori* whether commuting should be taxed or subsidized. On the whole, a negative sign seems to be the more plausible, particularly at density levels where w_f is negative.

8. HOUSING ESTATES

An alternative method for obtaining the full optimum when there are environmental externalities suggests itself. If the purchaser of living space is at the same time able to choose the local population density, the externality should be internalized, and the problem solved. This is, to some extent, what housing estates—that is, large-scale housing developments whose form is fixed before plots or dwelling-units are sold—achieve. Only rather large housing estates, with associated community services, parks, playgrounds, schools, etc., could achieve exactly what is wanted, and there are few cases where consumer choice in regard to such developments can be exercised; but the case is worthy of examination.

Suppose, then, that the land market consists of trading in 'estate membership': the seller offers an area of land a along with the assurance that the local population density will be f. There may be different sizes of plot within the same estate—but not, we shall see, in equilibrium. In equilibrium, since (in our simple model) everyone has the same tastes, representable by a utility function concave in land-area, there will in fact be no advantage in providing different plot sizes within the estate. Thus, we shall have a market in which the price of a plot of area a in an estate of average density $1/a$ at distance r from the centre is $P(a, r)$. Clearly, the owner of land on the circle of radius r will choose a so as to maximize

$$P(a, r)/a. \tag{64}$$

At the same time, a consumer with income m will choose c, a, and r so as to maximize

$$u(c, a, r, 1/a) \quad \text{subject to} \quad c + P(a, r) \leqslant m. \tag{65}$$

Consider what would happen if a price structure were given as follows:

$$P(a, r) = \frac{1}{\lambda} u(c^*(r), a, r, 1/a) - c^*(r) - \frac{\mu}{\lambda}. \tag{66}$$

It is clear that, with this land price function, a consumer is indifferent between alternative plot sizes, once he has chosen his r. Landowners will choose $a(r)$ so as to maximize

$$\frac{u(c(r), a, r, 1/a) - \lambda c^*(r) - \mu}{a}. \tag{67}$$

Thus (using (47)), we see that the allocations a and c^* (which are feasible if the income distribution is suitably chosen) maximize

$$\frac{u(c, a, r, 1/a) - \lambda c - \mu}{a} \tag{68}$$

for each r. Integrating over all r, we deduce that $\int u(r \, dr/a)$ is at least as great for this allocation as it could be for any other. Thus, the optimum has been achieved.

We have proved, then, that if the land market operates in terms of housing estates there exists a competitive equilibrium which is the optimum. It is interesting to note that, even with this form of realization, it is not necessary that utility be concave when the externality is taken into account. The reasons why only vestiges of such a market exist are perhaps reasonably obvious. (There are always substantial fixed costs associated with the existing pattern of land-use.) One would not expect a full optimum to be obtainable in this way. But the analysis suggests there may be some reasons for encouraging the common development of large land areas.

9. AN OPTIMUM GEOGRAPHY

Having worked out a theory of the optimum town, we can place optimum towns in a wider context, with more 'primitive' producers scattered between them, and ask what principles should determine the optimum size and number of the towns. By this approach, one may be able to provide an interesting analysis of the 'dual economy' and of its growth over time, and of related issues, such as the taxation and subsidy of agriculture. Here I shall do no more than sketch the theory for the simplest case.

Let us maintain the assumptions of identical tastes and a single commodity. In particular, capital will be ignored. Let us also make the peculiar assumption that land is not required for production even in the rural sector: this is done only to make calculations more transparent. Factors of production other than labour are, of course, easily incorporated into an analysis of this kind. It will also be convenient to neglect the costs of transporting commodities, since that must be easy to deal with too. Consider, then, a country of fixed area A and fixed population P. Production possibilities are given by a production function

$$Y = H(N) \tag{69}$$

for a single plant designed to employ N people in one location. In particular, production per head in rural areas, where people live and work in the same place and are separated from one another, is $h = H'(0)$. It is realistic to assume that H is convex for N not very large at least. We may take it that that is, in part, the explanation for towns. But it does not follow that all production should take place in towns: that is a matter we have yet to determine.

It is convenient to revert to the notation $W(Y, N)$, introduced in (7), for the maximum utility obtainable for a population of N, all working at one place, and enjoying, in aggregate, a quantity of goods, Y. Indeed, we shall extend the notation to $W(Y, N, B)$, where B is the area occupied by the town. We remarked earlier that the optimality equations hold whether or not the area of the town is circumscribed. The only difference is that the 'boundary conditions' (13) cannot apply. μ will be somewhat smaller so as to keep the whole population on a reduced area. With this notation, we can write the utility of the whole economy, when there are n towns, and country dwellers enjoy consumption c_0 and area a_0 each, as[4]

$$nW(C, N, B) + (P - nN)u(c_0, a_0, 0, 1/a_0). \tag{70}$$

Here C is the aggregate consumption of the population of a town, and we have the production constraint

$$nC + (P - nN)c_0 \leqslant nH(N) + (P - nN)h. \tag{71}$$

There is also an area constraint,

$$nB + (P - nN)a_0 \leqslant A \tag{72}$$

---

[4] In writing (70), we are assuming that all towns should be of the same size. It is possible that, with particular functions H, and values of total population P, one might want to have towns of unequal size. But this is presumably unlikely if the total population is at all large.

We want to maximize (70) subject to the constraints (71) and (72). It is easily seen that this requires

$$W_C = u_c^0, \tag{73}$$

$$W_B = u_a^0 - a_0^{-2} u_f^0, \tag{74}$$

$$W_N = u^0 - W_C(c_0 + H' - h) - W_B a_0 \tag{75}$$

(where the zero superfix indicates evaluation at $(c_0, a_0, 0, 1/a_0)$), and, treating n as a continuous variable (so that the number of towns must be large for the equation to be a good approximation),

$$W - NW_N - CW_C - BW_B + (H - NH'(N))W_C = 0. \tag{76}$$

This last equation is obtained by varying n and N together in such a way that nN remains constant. The consequent variation of C and B is then found from (71) and (72).[5]

We know that $W_C = \lambda$ and $W_N = \mu$. Clearly, W_B is the value of a unit of land added at the periphery of a town, i.e. $u_a - f^2 u_f$ evaluated for r equal to the radius of the town. Thus, (73), (74), and (75) are natural continuity conditions applying at the boundary between town and country. By using (76), we can throw light on the optimum size of town. We know that, within a town,

$$u - \lambda c - \lambda p(r)a + \lambda q(r) - \mu = 0. \tag{77}$$

Here we have substituted (47), and the definitions of the land price and commuter subsidy, into (48). If we multiply (77) by $rf(r)$ and integrate with respect to r from zero to the boundary of the town, we obtain

$$W - \lambda C - \lambda \int pr \, dr + \lambda \int qrf \, dr - \mu N = 0. \tag{78}$$

Combining (76) and (78) yields, on dividing by $\lambda = W_C$,

$$NH' - H = \int (p - p^0)r \, dr - \int (q^f - q^0 f_0)rf \, dr, \tag{79}$$

where $p^0 = u_a^0/\lambda$, the rural land price, and $q^0 = a_0^{-1} u_f^0/\lambda$, the 'base rate' of the commuter subsidy, applying to someone living where he works. We can state (79) in words as the requirement that

Marginal product − average product = average excess rent per man

− average excess commuter

subsidy per man. (80)

---

[5] When there is redistribution of consumer goods from town to country, or vice versa, the cost of transporting the goods may be an important consideration. It is interesting that, if redistribution of this kind is impossible or undesirable, our conditions remain unchanged, except that (73) must be dropped, and replaced by $C = H, c_0 = h$.

In each case, 'excess' refers to the comparison with the use of the town's land as a rural area.[6]

In the absence of the density externality, this principle is not too surprising. One may express it by saying that workers should be paid their marginal products (which will have to exceed their average products). There should then be income redistribution, involving no government surplus or deficit, except for a transfer of goods (possibly negative) to those living in rural areas. Incomes are spent on goods and on land rents. The transfer to be made to country dwellers is equal to total production, minus the cost of the land occupied by the town at rural land prices, minus the aggregate consumption of goods in the town.

Condition (79) will not always define the size of town uniquely. Since we are dealing with a nonconvex technology, we should not expect it to. A typical situation is illustrated in Fig. 8.2, where there are two different town sizes for which the first-order condition (79) is satisfied (not counting the zero size). One might guess that the larger town size of the two indicated in this case would be better, but I suspect that would not be correct in general. Similarly, the fact that (79) is satisfied for some size does not necessarily prove that towns ought to be

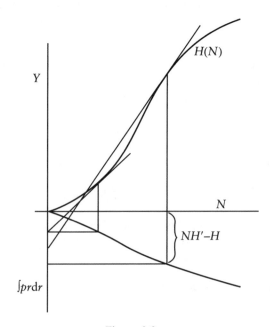

Figure 8.2.

<hr>

[6] David Starrett of Harvard has derived results similar to (79).

established. This involves a global comparison, which would have to be carried out directly (with the help, perhaps, of equation (78)).

One curious feature of the rule stated in (80) is the way in which the commuter subsidy term enters. If this truly is a subsidy, i.e. if q increases with r, the term is negative. This might lead to an optimal size of town greater than would have been proposed if the density effect had been neglected. It might even lead to an optimal size of town for which the marginal product of labour is less than the average product. To discover more about this, one will have to examine particular examples.

It does not seem to be possible to say anything about the optimum number of towns on the basis of the first-order conditions that we have derived. These conditions will, of course, help to determine the optimum number of towns. One may wonder whether it might not be optimal to establish so many towns that they cannot be fitted into the available land area with the circular form assumed in this paper. This will depend on the extent of the economies of scale available and the size of population. I am inclined to regard it as an unrealistic possibility, at least with the transport technology currently available. But this is another guess that should be checked in specific examples with 'realistic' numbers.

10. CAUTIONS AND CONCLUSIONS

It seemed to be worth while working through this simple model of land use in some detail, since it captures a number of considerations that are important for land planning. The assumptions of a single commodity and uniformity of tastes are, however, far from innocuous. When there are a number of different kinds of commodity, one is forced to consider the transportation of goods explicitly, and the shape of towns is likely to be rather different, and much more complicated. Diversity of tastes allows one to consider, for example, optimal diversity in the environment, as well as an association of different tastes with different locations. But it is not very likely that these complications would seriously upset the main conclusions of the paper:

(1) When, because of economies of scale in localized production, it is desirable to create centres of production with dispersed residence of the workers, some inequality of income distribution is (generally) desirable, even when individuals are identical.

(2) So long as there are no externalities, the optimum can be realized as a competitive equilibrium with a land market (provided that all uses of land, including transportation, are properly charged for).

(3) When there are environmental externalities, which can be represented as a dependence of utility on local population density, it is still possible to realize the optimum as a competitive equilibrium provided that there is

either a commuter subsidy (or tax), or a land market operating in terms of estate shares rather than independent plots.

(4) The optimum size of town can be characterized conveniently (though not uniquely) by the simple relationship that the excess of marginal over average productivity in the central plant should equal the average excess of land rents (per head) over what they would have been in the absence of the town, minus a correction if environmental externalities are present.

Nothing has yet been said about the large class of second-best problems that are important in this context. What, for instance, is the optimal policy when some land uses (such as roads) are not charged for, or when the income distribution is not optimal, or when redistribution by transfers between town and country is not feasible? These must be topics for further research. The model presented here may prove a convenient framework for that enquiry.

REFERENCE

Solow, R. M. and Vickrey, W. (1971) 'Land Use in a Long Linear City'. *Journal of Economic Theory*, December.

9

Population Policy and the Taxation of Family Size

1. THE POPULATION PROBLEM

1.1 Population is a difficult subject. Yet people have simple ideas about it. Many believe that the world's population is growing too rapidly; many believe it is already too large; a not inconsiderable number believe that overpopulation is *the* cause of much of the poverty and misery that exist. I suspect, however, that people generally jump to the conclusion that population is a great problem, and that they would be hard pressed to give a precise statement of the 'problem' and a detailed argument for massive state intervention in this area.

Two major arguments are frequently advanced. The first is that current rates of population growth cannot go on for ever, or even for many more decades, so that current birth rates must lead to indescribable disasters. This is an unsatisfactory argument, first, because the exact consequences are left obscure and the counterclaim that birth rates are bound to adjust in due course is not met; and second, because it has no implications for current action. The second argument is that most people in the world are ignorant of contraception, etc., and therefore ought to be told. This is a much more convincing argument, which I would largely accept. But the argument is insufficient to establish, for example, that methods for restricting the birth rate should be subsidized. It may well be that population policies can do more for human welfare more easily than other kinds of government action; but the arguments need thorough development, for population is a more difficult subject than is at first apparent.

1.2. In this paper, I want to discuss population policy primarily in terms of the natural policy for affecting population size—taxes and subsidies related to family size. The question to be addressed is under what assumptions it is

Reprinted from the *Journal of Public Economics*, Vol. 1 (1972), pp. 169–98 with permission from Elsevier Science. Earlier versions of part of the paper were presented in seminars at MIT, LSE, and the University of Essex. The paper has benefited greatly from the comments made there and in a research workshop at Oxford, and also from the stimulating and helpful suggestions of A. B. Atkinson, B. Fine, M. Morishima, and J. E. Stiglitz.

Readers may be interested in a very interesting discussion of the main influences on fertility in Hawthorn (1970). This book also contains a useful annotated bibliography.

desirable to tax families for increasing their size. One can conceive of more radical policies for affecting population size, by changing the social structure, and in particular severing the links between the consumption of parents and children, thus making possible punitive measures for restricting births. I shall keep within the conventional family framework. In that context, one can think of children as goods, as valuable in themselves and to their parents, and as affecting the group structure of the family. I shall assume that families are willing to trade this good off against other goods, preferring, if the terms are right, to restrict family size in order to ensure higher consumption for the existing family. I shall even express this assumption by the extreme postulate that families make their breeding decisions optimally. If it were to turn out that taxes or subsidies were, on that postulate, undesirable, it would become necessary to justify them on the ground of consumer irrationality—which is, of course, not implausible in the context.

It may be thought that, if children are goods that families (in some degree) choose to have, the case for attempting to affect these choices must rest on externalities. I suppose that most orthodox economists would take this view, that excessive population makes the environment unpleasant, and that parents should choose family size under the constraint of paying for these external diseconomies. But, without wishing to claim that the externality argument is irrelevant, I want to argue that we are dealing with a problem in 'second-best' welfare economics, so that, even if there were no externalities of the direct kind, there could be a case for special state intervention. This may be seen most clearly if we consider developing countries. The usual argument[1] in that case urges control of population on the grounds that per capita income can thereby be increased. Instead, one might argue that the marginal product of labour is so low that an extra individual who receives his marginal product will, on average, be so miserable that, even allowing for his value as child, companion, etc., it would be better if he did not exist. The first argument is too crude in looking only at per capita income, and ignoring the value of children as such. The second, in assuming that the additional person would receive his marginal product, is probably inconsistent with the facts, and certainly inconsistent with optimality.

If we are to consider optimal population policy, it should be considered in conjunction with optimal distribution policy. The existence of another person affects everyone through the distribution policy, since he will normally not be allowed to consume his marginal product, and his existence therefore changes the amount available for distribution to others. At the same time, the form of the distribution policy itself probably influences decisions about the number of

---

[1] Cf. Enke (1966). J. E. Meade, on the other hand, uses a more sophisticated criterion in his important discussion of optimum population (1955*a*, pp. 82–93, and 1955*b*, pp. 1–13). He restricts attention to what I shall call the utopian optimum and makes no allowances for the utility of having children. P. S. Dasgupta has pursued this line of analysis in the context of optimum growth (Dasgupta 1969).

children to have. It is the second consideration, whose importance is hard to judge, that leads to most of the difficulties in the models to be discussed in this paper.

If it is granted that family-size decisions are, to some extent, based on economic calculation, it will also be granted, perhaps, that the government may have good reason to differ from the family on the criterion to be employed. I shall argue later that there are, in this case, particularly good reasons why the State should follow a preference ordering inconsistent with the preferences of those who decide about family size. This affects government policy in ways that we shall want to consider.

1.3. The models to be discussed are very simple in form. The reader will be startled, for example, by the completely timeless nature of the analysis. One is inclined to think that population is an essentially dynamic topic, but the points that I have already suggested need analysis all arise in a timeless context. In any case, the dynamic formulations I have looked at seem to be too difficult for me. Another peculiarity of the analysis will be its emphasis on uncertainty about family size. It may be thought that observed differences in the number of children from family to family are primarily due to differences in fertility and differences in tastes, and that both are pretty well known to the family itself. For myself, I believe that uncertainty is not inconsiderable, particularly in developing countries. It should be remembered that differences in the average age at which a mother and father have children have a significant effect on population growth, and often on family size as well. It may be argued, however, that where uncertainty is greatest, deliberation in the choice of family size is least. This possibility, although it can hardly be so completely true as to render the following analysis inapplicable, should be borne in mind when we come to conclusions.

2. THE GENERAL MODEL

2.1. The population is assumed to consist of a very large number of separate families. Within a family, consumption (regarded as a single good during the analysis) is equally distributed. I use the notation

c = consumption per head within a family,

n = family size.

The total number of families is fixed; thus, fundamental changes in social structure are excluded from consideration. Family size is influenced by attempts to have children, represented by a variable N, which influences the probability distribution of possible family sizes. I define

$p(n, N, s)$ = probability of family size n,

where s is a parameter representing fertility. Families have preferences about family size which can be expressed by a von Neumann–Morgenstern utility function, so that, if families deliberately choose N,

$$N \text{ maximizes } Eu(c, n, N, t) = \sum_n u(c, n, N, t) p(n, N, s), \qquad (1)$$

where t is a parameter representing tastes. The choice of N depends upon s and t. Usually the choice will be made subject to c being a function of n, specified by the government.

The parameters s and t are distributed within the population according to a density function $f(s, t)$. Thus, the mean size of the population is

$$M = \iint \sum_n np(n, N, s) f(s, t) \mathrm{d}s\, \mathrm{d}t, \qquad (2)$$

and the mean level of aggregate consumption,

$$C = \iint \sum_n ncp(n, N, s) f(s, t) \mathrm{d}s\, \mathrm{d}t. \qquad (3)$$

If the number of families is large, actual population and aggregate consumption will, with high probability, be very close to C and M. For feasibility, it is necessary that the distribution of goods, given by the function $c(\cdot)$, should depend on actual population, a random variable. But this aspect is easily dealt with, and of negligible importance in an economy of many families. I therefore neglect it by assuming that production possibilities can be represented by a constraint

$$C \le H(M). \qquad (4)$$

It will be convenient to suppose that, for all s,

$$N = \sum_n np(n, N, s). \qquad (5)$$

Thus, N is not so much the family size aimed at as the average family size the decision-takers can expect to achieve. The two are presumably monotonically related. When there is no variability of tastes and fertility, I shall identify M and N.

2.2. The proper choice of social maximand requires careful consideration. At this stage, however, I shall simply suppose that the State accepts the maximand in (1) as measuring the family's welfare, and further that it accepts the utility function u (expressing risk preferences) as a cardinal measure of welfare for the evaluation of consumption allocations. That is, the State has objective function

$$W = \iint \sum_n upf(s, t) \mathrm{d}s\, \mathrm{d}t. \qquad (6)$$

2.3. This model presents us with a clear problem: to choose a policy for distributing consumption to people, under which a member of a family of size n gets $c(n)$, so that, subject to the production constraint (4), and the behaviour of families assumed in (1), W is maximized. I shall not attempt to solve this problem in its full generality, since it seems to be hard. Instead, I shall consider separately the cases where fertility varies, but not tastes, and there is no uncertainty (Section 3); where tastes, but not fertility, vary, and there is no uncertainty (Section 4); and where there is uncertainty about family size, but tastes and fertility are the same for everyone (Sections 5 and 6). One can see, in an intuitive way, how the separate considerations could be combined.

Since, even with the question split up in this way, it is not easy to solve the problem posed, and one is in any case interested in comparing the solution with the results of less sophisticated policies, I shall distinguish three different kinds of policies, and study their consequences:

(i) The *utopian optimum* is obtained if W is maximized by choice of c as a function of n, s, and t; and also N as a function of s and t. This maximization is subject only to the production constraint (4). In matters of procreation, families do what is desired of them, whether they desire it themselves or not.

(ii) The *free optimum* is the one we are really interested in, where c is chosen, by the State, as a function of n, and families are free to choose N, knowing perfectly what function $c(\cdot)$ will determine their consumption. The State is constrained by both (4) and the constraint that (1) holds for each t and s.

(iii) The *naive optimum* arises when the State ignores the operation of (1), although family-size decisions are in fact being taken on that basis. c is chosen as a function of n (by the State) so as to maximize W subject to (4) with the $N(s, t)$ treated as fixed parameters, although in fact $N(s, t)$ satisfies (1).

I shall take the point of view that the utopian optimum is unattainable, and that the naive optimum is a mistake. But when it is hard to solve for the free optimum, we may be able to determine the answer to an 'optimum propaganda' problem: in the utopian optimum, would families tend, from an individual standpoint, to wish for a larger or a smaller choice of N; or, alternatively, in the utopian optimum, would the State (if it knew the true circumstances) wish that families had chosen a smaller or larger N? Since in fact people can be influenced by considerations of public desirability, there is an element of realism in the optimum propaganda questions, quite apart from the help they may give to intuition about the free optimum.

2.4. The strategy of the paper is to begin by asking whether, when only fertility varies, the utopian optimum is in fact attainable. It will be shown that it may not be; and that, even when it is, the methods required show clearly that the utopian optimum will not be attainable when tastes vary or family size is uncertain. In the case of varying tastes, the analysis will concentrate almost entirely on the propaganda problems. Then, in Section 5, the same methods will be applied to the case of uncertainty. Finally, in Section 6, it will be found possible to obtain some interesting results about the free optimum for the uncertainty case.

3. VARIABLE FERTILITY

3.1. It seems that the utopian optimum should be attainable if families differ only in fertility, that is, if a family of type s can have any number of children not greater than s. One would think that there should be an ideal size of family, call it S_0, to be attained by the families that can attain it, the others having as many children as they are capable of. Consumption could be distributed in an ideal way to families with $s \leq S_0$, while families with $s > S_0$ would be promised zero consumption, with the result that no family would have $s > S_0$.

For a rigorous treatment, we have to make the following assumptions:

$$H(\cdot) \text{ is a concave function;} \tag{7}$$

$$v(G, N) = u\left(\frac{G}{N}, N\right) \text{ is concave in } G \text{ and } n. \tag{8}$$

I have here introduced $G = cN$ for family consumption, which is what the family actually obtains from the production sector of the economy, just as N is what it supplies to that sector. With these assumptions, it can be shown quite easily that the utopian optimum is attained when, for all s, G and N satisfy

$$v_G = \lambda, \qquad \text{a constant;} \tag{9}$$

$$v_N > -\lambda H' \quad \text{and} \quad N = S; \qquad \text{or} \qquad v_N = -\lambda H' \quad \text{and} \quad N \leq s. \tag{10}$$

The second possibility in (10) defines the ideal family size, S_0, which is given by

$$v_G(\overline{G}_0, S_0) = \lambda, \qquad v_N(\overline{G}_0, S_0) = -\lambda H'. \tag{11}$$

When $s \geq S_0$, $N = S_0$ and $G = \overline{G}_0$; when $s < S_0$, $N = s$, and G is obtained from (9).

This solution defines a policy relating G (or, equivalently, c) to N, $G = G_0$ (N). The policy will generate the *free* optimum if, when G is related to N in this way, families are willing to choose $N = s$ if $s \leq S_0$. (If $N > S_0$, the family is assigned zero consumption, or at least consumption sufficiently low to ensure that no family actually chooses $N > S_0$.) Families will be willing to act in this way if and only if utility is a nondecreasing function of N for $N \leq S_0$.

Now, using (9), it is easily shown that

$$\frac{\mathrm{d}}{\mathrm{d}N} v(G_0(N), N) = v_G G_0'(N) + v_N$$

$$= \frac{v_N^2}{v_{GG}} \frac{\partial}{\partial G}\left(\frac{v_G}{v_N}\right) \tag{12}$$

Clearly, this need not be positive for all $N \leq S_0$. It will be so if and only if the marginal rate of substitution of children for goods diminishes (remember $v_{GG} < 0$) as family consumption increases. This property of preferences may be expressed in terms of market behaviour: if a family faced prices for goods and for children (in the latter case, either positive or negative), an increase in other income would lead it to increase its demand for children.

This behavior may sound realistic, but it is certainly not overwhelmingly probable. If it does not hold the utopian optimum is not the free optimum; that is, it is unattainable.

It seems likely that the modification in the policy that would be required to attain the free optimum is simple. Over certain ranges of family size, the allocation of consumption would be determined in such a way as to ensure constant utility. I have not verified this rigorously. If the conjecture is correct, the free optimum in such a case has one feature that is very unsatisfactory: certain households are indifferent over a whole range of family-size choices. This is unsatisfactory because one can hardly suppose that the household free to choose will make just the choice implicit in the optimum policy, and yet the wrong choice is accompanied by no 'disequilibrium' that might correct it. In a sense, then, no optimum exists, although it is possible to be as nearly optimal as is desired.

Even if the utopian optimum is attainable, the required policy imposes an upper limit on family size by making consumption allocations to larger families sufficiently small for them never to occur. Because of varying tastes and randomness, such policies are not desirable in the real world. Thus, we have seen that, contrary to expectation, even the case of pure fertility variation may impose second-best problems on optimization. And in any case, it avoids the very features of the problem that cause most difficulty in the real world.

4. VARIABLE TASTES

4.1. The next case I want to examine has t as the only parameter varying from household to household. It should be particularly emphasized in this case, although it is true of all of them, that we are dealing with a labour supply problem. Households require consumption and supply people (or labour). It is interesting that, when economists think of labour supply, they are inclined to suppose that a perfectly egalitarian or utilitarian distribution of income (corresponding to our naive optimum) will lead to an undesirably small supply of labour, whereas, when thinking of population, they are inclined to think that naive redistribution will cause overpopulation. If there is any justification for such diversity of opinion, it is likely to lie in the correct choice of assumptions about consumption/labour and consumption/size preferences. We should be alert to this when considering the various optima. For ready comparison of the two cases, I shall express the utility function in the form $v(G, N)$, with $G = cN$. For a family of type t, utility is $v(G, N, t)$. The source of the orthodox intuitions may well be found in an opinion that $v_N > 0$ for the population case, whereas $v_N < 0$ if N is interpreted as labour supply of the usual kind. In fact, there is no obvious reason for supposing that, in our model, $v_N > 0$ at an optimum, naive or otherwise—more children may be good, but not if they have to share an unchanged level of family consumption. But it will be interesting to see whether the sign of v_N has something to do with the matter.

4.2. Consider the naive optimum, in which, since consumption is optimally allocated for given family sizes,

$$v_G = \lambda, \quad \text{a constant,} \tag{13}$$

for everyone. At the same time, a household of type t chooses N_t to maximize its own utility, granted that G is related to N by the function $G = G_2 (N)$ implied by (13); i.e. if $N > 0$,

$$v_G \, G_2'(N) + v_N = 0. \tag{14}$$

I suppose it is possible that no naive optimum exists, since (13) will define a policy $G_2(\cdot)$ only if N_t and t are monotonically related; but I shall ignore such cases. If, for some t, N is zero, $v_G \, G_2' + v_N$ may be negative. But in any case, we see that, so long as G_2' is positive, and it is very plausible that it should be, $v_N < 0$ for everyone at the naive optimum.

Nevertheless, it is possible that increases in N_t are desirable. Let us apply 'infinitesimal' changes dN_t to family sizes, accompanied by changes in consumption dG_t so as to ensure that production feasibility is maintained. The changes are desirable if total utility, $\int vf(t)dt$, is increased, so we perform the calculation

$$
\begin{aligned}
d\left[\int vf(t)dt\right] &= \int (v_G \, dG + v_N dN)f(t)\, dt \\
&= \lambda\left[\int d\, Gf(t)dt - \int G_2' dN f(t)\, dt\right] \\
&= \lambda \int (H' - G_2'(N_t))dN_t f(t)\, dt, \tag{15}
\end{aligned}
$$

where the last step follows from the assumption that production feasibility is maintained. Since λ is positive, it is desirable to increase N_t if and only if $G_2'(N_t) < H'$, the marginal product of labour. To determine G_2', we have to solve (13) and (14), using production feasibility, $\int G_2 f(t)dt = H(M)$, $M = \int N_t f(t)dt$ to eliminate λ.

When variations in labour supply arise from variations in effort and leisure, we may be inclined to use the simplification $v_{GN} = 0$, $v_{Gt} = 0$. Then (13) implies that $G_2' = 0 < H'$. In fact, no one would do unpleasant work, and it is scarcely surprising that increases in labour supply would be desirable.

Even in the labour-supply case, it is not implausible that $v_{GN} > 0$, in which case $G_2' > 0$, and if H' is small, increases in labour supply might not be desirable. When there are variations in family size, we surely want to assume that $v_{GN} > 0$. We might for example consider the special case

$$v(G, N) = u(c, N) = Nw(c, N) \qquad \text{with } w_{cN} = 0, \ w_{ct} = 0. \tag{16}$$

This captures the idea of the decision-taker aggregating the utilities of members of the household. It is still inadequate, but seems to be the only example that is simple to work out. Equation (16) implies that G/N is constant; i.e., $G = \gamma N$. γ is equal to $H(M)/M$. Thus, it is desirable to reduce all N_t if and only if

$$H'(M) < H(M)/M. \tag{17}$$

The assumption that the marginal product of labour is less than its average product may be implicit in the view that unconsidered redistributive policies encourage overpopulation. Inequality (17) confirms the need for this premiss in a particular case, but it is not in general likely to be either necessary or sufficient. This condition plays an important part in later parts of the paper. I shall discuss its plausibility in Section 8.

We see then that it is quite easy to reproduce the results intuition has suggested, but rather stringent special assumptions have been used, in particular the assumption that v_G is independent of t. This assumption means that households with a greater taste for children are regarded as deserving additional consumption as much as any other household of the same size and with the same total consumption. Perhaps it is not too bad an assumption.

4.3. It is interesting to look at the utopian optimum briefly with this assumption and the other assumption stated in (16). In the utopian optimum we have, in addition to (13), the conditions for optimal family sizes:

$$v_N = -\lambda H'. \tag{18}$$

With the assumptions $v = Nw$, $w_{cN} = w_{ct} = 0$, we may write

$$v = Na(c) + b(N, t). \tag{19}$$

From (13), we have $c = \gamma$, a constant, so that (18) yields

$$b_N(N, t) = -a(\gamma) + \gamma a'(\gamma) - \lambda H', \tag{20}$$

which is a constant. Since b is concave in N (this follows from the concavity of v), (20) tells us that N is an increasing function of t if and only if $b_{Nt} > 0$. This is an entirely reasonable conclusion, since it is equivalent in this special case to $v_{Nt} > 0$. But that is not a sufficient criterion for the result in general.

It is readily checked that households would not (in general) wish to adhere to the utopian optimum. One can analyse the direction in which they would want to deviate, with results essentially the same as those of the previous subsection.

4.4. The free optimum is particularly hard to analyse for this most important case of variable tastes. The analogy between labour-supply problems and the family-size problem shows us that, from a technical point of view, the choice of an optimal relationship between family size and family consumption is an 'optimum income tax' problem. An analysis of such problems may be found in Mirrlees (1971). That analysis may be applied to the present case. It may be shown, for example, that, if the free-optimum distribution policy is

$$cN = G = G_1(N), \tag{21}$$

then

$$0 \le G_1'(N) \le H' \qquad \text{for all } N; \tag{22}$$

and one may hope to gain some more precise impression of the optimum policy from detailed consideration of the optimality conditions; but the special examples of the income-tax paper are not relevant to the family-size case. A new investigation is therefore necessary, and I have not attempted it.

5. UNCERTAINTY OF FAMILY SIZE

5.1. Uncertainty is a feature one naturally associates with population and families. There is uncertainty about the date of marriage, the possibility of death, breakup, and remarriage, and the date at which children arrive. So long, however, as there is no risk of family size increasing beyond any desired level, these sources of uncertainty are, from the point of view of our analysis, variations in fertility. There would (in a world of uniform tastes) be no objection to policies that impose severe penalties on families that are too large if no one runs the risk of belonging to such a family.

But it is surely true in all parts of the world that there is *some* risk of family size being greater than intended, and in such a way that it is not possible to distinguish between cases of bad luck and cases of bad intention. In many parts of the world, these risks are considerable. There is a case, therefore, for including uncertainty in our models.

There is a further reason for concentrating analysis on the case where uncertainty is the only source of differences between families, in that it promises to be an easier case to analyse than the variable-tastes case, which would otherwise be the prime object of study. It is a convenient example in terms of which further issues can be discussed, such as the form of the criteria employed, and the main influences on the free-optimum policy. It may also be worth examining this case as a particular example of a general class of cases of 'moral hazard' and its implications for welfare economics, a class of cases that I hope to examine in more detail elsewhere.

5.2. When uncertainty alone is singled out, s and t do not vary. The welfare maximand is (returning to consumption per head as the consumption variable)

$$Eu = \sum_n u(c, n, N)p(n, N) \tag{23}$$

and the production constraint is

$$E(cn) = \Sigma\, cnp(n, N) \leq H(\Sigma\, np(n, N)) = H(En). \tag{24}$$

We shall continue the convention that $En = N \cdot u$ is supposed concave and increasing in c, and concave in N. Dependence on N may be thought of as utility derived from procreation as such. It might also reflect external economies in consumption arising from high population density, but that dependence would be treated as a parameter by the family. It will be recollected that the admittedly very special assumption that the authorities seek to maximize the same as private households is to be relaxed later. Distribution of consumer goods to families takes place after family size is known.

In the naive optimum, and also in the utopian optimum, all families must have the same marginal utility of total consumption:

$$u_c = \lambda n. \tag{25}$$

In Utopia, the marginal effect of a change in N along with the associated consumption changes is negligible:

$$\Sigma u_N p + \Sigma u p_N = \lambda(\Sigma cn p_N - H'(N)). \tag{26}$$

It is interesting to consider whether, if the utopian optimum were established, the rules for consumption distribution would make families wish they had more children. Since (25) implies that λ is positive, we may deduce from (26) that families would wish N to increase if and only if

$$\Sigma cn p_N > H'(N). \tag{27}$$

Since $\Sigma cnp = H(N) = \Sigma np(H/N)$, $cn - (H/N)n$ is, if not always zero, sometimes positive and sometimes negative. It is therefore instructive to write (27) in the form

$$\Sigma[c - (H/N)]\, np_N + H/N - H' > 0. \tag{28}$$

In making this transformation, I rely on the equation $\Sigma np_N = 1$, which is obtained by differentiating $\Sigma np = N$ with respect to N.

It may be presumed that p_N is negative for n less than some particular value, and positive for n greater than that value. A more restrictive assumption, but perhaps not a bad one, is that

$$q(n, N) = p_N/p \text{ is an increasing function of } n. \tag{29}$$

If (29) holds, it is easy to see that the first term in (28) is positive if c increases with n, i.e. if $c - (H/N)$ is initially negative and then positive. To prove the result, let n' be the largest value of n for which $c - (H/N)$ is negative, and $q' = p_N(n', N)/p(n', N)$. Then

$$\Sigma[c - (H/N)] np_N = \Sigma[c - (H/N)] n(p_N - q'p) > 0,$$

since by assumption (29) and the definition of q', we have a series of non-negative terms. We are led to

Proposition 1. *If (i) $q(n, N)$ is an increasing function of n,*
   (ii) the marginal product of labour is less than the average product, and

$$(iii) \; nu_{cn}/u_c > 1, \tag{30}$$

then the utopian optimum requires rules of consumption allocation under which families would wish to increase their size.

To complete the proof of the proposition, it is only necessary to check that (30) implies that c is an increasing function of n. From (25), we have

$$u_{cc} \frac{dc}{dn} + u_{cn} = \lambda = u_c/n. \tag{31}$$

Since, by concavity, $u_{cc} < 0$, (30) and (31) together imply that $(dc/dn) > 0$. The proof of the proposition is thus complete.   □

It will be noted that the conditions are somewhat stronger than required, since both terms in (28) have been made positive. But it is clear that the requirements are quite strong, perhaps stronger than one would have expected.

5.3. A similar proposition can be obtained for the naive optimum, which is a more natural standard for outcomes in the absence of deliberate population policy. In the naive optimum, we have, in addition to (25), the condition that families determine N so as to maximize their expected utility. The first-order condition for this is

$$\Sigma u_N p + \Sigma u p_N = 0. \tag{32}$$

At the same time, the second-order condition for maximization must hold:

$$\Sigma u_{NN} p + 2\Sigma u_N p_N + \Sigma u p_{NN} \leq 0. \tag{33}$$

With the naive optimum as starting point, the question to be considered is that of optimum propaganda: should families be persuaded to have more or fewer children? The technique to be followed is to consider an infinitesimal change in N, dN:

$$\begin{aligned}
d(\Sigma up) &= \Sigma(u_c dc + u_N dN)p + \Sigma up_N dN \\
&= \Sigma u_c dc \cdot p, \text{ by (32)} \\
&= \lambda \Sigma n dc \cdot p, \text{ by (25).}
\end{aligned} \tag{34}$$

Now production feasibility requires that $\Sigma cnp = H(N)$, so that we must have

$$\Sigma ndc \cdot p + \Sigma cnp_N dN = H'dN,$$

which with (34) implies that the change in utility is

$$d(\Sigma up) = (H' - \Sigma cnp_N)dN. \tag{35}$$

Thus, a reduction in family size is desirable if and only if

$$\Sigma c_2(n)np_N > H', \tag{36}$$

where c_2 is the naive optimum policy defined by (25). The condition takes the same form as (27), and the analysis following that condition holds in the present case also. Thus we have

Proposition 2. *If (i) $q(n, N)$ is an increasing function of n,*
(ii) the marginal product of labour is less than the average product, and

$$\text{(iii) } nu_{cn}/u_c > 1, \tag{30}$$

then, if the naive optimum is ruling, it is desirable that family size should be reduced.

5.4. In order to assess the plausibility or otherwise of condition (30), it may be helpful to write the utility function in the form

$$u = (1 - k + kn)w(c, n) \qquad (0 \le k \le 1). \tag{37}$$

w is to be thought of as the utility of a single member of the family in isolation. For this reason dependence on N is ignored. The number k varies with the weight given by the decision-maker to the utility of other members of the family. One can question whether, even if the decision-taker can be thought of as aggregating individual preferences in this separable way, his von Neumann–Morgenstern utility function would take the additive form. But the form is not intrinsically unreasonable, and allows us to compare the effects of greater or less 'selfishness' on the part of parents by varying k from one to zero.

So long as w is a suitable cardinal utility function both for risk choices and for the aggregation of individual preferences within the family, I would suggest that

$$w_{cn} < 0 \tag{38}$$

is a plausible assumption. I base this claim on the way in which the enjoyment of consumer goods and of other people in the same family compete for time, energy and attention.

From (36), we have

$$\frac{nu_{cn}}{u_c} = \frac{nw_{cn}}{w_c} + \frac{kn}{1-k+kn}.$$

It follows that, when (37) holds, (30) does not hold. Indeed, we can then show, exactly in the same way as above, that, if the marginal product of labour should exceed the average product, the utopian optimum creates conditions in which families wish they had fewer children, and in the naive optimum the State would like them to have more. The argument is stronger the smaller is k. On this basis, we are led to suspect that the conventional views are justified only if the marginal product of labour is considerably less than the average product.

6. THE FREE OPTIMUM UNDER UNCERTAINTY

6.1. As always, the free optimum is the difficult one to analyse, although the most interesting one. For it, the authorities seek maximization of

$$\Sigma up \text{ subject to } \Sigma cnp \leq H(N) \quad \text{and} \quad \Sigma up_N + \Sigma u_N p = 0. \tag{39}$$

Multipliers λ and μ are introduced for the two constraints and we obtain, differentiating with respect to c for each n, and with respect to N,

$$u_c - \lambda n + \mu u_{cN} + \mu u_c p_N/p = 0, \tag{40}$$

$$\lambda(H' - \Sigma cnp_N) + \mu(\Sigma u_{NN}p + 2\Sigma u_N p_N + \Sigma up_{NN}) = 0. \tag{41}$$

Because of the second-order condition for family utility maximization (33), (41) shows that the sign of μ/λ is the sign of $H' - \Sigma cnp_N$. Our previous discussion of this expression has shown that its sign depends, roughly speaking, on whether c is an increasing or a decreasing function of n. This in turn has to be deduced from (40), and depends therefore upon the sign, and magnitude, of μ/λ. Thus, a general analysis is awkward.

We can get some definite information if we make an assumption, which, although restrictive, defines interesting cases:

$$u = na(c) + b(n, N). \tag{42}$$

With this assumption, (40) becomes

$$\lambda/a'(c) = 1 + \mu p_N/p = 1 + \mu q. \tag{43}$$

Since p_N is sometimes positive and sometimes negative, λ is certainly positive. Thus, a being a concave function, c is an increasing function of μq, which we may write

$$c = g(\mu q). \tag{44}$$

We have

$$\Sigma cn p_N - H/N = \Sigma cn p_N - \Sigma n c p / N$$

$$= \Sigma n p \left(q - \frac{1}{N} \right) g(\mu q). \tag{45}$$

I shall show that, provided assumption (29), that q increases with n, is satisfied, this last sum has the same sign as μ.

Let n_1 be the largest n such that $q - 1/N$ is negative. Then, if $\mu > 0$,

$$\Sigma n p \left(q - \frac{1}{N} \right) g(\mu q) \geq g(\mu q(n_1)) \sum_{1}^{n_1} n p \left(q - \frac{1}{N} \right)$$

$$+ g(\mu q(n_1)) \sum_{n_1+1}^{\infty} n p \left(q - \frac{1}{N} \right), \tag{46}$$

since g is an increasing function of n when $\mu > 0$. Now

$$\Sigma n p \left(q - \frac{1}{N} \right) = \Sigma n p_N - \Sigma n p / N = 0.$$

Therefore we have

$$\Sigma n p \left(q - \frac{1}{N} \right) g(\mu q) \geq 0 \qquad \text{when} \quad \mu > 0, \tag{47}$$

and the same sum is, by a similar argument, non-positive when μ is negative. Writing $A(\mu)$ for this sum, we have, from (41) and (45),

$$\lambda(H' - H/N) = A(\mu) - \mu(\Sigma u p_{NN} + 2\Sigma u_N p_N + \Sigma u_{NN} p). \tag{48}$$

Because of the second-order condition for household maximization, the sign of the right-hand side of (48) is the sign of μ. Furthermore, it is clear from (43) that c is an increasing function of n if and only if $\mu > 0$. Thus we have proved

Proposition 3. *If u takes the form (42), c is an increasing, constant, or decreasing function of n according to whether the marginal product of labour, H', is greater than, equal to, or less than the average product of labour, H/N.*

Corresponding, but somewhat weaker, results can be obtained for a more general u, provided that $u_{cN} = 0$ and (29) holds. Suppose, for instance, that we are prepared to assume $H/N > H'$, and we want to know whether it is correct to deduce that $\mu < 0$. If, on the contrary, $\mu > 0$, and $w_{cn} > 0$ (where, as above, $u = nw$), it follows from (40) that c is an increasing function of n, and therefore $A > 0$. This, by (48), contradicts the initial assumption that $H/N > H'$. This, and a similar argument, establish.

Proposition 4. *(a) If* $u_{cN} = 0$, $w_{cn} > 0$, *and* $H/N > H'$, *c decreases with n. (b) If* $u_{cN} = 0$, $w_{cNn} < 0$, *and* $H/N < H'$, *c increases with n.*

6.2. These results enable us to obtain some qualitative information about the consumption–distribution policy under the free optimum. We need to consider a particular distribution of family sizes. A convenient assumption is that family-size follows a beta distribution (a discrete one), with M and t fixed:

$$p(n, N) = Q(r)(n - 1)^r (M + 1 - n)^{t-r}, \qquad n = 2, 3, \ldots, M, \qquad (49)$$

where the constant $Q(r)$ is determined so that $\Sigma p = 1$.[2]

The distribution has the advantage that its range is finite, and it can be skewed in either direction. In particular, one ought to be able to mimic actual distributions of family size fairly closely. The form of the distribution given in (49) has been chosen in such a way that the minimum family size is two (i.e. no children for two parents), and the maximum size is M. A change in N does not alter the range of the distribution: the effect comes entirely through r. A minor inconvenience of the distribution is that $Q(r)$ cannot be expressed analytically, nor can the dependence of r on N. However, the distribution is readily calculated. The case $M = 12$, $t = 12$, $r = 3$ is illustrated in Table 9.1. In this case, $N = 4.4$; i.e., the average family has 2.4 children. This distribution perhaps overstates uncertainty—certainly for the developing countries—but by increasing t one obtains distributions with less dispersion.

The particular parameter values would be important for calculating the free optimum in particular cases; but we can see the general shape of the optimum without going into so much detail. By differentiating (49), we obtain, writing Q' for the derivative of Q with respect to r, and N' for the derivative of N with respect to r,

$$q = \frac{p_N}{p} = \left(\frac{Q'}{Q} + \log_e \frac{n - 1}{M + 1 - n}\right) \frac{1}{N'}. \qquad (50)$$

N is certainly an increasing function of r. Therefore we may write

$$\frac{1}{u_c} = K + L\mu \log \frac{n - 1}{M + 1 - n}, \qquad (51)$$

where K and L are constants, independent of n, and L is positive.

Equation (51) displays clearly the manner in which u_c depends upon n. It will be noticed that the function $\log[(n - 1)/(M + 1 - n)]$ is steepest at its extremes,

---

[2] It might have seemed more elegant to use the continuous beta-distribution. This was avoided not so much because population size is a discrete variable, but because we would get into serious trouble with the basic equation (40) close to n for which p is zero. For example, p_N/p may be unbounded both below and above, and that makes nonsense of the equation. This kind of trouble is recurrent in the theory of moral hazard, but I prefer not to enter into a discussion of it unnecessarily.

Table 9.1. *Optimal distribution policies for the beta-distribution.*

No. of children $n-2$	$p(n,N)$	$a = \log c$ c	$a = -1/c$ c
0	0.063	1.140	1.068
1	0.213	1.061	1.030
2	0.279	1.010	1.005
3	0.229	0.969	0.984
4	0.135	0.934	0.966
5	0.058	0.900	0.949
6	0.018	0.866	0.931
7	0.000	0.831	0.912
8	0.000	0.790	0.889
9	0.000	0.739	0.860
10	0.000	0.660	0.812

so that deviations from the constant u_c that would be optimal in a utopian world become more marked as we go to unusually small and unusually large families. This is a rather curious result: in order to obtain an optimal population policy, the State should to some extent concentrate on severe discouragement of unusually large families, and give special encouragement of small families (i.e. with no children).

The nature of these policies may be made more vivid by considering the special case of utility (42) for particular functions $a(\cdot)$. We have $u_c = a'(c)$, so that it will be easy to calculate the optimal distribution function $c(n)$ for such utility functions as have $a = \log c$, or $a = -1/c$, for example. For particular utility functions and production possibilities, the optimal policies could take the form shown in Table 9.1. These policies correspond to negative μ. In the case of positive μ, the features of the policies are reversed, with c an increasing function of n.

One further point deserves mention, since it is rather surprising. The optimum policy requires that $1/u_c$ be symmetric around $n = 1 + \frac{1}{2}M$, regardless of the value of N. This is of course a feature of the special form of distribution we are using, but notable all the same.

7. CONFLICTING MAXIMANDS

7.1. There are many other aspects of population and its implications for the taxation of families, which if fully discussed would too greatly lengthen this paper. But I cannot leave the subject without saying something about the conflict between parental choice of family size and optimal population policy. In the rest of the paper, I have accepted without discussion a form of welfare maximand that accepts the household maximand; indeed, the two have been identified. I want to argue that this identification is (generally) inadmissible. To bring the conflict out clearly, let us suppose that household decisions are taken on the basis of the parents' preferences, which will be written $w(c, n)$. Dependence on N is ignored since it adds little to the argument.) Children are supposed to be identical with their parents, and consumption is supposed equally distributed within the household. The social valuation respects individual preferences, and is symmetric in individual utilities. From the social point of view, the probability distribution of family sizes gives the actual distribution of family sizes. To bring out the conflict, consider the case of an additively separable valuation, which must take the form

$$W = F(\Sigma nwp, N). \tag{52}$$

The manner in which F depends on N is a matter on which no very exact agreement is likely. I think the most appealing valuation[3] is simply

$$W_1 = \Sigma nwp, \tag{53}$$

but many would object to giving those who might exist a weight equal to those who do exist. An alternative valuation, lying at the other extreme of considering only those who do exist, seeks maximization of the average level of utility in the population:

$$W_2 = \Sigma nwp/N. \tag{54}$$

Although W_2 is somewhat clumsy, it does manage to evade the problem of defining a zero level of utility, being the level at which existence is only just worthwhile according to W_1. Addition of a constant to w does not change the ordering defined by (54).

7.2. Both W_1 and W_2 conflict with the household's decision, since the household seeks to maximize Σwp. The simplest way of bringing out the effect of this is to consider the naive optimum. It would be more satisfactory to analyse the free optimum and the effect of these new considerations on the free optimum policy, but that is harder and will not be attempted here. Instead, we ask whether a reduction in N would be desirable if the economy were naively optimal. In order to facilitate analysis, n will be supposed continuously variable, and distributed according to a density function

$$p(n, N) = \frac{1}{N} q\left(\frac{n}{N}\right). \tag{55}$$

Then it is readily verified that $p_N = -(1/N)(p + np_n)$.

In the naive optimum, parental choice of family size implies that

$$0 = \int wp_N dn = -\frac{1}{N} \int w \frac{d}{dn} (nf) dn = \frac{1}{N} \int \left(w_n - w_c \frac{w_{cn}}{w_{cc}}\right) nf dn, \tag{56}$$

---

[3] This is the valuation used by Meade (1955a).

where, in the last step, the government allocation rule $w_c = \lambda$ has been used. Now consider a variation dN in N. Since production continues to be feasible, we have

$$\int dc \cdot np\, dn + \int cnp_N dN \cdot dn = H' dN. \tag{57}$$

Then

$$
\begin{aligned}
d\left[\int nwp\, dn\right] &= \int nw_c dc \cdot p\, dn + \int nwp_N dN \cdot dn \\
&= \lambda \int dc \cdot np\, dn + \int nwp_N dN \cdot dn \\
&= \left[\lambda H' + \int n(w - \lambda c)p_N dn\right] dN, \text{ by} \tag{57} \\
&= \left[\lambda H' - \frac{1}{N}\int n(w - \lambda c)(p + np_n)dn\right] dN, \\
&= \left[\lambda H' + \frac{1}{N}\int (w - \lambda c + nw_n)np\, dn\right] dN, \\
&\quad \text{on integrating by parts} \\
&= \left[\lambda(H' - H/N) + \frac{1}{N}\int (w + nw_n)np\, dn\right] dN. \tag{58}
\end{aligned}
$$

Consider first the criterion W_1. Assume that

$$w_{cn} < 0, \quad \text{and } w \text{ is concave, so that} \quad w_{cc}w_{nn} > w_{cn}^2.$$

The concavity assumption implies that, w_c being constant, w_n is a decreasing function of n. Therefore, if $\int nw_n p dn$ is negative, $\int n^2 w_n p dn$ is negative, a fortiori. That $\int nw_n p dn < 0$ follows from (56), since $w_{cn} < 0$. Thus, our assumptions imply that when $H' < H/N$ and $\int nwp dn < 0$, a reduction in N will increase W_1. But to say that $W_1 = \int nwp dn < 0$ means that it would be better if the economy did not exist. Certainly this is a possible outcome, even though households are taking independent decisions: one cannot be seriously surprised that an unhappy person continues to exist, and it is possible to take the view, without ethical contortions, that the existence of a man who is contented, even happy, does not justify itself. However, it is an extreme view, though not it seems to me an implausible one, which claims the average inhabitant of Britain or the United States lives in such a way that it would be better that he did not exist. If this view is not taken, it can be seen from (58) that an increase in population may be desirable even when the marginal product is less than the average product. This would be all the more likely the less it is thought the value of lives derives from consumption.

7.3. In the case of W_2, we have, using (58),

$$\frac{d}{dN} W_2 = \lambda \frac{1}{N} (H' - H/N) + \frac{1}{N^2} \int n^2 w_n p \, dn, \tag{59}$$

which on our assumptions is certainly negative if $H' < H/N$. In this case the conflict between social aims and parental values tells definitely in the direction of rendering reductions in population more desirable. It is to be presumed that corresponding results will hold for the consumption allocation rules implied by the free optimum.

CONCLUSIONS

8.1. The best way to summarize the conclusions of the arguments is to consider what they imply for child allowances and tax allowances related to family size. Think of an economy in which the typical family consists of husband, who earns income in the labour market, wife, who works in the home, and children. It will be recognized that this picture ignores the considerable number of households that contain less than, or more than, a nuclear family; but these raise quite different questions which are not at issue here. The no-tax position is one in which each family has total consumption equal to the earnings of the husband plus the value of the wife's work within the home. If we do conclude in favour of policy that makes consumption per head fall with family-size, the connection with tax policy is not straightforward. The simple translation is that each man should receive an after-tax wage that is lower if he belongs to a larger family; but, for this to have the effects contemplated in the model, there would have to be a perfect capital market, enabling the present family to borrow against the future incomes of its children, or to rely on the future incomes of children to make saving less necessary. Realism requires that we should contemplate a system of child allowances 'financed by' the future earnings of the child. In the absence of an intertemporal model, which should make allowance for expectations about tax rates as well as other matters not discussed in the present paper, one can only guess that the sensible translation of an optimum policy that gives lower consumption per head to larger families is a system of child allowances, positive up to quite large families, but which fall with family size.

8.2. We have seen that, if differences in fertility are the sole cause of differences in family size, an optimum, in respect of population as well as the distribution of consumption, may possibly be obtained by changing after-tax earnings so as to equate the marginal utility of consumption in different families (paying due attention to the effect of family numbers on marginal utility, which, it was suggested, is probably negative). If aggregate population density has an external effect on utility, it is clear that procreation should be discouraged for that reason; but we saw that, even in the case of fertility variations, there may be a case for changing the structure of optimum taxation on account of population effects.

The second-best features become more important when we allow for variations in tastes. It is well recognized that taxes should not be pushed to the extreme of equalization if, as is likely, to do so would adversely affect the supply of labouring effort. But some weak confirmation was obtained for the conventional view that, in so far as changes in the labour supply arise from changes in population, the 'disincentive' effects of taxation are to be welcomed.

It is only in the last case, of uncertainty about family size, that actual numbers were obtained, and a fairly detailed analysis of the different optima in small space was possible. There the results are striking, and indeed quite surprising. If the aim is to discourage large families, it is accomplished by specially large reward to families with no children, and special large penalties to the few families that, by ill luck, are exceptionally large. On simplifying, but not absurd, assumptions, the criterion as to whether larger families should be rewarded or penalized proved to be quite simple: namely whether or not the marginal product of labour exceeded the average product. Evidence on this point will be discussed briefly below. I shall suggest that, of the two possibilities, it is more likely that the average product exceeds the marginal product.

8.3. Models in which there is uncertainty about family size are not very satisfactory. As was remarked in the introduction, deliberate choice of family size may be least when uncertainty is greatest; and in any case much of the uncertainty that exists should be regarded as variations in fertility, since actual decisions can be taken sequentially. Nevertheless, I tend to believe that the relevant level of inclination, effort, discipline, and education in developing countries will be influenced by the relation between economic prospects and family size; and that uncertainty about family size is a reason for not recommending grave penalties for those who exceed whatever is thought to be the ideal size. Much work remains to be done on the relation between simple models and realistic policies for developing countries.

Another advantage of the uncertainty case is that we can use it to explore a consideration of importance that is otherwise neglected in the formal economic literature—conflict of interest between parents and society as a whole. It is fairly well known that this kind of question raises special difficulties about the choice of welfare criterion. Without going very far, we have been able to gain some impression of the considerations and the directions in which they point.

As a further example of the convenience of this way of looking at population problems, I should like to comment on a suggestion made to me by Professor Morishima, that parental and family preferences of the kind we have been discussing are much affected by experience, so that a family will tend to prefer the size it actually attains. Of course, one could not claim that a family will always prefer the size actually attained; but even if it did, decisions about family size are not taken on that basis, and we are led to a new formulation in which preferences of one generation are determined by experience in the previous generation. The equilibrium is not one single value of N but a whole distribution of values, depending on the actual outcome in the previous generation. Using the uncertainty model, one obtains an analytically manageable but more complicated version, with qualitatively similar results to those discussed in the present paper. The model discussed here is far from capturing the full richness of family and population problems, but I suspect that the form of the model and the methods of analysis may be suggestive for richer versions.

8.4. The most notable feature of the analysis, and one which might be extended to more general assumptions, is that the answer to the main question, as to the direction in which the State ought to deviate from the utopian or naive optimum, has tended to turn on whether the average product of labour exceeds the marginal product or not. One might expect this answer if the economy's income were equally distributed; but we have been considering second-best problems where this may not be so. Since the relationship between average and marginal product has turned out to be important, some remarks on it are due.

There are two kinds of consideration, which seem to tell in opposite directions. First, there is the obvious relationship between aggregate production and the aggregate labour force. Whether the average product is greater than the marginal product or not turns on the balance between tendencies to increasing returns and tendencies to diminishing returns. The main source of increasing returns is probably in the provision of collective goods, represented in part by government expenditure on administration, defence and protection, social overhead capital, and so on, and in part by the diffusion of information. There are also economies in distribution and transportation that may accrue to larger populations. On the other hand, the fixed supply of land and its qualities may soon, if it does not already, create diminishing returns of at least equal amount. If one compared aggregate compensation for labour performed with the part of the national product available for private consumption and investment in most developed countries, one would probably be inclined to guess that the marginal product exceeds the average product. These figures are seriously biased, of course, in both directions. One is particularly aware of the inadequate social accounting for increased pressure on fixed resources, and some who believe themselves particularly in need of peace and space will weight this 'congestion' particularly heavily. Yet some of the most unpleasant manifestations of high population may be much diminished by appropriate government policies: I have in mind particularly the design of land use, and control of access to roads. On such general impressions and evidence as I am aware of, it would be hazardous to form definite conclusions as to which of the average and marginal products is now the greater. The distant future is perhaps another matter.

But there is another, more straightforward, consideration that may be taken to turn the balance. Although we have been discussing a timeless economy, we should not be unaware of the essentially temporal structure of these problems. If a family has an extra child, it must eat at once, but will work only in the future.

This consideration can be incorporated in our model without requiring a full dynamic treatment if we assume that additional members of a family are simply less productive than existing members. Now this may not always be true: older parents may represent a smaller quantity of human wealth than their children. Professor Atkinson has suggested to me that the need to provide consumption for the unproductive old may be as important as the need to provide for the unproductive young. It seems to be an important question whether the average date of consumption for a human comes before or after the average date of production, and I would like to see a careful analysis of the question. I suppose it is clear that, in those developing countries where the expectation of life is not as high as in the developed countries, consumption probably does tend to come before production on average. In those developed countries where the welfare state may relate the consumption of the aged to current standards of living, the balance might go the other way. But when I consider the extent of education and training in the developed countries, I am inclined to think that, the larger is N, the smaller will be the proportion of the population working at any time (at least if we assume that family size remains constant over time). Indeed, I suspect this tendency is so marked that it might justify reducing a first estimate of the marginal productivity by 25 per cent or more.

For these reasons, I think it not unreasonable to assume that the relationship $H' < H/N$ gives a fair representation of reality. But the matter is not at all as certain as popular views about the obvious seriousness of the population problem implicitly assume.

8.5. Even at the present level of simplicity, the analysis, with its special assumptions, and emphasis on $H' - H/N$, may have suggested some hesitation in accepting the view of secular religion that population must be cut at all costs, or the view, fortunately less popular, that redistribution to large families through family allowances is undesirable. But two important considerations have been ignored; genetics, and the long run. The genetic argument would claim that we have sufficient evidence to distinguish, with imperfect but adequate accuracy, between families likely to produce children of high social marginal productivity and those whose children will have low social marginal productivity. It is clear what implications this proposition has, in conjunction with the above analysis: the State would wish to subsidize production of people who are likely to contribute substantially to its tax revenues. The conclusion is unpalatable, and in any case the evidence and the argument require thorough research.

Finally, it has to be recognized that the argument for population control may rest on the presumption that parents are bad at predicting the future, and therefore do not know what kind of a life they are creating children to suffer. The extent to which this argument is plausible depends on the likelihood that economies will shift course in ways that individuals projecting the more obvious of past trends might fail to predict. Our parents probably thought the world would be worse now than it is; and it is quite possible that we think the chances of improvements in the conditions of life are greater than they are. Since there are no very convincing models of long-run economic development, economists are not in a position to decide these issues, and I doubt whether anyone else is.

REFERENCES

Dasgupta, P. S. (1969) 'On the Concept of Optimum Population'. *Review of Economic Studies*, 36, 295–318.

Enke, S. (1966) 'The Economic Aspects of Slowing Population Growth'. *Economic Journal*, 76, 44–56.

Hawthorn, G. (1970) *The Sociology of Fertility*. (London: Collier-MacMillan).

Meade, J. E. (1955a) *The Theory of International Economic Policy*, Vol. II, *Trade and Welfare* (Oxford University Press).

—— (1955b) Mathematical supplement to Mirrlees (1955a).

Mirrlees, J. A. (1971) 'An Exploration in the Theory of Optimum Income Taxation'. *Review of Economic Studies*, 38, 175–208.

10

Optimal Tax Theory: A Synthesis

1. INTRODUCTION

The main purposes of this paper are to unify some uncoordinated parts of the theory of optimal taxation, and to develop methods of analysis that can be quickly and easily applied to all kinds of optimal tax problems. The analysis is presented without attention to minor points of rigour (which I intend to treat elsewhere). As a result, the basic mathematical manipulations are relatively brief once the best ways of setting up the problems have been found. At the same time, a number of important details are treated in depth.

Theory can contribute to discussions about the levels of tax rates in a number of ways. It makes possible the calculation of optimal tax rates, to gain knowledge of how tax rates vary with objectives and possibilities. It shows how tax rates depend on certain indices (elasticities of various kinds, for example), thus indicating what form of evidence would be most useful and what influence that information would have on tax rates. It can formulate rules for optimal taxation which, though not expressed in terms of tax rates, may serve to attract attention to better measurements of the effects of economic policy. It can explore the consequences, for optimal tax rates or optimal taxation rules, of introducing considerations that have previously been absent or imperfectly present in models and policy discussions.

A number of papers have presented calculations of optimal tax rates under a variety of assumptions: Atkinson (1973), Mirrlees (1971), and Stern (1976) for income taxation; Atkinson and Stiglitz (1972) and Deaton (1975) for commodity taxation. I contribute nothing to that topic in the present paper, which is concerned with formulae for optimal tax rates, and optimal taxation rules. Rules for commodity taxation have been discussed in many papers, including Diamond and Mirrlees (1971), Mirrlees (1975), Ramsey (1927), and Stiglitz and Dasgupta (1971). Formulae involving optimal tax rates have been derived

Reprinted from the *Journal of Public Economics*, Vol. 6 (1976), pp. 327–58 with permission from Elsevier Science. Financial support by the National Science Foundation during its preparation is gratefully acknowledged. A preliminary version was presented at the Conference on 'Public Economics' at Kiryat Anavim, Israel, in June 1975. Parts of Section 3 are based on a paper 'Optimal Incentive Schemes' presented at the Berlin Conference on Incentives, September 1973. Valuable comments have been received from P.A. Diamond, Y-K Ng, Jesus Seade, and referees.

by Atkinson and Stiglitz (1972) for commodity taxes, and Mirrlees (1971) for a nonlinear income tax.

There is a striking contrast in this literature between the analysis and interpretation of first-order conditions, which is usually emphasized in work on commodity taxation, and the development (and numerical implementation) of formulae for marginal tax rates, which is characteristic of theories of optimal income taxation. This contrast seems to be quite basic to the theory of optimal taxation, as I shall argue in Section 2. Sections 2 and 3 are devoted to a relatively quick, and therefore non-rigorous, derivation of the main formal results in optimal tax theory, and a discussion of their interpretation. Section 4 outlines the conditions for a more general nonlinear theory.

The discussion of Section 3 raises the question of the interrelations between optimal commodity taxes and an optimal nonlinear tax on (say) labour incomes. In Section 5, first-order conditions for this case are derived, and discussed. This is the central part of the present paper. The analysis provides a unification of previous theories of optimal taxation, in that it covers linear (commodity) or fully nonlinear taxation, or any mixture of the two. This approach also enables one to derive a general 'Paretian' tax rule, corresponding to a result previously obtained (Mirrlees 1975) for the two-class case. The rule is a necessary condition that must hold independently of the welfare function used. Naturally, this rule is far from enough to determine the optimal tax system. Using the whole set of first-order conditions, I discuss the implications of optimizing the labour-income tax for optimal commodity taxes, and vice versa. In particular, one would like to be able to gain some impression of how the presence of commodity taxes bears upon the overall progression of the tax system, and on the progressivity of the labour-income tax. As yet, these implications are not entirely clear to me.

It is striking how easily the rules for the optimal provision of public goods can be obtained in the general setting introduced in Section 5, and how simple the rules are. They are derived in section 6.

Finally, in Section 7 it is shown how the various optimality conditions derived in the paper are particular instances of a general principle which is quite simple to formulate. This principle shows clearly how both efficiency and distributional considerations operate in the rules for optimal economic policy.

Apart from this 'fundamental principle', and the general 'duality' method used throughout, the most important particular new results of the paper are the following:

(1) the general conditions for optimal nonlinear taxes, derived in Sections 3 and 4;

(2) a set of conditions in simple form, depending only on production prices and consumer preference orderings, which must necessarily hold for any tax equilibrium which is Pareto-efficient among the set of all tax equilibria: these conditions are stated at their simplest in equation (39);

(3) the conditions for optimal linear taxes in the presence of optimal nonlinear taxes, derived in Section 5: these provide a strikingly simple criterion for assessing the optimal impact of commodity taxation when there is an income tax;

(4) the form of the condition for optimal income taxation in the presence of commodity taxes (optimal or not), also presented in Section 5;

(5) the conditions for optimal provision of public goods in the presence of an optimal income tax: these are given a neat and illuminating form, which has an interesting connection with the commodity-tax conditions just mentioned.

2. OPTIMAL TAXATION IN THE LINEAR CASE

In the theory of optimal commodity taxation, it has been usual to consider a finite population of households, whose net demands will here be denoted by vectors:

$$x^1, x^2, x^3, \ldots, x^H.$$

These households face prices q for commodities, with

$$q = p + t,$$

where p are producer prices and t are tax rates. Thus, each household has the same budget constraint, $q \cdot x \leq 0$. In the present paper, I assume the following:

(i) Production available to consumers is constrained by a production constraint,

$$p \cdot \sum_b x^b = A, \tag{1}$$

with p and A constant. This is not a serious restriction. The linear constraint can be thought of as a linear approximation to production possibilities in the neighbourhood of the optimum, in which case the producer prices p are to be regarded as marginal costs and marginal products. So long as first-order necessary conditions are at issue, it does not matter that p is constant. A fuller discussion of production is given in Diamond and Mirrlees (1971).

(ii) Pure profits, if any, are paid to the State. This excludes certain interesting issues that have been discussed in the literature, but allows us to concentrate on the main taxation issues without having to deal with producer taxation alongside consumer taxation.

(iii) An individualistic welfare function,

$$W = \sum_b u^b(x^b), \tag{2}$$

is to be maximized. The representation (2) is implied by complete separability of consumption by individuals, but is not necessary for most of the results of this paper, since only local changes are considered. Equation (2) simply represents a convenient choice of utility functions representing individual preferences so that the marginal weights attached to utility levels are all equal.

The first-order conditions for optimal choice of the tax rates t (or, equivalently, q) will be derived by duality methods. Let

$$m^h(q, u) \tag{3}$$

be the expenditure function for household h, i.e. the minimum expenditure required to attain utility u when prices are q. Then the (Slutsky) compensated demand functions for household h are

$$x^{ch}(q, u) = m_q^h, \tag{4}$$

where the subscript here and subsequently denotes differentiation. The utility level of household h will be denoted by v^h.

Then the optimal taxation problem can be expressed as

$$\max_q \sum_b v^b : \begin{cases} p \cdot \sum_b x^{cb}(q, v^b) = A, \\ m^b(q, v^b) = 0 \quad \text{(all } b\text{)}. \end{cases} \tag{5}$$

The second set of constraints here reflects the assumption that households have no lump-sum income or expenditure.

It is of the first importance to realize why the optimal commodity tax problem is best set without explicit reference to tax rates. Suppose q^* is the solution to the problem. Then $t^* = q^* - p$ are optimal tax rates. But the real equilibrium of the economy is unaltered if instead we have tax rates

$$t_p{}^* = \rho q^* - p \tag{6}$$

for any positive constant ρ. It follows that (except when no taxation is optimal) there is no answer to the question: which commodities should be taxed and which subsidised? The 'answer' varies with the arbitrary choice of a number ρ. A specific answer can be given if it is stipulated that some particular commodity is to have a zero tax rate; but that is usually an uninteresting device because there is no naturally untaxed commodity.

For this reason, one should not seek formulae for optimal tax rates in the general problem. One can hope to find equations identifying commodities whose net demand is encouraged, or discouraged, by the tax system, since these are real properties of the tax system, which remain invariant under the trivial change in tax rates described by (6). Having set the problem up as in (5), we shall find that such conditions appear almost immediately. The other advantage of this new way of setting up the problem is that it is more easily related to the problem of nonlinear taxation.

To obtain necessary conditions for the optimum in (5), introduce Lagrange multipliers for the constraints, and set the derivatives of the following expression with respect to $v^1, \ldots, v^H$, q (holding p constant) equal to zero:

$$L = \sum_h v^h - \lambda p \cdot \sum_h x^{ch}(q, v^h) - \sum_h \mu_h m^h(q, v^h). \tag{7}$$

Differentiating L with respect to v^h, we obtain

$$1 = \lambda p \cdot x_v^{ch} + \mu_h m_v^h. \tag{8}$$

Differentiation with respect to q, with p and the v^h constant, yields

$$\lambda p \cdot \sum_h x_q^{ch} + \sum_h \mu_h m_q^h = 0. \tag{9}$$

Using (4), and the symmetry of the Slutsky derivatives, we obtain from (9)

$$-\lambda \sum_h x_q^{ch} \cdot p = \sum_h \mu_h x^{ch}. \tag{10}$$

Now $x_q^{ch} \cdot q = 0$ by homogeneity. Therefore

$$-x_q^{ch} \cdot p = x_q^{ch} \cdot (q - p) = x_q^{ch} \cdot t$$
$$= \frac{\partial}{\partial \theta} x^{ch}(p + \theta t)|_{\theta=1}; \tag{11}$$

and we can write (10) in the form

$$\sum_h x_q^{ch} \cdot t = \frac{\partial}{\partial \theta} \sum_h x^{ch}(p + \theta t)|_{\theta=1} = \sum (\mu_h/\lambda) x^{ch}. \tag{12}$$

In words, the total substitution effects of a proportional change in all tax and subsidy rates should be proportional to a weighted sum of demands. We shall see that μ_h can be negative for some h. The weights in (12) are obtained from (8):

$$\frac{\mu_h}{\lambda} = \frac{(\lambda^{-1} - p \cdot x_v^{ch})}{m_v^h} = \frac{1}{(\lambda m_v^h)} - p \cdot x_m^h(q, 0)$$
$$= \frac{1}{\lambda m_v^h} + t \cdot x_m^h(q, 0) - 1, \tag{13}$$

where x^h is the uncompensated demand function, and x_m^h its derivative with respect to income. In words, the weight is the difference of a term proportional to the marginal utility of income, and the income derivative of the household's income net of taxes.

The above conditions were derived on the assumption that there is no lump-sum taxation. It is always possible to have lump-sum taxation (or subsidization) at a uniform rate. If this is done, the constraints $m^h = 0$ should be replaced by the constraint $m^h = b$, with the subsidy b free to be chosen. The analysis is then unchanged, except that differentiation of the Lagrangean with respect to b yields a further condition

$$\sum \mu_h = 0. \tag{14}$$

λ and μ_h were introduced as multipliers dual to the government's revenue constraint (which is equivalent to (1) for given household incomes) and the constraints on household income. Thus, λ is the social marginal utility of income transferred to household h, the production constraint being unchanged. Since the production constraint is $\sum m^h - \text{taxes} = A$, the increase in income involves a tax change. The social marginal utility of income, ignoring this tax change, is $\lambda + \mu_h$. Diamond (1975) calls this the social marginal utility of income. μ_h can be termed the *social marginal utility of transfer*.

The form of the first-order conditions (12) differs from those derived in Diamond and Mirrlees (1971). The other form is readily derived from (8) and (9) by eliminating μ_h: after some manipulation, one has

$$\lambda \frac{\partial}{\partial t} \sum_h t \cdot x^h (p + t, m) = \sum_h \frac{x^h}{m_v^h}. \tag{15}$$

In words, the revenue effects of tax changes should be proportional to welfare-weighted demands.

Of the two forms, (12) and (15), for the first-order conditions, we shall see that (12) corresponds best to the conditions for optimal nonlinear taxation.

Equation (12) is appealing chiefly because the left-hand side, $\sum x_q^{ch} \cdot t$, is a measure of the extent to which the tax system discourages a commodity. If the tax system is intensified, in the sense that all taxes and subsidies are changed proportionately, demands for commodities are subject to both income and substitution effects. The income effects, $-x_m^h x^h \cdot t$, are simply the income derivatives of demand times taxes paid. The total substitution effect is $\sum x_q^{ch} \cdot t$ (as can be seen from (12)). Since the income effect has nothing to do with the way the tax system bears on commodities individually, it should be ignored in assessing the effects of optimal taxes. Thus, we can reasonably introduce the following definition.

Under a tax system, the *index of discouragement* of commodity i is

$$d_i = \sum_h \sum_j \frac{\partial x_i^{ch}}{\partial q_j} t_j \bigg/ \sum_h x_i^h. \tag{16}$$

The first-order conditions for optimal commodity taxation can then be expressed as

$$d_i = \frac{\sum_h (\mu_h/\lambda) x_i^h}{\sum_h x_i^h},$$ (17)

where μ_h/λ is given by (13), and satisfies $\sum (\mu_h/\lambda) = 0$.

3. OPTIMAL NONLINEAR TAXATION

Linearity of the tax system plays an essential role in the previous section, because linearity defines control variables (q) for the optimization problem. With nonlinear taxation, the government can, in effect, impose any budget constraint it wishes on the members of population, the only restriction being that the constraint is the same for everyone. When policy options are extended in this way, it is best to consider a continuum population of households. Then one may avoid having as optimum policy an awkwardly shaped budget set with many corners. It is very restrictive, despite appearances, to describe the population by a single parameter n. Nevertheless, we must usually do so to get neat results. The analysis will be carried out for the one-parameter case, n being distributed with density function $f(n)$. The many-parameter case is outlined in Section 4.

For the nonlinear case, it is useful to identify a numeraire commodity. The notation is now that household n, with utility function $u(x, z, n)$, chooses a vector $x(n)$ of net demands for non-numeraire goods and a net demand $z(n)$ for numeraire; u is a nondecreasing function of all variables. We have to consider allocations in which

$$x(n), z(n) \text{ maximizes } u(x, z, n) \text{ subject to } (x, z) \in B,$$ (18)

where B is the budget set, describing the effect of taxes and subsidies in combination with producer prices. It should be noted that the consumption set of net demands feasible for the consumer may vary with n. This will be ignored in the following, where the set of definition of u is supposed the same for all n.

To reduce (18) to a more manageable form, the method of Mirrlees (1971) is generalized. The idea is that, if we define

$$v(n) = u(x(n), z(n), n),$$ (19)

(18) implies that

$$v(n) - u(x(n), z(n), n) = 0 \leq v(m) - u(x(n), z(n), m);$$ (20)

i.e., $m = n$ minimizes $v(m) - u(x(n), z(n), m)$. Consequently,

$$v'(n) = u_n(x(n), z(n), n).$$ (21)

When x and z are differentiable with respect to n, differentiation of (19) shows that (21) is equivalent to

$$u_x \cdot x'(n) + u_z z'(n) = 0,$$

which we can write more neatly if we introduce the marginal rate of substitution,

$$s(x, z, n) = u_x/u_z, \tag{22}$$

as

$$z'(n) + s(x(n), z(n), n) \cdot x'(n) = 0. \tag{23}$$

We also have a second-order condition from the minimization of $v - u$:

$$v''(n) \geqq u_{nn}(x(n), z(n), n). \tag{24}$$

This is equivalent (when x and z are differentiable) to

$$s_n(x(n), z(n), n) \cdot x'(n) \geqq 0. \tag{25}$$

To deduce (25) from (24), differentiate (21) with respect to n:

$$v''(n) = u_{nx} \cdot x'(n) + u_{nz} z'(n) + u_{nn}.$$

Applying (22), we have

$$u_{nx} \cdot x'(n) + u_{nz} z'(n) \geqq 0. \tag{26}$$

Equation (23) allows us to replace $z'(n)$ in this inequality:

$$u_{nx} - u_{nz} \frac{u_x}{u_z} \cdot x'(n) \geqq 0. \tag{27}$$

Since

$$\frac{\partial s}{\partial n} = \frac{u_{nx}}{u_z} - \frac{u_{nz} u_x}{u_z^2},$$

(27) is in turn equivalent to (25) (since $u_z > 0$ by assumption).

In an appendix to this paper, it is shown that (21), in conjunction with a condition a little stronger than (25),

$$s_m(x(n), z(n), m) \cdot x'(n) \geqq 0, \quad \text{all } m, n, \tag{28}$$

together imply that (18) holds for some budget set B. When there are only two commodities, this is a very satisfactory situation. Then $s_n \geqq 0$ is a sufficient assumption to ensure that (18) is equivalent to (21) and $z'(n) \geqq 0$. It is this circumstance that makes the income-tax problem studied in Mirrlees (1971) manageable.

In the many-commodity case, we can replace the consumer constraint (18) by the weaker condition (21). If the solution of that problem satisfies (28), then it is a solution of the basic problem. This gives us an easy check on a computed solution, but it is perfectly possible that $s_n \cdot x'(n)$ will vanish for certain ranges of n in the optimum. In that case a more detailed analysis than the one below would be required.

We shall now obtain necessary conditions for the problem

$$\max \int v(n)f(n)\mathrm{d}n : \begin{cases} \int [p \cdot x(n) + z(n)]f(n)\,\mathrm{d}n = A, \\ v'(n) = u_n(x(n), z(n), n). \end{cases} \tag{29}$$

Notice that production prices are based on z as numeraire. If labour is numeraire, $z(n)$ should be a negative number, being supplied by households, not demanded. Recollect that

$$v(n) = u(x(n), z(n), n), \tag{30}$$

and f is the density function describing the composition of the population. n is assumed distributed between 0 and ∞. In what follows, subscripts denote partial derivatives.

Having formulated the problem in this way, it will obviously pay to invert the utility function, writing

$$z(n) = \zeta(x(n), v(n), n). \tag{31}$$

In effect, this transformation is a 'duality trick', as we shall see in Section 5. Since (31) is derived from (30), we can calculate the derivatives:

$$\begin{aligned} \zeta_x &= -u_x/u_z = -s, \\ \zeta_v &= 1/u_z. \end{aligned} \tag{32}$$

Converting (29) into Lagrangean form, we set equal to zero the derivatives of

$$L = \int [(v - \lambda p \cdot x - \lambda \zeta)f + \mu v'(n) - \mu u_n(x, \zeta, n)] \, \mathrm{d}n.$$

Differentiating in turn with respect to $v(\cdot)$ and $x(\cdot)$, we obtain (noting that $u_{nx} + u_{nz} \cdot (-s) = u_z s_n$),

$$\left(1 - \frac{\lambda}{u_z}\right)f - \mu \frac{u_{nz}}{u_z} - \mu'(n) = 0, \tag{33}$$

$$\lambda(s - p)f = \mu u_z s_n. \tag{34}$$

The last term in (33) is obtained by first integrating by parts the term $\mu v'$ in L. This leaves an integrated part $\lim_{n \to \infty} \mu(n)v(n) - \mu(0)v(0)$. Differentiation with respect to $v(0)$ and $v(\infty)$ (this can be checked by a more careful analysis) yields the further conditions,

$$\mu(0) = 0, \qquad \mu(\infty) = 0. \tag{35}$$

Equation (34) holds only when $(x(n), z(n))$ is not up against the consumer's supply constraint. For example, the possibility of a zero labour supply is not allowed. Though this point must be considered for numerical calculations, it will be ignored here as not being of great importance.

The first, simplest, and most exciting feature of these first-order conditions is the set of equations (34), which are statements about marginal tax rates. If the numeraire is untaxed, and τ_i is the *marginal* tax rate on commodity i, the marginal price facing the consumer is $p_i + \tau_i$, which he will equate to s_i, the marginal rate of substitution between that commodity and numeraire. Equation (34) says that

$$\tau_i = \frac{v}{f} \frac{\partial s_i}{\partial n}, \qquad v = \mu u_z / \lambda. \tag{36}$$

To fix ideas for the moment, let n describe ability or willingness to work. Mathematically, this says that, as n increases, individuals find it easier to do additional work of the same productive value, so that for most goods s_i should be an increasing function of n. The exceptional goods are those whose marginal utility falls faster than the marginal disutility of labour. (Remember that labour is measured not in units of time but in units of equal marginal productivity.) Normally it is thought right that the tax system should bear more heavily on the more able. Thus, marginal tax rates are expected to be positive on most commodities. This being so, the numerical factor in (36) ought normally to be positive. In that case, our condition says that marginal taxes should be greater on commodities the more able would tend to prefer.

More explicitly, (36) implies that

$$\frac{\tau_i}{s_i} - \frac{\tau_j}{s_j} = \frac{v}{f} \frac{\partial}{\partial n}\left(\frac{s_i}{s_j}\right), \qquad v = \frac{\mu u_z}{\lambda}, \tag{37}$$

so that the question which commodity should be taxed more highly is answered by reference to the effect of an increase in n upon the slope of the individual's indifference curves.

This prescription is most agreeable to common sense; but it should be remembered that it is not true when only linear taxation is allowed. In that case, as we saw, more awkward statements about the effect of general tax changes on aggregate compensated demands must be made. It is the extra scope for policy allowed by nonlinearity that restores the 'common-sense' result.

Perhaps the most surprising feature of (34) is the strong implications that are independent of the welfare function assumed, or even the population distribution, namely (dividing the equations for different commodities)

$$\frac{s_i - p_i}{s_j - p_j} = \frac{s_{in}}{s_{jn}}.$$ (38)

Whether these equations hold can be tested by reference to indifference curves alone (and the way they vary with n). Therefore these equations must hold (for all i and j) *as a condition of Pareto efficiency*. If they do not hold, there exists a tax system which would make everyone better off.

Since $(\partial/\partial n)\tau_i = (\partial/\partial n)(s_i - p_i) = s_{in}$, (38) takes an even neater form:

$$\frac{\partial}{\partial n}\frac{\tau_i}{\tau_j} = 0.$$ (39)

Thus, *it is necessary for Pareto-efficiency* (*relative to the set of tax equilibria*) *that the ratios of marginal tax rates are locally independent of n*. Equation (39) is simple but mysterious. The τ_i are to be regarded as functions of x, z, and n. We ask what τ' would make an n-man choose the demands of an $(n + dn)$-man. The ratios of these τ' have to be the same as the ratios of the marginal tax rates the $(n + dn)$-man actually faces. This is a strong requirement. No intuitive explanation of the result has occurred to me.

Returning to (37), we see that the marginal tax rates on commodities i and j should be the same for all individuals if s_i/s_j is independent of n. This means that x_i and x_j enter the utility function through a subutility function which is the same for everyone. More generally, if a subset of commodities, represented by a vector x^1, enters the utility function in the following way,

$$u = U(a_1(x^1), x^2, z, n),$$ (40)

all the commodities in x^1 should be taxed at the same rate. In particular, when utility has this form with no commodities in the second group, it is optimal to have a tax schedule for the numeraire alone, with no taxes on other commodities. This notable result generalizes that obtained by Atkinson and Stiglitz (1976) for the additively separable case. It is true also when n is multidimensional.

The remaining task, in interpreting the optimality conditions, is to use equation (33) to get more precise information about the sign and magnitude of the multipliers $\mu(n)$. Let us first, to encourage intuition, assign a special symbol to the marginal utility of numeraire (e.g. the marginal disutility of labour value) which plays in the model much the role of the marginal utility of income in one- and two-good models:

$$\beta = u_z.$$ (41)

β is to be regarded as a function of x, z, and n; and β_n, for example, means the partial derivative of β with respect to n; but $\beta(n)$ and $\beta_n(n)$ mean $\beta(x(n), z(n), n)$ and $\beta_n(x(n), z(n), n)$ respectively.

There are two convenient ways of integrating (33) for μ. Integrating as it stands, and using the boundary condition $\mu(0) = 0$, we get

$$\mu(n) = \int_0^n \left[1 - \frac{\lambda}{\beta(m)}\right] \exp\left[\int_n^m \beta_n(m')/\beta(m') \cdot dm'\right] f(m)\, dm. \tag{42}$$

The alternative equation for μ is obtained by rewriting (33) in the form

$$\frac{d}{dn}(\beta\mu) - s_z \cdot x'(n) \cdot \beta\mu - (\beta - \lambda)f = 0. \tag{43}$$

The derivation of (43) is based on the calculation

$$\begin{aligned}
\frac{d}{dn}\beta &= \beta_n + \beta_x \cdot x'(n) + \beta_z z'(n) \\
&= \beta_n + u_{zx} \cdot x' + u_{zz}(-u_x \cdot x') \\
&= \beta_n + \mu_z \frac{\partial}{\partial z}\left(\frac{u_x}{u_z}\right) \cdot x' \\
&= \beta_n + \beta s_z \cdot x'.
\end{aligned} \tag{44}$$

Integration of (43) yields the formula

$$\beta\mu = \int_0^n [\beta(m) - \lambda] \exp\left[\int_m^n s_z \cdot x'(m')dm'\right] f(m)\, dm. \tag{45}$$

Equations (42) and (45) suggest two special cases that should be easy to handle, namely $\beta_n \equiv 0$ (which simplifies (42)), and $s_z \equiv 0$ (which simplifies (45)). Take the latter case. s is independent of z if and only if utility can be expressed in the form

$$u = U(a(x, n) + z, n). \tag{46}$$

This is the case where income effects vanish in ordinary consumer theory. If utility were to take this form, we should have

$$\beta\mu = \int_0^n [\beta(m) - \lambda]f(m)\, dm \tag{47}$$

and, from (44), $(d/dn)\beta = \beta_n$. Consequently $\beta_n \leq 0$ implies that $\beta(m)$ is non-decreasing. Let $\beta(n_1) = \lambda$. Then (47) implies that $\mu \geq 0$ when $n \leq n_1$. But $\mu = 0$ when $n = \infty$. Therefore $\beta\mu$ is equal to $-\int_n^\infty [\beta(m) - \lambda]f(m)dm$; and it follows that $\mu \geq 0$ for $n \geq n_1$ also.

What we have found is this: *in the no-income-effects case,*

$$\beta_n \leqq 0 \qquad (48)$$

is a sufficient condition for

$$\mu(n) \geqq 0. \qquad (49)$$

It will be recollected that the tax rules (34) then have their natural interpretation, for λ, f, and $u_z = \beta$ are all non-negative.

Condition (48), stating that the marginal utility of numeraire is a decreasing function of n, for fixed x and z, expresses the assumption that consumers with larger n are less deserving. We have now shown (cf. the discussion of (36) above) that in the no-income-effect case, it is indeed implied that the tax system should bear more heavily on those with greater ability. But in general, it seems that one cannot establish the result; for the last term in (44), $\beta s_z \cdot x'$, is quite likely to be positive. There are other special cases, notably the two-commodity case with normality, for which a theorem can be established (cf. Mirrlees 1971). Also, cases where μ is negative for some n are odd in other respects. Consider (34) again:

$$\lambda(s - p)f = \mu u_z s_n,$$

and multiply by x':

$$(s - p) \cdot x' = \frac{\mu u_z}{\lambda f} s_n \cdot x'. \qquad (50)$$

We know that $s_n \cdot x' \geqq 0$ (equation (25)); and that $s \cdot x' = -z'$ (equation (23)). Therefore

$$\mu < 0 \text{ implies } p \cdot x' + z' \geqq 0. \qquad (51)$$

If the numeraire is not taxed, $-z$ is the consumer's expenditure, and the total tax paid by an n-man is

$$T(n) = -z(n) - p \cdot x(n). \qquad (52)$$

It follows that

$$\mu < 0 \text{ implies } T'(n) \leqq 0. \qquad (53)$$

In words, μ is negative only if the tax system does not bear more heavily on consumers with greater n.

A number of economists have examined, usually for special cases, the implications for marginal tax rates of the boundary conditions that $\mu = 0$ at the ends of the skill distribution. Equation (34) suggests that marginal tax rates should be zero when $n = 0$ or ∞, provided that f does not tend to zero too rapidly. Phelps (1974) and Sadka (1974) have followed this idea for $n = \infty$, and more recently Seade (1975) has noticed a similar result for the lower end of the distribution. When the result holds at both ends, the tax system is neither progressive for all n, nor regressive. Calculations suggest to me that these end-results are of little practical value. When the conditions for their validity hold, it is usually true that zero is a bad approximation to the marginal tax rate even within most of the top and bottom percentiles.

4. MULTIPLE CHARACTERISTICS

In the previous section, the population was described by a single parameter. The power of this assumption is shown in the conclusion that marginal tax rates are proportional to $\partial s_i / \partial n$. Matters are not quite so simple when the population is described by a *vector n*. Let us suppose there are $I + 1$ commodities, and J parameters describing the population.

It will be recollected that, in the one-parameter case, consumer utility maximization implies that

$$v'(n) = u_n(x(n), z(n), n). \tag{54}$$

The argument leading to this conclusion is valid also for many parameters, and we therefore have

$$\frac{\partial v}{\partial n_j} = u_{nj}(x(n), z(n), n) \tag{55}$$

for each parameter. Thus we can read (54) as a vector equation. Similarly, we obtain from second-order conditions the implication that the matrix

$$\left[\frac{\partial x}{\partial n_j} \cdot s_{nk}(x(n), z(n), n) \right] \tag{56}$$

is non-negative definite. (This matrix is in fact symmetric, as one can deduce by differentiating (54) with respect to n.) The question then arises whether, as in the one-parameter case of (54), in conjunction with a condition similar to (56), equation (56) implies utility maximization subject to some budget constraint. Fortunately it does so, as I shall establish elsewhere. This allows an argument that in a large class of cases the constraint (56), or rather a stronger form analogous to (28) can be neglected in deriving the first-order conditions for constrained maximization.

In that case, we have to consider a Lagrangean,

$$L = \int [\{v(n) - \lambda p \cdot x(n) - \lambda s\} f + \{v'(n) - u_n(x, \zeta, n)\} \cdot \mu(n)] \, dn, \tag{57}$$

where integration is over the whole non-negative orthant in the space of parameter vectors n, and $\mu(n)$ is, for each n, a vector of multipliers commensurate with n. As before, ζ is the function of x, v, and n defined by $v = u(x, \zeta, n)$. Before differentiating L, we want to replace the term

$$\int v'(n) \cdot \mu(n)\, \mathrm{d}n = \int \cdots \int \sum_j \frac{\partial v}{\partial n_j} \mu_j(n)\, \mathrm{d}n_1 \ldots \mathrm{d}n_J$$

by something more convenient. This can be done by using a standard theorem in multidimensional calculus, which states that, for nice functions v, μ_1, $\ldots$, μ_J defined in a closed region D,

$$\int_D \sum_j \frac{\partial v}{\partial n_j} \mu_j\, \mathrm{d}n + \int_D v \sum \frac{\partial \mu_j}{\partial n_j}\, \mathrm{d}_n = \int_{\partial D} v\mu \cdot \mathrm{d}s, \tag{58}$$

where ∂D is the boundary of D, and $\mathrm{d}s$ is outward normal to this surface. This theorem allows us to write

$$L = \int [\{v - \lambda p \cdot x - \lambda \zeta\} f - v\nabla \cdot \mu - u_n \cdot \mu] \mathrm{d}n + \int_{\partial D} v\mu \cdot \mathrm{d}s, \tag{59}$$

with ∂D the boundary of the non-negative orthant, and $\nabla \cdot \mu$ a standard notation for the divergence $\sum_j \partial \mu_j / \partial n_j$.

Setting the derivatives of L with respect to $x(n)$ and $v(n)$ equal to zero as in the one-dimensional case, we get

$$(s - p)f = \frac{u_z}{\lambda} s_n \cdot \mu, \tag{60}$$

$$\nabla \cdot \mu + \frac{u_{zn}}{u_z} \cdot \mu = \left(1 - \frac{\lambda}{u_z}\right) f. \tag{61}$$

(Note that $s_n \cdot \mu$ is a vector with components $\sum_j (\partial s_i / \partial n_j) \mu_j$, and $u_{zn} \cdot \mu$ is defined similarly.) These equations are supplemented by boundary conditions on μ obtained by considering variations of v on the boundary of the orthant:

$$\mu_j = 0 \text{ when } n_j = 0, \infty. \tag{62}$$

No doubt a thorough analysis of these conditions would be quite complicated. The basic ideas are tolerably clear when $I \geq J$. First, one should consider the system of equations:

$$
\begin{aligned}
v &= u(x, z, n), \\
v' &= u_n(x, z, n), \\
(s - p)f &= \frac{u_z}{\lambda} s_n \cdot \mu.
\end{aligned}
\tag{63}
$$

There are $I+J+1$ of these equations. Consequently one can hope to solve for J variables μ_j/λ, the I variables x_i, and z, as functions of v, $v' = (\partial v/\partial n_1, \ldots, \partial f/\partial n_J)$, and n. Substituting in (61), one has

$$
\sum \frac{\partial}{\partial n_j} \mu_j(v, v', n) + \sum \frac{u_{znj}(x(v, v', n), z(v, v', n), n)}{u_z} \mu_j(v, v', n)
$$
$$
= \left(1 - \frac{\lambda}{u_z}\right) f. \tag{64}
$$

This is a second-order partial differential equation in v. It is to be associated with boundary conditions upon v and v' on the boundary of the non-negative orthants which are defined by (62). For this to make sense, (64) should be an elliptic equation. Methods for computing the solution of such partial differential equations with given boundary conditions are available. Once (64) has been solved for v, $x(n)$ and $z(n)$ can be obtained from (63), thus defining the desired budget set. (Seade has shown me the method does not work when $I < J$.)

It is interesting to note that the budget set so obtained will in general be of dimension $\min(I, J)$. So long as $J \leq I$, there is no reason why consumers of different types should not be choosing different consumption plans in the optimal equilibrium. Then the budget set defined as

$$
B = \{(x(n), z(n)) : n \geq 0\} \tag{65}
$$

is of dimension J.

But if $J > I$, this set has dimension I. This has to be true because, for any given vector x, any consumer would choose the largest z with (x, z) in B. Therefore B may be restricted to vectors (x, z) with a unique z for each x, and that is a set of dimension I. It can be confirmed that (54) implies $(x(m), z(m)) = (x(n), z(n))$ for all m such that

$$
s(x(n), z(n), m) = s(x(n), z(n), n), \tag{66}
$$

so that a $(J-I)$-dimensional set of consumers chooses each point of B. To prove this, one uses the symmetry of the matrix $v'' - u_{nn}$, which is equal to

$$
v'' - u_{nn} = u_z \sum_i \frac{\partial s_i}{\partial n_j} \frac{\partial x_i}{\partial n_k}. \tag{67}
$$

The details are left to the reader.

When $J < I$, the budget set B can be extended to an I-dimensional set without introducing new consumption vectors that any consumer would wish to choose. Then it can be expressed in the form

$$
z = c(x). \tag{68}
$$

In the case $J = 1$, where B is 1-dimensional, it is often possible to describe the optimal budget set in the 1-dimensional form

$$x_i = a_i(z), \quad i = 1, \ldots, I, \tag{69}$$

which may be preferable administratively. This requires, of course, that x_i and z are monotonically related in the optimum. It is only when $J > 1$ that some cross-dependence of tax rates is generally necessary for optimality.

The most important aspect of the conditions developed in this section, from the point of view of the previous section, is that the attractive simplicity of the marginal-tax-rate equation (36) has to some extent been lost in its generalized form (60). The signs of marginal tax rates can no longer be determined without prior knowledge of the multipliers μ_j. Correspondingly, the conditions for Pareto efficiency come from

$$\sum \mu_j \frac{\partial}{\partial n_j} \left(\frac{\tau_{i_1}}{\tau_{i_2}} \right) = 0, \tag{70}$$

and say that the $J \times (I - 1)$ matrix $[(\partial/\partial n_j)/(\tau_i/\tau_1)]$ has rank no greater than $J - 1$. This condition is empty when $J \geqq I$. A principal purpose of this section has been to warn that the results of the previous section depend for their relative simplicity on the one-parameter assumption. At the same time, it should be remembered that only models with a small number of parameters are likely to be of any use for the practical implementation of optimal tax theory.

5. OPTIMAL MIXED TAXATION

The results of the nonlinear approach to the theory of optimal taxation are interesting and promising. What should be emphasized is the contrast with the linear results, that the nonlinear conditions say some rather clear things about tax rates, whereas the linear conditions say something about demand changes. It is hard to resist the appeal of conditions where tax rates appear explicitly. But this is achieved at considerable cost. The form of budget constraint the government is supposed to be able to impose is extremely general, allowing progression or regression in the taxation of all commodities, at rates which can depend upon the consumption of different commodities. That is to say, the satisfaction of the first-order conditions must be expected to be inconsistent with a simple tax system, with constant tax rates, or even tax rates dependent upon the consumption of the commodity taxed alone. What worries me about this is not the difficulty of persuading government to adopt complicated tax systems, but the serious neglect of tax avoidance possibilities (by trade among consumers) which the comparison of these very general tax systems commits us to. In this section, I derive conditions for an optimal tax system in which some commodities (i.e. one at least) are subjected to nonlinear taxation, while the others are subject to constant tax rates. Thus, in particular, nonlinear taxation can be restricted to commodities in which retrading is impossible or perfectly observed.

The notation to be used in this section is:

x = vector of net demands for commodities subject to proportional taxation,
p = producer prices for these commodities,
q = consumer prices for these commodities,
z = vector of net demands for commodities subject to nonlinear taxation,
r = producer prices for these commodities.

The population is described by a single parameter n.

Define an expenditure function

$$m(q, z, v, n) = \min[q \cdot x : u(x, zn) = v]. \tag{71}$$

Then we can define a compensated demand function, in this case for the goods subject to proportional taxation only, with demand for the other goods given:

$$x^c(q, z, v, n) = m_q(q, z, v, n). \tag{72}$$

We are contemplating allocations in which, for each n,

$$x(n), z(n) \text{ maximize } u(x, z, n) \text{ subject to } (q \cdot x, z) \in B, \tag{73}$$

where B expresses the nonlinear taxation. For example, in the case where one good only is subject to nonlinear taxation, B would be described by $q \cdot x \leq wz - t(z)$, w being the price of that good.

As in the case of completely nonlinear taxation, we want to express (73) in a more readily manipulated form. To this end, define a partially indirect utility function,

$$u^*(q, y, z, n) = \max\{u(x, z, n) : q \cdot x \leq y\}. \tag{74}$$

Condition (73) is equivalent to

$$y(n) = q \cdot x(n), z(n) \text{ maximizes } u^*(q, y, z, n) \text{ subject to } (y, z) \in B, \tag{75}$$

$$x(n) \text{ maximizes } u(x, z(n), n) \text{ subject to } q \cdot xy(n). \tag{76}$$

We know already from Section 3, and also from the appendix to the paper, that (75) is equivalent to

$$v'(n) = u_n^*(q, y(n), z(n), n), \tag{77}$$

where

$$v(n) = u^*(q, y(n), z(n), n), \tag{78}$$

along with inequality constraints which can be neglected in a large class of cases. Condition (76) is equivalent to

$$
\begin{aligned}
x(n) &= x^c(q, z(n), v(n), n), \\
y(n) &= m(q, z(n), v(n), n).
\end{aligned}
\tag{79}
$$

As a result of these transformations, we address ourselves to the following problem:

$$
\max \int v(n) f(n) \, dn,
$$

subject to

$$
\begin{aligned}
&\int [p \cdot x^c(q, z, v, n) + r \cdot z] f \, dn = A, \\
&v'(n) = u_n^*(q, m(q, z, v, n), z, n).
\end{aligned}
\tag{80}
$$

From this simple form, the first-order conditions for optimal mixed taxation are readily derived. The Lagrangean is

$$
\begin{aligned}
L &= \int \{[v - \lambda(p \cdot x^c + r \cdot z)] f + \mu v' - \mu u_n^*(q, m, z, n)\} dn \\
&= \int \{[v - \lambda(p \cdot x^c + r \cdot z)] f - \mu' v - \mu u_n^*\} \, dn - \mu(0)v(0) + \mu(\infty)v(\infty).
\end{aligned}
\tag{81}
$$

The derivatives of L with respect to q, $v(\cdot)$, and $z(\cdot)$ are to be set equal to zero.

Optimizing first with respect to q, we obtain conditions for optimal commodity taxation:

$$
\lambda \int p \cdot x_p^c f \, dn + \int \mu(u_{nq}^* + u_{ny}^* m_q) dn = 0.
\tag{82}
$$

As usual, Slutsky symmetry implies that

$$
p \cdot x_q^c = (q - t) \cdot x_q^c = -t \cdot x_q^c = -x_q^c \cdot t.
\tag{83}
$$

To evaluate $u_{nq}^* + u_{ny}^* m_q$, we use the fact (Roy's theorem for the situation) that

$$
u_q^* + u_y^* x(q, y, z, n) = 0,
\tag{84}
$$

where $x(q, y, z, n)$ is defined as the x that maximizes $u(x, z, n)$ subject to $q \cdot x \leq y$. Equation (84) is an identity. Differentiating partially with respect to n, we get

$$
u_{nq}^* + u_{ny}^* x + u_y^* x_n = 0.
\tag{85}
$$

Substitution of (83) and (85) into (82) yields

$$\left(\int x_q^c f \, dn \right) \cdot t = - \int v(n) x_n(q, y(n), z(n), n) \, dn, \tag{86}$$

where

$$v(n) = u_y^* \mu / \lambda. \tag{87}$$

In Section 2, it was argued that $-\left(\int x_q^c f \, dn \right) \cdot t$ is a satisfactory measure of the extent to which commodity taxes discourage consumption of the different commodities. Equation (86) says that discouragement should be zero when $x_n = 0$. We shall see that v is normally non-negative in such cases as the model with n interpreted as ability. Then $x_{in} > 0$ implies that commodity i should be discouraged, while $x_{in} < 0$ implies that it should be encouraged.

This surprisingly simple criterion says that commodity taxes should bear more heavily on the commodities *high-n* individuals have relatively strongest tastes for. Notice that the criterion looks at the way in which demand change *for given income and labour supply* when n changes. The spirit of the criterion is more akin to the two-class criterion (Mirrlees 1975) than to that of Ramsey (1927). But it is surprising, and satisfactory, that it is expressed as an integral of $\partial x / \partial n$ rather than an integral of x.

Turning to the conditions for nonlinear taxation, we differentiate L (81) with respect to $z(n)$ and $v(n)$:

$$-(p \cdot x_z^c + r)\lambda f = \mu(u_{n\,y}^* m_z + u_{n\,z}^*), \tag{88}$$

$$\mu' + u_{ny}^* m_v \mu = (1 - \lambda p \cdot x_v^c) f, \tag{89}$$

$$\mu(0) = 0, \qquad \mu(\infty) = 0. \tag{90}$$

These equations correspond in a general way to (34), (33), and (35) above. The correspondence can be brought out more clearly if we define the marginal rate of substitution between y and z:

$$s = u_z^* / u_y^* = -m_x. \tag{91}$$

Then

$$s_n = u_{nz}^* / u_y^* - s u_{ny}^* / u_y^* = (u_{nz}^* + u_{ny}^* m_z)/u_y^*, \tag{92}$$

and

$$\begin{aligned} p \cdot x_z^c = q \cdot x_z^c - t \cdot x_z^c &= m_z - t \cdot x_z - t \cdot x_y m_z \\ &= -(1 - t \cdot x_y)x - t \cdot x_z. \end{aligned} \tag{93}$$

Note also that

$$m_\nu u_y^* = 1 \tag{94}$$

and

$$\begin{aligned}
p \cdot x_\nu^c = q \cdot x_\nu^c - t \cdot x_\nu^c &= m_\nu - t \cdot x_y m_\nu \\
&= (1 - t \cdot x_y)/u_y^*.
\end{aligned} \tag{95}$$

Introducing the results of these calculations into (88) and (89), and using definition (87), we obtain

$$[(1 - t \cdot x_y)s + t \cdot x_z - r]f = vs_n, \tag{96}$$

$$\mu' + (u_{ny}^*/u_y^*)\mu = [1 - (\lambda/u_y^*)(1 - t \cdot x_y)]f. \tag{97}$$

In order better to appreciate these equations, it should be recognized that $(1 - t \cdot x_y)s + t \cdot x_z - r$ is the total marginal tax rates on the z commodities, including both linear and nonlinear taxes.

When applying the theory of optimal income taxation to an economy with many commodities, one would use a utility function for disposable income and labour which assumes given prices for commodities. In both actual economies and optimized ones, these prices are not proportional to the social marginal costs of commodities. Conditions (96) and (97) show how one should allow for the differences. Calculations of optimal tax rates that have been done (e.g. Mirrlees 1971 and Stern 1975) do not allow for this, so it is interesting to consider in which direction the results have been biased, and whether these calculated optimal rates are closer to the optimal income tax or the optimal total tax rate (including commodity tax effects).

The interrelations of the various equations are so complicated that no general answer to these questions seems possible. But it is instructive to consider the special case,

$$u = U(a(x, n) + b(z, n)). \tag{98}$$

It will be recollected that, when $a_n \equiv 0$, it is optimal to have no commodity taxes (linear or nonlinear), so long as it is possible to tax the z-goods non-linearly (Section 3 above). That case is therefore of no interest for our present purpose. Instead, take the case where

a is homogeneous of degree one in x. $\tag{99}$

It is then easily seen that the functions $s(q, y, z, n)$ and $x(q, y, z, n)$ used in the theory above have the following properties:

$$s_y = 0, \tag{100}$$
$$x_y = x/y, \tag{101}$$
$$x_z = 0. \tag{102}$$

Also, in indirect form, $a = ya^*(q, n)$.

We need to know how $t \cdot x_y$ varies with n:

$$
\begin{aligned}
\frac{d}{dn} t \cdot x_y &= \frac{d}{dn} \frac{t \cdot x}{y} = \frac{t \cdot x_n + t \cdot x_y y' + t \cdot x_z \cdot z'}{y} - \frac{t \cdot x}{y^2} y' \\
&= \frac{t \cdot x_n}{y} + \frac{t \cdot x}{y^2} y' - \frac{t \cdot x}{y^2} y' \\
&= \frac{t \cdot x_n}{y}.
\end{aligned}
\tag{103}
$$

Now, from (86), we have

$$
\int vt \cdot x_n dn = - \int t \cdot x_q^c \cdot tf \, dn
\tag{104}
$$
$$
\geqq 0,
$$

by Slutsky. This suggests that, normally,

$$
v \frac{d}{dn} t \cdot x_y \geqq 0.
\tag{105}
$$

Trying to confirm that v is non-negative, we use the computation (following the argument that led to (49))

$$
\begin{aligned}
\frac{d}{dn} u_y^* &= u_{ny}^* + U''(ya^* + b)(y'a^* + b_z z')a^* \\
&= u_{ny}^*,
\end{aligned}
\tag{106}
$$

since $y' = -s \cdot z' = -(b_z/a^*) \cdot z'$. Also, note that

$$
u_{ny}^* = U'' \cdot (ya_n^* + b_n)a^* + U' \cdot a_n^*.
\tag{107}
$$

A variety of assumptions would make the left-hand side of (107) non-positive; for example, it is sufficient that

$$
\frac{zU''(z)}{U'(z)} \leqq -1, \qquad \frac{\partial}{\partial n}(a^*/b) \leqq 0.
\tag{108}
$$

Under these assumptions,

$$
\frac{d}{dn} u_y^* \leqq 0.
\tag{109}
$$

We also have (from (106), and the definition of v, (87))

$$
\frac{d}{dn} v = \left(\frac{u_y^*}{\lambda} - 1 + t \cdot x_y \right) f.
\tag{110}
$$

I shall show that, if (105) holds, $v \geq 0$ for all n. Suppose that, on the contrary, $v(n_1) < 0$. Since $v(0) = 0$, there exists n_2 such that $v(n_2) < 0$ and $v'(n_2) < 0$. Then, by (110), (105), and (109),

$$\frac{d}{dn}\left(\frac{1}{f}\frac{dv}{dn}\right) \leqq 0 \qquad \text{in a neighbourhood of } n_2.$$

Consequently, v' is non-increasing in the neighbourhood of n_2, and v decreases. This must hold, then, for all $n \geq n_2$, and we conclude that

$$v(n) < v(n_2) < 0, \qquad \text{for all } n > n_2. \tag{111}$$

This contradicts the condition that $v \to 0$ as $n \to \infty$.

Collecting arguments, we have shown that, on the reasonable postulate that (105) holds,

$$v \geqq 0, \qquad \text{(all } n) \tag{112}$$

$$\frac{d}{dn}(t \cdot x_y) \geqq 0 \qquad \text{(all } n). \tag{113}$$

Thus, the introduction of commodity taxes introduces an increasing term into the right-hand side of (110). Since v begins and ends at zero, this seems to mean that v should increase more slowly and then decrease more slowly than in the absence of commodity taxes; that is, v should be smaller.

The consequences of this for tax rates may be understood most clearly for the case of a simple income tax, where labour is the only commodity subject to nonlinear taxation. Taking labour as numeraire, $r = 1$ and $-z$ is labour supplied (z being a negative number). Let the income tax be $\theta(-z)$. Then the budget constraint is $y = -z - \theta(-z)$, and the consumer equates $s = u_z/u_y$ to $1 - \theta'(-z)$. Thus, the right-hand side of (96),

$$(1 - t \cdot x_y)s + t \cdot x_z - r = (1 - t \cdot x_y)(1 - \theta') + t \cdot x_z - 1$$

$$= -\frac{\partial}{\partial(-z)}[t \cdot x(q, -z - \theta, z, n) + \theta(-z)]$$

$$= -\text{marginal total tax on labour earnings.}$$

$$= -\tau, \text{say.}$$

Condition (96) says that

$$\tau = -vs_n, \tag{114}$$

and, if n represents ability, $s_n = (\partial/\partial n)(u_z^*/u_y^*)$ should be negative, since n-men find it easier to supply labour.

We find, then, that lower v implies lower τ: the tax system as a whole should, it seems, bear less heavily upon labour on the margin than one would suppose if commodity taxes were not allowed for. From the calculations above (noting that $x_z = 0$ in the special case we are dealing with), we have

$$\theta'(-z) = \frac{\tau}{1 - t \cdot x_y} - \frac{t \cdot x_y}{1 - t \cdot x_y}, \tag{115}$$

so that θ' should be yet smaller than τ, if commodity taxes are predominantly positive.

In the above argument, first, it was assumed that individuals had a special form of utility function; and, second, an unproved (but reasonable) conjecture was made at (105). It would be even harder to push through a corresponding argument for the general case. Yet the argument provides some reason for believing that the usual calculations of income tax rates are too high, not only because the commodity tax system does and should do some of the work of the income tax, but also because the varying pattern of demand with ability normally requires a lower marginal total tax on labour income. It would be interesting to know whether calculations for plausible cases would support this conjecture. Though strongly suggested by the equations, it is hard to understand intuitively.

It is worth noting one further feature of the first-order conditions, namely that they contain within them some necessary conditions for Pareto efficiency, which we can obtain by eliminating v from (86) and (96):

$$-\left(\int x_q^c f dn \right) \cdot t = \int \left[(1 - t \cdot x_y)s + t \cdot x_z - r \right] s_n^{-1} x_n f dn. \tag{116}$$

These relations are not easy to interpret as they stand. The main point is that the weighting function $v(n)$ appearing in the conditions for commodity taxation and for income taxation must be the same. Equation (116) could allow one to calculate optimal commodity tax systems once the optimal income tax was known, without further reference to the welfare function. It might be more interesting to use them as a means of identifying commodities which are affected in a grossly nonoptimal way by the tax system. But in this form, the efficiency conditions seem not much more than a theoretical curiosity.

This completes the discussion of mixed taxation. It is interesting to note that the optimality conditions (86), (96), and (97) contain within them *both* the conditions for optimality where full nonlinearity is possible, *and* the conditions where only linearity is possible. The theory of linear taxation is obtained simply by omitting z and ignoring (96). In this case $x_n = (d/dn)x$, and the right-hand side of (86) can be integrated by parts. The details will be left to the reader. The conditions for nonlinear taxation are obtained by letting x be one-dimensional. No control is then lost by setting $q = p$. Then (86) is irrelevant, and the remaining equations reduce to the theory of Section 3.

6. PUBLIC GOODS IN AN OPTIMAL MIXED SYSTEM

The point to be made in this section is a simple one. Let g be a public good, entering all utility functions (possibly trivially in some cases) and with production price π. In the Lagrangean (81), x^c, u_n^*, and m are now all functions of g as well as the other variables; and πg appears as an additional term in the production constraint, so that one subtracts $\lambda \pi g$ from the Lagrangean. Then differentiation with respect to g yields

$$\lambda \int p \cdot x_g^c f \, dn + \lambda \pi + \int \mu(u_{ng}^* + u_{ny}^* m_g) \, dn = 0. \tag{117}$$

By means of the usual manipulation in tax theory, we have

$$
\begin{aligned}
p \cdot x_g^c &= (q - t) \cdot x_g^c \\
&= m_g - t \cdot (x_g + x_y m_g) \\
&= -t \cdot x_g + (1 - t \cdot x_y) m_g.
\end{aligned} \tag{118}
$$

Furthermore, $m_g = -u_g^*/u_y^*$, and we want to define

$$\sigma = u_g^*/u_y^* = -m_g \tag{119}$$

as the marginal rate of substitution between income and the public good. Partial differentiation of (119) with respect to n gives

$$
\begin{aligned}
\sigma_n &= (u_{ng}^* - u_g^* u_{ny}^*/u_y^*)/u_y^* \\
&= (u_{ng}^* + u_{ny}^* m_g)/u_y^*.
\end{aligned} \tag{120}
$$

Using (118) and (120), we can write (117) in the form

$$\pi = \int (1 - t \cdot x_y)\sigma f \, dn + \int t \cdot x_g f \, dn - \int v\sigma_n dn. \tag{121}$$

This says that the supply of public goods should be at such a level that their marginal costs are equal to

(1) a sum of individual marginal rates of substitution for the public goods, reduced by a proportion equal to the derivative of commodity taxes with respect to income spent on them (for that individual) *plus*
(2) the derivatives of total commodity tax revenue with respect to the provision of the public goods, *less*
(3) a weighted sum of terms expressing how the personal value of the public good varies with n.

The first two parts of this expression give a direct estimate of the social value of the good, adding marginal rates of substitution in the usual way and making allowance for direct revenue effects. The last part of the expression corrects this estimate for distributional considerations. It uses the fundamental weighting factors $v(n)$, which played such an important part in the conditions for optimal taxation, and applies them to the quantities σ_n, which show how much preference for the public good varies with n. This is analogous to the way in which v multiplied s_n and x_n in the optimal tax conditions. In the normal case with $v \geq 0$, the correcting term is negative if the more able have a stronger preference for the public good, positive if the less able have. Thus, the rule encourages provision of public goods valued by the poor and discourages those valued by the rich. The existence of optimal taxes does not eliminate distributional considerations in the provision of public goods; but it does allow the distributional considerations to be analysed out and expressed as a separate contribution to (or deduction from) the marginal social value of the good.

It will be recognized that, in the one-parameter case, v can be deduced from the optimal taxes themselves through (96), and substituted in (121). Thus, we obtain a further set of welfare-independent conditions which are necessary for Pareto efficiency. In the case of zero commodity taxes (or fully nonlinear taxation), these conditions take a rather neat form:

$$\pi = \int \left(\sigma - \tau_i \frac{\sigma_n}{s_{in}} \right) f \, \mathrm{d}n, \tag{122}$$

where τ, the marginal tax on commodity i, is $s_i - p_i$. An alternative form is

$$\pi = \int \sigma \left(1 - \frac{\sigma_n/\sigma}{\tau_{in}/\tau_i} \right) f \, \mathrm{d}n. \tag{123}$$

In this form it is plain that the social value of the public good is enhanced when its value for some individual responds more sensitively to n than do his marginal tax rates.

7. THE FUNDAMENTAL PRINCIPLE OF OPTIMAL TAX THEORY

We have derived necessary conditions for the optimality of various economic policy variables. These conditions have an essentially simple common structure, which it is the purpose of this section to emphasize.

If an economic policy is optimal, there is no change in it which will leave total welfare unchanged and at the same time generate a net addition to government revenue. Consider a small change in some policy, δP, and associate with it income transfers to and from individuals which are designed to keep total welfare constant. These transfers may be analysed into two parts. First, an income transfer δy_1 made that would, if behavior did not change, leave each individual's utility unchanged: this transfer is pure compensation for the initial policy change. Since it is not in general possible to make these δy_1 transfers in a lump-sum manner, individuals would want to change their behavior to benefit from the structure of these transfers. We therefore institute a second set of income transfers δy_2, whose effect is to leave *total* utility unchanged, while removing the incentive to change behaviour arising from the first round of transfers. Specifically, we know that individuals always adjust their behavior in such a way that $v' = u_n$. Having chosen δy_1 so that $\delta v = 0$, δy_2 is now chosen so that $\delta v' = \delta u_n$.

These income transfers create changes $\delta y_1 + \delta y_2$ in government expenditures, which are partly offset by changes in tax revenue, δt_1, arising from the policy change δP, utility being kept constant, and δt_2, arising from the second-round income transfers δy_2.

If the policy were originally optimal, the net increase in government revenue does not increase whether the policy change is positive or negative. Thus,

$$\int (\delta y_1 - \delta t_1 + \delta y_2 - \delta t_2) f \, dn = 0. \tag{124}$$

δy_1 and δt_1 are easily computed from elementary considerations. Writing

$$m(v, P, n) = \text{income yielding utility } v \text{ for } n\text{-man when policy is } P, \tag{125}$$

$$t(v, P, n) = \text{tax revenue from } n\text{-man when he has utility } v \text{ and policy is } P, \tag{126}$$

we have

$$\delta y_1 = \frac{\partial m}{\partial P} \, \delta P = m_P \delta P, \tag{127}$$

$$\delta t_1 = \frac{\partial t}{\partial P} \, \delta P = t_P \delta P. \tag{128}$$

It remains to estimate $\delta y_2 - \delta t_2$. Remarkably, we find that

$$\int (\delta y_2 - \delta t_2) f \, dn = - \int v(n) \left(\frac{\partial}{\partial n} m_P \right)_{m,P} dn, \tag{129}$$

where m_P is differentiated with m, P held constant; and the multipliers v (normally non-negative) *are independent of the particular policy considered.* This is what we have been discovering in the previous sections of this paper. There we also found that v is the solution of the differential equation (rewriting (89))

$$u_y^* \frac{d}{dn} (v/u_y^*) + u_{ny}^* (v/u_y^*) = (1 - \lambda p \cdot x_v^c) f$$
$$= (1 - \lambda m_v + \lambda t_v) f, \tag{130}$$

Table 10.1.

Policy instrument	m_P	t_P
Proportional taxes	x	$\frac{\partial}{\partial t}(t \cdot x_q^c) = x_q^c \cdot t + x$
Public goods	$\sigma = u_g^*/u_y^*$	$\frac{\partial}{\partial g}(t \cdot x^c) = t \cdot x_g^c$
Nonlinear taxes	$s = u_z^*/u_y^*$	$\frac{\partial}{\partial x}(t \cdot x^c + p \cdot z)$

with $v = 0$ at $n = 0, \infty$. The function $u^*(y, P, n)$ is related to the compensation function m by

$$v = u^*(m, P, n). \tag{131}$$

Thus the fundamental principle is that we can assess the value of a policy by associating with an n-man three numbers:

(1) $m_P =$ pure compensation for the policy,
(2) $-t_P =$ reduction in taxes, at constant utility,
(3) $-(v/f)((\partial/\partial n)m_P)_{m,P} =$ distributional and incentive effects.

The total effect of the policy is measured by adding these numbers for everyone affected. For the three major policy tools examined in this paper we have Table 10.1. To appreciate the last row of the table, it should be understood that the instruments in the case of nonlinear taxes are best taken to be the demands $z(n)$ for the taxed commodities (marginal tax rates lead to very complicated equations which can only with considerable labour be reduced to the simple form).

The form in which commodity tax rules appear is also worth attention. For this case the cost of an increase in a commodity tax rate is

$$\int \left[x - (x_q^c \cdot t + x) - \frac{v}{f} x_n \right] f \, dn. \tag{132}$$

If there are no nonuniform policies (such as nonlinear taxes), $x_n = (d/dn)x$, and the last term can be integrated by parts, so that we have the form

$$\int x_q^c \cdot t f \, dn = \int v'(n) x \, dn, \tag{133}$$

which is essentially equation (12) of Section 2. In this case $v'(n)$ is the social marginal utility of income transfer.

In the general case, since v is the multiplier dual to the constraint

$$\begin{aligned}
0 &= (v' - u_n)/u_y \\
&= m_v v' + m_n \\
&= \left(\frac{\partial}{\partial n} m(v(n), P, n) \right)_P,
\end{aligned} \tag{134}$$

it is appropriate to call v the *social marginal utility of income difference*.

The striking feature of this analysis is that the distributional aspects of policy choice can be incorporated in a weighting function v, which then defines a simple differential operator to be applied to m_P. m_P is the old measure of social value, which ignores revenue effects and the desirable 'distortions' arising from distributional considerations. It is easy to see how to supplement it with an estimate of revenue effects; and we now have a simple general principle showing how the remaining adjustment should be made. The method can be applied without difficulty to other types of economic policy, such as quantity rationing, wherever the simple equilibrium model of this paper is thought to be appropriate.

Appendix

The following lemma will be proved, on the assumption that $u(x, z, n)$ is a twice differentiable function, increasing in z; and x, z are differentiable functions of n:

Lemma. *If*

$$v(n) = u(x(n), z(n), n), \qquad v'(n) = u_n(x(n), z(n), n), \tag{A1}$$

and, for all m, n,

$$s_m(x(n), z(n), m) \cdot x'(n) \geqq 0, \tag{A2}$$

then there exists B such that, for all n,

$$x(n), z(n) \text{ maximizes } u(x, z, n) \text{ for } (x, z) \in B. \tag{A3}$$

If (A3) holds, and (A1) holds, and for all n,

$$s_n(x(n), z(n), n) \cdot x'(n) \geqq 0. \tag{A4}$$

Recollect that $s = u_x/u_z$.

Proof. The second part of the theorem was proved in Section 3 following (19). For the first part, suppose on the contrary that there exist n_1, n_2 such that

$$u(x(n_1), z(n_1), n_2) > u(x(n_2), z(n_2), n_2). \tag{A5}$$

If $n_1 < n_2$ (a similar argument works if $n_1 > n_2$), (A5) implies the existence of n_3, $n_1 < n_3 < n_2$ such that

$$\frac{\partial}{\partial n} u(x(n), z(n), n_2) < 0 \qquad \text{at } n = n_3. \tag{A6}$$

This derivative is equal to

$$u_x(x(n_3), z(n_3), n_2) \cdot x'(n_3) + u_z z'(n_3)$$
$$= u_z[s(x(n_3), z(n_3), n_2) \cdot x'(n_3) + z'(n_3)].$$

Therefore

$$s(x(n_3), z(n_3), n_2) \cdot x'(n_3) + z'(n_3) < 0. \tag{A7}$$

But (A1) implies that

$$s(x(n_3), z(n_3), n_3) \cdot x'(n_3) + z'(n_3) = 0. \tag{A8}$$

Since $n_3 < n_2$, (A7) and (A8) imply the existence of n_4, $n_3 < n_4 < n_2$, such that

$$s_n(x(n_3), z(n_3), n_4) \cdot x'(n_3) < 0, \tag{A9}$$

contradicting (A2).

This proves that (A3) holds with B defined as the set of $(x(n), z(n))$ as n runs through all values. Thus, the lemma is proved. $\qquad\qquad\qquad\qquad\square$

REFERENCES

Atkinson, A.B. (1973) 'How Progressive should Income Tax Be?' In J.M. Parkin and A. Nobay (eds.), *Essays in Modern Economics* (Macmillan, New York).

—— and Stiglitz, J.E. (1972). 'The Structure of Indirect Taxation and Economic Efficiency'. *Journal of Public Economics*, 1, 97–119.

—— and (1976) 'The Design of Tax Structure: Direct versus Indirect Taxation'. *Journal of Public Economics*, 6, 55–75.

Deaton, A.S. (1975) 'Equity, Efficiency and the Structure of Indirect Taxation'. Mimeo, University of Cambridge.

Diamond, P.A. (1975) 'A Many-Person Ramsey Tax Rule'. *Journal of Public Economics*, 4, 335–42.

and Mirrlees, J.A. (1971) 'Optimal Taxation and Public Production'. *American Economic Review*, 61, 8–27 and 261–78.

Mirrlees, J.A. (1971) 'An Exploration in the Theory of Optimal Income Taxation'. *Review of Economics Studies*, 38, 175–208.

—— (1972) 'On Producer Taxation'. *Review of Economic Studies*, 39, 105–11.

—— (1975) 'Optimal Commodity Taxation in a Two-Class Economy'. *Journal of Public Economics*, 4, 27–33.

Phelps, E.S. (1973) 'Taxation of Wage Income for Economic Justice'. *Quarterly Journal of Economics*, 87, 331–54.

Ramsey, F.P. (1927) 'A Contribution to the Theory of Taxation'. *Economic Journal*, 37, 47–61.

Sadka, E. (1976) 'On Income Distribution, Incentive Effects and Optimal Income Taxation'. *Review of Economic Studies*, forthcoming.

Seade, J. (1975) 'Progressivity of Income Taxation'. Mimeo, Oxford University.

Stern, N.H. (1976) 'On the Specification of Models of Optimum Income Taxation'. *Journal of Public Economics*, 6, 123–62.

Stiglitz, J.E. and Dasgupta, P.S. (1971) 'Differential Taxation, Public Goods and Economic Efficiency'. *Review of Economics Studies*, 38, 151–74.

11

The Theory of Optimal Taxation

1. ECONOMIC THEORY AND PUBLIC POLICY

A good way of governing is to agree upon objectives, discover what is possible, and optimize. At any rate, this approach is the subject of optimal tax theory. From this point of view, 'optimal tax theory' is an unduly narrow term to describe the subject, but it is neater than 'theory of optimal public policy'. In any case, I shall not be discussing the optimization of macroeconomic models, which are used to treat several aspects of public policy. Much—though not all—of what has so far been done in optimal tax theory uses the standard model of competitive equilibrium, with rational consumers and profit-maximizing, price-taking firms. In this way, one avoids debate about the dubious relationships of disequilibrium macroeconomics or oligopoly theory, and concentrates on essentials.

The central element in the theory is information. Public policies apply to individuals only on the basis of what can be publicly known about them. There is little difficulty about paying the same subsidy to every individual in the economy: there is not much more difficulty in making the subsidy depend on age. Uniform positive taxes may be a little more difficult. Taxes and subsidies proportional to trade in specified goods or services may also be difficult to administer with perfect accuracy. But, subject to some minor imperfections, we can take it that most such taxes use information that is cheaply and publicly available. Not all conceivable public policies have this convenient property. One of the basic theorems of welfare economics asserts that, where a number of convexity and continuity assumptions are satisfied, an optimum is a competitive equilibrium once initial endowments have been suitably distributed. To make such a distribution requires, in general, complete information about individual consumers, for the transfers must be lump-sum in character, that is, independent of the individual's behaviour. It is generally agreed by economists that the lump-sum transfers necessary to achieve an optimum are scarcely ever feasible.[1] There is no way of obtaining the information about individuals

Reprinted from *Handbook of Mathematical Economics*, Vol. 3, K.J. Arrow and M.D. Intriligator (eds.), (Amsterdam: North-Holland, 1986), with permission of Elsevier Science.

[1] Hahn (1973) asserts that lump-sum taxation has in fact been used. This is true, though his examples are bad ones; but it is beside the point. The question is whether *optimal* lump-sum transfers are possible.

that is required except in a society of individuals who are truthful regardless of selfish considerations. A theorem supporting this view is given in Section 3 below.

Widespread agreement among economists that optimal lump-sum taxation is impossible in practice came long before analysis of optimal non-lump-sum taxation. This is surprising. Possibly too many economic theorists were chiefly interested in the supposed merits of the undistorted competitive price system; but socialist economists did not fill the gap. Perhaps distaste for the welfare function was a more effective barrier to progress. It is true that Bergson and Samuelson used welfare functions in their work on the fundamentals of welfare economics. But those more closely concerned with policy issues would not have thought the welfare function, embodying interpersonal comparisons of welfare, a practical tool of analysis. In this century, economists have usually referred to analyse empirical propositions of doubtful validity rather than analyse the consequences of value judgements, even when these might have been expected to command more widespread agreement.

There are, it seems to me, only two promising approaches to making well-based recommendations about public policy. One is to use a welfare function of some form and develop the theory of optimal policy. The other is to model the existing state of affairs in some manageable way, and on that basis to display the likely effects of changes in government policy, these effects being displayed in sufficient detail to make rational choice among alternative policies possible. If a welfare function were used to evaluate the changes predicted, the second approach would come fairly close to the first, and in fact there is then a close theoretical relationship. But the second method could concern itself with presentation of effects rather than their evaluation. For example, the effects of policy changes on income distribution can be presented graphically. This approach is open to many objections as it is practised, and it is not easy to see how these faults could be avoided. In the first place, the particular way of presenting effects is not the outcome of systematic analysis, but is chosen quite informally. Secondly, the presentation is liable to divert attention completely from matters that could be important. In the income-distribution example, people presented with income-distribution pictures are unlikely to consider how these judgements should be affected by differences in relative prices. Thirdly, summary variables may be used which no plausible welfare judgements would validate. The use of Gini coefficients in the presentation of income-distribution effects is, I think a case in point.[2] The user of such figures is all too likely to regard bigger as better. The fact that the summary variable is precisely intended not to be a welfare function, or an argument in a welfare function, is no help in avoiding misuse.

There are then some practical arguments in favour of using welfare functions to analyse public policy. But unless there are stronger cases for some welfare

---

[2] Sen (1973, pp. 29–34) makes a moderate case for this measure.

functions than for others, the formal derivation of properties of welfare-maximizing policies is a pointless exercise. It turns out that some of these properties are independent of the welfare function; but optimal policies are not. For much of the theory, one must bear in mind what kind of welfare function is likely to be satisfactory. Furthermore, some of the most interesting results obtainable in this area are numerical calculations for specific welfare functions. For this reason, too, optimal tax theory is a field where econometric work is of considerable interest to the theorist, and the needs of theory are a guide to the econometrician.

The models to be discussed are firmly based on a distinction between public and private information. The government deals with an economy of consumers, producers, and possibly other corporate institutions, such as charitable bodies. These private individuals and institutions may know things the government does not know, such as a specific person's income-earning potential. The simplest assumption is that, in respect of such individual characteristics, the government either observes and knows the precise truth, or knows nothing to distinguish the individual from anyone else. Thus, we usually exclude the realistic possibility that the government could at a cost improve its information; or that the government has information about individuals that is not completely reliable. But the theory can be expected to throw light on the magnitude of the gain from additional information of this kind. Something will be said about the use of imperfect lump-sum taxation, based on individual characteristics observed with errors, in Section 3.

Another aspect of public policy omitted from the basic models is the evasion and enforcement of government policies. From one point of view, the problem of enforcement is one of getting information. A firm reports its profits and pays tax accordingly: the profit tax is a policy tool that relates tax payment to reported profits. Actual profits may or may not be equal to reported profits; so there are other rules relating tax payments—this time known as fines and imprisonment—jointly to reported profits and a more accurate measurement of actual profits made, at a cost, by government agents. Again, in certain countries, what the government servants report actual profits to be may be influenced by bribes. This brings in another set of considerations, where transactions are necessarily personal, unlike transactions in the standard competitive model. Since, in the basic optimal tax models, states of information are fixed, personal transactions, whose terms are specific to the individuals involved, need not be considered. But transactions of this kind—which are common in the real world, particularly in the capital market—would be an important subject of study in a complete theory of the administration, enforcement, and evasion of the tax system.[3]

---

[3] A more straightforward treatment of administrative costs has been initiated by Heller and Shell (1974).

The range of public policy contemplated in optimal tax theory is quite wide. Besides taxes and subsidies themselves, which may be related to any transactions between individuals, firms, other corporate bodies, foreign countries and individuals, and government and its agencies, the theory should also be prepared to encompass the use of quantity controls and restrictions, and the control of information flows, for example in training programmes or public advice. Also, the government and its agencies can make expenditures or set up productive activities itself. Public expenditures may be undertaken to meet international obligations, or to benefit individuals, corporate bodies, or groups of these. A first requirement of the theory is that one finds a convenient, simple notation that will encompass all such policy variables without unduly complicating the analysis. In fact, despite the range of possible policies, the basic relationships are usually quite simple and similar. It is good to cultivate the art of seeing specific policy instruments as instances of the general possibilities of policy whose modelling we are to discuss.

It will be noticed that the list of policy instruments in the previous paragraph does not include certain policies which rely for their operation on disequilibrium states of the economy. Deficit finance, price control, and wage and income policies are instances of non-equilibrium policies. It should be possible to apply the methods of optimal tax theory also to models allowing disequilibrium.[4] This seems to be an interesting area for further research.

In the next section, the common mathematical form of optimal tax problems will be explained, and certain basic features and issues discussed. In subsequent sections, we shall look at a variety of cases. After dealing with lump-sum taxation in Section 3, we examine linear taxation in Sections 4 and 5. Sections 6 and 7 are devoted to the theory of income taxation and nonlinear taxation generally. The discussion is concluded largely in terms of taxes and subsidies. Models with individual uncertainty about the effect of policies are discussed briefly in Section 8. Some remarks and results about computation and approximation are collected in Section 9. After some concluding remarks, constituting Section 10, Section 11 provides some brief notes on the literature.

This paper does not contain a thorough survey of the literature on optimal tax theory. Neither the time nor the facilities for such a survey were available. It is rather an account of what seem to me the fundamental parts of the theory, with emphasis on the mathematical problems. Much of the published literature deals with economies in which all individuals are identical. Since this case does not seem to me especially interesting or useful, it will not be given much attention. Interesting and important areas which are neglected are the analysis of an international economy, where the impossibility of lump-sum transfers should have many interesting consequences, and the study of variable population.

---

[4] Dixit (1976) has looked at some issues in a temporary equilibrium model.

2. OPTIMIZATION SUBJECT TO MAXIMIZATION CONSTRAINTS

Problems in optimal tax theory have a characteristic form. To bring this out, consider three typical models.

In the first, the government sets commodity taxes $t = (t_1, \ldots, t_n)$ proportional to trade in the n commodities. Producers face prices $p = (p_1, \ldots, p_n)$, and their production activity is uniquely determined by these prices. Writing y for the aggregate net production vector, and x^h for the net demand vector of consumer h (there being H consumers), market-clearing requires

$$\sum_{h=1}^{H} x^h = y(p). \tag{1}$$

At the same time, consumers maximize utility, and we have, for $h = 1, 2, \ldots, H$,

$$\left. \begin{array}{l} x^h \text{ maximizes } u^h(x) \\ \text{subject to: } (p + t) \cdot x \leq b^h(p) \\ \text{and } \quad x \in X_h \end{array} \right\}, \tag{2}$$

where b_h is the profit income of the consumer, which in the absence of profit taxation is simply a function of p; and X_h is the consumption set of consumer h, u^h his utility function.

A rather general form for the welfare function that government seeks to maximize is

$$W(x^1, x^2, \ldots, x^H).$$

In the problem outlined, W is to be maximized subject to the constraints (1) and (2). The first of these constraints is of familiar type. The second group of constraints looks quite unlike those encountered in elementary constrained maximization problems, for it involves maximization itself with respect to some of the variables, in this case the x^h, while other variables p and t are parametric.

It will be noticed that, when the u^h are strictly concave and the X_h convex, the apparently complicated form of (2) is of no great consequence, because we can write

$$x^h = x^h(p + t, b^h(p)),$$

just as the supply functions $y(p)$ may be derived from profit maximization. This feature is specific to problems with linear taxation.

The second problem makes a common, but generally unsatisfactory, assumption that all consumers react in the same way to the government's policy variables. The government provides a facility, such as education, to some homogeneous groups of consumers. The supply of the facility is measured by a real number z which happens to be equal to its cost. The cost is met from the taxes paid by the beneficiaries, and taxes T_0 obtained from the rest of the community. The tax paid by the beneficiaries is a function $T_1(y)$, of their labour supply y. This function is to be taken as given. The welfare function has as arguments the utility $u(y, z)$ of beneficiaries, and the tax T_0 paid by the rest of the community. Thus, the problem is

$$\underset{y, z, T_0}{\text{maximize}} \ W(u(y, z), T_0), \tag{3}$$

$$\text{subject to:} \quad z = T_0 + T_1(y), \tag{4}$$

$$\text{and } y \text{ maximizes } u(y, z). \tag{5}$$

This problem is a rather special and artificial one, but shows how naturally a maximization constraint arises. In this case there would be no reasonable presumption that u be strictly concave in y for all z, and therefore no reason to suppose that we can replace (5) by writing $y = y(z)$.

The third problem is that of optimal income taxation, where there are two commodities, a consumption good and labour, and the population is an infinite one where individuals are characterized by a continuous parameter h, distributed with density function f. The income tax takes a net amount $t(wy)$ of consumption good from a consumer who supplies labour y, the wage rate being w. Consumer h has utility $u(x, y, h)$, x being his consumption, and $x = wy - t(wy)$. The welfare function is

$$W = \int u(wy - t(wy), y, h) f(h) \, dh. \tag{6}$$

This is to be maximized subject to the constraints that

$$y(h) \text{ maximizes } u(wy - t(wy), y), \tag{7}$$

for all h; and the production constraint

$$\int [wy - t(wy)] f(h) \, dh \leq G\left(\int yf(h) \, dh\right). \tag{8}$$

Furthermore, the wage is the marginal product of labour:

$$w = G'\left(\int yf(h) \, dh\right). \tag{9}$$

In this formulation it has been assumed that all profits go to the government: otherwise the consumer's budget constraint would have to be modified.

Each of these problems can be written in the form

$$
\left.
\begin{aligned}
&\text{maximize } W(x, z) \\
&\text{subject to: } (x, z) \in A \\
&\text{and } x \text{ maximizes } U(x', z) \\
&\text{subject to: } x' \in X(z)
\end{aligned}
\right\}.
\tag{10}
$$

Generally, the set A represents technological feasibility, and the relationship between production and prices. The maximization constraint represents consumer and producer behaviour. The set $X(z)$ is the intersection of the set of definition of the function $U(\cdot, z)$ and other constraints imposed by government.

There could be many maximization constraints, but in each of the above problems they can be written as one. For instance, in the third example, the function $y(h)$ is chosen to maximize

$$
\int u(wy - t(wy), y) f(h) \, \mathrm{d}h,
$$

and this single maximization encompasses the behaviour of all consumers. This is possible because of the absence of consumption externalities. It will also be noticed that in this case the constraint imposed on consumers by taxation is incorporated into the utility function, and the set $X(z)$ is simply the set of $y(h)$ that are consistent with non-negative consumption and labour, i.e. that satisfy $0 \le y(h)$, $t(wy(h)) \le wy(h)$. It usually seems best so to transform a problem that the sets $X(z)$ reflect only consumption feasibility, and can often be understood implicitly from finiteness of the function U. It will be seen below that transformations of problems into convenient form play an important part in the theory. The first and third problems, as set out above, are not in a good form for mathematical analysis; in fact, they are much simpler than they look when the economics is first set up mathematically.

In some cases the control variables z and the behavioural variables x are numbers or vectors in finite-dimensional vector space. In other cases, such as our third problem, they are functions, (z might even be a subset of finite- or infinite-dimensional space, but I know of no problem that has been analysed directly in this form.)

Granted that (10) is the form of problems in optimal tax theory, we have to deal with two issues. The first is that concavity of W and convexity of A are not usually implied by the natural assumptions of the problem. Therefore theorems of concave programming are not applicable, and first-order conditions for optimality are unlikely to be sufficient conditions. These issues will be taken up as they appear in the various models: the optimal tax theorist must always bear them in mind, and look for ways of circumventing them.

The second issue is the nature and treatment of the constraint that (leaving $X(z)$ to be understood)

$$
x \text{ maximizes } U(x', z).
\tag{11}
$$

If U is differentiable and strictly concave, (11) is equivalent to

$$U_x = 0, \tag{12}$$

which can be handled as a normal set of constraints, although it is unlikely to define a convex set. But that takes us back to the first issue. In many interesting cases, U is not concave in x, at least not for all z: this is so for the second and third examples above.

There are two ways of handling (11). We could replace (11) by the rather large set of constraints, with new variables:

$$U(x, z) \geq (x', z), \qquad \text{all } x'. \tag{13}$$

In almost all interesting cases, this is an uncountable infinity of inequalities, which may therefore be delicate to handle; but the reduction to (13) can be useful. The alternative method is to examine directly the set of (x, z) defined by (11).[5]

It may be helpful to do this first for a special case (which has no economic significance).

Example 1. x and z are scalars.

> Find z to maximize $- (x - 1)^2 - (z - 2)^2$
>
> subject to: x maximizes $\quad U(x, z) = z e^{-(x+1)^2} + e^{-(x-1)^2}$.

We begin by describing the constraint set. The first-order condition for maximization with respect to x is

$$z(x + 1)e^{-(x+1)^2} + (x - 1)e^{-(x-1)^2} = 0;$$

i.e.,

$$z = \frac{1 - x}{1 + x} e^{4x}. \tag{14}$$

For x between 0.344 and 2.903 there are three values of x satisfying (14), and it still remains to discover which of them actually does the maximizing.

---

[5] The recently developed branch of differential topology known as catastrophe theory (based on work of R. Thom) studies the set of (x, z) such that $U_x = 0$, and particularly the set of z for which the local behaviour of x satisfying $U_x = 0$ is especially noteworthy. The study of the set of (x, z) such that x maximizes U is in some ways closely related. Bröcker (1975, p. 145) refers to the *Maxwell convention* as describing this kind of problem. But the features of these sets that are of interest in optimization are, by and large, quite different from those that are of interest in the dynamic analysis of systems, which has so far been the main motivation of catastrophe theory. In particular, the *catastrophe points* z at which $\det U_{xx} = 0$ are rather unimportant optimizations.

To settle this, we observe that

$$U(z, x) - U(z, -x) = (z - 1)(e^{-(x+1)^2} - e^{-(x-1)^2})$$
$$= -(z - 1)(e^{4x} - 1)e^{-(x+1)^2},$$

so that, for fixed $z > 1$, U is less for positive x than for negative; while if $z < 1$, U is greater for positive x than for negative. Therefore the maximum of U occurs for positive x when $z < 1$, for negative x when $z > 1$. In either case (as is readily verified) this identifies the desired solution of (14) uniquely. The points of the locus (14) for which x maximizes U form two closed connected subsets of the locus. When $z = 1$, U is maximized by $x = \pm 0.957$.

It is clear, by sketching contours $(x - 1)^2 + (z - 2)^2 = $ constant in a diagram, that the solution of the maximization problem is

$$x = 0.957, \qquad z = 1.$$

This solution is not obtained if one treats the problem as a conventional constrained maximization problem with the first-order condition (14) as constraint. The Lagrangean is then

$$-(x - 1)^2 - (z - 2)^2 + \lambda\left(z - \frac{1 - x}{1 + x}e^{4x}\right).$$

whose derivatives are zero when

$$2(z - 2) = \lambda,$$

$$2(x - 1) = \frac{4x^2 \cdot 2}{(1 + x)^2}e^{4x}\lambda,$$

$$z = \frac{1 - x}{1 + x}e^{4x},$$

i.e. when

$$z = \frac{1 - x}{1 + x}e^{4x},$$

$$2z(2 - z) = \frac{(1 - x^2)^2}{(1 + x)(2x^2 - 1)}.$$

There are three solutions:

    (I) $x = 0.895$, $z = 1.99$;
    (II) $x = 0.420$, $z = 2.19$;
    (III) $x = -0.980$, $z = 1.98$.

The first clearly gives the largest value for the maximand, $-(x - 1)^2 - (z - 2)^2$, but our previous analysis shows that x does not maximize $U(x, z)$ for this value of z. As a matter of fact, x is a *local* maximum, but not a *global* maximum. The second solution is ineligible on all possible grounds: x is a local minimum of $U(x, z)$. The third solution, on the other hand, has the property that x is a global maximum of $U(x, z)$, so that it does satisfy the constraint of the original problem. But it is not the solution of that problem, and indeed gives a much lower value of the maximand than is actually possible.

This example shows that it is not legitimate to attempt to solve the problem by substituting first-order conditions for the maximization constraint. Furthermore, and this deserves emphasis, the example, though complicated, is in no sense special. Any moderate variation of the functions involved yields a problem with the same properties.

In order to understand the form of the set[6]

$$M = \{(x, z) : x \text{ maximizes } U(x', z)\},$$

in general, we should take U to be a smooth (C^∞) function on $(m+n)$-dimensional Euclidean space. We do not want to examine M for all possible smooth U, but for 'almost all' U, excluding pathological or special cases. In general, for each z, U has a finite number of distinct maxima, $x_i(z)$ $(i = 1, \ldots, r)$. Provided that the matrix U_{xx} of second derivatives is of full rank m at each of these maxima, the x_i are smooth mappings of z. Then

$$U(x_i(z), z) - U(x_1(z), z) = 0, \qquad i = 2, \ldots, r, \tag{15}$$

and also

$$U_x(x_i(z), z) = 0, \qquad i = 1, \ldots, r. \tag{16}$$

Regarding (15) and (16) as equations for $z, x_1, \ldots, x_r$, we have $r - 1 + rm$ equations and $n + rm$ unknowns. That is to say, the set of $(z, x_1(z), \ldots, x_r(z))$ is contained in the inverse image of $(0, \ldots, 0)$ by the mapping

$$(z, x_1, \ldots, x_r) \to (U(x_2, z) - U(x_1, z), \ldots, U(x_r, z) - U(x_1, z), \ldots,$$
$$U_x(x_1, z), \ldots, U_x(x_r, z)),$$

from E^{n+rm} to E^{r-1+rm}. For almost all functions U, $(0, \ldots, 0)$ should be a regular value of this mapping when $x_1, \ldots, x_r$ are distinct. Provided that is the case, there will be a $(n - r + 1)$-dimensional neighborhood of $(z, x_1, \ldots, x_r)$ that also maps into $(0, \ldots, 0)$. In other words the set of z for which U has r distinct maxima is of dimension $n - r + 1$; and the corresponding subset of M has the same dimension. In particular, there are no z with $r > n + 1$, i.e. more than $n + 1$ maxima, for general U.

---

[6] The discussion of M owes a great deal to discussions with Kevin Roberts, who formulated the theorem about the essential maximum to the number of maxima recorded below.

In Mirrlees and Roberts (1980), written after the present chapter, the following theorem was proved:

For almost all[7] C^∞ functions U, the number of distinct maxima is less than or equal to $n+2$ for all z, and the dimension of the set of points of M corresponding to z with r distinct maxima is less than or equal to $n+1-r$.

It should not be supposed that, since dimension falls with the number of distinct maxima, points with a single maximum are almost certain to give the answer in actual optimization problems. Points (x, z) corresponding to r maxima essentially form the boundary to the set of (x, z) corresponding to $r-1$ maxima. Thus, broadly speaking, the solution to an optimizing problem is just as likely to be a value of z with many maxima as with few, subject to the overall bound $n+2$.

The economic significance of this is that an optimum may well leave consumers indifferent among several options, only one of which the government would like to see chosen. Also, the optimum can easily be something of a corner solution. To bring this out, consider how one would have to solve a general problem of the form

$$\left.\begin{array}{l} \text{maximize } W(x, z) \\ \text{subject to: } G(x, z) = 0 \\ \text{and } x \text{ maximizes } U(x, z) \end{array}\right\}. \tag{17}$$

Using the theorem stated above, we can express this in a more convenient form for almost all U. Not only do we know that when x maximizes $U(x, z)$, $U_x(x, z) = 0$, but also, there are only a finite number of x' that maximize U, and these also satisfy $U_x = 0$. Thus, x maximizes U if and only if $U_x = 0$ and

$$\left.\begin{array}{l} U(x, z) \geq U(x', z), \quad \text{all } x' \\ \text{such that: } U_x(x', z) = 0 \end{array}\right\}, \tag{18}$$

and we can have equality in the constraints (18) for at most $n+2$ values of x'. In this way we can replace the constraint 'x maximizes U' by a finite number of equations and inequalities. The problem can therefore be treated as a standard Kuhn–Tucker problem.

Provided that certain regularity conditions are satisfied, it is necessary, for (x, z) to be an optimum, that there exist a scalar λ, an m-vector μ, and scalars v', one for each x' satisfying $U_x = 0$, such that

$$L(x, z) = w + \lambda G + U_x \cdot \mu + \sum v'\{U(x, z) - U(x', z)\} \tag{19}$$

---

[7] The set of such functions contains a countable intersection of open dense sets in the Whitney or strong topology.

have zero derivatives with respect to x and z. The summation is over all x' satisfying $U_x = 0$, and each $v' \geq 0$ with strict inequality only if $U(x, z) = U(x', z)$. Differentiation of L yields

$$W_x + \lambda G_x + U_{xx} \cdot \mu = 0, \tag{20}$$

$$W_z + \lambda G_z + U_{xz} \cdot \mu + \sum v'\{U_z(x, z) - U(x', z)\} = 0. \tag{21}$$

Equation (20) has simplified because the last terms drop out, as $U_x(x, z)$ and $U_x(x', z)$ both vanish.

In principle, the equations we have found are enough to determine a finite number of solutions, one of which is the optimum. The chief difficulty is that the set M and its structure must be known before (21) can be found explicitly. To use the Lagrangean method, we would need to try successively z for which the maximim is unique (when the last terms drop out), then z with two maxima, and so on until all possibilities have been tried. Unfortunately, the determination of the set M of maxima for every z must usually be difficult and requires much computation.

Nevertheless, certain lessons can be drawn. Granted the difficulties in handling the general problem, it is important to find conditions under which it simplifies, particularly under which one can be sure that the optimum occurs where there is a unique maximum for U. It is also important not to be lulled into believing that solutions in these cases have a character that is universally applicable.

One of the most striking features of these problems is that, as the number of control variables (the dimension of z) increases, the possible extent of consumer indifference in the optimum increases. This suggests that, when the government policies are functions, i.e. infinite-dimensional, it can be optimal for consumers to have continuous ranges of indifference. It can even be the case that this idea simplifies the task of solution, because indifference over a range determines the form of optimal policy over the range; just as knowledge that the optimum is at an $(n + 2)$-maximum virtually determines optimal z in the class of problems we have been discussing. On occasion, it is possible to discover quite easily conditions sufficient to imply that the optimum has this form.

3. LUMP-SUM TRANSFERS

In this and the following sections, a common model will be used. It will be useful to establish notation.

$x^h =$ net demand vector (i.e. consumption net of endowment) of consumer,
u^h, $X^h =$ utility function and consumption set of consumer h.

Either there are a finite number of consumers H, or h is continuously distributed and non-negative with density function f.

> y = aggregate net supply vector of private producers,
> Y = aggregate production set,
> y^j = net supply vector of producer j,
> Y^j = production set of producer j,
> z = net supply vector of government, being the public production vector minus the public consumption vector,
> Z = set of feasible z,
> q = prices faced by consumers,
> p = prices faced by private producers.

It will be assumed that u^h is differentiable and concave and X^h convex. This is rather stronger than assuming convex preferences, but convenient. Private production sets are convex unless otherwise stated. Each u^h a strictly increasing function of its arguments.

Let the welfare function be individualistic, i.e.

$$W = \Omega(u^1, \ldots, u^H) \tag{22}$$

in the case of a finite population. W is smooth and an increasing function of all u^h. It is interesting first to analyse the problem when all possible policies are available to government, partly because we can introduce some techniques that prove useful later. If all policies are possible, the government can impose on each consumer separately a budget set $B^h(p)$, and have each producer maximize profits. (There is no interest here in considering more general forms of production control.) Then the constraints in the optimization are

$$\left.\begin{array}{l} x^h \text{ maximizes } u^h(x) \\[4pt] \text{subject to: } x \in B^h(p) \cap X^h \end{array}\right\}, \tag{23}$$

$$\left.\begin{array}{l} y^j \text{ maximizes } p \cdot y \\[4pt] \text{subject to: } y \in Y^j \end{array}\right\}, \tag{24}$$

$$\sum_h x^h = \sum_j y^j + z, \tag{25}$$

$$z \in Z. \tag{26}$$

By the fundamental theorem of welfare economics, it is known that the solution to this complicated looking problem takes the simple form (when every consumer is in the interior of his consumption set at the optimum) of

$$B^h(p) = \{x : p \cdot x - b^h\}, \tag{27}$$

where the scalars b^h satisfy

$$\sum_h b^h = \sum_j p \cdot y^{j^*} + p \cdot z^*, \tag{28}$$

y^{j^*} and z^* being the optimal values of y^j and z.

Using the indirect utility function, we state a rule for the optimal lump-sum transfer b^h. Let

$$v^h(q, b^h) = \max\{u^h(x) : q \cdot x \le b^h, x \in X^h\} \tag{29}$$

and

$$V(q, b^1, \ldots, b^h) = \Omega(v^1(z, b^1), \ldots, v^H(q, b^H)). \tag{30}$$

Then optimal $b^* = (b^{1^*}, \ldots, b^{H^*})$ maximizes

$$V(p, b) \text{ subject to the constraint (28).} \tag{31}$$

The first-order condition for this is that

$$\partial V / \partial b^h = \lambda, \qquad h = 1, \ldots, H, \tag{32}$$

for some scalar λ. This familiar condition may also be expressed by using the expenditure function

$$E^h(q, u^h) = \min \{q \cdot x : u^h(x) \ge u^h\}. \tag{33}$$

With this notation we can say that optimal utility levels $u^* = (u^{1^*}, \ldots, u^{H^*})$ maximize

$$\Omega(u) \quad \text{subject to:} \sum_h E^h(p, u^h) \le \sum_j p \cdot y^{j^*} + p \cdot z^*. \tag{34}$$

The assumption that $u^h(x)$ is a concave function implies that E^h is a convex function of u^h: $E^h_{uu} \ge 0$. The first-order conditions for (34) are

$$\partial \Omega / \partial u^h = \lambda E^h_u. \tag{35}$$

The objections to assuming it possible to make b^h a function of h are, first, that consumers may not choose to give the government correct information about their utility functions; and, second, that, even if consumers were willing to tell the truth, it would be costly to obtain the information. These objections will each be formalized.

To capture the first objection, we need a formulation of welfare with more content. The most powerful welfare functions are those based on the idea that individuals are basically the same, but vary in endowment, abilities, and sensibilities. These differences can be taken to be differences in the significance of trade for utility. A simple formulation (ignoring differences in material endowment) is

$$u^b(x) = u(b_1 x_1, \ldots, b_n x_n), \tag{36}$$

with the consumer described by n parameters $b_1, \ldots, b_n$. If, for example, commodity n is labour, and labour has disutility, larger b_n means labour is harder, or, equivalently, the ability (or inclination) to provide labour is less. Similarly, b_1 can represent the ability to appreciate wine. If individuals are identical, welfare ought to be a symmetrical function of utilities. For concreteness and convenience, take an additive function

$$\Omega(u) = \int u^b f(b_1, \ldots, b_n) db_1, \ldots, db_n. \tag{37}$$

If the government must rely completely on individual report for its knowledge of an individual's b, and individuals are truthful only when they do not lose by it, either B^b must be independent of b (so that the government does not use observations of b), or u^b must be independent of b. We shall see below that, under some plausible assumptions, the latter is the better alternative. It may be more interesting to suppose that the government can obtain information about b by some form of testing. The leading examples are abilities, where an individual can easily pretend to less ability than he truly has, but would find it difficult to prove he has more. (Uncertainties of observation will be mentioned later.) Supposing then that individuals can misreport b_i only by claiming it is greater than in fact it is, an b_i-dependent policy can be administered only if, in the outcome,

$$v(b) = u^b(x^b) \tag{38}$$

is a non-increasing function of b_i. The following result is then of interest.

Theorem 1. *Let the utility function be (36), and the welfare function additive. In the first-best optimum, v is an increasing function of b_i if commodity i is always a normal (i.e. not an inferior) commodity.*

Proof (illustrating the convenience of the expenditure function in these problems). We have seen that, at the optimum,

$$E_u^b(p, v(b)) = \lambda. \tag{39}$$

With the utility function (36), E^b takes the form

$$E^b(p, u) = E\left(\frac{p_1}{b_1}, \ldots, \frac{p_n}{b_n}, u\right). \tag{40}$$

Therefore differentiation of (39) with respect to h_i yields

$$E_{uu} \frac{\partial v}{\partial h_i} - E_{ui} \frac{p_i}{h_i^2} = 0.$$

Thus,

$$E_{uu} \frac{\partial v}{\partial h_i} = \frac{p_i}{h_i} \frac{\partial}{\partial_u} x_i^c, \tag{41}$$

where $x_i^c = (\partial/\partial p_i) E^h$ is the compensated demand function for commodity i. Normality means that $(\partial/\partial u) x_i^c > 0$; and concavity of u implies $E_{uu} > 0$. Therefore (41) implies $\partial v/\partial h_i > 0$, as claimed. $\qquad\square$

This theorem shows how unlikely it is that optimal lump-sum taxation is feasible. But the constraint that v be a non-increasing function of the h_i still implies that all taxation should be lump-sum in character. It does not, in all circumstances, imply that utility should be the same for everyone. The next result includes one of the cases where equal utility is optimal. We go back to a more general form for u^h.

Theorem 2. *Let welfare be individualistic, and consumers be characterized by m parameters $h_1, \ldots, h_m$. If it is required that utility be a non-increasing function of the h_i, the optimal budget sets have the form*

$$B^h = \{x : p \cdot x \le b^h\}.$$

If $m = 1$, and the marginal utility of income at constant prices is a non-decreasing function of h_1, all consumers have the same utility at the optimum.

   Proof (illustrating the use of indifference surfaces; and of convexity inequalities). Let $\xi(x_2, \ldots, x_n, u, h_1, \ldots, h_n)$ be the amount of commodity 1 required to provide utility u when $x_2, \ldots, x_n$ are trade levels in the other commodities; $\xi = \infty$ if u is unattainable; $\xi = 0$ if $x_2, \ldots, x_n$ are already enough to provide more than u. With this notation, the constraints in the optimization problem take the form

$$v(h) = v(h_1, \ldots, h_m) \quad \text{is non-increasing in all arguments,} \tag{42}$$

$$x = y + z, \tag{43}$$

$$y \text{ maximizes } p \cdot Y, \tag{44}$$

$$x_1 = \int \xi(x_2(h), \ldots, x_n(h), v(h), h) f(h) \, dh_1, \ldots, dh_m, \tag{45}$$

$$x_i = \int x_i(h) f(h) \, dh_1, \ldots, dh_n, \qquad i = 1, \ldots, n. \tag{46}$$

We may as well assume that Y admits free disposal, since extra production can be used to increase utility, and therefore welfare, without breaking constraint (42). Fixing v and z at their optimal levels, consider x, defined (45) and (46), as the functions $x_2(\cdot), \ldots, x_n(h)$ vary. We shall never obtain a point $x - z$ in the interior of Y, because if we did it would be possible to change v in such a way as to increase welfare. Therefore the interior of Y does not intersect the set of points $x - z$ with $x_1 \geq \int \xi f d^n h$, $x_i \geq \int x_i(h) f d^n h$. This latter set is convex, since preferences are convex. Therefore we can separate by a hyperplane yielding prices p. These prices satisfy (44), and we also have

$$p_1 \xi(x_2(h), \ldots, x_n(h), v(h), h) + \sum_{i=2}^n p_i x_i(h) = \max_x \qquad (47)$$

for almost all h at the optimum. We may as well satisfy it for all h. Equation (47) implies that $\partial \xi / \partial x_i = -p_i/p_1$ $(i = 2, \ldots, n)$, i.e. that consumers maximize utility subject to budget constraints of the form stated in the theorem.

To prove the second part of the theorem, introduce the expenditure functions $E(p, v(h), h)$, with a single parameter h. Let u^* be the maximum constant utility level consistent with the optimum output levels, and let $v(\cdot)$ be a non-increasing function, which is also consistent with these output levels, consumers always facing prices p. Then

$$\int E(p, u^*, h) f d^n h = \int E(p, v, h) f d^n h. \qquad (48)$$

Since E is a convex function of v,

$$E(p, u^*, h) - E(p, v(h), h) \leq E_u(p, u^*, h)(u^* - v(h)). \qquad (49)$$

Let h_0 be the largest value such that $v(h) \geq u^*$. (If there is none such, u^* yields more welfare than v.) Then, since, by assumption, E_u is a non-increasing function of h,

$$E_u(p, u^*, h)(u^* - v(h)) \leq E_u(p, u^*, h_0)(u^* - v(h)). \qquad (50)$$

Combining (49) and (50), and integrating over h,

$$\int E(p, u^*, h) f d^n h - \int E(p, v, h) f d^n h$$

$$\leq E_u(p, u^*, h) \left\{ \int u^* f d^n h - \int v f d^n h \right\}.$$

Since, by (48), the left-hand side is zero, $\int u^* f d^n h \geq \int v f d^n h$. Therefore, as claimed, the optimum has constant utility. $\qquad \square$

This last argument fails with more than one parameter because there may be no h_0 for which (50) holds. Conditions can be found that imply constant utility, but it looks as if there are cases where it is not optimal. When it is, the theorem implies that it is better to have constant utility than any budget set that is the same for all h. I do not know whether this is always true.

It is obviously unreal to suppose that a government can get perfect information about individual characteristics even when individuals have nothing to lose by reporting it. We can consider a model in which these characteristics are imperfectly observed by government.[8] For simplicity, suppose the population characterized by a simple parameter, h. An individual seems to the government to have characteristic k, but knows he has characteristic h. The distribution of h and k, which is not degenerate, is described by a joint density function $f(h, k)$. With an additive welfare function, and indirect utility function $v(p, b, h)$, welfare in a competitive equilibrium is

$$W = \iint v(p, b(k), h) f(h, k) \, dh \, dk. \tag{51}$$

Aggregate demand is

$$\iint x(p, b(k), h) f(h, k) \, dh \, dk. \tag{52}$$

Theorem 3. *Let v_b be a strictly monotonic function of h (for each p and b); and let there be a commodity, say $i = 1$, for which x_1 is a strictly monotonic function of h. If the frontier of Y is smooth, then no competitive equilibrium with only lump-sum taxation is optimal.*

Proof. We first determine optimal lump-sum transfers given that there are no other taxes. The derivative of welfare with respect to $b(k)$ is

$$W_k = \int v_b(p, b(k), h) f(h, k) \, dh.$$

The derivative of $p \cdot y$ with respect to $b(k)$ is

$$p \cdot \int x_b(p, b(k), h) f(h, k) \, dh = \int f(h, k) \, dh.$$

Since Y is smooth at y, transfers b are optimal if and only if W_k is proportional to $\int f(h, k) \, dh$. Thus, for some λ,

$$\int v_b(p \cdot b(k), h) f(h, k) \, dh = \lambda \int f(h, k) \, dh. \tag{53}$$

With optimal transfers, λ is the change in W made possible (by changing b) if $p \cdot y$ is changed by a unit.

---

[8] The material on imperfect lump-sum taxation is joint work with Peter Diamond.

It will now be shown that a change in p_1 (corresponding to commodity taxation of the first commodity), along with appropriate changes in b, can increase welfare. The derivative of W with respect to p_1 is

$$\int\int \frac{\partial v}{\partial p_1} f \, dh \, dk = -\int\int v_b x_1 f \, dh \, dk.$$

The derivative of aggregate demand is $\int\int(\partial/\partial p_1)xf \, dh \, dk$, whose value at prices p is

$$p \cdot \int\int \frac{\partial}{\partial p_1} xf \, dh \, dk = -\int\int x_1 f \, dh \, dk.$$

It will be shown that

$$\int\int v_b x_1 f \, dh \, dk \neq \lambda \int x_1 f \, dh \, dk. \tag{54}$$

It follows that it cannot be optimal for p_1 to be the consumer price for commodity 1. This will prove the theorem.

To demonstrate (54), we use (53) to obtain

$$\int\int (v_b - \lambda) x_1 f \, dh \, dk = \int\int (v_b - \lambda) \{ x_1(p, b(k), h) \\ -x_1(p, b(k), h_k) \} f \, dh \, dk, \tag{55}$$

where we can define h_k by $v_b(p, b(k), h_k) = \lambda$. Since $v_b - \lambda$ is strictly monotonic, and so is x_1, for each k, the right-hand side of (55) is not zero. This proves (54) and completes the proof of the theorem.

The assumption that the private production set has a smooth frontier merely excludes pathological cases. The general lesson is that imperfect information normally implies that non-lump-sum taxation ought to be used. In the model here, it would usually be desirable to use lump-sum transfers as well. There is one problem with lump-sum taxation based on inaccurate information which is of great practical importance and is hidden by the model, or at least the way it has been handled. Suppose, to fix ideas, that consumer prices are p. One would anticipate that for certain values of h and k there will be no feasible consumption plan satisfying $p \cdot x \leq b(k)$. Men of high ability should pay large taxes: what should be done about men of apparently high ability who are unable to earn much, and how can those be distinguished who simply do not feel like it?

Throughout this section, and throughout subsequent sections, it is assumed that the government is well informed about the population, as a statistical aggregate. The government may be unable to use information about an individual as a basis for applying policy to him, but the construction of policies is based on knowledge of his characteristics. This dichotomy between individual and statistical information cannot be strictly justified. In a small population, any information an individual gives affects his own fate. This leads to the theory of preference revelation,[9] which is however of no value to the student of public policy, since it uses only the uselessly weak criterion of Pareto efficiency. A welfare-theoretic treatment of the issues, using a Bayesian formulation, would be of interest. But for large populations, it seems reasonable to use a model in which there is fixed prior information about the distribution of characteristics in the population. It is unlikely that for most policy issues this will give misleading results.

It will now be assumed that there is no information basis for lump-sum taxation, because we thereby concentrate attention on the central difficulties. Lump-sum taxation is easily introduced into the theory. Something will be said about this later.

4. PRODUCERS AND EFFICIENCY

In the standard general model of competitive equilibrium, consumers are related to producers in two ways: as traders, and as owners receiving pure profits. If there are constant returns to scale in private production, equilibrium profits are zero. We shall make this assumption for the present and return to it below. In the absence of profits, consumers are completely described by their utility functions, consumption sets, and budget constraints. If government has no information allowing it to discriminate among individuals, the budget set B, consisting of those demand vectors that are available to the consumer, is the same for all individuals. For example, if there are commodity taxes proportional to trades and a uniform lump-sum tax (often called a poll tax or subsidy), the budget set is

$$B = \{x : q \cdot x \leq b\}, \tag{56}$$

where $q = p + t$. Notice the important point that we can regard q and b as the control variables rather than t and b. In general, B can be taken to be the control variable rather than B as a function of p.

In Sections 6 and 7 we shall analyse cases where the government is not further constrained in its choice of B, which may be defined by linear inequalities as in (56), or some more general set. In most of optimal tax theory, B has been assumed subject to constraint, for example that it be linear, or even more severely constrained, with some commodities untaxed. In the present section, it is not the choice of B that is the focus of interest, but the control of private producers and the choice of government expenditures and production plans. The rules that should govern these choices depend on the

---

[9] See Groves and Ledyard (1977).

extent to which the government is constrained in the control it can apply to consumers. One of the lessons of optimal tax theory that matters most in practice is that optimal production rules are not as much affected by the existence of constraints on consumer taxation, and in particular on lump-sum taxation, as might once have been thought.

Theorem 4 (Efficiency Theorem for Linear Taxation). *Let the welfare function be individualistic. If the government is constrained to use linear taxation, i.e. to choose a budget set of the form (56), then at the optimum, $y + z$ is in the frontier of the aggregate net production set $Y + Z$. This result is true even if it is possible to subject producers to differential commodity taxation.*

Proof (simple topology). Suppose first that all production is under government control, so that the optimization problem is

$$
\left.
\begin{aligned}
&\text{maximize } W \\
&\text{subject to: } \sum_b x^b \in Y + Z \\
&x^b \text{ maximizes } u^b(x) \text{ for } x \in X^b \\
&\quad\quad \text{and} \quad q \cdot x \le b
\end{aligned}
\right\}.
\tag{57}
$$

Under our concavity assumption, the maximizing x^b is a continuous function of q and b. If the solution to the problem is q^*, b^*, no welfare-increasing variation of q and b yields feasible aggregate demands. In particular, if $b > b^*$ and q^* remains fixed,

$$
\sum x^b(q^*, b) \notin Y + Z.
$$

Since Σx^b is continuous in b, it follows that

$$
y^* + z^* = \sum x^b(q^*, b^*) \in \text{ frontier of } Y + Z.
$$

This implies that y^* is in the frontier of Y, and, by convexity, that there exists p such that y^* maximizes $p \cdot Y$. Therefore the optimum for problem (57) is also the optimum for the more constrained optimizations where production is private and competitive with or without differential taxation. This proves the theorem.

The proof of the theorem is pretty trivial. The result obviously holds whenever the range of budget sets that can be imposed on consumers by government is sufficiently wide that arbitrarily small expansions of any budget set are possible. In particular, the addition of new tax and control possibilities leaves the conclusion unaffected. The importance of the result is that it implies simple rules for shadow prices. There are shadow prices s for z^* in the frontier of Z if Z is convex and s are support prices at z^*, i.e. z^* maximizes $s \cdot Z$;

or if the frontier of Z is smooth at z^*, and s defines a tangent hyperplane at z^*. In either case, we have:

Corollary. *Under the assumptions of Theorem 4, optimal public net production z^* is in the frontier of Z, and if shadow prices exist, there are shadow prices which are equal to producer prices at the optimum.*

The theorem and its corollary imply that, when the assumptions of constant returns, competitive conditions for private production, unconstrained linear taxation, and individualistic welfare are satisfied, there should be no taxation of intermediate goods, i.e. of trade between producers, and that public and private discount rates for production decisions should be the same.

It is interesting to enquire what happens to the efficiency result when the assumptions of the theorem are relaxed. Individualistic welfare is not an issue: it would be hard to devise interesting welfare assumptions for which the result did not hold. I shall comment on non-constant returns, non-competitive conditions, and tax constraints in turn.

If private producers do not have constant returns, we can restore constant returns by defining new dummy commodities, a fixed factor for each producer, owned by consumers in the same proportions as they have shares in the firm.[10] In other words, the firm is itself regarded as a commodity. Since these fixed factors do not affect utility, utility functions are not strictly concave in terms of all commodities, but supplies are continuous functions, provided we make the usual assumption that consumers are prepared to supply even when the price is zero.[11] Then the theorem remains valid. This means that efficiency holds if the fixed factors can be taxed independently, or, equivalently, if profit taxes are levied at possibly different rates on different firms.

If all profits have to be taxed at the same proportional rate, the relative value of different shares to the consumer is the same as the relative values of the firms, measured in producer prices. Thus, the budget sets that can be imposed on consumers are constrained by the producer prices ruling. (Taxation on transactions between firms can restore the effect of firm-specific profit taxation, but this also violates the uniform treatment of firms.) A similar point might be made about the difficulty of taxing labour income derived from different firms at different rates, although labour for different firms should often be treated as different commodities. The fixed-factor aspect of

---

[10] Avinash Dixit has encouraged me to take this approach.

[11] If a firm that could exist does not, it may be hard for the government to take advantage of its potential existence in setting taxes and subsidies. If it cannot, it is possible to construct examples in which the optimum is inefficient. There are even examples where no optimum exists. See Mirrlees (1972). In that paper, I also discuss briefly the case of what are there called managerial inputs. In the terminology used above, it is assumed impossible to distinguish between the managerial input and the fixed input for tax purposes. In this case efficiency is generally undesirable. Hahn's (1973, p. 104) argument to the contrary is fallacious because it ignores the effect of price changes on the marginal profitability of managerial effort.

the issue is really beside the point. In any case, profits can be interpreted as the return to the initial entrepreneur or inventor who set up the firm (and perhaps took his gains by floating the firm as a corporation). Then they are returns to a variable factor, and not particularly different from prices in any other market.

What comes out of this discussion is the importance of the assumption that consumer prices (or equivalently tax rates) can be chosen independently of producer prices. Governments do not act as though this were true. Then the efficiency theorem is not valid—though it may be a good approximation.

Non-competitive behaviour by firms does not change the efficiency theorem, but rather its interpretation, provided that any profits can be taxed as desired. In this case Y should be interpreted not as the production set of private producers but as the set of net supply vectors that can be elicited as producer taxation and other government controls vary. Then shadow prices for government production decisions can be obtained as the tangent hyperplane to the new set Y, and will not in general be simply related to producer prices.

Constraints on the tax powers of government have been much analysed in the literature.[12] We have seen that they may be implied by uniform tax treatment of producers. Many of the constraints dealt with in the literature are introduced without any compelling reason. The non-taxability of certain commodities and the imposition of profit constraints on public producers may be instanced. By and large, these constraints are a way of capturing administrative considerations rather than limitations imposed by lack of information. Ideally, a theory of administration and implementation would be developed before considering what are the most relevant and interesting constraints on taxation to model.

Another reason why tax constraints are important is that governments are often prepared to seek advice on public production and expenditure decisions when they are not prepared, in the medium run, to change a tax system whose form they believe to be constrained by its political image, and perceived effect on particular groups. The last result of this section gives some information about shadow prices under circumstances where the efficiency theorem does not apply. It takes as premiss the optimality of efficiency within the public sector, which is probably valid under very general circumstances, since some policy change would almost always increase welfare if the resources were available, though no theorem on this point seems to be available.

Theorem 5. *Let policy possibilities be constrained only by producer prices (not quantities). Suppose that for any optimum, z^* is in the frontier of Z. If y^0 is the production vector for a competitive, constant returns producer in the optimum,*

---

[12] Dasgupta and Stiglitz (1971). Guesnerie (1975) deals with non-competitive producer behaviour. The shadow price theorem (Theorem 5) comes from Diamond and Mirrlees (1976).

there exist shadow prices s for z^* such that

$$s \cdot y^o = 0. \tag{58}$$

Proof. Let θ be a real number such that $|\theta| < 1$. If the producer who has been singled out produced θy^o and the public sector produced $z^* + (1 - \theta)y^o$, there would be no change in policies and no effective change in equilibrium. Then welfare is unchanged. The producer in question is perfectly willing to produce θy^o instead of y^o. Thus, $z^* + (1 - \theta)y^o$ would be another optimum for public production if it were feasible. It follows that

$$z^* + (1 - \theta)y^o \in \text{frontier of } Z, \qquad |\theta| < 1.$$

Therefore there exists a tangent hyperplane at z^* containing all vectors $z^* + (1 - \theta)y^o$. Let the shadow prices defined by this hyperplane be s. Then $s \cdot y^o = 0$, as was claimed.

This result is of use wherever there are a number of sectors which can be adequately modelled as constant-returns competitive sectors. It implies in particular that shadow prices of commodities traded at fixed prices in world markets are proportional to border prices, a result useful in benefit–cost analysis. It must be emphasized that (58) is not applicable if in the optimum the constant returns firm should close down: it is not always valid to use y^o derived from input–output tables for an existing economy.

5. LINEAR TAXATION

As we have seen, there is no loss of generality in assuming that private-sector producers have constant returns to scale. With this assumption, the efficiency theorem (Theorem 1) means that the optimal choice of linear taxation is achieved by finding q^* and b^* that maximize $V(q, b)$ subject to $x(q, b) \in Y + Z$, where $x(q, b)$ is the aggregate net demand function of consumers. It must be emphasized that $q \geq 0$ in this optimization. If production sets had smooth frontiers, there would be a unique shadow price vector s associated with $x^* = x(q^*, b^*)$. Since in that case the aggregate production frontier is approximately given by $s \cdot y = s \cdot x^*$ in the neighbourhood of the optimum, we would expect that the derivatives V_q and V_b should be proportional to $s \cdot x_q$ and $s \cdot x_b$ at the optimum, provided the optimum is not on the boundary in price space, i.e. q^* is strictly positive.

To obtain a general theorem yielding these conditions, we need certain regularity conditions. A fairly simple one will be used here: we introduce the following assumption, which says, in a rather strong way, that inefficiency is feasible in the neighbourhood of the optimum:

(I) There exists y^o in the relative interior of Y and continuously differentiable functions $q^o(\theta)$, $b^o(\theta)$ defined for $0 \leq \theta \leq 1$ such that $q^o(\theta) \geq 0$ and

$$x(q^o(\theta), b^o(\theta)) = (1 - \theta)x^* + \theta y^o. \tag{59}$$

Notice that $q^o(0) = q^*$, $b^o(0) = b^*$. When $q^* \gg 0$ (i.e. $q_i^* > 0$ for all i), (I) is implied simply by the assumption:

(J) The matrix $(x_q(q^*, b^*), x_b(q^*, b^*))$ is of full rank.

(J) implies that all x in a neighborhood of x^* correspond to some (q, b) with $q \geq 0$; and (I) is therefore trivially satisfied, provided that Y consists of more than a single point. This assumption (J) is a fairly acceptable one, which would be satisfied in almost all cases,[13] but it is insufficient when q^* has zero components. Assumption (I) is by no means the weakest assumption that would work in the following theorem, but it yields a fairly simple proof, and problems not satisfying it are unlikely to arise in practice.

Theorem 6. *Let V and x be continuously differentiable functions of q and b for $q \geq 0$, and Y a convex set. If q^*, b^* maximize V subject to $x \in Y$, and assumption (I) is satisfied, there exists a non-zero vector s and a scalar λ such that*

$$x^* \text{ maximizes } s \cdot Y \tag{60}$$

$$V_q(q^*, b^* \leq \lambda s \cdot x_q(q^*, b^*), \tag{61}$$

$$V_b(q^*, b^*) = \lambda s \cdot x_b(q^*, b^*). \tag{62}$$

Since V and x are homogeneous of degree zero in q and b,

$$[V_q - s \cdot x_q] \cdot q + [V_b - s \cdot x_b]b = 0.$$

Therefore, q^* being non-negative, (61) and (62) imply that

$$\frac{\partial V}{\partial q_i}(q^*, b^*) = s \frac{\partial x}{\partial q_i}(q^*, b^*) \qquad \text{when} \quad q_i^* > 0. \tag{63}$$

Proof. We work in the smallest linear manifold L containing Y. Let C be the cone of non-zero vectors s in L such that x^* maximizes $s \cdot Y$. Since y^o is in the interior of Y in L, $s \cdot y^o < s \cdot x^*$ for all s in C. Now (59) implies, differentiating with respect to θ and setting $\theta = 0$, that

$$x_q(q^*, b^*)q^{o'}(0) + x_b(q^*, b^*)b^{o'}(0) = y^o - x^*. \tag{64}$$

$q_i^{o'}(0) \geq 0$ for any i such that $q_i^o(0) = q_i^* = 0$. By multiplying $q(\theta)$, $b(\theta)$ by a positive scalar if necessary (which does not change $x(q(\theta), b(\theta))$), we can ensure that $q_i^{o'}(0) \geq 0$ for all i. Thus, (64) implies that there exists $a^o \geq 0$ and α^o such that

$$x_q^* \cdot a^o + x_b^* \alpha^o = y^o - x^*.$$

---

[13] (J) is not satisfied when there are fixed factors, but (I) generally is.

Since $s \cdot y^o < s \cdot x^*$ for all s in C, this implies that

$$s \cdot x_q^* \cdot a^o + s \cdot x_b^* \alpha^o < 0, \qquad s \in C. \tag{65}$$

This inequality will prove to be of crucial importance in the proof.

Consider smooth functions $q(\theta)$, $b(\theta)$ $(0 \le \theta \le 1)$ such that $q(0) = q^*$, $b(0) = b^*$, $a = q'(0) \ge 0$, $\alpha = b'(0)$. If

$$V_q(q^*, b^*) \cdot a + V_b(q^*, b^*) \cdot \alpha > 0, \tag{66}$$

$V(q(\theta), b(\theta)) > V(q^*, b^*)$ for all small θ. Consequently

$$x(q(\theta), b(\theta)) \notin Y.$$

It follows that, for some $s \in C$,

$$s \cdot x_q(q^*, b^*) \cdot a + s \cdot x_b(q^*, b^*) \alpha \ge 0. \tag{67}$$

Thus, (66) implies (67) for some $s \in C$. Equivalently,

$$s \cdot x_q^* \cdot a + s \cdot x_b^* \alpha < 0, \qquad \text{all} \quad s \in C, \qquad \text{and} \quad a \ge 0, \tag{68}$$

implies

$$V_q^* \cdot a + V_b^* \alpha \le 0. \tag{69}$$

Suppose it were only true that

$$s \cdot x_q^* \cdot a + s \cdot x_b^* \alpha \le 0, \qquad \text{all} \quad s \in C, \qquad \text{and} \quad a \ge 0, \tag{70}$$

Then for any positive number γ, (68) is satisfied by $a' = a + \gamma a^o$ and $\alpha' = \alpha + \gamma \alpha^o$. This follows from (65). Then (69) holds for a' and α'. Letting $\gamma \to 0$, we see that (69) also holds for a and α.

Since (70) implies (69), we can apply the duality theorem for convex cones to deduce that the vector (V_q^*, V_b^*) is in the closure of the cone

$$D = \{(s \cdot x_q^* - d, s \cdot x_b^*): s \in C, d \ge 0\}.$$

In other words, there exists a scalar λ and $s \in C$ such that

$$V_q^* \le \lambda s \cdot x_q^*, \qquad V_b^* = \lambda s \cdot x_b^*.$$

The scalar λ must be inserted to allow for the (exceptional) possibility that $\lambda = 0$. $\qquad\qquad\square$

Most of the literature on optimal commodity taxation is concerned with manipulating and interpreting the first-order conditions of this theorem.

Many papers have been written on the case of identical consumers (with identical endowments) with $b = 0$. Since it is hard to see why b must be zero, this case seems to be of little practical interest. In the case of identical consumers, the conditions obtained by using the direct utility function and constraining maximization by the first-order conditions for consumer choice are of some interest, particularly for additively separable utility,[14] but the indirect utility approach seems to be much more useful for the many-consumer economy.

The chief manipulations used in interpreting (61) and (62) are the following. If welfare is individualistic,

$$V(q, b) = \Omega(v^1(q, b), \ldots, v^H(q, b)),$$

and, writing Ω_h for $\partial\Omega/\partial v^h$,

$$V_q = \sum \Omega_h v_q^h = -\sum \Omega_h v_b^h x^h = -\sum \beta_h x^h, \tag{71}$$

where $\beta_h = \Omega_h v_b^h$ is often called the 'welfare weight' or 'marginal social utility of income'. Equation 71 says that $-V_q$ is a weighted sum of demands. One also finds that

$$V_b = \sum \beta_h. \tag{72}$$

Thus, $-V_q/V_b$ is a weighted average of demands, and this interpretation encourages one to divide (61) by (62).

The right-hand sides of (61) and (62) can be written, interpreting $q - s = t$ as tax rates, as

$$s \cdot x_q = -(q - s) x_q - x$$
$$= -\frac{\partial}{\partial t}[t \cdot x(s + t, b) - b], \tag{73}$$

$$s \cdot x_b = -(q - s) x_b + 1$$
$$= -\frac{\partial}{\partial b}[t \cdot x(s + t, b) - b]. \tag{74}$$

Writing

$$T(t, b, s) = t \cdot x(s + t, b) - b, \tag{75}$$

for the net revenues of government, (73) and (74) can be written as

$$s \cdot x_q = -T_t, \qquad s \cdot x_b = -T_b,$$

---

[14] Atkinson and Stiglitz (1972).

and the first-order conditions (61) and (62) become

$$\sum \beta_h x^h \geq \lambda T_t, \tag{76}$$

$$\sum \beta_h = -\lambda T_b. \tag{77}$$

Assuming $q \gg 0$, $\lambda > 0$ for emphasis, and dividing (76) by (77),

$$\sum \beta_h x^h \Big/ \sum \beta_h = (\partial b/\partial t)_T \text{ constant}. \tag{78}$$

In words, the welfare-weighted average of demands should be equal to the constant-revenue effect of tax rate changes on the general subsidy b.

Another manipulation should be mentioned, though it may have been overrated. Writing x^{ch} for the compensated demand functions, we have

$$
\begin{aligned}
s \cdot x_q^h &= -(q - s)\, x_q^h - x^h \\
&= -t \cdot x_q^{ch} + t \cdot x_b^h x^h - x^h \\
&= -x_q^{ch} \cdot t - (1 - t \cdot x_b^h) x^h,
\end{aligned}
\tag{79}
$$

by Slutsky symmetry. Now $x_q^{ch} \cdot t$ is, to a first-order approximation, the changes in demands brought about by the introduction of taxes, provided income effects are ignored. One can also interpret $x_q^{ch} \cdot t = [(\partial/\partial\theta)x^{ch}(s + \theta t, b)]_{\theta=1}$ as showing the effects on compensated demand of intensification of the tax system. Thus, (61) implies that

$$\sum_h \left\{\beta_h - \lambda\left(1 - t \cdot x_b^h\right)\right\} x^h \geq \sum_h x_q^{ch} \cdot t. \tag{80}$$

The welfare weights on demands are here modified to take account of the revenue effects of changes in the consumer's lump-sum income. Equation (62) implies that

$$\sum_h \left\{\beta_h - \lambda\left(1 - t \cdot x_b^h\right)\right\} = 0. \tag{81}$$

It follows from (81) that the left-hand side of (80) is the covariance of x^h, and the adjusted weights (called the *social marginal utility of income* by Diamond),

$$\gamma_h = \beta_h - \lambda(1 - t \cdot x_b^h). \tag{82}$$

Among the problems in this area that seem to be of theoretical interest, mention should be made of separability questions, as to the conditions under which some commodities should be untaxed, or groups of commodities taxed at the same rates. In this connection, it is important to notice that in the model there are always many equivalent tax systems. If q^*, b^*, and s are optimal consumer prices and subsidy and shadow prices, it is optimal to set producer prices

$$p = \mu s,$$

and tax rates

$$t = vq^* - \mu s,$$

while paying a general uniform subsidy

$$b = vb^*.$$

This tax system is optimal for any positive μ and v. In general, any commodity can be made an untaxed commodity by suitable choice of μ and v. If the natural interpretation of a problem, e.g. untaxed fixed factors representing the absence of profit taxation, imposes part of the normalization, the tax system can no longer be chosen so freely. This point has sometimes led to confusion and error.

It is also interesting to enquire how the optimal tax rules are altered when there are constraints on the choice of linear tax systems, for example when certain goods cannot be taxed. In such problems, the private producers may, and usually should, face prices that are not proportional to shadow prices s, and it is useful to speak of consumer taxes $q - s$ and producer taxes $p - s$, although the constraint may take the form of requiring that they be equal for certain commodities.[15]

In the model discussed, there has been no dependence of consumer utilities on public expenditures, that is, no role for what are called public goods. If such expenditures are the sole responsibility of government, and their provision is not associated with new controls on consumers, they are easily accommodated in the model. We simply write $V(q, b, g)$, $x(q, b, g)$, where g is public consumption expenditure. The same methods as were used to establish the first-order conditions for optimal taxation prove that it is necessary for optimality that

$$V_g = \lambda(s \cdot x_g + s). \tag{83}$$

If welfare is individualistic, this can be rewritten, as before,

$$\sum \beta_h m^h = \lambda(-t \cdot x_g + s),$$

where $m^h = -(\partial b^h / \partial g)_{uh \text{ constant}}$, is the marginal value of the public expenditures at constant q. Thus, at the optimum,

$$s = \frac{1}{\lambda} \sum \beta_h m^h + t \cdot x_g. \tag{84}$$

---

[15] Dasgupta and Stiglitz (1971). This work is clarified, and to some extent corrected, by Munk (1977).

The revenue effect could in practice by very important. A revenue gain arising from provision of the good strengthens the case for it.

6. NONLINEAR TAXATION IN A ONE-DIMENSIONAL POPULATION

So long as the government is constrained to choose linear tax systems, consumers, provided they have convex preferences, have well-defined consumption choices, so that the maximization constraint defines a nice set. If there is no constraint on the tax system, other than independence of individual information, it may be desirable to impose a budget set which leaves some consumers indifferent among widely different consumption plans. For a finite population we intuitively expect that this will be optimal. The most able consumer need be no better off than if he did the same as the next most able consumer, but in general the government would want him to do something different, i.e. choose a different point on the same indifference surface.

The case of a large finite population seems unlikely to be of much interest, because computation would be extremely demanding. Accordingly, we go to the continuum case, where under some circumstances it is to be expected that the optimum budget set can be defined by nice functions. The population is described by a non-negative scalar parameter h with density function f. The allocations that can be brought about by government policy are given by

$$x(h) \text{ maximizes } u(x, h) \quad \text{for} \quad x \in X^h \cap B, \tag{85}$$

for some set B. The first task is to find more manageable control variables than the set B. One way of doing this would be to single out a numeraire good and express B by the inequality

$$x_1 \le c(x_2, \ldots, x_n). \tag{86}$$

This approach turns out to be extremely complicated, and an alternative must be devised. The difficulty with using the function c in (86) as the control variable seems to be that variations in it can have complicated effects on the variables of the problem.

An approach that is manageable is to define the function

$$v(h) = \max\{u(x, h) : x \in X^h \cap B\}, \tag{87}$$

and use an 'envelope theorem' for it. If the maximizing x is a differentiable function of h, and $x(h)$ is always in the interior of X^h,

$$v(h_1) \ge u(x(h_2), h_1), \tag{88}$$

at least for h_2 near h_1. This is because, B being independent of $h, x(h_2)$ is available to a consumer of type h_1 if he wants it. Inequality (88) implies that, as h_1 varies, $v(h_1) - u(x(h_2), h_1)$ attains a local minimum (which happens to be zero) when $h_1 = h_2$. It follows that

$$v'(h) = u_h(x(h), h). \tag{89}$$

If (89) were equivalent to (85) for some B, we should have reduced our maximization constraint to a simple differential equation, which ought not to be too difficult to handle; and is in any case the kind of constraint met with in control theory.

The argument leading to (89) leaned heavily on the unwarranted assumption that $x(h)$, and consequently $v(h)$, is a differentiable function of h. There were also some loose ends about the consumption sets. A precise lemma is needed. Before stating it, some standing assumptions about utility functions and consumption sets are introduced. These lay down some standard properties, and insist that as h increases the consumption set expands in a very regular way.

(C$_1$) u is a continuously differentiable function of x and h, concave in x.
(C$_2$) X^h is a convex set; and for all $h, k, k > h$, the closure of X^h is contained in X^k.
(C$_3$) For all x in X^h there exists $\epsilon > 0$ such that $x \in X^k$ when $|k - h| < \epsilon$.
(B) $X^h \cap \{x: u(x, k) \le u(x^o, k)\}$ is bounded if $h < k$, and $x^o \in X^k$.

The first assumption requires no comment, nor does the first part of (C$_2$). The second part says that X^h is a non-decreasing function of h and actually increases along any 'open' part of its boundary. (C$_3$) requires that X^h vary continuously with h and that 'closed' parts of the boundary remain fixed. The last assumption is a little weaker than the requirement that indifference hypersurfaces be bounded. It allows the possibility that the indifference hypersurface $u(x, k) = u(x^o, k)$ is asymptotic to an 'open' part of the consumption frontier, but only if that part of the frontier is moving outwards, even at infinity.

The assumptions are satisfied, for example, by a function u satisfying (C$_1$) with $X^h = \{-h < x_1 \le 0, x_i \ge 0, i = 2, \ldots, n\}$, and all indifference surfaces cutting the coordinate planes $x_i = 0$ when $i = 2, \ldots, n$. (Think of commodity 1 as labour.) In effect, bigger h is now taken to mean greater ability, unlike the special cases in Section 3 where it was convenient to use the opposite convention.

Assumption (B) is unduly strong, but it is hard to see how to prove the result we want without something like it.

Lemma 1. *Let the above assumptions hold. If there exists B such that, for all h, $x(h)$ maximizes $u(x, h)$ for $x \in X^h \cap B$, and $v(h) = u(x(h), h)$,*

$$v(h) - v(0) = \int_0^h u_h(x(k), k)\, dk. \tag{90}$$

Proof. Let $\eta > 0$. It will first be shown that the set

$$A = \{(x(k), k') : 0 \le k, k' \le h + \eta\}$$

is bounded. Let $h_1 > h + \eta$. Since for all k, $x(k) \in B$, and $x(k) \in X^{h_1}$ for $k \le h + \eta$,

$$u(x(k), h_1) \le u(x(h_1), h_1), \qquad k \le h + \eta.$$

Therefore

$$x(k) \in X^{h+\eta} \cap \{x : u(x, h_1) \le u(x(h_1), h_1)\},$$

and is bounded, by assumption (B). Thus the set A is bounded. It follows that the partial derivative $u_h(x(k), k')$ is bounded in A, and thence, by the mean value theorem, that

$$\alpha_\epsilon(k) = \tfrac{1}{3}\{u(x(k), k + \epsilon) - u(x(k), k)\}$$

is bounded for $0 \le k \le h$, $|\epsilon| < \eta$, $k + \epsilon \ge 0$.

Since $\alpha_\epsilon(k) \to u_h(x(k), k)$ as $\epsilon \to 0$, Lebesgue's theorem on bounded convergence implies that

$$\lim_{\epsilon \to 0} \int_\eta^h \alpha_\epsilon(k)\, dk = \int_\eta^h u_h(x(k), k)\, dk. \tag{91}$$

Now

$$\epsilon \int_\eta^h \alpha_\epsilon(k)\, dk = \int_\eta^h \{u(x(k), k + \epsilon) - u(x(k), k)\}\, dk$$

$$\le \int_\eta^h \{v(k + \epsilon) - v(k)\}\, dk$$

$$= \int_0^\epsilon \{v(h + x) - v(\eta + x)\}\, dx.$$

Therefore

$$\lim_{\epsilon \to 0+} \frac{1}{\epsilon} \int_0^\epsilon \{v(h + x) - v(\eta + x)\}\, dx$$

$$\ge \lim_{\epsilon \to 0} \int_\eta^h \alpha_\epsilon(k)\, dk$$

$$\ge \lim_{\epsilon \to 0-} \frac{1}{\epsilon} \int_0^\epsilon \{v(h + x) - v(\eta + x)\}\, dx.$$

The left-hand and right-hand limits exist and are both equal to $v(h) - v(\eta)$, since v is a continuous function. Therefore, from (91), we have

$$v(h) - v(\eta) = \int_{\eta}^{h} u_h(x(k), k)\, dk.$$

Finally we let $\eta \to 0$, and the lemma is proved.

The strategy that will now be followed is to use the lemma to prove that certain conditions are *sufficient* for optimality. Naturally this can be proved only under rather strong assumptions on the utility function; but, since sufficiency theorems are of the first value in doing computations, the restrictions are worth their cost. To motivate the sufficiency conditions, I shall first derive them in a rather heuristic way.

We saw in Section 3 that, under plausible assumptions, the first-best optimum requires that utility decrease with ability. This suggests that the constraint (90), which (partially) expresses the constraint that B be uniform, works as an inequality preventing $v(h)$ from being too low in relation to $v(0)$,

$$v(h) - v(0) - \int_{0}^{h} u_h(x(k), k)\, dk \geq 0. \tag{92}$$

In this form it is a linear constraint in v. If we are to apply the ideas of programming theory to obtain sufficient conditions, the left-hand side of the inequality should be a concave function of the control variables. This suggests that we treat $v(\cdot)$ as one of the control variables, and eliminate one of the commodities. Specifically, let us treat commodity one as numeraire, denoting it by ξ, and write x' for the vector of commodities 2 to n. Then ξ is defined as a function of x', v and h by

$$v = u(\xi, x', h). \tag{93}$$

It is readily shown that (C_1) implies that ξ is a *convex* function of x' and v, and a (62) implies that function of all the variables.

With this transformation, v and x' are to be regarded as the control variables. The assumption that will let the sufficiency theorem go through is

(CON') $u_h(\xi(x', v, h), x', h)$ is a convex function of x and v.

As it stands this is not in satisfactory form. It is equivalent to:

(CON) For any vector a, $(\partial/\partial h)(a \cdot u_{xx}(x, h) \cdot a/u_{\xi}(x, h)) \geq 0$.

In words, this states that the degree of concavity of u (which is measured by $-a \cdot u_{xx} \cdot a$) does not increase, relative to the marginal utility of numeraire, when h increases. The condition is numeraire-dependent. To have the best chance of applying the sufficiency theorem successfully, one should choose as numeraire a commodity such that $u_{\xi h}/u_{\xi}$ is as large as possible, i.e. the commodity for which $\partial(u_{x'}/u_{\xi})/\partial h \leq 0$.

To prove that (CON') and (CON) are equivalent, one makes a routine change of variables. Writing $w = (v, x')$, $x = (\xi, x')$, and $\psi(w, h) = u_h(x, h)$, we have $u_{hxx} = w_x \cdot \psi_{ww} \cdot w_x + \psi_w \cdot w_{xx}$ (subscripts denoting differentiation). It is easily seen that $\psi_w \cdot w_{xx} = (u_{h\xi}/u_\xi)u_{xx}$. Thus, ψ_{ww} is positive semi-definite if and only if

$$u_{hxx} - \left(\frac{u_{h\xi}}{u_\xi}\right)u_{xx} = u_\xi \frac{\partial}{\partial h}\left(\frac{u_{xx}}{u_\xi}\right)$$

is positive semi-definite. The equivalence of (CON) and (CON') follows at once.

Assume an additive welfare function $\int vf\, dh$, and consider the problem

$$\left.\begin{array}{l}\text{maximizes } \displaystyle\int vf\, dh \\[2ex] \text{subject to (92) and } \displaystyle\left(\int \xi(x', v, h)f\, dh, \int x'f\, dh\right) \in Y\end{array}\right\}. \tag{94}$$

Following our work on the linear problem, it should be legitimate to replace the production constraint (94) by

$$\int \{\xi(x', v, h) + s' \cdot x'\}f\, dh \leq \alpha, \tag{95}$$

where the shadow price of numeraire has been set at unity, and s' are the shadow prices of the other commodities.

If Lagrange's method of undetermined multipliers is applicable, we can find conditions for optimality by setting equal to zero the derivatives of the Lagrangean

$$L = \int vf\, dh - \lambda \int \{\xi + s' \cdot x'\}f\, dh + \int \mu(h)\left\{v(h) - v(0) - \int_0^h u_h\, dk\right\}dh,$$

where λ should be positive. The sign of $\mu(h)$ will be considered later. If we reverse the order of integration in the double integral, we obtain

$$L = \int_0^\infty \left\{(v - \lambda\xi - \lambda s' \cdot x')f + \mu v - \mu v(0) - \int_h^\infty \mu(k)dk \cdot u_h\right\}dh. \tag{96}$$

On differentiating with respect to $x'(h)$, we have

$$\lambda(\xi_x + s')f + \int_h^\infty \mu\, dk(u_{h\xi}\xi_{x'} + u_{hx'}) = 0, \tag{97}$$

provided that $\xi(h)$, $x'(h)$ is in the interior of X^h. If it is on the boundary, we have an inequality (e.g. for people who do not choose to work). Differentiation with respect to $v(h)$ yields

$$(1 - \lambda\xi_v)f + \mu - \int_h^\infty \mu \, dk \cdot u_{h\xi}\xi_v = 0, \tag{98}$$

and differentiation with respect to $v(0)$,

$$\int_0^\infty \mu \, dh = 0. \tag{99}$$

Consider the sign of μ. In the light of (99), we cannot want to have $\mu \geq 0$. But we see from (96) that L is a concave function of the control variables provided that

$$M(h) = \int_h^\infty \mu \, dk \geq 0, \tag{100}$$

for all h. This completes the heuristic derivation of first-order conditions, except for some suggestive simplifications. We note that

$$\xi_v = 1/u_\xi, \tag{101}$$

$$\xi_{x'} = -u_{x'}/u_\xi, \tag{102}$$

which suggests we define the marginal rates of substitution, or marginal consumer prices as

$$q = q(\xi, x', h) = -\xi_{x'} = u_{x'}/u_\xi. \tag{103}$$

Also

$$u_{h\xi}\xi_{x'} + u_{hx'} = u_\xi \frac{\partial}{\partial h}\left(\frac{u_{x'}}{u_\xi}\right) = u_\xi q_h. \tag{104}$$

These formulas are used to obtain the conditions in the sufficiency theorem.

Theorem 7. Assume (C_1), (C_2), (C_3), (B), and (CON). Let the allocation $\xi^*(\cdot)$, $x'^*(\cdot)$, and s', v and $\mu(\cdot)$ satisfy the following conditions:

$$(\xi^*(h), x'^*(h)) \in X^h, \qquad \text{for all } h. \tag{105}$$

For all h, k, such that $(\xi^*(k), x'^*(k)) \in X^k$,

$$u(\xi^*(k), x'^*(k), h) \leq u(\xi^*(h), x'^*(h), h), \tag{106}$$

$$\left(\int \xi^* f dh, \int x'^* f dh\right) \text{ maximizes } (1, s') \cdot Y. \tag{107}$$

$$\{q(\xi^*(h), x'^*(h), h) - s'\}f(h) = u_\xi^* q_h^* \int_h^\infty \mu \, dk \tag{108}$$

(for consumers in the interior of X^h, and an appropriate boundary condition in other cases),

$$u(h) - \frac{u_{h\xi}{}^*}{u_\xi{}^*} \int_h^\infty \mu \, dk = \left(\frac{1}{u_\xi{}^*} - v \right) f, \tag{109}$$

$$v > 0, \quad \int_h^\infty u \, dk \geq 0 \quad \text{all } h, \tag{110}$$

$$\int_0^\infty u \, dk = 0. \tag{111}$$

Then the given allocation is an optimum.
In this statement, v is $1/\lambda$ and μ replaces μ/λ in (97)–(100).

Proof. The argument is a routine calculation based on the assumed concavity properties. We consider an alternative allocation satisfying the constraints of the problem, i.e.

$$\xi(h), x'(h) \text{ maximize } u(\xi, x', h),$$
$$\text{subject to: } (\xi, x') \in X^h \cap B, \tag{112}$$

$$\left(\int \xi f \, dh, \int x' f \, dh \right) \in Y, \tag{113}$$

and show that ξ^*, x'^* provides utility at least as great. (It is a feasible allocation by (105), (106), and (109).)

Lemma 1 implies that

$$v(h) - v(0) - \int_0^h u_h(\xi(k), x'(k), k) dk = 0, \tag{114}$$

$$v^*(h) - v^*(0) - \int_0^h u_h(\xi^*(k), x'^*(k), k) dk = 0. \tag{115}$$

Equation (114) follows from (112), and (115) from (106) (where the set B^* consists simply of all $\xi^*(h), x'^*(h)$). Subtracting (115) from (114), multiplying by $\mu(h)$ and integrating from 0 to ∞, we get

$$\int_0^\infty \left\{ \mu(v - v^*) - \mu \int_0^h (u_h - u_h{}^*) \, dk \right\} dh = \{v(0) - v^*(0)\} \int \mu \, dk$$
$$= 0 \text{ by } (111)$$

Reversing the order of integration, we deduce that

$$\int \mu(v - v^*)\,dh = \int_0^\infty \int_h^\infty \mu\,dk(u_h - u_h^*)\,dh$$

$$\geq \int_0^\infty \int_h^\infty \mu\,dk\left\{\frac{u_{h\xi}^*}{u_\xi^*}(v - v^*) + u_\xi^* q_h^*(x' - x'^*)\right\}dh, \quad (116)$$

by using (110) and (CON), and using our earlier calculations for the partial derivatives of u_h with respect to v and x'.

Combining (116) with conditions (108) and (109), we obtain

$$\int \left(\frac{1}{u_\xi^*} - v\right)(v - v^*)f\,dh \geq \int (q^* - s') \cdot (x' - x'^*)f\,dh$$

$$\geq \int q^* \cdot (x' - x'^*)f\,dh + \int (\xi - \xi^*)f\,dh, \quad (117)$$

by (107). Since ξ is a convex function of v and x',

$$\xi - \xi^* \geq \xi_v^*(v - v^*) + \xi_{x'}^* \cdot (x' - x'^*)$$

$$= \frac{1}{u_\xi^*}(v - v^*) - q^* \cdot (x' - x'^*).$$

Combining this with (117), we have finally

$$-v\int (v - v^*)f\,dh \geq 0. \tag{118}$$

Since $v > 0$, this implies that $\int v^* f\,dh \geq \int vf\,dh$. $\qquad\square$

The two problems with this theorem are, first, that (CON), expressing decreasing concavity of u, is a little obscure though not implausible; and, second, that, even when (CON) is satisfied, there may not exist any allocation satisfying the conditions of the theorem. As to the first problem, it is useful to note certain special cases where (CON) holds. If u has the form

$$u = u_1(x', h) + u_2(\xi),$$

convexity of u_{1h} with respect to x' is equivalent to (CON), and it is readily checked whether or not this holds. If u has the form

$$u = u_1(x') + u_2(\xi, h),$$

it is sufficient for (CON) that u_{2h} be an increasing convex function of ξ (since ξ is itself convex in x' and v).

In this context it is also interesting to note that the theorem can be generalized by assuming a welfare function

$$W = \int G(v)f\,dh,$$

with G concave, increasing, i.e. by taking a monotone transform of utility before using Lemma 1. The only change in the theorem is that v is replaced by $vG'(v^*(h))$. By this transformation to a new utility funciion, u_h, may sometimes be made convex when it would not otherwise have been.

The second problem, that it may be impossible to satisfy the conditions of the theorem, arises because there are allocations satisfying (90) that are not utility-maximizing allocations. One would expect to be able to satisfy the conditions if (90) replaced the stronger condition (105), but that may not be what one wants.

To check whether or not a particular allocation $x(h)$ as h varies maximizes utility for some constant budget set B, the following partial converse to Lemma 1 is useful:

Lemma 2. *Suppose that, for all h,*

$$\begin{aligned}
&x(h) \in X^h, \\
&v(h) = u(x(h), h), \\
&v(h) - v(0) = \int_0^h u_h(x(k), k)\, \mathrm{d}k, \\
&u_h(x(k), h) \text{ is a non-decreasing function of } k,
\end{aligned} \tag{119}$$

for k such that $x(k) \in X^h$. Then there exists B such that, for all h, $x(h)$ maximizes $u(x, h)$ for $x \in B \cap X^h$.

Proof. It is sufficient to show that, for all h, h_0 such that $x(h_0) \in X^h$, $u(x(h), h) \geq u(x(h_0), h)$. Since $u_h(x(k), h)$ is non-decreasing in k, we have

$$\begin{aligned}
u(x(h), h) - v(h_0) = \int_{h_0}^h u_h(x(k), k)\, \mathrm{d}k &\geq \int_{h_0}^h u_h(x(h_0), k)\, \mathrm{d}k \\
&= u(x(h_0), h) - u(x(h_0), h_0),
\end{aligned}$$

proving the lemma.   □

When x is (62) implies that, a routine calculation shows that (119) is equivalent to

$$q_h'(x(k), h) \cdot \frac{\mathrm{d}}{\mathrm{d}k} x'(k) \geq 0.$$

It is interesting to compare this with a form of the second-order necessary condition for maximization (also easily proved),

$$q_h'(x(h), h) \cdot \frac{\mathrm{d}}{\mathrm{d}h} x'(h) \geq 0.$$

In the two-commodity case, and particularly in the simple optimal income-tax problem, x' is a scalar. Suppose that h can be measured in such a way that

$\partial(u_{x'}/u_\xi)/\partial h < 0$. Then both necessary and sufficient supplements to the envelope condition (90) have the simple form that x' be a non-increasing function of h, and, equivalently, that ξ be a non-decreasing function of h. In general, the class of allocations consistent with the maximization constraint cannot be so easily identified.

Suppose now that an attempt to apply the sufficiency theorem fails because we cannot find a solution satisfying (106). Then it must be realized that we should not have neglected the other constraints on maximizing allocations (besides the condition (90) of Lemma.) It must also be the case that $v(h)$ does not become smaller than $u(x(h_1), h)$ as h increases from h_1. It might be optimal to have $v(h)$ just remaining equal to $u(x(h_1), h)$ over some interval $[h_1, h_2]$. Then we must allow for the additional constraint $v(h) \geq u(x(h_1), h)$ in our maximization problem. This introduces a new term $\int_{h_1}^{h_2} \rho(h)\{v(h) - (\xi(h_1), x'(h_1), h)\}dh$ into the Lagrangean, with $\rho(h) \geq 0$. If $[h_1, h_2]$ is the whole interval on which the additional constraint binds, we see at once that, since $\xi(h_1), x'(h_1)$ occurs predominantly in the new term of the Lagrangean,

$$\int_{h_1}^{h_2} \rho(h)u_\xi(x(h_1), h)\{q(x(h_1), h_1) - q(x(h_1), h)\}dh = 0. \tag{120}$$

It is further found that condition (108) is unchanged, while condition (109) becomes

$$\rho(h) + \mu(h) - \frac{u_{h\xi}^*}{u_\xi^*} \int_h^\infty \mu \, dk = \left(\frac{1}{u_\xi^*} - v\right)f. \tag{121}$$

One can prove in the same way as before that, if the conditions of the theorem hold on intervals where $v(h) > u(x(h_1), h)$ and the modified conditions ((121) replacing (109), and (120) added) hold on intervals where $v(h) = u(x(h_1), h)$, an optimum has been found.

In the two-commodity case, $v(h) = u(x(h_1), h)$ and $v'(h) = u_h(x(h), h)$ generally imply that $x(h)$ is constant. Thus, these awkward intervals correspond to bunching of consumers, many of whom choose the same demands. In the many-commodity case, this need no longer be so.

Returning to the conditions of the theorem, we see that (108) strongly suggests that $x(h)$ is a continuous function of h. This seems to be correct under assumption (CON). It appears that discontinuities occur only when assumption (CON) is violated. When it is violated, we can no longer hope to use sufficient conditions for an optimum, but must make do with necessary conditions. For these we can rely on Pontrjagin's Maximum Principle, suitably generalized to take account of possible discontinuities.[16] The conditions given in the theorem are then necessary conditions for an optimum.

---

[16] Relevant results and methods can be found in Swinnerton-Dyer (1959).

The conditions for optimal nonlinear taxation are interesting in a number of ways. Condition (108) is the most striking, for it not only shows that the effective marginal tax rates on consumer h have the signs of $\partial q/\partial h$, but also gives a simple formula relating different marginal tax rates,

$$\frac{q_i - s_i'}{q_j - s_j'} = \frac{q_{ih}}{q_{jh}}. \tag{122}$$

The general principle is that the proportional marginal tax rate $(q_i - s_i')/q_i$, or equivalently $(q_i - s_i')/q_i$, should be higher for commodity i than for commodity j if and only if $(\partial/\partial h)(\mu_i/u_j) > 0$, i.e. when the marginal rate of substitution would be increased by an increase in h. This suggests a theorem of Atkinson and Stiglitz (whose formal proof is omitted here):

Theorem 8. *If utility takes the form*

$$u(x, h) = U(u_1(x'), u_2(\xi, h)),$$

the optimal allocation can be obtained by imposing a budget constraint of the form

$$p \cdot x' \leq c(\xi). \tag{123}$$

It is interesting to note that the analysis of this section can also be done in a fully dual way,[17] treating marginal prices q and utility as control variables. We can think of offering consumers a set of linear budget constraints C instead of a set of demand vectors. Writing $E(q, u, h)$ for the expenditure function, and $v(q, b, h)$ for the indirect utility function, we can set up the problem as maximization of $\int u(h)f(h)dh$ subject to

$$\left.\begin{array}{c} \int E_q(q(h), u(h), h)f(h)\,dh \in Y \\ q(h), E(q(h), u(h), h) \text{ maximizes } v(q, b, h) \\ \text{subject to: } (q, b) \in C \cap Q^h \end{array}\right\} \tag{124}$$

where Q^h is the set of linear budget constraints that are consumption-feasible.

The entire previous analysis can be applied to (124), and we obtain as first-order conditions

$$\mu(h) - \frac{v_{bb}^*}{v_b^*}\int_h^\infty \mu\,dk = \left(\frac{1}{v_b^*} - v\right)f, \tag{125}$$

$$-s \cdot x_q^c f = v_b^* x_h \int_h^\infty \mu\,dk, \tag{126}$$

---

[17] This approach is due to Kevin Roberts.

where x_b is the derivative of demands holding q and b constant. In fact, (125) is exactly the same equation as (109); (126) does not look the same as (108), but the two can easily be shown to be equivalent, by using the equation

$$x_q^c \cdot q_b = -x_b,$$

which can be obtained by differentiating the equations $x^c(q(x, b), u(x, b), b) = x$ and $x^c(q, v(q, b, b), b) = x(q, b, b)$ with respect to b.

Equation (126) has an interesting similarity to the first-order conditions for optimal linear taxation, for they can be expressed (cf. (79)) in the form

$$-\int s \cdot x_q^c f \, db = \frac{1}{\lambda} \int (v_b - s \cdot x_b) x f \, db. \tag{127}$$

If we write (126) in the form, obtained by using $q \cdot x_q^c = 0$ and Slutsky symmetry,

$$x_q^c \cdot (q - s) = \left(v_b{}^* \int_b^\infty \mu \, dk \right) x_b / f(b), \tag{128}$$

it says that the approximate compensated effect on consumer b's demands of imposing the optimum tax system is proportional to the derivative of demands with respect to the population percentile.

It is worth emphasizing that this dual approach to the problem provides a technique that allows us to apply nonlinear taxation to some groups of commodities while applying only proportional taxes to others, for it is very easy to insist that some q_i be independent of b.[18]

Finally, to mention the obvious, (109) would in practice be treated as a differential equation in $\int_b^\infty \mu \, dk$. It is written in the form above to allow for the possibility that μ is discontinuous, and that happens only where x is discontinuous.

7. M-DIMENSIONAL POPULATIONS

Although the one-dimensional population is an extremely useful model for computations and examination of particular issues, it is not, in that respect, an accurate representation of reality. Theorem 7 can be generalized to the m-dimensional case, with m parameters $b_1, \ldots, b_m$ ranging over the non-negative orthant. The function $\mu(b)$ becomes an m-dimensional vector field, and the main equations of the theorem become

$$(q - s')f = u_\xi s_b' \cdot M = u_\xi \sum_1^m \frac{\partial s'}{\partial j_j} M_j,$$

---

[18] The problem was solved by a different method in Mirrlees (1976).

where

$$M_j = \int_{h_j}^{\infty} \mu_j(h_1, \ldots, h_{j-1}, k, h_{j+1}, \ldots, h_n) \, dk, \tag{129}$$

and

$$\sum_1^m \mu_j - \frac{1}{u_\xi} u_{\xi h} \cdot M = \left(\frac{1}{u_\xi} - v\right) f \tag{130}$$

(ignoring corner solutions). In the case where μ (and x) vary continuously, (130) can be written

$$\Delta M - \frac{1}{u_\xi} u_{\xi h} \cdot M = \left(\frac{1}{u_\xi} - v\right) f,$$

where $\Delta M = \sum \partial M_j / \partial h_j$ is the divergence of M. The boundary conditions in terms of M (which should be non-negative for the sufficiency theorem to go through) are

$$\begin{aligned} M_j &= 0 &\text{when} \quad h_j &= 0, \\ M_j &\to 0 &\text{as} \quad h_j &\to \infty. \end{aligned}$$

The above equations will not be derived here. Lemma 1 is easily generalized to the m-dimensional case, carrying with it the important fact that u_h is an integrable vector field. Then the equation $v(h) - v(0) = \int_0^h u_h dk$ is brought in as a constraint in m different ways, following m different rectangular paths of integration, to enforce integrability on the solution to the optimization problem. The m Lagrangean functions μ_i correspond to these m constraints.

To find an optimum, we would look for a solution to the system of equations, in the functions v, x', $M_1, \ldots, M_m$ of $h = (h_1, \ldots, h_m)$:

$$u_\xi s_h' \cdot M = (q - s') f, \tag{131}$$

$$\Delta \cdot M - \frac{1}{u_\xi} u_{\xi h} \cdot M = \left(\frac{1}{u_\xi} - v\right) f, \tag{132}$$

$$\Delta v = u_h, \tag{133}$$

$$M_j = 0 \quad \text{when} \quad h_j = 0, \infty. \tag{134}$$

M occurs in these equations only where it is shown explicitly (133) is the generalized envelope theorem. When $m < n$, i.e. the number of characteristics is less than the number of commodities, (131)–(134) can be reduced to a second-order partial differential equation for v with mixed boundary conditions specifying the values of functions of v and Δv where $h_j = 0, \infty$. To do this, we would first solve (131) for x' as a function $x'(M, v, h)$ of M, v and h. In general, this is a mapping of full rank from M to x', provided $m < n$; and so is the mapping from x', M, h, v to Δv given by (133). Consequently, the mapping from M to Δv obtained from (133) and $x'(M, v, h)$ can be inverted, giving M as a function of Δv, v and h. Substitution in (132) gives the promised equation for v.

This procedure breaks down when $m \geq n$. In that case one can eliminate v and x' from (131) and (132) to obtain v as a function of $\Delta \cdot M$, m, and h. Substitution in (133) yields a second-order system of m partial differential equations for the m functions M_j, with boundary conditions specified in (134). Even when $m = n = 2$, these look hard to handle. But there are many aspects of the solution one would like to know about. Since the budget set frontier is $(n-1)$-dimensional and the population m-dimensional, any point (ξ, x') is chosen by an $(m-n+1)$-dimensional set of people. One would like to know what these sets are like. Since (131) no longer gives any information about marginal tax rates if nothing is known about M, it is now a much deeper question: how to characterize the commodities that should be most heavily taxed. It would be interesting to enquire what special structure of the utility function, as a function of h particularly, would simplify the equations and yield information about the solution. One would like to use that to indicate what should guide us in setting up one-parameter models for practical work.

In the model with large m, the boundary conditions (134) seem to play a very important part in determining the solution. This means that the economist's instinct to rely on differential first-order conditions to derive properties of the solution is no help in these cases. I think this is the root difficulty in making the m-dimensional model produce any results.

8. CONSUMER UNCERTAINTY

In all the models considered, consumers have been perfectly informed about themselves and the possibilities open to them. There has been no uncertainty about taxes or prices, or about the circumstances in which these taxes and prices will apply. There is a large range of unexplored problems here. The only case for which much is known is that in which individuals all make their decisions in advance of knowing the states of nature that distinguish them. This is the case of pure moral hazard. Denoting the initially unknown state of the consumer—his future ability, health, or luck—by θ, and the observed outcome on which government policy can be based—wage, retirement date, or prize—by y, we assume a functional relationship

$$y = g(\theta, x), \tag{135}$$

where x is the consumer's choice variable. On the basis of y, government delivers

$$z = \zeta(y) \tag{136}$$

to the consumer, who chooses x to maximize

$$Eu(\zeta(g(\theta, x)), x). \tag{137}$$

There is a resource (or revenue) constraint, which for a large identical population with independent and identically distributed states θ can be written in the form

$$Eh(y, \zeta(y), x) = 0, \tag{138}$$

where y is given by (135). The leading case is that in which expected utility is also the government's maximand, though other welfare functions are also of interest.

I shall not go into the methods of analysing this kind of problem. It is a problem in which the general issues raised in Section 2 loom large; and one further issue arises which I have not discussed earlier. Since the set defined by the maximization constraint can be complicated and difficult to work with, it is best to look for cases in which certain kinds of fairly simple solutions exist. There are three (if the maximization constraint is not inessential).

(1) There are problems where the solution is a function ζ for which the expected utility function is known to be a concave function of x. In such a case, the maximization constraint is equivalent to its first-order condition, and the optimization can then be treated by Kuhn–Tucker methods. It is usually quite easy to see for what functions ζ, Eu is concave in x: to get an adequately large class, one may have to specialize the utility function. The difficulty is to find conditions under which one can be sure in advance that the optimum ζ falls into this class. This requires a direct argument that any other ζ can be improved upon.

(2) Following the discussion in Section 2, it is a real possibility that expected utility should have up to $m + 1$ global maxima, where m is the dimensionality of the available set of policy functions ζ. If all functions (analytic, integrable, or whatever) are available, a continuum of global maxima is a possible optimum, not only in exceptional cases. It is therefore a good idea to look for cases in which

$$Eu(\zeta(g(\theta, x)), x) = u_0 \tag{139}$$

is a constant at the optimum. It may not be very difficult to find under what conditions such a policy is optimal, and when it is, both computation and further analysis are relatively easy.[19]

---

[19] An example of special economic interest is treated by Diamond and Mirrlees (1977).

(3) In cases where utility is unbounded, which may be useful approximations to reality, it is possible that no optimum exists, because government can always increase expected utility by reducing the level of reward to some low probability set of possible outcomes. It is obvious that minimum reward is an optimal policy when effort is then increased so that events with minimum reward do not occur. In most of the interesting cases, effort can never ensure that disastrous outcomes will never happen. Yet it can be (nearly) optimal to impose extremely severe 'punishment' when these events do occur. Solutions of this form can occur in perfectly reasonable models, which contrast sharply in this respect with models where there is no consumer uncertainty. The possibility of providing incentives, usually sticks rather than carrots, through the consequences of rare events is of considerable interest, and should be examined in all cases.[20]

These three possibilities seem to exhaust the manageable solutions to problems with consumer uncertainty; but they do not by any means exhaust the possible solutions. It may be that some of the most interesting results in this area will come from identifying the borderlines between the different classes of optimum rather than by attacking the optimization problem directly.

9. COMPUTATION AND APPROXIMATION

A major aim of optimal tax theory is to obtain numerical information about optimal policies. In most of these problems, non-concavity is an important intrinsic property, and first-order conditions may not determine the optimum uniquely, even when the more intractable problems of non-connected constraint sets explained in Section 2 do not occur. For example, in the simple linear income-tax problem, where there are two tax parameters in a simple two-commodity world, we have essentially a one-variable maximization, but it must be carried out by explicit search over the possible range, not by hill-climbing, or solving first-order conditions.[21] As soon as additional parameters are introduced, computational problems begin to be severe. Even the standard, and empirically oversimple, linear expenditure system, when labour is included, leads to non-concave problems. It would seem that optimal tax theory can contribute to the computation of optimal commodity taxes chiefly by narrowing down the range of tax rates it is sensible to try.

A major advantage of the nonlinear theory is, therefore, that there is a sufficiency theorem, such that solution of certain differential equations is sufficient to give an optimum, provided a basic condition is satisfied. When the population is more than one-dimensional, the computational problems again become severe. However, one-dimensional models would seem to be a

[20] See Mirrlees (1974) for an example.

[21] Stern (1976) discusses and carries out computations for the optimal linear income tax.

promising tool for computing optimal commodity taxes for many-commodity models, provided an empirically acceptable model can be devised. Of course, if the model of Theorem 8 is applicable, and on present knowledge it seems as good as any other, optimal tax calculations are reduced essentially to a two-commodity income-tax problem, which poses no insurmountable computational difficulties.

Since, in general, computation and simulation are not particularly easy (and this is even more true of the models mentioned in Section 8), other techniques of numerical exploration can be useful. It seems to be illuminating to set up a number of questions as approximation problems, asking for properties of the optimum when certain parameters are small. I have been able to obtain approximate formulae for optimal commodity taxes when the distribution of characteristics in the economy has a low variance, and when the degree of inaccuracy in observations used for lump-sum taxation is small; but there is not space to develop these calculations here.

In a similar vein, it is interesting to analyse the asymptotic form of non-linear optimal tax policies for very high (or very low) values of the characteristics. But this often gives inaccurate, or even seriously misleading, information.[22] Indeed, it is a general principle of work on approximations that one should try to discover something about the accuracy of the approximations. It would be valuable to show that certain classes of approximations are tolerably accurate by carrying out complete calculations in a few representative cases. This may even be the best line to follow for calculating optimal commodity taxes.

10. IN CONCLUSION

Computational and empirical issues seem likely to loom large in optimal taxation in future. It is not always easy to devise simple models that are simple enough to be manageable theoretically and rich enough to be empirically relevant. Like growth theory and planning theory, to instance only two examples in the recent history of economics, optimal tax theory has fairly quickly reached a stage where good theorems may be hard to come by, while the theory contains many suggestions or possibilities for practical implementation.

Yet there is still much theoretical work to be done, and the best theorems may be still to come. The whole area of consumer uncertainty where consumers are not identical remains to be explored. Little has been done on variations in population size. Aspects of the real world, like overtime rates, discrete labour choices, misperceptions, and, above all, disequilibria, could be incorporated in manageable models. International issues, such as tax agreements and treaties, or incentives acting upon countries (e.g. aid agreements), could be examined. Problems of tax evasion and administration have only begun to be looked at.

---

[22] The optimal income-tax problem analysed by Mirrlees (1971) provides examples of this.

This account of optimal tax theory has by no means covered all the theoretical work that has been done. On the contrary, it has concentrated on certain fundamental models, and the methods for solving them, and has said rather little about properties of the solutions. I conclude with a few notes on the literature, to guide the reader to what has been said about the topics taken up here.

11. NOTES ON THE LITERATURE

Optimal tax theory began with Ramsey (1927), who solved the problem of raising revenue by commodity taxes from a single consumer. Pigou (1947) discussed Ramsey's solution, but the next contributions published were those of Boiteux (1956), Corlett and Hague (1953–4), and Meade (1955). Boiteux still assumed lump-sum taxation, as it happens quite unnecessarily, and looked at optimal pricing by public enterprises subject to a budget constraint. This is essentially equivalent to Ramsey, but Boiteux introduced the use of indirect utility functions. Corlett and Hague considered a special case of the problem of improving matters by introducing taxes where none were before, and Meade solved the corresponding optimization problem. Work on discount rates for public investment during the 1960s often implicitly assumed imperfections, such as absence of lump-sum taxation, but general models of optimal taxation seem not to have appeared before 1970. Several contributions appeared at the beginning of the 1970s. Baumol and Bradford (1970), Diamond and Mirrlees (1971), Feldstein (1972), and Kolm (1970) may be mentioned among many. Diamond and Mirrlees introduced the many-consumer economy without lump-sum taxes, stated and proved the efficiency theorem, provided a discussion of existence, and gave a case where the optimum can be obtained explicitly. An application of this work to the measurement of national income is presented in Mirrlees (1969).

This work and later contributions are discussed in a brief survey by Sandmo (1976), which includes a useful bibliography. Sandmo's paper forms part of a symposium in the July–August issue of the *Journal of Public Economics*, which contains several useful papers. Much of the recent work in optimal tax theory has appeared in that journal.

I conclude with a few selected references for the individual sections. The references provided are by no means complete, even for the period to 1977 when the chapter was written. Two valuable books containing extensive accounts of optimal tax theory have appeared: Atkinson and Stiglitz (1980), and Tresch (1981).

Section 2

The material presented here has not previously appeared in print. Problems of the type discussed were classified in Spence and Zeckhauser (1971). Some of the difficulties arising from the maximization constraint were noticed in Helpman and Laffont (1975). On evasion see Srinivasan (1973).

Section 3

The treatment of lump-sum taxation as based on individual information is related to the work on 'signalling' and 'screening': Spence (1973) and Stiglitz (1976). Some aspects were mentioned in Mirrlees (1974).

Section 4

Efficiency and other shadow-price results are important for cost–benefit analysis: Diamond (1968), Little and Mirrlees (1974), and Dasgupta and Stiglitz (1974) may be consulted. Efficiency when there are positive profits was first discussed in Dasgupta and Stiglitz (1972). See also Mirrlees (1972).

Section 5

In addition to the works referred to above, the following should be mentioned: Dasgupta and Stiglitz (1971), Atkinson and Stiglitz (1972), Diamond (1975), and Atkinson and Stiglitz (1976). Dixit (1975) and Guesnerie (1977) discuss the welfare effects of commodity tax changes.

Section 6

A special case of nonlinear taxation, with extensive results and numerical calculations, is given in Mirrlees (1971). Theorem 7 above generalizes the result that underpinned that paper, a result that never seemed worth publishing for a special case. The more general model is discussed under differentiability assumptions in Mirrlees (1976). See also Atkinson (1973), Phelps (1973), Atkinson and Stiglitz (1976), Sadka (1976), and Seade (1977). An interesting approach, concerned not with optimality but with bargaining, is Aumann and Kurz (1977).

Section 7

The optimality conditions were given in Mirrlees (1976). Mirrlees and Spence have work in progress on special cases of optimization with many characteristics.

Section 8

The papers by Mirrlees (1974), where the inadequacy of treating first-order conditions as constraints is not adequately appreciated, and Helpman and Laffont (1975), referred to above, are relevant here. Diamond and Mirrlees (1977) give a fairly full explicit analysis of an interesting special case, where the consumer chooses retirement, and the government the social insurance system.

REFERENCES

Atkinson, A. B. (1973), 'How progressive should income tax be?' In M. Parkin (ed.), *Essays in Modern Economics*. (London: Longmans, pp. 90–109).

—— and Stiglitz, J. E. (1972), 'The structure of indirect taxation and economic efficiency', *Journal of Public Economics*, 1, 97–119.

—— and —— (1976), 'The design of tax structure: direct versus indirect taxation'. *Journal of Public Economics*, 6, 55–75.

—— and —— (1980), *Lectures on Public Economics*. (New York: McGraw-Hill).

Aumann, R. J. and Kurz, M. (1977), 'Power and taxes', *Econometrica*. 45, 1137–62.

Baumol, W. J. and Brandford, D. F. (1970), 'Optimal departures from marginal cost pricing'. *American Economic Review*, 60, 265–83.

Bröcker, T. H. (1975), *Differential Germs and Catastrophes*. (Cambridge: Cambridge University Press).

Boiteux, M. (1956), 'Sur la gestion des monopoles publics astreint à l'équilibre budgétaire'. *Econometrica*, 24, 22–40.

Corlett, W. J. and Hague, D. C. (1953–4), 'Complementarity and the excess burden of taxation'. *Review of Economic Studies*, 21, 21–30.

Dasgupta, P. and Stiglitz, J. E. (1971), 'Differential taxation, public goods and economic efficiency'. *Review of Economic Studies*, 38, 151–74.

—— and —— (1972), 'On optimal taxation and public production'. *Review of Economic Studies*, 39, 87–104.

—— and —— (1974), 'Benefit–cost analysis and trade policies'. *Journal of Political Economy*, 82, 1–33.

Diamond, P. A. (1968), 'The opportunity costs of public investment: a comment'. *Quarterly Journal of Economics*, 82, 682–6

—— (1975), 'A many-person Ramsey tax rule'. *Journal of Public Economics*. 4, 335–42.

—— and Mirrlees, J. A. (1971), 'Optimal taxation and public production I–II'. *American Economic Review*, 61, 8–27, 261–78.

—— and —— (1976), 'Private constant returns to scale and public shadow prices'. *Review of Economic Studies*, 43, 41–8.

—— and —— (1977), 'A model of social insurance with retirement'. *Journal of Public Economics*, 10, 295–336.

Dixit, A. K. (1975), 'Welfare effects of tax and price changes'. *Journal of Public Economics*, 4, 103–24.

—— (1976), 'Public finance in a Keynesian temporary equilibrium'. *Journal of Economic Theory*, 12.

Feldstein, M. S. (1972), 'Distributional equity and the optimal structure of public prices'. *American Economic Review*, 62, 32–6.

Groves, T. and Ledyard, J. (1977), 'Optimal allocation of public goods: a solution to the "free-rider" problem'. *Econometrica*, 45, 783–810.

Guesnerie, R. (1975), 'Production of the public sector and taxation in a simple second best model'. *Journal of Economic Theory*, 10, 127–56.

Guesnerie, R. (1977), 'On the direction of tax reform'. *Journal of Public Economics*, 7, 179–202.

Hahn, F. H. (1973), 'On optimum taxation'. *Journal of Economic Theory*, 6, 96–106.

Heller, W. P. and Shell, K. (1974), 'On optimal taxation with costly administration'. *American Economic Review*, Papers and Proceedings, 64, 338–45.

Helpman, E. and Laffont, J.-J. (1975), 'On moral hazard in general equilibrium theory'. *Journal of Economic Theory*, 10, 8–23.

Kolm, S. Ch. (1970). *La Theorie des contraintes de valeur et ses applications*. (Paris: Dunod).

Little, I. M. D. and Mirrlees, J. A. (1974), *Project Appraisal and Planning for Developing Countries* (London: Heinemann New York: Basic Books).

Meade, J. E. (1955), *Trade and Welfare*. (London: Oxford University Press).

Mirrlees, J. A. (1969), 'The evaluation of national income in an imperfect economy'. *Pakistan Development Review*, 9, 1–13.

—— (1971), 'An exploration in the theory of optimum income taxation'. *Review of Economic Studies*, 38, 175–208.

—— (1972), 'On producer taxation'. *Review of Economic Studies*, 39, 105–11.

—— (1974) 'Notes on welfare economics, information, and uncertainty'. In M. Balch, D. McFadden, and S. Wu (eds.), *Essays in Equilibrium Behavior under Uncertainty*. (Amsterdam: North-Holland).

—— (1976), 'Optimal tax theory: a synthesis'. *Journal of Public Economics*, 6, 327–58.

—— and Roberts, K. W. S. (1980), 'Functions with multiple maxima'. Mimeo, Nuffield College, Oxford.

Munk, K. J. (1978), 'Differential taxation and economic efficiency reconsidered'. *Review of Economic Studies*.

Phelps, E. S. (1973), 'Wage taxation for economic justice'. *Quarterly Journal of Economics*, 87, 331–54.

Pigou, A. C. (1947), *A Study in Public Finance*, 3rd edn. (London: Macmillan; first published 1928).

Ramsey, F. P. (1927), 'A contribution to the theory of taxation'. *Economic Journal*, 37, 47–61.

Sadka, E. (1976), 'On income distribution, incentive effects and optimal income taxation'. *Review of Economic Studies*, 43, 261–7.

Seade, J. K. (1977), 'On the shape of optimal tax schedules'. *Journal of Public Economics*, 7, 203–35.

Sen, A. K. (1973), *On Economic Inequality*. (Oxford: Clarendon Press).

Spence, M. (1973), 'Job market signalling'. *Quarterly Journal of Economics*, 87, 355–79.

—— and Zeckhauser, R. (1971), 'Insurance, information, and individual action'. *American Economic Review*, 61, 380–7.

Srinivasan, T. N. (1973), 'Tax evasion: a model'. *Journal of Public Economics*, 2, 339–46.

Stern, N. H. (1976), 'On the specification of models of optimum income taxation'. *Journal of Public Economics*, 6, 123–62.

Stiglitz, J. E. (1975), 'Information and economic analysis'. In M. Parkin and A. R. Nobay (eds.), *Current Economic Problems*. (Cambridge: Cambridge University Press).

Swinnerton-Dyer, H. P. F. (1959), 'On an extrenal problem'. *Proceedings of the London Mathematical Society*. (London: LMS).

Tresch, R. W. (1981), *Public Finance: A Normative Theory*. (Plano Texas: Business Publications).

12

Migration and Optimal Income Taxes

1. MIGRATION

High tax rates encourage emigration. The resulting loss of tax revenue is widely believed to be an important reason for keeping taxes down. If, as Bhagwati (1980) has proposed, the emigrants' foreign incomes were taxed, there would be two advantages to the domestic government: emigrants would contribute to tax revenues, and tax rates could be higher. There are also implications for other taxes and subsidies. In particular, education would become a better investment for the State, and should therefore be subsidized to a greater extent. Bhagwati and Hamada (1982) have shown that, in a simple model, foreign and domestic incomes should be taxed at the same rate, namely (nearly) 100 per cent. The assumptions of that model lead perhaps too directly to the conclusion. Income is the outcome of education, in the same way that a firm's profits are the outcome of its investments, consumers wishing to maximize discounted net income less education costs. Thus, nearly full taxation of the return, and nearly full subsidization of the capital cost, induces individuals to do what the State would like, with essentially all costs and benefits accruing to the State. Fundamental reasons for less than full taxation are absent from the model, and one wonders whether the conclusion that the same tax rates should be levied on domestic and foreign incomes would hold in a more realistic model.

The model also ignores the possibility of emigrants severing themselves completely from their country's tax system. One might perhaps think it obvious that this is a reason for reducing the foreign-income tax rate relative to domestic tax rates, a point possibly too obvious to be worth exploring formally.

This paper examines the optimal taxation of foreign incomes by LDCs in models that may be a little more realistic than the Bhagwati–Hamada model.

Reprinted from the *Journal of Public Economics*, Vol. 18 (1982), pp. 319–341, with permission from Elsevier Science. It is a revised version of a paper entitled 'Optimal foreign-income taxation' that was presented at a Conference on 'The Exercise of Income Tax Jurisdiction over Citizens Working Abroad', under the auspices of the National Institute of Public Finance and Policy, New Delhi, January 1981. I am grateful to the sponsors of the conference for providing the occasion for the paper. Valuable comments were provided by Peter Diamond and other participants in the conference, and at a seminar in University College, London. I am particularly grateful to two referees who provided useful comments and identified serious errors in the previous version of this chapter.

Although only special cases are solved explicitly, the results for these cases tend to support the case for high taxation of foreign earnings. It should be emphasized that the arguments apply only to LDCs with governments whose expenditures benefit the generality of the population. As a preliminary, Section 3 is devoted to the theory of optimal taxation when foreign earnings are not taxed.

It should be emphasized at the outset that the income taxes and subsidies appearing in the models correspond to all taxes on incomes *and expenditures* in the real world. If it were desirable to tax foreign earnings at the same rate as domestic earnings, the foreign-income rate should include an element corresponding to such taxes as sales tax, value-added tax, and import duties.

A second simplification I have allowed myself is to ignore all intertemporal considerations, and even to pretend that individuals earn income either at home or abroad, but not both. These are not satisfactory assumptions, but models allowing migration to be temporary or permanent, and to take place part of the way through the working life, seem to become complicated very quickly. In Section 4, where the discussion is conducted heuristically, it is possible to allow for partial migration.

2. CRITERIA

Three different criteria occur to people thinking about migration, depending on the group whose welfare is to count. The first criterion attempts to restrict the group to those who do not migrate. This is hardly satisfactory. Some of those who do not migrate may have wished to do so; some who do migrate may do a great deal for their country of origin, such as sending home remittances. It is therefore hard to see how a loyalty criterion could be implemented. The fact that many countries do so little to tax emigrants, temporary or permanent, suggests that governments are not guided by a loyal-citizen criterion. Since it is morally unattractive, we should be pleased to be able to reject it. An alternative interpretation of the criterion is that the government should restrict taxation (and benefits) to voters. That opens the question: Who should be voters? But, whether the voters are all nationals, or one colonel, we should be prepared to argue that they ought to vote in the interests not only of one another, but of others, if that seems to be right.

The second criterion defines the relevant group as that of nationals, whether working in the country or not. 'Nationals' had better be understood in a nonlegal sense, since the group is otherwise endogenous, the extent to which people change nationality being influenced by economic variables. Perhaps the best definition is nationality at birth, though even that is not always well-defined. This criterion, like the first, is unsure what to do about immigrants. Strictly speaking, they are excluded; but I hope few of us believe that is morally right. Yet the alternative of including all who would, or might, like to immigrate is not consistent with the spirit of the criterion.

The third main possibility is to include all humans. Criteria that do so are surely morally defensible, but they may be thought not to be what an adviser to a democratic state is expected to be guided by. The network of double-tax agreements, and the allowances for foreign-income tax provided by many countries, suggest that the conclusion is too hasty. Totally to neglect the welfare of citizens of other countries is not acceptable as explicit policy motivation.

In the case of LDCs, one might reduce possible conflict between the national and world welfare functions by insisting that marginal income for those living in the countries to which emigrants go have a negligible weight in the world welfare function because of their high incomes. Specifically, it would then be permissible to neglect the effect on their incomes of changes in their governments' tax revenue, brought about by changes in emigration. These effects are in principle substantial, and can be neglected only if there is some reason to regard the welfare change as negligible. One can also often neglect immigration as negligible, simply because incomes are too low to encourage it. In the present paper, effects on foreigners are neglected on these grounds. But it is not always permissible to do so. Doctors and engineers may migrate from one poor country to another. There are LDCs where the use to which government revenues are put is not such as to make one assign them more weight than government revenue in a typical industrial country.

3. NO TAX ON FOREIGN INCOMES

The easiest theory of optimal income taxation is that for an economic model where each individual's productivity—here identified with his wage—is identifiable and fixed, though his inclination to migrate is unknown. An individual of productivity n receiving after-tax income $x(n)$ has utility

$$v(n) = u(x(n), n). \tag{1}$$

The number of such individuals who remain in the economy is $f(v(n), n)$, an increasing function of v. A small change in $x(n)$, δx, induces a few people more or less to emigrate, but they are almost indifferent between staying and going. Assuming that this indifference correctly reflects what they will or would experience, the impact on total utility is

$$u_x \delta x \cdot f(c(n), n). \tag{2}$$

Notice that this argument neglects the effects upon those living in the foreign economies of resulting changes in tax revenue there.

The impact of δx on tax revenue in the domestic economy is, since by assumption marginal productivities do not change, to reduce it by

$$\delta x \cdot f(v(n), n) + (x - n)f_v \cdot u_x \cdot \delta x. \tag{3}$$

For optimality, (2) and (3) must be in constant proportion as n varies. Thus,

$$u_x f = \lambda f + \lambda(x - n)f_v u_x \tag{4}$$

for some constant λ. The constant is to be determined by the economy's budget constraint. Information about propensities to migrate is conveniently expressed by the *elasticity of numbers with respect to after-tax income*:

$$\eta = \frac{x f_v u_x}{f}. \tag{5}$$

With this notation, (4) can be rewritten as

$$\frac{n - x}{x} = \frac{1}{\eta}\left(1 - \frac{u_x}{\lambda}\right). \tag{6}$$

The left-hand side is tax as a proportion of after-tax income.

In general, η is a function of n as well as x, so that (6) is not an explicit formula for the optimal tax rates. When η is constant, it is easily solved. For example, if

$$\eta = 0.5, \qquad u = t(n) - \frac{1}{x}, \tag{7}$$

then (6) becomes

$$n = 3x - \frac{2}{\lambda x}. \tag{8}$$

Thus, writing $\lambda = 12/a$,

$$x(n) = \tfrac{1}{6}[n + (a + n^3)^{1/2}]$$

and

$$\frac{x}{n} \to \frac{1}{3} \qquad (n \to \infty).$$

In this case x is a convex function of n. There is a minimum consumption level, depending on the resource constraint, and the marginal tax rate falls from 5/6 on the lowest incomes to 2/3 on the highest. This example suggests that rather high tax rates are justifiable even if the propensity to migrate is quite large. Of course, other sources of labour supply elasticity have been neglected.

To help intuition about η, consider the following situation. Denote foreign earnings, net of foreign tax, by m, and suppose that m, n are jointly distributed in the population with density $g(m, n)$. (One might well suppose that a nonzero proportion of people with home wages n have no foreign opportunities, i.e. $m = 0$; but it is simpler to neglect that here, for it makes no essential difference to the analysis.) Suppose, furthermore, that working abroad involves the same disutility of labour for anyone as working at home and is equivalent to multiplying after-tax income by $\gamma < 1$: i.e. an (m, n)-person who works abroad has utility $u(\gamma m, n)$.

Then the number of n-people who decide not to migrate is

$$f(v, n) = \int_0^M g(m, n)\, dm, \tag{9}$$

where $M = M(v, n)$ is defined by

$$u(\gamma M, n) = v. \tag{10}$$

From (9) we have

$$f_v = g(M, n)M_v$$
$$= \frac{g(M, n)}{\gamma u_x(\gamma M, n)}.$$

In formula (5), η is defined in terms of $u_x(x, n)$, where x is after-tax income of an n-person, satisfying $u(x, n) = v$. By (10), $\gamma M = x$. Consequently,

$$\eta = \frac{x f_v u_x}{f} = \frac{xg}{\gamma f}$$
$$= Mg(M, n) \bigg/ \int_0^M g(m, n)\, dm. \tag{11}$$

It is to be expected that under any tax schedule, and in particular the optimum, η will vary to a substantial extent with n. To explore this, it is worth analysing another specific example. Let

$$u(x, n) = u_1(x) + t(n). \tag{12}$$

Let $\log m$ and $\log n$ be distributed according to a binormal distribution with means zero and variances σ_m^2 and σ_n^2 and correlation coefficient ρ, so that $g(m, n)$ is proportional to

$$\frac{1}{mn} \exp\left[-\frac{\mu^2 - 2\rho\mu v + v^2}{2(1 - \rho^2)} \right],$$

where

$$\mu = \frac{\log m}{\sigma_m}; \qquad v = \frac{\log n}{\sigma_n}.$$

The restriction to zero means is no real restriction: different means can be accommodated by varying the parameter γ.

With a little manipulation, we find, using (11), that

$$\eta = \frac{1}{\alpha}\frac{1}{\psi(\zeta)}; \qquad \alpha = \sigma_m\sqrt{(1-\rho^2)}, \tag{13}$$

where we define

$$\psi(\zeta) = e^{(1/2)\zeta^2} \int\limits_{-\infty}^{\zeta} e^{-(1/2)z^2} dz \tag{14}$$

$$\zeta = \frac{\mu - \rho v}{\sqrt{(1-\rho^2)}} = \frac{1}{\sqrt{1-\rho^2}} \left[\frac{\log M}{\sigma_m} - \frac{\rho \log n}{\sigma_n} \right]. \tag{15}$$

ψ is an increasing positive function, approximately $1/(1-\zeta)$ for $\zeta < -3$ ($\psi(-3) = 0.305$), and approximately $\sqrt{(2\pi)}e^{(1/2)\zeta^2}$ for large ζ.

The optimal-tax formula (6) for this case is,

$$\frac{n}{x} - 1 = \alpha\psi(\zeta) \, (1 - u_1'(x)/\gamma). \tag{16}$$

Recollect that by (10), $M = x/\gamma$, and this should be substituted in (15):

$$\zeta = \frac{1}{\alpha}\log(xn^{-\tau}\gamma); \qquad \tau = \rho\sigma_m/\sigma_n. \tag{17}$$

To gain some qualitative insight, we shall analyse the implications of (16) for small and large n in turn. But notice first that, if we define x_0 by

$$u_1'(x_0) = \gamma, \tag{18}$$

(16) is satisfied when $x = x_0$ and $n = x_0$. Thus,

$$x(x_0) = x_0. \tag{19}$$

By concavity of u, $x < n$ for $n > x_0$ (income taxation) and $x > n$ for $n < x_0$ (income subsidization).

As $n \to 0$, one expects that x tends to a positive limit. I can show that it does, provided that $\lim_{x \to 0} u_1 = -\infty$. This seems a reasonable assumption to make, and it will be assumed. If $\lim x$ is positive as $n \to 0$, the left-hand side of (16) tends to -1. Also, by (17), $\zeta \to \infty$; and ψ therefore tends to infinity. It follows from (16) that $u_1'/\gamma \to 1$ as $n \to 0$, i.e.

$$x(0) = x_0. \tag{20}$$

Before further comment on the joint significance of (19) and (20), consider n large. To avoid a lengthy analysis, assume that ζ tends to a limit, possibly $\pm\infty$, and consider the three possibilities.

(i) $\zeta \to -\infty$. Then $\psi \sim -1/\zeta$, and (16) implies that

$$-\alpha \log \frac{xn^{-\tau}}{\gamma} \left(\frac{n}{x} - 1 \right) \to 1$$

if $x \to \infty$, or is bounded above in any case. Since $xn^{-\tau} \to 0$, $n/x \to 1$. These two statements can be consistent only if $\tau > 1$, and then we have

$$x \sim n - \frac{1}{\alpha(\tau - 1) \log n}. \tag{21}$$

(ii) $\zeta \to \bar{\zeta}$. Then $x \sim \gamma e^{x\bar{\zeta}} n^{\tau} \to \infty$, and from (16),

$$\frac{x}{n} \to [1 + \alpha\psi(\bar{\zeta})]^{-1}. \tag{22}$$

These statements can be consistent only if $\tau = 1$, and then we have

$$[1 + \alpha\psi(\bar{\zeta})]\gamma e^{x\bar{\zeta}} = 1. \tag{23}$$

(iii) $\zeta \to \infty$. Again $x \to \infty$, and (16) implies that $n/x \to \infty$. With $xn^{-\tau} \to \infty$, this requires $\tau < 1$. We have $\psi \sim \sqrt{(2\pi)}e^{(1/2)\zeta^2}$ as $\zeta \to \infty$. Therefore

$$\sqrt{(2\pi)}\alpha \frac{x}{n} \exp\left[\frac{1}{2\alpha^2} \left\{ \log\left(\frac{xn^{-\tau}}{\gamma} \right) \right\}^2 \right] \to 1.$$

Taking logarithms,

$$\frac{1}{2\alpha^2} \left\{ \log\left(\frac{xn^{-\tau}}{\gamma} \right) \right\}^2 + \log\left(\frac{x}{n} \right) \to -\log\{\alpha\sqrt{(2\pi)}\}.$$

Since $\log(x/n) = \log(xn^{-\tau}) - (1 - \tau)\log n$, and $xn^{-\tau} \to \infty$, we deduce, on dividing by $\{\log(xn^{-\tau}/\gamma)\}^2$, that

$$\frac{(1 - \tau) \log n}{\{\log(xn^{-\tau}/\gamma)\}^2} \to \frac{1}{2\alpha^2}.$$

Taking square roots, we obtain

$$x \sim \gamma n^{\tau} \exp[\alpha\sqrt{(2(1 - \tau) \log n)}]. \tag{24}$$

In summary, we have shown that $x/n \to 1$, and the marginal tax rate therefore tends to zero, when $\rho\sigma_m/\sigma_n = \tau \geq 1$; but that $x/n \to 0$, and the marginal tax rate tends to one when $\rho\sigma_m/\sigma_n < 1$. The latter case is perhaps the most realistic. In the lower range of n, where incomes are subsidized, we have found that $x = x_0$ both at $n = 0$ and at the zero-tax level. Thus, x is a *decreasing* function of n near $n = 0$. In the setting of the problem, it was supposed, unreasonably, that it would be possible, if desirable, to have after-tax income a decreasing function of before-tax income. Since we have found that it is optimal to exploit this freedom in a model with no elasticity of labour supply other than through migration, we should really modify the problem at least by requiring x to be a nondecreasing function of n. If we do so, it is optimal to have x constant for an initial range of n. In this model it is optimal to have a marginal tax rate of 100 per cent on the lowest range of incomes.

4. THE FOREIGN INCOME TAX: GENERAL CONSIDERATIONS

From the point of view of the worker, domestic labour and foreign labour are substitutes. Therefore if one is taxed, both should be. From the general theory of nonlinear taxation (see, for example, Mirrlees 1976) we know that the marginal rate of tax on one commodity should be greater than the marginal rate on another if the marginal rate of substitution of the first for the second increases with ability. The result is independent of the distribution of ability, but it does depend on the assumptions (among others) that ability can be characterized one-dimensionally, and that individual consumers use some of each of the commodities. We therefore cannot apply the theorem automatically. It is plausible that more able people find it easier to substitute a dollar of foreign earnings for a dollar of home earnings, and therefore plausible that foreign income should be taxed at a higher rate than domestic income. But this is not a strict implication of the theorem. In particular, one may well wonder whether the presence of opportunities for earning untaxed foreign income may not so affect the marginal rate of substitution between taxed foreign income and home income as to greatly weaken the result.

This issue is worth exploring formally, despite the highly restrictive assumption that abilities in the population can be characterized by a single real variable. Consider, then, a model in which a typical consumer has utility function

$$u(x, y, y', z, n),$$

where

    x = income after tax,
    y = foreign earnings net of tax, subject to domestic tax,
    y' = foreign earnings net of tax, not subject to domestic tax, and
    z = domestic earnings before tax.

Recollect that in this kind of model one identifies earnings, before deduction of the taxes that are to be determined, with labour supplied by the consumer. Foreign tax rates being fixed throughout the analysis, we can use variables for foreign income that are net of tax collected by foreign governments, n is the consumer's 'ability'.

The tax policy of the domestic government makes x a function of y, y', and z of the form

$$x = c(y, z) + y'.$$

We know, from the theorem alluded to above, that in a model where there is no untaxable commodity the difference between the marginal tax rates on two income sources (as a proportion of before-tax income from the source) has the opposite sign to the partial derivative with respect to n of the ratio of the marginal utilities of the two income sources. In the present model that means that foreign income is taxed at a higher marginal rate than domestic income under the optimal system if

$$\frac{\partial}{\partial n} \frac{u_y(x, y, z, n)}{u_z(x, y, z, n)} < 0. \tag{25}$$

This is the correct result when there is no untaxed commodity. We can deduce the corresponding result when the untaxed income source y' is introduced. The consumer chooses y' to maximize

$$u(c(y, z) + y', y, y', z, n).$$

Denoting the maximized utility by $\bar{u}(c, y, z, n)$, the above result now applies to the utility function $\bar{u}$. By the envelope theorem,

$$\bar{u}_y = u_y(c + y', y, y', z, n),$$
$$\bar{u}_z = u_z(c + y', y, y', z, n),$$

where y' is the function of c, y, z, n defined by the fact that it maximizes u. Define

$$s(c, y, y', z, n) = u_y/u_z.$$

We have to consider the partial derivative of s with respect to n, taking account of the dependence of y' on n. Thus, foreign income should be taxed more highly at the margin than domestic income if

$$s_n + s_{y'} \frac{\partial y'}{\partial n} < 0. \tag{26}$$

It seems likely, as remarked above, that s, being willingness to substitute home for foreign earnings, would have a negative partial derivative with respect to n: $s_n < 0$. It also seems plausible that y' would increase with n, given y and z and c. But it does seem reasonable that y' should have the opposite effect on s from n, i.e. that $s_{y'} > 0$. In this case the presence of an untaxed source of income does seem to be a good reason for having a lower marginal tax rate on the source for which it is a closer substitute.

The case for supposing that the partial derivative of s with respect to untaxable foreign income y' is positive is by no means overwhelming. One way of thinking about this question is to consider the special case

$$u = u_0(x) + u_1(z/n) + u_2(y/n) + u_3(y'/n), \tag{27}$$

where u_1, u_2, and u_3 might be thought of as utility arising from labour activity in successive subperiods of the consumer's life. In this particular case, it is evident that s, being the ratio of the derivatives of u_1 and u_2, is independent of y'. Consequently, by (26), the condition for higher tax on foreign income is simply that s_n be negative, a condition that, as we have remarked, seems quite plausible. The form (27) may not seem particularly plausible, with consumption separated from labour and allocated over the lifetime independently of labour. An additively separable utility function for consumption and labour is quite commonly used, and is at least not evidently absurd. The implicit assumption of a rather perfect capital market is much more unrealistic, but there is no reason to think that a more detailed treatment of intertemporal consumption would affect the presumption about $s_{y'}$ one way or the other. One influence neglected by the additive form (27) is the way that experience of working abroad may make the transition to complete independence from the home country, severing the tax link, more palatable. Like all intertemporally additive utility functions, it supposes that the influence of recent circumstances is no different from the influence of earlier experiences. The best case for supposing that $s_{y'}$ is positive is that working abroad may tend to make the home country, its needs, and the obligations it imposes less vivid and compelling.

For the more general case, where consumers differ in more than one dimension of ability, where for example their earning capacity may not be highly correlated with their earning capacity at home, no result as conveniently applicable as (25) is available. A simple generalization of the Atkinson–Stiglitz theorem (Atkinson and Stiglitz 1976) tells us that foreign and home income should be taxed at the same rate if the consumer's utility function takes the form

$$u(\phi(x, y, z), x, n_1, n_2, \ldots). \tag{28}$$

In this case the marginal rate of substitution between y and z is the same for everyone who has the same x, y, and z. Unfortunately, (28) is not a particularly plausible form in our context. That does not imply that the two sources of income should be taxed at different rates. It does not seem to be worth pursuing the impact of a nontaxable income source y' on the Atkinson–Stiglitz result in the present context, interesting though the question is, more generally.

From a heuristic discussion like this, one should not draw firm conclusions. But I think it shows that the 'common-sense' belief that taxes on foreign income ought to be low because it is easy to change citizenship, or cheat, is not very well founded. There may be other offsetting arguments for taxing foreign income at a higher rate. In any case, escape to nontaxed status, whether legally or illegally, may often be as easily available to the home earner as to the foreign-income earner. Escape routes do often provide a case for lower tax rates. One must assess their bearing on different kinds of earnings rather carefully before concluding that they provide a case for low foreign-income tax rates.

5. A MODEL OF FOREIGN INCOME TAXATION

The rather general model indicated in the previous section is, it seems, hard to get detailed results from. Qualitative results are quite interesting, but quantitative ones are a better basis for policy discussion, however preliminary. In this section I extend the model used in Section 3 to the case where foreign income can, sometimes, be taxed by the home country. From the previous analysis, we found that it might be optimal, under special circumstances, to have a tax system under which after-tax domestic earnings decrease with earnings, while foreign after-tax earnings increase. That is a mildly interesting curiosity, but hardly realistic. The model omitted labour-supply elasticity which surely exists. One simple way of bringing it in is to introduce the possibility of untaxed labour, as in Section 4. The model is therefore generalized as follows.

Imagine a country whose citizens can choose (i) to stay in the country as income-tax payers, (ii) to work abroad, report their incomes to the home government, and pay income tax at a different rate, or (iii) not to pay income taxes to the home government. They vary in their abilities to earn income in these three categories, and in their willingness to sever legal connections with the home country. This conception is expressed by supposing that people of given income-earning ability would choose the one of the two taxable possibilities that provides greatest utility; but that a proportion depending on the utility thus available will prefer nontaxable status. We then have to identify the tax policies that maximize total utility, subject to the home government's budget constraint.

The next few pages are devoted to the mathematical analysis of this problem. Conditions characterizing the optimum for nicely behaved situations are stated as the Solution at the end of the section. These take the form of a pair of differential equations and corresponding initial conditions. The equations are not as readily interpreted as (6) above, although a sympathetic eye would see a resemblance to the previous equation (particularly in the specialized form (16)). Numerical solution would be possible, though there are difficulties which will be alluded to below. Rather than pursue that approach, we turn in the final section to the analysis of special cases for which substantial information may be obtained.

In the present section, notation is first established, then a Lagrangean for the problem set up. The Lagrangean is a double integral, in the space of home and foreign incomes. First-order conditions are obtained by considering the subpopulation with a particular home income, and choosing the utility level for those who choose to be taxable at home with due regard to the effects on migration. This procedure yields an equation for the derivative with respect to utility of the taxable foreign income of someone indifferent about migrating. A similar procedure yields another equation for the derivative of home income with respect to utility. These conditions provide the two differential equations. The initial conditions are obtained by careful attention to those who have the lowest foreign-income earning ability.

An individual who works at home in an occupation that attracts tax has productivity n. If he worked abroad with taxable status, his income net of foreign tax would be m. Taxes exist—and are to be chosen optimally—that provide him with utility $u_h(n)$ if he stays at home, $u_f(m)$ if he works abroad. This formulation embodies the assumption that the government cannot know what an individual's income would have been had he gone abroad instead of staying at home, or vice versa. An individual of type (m, n) who chooses to remain a taxpayer gets utility

$$v = \max\{u_h(n), u_f(m)\}. \tag{29}$$

In equilibrium, $f(m, n, v)$ of such people choose to remain taxable, the others emigrating for good and severing their tax liability to the home government, or indulging in other untaxable activities, where they have greater utility. To be more precise, f is a density function for m and n.

The after-tax earnings that people require to achieve specified levels of utility are given by convex increasing functions:

$$\begin{aligned} y(m) &= Y(u_f(m)), \\ z(n) &= Z(u_h(n)), \end{aligned} \tag{30}$$

where y refers to foreign earnings, after deduction of home tax, and z to home earnings, net of tax. Notice that this notation differs from that used in the previous section, where y and z referred to earnings before deduction of home tax.

Let H be the set of (m, n) for which $u_h \geq u_f$, and F the set for which $u_h < u_f$. Then the State's tax revenue is

$$\begin{aligned} T = &\iint\limits_{H} [n - z(n)] f(m, n, u_h(n)) \, dm \, dn \\ &+ \iint\limits_{F} [m - y(m)] f(m, n, u_f(m)) \, dm \, dn. \end{aligned} \tag{31}$$

This formulation assumes that the indifferent stay at home. One would suppose that they form a set of measure zero, so that the convention is of no significance.

The total utility of (m, n)-people who leave the tax system is

$$\int_v^\infty w f_w(m, n, w)\mathrm{d}w = \Omega(m, n, v) \tag{32}$$

as a definition. Welfare will be measured by total utility. The welfare of the whole relevant population is

$$W = \iint_H [\Omega(m, n, u_b) + u_b f(m, n, u_b)]\mathrm{d}m\,\mathrm{d}n$$
$$+ \iint_F [\Omega(m, n, u_f) + u_f f(m, n, u_f)]\mathrm{d}m\,\mathrm{d}n. \tag{33}$$

Our problem is to find how to maximize W subject to the government budget constraint, for which a multiplier λ is introduced. Thus, we seek to maximize $W + \lambda T$ by choice of the functions u_b and u_f. It is convenient to write $W + \lambda T$ in the form

$$L = \iint_H \phi(m, n, u_b(n))\,\mathrm{d}m\;\mathrm{d}n + \iint_F \psi(m, n, u_f(m))\mathrm{d}m\,\mathrm{d}n, \tag{34}$$

where

$$\phi(m, n, v) = \Omega(m, n, v) + [v + \lambda(n - Z(v))]f(m, n, v),$$
$$\psi(m, n, v) = \Omega(m, n, v) + [v + \lambda(m - Y(v))]f(m, n, v). \tag{35}$$

The inverse utility functions Z and Y are central to the analysis. It is assumed that, offered the same after-tax income at home and abroad, anyone would choose to remain in his own country, which is equivalent to

$$Y(v) > Z(v), \qquad \text{for all } v. \tag{36}$$

A further reasonable assumption is that

$$Y'(v) \geqq Z'(v), \qquad \text{for all } v. \tag{37}$$

The problem to be solved is not immediately of standard type, since the region of integration is divided up in a rather inconvenient way. Necessary conditions for maximization will be found by first considering the choice of the function u_b, given that u_f has already been chosen, and afterwards reversing the role of the two functions. Before doing that we shall make one further modification in the problem. When considering a model with taxation only of domestic incomes, we found that, under optimal taxes, it might be the case that utilities decrease with productivity over certain ranges. We noted that such an arrangement is not likely to be feasible. In the model we are now considering, it would also be somewhat intractable to allow utility to decrease with income. Let us therefore constrain u_f and u_b to be nondecreasing functions. Let us also make the reasonable (and justifiable) assumption that they are continuous functions.

Define a function M inverse to u_f. Specifically,

$$M(v) = \max\{m : u_f(m) \leqq v\}. \tag{38}$$

Like u_f, M has to be a nondecreasing function. The region of (m, n)-space that we call H, where people would choose to work in the home country, can now be defined by the inequality

$$m \leqq M(u_b(n)). \tag{39}$$

It follows that we can write the integral L as $\int L(n)\mathrm{d}n$ with

$$
\begin{aligned}
L(n) = &\int_0^{M(u_b(n))} \phi(m, n, u_b(n))\, \mathrm{d}m \\
&+ \int_{M(u_b(n))}^{\infty} \psi(m, n, u_f(m))\, \mathrm{d}m.
\end{aligned}
\tag{40}
$$

We must choose the function u_b as the nondecreasing function that maximizes L. It would be nice if we could, for each n, choose $u_b(n)$ so as to maximize $L(n)$, given in (40), and then find that the resulting u_b is a nondecreasing function of n. It turns out that our model is simple enough for this to be true. We shall not take the space to prove this rigorously. Another point is worth making rigorously. We can show that

$$u_b(0) > u_f(0). \tag{41}$$

To prove this we simply have to show that it is never desirable to have $M(u_b(n)) = 0$. We see from the definitions (35) that

$$\phi(m, n, u) - \psi(m, n, u) = \lambda f(m, n, u)(Y - Z - m + n) \tag{42}$$

is positive when $m = 0$. Therefore small positive M in (40) always yields a larger value of $L(n)$ than having $M = 0$. This proves (41). We may therefore define the minimum utility level by

$$\omega = u_b(0). \tag{43}$$

People with m less than $M(\omega)$ never work abroad and pay tax. We define

$$m_0 = M(\omega). \tag{44}$$

Below this level of m the choice of u_f has no effect, and we can therefore restrict attention to the choice of the function for $m \geq m_0$.

The first-order condition for the choice of $u_h(n)$, when M is differentiable at that value of u, is obtained from (40) by differentiation:

$$[\phi(M(u), n, u) - \psi(M(u), n, u)]M'(u) = - \int_0^{M(u)} \phi_u(m, n, u)\, dm. \tag{45}$$

Notice that we have used the fact that $u_f(M(u)) = u$. The statement that (45) holds at $u = u_h(n)$ can be expressed equivalently as the statement that it holds when $n = N(u)$. In an exactly similar way, we get the first-order condition for $u_f(m)$ when the function N inverse u_h is differentiable at $u = u_f(m)$, and u_f is strictly increasing in m:

$$[\phi(m, N(u), u) - \psi(m, N(u), u)]N'(u) = \int_0^{N(u)} \psi_u(m, n, u)\, dn. \tag{46}$$

This holds when $m = M(u) > m_0$. As in the previous case, it turns out that u_f is strictly increasing in the relevant range $m \geq m_0$, and the constraint that it be nondecreasing is therefore satisfied.

Finding conditions that determine the numbers ω and m_0 is the familiar task of finding terminal conditions in calculus of variations problems. It is most straightforward if ϕ and ψ do not vanish when $n = 0$, nor do their derivatives and difference. A heuristic derivation is as follows.

Consider small changes in the u_f function near m_0. The effect is to move a few marginal people with $n = 0$ into or out of the domestic economy: the change in L is proportional to $\phi(m_0, 0, \omega) - \psi(m_0, 0, \omega)$. At the optimum, this expression must be zero. Using (42), this implies

$$m_0 = Y(\omega) - Z(\omega). \tag{47}$$

With a little trouble, it can be shown that this is also a valid condition when f tends to zero as n tends to zero.

Now consider the effect of changing $u_h(0)$ by a small amount, while leaving other utility levels the same (except, necessarily, for n very close to zero). The effect on L is proportional to

$$\int_0^{m_0} \phi_u(m, 0, \omega)\, dm, \tag{48}$$

which therefore must vanish. It would vanish automatically if ϕ_u were zero when $n = 0$, but it is then possible to get an essentially similar condition, which will be noted below.

It only remains to replace the functions ϕ and ψ by their definitions (35). We have

$$\phi_u = [1 - Z'(u)]f + \lambda[m - Z(u)]f_u \qquad (49)$$

and a similar expression for ψ_u. Using these, we have the following solution.

Solution. *The functions M and N are given by*

$$(N - M - Z + Y)f \, M'(u) = - \{\rho - Z'(u)\} \int_0^M f \, dm$$

$$\qquad (50)$$

$$- (N - Z) \int_0^M f_u \, dm,$$

$$(N - M - Z + Y)f \, N'(u) = \{\rho - Y'(u)\} \int_0^N f \, dm$$

$$\qquad (51)$$

$$+ (M - Y) \int_0^N f_u \, dn,$$

which hold for $u > \omega$, with

$$M(\omega) = Y(\omega) - Z(\omega), \text{ called } m_0,$$
$$N(\omega) = 0, \qquad (53)$$
$$\frac{\rho - Z'(\omega)}{Z(\omega)} = \lim_{n \to 0} \left\{ \int_0^{m_0} f_u(m, n, \omega) dm \Big/ \int_0^{m_0} f(m, n, \omega) dm \right\}.$$

The optimal relationships between income before and after taxes, $z(n)$ and $y(m)$, are deduced from the equations

$$z(N(u)) = Z(u); \qquad y(M(u)) = Y(u).$$

Equations (50) and (51) are translations of (45) and (46), using (42) and (49). The number ρ is $1/\lambda$, and is determined by the resource constraint. Equation (53) is given in the more general form that is valid when f and f_u vanish at $n = 0$. (Essentially, this comes from the principle that the multipliers in a calculus-of-variations problem of Pontrjagin type should tend to zero as rapidly as possible.)

Notice that, because of the initial conditions, (50) and (51) yield expressions of the form '0/0' for $M'(\omega)$ and $N'(\omega)$. These initial derivatives have to be found by l'Hôpital's rule. This makes general analysis of the solution difficult. But there is a class of examples that is more amenable, and which seems to be general enough to be interesting.

6. A SPECIAL CASE

Define

$$F(M, W, u) = \int_0^M \int_0^N f(m, n, u)\,dm\,dn. \tag{54}$$

Unfortunately, this function has no very natural economic interpretation: it is the number with earning ability $(m, n) \leq (M, N)$ which would choose to remain taxable if all of them were offered the same utility u. Using the definition, we have

$$F_M = \int_0^N f\,dn, \qquad F_N = \int_0^M f\,dm,$$

$$F_{Mu} = \int_0^N f\,dn, \qquad F_{Nu} = \int_0^M f_u\,dm,$$

$$F_{MN} = f,$$

which allow us to write the basic equations, (50) and (51), a little more briefly.

The real advantage of this new function emerges if it takes the special form:

$$F(M, N, u) = F(G(M, N), u). \tag{55}$$

Using the notation F for both functions should occasion no confusion. The new F may be taken to be increasing in G, which is increasing in M and N. Equations (50) and (51) can now be written

$$(N - M - Z + Y)f\,M' = -[(\rho - Z')F_G + (N - Z)F_{Gu}]\,G_N, \tag{56}$$

$$(N - M - Z + Y)f\,N' = [(\rho - Y')F_G + (M - Y)F_{Gu}]\,G_M. \tag{57}$$

From these it follows that

$$(N - M - Z + Y)f\frac{dG}{du} = -[(Y' - Z')F_G + (N - M - Z + Y)F_{Gu}]G_M\,G_N,$$

which can be rewritten

$$(N - M - Z + Y)\left(f\frac{dG}{du} + F_{Gu}\,G_M\,G_N\right) = -(Y' - Z')F_G\,G_M\,G_N. \tag{58}$$

We know that G is an increasing function of u, and that G_M, G_N, F_G, and F_{Gu} are all positive. (Note that $F_{Gu}G_M = F_{Mu} > 0$.) Furthermore, $Y' \geq Z'$. Equation (58) therefore implies that

$$N - M - Z + Y \leq 0;$$

i.e.

$$N(u) - Z(u) \leq M(u) - Y(u). \tag{59}$$

This proves the following:

Proposition. *If F can be written in the separable form (55), the tax optimally paid by a person who earns taxed income at home is not greater than that paid by a person of equal utility who earns taxed income abroad.*

The point of the separability condition is that it is general enough to allow a greater propensity to leave the tax system for people with high foreign earning power m, compared to those with relatively high home earning power n. This can be done by making G more sensitive to variations in M than in N; but we are then forced to make possibly unacceptable assumptions about the underlying distribution of m and n. The condition is however a strongly sufficient one.

A further result is obtained by going back to (56) and (57). It is convenient to define

$$\gamma = F_G / F_{Gu}. \tag{60}$$

Corollary. *Under the above assumptions,*

$$N \geq Z + \gamma(Z' - \rho), \tag{61}$$

$$M \geq Y + \gamma(Y' - \rho). \tag{62}$$

These conditions place lower bounds on the optimal tax rates if we are prepared to estimate the magnitudes of ρ and γ.

It will be evident from the above discussion that in one very special case it is easy to calculate optimal tax schedules, namely when

$$Z(u) = Y(u) - K \tag{63}$$

for some constant, K. Equation (63) means that migration is equivalent to a constant income loss K, independent of income levels. This assumption presumably seriously overstates the relative willingness of the rich to migrate. It implies that $Z' = Y'$. Then the inequalities (59), (61), and (62) just derived become equalities, and the optimal taxes are defined by

$$N = Z + \gamma(Z' - \rho), \tag{64}$$

$$M = Y + \gamma(Y' - \rho) = N + K, \qquad \text{by (63).} \tag{65}$$

From these equations we can deduce that a home earner should pay more than a foreign earner with the same income. Since at equal utility $M > N$, equal income implies that the home earner is better off: $u_h > u_f$. Therefore, by concavity of utility which is equivalent to convexity of Z and Y, $Z'(u_h) > Z'(u_f) = Y'(u_f)$. With $N(u_h) = M(u_f)$ in (64) and (65), we then have

$$Z(u_h) < Y(u_f), \tag{66}$$

showing that the home earner pays more tax at all levels of income. It will be appreciated that this result depends on the extreme assumption that $Y(u) - Z(u)$ is constant. If, instead, it is an increasing function of u, the tax on the foreign earner can be greater even at equal incomes.

As an illustrative example, suppose that

$$U_h(x) = -\frac{1}{x}; \qquad U_f(x) = -\frac{1}{x - K},$$
$$f(m, n, u) = h(m, n)(-u)^{-\eta}. \tag{66}$$

Easy calculations yield:

$$\gamma = (-u)/\eta,$$
$$Z(u) = 1/(-u),$$
$$Y(u) = 1/(-u) + K.$$

From these equations, we have

$$Z'(u) = Z^2; \qquad \gamma = 1/(\eta Z).$$

Substitution in (64) then tells us that $z(n)$ is given by solving

$$n = \frac{1 + \eta}{\eta} z - \frac{\rho}{\eta} \frac{1}{z}. \tag{67}$$

Disposable income of foreign earners is given by

$$y(m) = z(m - K) + K. \tag{68}$$

To determine m_0 and ω, we use the auxiliary conditions in the Solution above. From (53),

$$\frac{\rho - 1/\omega^2}{1/(-\omega)} = \frac{\eta}{-\omega},$$

which simplifies to

$$\omega = \left(\frac{1+\eta}{\rho}\right)^{1/2}. \tag{69}$$

The other condition yields:

$$m_0 = Y(\omega) - Z(\omega) = K. \tag{70}$$

These results are consistent with (67) and (68), with

$$z(0) = y(m_0) = \left(\frac{\rho}{1+\eta}\right)^{1/2}. \tag{71}$$

From (67), it can be seen that the marginal tax rate

$$1 - z'(n) \to \frac{1}{1+\eta} \tag{72}$$

as $n \to \infty$. The same result holds for foreign incomes. Notice that the details of income distribution incorporated in the function h affect results only through ρ.
   A numerical solution for the case

$$K = 1, \qquad \eta = \tfrac{1}{2}, \qquad \rho = \tfrac{3}{2}$$

is shown in Figure 12.1.

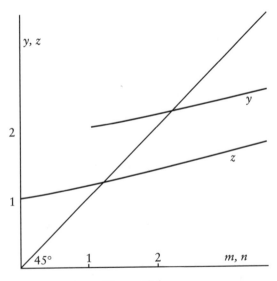

Figure 12.1.

7. CONCLUSIONS

The final numerical example made several assumptions. One, very favourable to home taxes being higher than taxes on foreign income, was that the cost of working abroad is equivalent to a reduction of income independent of income actually enjoyed. Another, which is probably favourable to the opposite conclusion, was that the distribution of incomes is described by a density function of the multiplicative form $h(m, n)q(u)$. This means that, among people enjoying the same utility, the propensity to migrate is the same for those with relatively high n as for those with relatively high m. The basic structure of the model used tends to have the latter work abroad, the former at home; and it may seem that a change in prospective utility would be more likely to induce those working abroad to give up citizenship, through either taste or opportunity. Yet we have seen that a more general assumption works in much the same way, yielding the result that those working abroad pay higher taxes than people provided with equal utility working at home.

Taking these results with the general ideas presented in the opening section of the paper—that an income tax on foreign earnings should include an element corresponding to expenditure taxes at home, and that the relative magnitude of the optimal taxes depends on the degree of substitutibility of home and foreign taxable earnings with untaxed alternatives—it seems that it may well be desirable to institute substantial income taxes on foreign earnings, if only the narrowly economic considerations incorporated in our model are relevant.

REFERENCES

Atkinson, A. B. and Stiglitz, J. E. (1976) 'The Design of Tax Structure: Direct versus Indirect Taxation'. *Journal of Public Economics*, 6: 55–75.

Bhagwati, J. (1980) 'Taxation and International Migration: Recent Policy Issues. Paper presented at the Conference on U.S. Immigration Issues and Policies, Chicago.

——and Hamada, K. (1982) 'Tax Policy in the Presence of Emigration'. *Journal of Public Economics*, 18.

Mirrlees, J. A. (1976) 'Optimal Tax Theory: A Synthesis'. *Journal of Public Economics*, 6, 327–58.

13

Taxing Uncertain Incomes

1. UNCERTAIN INCOMES AND UNCERTAIN TAXES

People deciding what labour to supply are uncertain what labour income their efforts will produce, particularly when the results are delayed, as with training and career choices. This fact is relevant to optimal income redistribution. It is not easy to guess whether such uncertainty is a reason for higher or lower marginal tax rates. That is the issue I want to address.

The question of optimal taxation when consumers are uncertain about income is a case of moral hazard, and has been examined as such by Varian (1980). A somewhat complex simple example was studied in detail by Diamond, Helms and Mirrlees (1980): in that paper, we explored the issues by means of numerical solutions. In the present paper I shall be looking for qualitative results, in a straightforward modification of the simple linear income tax model.

First, I develop approximations to the optimal linear tax schedule, when individuals have partial information about the relationship of their income to their effort. These approximation results give some insight into the magnitude of optimal tax rates in the standard model. Then, with the extent of inequality in *ex post* wage rates given, the proportion of that inequality that reflects *ex ante* uncertainty is allowed to vary. The approximate results are used to assess the influence of this proportion on the optimal tax schedule.

It should be emphasized that the linear income tax is not, in a more general sense, an optimal policy within the simple model of labour supply that will be used. When individuals each know something about the return to their effort, but are also uncertain, it is theoretically better to provide them with an *ex ante* choice of tax schedules. People with different expected wages would choose different schedules. People with the same expected wage, and therefore the same schedule, will in the outcome have different labour supply and therefore different incomes. Policies of this kind clearly generalize the provision of a single tax schedule, without choice. The richer policy structure makes it possible to provide better insurance and better effort incentives simultaneously and is superior to the kind of tax policy we are accustomed to,

This chapter first appeared in *Oxford Economic Papers*, Vol. 42 (1990), pp. 34–45. Support from the US National Science Foundation is gratefully acknowledged. I am also grateful for the helpful comments provided by a referee.

where everyone is subject to the same schedule. That possibility will not be further considered in the present chapter. I hope to compare this more complex optimal tax policy with those considered here in subsequent work. The restriction that the State must use a single income tax schedule applying to everyone simplifies the analysis.

The purpose of the chapter is to estimate approximately optimal tax rates, for economies with a small degree of inequality. Suppose that the tax schedule must be linear. Then one can, by relatively straightforward techniques, obtain approximations to the optimal marginal tax rate. This chapter deals with the crudest approximation to optimal taxes, correct to the first order in a small parameter describing the degree of inequality in the population. For such an approximation, the restriction to linear schedules is probably not significant.[1] One can anticipate that tax rates calculated to be optimal even to this degree of accuracy would achieve welfare quite close to its maximum. They can be regarded as 'nearly optimal', and provide some degree of guidance about the influence of parameters on optimal taxes.

The first part of the chapter deals with uncertainty about the payment the labour market will make for work. Individuals may also be uncertain about the amount of tax that they will pay. Uncertainty about tax liabilities is likely to be particularly significant in developing countries, where it may be especially difficult to estimate individual income, especially when it should include the fruits of unmarketed labour; but it is not unimportant in developed ones. It is relatively easy to apply the same methods of analysis to an economy where there is uncertainty about the way income will be observed and assessed for tax and subsidy purposes; or, more generally, about the relationship between tax or subsidy and any particular level of true income. That will allow us to consider what influence errors in the observation of incomes should have on optimal tax rates. I pose the question in the form: assuming a fixed distribution of observed wage rates, how should the extent to which observed inequality is believed to reflect errors in observation of income by the tax authority affect judgements about the optimal tax rate?

2. NEARLY OPTIMAL TAXES

First, we need a theory of nearly optimal linear taxes, for the standard case with no uncertainty. Conditions for the general *n*-commodity optimal tax system are well known (Atkinson and Stiglitz (1980) provide an exposition); and we shall see that they can be made to yield a convenient formula for

---

[1] The linear tax system is an approximation to the optimal nonlinear system in the neighbourhood of average consumption levels. It would not be a good approximation if the optimal nonlinear system had a kink at the average consumption levels. In that case one should find that a piecewise linear schedule is superior to a linear one, even at this crude order of approximation. This seems unlikely when demand functions are sufficiently smooth, but it is possible.

nearly optimal taxes. The sense of 'nearly' is that the degree of inequality in the population is taken to be small. The population is also taken to be one-dimensional, in the sense that utility varies from person to person in a way that can be represented by a single parameter. It is obvious how to generalize the results, but there is no need to do so here, since the general results will be applied to a special model. I am going to concentrate on the simplest interesting model of a redistributive tax system, in which individuals have the same utility function in terms of consumption and work, and differ only in the wage they receive for work. This model allows us to concentrate attention on the central question of the direction and magnitude of the influence of uncertainty considerations on the optimal degree of redistribution.

The following notation is used:

p = vector of producer prices
t = vector of specific tax rates
b = uniform lumpsum income
n = index describing individuals
$v(p + t, b, n)$ = indirect utility function
$x(p + t, u, n)$ = *compensated* net demands
g = vector of public net expenditure.

I use a utilitarian welfare function, the sum of individual utilities. The notation $\mathscr{E}f$ means the average of a function f over the population.

Before approximating, we need the first-order conditions for optimality. There are dozens of ways of deriving them: here is one that is a bit tricky, and gets quickly to what I want.

$$\text{maximize}_{t, b} \quad \mathscr{E}v(p + t, b) \tag{1}$$
$$\text{subject to:} \quad t \cdot \mathscr{E}x(p + t, v(p + t, b)) - b = p \cdot g.$$

Use a multiplier λ for the constraint, and differentiate with respect to t and b, ignoring the possibility of corner conditions:

$$\mathscr{E}[-v_b x + \lambda x + \lambda t \cdot x_p + \lambda t \cdot x_u \cdot (-v_b x)] = 0, \tag{2}$$

$$\mathscr{E}[v_b + \lambda t \cdot x_u v_b - \lambda] = 0. \tag{3}$$

Condition (2) uses Roy's identity for the derivative of the indirect utility function with respect to prices. This equation can be written as a kind of formula for optimal tax rates,

$$t \cdot \mathscr{E}x_p = \mathscr{E}\left[\left(\frac{v_b}{\lambda} - 1 + t \cdot x_u v_b\right)x\right]. \tag{4}$$

By (3), the scalar expression multiplying the vector x has mean zero. Therefore we can write, in a similar way to Diamond's (1975) covariance condition,

$$t \cdot \mathscr{E}x_p = \text{cov}\left(\frac{v_b}{\lambda} + t \cdot x_u v_b, x\right). \tag{5}$$

Suppose that var(n) is small. The covariance of two functions of a random variable n is approximately equal to the var(n) times the product of the derivatives of the two functions, evaluated at $\mathscr{E}n$. We use this fact to estimate the right-hand side of (5).

Notice first that t can be assumed to be small, relative to prices. When var(n) $= 0$, there is no inequality, and the optimum has $t = 0$. To be more precise, this is one of the tax optima: one can have producer prices and consumer prices proportional rather than equal, which means that all tax rates are the same; but that is equivalent to an equilibrium with all tax rates zero. Therefore when var(n) is small, the optimal t can be taken to be small (although there are other optimal tax equilibria where they are not small). For example, if one commodity is not taxed, other tax rates will be small relative to the corresponding prices. Since t is small, the derivative of $(t \cdot x_u)v_b$ with respect to n is small, and can be neglected, relative to the derivative of v_b/λ, Also, by (3), λ is approximately $\mathscr{E}v_b$, which is approximately v_b evaluated at $\mathscr{E}n$.

From these considerations, we obtain

$$t \cdot x_p \cong \text{var}(n) \frac{v_{bn}}{v_b} x_n. \tag{5'}$$

All terms are evaluated at the mean value of n, $\mathscr{E}n$. Furthermore, we can evaluate the matrix x_p, the vector x_n, and the scalar v_{bn}/v_b at producer prices p and a lump-sum income $-g$. The reason is that replacing $p + t$ by p, and b by $-p \cdot g$, changes the various elements in the formula by amounts of the same order as the tax rates t, which are of order var(n), and therefore does not affect the validity of (5), in which terms of order $[\text{var}(n)]^2$ are neglected. Notice that the differences between b and $-p \cdot g$ is $t \cdot \mathscr{E}x$, which is of the same order of magnitude as t.

x_n in formula (5) is the total derivative of $x(p, v(p, b, n), n)$ at the average n, best written as $x_n(p, b, \mathscr{E}n)$: it is the derivative of the uncompensated demand functions with respect to n. The matrix x_p, on the other hand, is the matrix of compensated price derivatives. These equations can be solved if any one tax rate is set equal to zero to obtain approximately optimal tax rates on other commodities.

The formula (5) for nearly optimal taxes has been obtained on the assumption that no corner conditions apply in the first-order conditions. It may be accepted that optimal consumer prices will not usually be zero, but the assumption that lump-sum income b is nonzero needs some justification. In effect, we have been discussing optimal taxation with no constraint on b. When var(n) is small, we have seen that b is approximately $-p \cdot g$. In most realistic cases, this will be negative. Application of formula (5) would set tax rates at levels too low to meet public expenditure: it is implicit in the formula that a lump-sum tax will then be imposed to cover the deficit.

Although it has been assumed that var(n) is small, that does not imply that there are no individuals with a value of n far from its mean. Small n might mean that the individual has little property or low-productivity labour. Someone with small enough n could be unable to pay the implied lump-sum tax: it could violate feasibility for such people. That is the realistic case. If, in the simple labour supply model we shall be using later in the paper, the wage rate n were distributed throughout the real axis, feasibility for all consumers would require that b be positive. The procedure followed above would then be invalid. In fact, the correct first approximation to optimal taxes is the Ramsey taxes for a single consumer with n equal to $\mathscr{E}n$.

This problem, though formally a real one, is a problem created by assuming a linear tax system. If nonlinearity is allowed, it is easy to arrange that all consumers can survive when people at average income levels face the taxes given by (5). In the consumption/labour model, that is achieved by making the marginal tax rates small for most people, but quite high for people with low incomes. In welfare terms, there are so few people with small n that they can be ignored, provided that (as is optimal) they are granted positive minimum income, in effect a positive lump-sum income if they do no work. Granted that, we can, to a first approximation, ignore low-income groups. The approximation formula (5) is to be interpreted as giving marginal tax rates for the large majority of the population. To this order of approximation, even quite large changes to the taxes paid by people at the extremes of the income distribution do not matter significantly.

3. INCOME TAX

Now apply these results to the two-commodity linear income-tax model with n the productivity of a person.[2] In this model, utility is a function of labour supply y and consumption. Labour supply by an individual of type n yields output (efficiency units of labour) ny. It is convenient to introduce the normalization,

$$\mathscr{E}n = 1. \tag{6}$$

Let there be no tax on the consumption good. Then there is only one tax rate t, so that the linear equations (5) will be easy to solve. $-ny$ corresponds to x in the approximation formula; v and y are functions of b and $(1-t)nw$, where w is the producer price of labour in efficiency units:

$$v = v((1-t)wn, b); \qquad x = -ny((1-t)wn, b). \tag{7}$$

---

[2] The analysis of this case by Dixit and Sandmo (1977) is particularly neat.

From these, using Roy's identity, which for labour is $v_1 = yv_b$, we obtain

$$v_{bn} = (1 - t)w(v_{bb}\, y + v_b y_b), \tag{8}$$

$$-x_n = y + (1 - t)wny_1, \tag{9}$$

$$-x_p = (1 - t)wn^2 y_1 - n^2 y_b\, y. \tag{10}$$

Equations (8) and (9) are obtained straightforwardly by differentiation of v and x in (7). In (10), the matrix $-x_p$ becomes simply a scalar, the compensated derivative of ny with respect to w. The uncompensated derivative is $n \cdot (1 - t)n \cdot y_1$, and the income effect is $(ny_b)(ny)$: from these we obtain (10).

It is then found, by direct substitution in (5), that a nearly optimal marginal tax rate is

$$t = \mathrm{var}(n)y^2 \left(\frac{v_{bb}}{v_b} + \frac{y_b}{y}\right)\left(1 + \frac{wy_1}{y}\right)(y_1 - y_b\, y)^{-1}. \tag{11}$$

I find it helpful to introduce the following elasticities:

$$\eta_0 = -(wy + b)\frac{v_{bb}}{v_b}, \tag{12}$$

the elasticity of the marginal utility of income with respect to full income;

$$\eta_i = -(wy + b)\frac{y_b}{y}, \tag{13}$$

the elasticity of labour supply with respect to full income; and

$$\eta_w = w\frac{y_1}{y}, \tag{14}$$

the elasticity of labour supply with respect to the (marginal) wage rate.

With these definitions, and replacing b by $-g$, g being public spending, we obtain the formula we have been seeking:

$$t = \mathrm{var}(n)\frac{(\eta_0 + \eta_i)(1 + \eta_w)}{n_i + (1 - g/wy)\eta_w}. \tag{15}$$

It is legitimate to replace b by $-g$ because $b + g$ is equal to tax revenue, and that is of order $\mathrm{var}(n)$. The replacement therefore makes no difference to an approximation that is valid only to order $\mathrm{var}(n)$.

The formula simplifies dramatically if η_w happens to be 0 (i.e. if income and substitution effects happen to balance for labour supply at the optimum):

$$t = \mathrm{var}(n)\left(\frac{\eta_0}{\eta_i} + 1\right). \tag{16}$$

One can best understand the determination of the optimum tax rate by starting from this version of the nearly-optimal rule. η_0 is a measure of inequality aversion, while η_i is a measure of the effectiveness of incentives in augmenting labour supply. The optimal tax rate is an increasing function of their ratio, and also of the extent of inequality.

In the more general formula (15), it can be seen that the optimal marginal tax rate may be an increasing or a decreasing function of η_w, for g is necessarily less than wy, total production. This indicates that greater responsiveness of labour supply to the wage rate can be a reason for a larger tax rate (given the level of the income effects), an unexpected result.

It will be noticed that t is not zero when $\eta_0 = 0$. In a way, that is because η_0 is not an entirely satisfactory measure of inequality aversion. But there presumably cannot be such a measure for the two-good economy that works as simply and neatly as the corresponding measure for a one-good economy. If one considers the example of a utility function $c(1-y)$ ($c=$ consumption, $y=$ labour), which appears to be equality-neutral, one finds that $\eta_0 = 0$ for large b, but $\eta_0 < 0$ for an average income household, especially when $b < 0$. In any case, a tax rate of zero is not in general optimal with that particular utility function.

4. INCOME UNCERTAINTY

Now suppose that, when y is chosen, productivity is still subject to a multiplicative error m (with mean 1):

$$y \max \mathscr{E}_m u(b + (1 - t)mnwy, y),$$

where u is the direct utility function, and $\mathscr{E}_m$ means the expectation operator with respect to the random variable m; m is taken to be distributed independently of n in the population. Again, we define indirect utility and labour supply functions, but Roy's identity, $v_1 = yv_b$, no longer holds: it is replaced with the formulae (18) below. With that modification in the analysis, and assuming the variance of m is small, as well as the variance of n, we get a formula for the optimal tax rates by the same methods.

The indirect utility function is now

$$v((1 - t)nw, b) = \max_y \mathscr{E}_m u(b + (1 - t)mnwy, y). \tag{17}$$

Consequently,

$$v_2 = \mathscr{E}_m u_1; \qquad v_1 = y \cdot \mathscr{E}_m m u_1 \tag{18}$$

with $y = y((1 - t)nw, b)$. The Lagrangean is

$$\mathscr{E}[v - \lambda(b - tnwy)]. \tag{19}$$

When we differentiate with respect to b and tw, and set the derivatives equal to zero, we get

$$\mathscr{E}[v_2 - \lambda + \lambda tnwy_2] = 0, \tag{20}$$

$$\mathscr{E}[n(v_1 - \lambda y + \lambda tnwy_1)] = 0. \tag{21}$$

Following essentially the same method as earlier, we multiply (20) by $\mathscr{E}(ny)$ and subtract the result from (21):

$$t \cdot w\mathscr{E}\{n[y_1 - y_2\,\mathscr{E}(ny)]\} = \frac{1}{\lambda}\,\mathscr{E}[n(y\mathscr{E}v_2 - v_1)].$$

The term multiplying t on the left is approximately equal to $w(y_1 - y_2y)$, the value of the random variable at $n = 1$. Therefore we can write

$$t \cdot w(y_1 - y_2y) = \frac{1}{\lambda}\{\mathscr{E}[n(yv_2 - v_1)] - \text{cov}\,(ny, v_2)\}. \tag{22}$$

The new term here is $(1/\lambda)\mathscr{E}[ny(yv_2 - v_1)]$: apart from that, we would simply recover the approximation (11) from this equation. Making use of (18),

$$yv_2 - v_1 = y \cdot \mathscr{E}_m[(m - 1)u_1].$$

When var(m) is a small,

$$
\begin{aligned}
\mathscr{E}_m[(m - 1)u_1] &\cong \text{var}(m)\frac{d}{dm}u_1\,|_{m=1} \\
&= \text{var}(m)(1 - t)nwy \cdot u_{11}[b + (1 - t)nwy, y] \\
&\cong \text{var}(m)nwy \cdot v_{22}.
\end{aligned}
\tag{23}
$$

Therefore, to this order of approximation,

$$\mathscr{E}\{ny \cdot \mathscr{E}_m[(m - 1)u_1]\} \cong \text{var}(m)wy^2 \cdot v_{22}. \tag{24}$$

Modifying the previous formula, (11), by introducing (24), and then using the elasticities defined above, we get an approximation to the optimal tax for the extended model. Writing var(n)t_c for the optimal tax rate when there is no uncertainty and the distribution of productivities is var(n), we have

$$t = \text{var}(n)\,t_c + \text{var}(m)\,\frac{\eta_0}{\eta_1 + (1 - g/wy)\eta_w}$$

or, explicitly,

$$t = \frac{\text{var}(n)(\eta_0 + \eta_1)(1 + \eta_w) + \text{var}(m)\eta_0}{\eta_1 + (1 - g/wy)\eta_w}. \tag{25}$$

To see how the consideration of uncertainty affects optimal taxes, we should think of the dispersion of $m \cdot n$ as being given, and look at the effect of changing the relative dispersion of m and n. Since both variances are taken to be small, we may as well take $\text{var}(n) + \text{var}(m)$ as given and vary the ratio of the two variances. More income uncertainty means a lower marginal tax rate (to this order of approximation) if and only if

$$(\eta_0 + \eta_1)(1 + \eta_w) > \eta_0,$$

i.e. if

$$\eta_w > -\frac{\eta_1}{\eta_0 + \eta_1}. \tag{26}$$

Only when an increasing marginal wage rate would have a substantially negative effect on labour supply does greater income uncertainty imply a higher marginal tax rate.

The conclusion is that, normally, income uncertainty is probably a reason for somewhat lower income-tax rates. In the special, and perhaps central, case, $\eta_w = 0$, we have the simpler formula

$$t = [\text{var}(n) + \text{var}(m)] \frac{\eta_m}{\eta_i} + \text{var}(n), \tag{27}$$

which proposes an income-tax rate equal to the variance of *ex post* incomes, times the ratio of our index of inequality aversion to our measure of the income effect on labour supply, plus the variance of *ex ante* incomes.

5. UNCERTAIN ASSESSMENT

Next consider tax uncertainty. Model it by supposing that true income wny is observed by the tax authority as $m \cdot wny$. Then consumption is $wny - twmny = (1 - mt)wny$, and

$$y \max \mathscr{E}_m u[b + (1 - mt)nwy, y].$$

Observe that this makes good sense only if the range of the random variable m is not too large: m must be bounded above if we are to be sure that positive tax rates can be levied without placing some consumers in an impossible position. For example, we can suppose that the tax authorities may fail to observe some parts of true income nwy. Then m would be bounded above by 1. In order to use our normalization that $\mathscr{E}_m m = 1$, we would multiply m by an appropriate constant. In that case, our optimal tax rate t is the rate applied not to the part of income that is observed, but to that part divided by the average proportion of income that is observed.

With the new model, indirect utility must be written as a function of three variables:

$$v(t, nw, b) = \max_y \mathscr{E}_m u[b + (1 - mt)nw \cdot y, y]. \tag{28}$$

Labour supply y must also be written as a function of t, nw, and b. From (28), we find, using the envelope theorem, that

$$v_b = \mathscr{E}_m u_1, \qquad v_b = -nwy \cdot \mathscr{E}_m m u_1. \tag{29}$$

These formulae correspond to (18) in the previous section. The calculations go through much as in that section, yielding

$$(y_t + wy_b y)t \cong \frac{1}{\lambda}[\text{cov}(ny, \mathscr{E}_m u_1) + \mathscr{E}\{ny \cdot \mathscr{E}_m[(m - 1)u_1)]\}. \tag{30}$$

As before, $\mathscr{E}_m u_1$ differs from $u_1(b + wny, y)$ by an amount of the same order of magnitude as t, i.e. of order var(n). We may therefore replace $\mathscr{E}_m u_1$ by u_1 (which is v_b for the model without income uncertainty) in the first term on the right-hand side. That term then gives var(n)t_c, as in the previous section.

When we come to calculate $\mathscr{E}_m[(m - 1)u_1]$, we notice that the derivative of u_1 with respect to m is now $- twny \cdot u_{11}$, which is the same order of magnitude as t. Therefore if var(m) is small, of the same order of magnitude as var(n), the term incorporating $\mathscr{E}_m[(m - 1)u_1]$ is of a smaller order of magnitude, and should be neglected in calculating the nearly optimal tax rate. In other words, the tax rate that is nearly optimal for the model without any tax uncertainty is also optimal for the model with tax uncertainty. On consideration, that should not be surprising: if taxes are small, proportionally small errors in taxation should have no significant effect on optimal taxation. There is one important modification to this conclusion, already alluded to. It is the tax rate on expected income that should be (nearly) the same with small errors of observation as without. If observed incomes are on average lower than actual incomes, the tax rate should be increased proportionately to compensate.

6. LARGE ERRORS IN INCOME MEASUREMENT

One would still like to know about larger errors in the assessment of income. We can use the methods of approximate analysis to deal with the case where errors in income measurement are substantial, but the degree of inequality in skills is sufficiently small to warrant the use of nearly optimal taxes. It must be emphasized that in this case almost all observed inequality in incomes will be the result of errors of observation, not differences in earning capacity. Nevertheless, the underlying inequality of true earnings has an important influence on the optimal tax.

When var(m) is not small, but var(n) is small, tax rates are small, of order var(n). To see that, consider the right-hand side of (30). The first term is a covariance, therefore of order var(n). The second term vanishes when $t = 0$, since $\mathscr{E}m = 1$, and u_1 is independent of m when $t = 0$. Therefore, for small t, that second term is proportional to t. Thus, (30) shows that t is proportional to var(n) when var(n) is small.

Now consider the right-hand side of (30) in more detail, so as to derive an approximate formula for t. The first term on the right-hand side of (30) is, as we have seen, the same as in the model without income uncertainty: that argument did not depend on var(m) being small. We can now estimate the second term in the formula without assuming that var(m) is small.

We have, to the same order of approximation as before,

$$\mathscr{E}\{ny \cdot \mathscr{E}_m[(m-1)u_1]\} \cong y(0, w, 0)\mathscr{E}_m[(m-1)u_1(b + (1-mt)wy, y)]$$

$$+ \operatorname{var}(n) \frac{\mathrm{d}}{\mathrm{d}n}(ny) \frac{\mathrm{d}}{\mathrm{d}n} \mathscr{E}_m[(m-1)u_1], \qquad (31)$$

where both the derivatives with respect to n are calculated at $n = 1$.

I first show that the second term on the right-hand side of (31) can be neglected, because the derivative of $\mathscr{E}_m[(m-1)u_1]$ is of the same order of magnitude as t. To establish that, differentiate inside the expectation. The derivative of $u_1 = u_1(b + (1-mt)nwy, y)$ with respect to n is

$$(1 - mt)wy \cdot u_{11}(b + (1-mt)nwy, y)$$
$$= wy \cdot u_{11}(b + wy, y) + \text{terms of order } t \text{ and greater.} \qquad (32)$$

Multiplying by $(m-1)$ and taking the expectation, the first term in the expansion drops out, since $\mathscr{E}_m m = 1$. Therefore the result is of order t, as claimed.

Turning to the first term on the right-hand side of (31), and expanding in powers of t, we obtain

$$\mathscr{E}\{ny, \mathscr{E}_m[(m-1)u_1]\} \cong y(0, w, 0)\mathscr{E}_m\{(m-1)[u_1(b+wy, y) - mtwy \cdot u_{11}]\}$$
$$= -\operatorname{var}(m)wy^2 \cdot u_{11} \cdot t, \qquad \text{since } \mathscr{E}[m] = 1.$$

Using this approximation in (22), we find that the formula for the model without uncertainty is to be modified by changing the denominator of expression (15), which now reads

$$t = \operatorname{var}(n) \frac{(\eta_0 + \eta_1)(1 + \eta_w)}{\eta_1 + (1 - g/wy)\eta_w + \eta_0 \operatorname{var}(m)}. \qquad (33)$$

From this formula, we see that the nearly optimal marginal tax rate is unambiguously reduced by the presence of tax uncertainty. It is reduced by more, the more desirable it is to have redistribution, that desire being measured by the elasticity of marginal utility of income η_0. This result is what one would expect. But formula (19) implies that t itself may be a decreasing function of η_0, certainly if var(m) is greater than or equal to 1. It appears therefore that, when there is great uncertainty in the operations of tax assessment, those of us who would assign greatest weight to the needs of the poor should, under certain circumstances, favour less redistributive action. The conclusion is the result of assuming that there is much more inequality of observation than underlying inequality. In these circumstances, the worst off are predominantly those who are unlucky enough to seem to have relatively high incomes, and therefore pay high tax. Taxation has the effect of randomizing after-tax income, with a considerable welfare cost for an inequality-averse society.

7. CONCLUSION

Formulae have been derived for optimal taxation, formulae that are only approximately valid, for any economy described by a single individual parameter. They help to understand the bearing of the different competing considerations on the desirability of redistributive tax policies. The basic formula is the multi-product result, (5), which shows that compensated demand changes should be approximately proportional to rates of change of demands with respect to the parameter. Application of that formula to the simple income-tax model yields a formula (15) involving three elasticities, measuring inequality aversion, and the responsiveness of labour supply to income and wage changes, and the ratio of public expenditure to total output. Among interesting features of the formula, it is notable that the nearly optimal marginal income-tax rate may increase or decrease with the public expenditure requirement, depending on whether (for an average member of the population) labour supply increases or decreases when the wage increases.

When the consumer is uncertain about labour income, a further term is introduced into the nearly optimal tax formula, which now takes the form (25). It is found that, unless labour supply decreases with increasing wages at a quite substantial rate, a model in which larger part of the inequality of wages is unknown to the individual at the time when labour decisions are taken, implies a lower nearly optimal tax rate on labour incomes.

Finally, we considered a model in which observations of income by the tax authority are uncertain. These errors of observation are found to be of smaller importance than other considerations that bear on the choice of optimal tax systems, except when the errors are large, much larger than underlying inequality of true incomes. In this last case, formula (33) displays the modification required in the earlier nearly optimal tax formula (15): it implies a lower marginal tax rate on expected incomes, although, if incomes tend to be underestimated, that rate would have to be marked up correspondingly.

REFERENCES

Atkinson, A. B. and Stiglitz, J. E. (1980) *Lectures on Public Economics* (New York: McGraw Hill).

Diamond, P. A. (1975) 'A Many Person Tax Rule'. *Journal of Public Economics*, Vol. 4, pp. 335–42.

——Helms, J., and Mirrlees, J. A. (1980) 'Optimal Taxation in a Stochastic Economy: a Cobb–Douglas Example'. *Journal of Public Economics*, Vol. 14, pp. 1–30.

Dixit, A. K. and Sandmo, A. (1977) 'Some Simplified Formulae for Optimal Income Taxation'. *Scandinavian Journal of Economics*.

Varian, H. R. (1980) 'Redistributive Taxation as Social Insurance'. *Journal of Public Economics*, Vol. 14, pp. 49–68.

PART III

PUBLIC EXPENDITURE

14

Arguments for Public Expenditure

1. IS PUBLIC EXPENDITURE TOO HIGH?

In Britain now, the weight of opinion in economic debate tends to the view that the government is spending too much. The case for this view is forcefully put by Bacon and Eltis in their recent book, *Britain's Economic Problem: Too Few Producers*. They particularly emphasize the rapidly rising proportion of government spending in the national income. That government activity has been playing an increasing role in the economy is indisputable. The percentage of the labour force employed by central and local government has risen from less than 16 in 1965 to more than 21 in 1975. That is a remarkably rapid increase, which could hardly fail to elicit opposition. But rapid changes, even when they are opposed, and even when they were not clearly envisaged or intended, may nevertheless be desirable.

A case might be made that, at least in the British case, the most recent growth in public expenditure has been undesirable: there is now widespread objection to the reduction in disposable incomes that is accompanying it, while opposition to public spending cuts comes almost entirely from those who believe their incomes and employment threatened rather than from the beneficiaries of the expenditures. I do not find this case very convincing. Nothing that can be thought to reflect real feeling and experience shows clearly that the reduction in disposable real incomes has been very unpleasant for most people. Nor do the processes of income bargaining seem to have been more difficult in the period of falling incomes than in the previous period of rising ones. On the other side of the balance, consumer objection to cuts in health, educational, and social services may be lacking simply because most people are badly informed about their nature and impact. Even if, more plausibly, there are considerable gains in efficiency to be had from larger classes, shorter hospital stays, and reduced administration, that fact would not, in itself, show that the level of public services, or even expenditure on them, should be reduced.

It is not in any case satisfactory to rely on such impressionistic and anecdotal argument. If we are to make well-grounded judgements about the size of government spending, a theory is required and we have to see what the theory

This chapter was first published in M. J. Artis and A. R. Nobay (eds.), *Contemporary Economic Analysis* (London: Croom Helm, 1978). Reproduced by kind permission of Taylor and Francis Books Ltd.

seems to suggest in the particular circumstances of the country. This is not one of those questions on which economists can easily show that the economy has obviously gone wrong. In the past, there have been questions like that: widespread unemployment, and protection at the expense of employment in less developed countries, are two of the classic examples. In the case of public expenditure, nothing could be less immediately evident than its optimality or lack of it. One need know little of history to reject the view that what is being done was deliberately chosen, and must therefore be optimal from some reasonable man's point of view. What is, is accident. It is legitimate to dig a little deeper, and consider what kinds of reasons might properly be advanced in criticism or support of this adventitious status quo.

What does welfare economics offer us in the way of arguments bearing on the optimality of public expenditure? There are two main classes of public expenditure: direct spending by government departments on goods and services, and subsidies in money or kind provided to private persons. Consequently there are two existing theories that ought to be able to help us: the theory of public goods, and the theory of optimal taxes, which is at the same time necessarily a theory of optimal subsidies. In the theory of optimal taxation, the revenue requirements of the State, to be used for expenditures on defence, crime prevention, and the like, are taken as given. In the theory of public goods, the rules for the optimal provision of these activities are discussed. In what follows, I shall make greatest use of optimal tax theory, in its simplest form, optimal (linear) income tax theory: I shall be using it back to front, focusing on optimal subsidies rather than on the tax rates that are usually in the forefront of discussion.

Public good theory should be in our minds too, and here I want to depart from the usual terminology, at least for the purposes of this chapter. These goods and services to which one would expect public good theory to be applied will be termed 'social goods'—goods that are of social, rather than individual, concern. This is done to avoid confusion between the way people benefit from goods, and the way in which the goods happen to be provided to people, Of course many commodities that are not social goods are publicly provided, and there may be strong arguments for so doing.

At a methodological level, my main focus is on the relation between the models that have been developed in public economics—models which are, in a sense, rather simple—and an actual economy, namely the United Kingdom in recent years. These models are characterized by the use of variables which have no precise counterpart in the real economy. In linear income tax theory, for instance, there is a homogeneous kind of labour, and there is a uniform marginal tax rate on labour income, and a uniform subsidy paid to everyone. An econometrician might use such a theory to guide him in setting up a system of equations relating actual numerical observations; but for some purposes his success or failure turns on the fit of the stochastic model so constructed of real variables. The theoretical economist attempts to picture reality by variables which, like capital in the one-good growth model, need have no direct counterpart in the real world. To use his model, he must use actual measurements to construct figures that correspond in some degree to the variables in the model. There is, I think, a difference of spirit here, though it may often come to the same thing in the end. I hope to show that there is considerable interest and value in keeping the basic model simple and measuring reality in such a way that, for a little while, it looks quite like the model.

2. OPTIMAL INCOME TAX THEORY

In the theory of linear income taxation, it is assumed that every person in the economy faces a budget constraint of the form

$$x = ay + b,$$

where x is his after-tax income, inclusive of subsidies, and y his income before tax. The lump-sum subsidy b is the same for everyone, and $t = 1 - a$ is the marginal tax rate on income. The simplest model that seems to picture reality, and the one to which most attention has been devoted, is that in which individuals earn different wages per unit of effort, w, and have utility

$$u(x, y/w).$$

w is often referred to briefly as ability, though other words, like 'success' or 'drive', might be appropriate.

N being the number of individuals in the population, $B = bN$ is the total of subsidy payments, which have to be met out of the proceeds of income taxation, after meeting government's revenue requirements for its own expenditures, R. R is to be taken net of any profits received by government, and includes subsidies paid to producers. The government's budget constraint is

$$B + R = tY,$$

where $Y = \Sigma y$ is the total labour supply from the population.

As a matter of pure theory, the linear income tax model is a special case of the theory of optimal commodity taxation, the commodity here singled out for taxation being labour. For a quick clear account of optimal tax theory, one can read Sandmo (1976). The interest of the special case lies entirely in the possibilities for explicit computation, and the obvious correspondence, at a crude level, with interesting policy issues about the level of income tax rates. Non-linear income tax theory allows one to consider issues about the degree of progression or regression that might be justified in an income tax schedule. But since I want to concentrate on the expenditure side here, the linear tax model may do fairly well for the purpose.

We all know that an increase in the tax rate t by itself need not make people less inclined to work or work hard: for most people it probably has the opposite effect. But it is not optimal to increase t as much as possible, because there are income effects which do adversely affect incentives. So long as an increase in t would increase labour supply, it increases tax revenue, and therefore makes possible an increase in the lump-sum subsidy b: that is, indeed, the purpose of increasing t. This increase in b normally reduces labour supply, partly counteracting the effect of the increased marginal tax rate.

The possibilities can be shown most clearly in a diagram with community offer-curves, which show the aggregate labour supply and aggregate disposable income as the marginal tax rate changes. In Fig. 14.1, I have drawn these offer curves for different values of b. For simplicity, aggregate production possibilities are taken to be linear, and define the line RA_1A_2 whose equation is $X = \overline{w}Y - R$, where $\overline{w}$ is the average wage rate. The community offer curves have the shape shown because when $t = 1$ there is no selfish reason for anyone to work, and it is well established empirically that, at wage rates that are not very low, labour supply diminishes with increases in the wage. The point A_1 corresponds to the largest possible value of $b, \overline{b}$, and therefore represents what is usually called the Rawlsian optimum, where the worst-off member of the community has the highest possible utility. When some weight is given to everyone's welfare, and not much weight to inequalities in utility as such, the optimum equilibrium of the economy is another point on the production frontier to the right of A_1, such as A_2. It may well be on the backward-sloping part of the community offer curve.

In passing, it should be noticed how clearly the diagram brings out the effect of an increase in the government revenue requirement R, since that is simply a downward parallel shift of the production frontier RA_1A_2. It is very likely to require a substantial reduction in b: but it may not imply that an increase in t is desirable.

The diagram also helps to highlight some of the theoretical difficulties that should be faced in estimating labour supply functions. The community offer-curves that I have drawn, and which seem to me extremely plausible, do not correspond at all well to linear or log-linear labour supply functions in terms of a and b. It would be better to use data to estimate utility functions directly (or some other representation of preferences, such as the expenditure function) than to impose some simple functional form for the labour supply function itself. But it is not so easy to select a plausible form for the utility function.

The calculations of optimal income taxes that I shall use are those published by Stern (1976), which are based on a CES utility function, for which the elasticity of substitution between consumption and leisure is one-half, and the assumed distribution of wage rates is consistent with UK data. This utility function is not totally absurd, and may fit available empirical

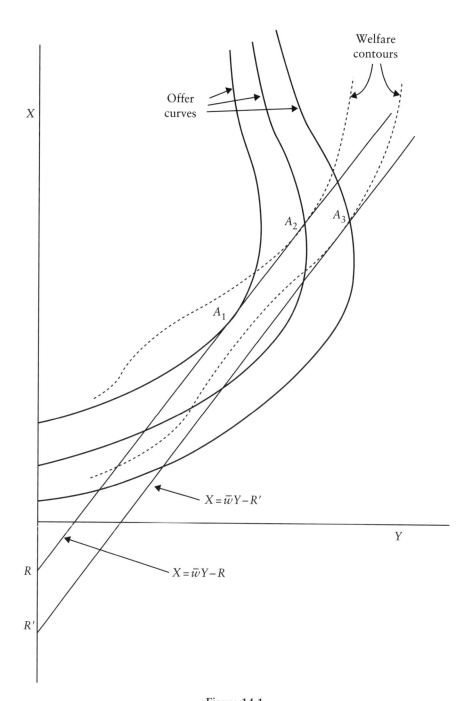

Figure 14.1.

studies quite well; but it predicts an unrealistically low labour supply at high wage rates. This means that the community offer curves have too great a backward slope in their upper reaches. One would guess that the calculated optimum tax rates are biased upwards as a result, since the labour-encouraging effects of high tax rates are exaggerated; but guessing is probably rather unreliable in this area.

In the optimal income tax model, the two categories of government expenditure, b and R, play very different roles. One begins by thinking of R as expenditures on public goods, in the usual sense, and on international obligations or necessities. On the assumption that the government has good, or at least fairly good, reasons for its choice of expenditures like these, and in the knowledge that macroeconomic analysis of this kind is not going to throw any light on these or other reasons for the choice of R, we take it as given. Then the choice of b and t is made to give the distributionally best way of financing these expenditures. Implicit in this procedure is the idea that, if different values of R were considered, consumer preferences as between consumption and work would remain unaffected: and so would interpersonal comparisons.

There is, I suppose, no necessity that social goods should act on utility without affecting preferences. Indeed, one can think of social goods that are close substitutes for individual consumption, such as research into reducing the cost of making bread. Once the general form of the model has been chosen, it would be best to regard such expenditures as part of b rather than part of R. Nevertheless, it does strike me as plausible that the distinction between social goods, which are jointly consumed, enjoyed, or endured, and individual goods, whose consumption is exclusive, coincides fairly well with the distinction between two kinds of consumption that affect utility independently. It is perhaps less plausible that changes in the provision of social goods leave interpersonal comparisons, as expressed for example by relative marginal utilities of individual consumption, unaffected: but I shall continue to accept this part of the standard model too, for the purposes of this chapter.

3. THE UK GOVERNMENT AS A LINEAR TAX SYSTEM

In order to relate a particular economy to the simple income-tax model, we have to classify actual expenditures into the categories used by the model. The task is made especially difficult by the rather delicate distinctions on which the categories of the model turn. As soon as one thinks hard about the problems—for example, about what period of time is supposed to be represented by the model—one feels that there are too few commodities in the model. I propose to deal with this particular problem of the time period in the simplest possible way, by classifying the expenditure of the net national income in a single year. Investment expenditures are to be thought of as providing consumption in the future, and that consumption is to be thought of as substitutable for present consumption. It is not a very good assumption, but then the level of savings in our economy is rather low, so that alternative procedures could hardly make much difference to the outcome.

The source of data is the 1977 National Income Blue Book. Using that, I have classified data for government tax and expenditure for four different years—1966, and the three most recent years for which data are available. It is well to remind ourselves at the outset that these data are subject to considerable errors, particularly for the most recent years. The magnitude of revisions from one year to the next, and the reconciliation entry 'residual error', suggest that there may be errors of up to £1,000 million in national income, and smaller, though substantial, errors in the components of national income. In the tables below, figures are rounded to the nearest £100 million; but that suggests greater accuracy than the figures possess. These errors may, paradoxically, reassure us a little in making some of our more adventurous estimates.

The economic activities of government are to be described by three numbers: T, the total of taxes, less subsidies, which varies with income and expenditure; B, the total of lump-sum subsidies; and R, the total expenditure of government on social goods. For ease of comparison with the income tax model, we shall want to regard all the taxes included in T as applying to income. Thus, the tax base will be taken to be national income measured at market prices, which I denote by Y. Wherever investment expenditures occur, they are included net of depreciation, which is calculated by assuming net investment is the same proportion of gross investment for all categories of expenditure.

Estimates of T are derived in Table 14.1. In principle, those elements of, or charges on, government revenue that vary with individual earnings and expenditure, and only those, are to be included. Among taxes, the most doubtful items are taxes on unearned income and profits, and taxes on capital. Taxes on rents, interest, and profits, and on capital gains (which the Blue Book quaintly classifies as taxes on capital), are included in T on the grounds that a large part of income from capital is the result of the individual's own saving, so that taxes on this income are, in effect, taxes on expenditure upon future goods and services, which is as much a kind of expenditure as any other. In other words, taxes on income derived from one's own savings reduce the value of one's pre-tax earnings, and this disencentive effect justifies inclusion in T. In the case of taxes levied on income from inherited capital, this argument may not seem to apply, but on the margin, one's capital is one's own saving, and the point of the calculation is to estimate, very roughly, the aggregate marginal tax rate on an average person; so these taxes should be included too.

Table 14.1. *Taxes and subsidies related to income and expenditure*

	(£'000 million)			
	1966	1974	1975	1976
Taxes on income	4.6	12.5	16.5	18.7
Taxes on expenditure	4.0	8.4	10.2	12.1
National insurance	0	5.0	6.8	8.4
Rates	1.4	3.1	4.0	4.5
Taxes on capital	0.3	0.9	0.8	0.9
Subsidies and transfers, excluding housing	−0.5	−2.7	−3.4	−2.7
Public corporations, net loss[a]	−0.1	−1.3	−1.1	−1.3
Expenditure on roads	−0.4	−1.0	−1.3	−1.4
	9.3	24.8	32.5	39.3
Adjustment for tax allowances[b]	2.7	7.1	8.4	9.5
Adjustment for means-tested benefits[c]	0.1	0.4	0.4	0.6
Total	12.1	32.3	41.3	49.3

[a] This is the undistributed income of public corporations, less capital consumption and stock appreciation.
[b] The working population has been approximately 25 million. This is multiplied by the married man's income tax allowance for the tax year beginning in each year, and the result multiplied by the standard rate of income tax (adjusted for earned income relief in 1966).
[c] This is a notional figure to make some allowance, probably too small, for benefits that are income-related. The chief examples are rent rebates and student grants. A corresponding amount is added to the total for subsidies not related to income and expenditure in Table 14.2, where the benefits mentioned also appear.

Source: CSO, *National Income and Expenditure, 1966–1976* (HMSO 1977), tables 7.1, 7.2, 8.2, 6.3 (for public corporations), with adjustments for capital consumption from table 11.9.

The taxation of gifts and inheritance directly is a different matter. It could be argued that a rational man would find the proceeds of an extra year's work less attractive if any part of it that is gifted to others is subject to tax. But this is a seriously incomplete argument, since gifts must be expected to have substantial income effects upon recipients. It seems to me that, just as gifts concern two people (at least), so taxes on gifts and inheritance have double effects, being expenditure-related taxes from the point of view of the giver, and lump-sum taxes (more or less) on the receiver. If I were to take this position consistently, I should have to regard households as receiving the total of gifts as lump-sum payments additional to the earnings represented by the national income, and to treat the taxes not only as expenditure-related taxes on the giver, to be included in T, but also as lump-sum taxes on the recipient, to be included in B, as a negative item. I have no basis for estimating the total of gifts and inheritance, so a simpler approach must be taken. In effect, one has to ignore the bad distributional and incentive effects of the receipt of private transfers. The fact that there are taxes, though not very large ones, diminishes the importance of what the model thereby neglects; but one would give quite the wrong impression if these taxes were included as a negative part of B. If the model is ignoring the effects of inheritance, then one had better ignore the effect of death duties and capital transfer tax on the recipients of the transfers. Accordingly, taxes on capital are entirely included in T. The question is an extremely interesting, and not unimportant, one, which still lacks thorough theoretical analysis. But, as with many of the other interesting points highlighted by the attempt to fit simple tax models to the real world, the total picture will not be greatly affected by the particular convention we happen to adopt.

National insurance contributions should be included in T in so far as they vary with income. This has been more or less the case in recent years, but in 1966 was true only of what were called graduated contributions. Graduated contributions were associated with immediate rights to future pension, and can plausibly be regarded as compulsory saving. Though there would in general be an element of taxation in any compulsory saving scheme, it seems reasonable to regard this element as negligibly small in the present instance. The current national pension scheme, on the other hand, involves a relationship between earnings in any particular year and ultimate benefits which is weak, and likely to be unperceived, as yet. Accordingly, no national insurance contributions or benefits are classified as income-related in 1966, graduated contributions being regarded as exactly balanced by perceived benefits, and all other contributions assigned as a negative item in B. All national insurance contributions in 1974–6 are classified as income-related taxes, and included in T.

The various subsidies and transfers included in T seem to be mainly subsidies to industry, both public and private. In so far as the effect is to make some goods and services cheaper than would otherwise have been the case, these subsidies should evidently be negative items in T. But subsidies that merely keep inefficient production activity in being are either a straightforward waste of resources (a tribute to mistaken theories of employment, and to marginal constituencies), or subsidies analogous to unemployment benefits. In the first case, the subsidies should be classified as government expenditure on social goods, however uncomfortable one may be with the description. In the second case, they would be lump-sum subsidies, classified under B. It would require careful consideration, industry by industry, to make a reasonable classification of these subsidies and transfers, and of the net losses of public corporations, about which similar issues arise. Since a large proportion of the subsidies is to food and agriculture, and to nontraded goods, I would expect most of them to be classified as expenditure-related subsidies, and have accordingly classified all subsidies in that way here. But it should be remembered when we come to consider the historical record, and to compare with the theory of optimal income taxation, that T could

have been considerably underestimated, especially for recent years, as a result
of adopting this convention.

Expenditure on roads has also been regarded as an expenditure-related
subsidy, because the benfits of the road system accrue to a large extent, directly
and indirectly, in proportion to expenditures, for example on travel. This
may be the wrong way to treat public lighting and some urban roads: some of
these expenditures should perhaps be regarded as expenditures on social
goods. But there seems to be no easy way of incorporating this distinction in
the figures, and the social element would not be very large. Perhaps we may
regard this error as being offset by the other elements in government expenditure which do to some extent benefit people in relation to their income, but are
here classified as entirely social expenditures. Expenditure on external relations
(much concerned with commerce), and to some extent defence expenditures,
are cases in point.

If it were not for tax allowances, people would pay much more income
tax. Since, for standard-rate income taxpayers, the reduction in tax liability
arising from tax allowances is independent of income, this amount should
be regarded as part of B, and the amount of income-related tax increased
accordingly. A rough estimate of the extent to which income tax liability is
reduced by tax allowances is entered in the table as an 'adjustment for tax
allowances'. The married man's allowance was applied to a rough estimate
of the total population of taxpayers, on the grounds that single persons'
allowances and child allowances together may more or less cancel out. In any
case, the figure arrived at is a rough one, though accurate enough for my
purposes.

In a similar way, we should make some allowance for means-tested benefits,
since their effect is to introduce additional marginal taxes on income (or
whatever is the basis for estimating means). What one should do about
means-tested benefits depends upon the particular formula used in determining the level of benefits. Rather than carry out the considerable work of discovering and applying these formulae, I have entered notional amounts in
the table, which are roughly the total of rent rebates and student grants in
these years. The figures are small in the total picture, but entered as signals
that it would be interesting to look into the matter in detail.

In Table 14.2 are collected those items of government expenditure the
benefits from which are not related to the individual's income or expenditure,
but which are not expenditures on social goods such as parks and police. One
must obviously include all items which are simple monetary transfers to individuals, and are not related to what they do. In fact, most such transfers
require some qualification or other. Disability benefits may be largely independent of the individual's behaviour, but even they are not entirely independent of what the person has decided to do. Family allowances might affect
decisions to have children. Unemployment benefit almost certainly does
affect willingness to search for and move to employment, to a greater extent

Table 14.2. *Subsidies not related to income and expenditure*

	(£'000 million)			
	1966	**1974**	**1975**	**1976**
Health service	1.3	3.8	5.1	6.0
Education	1.5	4.0	5.8	6.4
Other social services	0.2	1.1	1.5	1.9
Social security benefits and other grants (net)	1.3	7.9	10.4	12.9
Housing subsidies	0.2	0.6	0.9	1.2
	4.5	17.5	23.6	28.4
Adjustment for tax allowances[a]	2.7	7.1	8.4	9.5
Adjustment for means-tested benefits[b]	0.1	0.4	0.4	0.6
	7.3	25.0	32.4	38.5

[a] See n. b of Table 14.1.
[b] See n. c of Table 14.1.
Source: as for Table 14.1.

than would transfer payments made to everyone regardless of employment status. I am inclined to think that this last item should be treated in a way much like means-tested benefits, but have adopted the conventional viewpoint and pretended that unemployment benefits are effectively lump-sum subsidies. Tax allowances, which are also treated as lump-sum payments, have the opposite effect, of encouraging search for paid employment, but they also have been treated as lump-sum subsidies. The absence of pure lump-sum subsidies is, after all, one of the most striking and curious features of real-world economies.

The figure for social security benefits and other grants in the table is net of contributions that are lump-sum in operation. Specifically, in 1966 national insurance contributions other than graduated contributions have been subtracted from benefits and grants to obtain the final figure.

Expenditures on health, education, and housing have been included as part of *B* because, though they are free provision of certain commodities rather than monetary subsidies, they are, in principle, provided independently of the person's income or expenditure. At the same time, it seems more correct to regard them as commodities analogous to consumer goods like food and clothes than as social goods. These are the kinds that, if they are not provided by the State, people work to provide for themselves and their families, as they work to provide food and clothes. The reasons, to which I shall come, why these commodities are provided to a large extent by the State rather than the individual are not relevant to the distinction that guides our classification, the distinction between lump-sum and income-related receipts. It is true that there are some health expenditures which have the character of social goods, expenditure on vaccination being the most obvious one; but these must be such a small item that I have not troubled to identify them. Similarly, there may be social benefits from education, if, for example, there is anything in the idea that better-educated voters bring about more intelligent political decisions. But the real question is whether and to what extent expenditures on health and education replace private spending that would otherwise have taken place (and consequently have the same kind of disincentive effects as a monetary lump-sum subsidy). In both cases, I suppose that public expenditure goes beyond, and in the case of education markedly beyond, the levels that would have been privately chosen. But much the larger part of these expenditures must represent substitution for private expenditures, and, lacking a basis for estimating the part that does not, I have included the whole in B. Similarly, in the case of housing, public provision goes beyond what would have been privately provided; but in that case, it seems likely that the total of explicit subsidies which are entered in the table understate the extent of public subsidy.

Table 14.3 contains the remaining government expenditures that have not already appeared in Tables 14.1 and 14.2. The main elements are defence expenditure, public administration, and the police; foreign aid and support of the arts also appear here. As we have just seen, there are some elements of education and housing that ought to be included in R, not B, but which do not appear because there was no basis for estimating them. At a guess, I suspect the figures in Table 14.3 should not be increased by more than 10 per cent to allow for these omissions.

The outcome of these calculations is collected in Table 14.4. This is a convenient point at which to comment on some general aspects of the calculation: the treatment of the national debt and interest on it, what should be done about economies of scale, and the meaning of the government deficit, $D = R + B - T$, as derived from these figures.

Interest payments by the government have not been included as an expenditure of government on the grounds that they are part of a borrowing

Table 14.3. *Public expenditure on social goods*

	(£'000 million)			
	1966	1974	1975	1976
Current expenditure on goods and services, excluding roads and social services	3.3	7.7	10.1	11.8
Net investment expenditure for same purposes	0.4	0.9	0.9	0.9
Current grants overseas	0.2	0.3	0.3	0.4
Total	3.9	8.8	11.2	13.4

Source: As for Table 14.1.

Table 14.4. *Tax and expenditure: the overall picture*

	(£'000 million)			
	1966	1974	1975	1976
Net national product at market prices, Y	35.2	75.0	93.4	109.9
Taxes,[a] T	12.1	32.3	41.3	49.3
$t = T/Y$	3.4	0.43	0.44	0.45
Subsidies,[b] B	7.3	25.0	32.4	38.5
B/Y	0.21	0.33	0.35	0.35
Expenditure on social goods,[c] R	3.9	8.8	11.2	13.4
R/Y	0.11	0.12	0.12	0.12
Government deficit, $R + B - T = D$	−0.9	1.5	2.3	2.6
D/Y	−0.3	0.02	0.03	0.02

[a] As defined in Table 14.1.
[b] As defined in Table 14.2.
[c] As defined in Table 14.3.

Source: *National Income Blue Book*, table 1.1, and Tables 14.1–14.3.

transaction carried out on the open market, and are therefore analogous to other trading activities of government: they apparently involve no element of subsidy, social expenditure, or tax. Yet, as we all know, government lending and borrowing does have effects on the economy, which the government ought to consider. If the government had borrowed less in recent years, there might have been more capital investment. This is the question concerning how large the government deficit ought to be, and does not affect the way it should be measured. Therefore neither changes in national and local authority debt, nor interest payments on it, should be included in R, B, or T.

Economies of scale pose an awkward problem for such a calculation as has been done above, because they exist, and are in some industries substantial, and yet there is no easy way of measuring them in the aggregate. Suppose that economies of scale are substantial in public corporations. Then the losses which these corporations are running, and are allowed to run, may reflect the difference between average cost and marginal cost, the desirable Pigovian subsidy to industries with decreasing costs. If this were so—and I have no reason to think that the actual magnitude of these losses and of subsides to nationalized industries bears any relation to optimal Pigovian subsidies—the losses are items of social expenditure which the government ought to meet, and should therefore be classified as positive items in R rather than negative items in T. Similarly, if in some private industry there are increasing returns, the price charged by firms in the industry will exceed marginal cost, and consumers are therefore paying a price that exceeds marginal cost by more than has already been allowed for. Implicitly, there is a tax on the products of the industry, and a subsidy to the firms in the industry just equal to that tax. The tax would require an item in T, the subsidy an item in R. Thus, overall, the effect of economies of scale is that T should be greater, and R also greater by the same amount. For public-sector industries with decreasing returns, the argument would go the other way, and this would not be an unimportant item either. But there is no reason to think that the two should cancel one another, and it seems fairly clear that increasing returns are nowadays more important overall than decreasing returns. Increasing returns might apply to the production of a third of the national product; and on average one might reasonably expect average cost to exceed marginal cost by something of the order of 10 per cent. Therefore I am inclined to believe that the largest adjustment one should be prepared to make for increasing returns is £1 billion in 1966 and £3 billion in 1976. This would be added to both T and R. These figures could easily be much too large.

The government deficit which has been estimated by drawing up these tables is the extent to which, by intertemporal transactions, the government has arranged to spend more or less than its tax revenue in any particular year. The interesting question is whether, in years of surplus like 1966, expenditure on social goods is unusually low, taxation is unusually high, or the redistribution of revenues is unusually low. In 1964–76 we find the government, at a time when borrowing has been very cheap in real terms, spending more than it receives. I shall interpret this as a decision that, instead of having to pay for R out of the surplus from the redistributive tax system, only $R - D$ need currently be met in this way. On this view, R represents expenditures which are fixed more or less independently of the current cost of funds. Clearly, this is going too far, and the reader can make allowances.

4. THE HISTORICAL RECORD AND SOME OPTIMA

When one looks at Table 14.4, the most striking thing the figures say is that expenditure on social goods has not, as a proportion of national income, grown significantly during the period considered. (The reader may like to be reminded that real national income has grown by 20 per cent between 1966 and 1976.) Whatever the inaccuracies in the data, and the imperfections in the way they have been used, I think we are driven to the conclusion that the growth of the public sector cannot be interpreted as a shift from individual to collective consumption, as either new recognition of the value of collective goods, or neglect of what individuals value at the expense of social affluence.

There has been a very substantial increase in the redistributive effects of the tax system. Tax rates have risen greatly—by nearly one-third in only ten years—and the proceeds have been used redistributively, to provide individuals directly with what they might have done themselves. We must not immediately conclude that government is doing much more for equality now than in 1966. These figures tell us nothing about the distribution of lump-sum benefits within the population. All we know is that the benefits are not perceived as related to the individual's income. Nevertheless, educational expenditures are not equally distributed, nor are the other social services. What one gets depends on where one is born, and where one lives. Tax rates too impinge unequally. The large increase comes from an increase in the numbers and incomes covered by income tax (so that now hardly anyone faces a zero marginal income tax rate) and the introduction of value added tax. National insurance contributions have also increased substantially, and have been transformed into an effective tax on incomes. The only substantial reduction in taxation relative to national income is in taxes on tobacco, which have fallen from 0.29 per cent of national income to 0.16 per cent. (VAT would be a partial offset.) This latter item apart, we should, I think, approve of the increase in marginal tax rates on incomes which previously escaped taxation, even though, as is often said, it has greatly increased the unpopularity of taxes among the unthinking.

We should be aware not only of the redistributive effects of this very considerable change in the government of the economy, but also of the incentive effects implicit in the change. On average, marginal tax rates have risen greatly, and that may or may not discourage work, but they cannot have risen so far as to diminish the tax revenue collected. What is more important is the reverse of the tax increase, the increase in lump-sum income, which, unless it is to a great extent an increase in the provision of undesired and untradable goods, must have had considerable disincentive effects. I am disinclined to believe that these expenditures represent to any great extent the provision of goods and services that people do not want, but it is possible that a large part of the growth represents increased inefficiency in providing the services: excessive administration of hospitals and of education, spending on new medical treatments or new educational ideas that are in fact no improvement, paying local government officials more than is necessary for less than should be expected. But these are, mostly, lump-sum subsidies however you look at them. More teachers means either more education for our children, or shorter hours for our teachers. In the latter case it is as much a gift unrelated to effort as in the first. It is perhaps a less desirable redistribution of income in the second case.

Undesirable disincentive effects must be considered in relation to the good redistribution that the same policies make possible. The question is: has redistribution in Britain now gone too far? The only way we can approach an answer is to work out what the optimal degree of redistribution is in a simple model that pictures the real economy with adequate accuracy. Stern in his paper uses a model in which all consumers have utility function,

$$u(x,z) = \frac{1}{\nu}[(1-\alpha)x^{-\mu} + \alpha(1-z)^{-\mu}]^{-\nu/\mu},$$

where x is disposable income, z is the proportion of time available for working that is actually worked, and $\epsilon = 1/(1+\mu)$ is the elasticity of substitution. The sum of utilities is maximized; so the parameter ν, representing our assessment of the rate at which marginal utilities fall off with increasing income, expresses the degree of urgency that is to be attached to redistribution. Stern takes $\epsilon = \frac{1}{2}$ to be a realistic value, on the basis of available data. The data do not give a very precise estimate, and this value does imply an unrealistic relationship between the working hours of, say, highly skilled and unskilled workers in our economy. I would prefer a formulation of the utility function that assumed consumers do not like to work less than a certain amount, and took a value of ϵ closer to unity. Therefore, I have considered the outcome of Stern's calculations for both $\epsilon = \frac{1}{2}$ and $\epsilon = 1$. $\nu = 1$ seems to me to take a reasonable, but moderate, view of the way in which the value of income varies from poor to rich. At any rate, I do not think it overstates the case for redistribution of incomes. Stern chose the remaining parameter α in such a way that the average individual has $z = 2/3$.

In Table 14.5, I give calculations of optima derived from Stern's paper. For most cases, Stern gives only the optimal marginal tax rate, and not the optimal subsidy rate, and he has done computations at only rather large intervals of R. It has therefore been necessary to do some crude interpolation to get the results I want. But the main point is evident from Stern's calculations: that the optimal marginal tax rate does not vary very rapidly as R is changed. If, for whatever reason, the government wishes to raise a larger surplus through the tax system, it should do that mainly through a reduction in the

Table 14.5. *Elasticity of substitution: optima*

R/Y	Elasticity of substitution	
	0.5	1
0	$t = 0.43$, $B/Y = 0.43$	$t = 0.29$, $B/Y = 0.29$
0.1	$t = 0.46$, $B/Y = 0.36$	$t = 0.32$, $B/Y = 0.21$
0.2	$t = 0.49$, $B/Y = 0.29$	$t = 0.34$, $B/Y = 0.14$

Notes: From the tables in Stern's paper, one gets optimal tax rates for $R/Y = 0$ and 0.2 in the case where the elasticity of substitution is 0.5, and for $R/Y = 0$ and 0.22 when the elasticity of substitution is 1. Other optimal tax rates are then obtained by simple linear interpolation, and B/Y deduced as $t - (R/Y)$. As explained in the text, the results given are for cases where the elasticity of marginal utility with respect to income is 2.

Source: Stern (1976).

lump-sum subsidy, and to only a limited extent by increasing the marginal tax rate. The reason is that a reduction of the lump-sum subsidy has greater incentive effects than an increase in the tax rate.

If, referring to Table 14.4, we take it that in 1976 the government wanted to raise a surplus of $R - D$ from the tax system, we have $(R - D)/Y = 0.10$, and from Table 14.5 we find that the optimal t is 0.46 if the elasticity of substitution is $\frac{1}{2}$, 0.32 if the elasticity of substitution is 1. Correspondingly, lump-sum subsidies should be 36 per cent, or 21 per cent of national income, compared with the 35 per cent calculated in Table 14.2.

Believing that the elasticity of substitution is probably rather greater than $\frac{1}{2}$, I would take the view, from this calculation, that the actual degree of redistribution is a little too large, but a reasonable man could well believe that it is just right, or perhaps too little. We should also consider what would happen to this comparison if some of the adjustments one might make in the picture of the UK economy to allow for increasing returns, or for social elements in such expenditures as education, were made. To allow for increasing returns, we might increase R/Y by 0.03 and t by the same amount. Interpolating in Table 14.5, we find that $R/Y = 0.13$ implies $t = 0.47$ or 0.33, and $B/Y = 0.34$ or 0.20. This should be compared with 'actual' $t = 0.48$ and $B/Y = 0.35$. The case for believing that redistribution has gone a little too far is strengthened. If we move some expenditure from B to R, we do not increase our estimate of the actual t, and the case for less redistribution is weakened. Moving agricultural subsidies from T to B would increase the apparent degree of redistribution in the economy.

We find then that our assessment of recent years must be, in the present state of knowledge, somewhat ambiguous. On the other hand, it does seem very likely that the degree of redistribution was too low in 1966, and that it moved thereafter in the right direction. It may now have gone a little too far.

5. CONCLUSIONS

It has been my main purpose to direct attention to the relevant considerations we must attend to if we are to get any kind of answer to the question: is public expenditure too high? We have noticed that a large part of public expenditure must be regarded as the provision of private goods for individual consumption, and therefore as part of the redistributive policies of government. There is a little more to be said about this.

If we reject the 'public good' argument for the public provision of medical care, housing, and education, as I think we must, we should not suppose that we have disposed of all possible arguments for their public provision. Indeed, we know well that the real argument is a paternal one: that individuals, for one reason or another, make poor consumption decisions about these goods and services. Some of the reasons have to do with the bias or incompetence of decisions that parents make on behalf of their children, some with the impossibility of presenting most people with the relevant information in a way that will enable them to make satisfactory decisions. In recent years, as a result of our experience with the quality of government decisions in these areas, many of us have become more doubtful that what consumers do badly, governments do better. But it would be a foolish person who claimed that in these areas consumers do make the right choices. I incline to think that there is a better chance of persuading governments to spend more wisely in these areas than of persuading them to give up their role as providers of education, medical care, housing, and insurance; but that is no very great claim about the power of rational argument.

Recognizing that there is a good argument for paternalism, we shall have to agree that, when a specific subsidy is both a subsidy and a way of improving consumer decisions, it is doubly good, and that, up to some level, this consideration may actually strengthen the case for subsidies, and make more redistribution desirable than would otherwise be the case. The fact that these expenditures are somewhat unequally distributed, as we have noted, suggests something different: that this aspect of public expenditure should not be seen as a perfect substitute for straightforward monetary subsidies. There is surely a very strong case for a thorough reconstruction of the subsidy side of the fiscal system, replacing many parts of the system by pure credits, to be paid regardless of income, employment status, educational activity, or whatever. If it were found, after further research on labour supply, that a yet greater degree of redistribution is desirable, it would seem to be a mistake to assume that it should be achieved by a uniform expansion of all parts of what I have classified as *B*. On the contrary, it seems likely that many of the specific expenditures have already become as large as they should, or may already be too large, and that any further redistribution ought to be in purely monetary terms.

As for commodities to which the theory of public or collective goods can be applied, it is striking how few and, measuring by expenditure, unimportant they are. Defence expenditures cannot be analysed very effectively in this way, nor can expenditures on social goods which are provided because it is right to do so, rather than as collectively consumed goods: aid to developing countries is the chief example, which would be none (or very little) the less desirable if no British citizen got any pleasure from it. Because of the way in which optimal income-tax analysis is carried out, the right level of expenditures on social goods determines the overall optimal pattern of public expenditures, and we have not discussed whether it is currently optimal. I do not have the information that would enable me to do so. But it is interesting to consider whether we would expect the optimal proportion of social expenditures in national income to rise or fall over time. One of the arguments wielded by Bacon and Eltis is that technological change, economies of scale, and investment possibilities together imply that the relative cost of private goods, compared with social goods, tends to fall over time. They correctly deduce from this proposition, which I suppose is likely to be true, that an economy in which resources are being moved from private-good to social-good production will have a lower growth rate than one in which the movement goes the other way. But there is more to life than growth. To decide whether or not it is desirable to move resources between social goods and private goods, we must compare the marginal social value of the social goods with the cost to individual consumers of raising more revenue to pay for them.

The cost of the revenue is the cost of reducing the lump-sum subsidies received by individual households. Consider a household whose indirect utility function is $v(q,b)$, where q is the vector of prices of private goods, and b is the lump-sum income. To fix attention on the right questions, let us take a social good as numeraire, so that b is measured in terms of the social good. The hypothesis is that the prices of private goods, q, are falling over time. We have to consider what would happen to the marginal utility of lump-sum income as a result. Denote by v_b the partial derivative of v with respect to b. Then,

$$\frac{d}{dt} v_b = v_{bq} \dot{q} + v_{bb} \dot{b},$$

where dots denote differentiation with respect to time. From Roy's identity, we know that $v_q = -v_b x$, where x is the vector of demands for private goods. Differentiating with respect to b, we obtain

$$v_{qb} = -v_{bb}x - v_b x_b.$$

Substituting in the equation for the rate of change of the marginal utility of income, we find that

$$\frac{d}{dt} v_b = -v_b[\dot{q} \, (x_b - \gamma x/b) + \gamma(\dot{b}/b)],$$

where $\gamma = -bv_{bb}/v_b$ is the elasticity of marginal utility of income with respect to income. Let n_i be the income elasticity of demand of commodity i. Then this last formula can be written as

$$\frac{d}{dt}v_b = -v_b \left[\sum \dot{q}_i x_i(n_i - \gamma)/b + \gamma(\dot{b}/b)\right].$$

This kind of formula, or at least the principles it embodies, should be fairly familiar. Let us apply it to the question at issue. By hypothesis, all the $\dot{q}_i < 0$. If, then, all the n_i are greater than γ, and $\dot{b} = 0$, it will follow that v_b increases with time, so that diverting resources from private goods through the tax system is becoming more expensive. But if, on the contrary, the n_i are generally less than

γ, v_b will fall over time so long as b is not falling. Which of the two cases is more plausible? The expenditure-weighted average of income elasticities of demand is unity, so that some of the n_i are greater than one, and others less than one. γ, on the other hand, is $1 + v$ in the notation of the Stern example that we used above, so that in that example $\gamma = 2$. More generally, I think that most people's values would support a value of γ greater than one. Consequently, in normal cases we should expect v_b to fall over time, so that we should shift resources towards social goods. From this point of view, one of the more disturbing features of recent British economic history is that expenditure on social goods has not been a rising proportion of the national income.

The arguments that have been advanced in criticism of the current level of public expenditure in the UK do not look very strong in the light of our examination. At the very least, they would have to depend upon special assumptions and values which many of us do not accept. A purely economic case against the current role and activity of government has not been made. Our analysis suggests that, in the aggregate, the government's performance does not look too bad.

But this certainly does not mean it has been good. It means only that the current faults of economic government are not to be seen in the aggregate long-run picture. In small matters, a great deal is wrong; and in total I suspect that these small mistakes, which happen to be invisible in the aggregate figures, are of considerable importance. A number of what I take to be errors in the small have already been alluded to. Any list should include unduly low taxes on many public-sector products, unduly high taxes on petroleum products, totally unreasonable taxation of income derived from capital (which should however be reduced only in conjunction with measures equivalent to a progressive capital levy), some excessively high marginal tax rates on earnings, inefficient methods of getting basic subsidies to those for whom they are intended, and almost everything to do with housing. Also, national insurance benefits could be made to have larger positive incentive effects. I choose these points more or less at random, to avoid ending on a complacent note.

In closing, one other point should be made. The tables I have given were put together in a few spare evenings and weekends. Those who know the National Accounts inside out, and are experienced in working with them, could do a much better job; and I think it would be interesting to examine a longer period in much the way I have sketched for the few years considered in this paper. The sort of classification I have attempted requires a good deal of guesswork and economic reasoning. It would not lend itself to the kind of 'objective' procedures which have become established in national accounting. But I doubt whether government statisticians are always content with the role of automatons, and wonder whether they might not find such an exercise as this one interesting. The results would certainly interest the rest of us.

REFERENCES

Bacon, R. W. and Eltis, W. A. (1976) *Britain's Economic Problem: Too Few Producers.* London: Macmillan.

Stern, N. H. (1976) 'On the Specification of Models of Optimum Income Taxation'. *Journal of Public Economics*, Vol. 6 (1,2), pp. 123–62.

15

Optimal Taxation and Government Finance

In his *Theory of Public Finance* (1959), Musgrave shaped his subject, and our subject, in terms of the three objectives of policy: allocation, distribution, and stabilization. Economic government was analysed in terms of three branches of the imaginary fiscal department, dealing with these three groups of objectives. More than two hundred pages of the book were devoted to the study of stabilization, which we would now call macroeconomic policy. In a much more recent text, Atkinson and Stiglitz's *Lectures on Public Economics* (1980), macroeconomic policy is excluded. Specialization has increased, and public economics, even public finance, is taken to refer to allocation and distribution. Stabilization is left to the macroeconomists and their textbooks. It is interesting, though, that the most recent major text on macroeconomics, the one by Blanchard and Fischer (1989), devotes a single, concluding chapter to monetary and fiscal policy issues.

This bifurcation of public finance is not mere subdivision and specialization as the organism expands. It reflects developments in economists' ways of thinking about different aspects of public finance that may not be easily reconciled. A key issue is the basis for judgment, the treatment of objectives in analysing economic policy. As Musgrave asserted, 'There is no simple set of principles, no uniform rule of normative behaviour that may be applied to the conduct of public economy. Rather we are confronted with a number of separate, though interrelated, functions that require distinct solutions' (1959, p. 5). He went on to deal with a multiplicity of objectives, analysing each aspect of public finance in terms of those objectives that seemed most apposite—merit wants, utilities, inflation, and the aggregate level of activity.

The purist welfare economics approach to public economics cannot easily accept this pluralist method. That is one reason why macroeconomics appears to play so little part in optimal tax theory, which nevertheless purports to be (potentially, one must say) a complete analysis of policy. It is interesting to see how Blanchard and Fischer deal with this issue of objectives: 'Evaluating the full-fledged social welfare function, which is likely to depend on the utilities

Reprinted by permission of the publisher from "Optimal Taxation and Government Finance" by J. A. Mirrlees in *Modern Public Finance*, edited by John Quigley and Eugene Smolensky, pp. 213–231, Cambridge, Mass.: Harvard University Press, ©1994 by the President and Fellows of Harvard College.

of current and prospective members of society, under alternative policies, rapidly becomes analytically untractable. Thus we often have to rely on a simpler objective function, a *macro welfare function*, defined directly over a few macroeconomic variables such as output, unemployment, inflation, or the current account' (Blanchard and Fischer 1989, p. 568). They then proceed to discuss policy issues in terms of a quadratic loss function, whose arguments are the rate of inflation and the level of output. As has often been remarked, it is difficult to find a basis for the numerical specification of such a loss function (other than impressions of the relative importance politicians assign to inflation and aggregate activity); and the procedure ignores serious issues of measurement and principle—What price index matters? Is it the rate of inflation or fluctuations in the rate of inflation that matters? What kinds of unemployment matter, and how much? It is much easier to ask such questions than to establish a framework for analysing them systematically.

There have been notable analyses of what may be regarded as macroeconomic questions, using an optimal tax framework—by Phelps, and by Lucas and Stokey, for example. The main macroeconomic aggregates can, after all, be seen as manifestations of general microeconomic equilibrium. It is customary to view the effects of unanticipated inflation as a tax on money; and unemployment can be modelled as the outcome of preferences for leisure, influenced by the tax/subsidy/social insurance system. But it better represents the current state of public finance to contrast general equilibrium optimal tax theory, using a microeconomic welfare function, with analyses of fiscal and monetary policy based on some kind of tradeoff between macroeconomic variables that do not easily relate to microeconomic categories.

At a relatively crude level, it is interesting that inflation, or at least inflation at more than a few percentage points per year, is widely regarded (particularly by noneconomists) as highly undesirable, although it is difficult to make a precise case for this judgement. Presumably the social cost of inflation cannot be fully derived from the kind of welfare function that is used in microeconomic analyses of policy. At least there is little in the way of highly articulated models connecting microeconomic welfare functions and the costs of inflation (or unemployment, for that matter). The pain of disappointed anticipations and costly money is only part of what is supposed to constitute the undesirability of inflation (although there are still many quite long-term contracts denominated in money). It is believed, rather, that political effects—unreasoned dislike by people at large, or panic and painful reactions by public authorities—are in some sense costly, in ways that are difficult to compare with microeconomic costs and benefits but that may be substantial all the same.

These general remarks are not a preface to an integrated treatment of the issues of macroeconomic finance within a general theory of public finance. This chapter simply looks at two issues that arise in government budgetary decisions, and looks at them from the standpoint of optimal tax theory—a thoroughly microeconomic way of analysing public policy. These are issues in macroeconomics that microeconomic techniques can fairly easily address. Neither involves the price level. Only the first touches on large-scale imbalances between supply and demand. The first topic is the central issue of budget balance: the choice of policy variables when there is uncertainty about the effects of taxes and the costs of expenditure programmes. The second is the question of assessing the cost of funds raised through taxes, for public expenditure projects.

1. BUDGET BALANCE AND OPTIMAL TAXES

A fully articulated theory of optimal taxes in a general equilibrium model may be taken to be a theory of all policy, leaving no room for a macroeconomic theory of policy. In this part, I want to explore some of the limitations of that view. In brief, the argument is that setting optimal taxes and expenditure plans, according to the ideas of optimal tax theory, will, under certain circumstances, lead to disequilibrium. The relationship between the disequilibrium and actual outcomes and the way it is influenced by policies are not readily analysed by the techniques of welfare economics. It may be best to analyse these policy issues in ways that are quite different from the welfare function method, just as particular numerical methods (in mathematics, physics, and engineering) are not selected by finding the method that maximizes some well specified objective function.

First, we need a model—the standard general equilibrium model with taxes. We consider an economy in which all taxes and subsidies are proportional to the consumption or supply of various commodities, except that there is also a uniform head tax or subsidy. It is well known that such a tax system is incentive-compatible, since it requires for its operation only information that is generated by ordinary economic behaviour. Though in reality there is scope for further refinement of the tax system (by having some nonlinear taxes, and by discriminating on the basis of unchangeable observable characteristics), these possibilities will be ignored in order to keep the structure of the model as simple as possible. Also for the sake of simplicity, assume there are no private-sector pure profits, at least in equilibrium. This amounts to supposing that there are no economies of scale—untrue of course, but some model other than perfect competition would be needed if we allowed for economies of scale—and that all possible sources of decreasing returns have become tradeable assets, and can be subject to taxation.

We shall consider policy issues for this economy, judging the policies by their impact on a measure of welfare, which is taken to be a sum of the utilities of individual households. The policy questions could be discussed with a more general or different form of welfare function. The additive form keeps the conditions for optimality somewhat simpler. Whether it is a reasonable form has been much discussed. On the whole, I find it so.

We shall be dealing with public expenditure, and must take account explicitly of the way that public expenditures affect utility. Specifically, let us treat all public expenditures as public goods, affecting (possibly) every household's utility. The following notation will be used: household h's utility is $v(q, b, z)$, where $q =$ the vector of consumer prices, $b =$ lump-sum income, and $z =$ the vector of public goods. Household's net demands are $x^h(q, b, z)$. *Aggregate* production possibilities are described by an equation $F(y, z) = 0$ in terms of an aggregate net production vector y, available for private consumption, and z. There are constant returns to scale. This way of putting things leaves the production technology for public goods implicit, but simplifies the notation. All functions are assumed to be differentiable.

Provided that competitive conditions prevail, we can describe optimal policy for this economy fairly easily: this is the first task of optimal tax theory.[1] The general idea is that producers face prices $p = q - t$, where t is the vector of tax rates; and that choosing tax rates optimally is equivalent to choosing q optimally. We can therefore say that an equilibrium with optimal taxes satisfies

$$q, b, z \max \sum_h v^h(q, b, z), \text{ subject to } F\left(\sum_h x^h x(q, b, z), z \right) = 0. \qquad (1)$$

This statement does not involve producer prices or tax rates explicitly. In competitive equilibrium, producer prices will be proportional to the derivatives of F. Optimal q and b are determined only up to multiplication by a positive constant, and the same is true of p. There are therefore many equivalent systems of optimal tax rates t, corresponding to different consumer and producer price levels.

When we go on to obtain first-order conditions for optimal taxes and expenditure levels, we should allow for the possibility of corner solutions, with some consumer prices being zero, but that does not seem to be an important possibility in the standard model with complete markets. It will be assumed that the optimum is not a corner solution. One expects that, realistically, the optimal b will be positive. The variable b corresponds to the effect of income-tax-deductible allowances in real-world tax systems.

The first-order conditions for optimality can be written[2]

$$\frac{\sum_h v_b^h x_h}{\sum_h v_b^h} = \frac{p \sum_h x_q^h}{p \sum_h x_b^h}, \qquad (2a)$$

---

[1] Atkinson and Stiglitz (1980) provide an account of the theory.

[2] Using a multiplier λ for the constraint $F(y, z) = 0$, we set the derivatives of $\sum_h v^h - \lambda F$ equal to zero. The derivative of v^h with respect to q is $-v_b^h x^h$, by Roy's famous identity. The derivative with

where p are producer prices, proportional to the derivatives of F with respect to y; and

$$\frac{\sum_b v_b^h m_h}{\sum_b v_b^h} = \frac{p \sum_b x_z^h + r}{p \sum_b x_b^h}, \tag{2b}$$

where m_h is the vector of marginal rates of substitution between the public goods and income for household h, and r is the vector of producer prices for public goods. The terms p and r can of course be thought of as marginal costs in terms of some arbitrary unit of account.

Conditions (2b) will be used intensively in Section 2. Conditions (2a) are one form of the conditions for optimal taxation. They are, as written, highly implicit, and various other forms of the conditions have been given over the years—notably the covariance form proposed by Diamond (1975), which emphasizes the convariance between demands and marginal utilities, already apparent in the product form of the left-hand side of (2a).

The left-hand side of (2a) is naturally interpreted as a welfare-weighted average of demands. The right-hand side is equal to the derivative of the general lump-sum subsidy b with respect to tax rates, holding government net tax revenue (and producer prices) constant. To show this, one uses the consumer budget constraint, and introduces tax rates explicitly as $t = q - p$. One particularly appealing form for the conditions comes fairly directly from (2a),[3] using consumer budget constraints, which imply $q \cdot x_q^h = x_h$ and $q \cdot x_b^h = 1$, and can be written in a more summary notation:

$$t(\bar{x}_q + \bar{x}_b x^*) = x^* - \bar{x}, \tag{2c}$$

where x^* is the welfare-weighted average of demands and $\bar{x}$ is the unweighted average of demands. The matrix post-multiplying t is singular; and that is right, because optimal t is indeterminate. The taxes can be made determinate by selecting a particular commodity arbitrarily as untaxed numeraire. Despite the indeterminacy, (2c) gives the right flavour: the level of tax rates tends to be inversely proportional to certain modified demand elasticities, and directly

---

respect to z is, by definition of marginal rates of substitution m, $v_b^h m^h$. We therefore get the three equations

$$-\sum_b v_b^h x^h = \lambda F_y \sum_b x_q^h, \quad \sum_b v_b^h m^h = \lambda \left[F_y \sum_b x_z^h + F_z \right], \quad \sum_b v_b^h$$
$$= \lambda F_y \sum_b x_b^h,$$

which yield (2a) and (2b) on dividing the first and second by the third, and using $p = \mu F_y$, $r = \mu F_z$ for some scalar μ.

[3] The consumer budget constraints $q \cdot x^h = b$ imply, on differentiating with respect to q and b, $q \cdot x_q^h = -x$ and $q \cdot x_b^h = 1$. Consequently $t \cdot x_q^h = (q - p) \cdot x_q^h = -x^h - p \cdot x_q^h$; and $t \cdot x_b^h = (q - p) \cdot x_b^h = 1 - p \cdot x_b^h$. Averaging over the population, and defining $x^* = \Sigma_h v_b^h x^h / \Sigma_h v_b^h$, we get equation (2c) in the text.

proportional to the relative unimportance of the commodity to those who have high welfare weights (at the optimum).

These first-order conditions for q, b, and z at least provide us with a way of organizing our ideas about the various considerations that influence optimal policy levels, and can sometimes be made to tell us something about magnitudes. Section 2 will provide an illustration of the use of these conditions to deal with particular policy questions. Macroeconomic considerations are trivial in the model as set out. Government budget balance (over all time in an intertemporal version of the model) is implied by equality of supply and demand in all markets. This aspect becomes more interesting when we recognize that there is in reality uncertainty about demand and supply conditions, with policy variables set *ex ante*—that is, before the state of nature is fully known.[4] Uncertainty can be incorporated into the model by having x_h and F depend on the state of nature s, and assuming that there is uncertainty about s when policy variables are chosen (and announced).

In reality, of course, there is a time dimension to demand and supply, and policy variables can change over time, responding to changing information as well as predicted changes in the economy. However that may be, if the government calculates optimal policy variables from (1), or a generalization of it allowing for intertemporal developments, and then implements the calculated policy variables, the outcome will be random; and indeed, there may not be an equilibrium, in which case the outcome is not described by the model as we have set it out. Randomness would not in itself seem to pose any great difficulties for an optimizing approach. Indeed, there is a literature on the desirability of tax smoothing that has the government budget surplus or deficit, and tax rates, vary over time in response to changing circumstances. Existence of equilibrium is more of a problem.

It is worth examining this more closely. What happens depends on whether or not there are elements in the tax system that are indexed to prices. Suppose first that the tax system is wholly unindexed. That is not at all realistic, of course. On the basis of an optimizing calculation, the government sets specific taxes t, so that consumer prices and producer prices must be related by $q = p + t$. The variables z and b are also set as specific numbers. Suppose these were calculated to be consistent with equilibrium when demand functions and production possibilities took some particular form. Now we ask whether, when these functions have changed, there is an equilibrium with markets clearing—that is, whether there are prices p such that

$$\sum_h x^h(p + t, b, z) = y \text{ maximizes } p \cdot y, \text{ subject to } F(y, z) = 0. \tag{3}$$

---

[4] Some policy variables are set later in the day than others. So far as I know, all tax and subsidy rates are set in advance, though I dare say there may have been one or two occasions where a tax rate was changed retrospectively. But it may be useful to identify some policy variables as being (relatively) *ex post*. Automatic stabilizers will be discussed briefly below.

There are here as many equations as there are commodities, and as many unknowns as commodities (namely the producer prices), but that does not guarantee the existence of equilibrium. There is no general existence theorem available for a system of equations like this, describing an economy with given specific taxes. The simplest case, of a two-good model, shows that there can be a problem with existence. For given tax rates, we find that public expenditure plans z can be too large for equilibrium to be possible.

Let us call the two commodities consumption and labour, and denote them by c and l. Production possibilities are $c + z = l$. Suppose the government tries to implement the optimum with a tax t on purchases of consumption. If there is to be equilibrium with H consumers, producer prices for the two goods must be equal. (I take it that there must be some production.) Let the prices be (p, p). The budget constraint for each consumer takes the form

$$(p + t)c = py + b. \tag{4}$$

As p varies from very small to very large, the consumers' aggregate choice of (L, L) follows a curve connecting $(Hb/t, 0)$, the choice when $p = 0$, to, say, (C', L'), the choice when the budget constraint is $c = y$, corresponding to $p = \infty$ (see Fig. 15.1). If z is large enough, the curve will not cut the production frontier.

In this example, we find that fluctuations in the underlying state of the economy could make the planned level of the public good so large as to be infeasible—not technically infeasible, but such that no possible prices could bring about an equilibrium with that level of the public good. In other states, there would be an equilibrium. The price level would have to vary to bring it about. In some states of nature, the required price changes would be large. Price stickiness is then likely to be important. A macroeconomist would recognize the importance of allowing for price stickiness in assessing the impact of policies. The point is that in some states of nature the impact of price stickiness may be considerable, and disequilibrium the right conclusion.

Even if fluctuations were sufficiently small that an equilibrium would always exist, the optimal taxation problem is incorrectly formulated if we take it to have the form (1) with the v^h replaced by their expected values. To get the correct formulation, denote the state of nature by s. The government should choose t, z, and b to maximize

$$\sum_h E[v^h(p(s) + t, b, z, s)],$$

$$\text{subject to } F\left(\sum_h x^h(p(s) + t, z, s), z, s\right) = 0 \text{ for all } s. \tag{5}$$

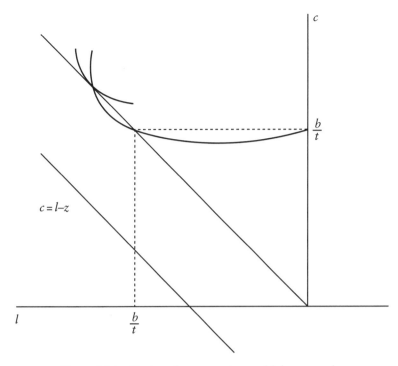

Figure 15.1. *Choice of consumption and labour supply*

(E is the expectation operator, averaged over states *s*.) The multiple resource constraints would be handled by state-dependent shadow prices. These can be interpreted as shadow prices on government revenue in different states of nature; but they do make the tax rules less transparent.

Formulation (3) has made an illegitimate assumption in supposing that equilibrium will always exist. Nonexistence is even more likely when taxes are indexed to prices. The value of labour-income tax allowances, for example, is proportional to wage rates, and sales taxes and property taxes are proportional to the corresponding prices. The extreme case is when all taxes are proportional to prices. In that case, we can write

$$q = Tp, \qquad b = \beta p_0, \tag{6}$$

where T is a diagonal matrix of proportional tax rates, β is a scalar, and p is some appropriate price. Equilibrium requires that

$$\sum_h x^h(Tp, \beta p_0, z) = y \text{ maximize } p \cdot y, \text{ subject to } F(y,z) = 0. \tag{7}$$

Now both consumer demands and producer supplies are homogeneous of degree 0 in producer prices p. With n commodities, there are in effect $n-1$

degrees of freedom, and the Walras's Law is not available to make sure that the nth market clears when all the others clear.

In this model, we can expect that, if one of the policy variables, say β, or the level of z, could vary *ex post*, equilibrium would be possible. An assumption of that kind was made in a paper by Diamond and myself (1974) on shadow pricing for public-sector decisions in an economy where tax rates, not being optimal, were largely fixed; we assumed rather arbitrarily that government policy variables had just enough flexibility to ensure that equilibrium was always possible. That is making the economy march to the modeler's convenience. It is tempting to say that this non-equilibrium problem is a reason for not having fully indexed tax systems; but we have seen that, even without indexing, there may be existence problems, though of a weaker kind.

An alternative view of the matter is that we have here found, lurking in the microeconomic optimal tax model, some aspects of the macroeconomic problems of adjustment and stabilization; and that welfare maximization is not a satisfactory way of analysing the policy issues in this context. What we want are means of adjustment that will bring the economy rapidly to equilibrium, without serious side-effects. It appears to be difficult to compare different budgetary adjustment processes on the basis of their impact on a welfare function like the one used above.

Compare what is at issue with the business of selecting a numerical algorithm to solve an equation. In choosing such an algorithm, we base our selection not on an optimizing analysis but on a number of desirable properties, such as rapid convergence, applicability to a wide range of functional forms, and so on. Although we want to make a rational choice, we are unable to formulate the choice problem as an optimization; we fall back on considering multiple objectives, and not measuring them very precisely either.

When policies are set *ex ante*, and disequilibrium ensues, the actual outcome is the result of adjustments whose welfare cost is hard to assess. There could be automatic stabilizers in the tax system, taking up some of the strain. The question that arises is whether automatic stabilizers would be better than leaving the system to adjust: in cases where disequilibrium cannot be removed without change in the policy parameters, one must assume that automatic stabilizers would be an improvement. Then we want to know which taxes and expenditures should be adjusted *ex post*, and in response to what observations. Properties like rapid convergence and robustness to variations in behaviour and technology are, plausibly, more important than the effect on welfare in the steady-state outcome for a particular model. In effect, we want a kind of analysis that would be complementary to the microeconomic analysis used in most of the tax literature.

2. THE COST OF GOVERNMENT FINANCE

The second topic to be addressed is a more straightforward one. It is the question whether there is a good general argument against public expenditure on the grounds of the distortionary cost necessarily involved in financing the expenditures by tax revenues. Several notable papers have addressed the issue. Until recently, the literature suggested that the argument is valid on the whole, though not completely general.[5] It deserves further consideration. It is a question concerning the broad balance of public activity, to which nevertheless the techniques of microeconomics can be directly applied.

Pigou long ago claimed that the existence of distortionary taxes, which he recognized as essential, and whose necessity is a central feature of optimal tax theory, was a reason for not 'carrying public expenditures as far' as would be done if the simple rule equating marginal cost to marginal benefit of consumers were applied. This issue was carefully treated by Atkinson and Stern (1974), following an earlier examination of the question by Dasgupta and Stiglitz (1971), who had seen that Pigou's claim was not necessarily correct in an optimal tax framework. It is still generally held that the existence of distortion is a reason for imposing a premium on the cost of public funds when considering possible public expenditures, and therefore for lower levels of public expenditure than would have been optimal in a first-best world.[6] Indeed, Atkinson and Stern's analysis gave some support for the view, since they show that, in an interesting local sense, the optimal level of public goods is less in the second-best than in the first-best.[7]

Atkinson and Stern study a Ramsey economy, where consumers are identical and there is no lump-sum tax. The issue really needs to be considered in the context of a multiperson economy, with a uniform lump-sum subsidy or tax chosen optimally alongside commodity taxes. It is true that in actual economies there is nothing that corresponds exactly to a uniform lump-sum subsidy; but personal tax allowances are not dissimilar in effect for those not on the lowest incomes, and welfare payments apply to many on the lowest incomes.

---

[5] A paper by J. D. Wilson (1991) has now appeared which, like this chapter, considers the question for an economy in which the government is allowed to use a uniform lump-sum subsidy. Wilson's analysis covers some of the same ground as this one, concluding that the cost of public expenditure may well be less in a second-best economy than in one with first-best taxation. On the question which kind of tax environment would justify the higher level of public expenditure, Wilson obtains definite results for two interesting examples. Below, I obtain general results valid only for economies with a small degree of inequality. Our results are therefore complementary.

[6] An interesting example is Ballard, Shoven, and Whalley (1985), where the premium on the cost of public expenditure is estimated for the United States, with a computable general equilibrium model of Ramsey type.

[7] Their proposition concerns a two-good economy with identical consumers, for whom the utility of a public good is additively separable from the utility of private goods. In this economy, there is a fixed level of lump-sum tax. Commodity taxes and the level of expenditure on the public good are chosen optimally. The optimal level of public-good expenditure is shown to be a decreasing function of the lump-sum tax, in the neighbourhood of the optimal lump-sum tax (that is, the amount required to finance the public good). The restriction to a two-good economy is in fact unnecessary: the same proposition is true whatever the number of goods in the economy. Since the interesting model is the many-person economy discussed in the text, I omit the proof for that more general case.

The existence of these taxes and subsidies must considerably modify the intuitive Pigovian argument, since it is not necessary to raise revenue for additional public expenditure by distortionary taxation: if desirable, it can be done by reducing the uniform lump-sum subsidy. Indeed, one can argue that the existence of a nondistortionary tax allows the cost of raising revenue to be assessed entirely by that yardstick, since on the margin all sources are equally good. I shall show how it is possible to interpret the conditions for optimal public good provision in that way. But that is not the whole story, for the structure of second-best taxation certainly does affect the value to people of public expenditures.

There are two ways of approaching the issue. One is to interpret the first-order conditions for optimality in such a way that one can see to what extent the rule for pricing public goods may differ from the first-best (Samuelson) rule for the optimal provision of public goods. When we do that, it will be seen that aggregating private marginal evaluations of the public good does not necessarily overstate the marginal value of the public good when the distortionary effects of financing are properly allowed for.[8] The other way of addressing the issue tries to compare the second-best optimal level of public good provision with the first-best. I shall state and prove a proposition somewhat analogous to the Atkinson–Stern proposition for the Ramsey economy. One implication is that, in the many-person case, the second-best optimal level of provision can easily be greater than the first-best level.

Recall the rule for optimal provision of a public good in a first-best world. Samuelson showed that it is a necessary condition for optimality that the marginal cost of the public good be equal to the sum of individuals' marginal rates of substitution of the public good for the numeraire. In terms of our notation, that means

$$r = \sum_b m, \tag{8}$$

provided that the producer-price level is such that q (which must be proportional to p) is equal to p. Notice particularly that the formula needs the assumption that consumer and producer price levels are the same. Of course when there are no taxes, that is inevitable. But if there were perfectly neutral taxes, levied at the same proportional rate on every commodity (amounting to subsidies on goods sold by households), the real equilibrium would be the same, but condition (8) would no longer hold. We would recover (8) by insisting that public good prices and marginal rates of substitution should be measured in terms of the same numeraire.

---

[8] King (1986) has also examined the conditions for optimal provision of public goods in the many-person optimal tax model. He derives them in a different form from the one used here. I comment on his interpretation below.

When tax rates vary from commodity to commodity—as they must if revenue is to be raised—it is tempting to take as numeraire something that is not taxed; but there is no reason why that choice would make aggregate marginal rates of substitution equal to public good marginal costs. To see precisely what is required, we want to compare (8) with some form of the first-order condition for optimal public good provision in the second-best world. The condition stated above as (2*b*) is equivalent to

$$(1 - t \cdot \bar{x}_b)Hm^* = -Ht \cdot \bar{x}_z + r, \tag{9}$$

where m^* is the welfare-weighted average marginal rate of substitution in the consumer population, H is the number of consumers, and, as before, $\bar{x}$ is average consumer demand, so that $t \cdot \bar{x}_b$ and $t \cdot \bar{x}_z$ are the effects of lump-sum income and public good expenditure on commodity tax revenue per head. It is not immediately clear how one can compare (8) and (9), though they can both be thought of as equations for r. For more convenient comparison, write (9) as

$$r = Hm^* - Ht \cdot (\bar{x}_b m^* - \bar{x}_z). \tag{10}$$

The first term in (10) corresponds naturally to the aggregate of marginal rates of substitution in (8): it is the welfare-weighted aggregate. What can we say about the other term? Notice that (8) holds only when producer and consumer price levels are in a particular relation to each other (namely, equality), whereas (10) is valid independently of these price levels. This suggests that the second term in (10), involving tax rates which vary with the relative consumer and producer price levels, is there only to allow for a possible difference in price levels. Indeed, it could well be zero.

On the whole, one would expect the elements of the vector $\bar{x}_{bm}^* - \bar{x}_z$ to be positive. If, for example, demands are independent of the level of public good provision, $\bar{x}_z = 0$; if goods and services are normal, $\bar{x}_b$ is a positive vector; and if the public goods are desired, m^* is positive, too. Therefore, when taxes are primarily on consumer goods, and the elements of t are therefore mainly positive, the second term in (10) would make r less than welfare-weighted aggregate marginal rates of substitution. In effect, marginal rates of substitution would be higher because of the higher consumer price level, and we should adjust for that before comparing r with marginal costs in producer price terms. In the opposite case, with tax revenue primarily from taxation of factors (such as the income tax), the opposite conclusion would hold: in that case, most of the components of the vector t would be negative, corresponding to taxation of commodities supplied by households.

Indeed, one can say that (9) expresses the simple idea that, when we ask consumers (or guess on their behalf) what some public expenditure would be worth to them 'in cash', we should adjust the answer to allow for consumer prices being higher (or lower) than producer prices because of taxes, and the price indexes should use as weights income-marginal expenditure shares. The other term on the right of the equation simply allows for direct tax revenue effects of changing public expenditure. It would not be right to make any further adjustment to allow for 'distortion'.

In a recent paper, Mervyn King (1986) derives an equation equivalent to (9), but analyses it into parts, one of which he calls the Pigou term, which he claims reflects the distortion from raising extra revenue. I believe this is a misinterpretation. Since it is possible to write the conditions in the form (9), we can see that distortion really plays no part in assessing marginal benefits. King does derive the price-level adjustment principle I have just described for the special case of a linear income tax system in an economy where the public good is neither a complement nor a substitute for leisure.

These first-order conditions do not tell the whole story. It is still possible that the real outcome of optimal policies when the government must use distortionary taxes to raise revenue will have lower levels of public good provision than would an economy with perfect lump-sum taxation. I do not know how to give anything like a full answer to that question, but it is possible to throw some light on it by looking for an approximate answer, in a certain sense.

To start with, we know that in an economy without inequality, in which all consumers are identical and in which a uniform lump-sum subsidy is available as a policy tool, the first-best and second-best optima coincide. It should be possible to find out how the optimal levels of public good provision vary as the degree of inequality varies, at least for small inequality. To keep matters reasonably simple, suppose that there is only one kind of public good. Denoting optimal public good provision in the first-best and second-best cases by z_1 and z_2 respectively, we let them depend upon a parameter α that describes the degree of underlying inequality in the economy, with $\alpha = 0$ meaning identical consumers. We have $z_1(0) = z_2(0)$. We try to calculate the derivatives with respect to α at $\alpha = 0$. If we find that $z_1'(0) > z_2'(0)$, it will follow that $z_1(\alpha) > z_2(\alpha)$, at least for all sufficiently small α.

This approach attempts to make the desired comparison between optima in distorted and undistorted economies for at least some economies— namely, those that have a small degree of underlying inequality—when we do not know how to make the comparison for all economies. It turns out that the result is ambiguous. That ambiguity is perhaps the most interesting feature of the result, for it shows that, contrary to the intuitions I have been discussing, there is no general presumption that the existence of distortions is a reason for adding a premium to the apparent cost of public expenditures.

This conclusion supports the argument that, on the margin, we may think of public expenditures as being financed by any particular tax—for example, the general lump-sum subsidy, which is not distortionary. Although it is optimal to have distortionary taxation, this is for distributional reasons, and does not imply that marginal increases in the public expenditure requirement would or should increase rather than decrease 'aggregate distortion'. But it turns out that, even in economies with small underlying inequality, the conditions for either sign of the comparison are not readily interpreted. It would seem that no simple intuitive principle is available.

A slight change of notation is convenient. Individuals in the model are indexed by a variable n and have indirect utility functions $v(q,b,z,n)$. The variable n is distributed in the population with mean μ and variance α. The variable v is taken to be strictly concave in b and z. The idea is that we can find approximations to the first-best and second-best levels of public expenditure z when α is small. To do this, we suppose that the distribution of individual characteristics n is parametrized by α. So long as the density of the distribution depends nicely on α, the precise distribution does not matter.

The remainder of this section is devoted to proving the following result:

Proposition. *Assume that the utility of a public good is additively separable from the utility of private goods. Then, for a small degree of underlying inequality, the optimal level of provision for the public good is greater under optimal second-best taxation than in the first-best if*

$$\frac{v_{bbn}}{v_{bn}} > \frac{1}{2}\frac{v_{bbb}}{v_{bb}}$$

In the opposite case, the second-best level is less.

Note that the condition given is equivalent to requiring that $-v_{bb}/v_{bn}^2$ be a decreasing function of b for given n.

Given z, taxes are chosen optimally. That includes lump-sum taxation, whether uniform in the second-best case or perfectly discriminating in the first-best. Total utility resulting is $W(z,\alpha)$. The first-order condition for optimal z is then $W_z(z,\alpha)=0$, from which we deduce

$$W_{zz}(z,0)\,\frac{\mathrm{d}z}{\mathrm{d}\alpha}\bigg|_{\alpha=0} = -W_{z\alpha}(z,0). \tag{11}$$

This is true for both the first-best economy and the second-best economy. $W(z,0)$—maximized utility when everyone has $n=\mu$—is the same in the first-best and the second-best, since discriminating lump-sum taxation is not required. Therefore, $W_{zz}(z,0)$ is the same in the two cases. By our concavity assumption, it is negative. Thus, (11) implies that z_1–z_2, the difference between public good supply in the first-best and second-best cases, is an increasing function of α at $\alpha=0$ if and only if $W_{z\alpha}$ is greater for the first-best economy than for the second-best. To prove the proposition, we shall calculate $W_{z\alpha}(z,0)$ for these two cases.

The strong simplifying assumption that utility is separable between public and private goods is needed to get a manageable expression for $W_{z\alpha}(z,0)$ in the first-best case. The analysis for the second-best case does not need the simplification. With additive separability, we can write average utility in the population as $\mathrm{E}v(q, b, n) + g(z)$, where E is the expectation operator for the random variable n, and where net demands per person are $\mathrm{E}x(q, b, n)$, independent of z. Since there is only one public good, we may as well take its producer price to be 1. We shall measure it per capita, so that the resource constraint can be written (locally) as $p\mathrm{E}x(q, b, n) + z = 0$.

Consider the optimum with uniform lump-sum taxation. We have

$$W(z, \alpha) = \max_{q, b}[\mathrm{E}v(q, b, n) + g(z) \,|\, p \cdot \mathrm{E}x(q, b, n) + z = 0]. \tag{12}$$

Introduce a Lagrange multiplier λ for the constraint, so that at the optimum

$$\mathrm{E}v_b = \lambda p \cdot \mathrm{E}x_b \tag{13}$$

(we shall not need the first-order conditions for q), and

$$W_z(z, \alpha) = g'(z) - \lambda, \tag{14}$$

where λ, q, and b all depend on α and z. When $\alpha = 0$, then $q = p$ and $b = -z$ are the values that maximize (12); for, with identical consumers, public spending can be financed optimally by a lump-sum tax. The variables q and b are determined only up to multiplication by a positive scalar. As α varies, choose particular maximizing $q = q(\alpha)$ and $b = b(\alpha)$ so that they are differentiable functions of α.

From (14), $W_{z\alpha}(z, 0) = -\lambda'_\alpha(z, 0)$. The derivative of λ can be calculated using (13). To do this, we need to obtain the derivatives of $\mathrm{E}v_b$ and $p \cdot \mathrm{E}x_b$ with respect to α, evaluated at $\alpha = 0$.

To calculate the derivatives, we can use the general proposition that, for any nice function f,

$$\mathrm{E}f(\alpha, n) \cong f(0, \mu) + f_\alpha(0, \mu)\alpha + \frac{1}{2}f_{nm}(0, \mu)\alpha,$$

and consequently

$$\frac{d}{d\alpha}\mathrm{E}f(\alpha, n)\bigg|_{\alpha=0} = f_\alpha(0, \mu) + \frac{1}{2}f_{nn}(0, \mu).$$

The derivative of $\mathrm{E}v_b$ at $\alpha = 0$ is calculated by setting $f(\alpha, n)$ equal to $v_b(q(\alpha), b(\alpha), n)$, and using the facts, already noted, that $q(0) = p$ and $b(0) = -z$. We immediately obtain

$$v_{bq}(p, -z, \mu)q'(0) + v_{bb}(p, -z, \mu)b'(0) + \frac{1}{2}v_{bnn}(p, -z, \mu). \tag{15}$$

Since $v_q = -v_b x$, we have $v_{bq} = -v_{bb}x - v_b x_b$, and the first two terms in (15) can be written

$$v_{bb}(b' - x \cdot q') - v_b x_b \cdot q'.$$

This expression simplifies further, since we can show that $b' = x \cdot q'$. To do so, we use the fact, implied by the resource constraint, that $p \cdot \mathbf{E}x$ is constant as α varies. Differentiating, we have

$$p \cdot x_q(p, -z, \mu)q'(0) + p \cdot x_b(p, -z, \mu)b' + \frac{1}{2}p \cdot x_{nn}(p, -z, \mu) = 0.$$

The coefficient of q' is $-x$, the coefficient of b' is 1, and the last term is 0—all because of the budget constraint $p \cdot x(p, b, n) = b$. Consequently, $b' - x \cdot q' = 0$, as claimed. We then have the following expression for the desired derivative:

$$\frac{d}{d\alpha}\mathbf{E}v_b\bigg|_{\alpha=0} = -v_b x_b \cdot q'(0) + \frac{1}{2}v_{bnn}. \tag{16}$$

We also need to calculate the derivative of $p \cdot \mathbf{E}x$ with respect to α. Using the same method, this time with $f(\alpha, n) = p \cdot x_b(q(\alpha), b(\alpha), n)$, the derivative is found to be

$$p \cdot x_{bq}(p, -z, \mu)q'(0) + p \cdot x_{bb}(p, -z, \mu)b'(0) + \frac{1}{2}p \cdot x_{bnn}(p, -z, \mu). \tag{17}$$

This expression simplifies, since the identity $p \cdot x_b(p, b, n) = 1$ yields, on differentiation, $p \cdot x_{bp} = -x_b$, $p \cdot x_{bb} = 0$, $p \cdot x_{bnn} = 0$. Therefore,

$$\frac{d}{d\alpha}p \cdot \mathbf{E}x_b\bigg|_{\alpha=0} = -x_b \cdot q'(0). \tag{18}$$

We can now use (16) and (18) in differentiating equation (13):

$$\frac{1}{2}v_{bnn} - v_b x_b \cdot q' = -\lambda x_b \cdot q' + \lambda', \tag{19}$$

where we have used the fact that $p \cdot \mathbf{E}x_b = p \cdot x_b(p, -z, \mu) = 1$ at $\alpha = 0$. Note finally that $\lambda = v_b$, and we have the result

$$W_{z\alpha}(z, 0) = -\frac{1}{2}v_{bnn}(p, -z, \mu) \text{ for the second-best.} \tag{20}$$

Surprisingly, the formula for this cross-derivative is more complicated for the first-best economy. In that case, lump-sum income is a function $b(n)$ of individual characteristics, and is chosen in such a way that marginal utility is the same for everyone. Define a function $B(n, \lambda)$ by the equation

$$v_b(p, B(n, \lambda), n) = \lambda. \tag{21}$$

The resource constraint requires that

$$EB(n, \lambda) + z = 0. \tag{22}$$

For the same reason as before, we need to evaluate the derivative of λ with respect to α at $\alpha = 0$. Differentiating (22) yields

$$B_\lambda(\mu, \lambda(0))\lambda'(0) + \frac{1}{2} B_{nn}(\mu, \lambda(0)) = 0. \tag{23}$$

From (21), $B_\lambda = 1/v_{bb}$; and $v_{bb}B_n + v_{bn} = 0$, so that $v_{bb}B_{nn} + v_{bbb}B_n^2 + 2v_{bbn}B_n + v_{bnn} = 0$. Multiplying (23) by v_{bb}, we obtain the desired result: for the first-best economy,

$$W_{z\alpha}(z, 0) = -\frac{1}{2} v_{bnn}(p, -z, \mu) - v_{bbn}B_n - \frac{1}{2} v_{bbb}B_n^2, \tag{24}$$

where $B_n = -v_{bn}/v_{bb}$. Comparing (20) and (24), and using (11), we deduce that optimal z is larger in the second-best case if

$$v_{bbn}B_n + \frac{1}{2} v_{bbb}B_n^2 > 0.$$

Rewriting this condition somewhat, dividing by the negative number $B_n^2 v_{bb}$, leads to the condition given in the proposition. Optimal public good provision is greater in the second-best case than in the first-best if

$$\frac{v_{bbn}}{v_{bn}} > \frac{1}{2} \frac{v_{bbb}}{v_{bb}}. \tag{25}$$

We have assumed that $v_{bb} < 0$. Notice that B_n is the rate of increase of lump-sum income in a first-best equilibrium. If n were the individual wage rate, and labour supply were normal, B would be negative—that is, it is reasonable to assume that $v_{bn} < 0$. The two third derivatives in (25) are not readily signed, though most utility functions used satisfy $v_{bbb} > 0$. I conclude that the comparison is ambiguous.

Condition (25) can be expressed in terms of a familiar object, the coefficient of absolute inequality aversion ('inequality' seems a better qualifier than 'risk' in this context), $A = -(v_{bb}/v_b)$. The derivatives of A with respect to b and n can be written

$$A_b = A^2 + A \frac{V_{bbb}}{v_{bb}}, \qquad A_n = -\frac{v_{bn}}{v_b} \left(A + \frac{v_{bbn}}{v_{bn}} \right).$$

We may reasonably expect that A is a decreasing function of both n and b. As noted already, $v_{bn} < 0$. Making these assumptions, straightforward substitutions transform (25) into

$$2\,\frac{v_b}{v_{bn}}\,A_n + A + \frac{A_b}{A} < 0. \tag{26}$$

The first two terms are positive, the third negative. Optimal public expenditure is higher in the second-best case if $-A_b/A$ is relatively large: for example, if A is small.

It is disappointing, but not surprising, that one should not be able to find a really simple, easily checked criterion for lower public expenditure in a second-best economy. The main lesson of the analysis is that we cannot easily tell which way the balance goes. The useful result, though more superficial, is the first-order condition for optimality of public good provision. Will someone now estimate relative consumer and producer price levels, using the income-marginal expenditure weights, and (a more challenging problem) the effect of public expenditures on tax revenues?

PART IV

CONTRACT THEORY

16

The Optimal Structure of Incentives and Authority within an Organization

1. INTRODUCTION

The usual idea of an organization is that it is a group of people (or roles) within which a structure of authority is defined. In other words, the actions of each member of the organization are constrained by certain of the decisions made by other members. Simon (1957) has developed this view, and it has been taken up more recently by Arrow (1974). Simon and Arrow, in common with many political theorists, emphasize the existence and desirability of limits on authority, which are termed 'responsibility'. More generally, it is clear that relations of authority can, and usually do, operate in both directions between any two members or subgroups within an organization. But, even allowing for this, the possibilities of organizational structure are perhaps rather richer than those suggested by the term 'authority', as Marschak and Radner (1972, p. 313) have indicated. In their work on the 'theory of teams', they choose to concentrate on a different, though related, aspect of organizations—the diversity of information available to the members. At the same time, they narrow their attention, and propose a correspondingly narrow definition of 'team', to organizations whose members have common preferences. Some authors have talked more loosely of teams as groups of people who together can achieve more than if they act separately (Mirrlees 1972a; Alchian and Demsetz 1972). Where such a coalition is possible, one can consider the possibility of the group's agreeing to work together without setting up a system of authority. Alchian and Demsetz propose a model of the firm in which the function of the management hierarchy is simply to measure the labor input of members of the group,

This chapter is reprinted from the *Bell Journal of Economics*, Vol. 7 (1976), pp. 105–31.

I am most grateful to Oliver Williamson for suggesting the subject and inviting me to present the paper at the symposium on 'The Economics of Internal Organization', which was held at the University of Pennsylvania, 19–21 September 1974. The symposium was supported by grants from the National Science Foundation (NSF-GS-35889X) and the General Electric Foundation. I am grateful to the participants in that conference for their comments on the first draft of the paper, and particularly to Michael Spence, whose perception of a serious error, and constructive suggestions, stimulated a complete revision of Section 2.

payments being in accordance with contractual agreement. They even seem to claim that this is the only model appropriate to firms, and that author-itative relationships do not occur.

This last claim cannot be accepted, but it may be agreed that there are interesting possibilities of organization which one would find difficult to describe in terms of authority, and that these possibilities can be applied to the same production possibilities as can more authority-based modes of organ-ization. The common feature is personal relationship between members of the group, with an established pattern of interaction. Thus conceived, organiza-tions may include sharecropping tenancy of a man's land, or even bank lending; for in these cases the contract governing the use of the lender's asset is based on personal information, and may specify aspects of individual behavior (cf. Cheung 1968; Stiglitz 1974). Indeed, there is no sharp line to be drawn between perfect-market relationships and intra-organization relationships: arrangements may vary in a continuous manner from pure trading at an exogenously established price to near perfect obedience by one party to the command of the other. One wants to consider the whole of this spectrum, so as to explain actual organizational structures, and prescribe better ones.

It is hard to specify the spectrum of possible economic relationships in a way that begins to be adequate. In this paper, I make the task easier by completely ignoring all bargaining. It might be thought that this ignores too much; but there are interesting suggestions in the literature, including some already mentioned, which avoid game theory. For example, Williamson (1970) advances a model of organizations, based on imperfect communica-tion, from which is derived an optimum size of firm even when the techno-logy exhibits constant or increasing returns to scale. The models to be developed in the present paper provide a similar theory, based on a more detailed theory of the relationships between the parties involved, but with rather different consequences.

In these models, the members of the organization have different interests, and behave in accordance with their own interests. We are therefore not dealing with a team in the Marschak–Radner sense. Members of the organ-ization take independent, but related, decisions. Thus, though related to Wilson's theory of syndicates (1968) (where diverse individuals share in the consequences of a single decision), our theory is essentially different. The models are closely related to the theory of land tenure systems (mentioned above), the theory of agency (Ross 1973), and models of behavior subject to moral hazard (Pauly 1968; Zeckhauser 1970; Spence and Zeckhauser 1971). This being so, it is as well to repeat the point that Arrow has made about the theory of moral hazard (1971, p. 220), that, in situations where moral hazard arises, there is, potentially, general advantage in moral beha-vior, i.e. behavior not motivated by narrow self-interest; and that such behavior occurs. The models used in this paper assume that contracts, explicit and implicit, are exploited by the parties in their own interest, so that promises and claims about unobservable behavior, for instance, are not admissable. A theory that overemphasizes self-interested behavior in this way deserves to fail in predicting various features of actual organizations; but it would be surprising if it were wholly irrelevant.

The aim of the models in this chapter is to explain the distribution of incomes within the firm, to explain the existence of authoritative relationships, and to derive a hierarchical structure and investigate its effects on production. Naturally much of this program is imperfectly worked out, and important elements are missing. Throughout, uncertainty plays an essential role. There may be uncertainty about the tasks (or the value of the tasks) that any member of the organization will be undertaking, about his capability to undertake these tasks, and about the way in which he will undertake or has undertaken these tasks. Uncertainties of these kinds suggest an analogy with the theory of public finance, where the government is assumed to have limited information about the characteristics of the population it rules. Section 2 develops the theory of a profit-maximizing organization, which has imperfect information about the qualities of its workers when they are recruited, and uses the model to elucidate the relevance of incentive considerations to payment schedules. The model assumes, however, that workers are perfectly able to predict their own activity and rewards within the organization. It is therefore impossible to discuss many interesting questions, particularly the structure of authority.

These issues are taken up in Sections 3–5, where the models allow some scope for imperfect reward administration and monitoring. Section 3 deals with the organization that, from the point of view of this chapter, seems to be the simplest: an organization consisting of two members, one of whom is subordinate (in a sense to be made precise) to the other. This example is helpful in allowing one to model and explore the various kinds of uncertainty mentioned above. The model is then extended to become a two-level organization in Section 4, and a multilevel organization in Section 5. In Section 6—where we return to a less technical level after the mathematical complications of the previous three sections—features of the models are briefly related to the concepts of control-loss and control-span and their consequences. Section 7 summarizes the argument.

2. THE PAY STRUCTURE FOR UNKNOWN ABILITIES

It is commonly asserted that one reason for the hierarchical pay structure within organizations is to be found in the incentives they provide. The person whose work is found good is promoted, and the managers and owners of the organization are thus enabled to discover which members of the organization do good work. None of this makes sense for the firm in perfect competition. But that is because perfect competition assumes that the properties, including the abilities, of each potential worker are public knowledge.

For incentives to have a role, it is necessary that the management have only imperfect information about the abilities and willingness of men and women to work: then they are interested in the way that a structure of wages and salaries elicits much valuable activity from the able and the energetic, while allowing others to choose a more moderate work level and position. It may suit to pay more than the market requires. At any rate, it appears that consideration of the incentives created by the pay structure should be an important element in explaining it.

To explore these matters, a reasonably simple and extreme model is suggested. In it, workers are completely aware of their own abilities, and choose how hard to work on that basis. Employers, on the other hand, cannot distinguish among job applicants, and therefore set pay schedules which are applied to all comers. There are many firms in the economy, all wanting to maximize profits. The behavior of workers, which they determine themselves in the light of the pay structure, is assumed to determine the firm's output. Thus, there is no explicit role for authoritative relations, and the model looks much like the orthodox monopsony model with the firm setting prices and the workers choosing labor supply. The case of a perfectly elastic supply of workers to the firm will, however, be discussed, as well as the monopsonistic case. The question to be chiefly considered is the relation, in equilibrium, between the wages which workers of different skills receive and their marginal productivities.

Technologies

Production possibilities will be assumed to take a form which considerably generalizes the special model which has been used in recent years to analyze the corresponding problem in public finance: that of optimal income taxation. The generalization does not greatly affect the details of the analysis, except at one important point; but it is important to establish that the analysis applies to a model wherein a hierarchical structure of employment is natural, since that is the object of study in this chapter.

Each firm in this model produces a single kind of output, in amount y, with fixed factors (which are ignored notationally) and different kinds of labor. The work done by a worker is denoted by z: different workers choose to provide different z. z is a measure of the quantity and quality of work, one-dimensional for simplicity. Output is taken to be a function of the *distribution* of z. This is best illustrated by some examples, where z is distributed as a continuous variable with density function f:

$$y = H\left(\int zf(z)\mathrm{d}z\right), \tag{1}$$

$$y = h\exp\left(\int \alpha(z) \, \log \, f(z)\mathrm{d}z\right), \tag{2}$$

$$y = H\left(\int \alpha(z)H^{-1}(f(z))\mathrm{d}z\right),\tag{3}$$

or

$$y = G\left(\int_{z\in A} \beta(z)f(z)\mathrm{d}z, \int_{z\in A} \gamma(z)f(z)\mathrm{d}z\right).\tag{4}$$

Equation (1) is the function that has usually been used, for simplicity, in income-tax theory, where the contributions of different workers are perfectly substitutible for one another; (2) generalizes the Cobb–Douglas production function to a continuum of inputs; (3) is a more general class, including (1), (2), and the generalized CES function as special cases; (4) captures the notion that workers may be used in either of two different kinds of activity (e.g. manual or supervisory), the levels of each contributing to total output through the function G. This last form is particularly worthy of attention because it can capture the idea that some workers are promoted after a time when the employer has acquired sufficient information about their working performance; and promotion is to a different kind of activity. This kind of arrangement is frequently mentioned as a reason for paying supervisory workers more: it can provide an incentive for those in less senior occupations to work hard. One of our aims is to check this argument. Perhaps a more precise statement of the situation would be

$$y = G(b + \lambda c, (1-\lambda)c), \qquad b = \int_{z\in A} \beta f\,\mathrm{d}z, \qquad c = \int_{z\notin A} \gamma f\,\mathrm{d}z,\tag{4a}$$

where λ is the (discounted) proportion of career spent in the 'lower' occupation.

One wants to extend these definitions to general distributions of z, where, say, a nonzero proportion of the labor force all supply the same value of z. The extension is done by continuity. For example, in case (2), a group of workers concentrated at a single value of z has no effect on output.

The assumption that output depends only on work levels, z, and not on ability, n, distinguishes this model from that of Spence (1973) and others, where a worker's productivity also depends on n. This dependence is crucial for Spence's results. Work by Rothschild and Stiglitz on Spence's model shows that the n-independent productivity assumption is important for the results to be proved below.

In each of the examples above (with suitable differentiability of the unspecified functions), output is a differentiable function of labor inputs. This means, in the present context, that, when the distribution f depends differentiably on a parameter ϵ, there exists a function p such that, if y is the output resulting from f,

$$\frac{\mathrm{d}}{\mathrm{d}\epsilon}\,y = \int p(z)\frac{\partial}{\partial\epsilon}\,f(z, \epsilon)\mathrm{d}z.\tag{5}$$

$p(z)$ is, in a natural sense, the marginal product of a worker providing work z. Note that in general (i.e. apart from the simple case (1)) p depends on $f(\cdot)$, the distribution of z within the labor force. It will be assumed in what follows that p exists.

Workers

Members of the labor force are characterized by a single parameter n. When faced with a payment schedule $w(z)$, a worker of type n chooses $z(n)$ so as to maximize a function, strictly concave in w and z,

$$u(w(z), z, n). \tag{6}$$

$w(z)$ is to be thought of as the present value of earnings in the firm, possibly through a series of promotions, if the worker behaves in the way described by z. It is assumed that $u_w > 0$, $u_z < 0$, $u_n > 0$. Though other interpretations are possible, n will here be interpreted as 'skill'. The maximization of (6) implies, if everything is differentiable, and z nonzero, that

$$u_w w'(z) + u_z = 0. \tag{7}$$

This can be written in the form

$$w'(z) = s(w, z, n), \tag{8}$$

where $s = -u_z/u_w$ is the marginal rate of substitution. The interpretation of n as skill suggests that we assume $s_n < 0$. The distribution of skills, n, within the labor force of the firm is described by a density function $\phi(n)$.

An alteration of the pay schedule w changes the function $z(n)$. We must see how this change affects output, the labor force being given. Let F be the distribution function of z. Then $F(z(n))$ is unchanged, so that variations in F and z are related by

$$\delta F(z) + F'(z)\delta z(n) = 0;$$

i.e.

$$\delta F = -f(z)\delta z(n). \tag{9}$$

From (5), $\delta y = \int p(z)\delta F'(z)dz = -\int p'(z)\delta F(z)dz$, integrating by parts. Therefore, using (9),

$$\delta y = \int p'(z)\delta z(n)f(z)dz$$

$$= \int p'(z(n))\delta z(n)\phi(n)dn. \tag{10}$$

The specification of the model is now complete, except for the conditions of supply of workers to the firm. The whole spectrum of possibilities will be considered, from the firm with a given labor force to the firm facing a perfectly elastic supply of workers. The case of perfectly elastic supply is where workers of type n are available to the firm provided they are assured of some threshold utility level (their supply price). Formally, the firm will be said to operate in a competitive labor market when it can recruit and keep workers of type n if and only if

$$\max_{z} u(w(z), z, n) \geq \bar{u}(n). \tag{11}$$

$\bar{u}(n)$ will be the utility available to the worker of type n in alternative employment. If all inequalities (11) hold, the firm knows that each recruit is drawn at random from a population with a given distribution described by $\phi(n)$. If some are violated, the recruit is drawn from that part of the population where (11) is satisfied. The extension of the model to an intermediate case, to be called the monopsonistic case, will be explained later.

The analysis proceeds by means of a series of propositions, the third of which is followed by an important remark.

Proposition 1. *For a firm operating in a competitive labor market, with a pay schedule which satisfies (11), in equilibrium,*

$$\int \{p(z) - w(z)\}\phi(n)\mathrm{d}n = 0. \tag{12}$$

Proof. Consider the effect of recruiting one more worker into the firm. The expected change in output per recruit is, by (5),

$$\int p(z)f(z)\mathrm{d}z = \int p(z(n))\phi(n)\mathrm{d}n,$$

where $z(n)$ is the work level chosen by a worker of type n. The average labor cost per recruit is

$$\int w(z)f(z)\mathrm{d}z = \int w(z(n))\phi(n)\mathrm{d}n.$$

It is clear from these two equations that equilibrium is possible only if (12) holds. □

In a competitive equilibrium, all firms (at least if identical) pay the same wage schedules, and the constraints (11) hold with equality. Rather than attempt to approach the question of the shape of the equilibrium pay schedule under these conditions directly, I look first at what is, in effect, the opposite extreme. This is a firm that has a given labor force; with the supplementary consideration that workers would leave if wages fell too low, a constraint that will not apply to most of them in equilibrium.

Proposition 2. *If a firm maximizes profits for a given labor force, subject to the constraints (11), and if, for all n,*

$$u(p(z(n)), z(n), n) \geq \bar{u}(n), \tag{13}$$

then for all n

$$w(z(n)) \leq p(z(n)). \tag{14}$$

Proof. For simplicity, proof is confined to the case where a density $f(z)$ exists. Suppose, in order to obtain a contradiction, that the firm has a wage schedule satisfying

$$w(z) > p(z), \qquad \text{for } a < z < b, \tag{15}$$

with $w = p$ at $z = a$, b. Construct a family of schedules $w(z, \epsilon)$ depending differentiably on ϵ, with

$$\left.\begin{aligned}
w(z, 0) &= w(z) \\
w(z, \epsilon) &= w(z) && \text{when } z \leq a \text{ and } b \leq z \\
w_\epsilon(z, \epsilon) &< 0 && \text{when } a < z < b \\
w_z(z, \epsilon) &= w_z(z) && \text{when } z = a, \, b.
\end{aligned}\right\} \tag{16}$$

This variation of the pay schedule is illustrated in Fig. 16.1. Expressions (13) and (16) imply that, for all small enough ϵ,

$$u(w(z(n), \epsilon), z(n), n) > \bar{u}(n) \qquad (a < z(n) < b).$$

Therefore, the proposed variation is consistent with the constraints (11), and has no effect on the membership of the labor force.

The variation is to be chosen in such a way that a density function $f(z, \epsilon)$ exists for the distribution of work levels, and so that $f(z, \epsilon)$ is a differentiable function of ϵ. That is why we must insist, in (15), that w remains a smooth function of z as ϵ increases.

Applying equation (5), we have

$$\begin{aligned}
\frac{d}{d\epsilon} \left\{ y - \int w(z, \epsilon) f(z, \epsilon) dz \right\} &= \int [(p - w) f_\epsilon - w_\epsilon f] dz \\
&= \frac{d}{d\epsilon} \int (p - w) f(z, \epsilon) dz \\
&= \frac{d}{d\epsilon} \int \{ p(z(n, \epsilon)) - w(z(n, \epsilon), \epsilon) \} \phi(n) dn,
\end{aligned}$$

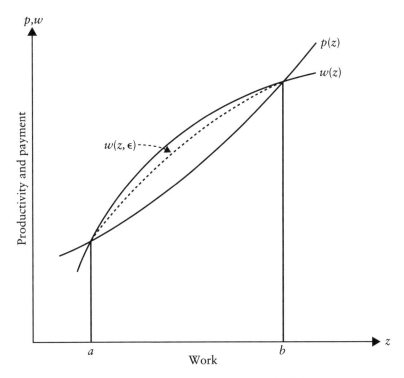

Figure 16.1. *Variation of the pay schedule*

where $z(n, \epsilon)$ is the work-level chosen by an n-worker when faced with $w(\,\cdot\,, \epsilon)$. Therefore, the firm would like to increase ϵ if for each n

$$\frac{\partial}{\partial \epsilon} \{p(z(n, \epsilon)) - w(z(n, \epsilon), \epsilon)\} > 0. \tag{17}$$

In order to calculate this expression, we need to know the partial derivative of $z(n, \epsilon)$ with respect to ϵ. A worker of type n chooses z so that $w' = s$ (equation (8)). Differentiating this relationship partially with respect to ϵ, one obtains

$$w'_\epsilon + w'' \cdot z_\epsilon = s_w(w_\epsilon + w' \cdot z_\epsilon) + s_z \cdot z_\epsilon,$$

where the ϵ-subscript denotes differentiation: w'_ϵ, for example, means $\partial^2 w/(\partial \epsilon \partial z)$. From this, it follows that

$$z_\epsilon = \frac{w'_\epsilon - s_w \cdot w_\epsilon}{s_w \cdot w' + s_z - w''}. \tag{18}$$

Using this result, we have

$$\begin{aligned}
\frac{\mathrm{d}}{\mathrm{d}\epsilon}(w-p) &= w_\epsilon + (w'-p')z_\epsilon \\
&= \frac{(w'-p')w'_\epsilon + (s_w p' + s_z - w'')w_\epsilon}{s_w w' + s_z - w''},
\end{aligned} \tag{19}$$

using (18) to substitute for z_ϵ. We want to be able to choose w_ϵ satisfying (16) in such a way that this expression is negative.

Utility maximization implies that the denominator in (19) is non-negative, for this is the condition that the indifference curve lie (locally) above the budget constraint $w(z)$. Let us assume slightly more:

$$s_w w' + s_z - w'' > 0 \qquad (a \le z \le b). \tag{20}$$

Other (exceptional) cases are presumably easily dealt with. If we now try defining $w(\cdot,\epsilon)$ by

$$w_\epsilon = -(w-p)^r \qquad (a \le z \le b) \tag{21}$$

with $r > 1$, it is readily checked that (16) is satisfied; and substitution in (19) yields

$$\begin{aligned}
\frac{\mathrm{d}}{\mathrm{d}\epsilon}(w-p) = -\frac{(w-p)^{r-1}}{s_w w' + s_z - w''} \{ r(w'-p')^2 \\
- s_w(w-p)(w'-p') + (w-p)(s_w w' + s_z - w'') \}.
\end{aligned}$$

The expression within braces is a quadratic form in $w'-p'$, and therefore is positive definite if

$$4r(s_w w' + s_z - w'') > s_w^2(w-p). \tag{22}$$

Because of our assumption (20), we can find r to satisfy (22) for all z in the interval. Therefore, the variation defined by (21) does have the desired property when r is chosen large enough.

Thus inequality (17) is established, and it follows that the original payment schedule cannot have been profit-maximizing for the firm. The proposition is proved.   □

This proposition is best appreciated if we consider one firm in an environment of other firms all paying less than the marginal products for laborers. For this situation, the proposition asserts that the firm will not choose to pay any of its workers more than his marginal product. Thus, we may say that incentive considerations in themselves give no reason for paying anyone more than his marginal product. If any worker is to be paid more than his marginal product, it must be by reason of some constraint imposed on the firm. It is not easy to see where such a constraint could come from in an industry of like firms. Indeed, in a special case, a much stronger result can be proved.

Proposition 3. *Under competitive conditions, with production possibilities available to each firm described by*

$$y = H\left(\int zf(z)\mathrm{d}z \right),$$ (1)

in equilibrium,

$$w(z) = p(z) = H'\left(\int z(n)\phi(n)\mathrm{d}n \right)z.$$ (23)

Proof. In equilibrium with a competitive labor market, all firms have the same pay schedule, and $\bar{u}(n) = \max_z u(w(z), z, n) = u(w(z(n)), z(n), n)$. It will first be shown that, for this pay schedule, $w(z) \le p(z)$ for all z. The reason is essentially simple: any firm constrained (by competition) to pay more than the marginal product for some work level z_0 can increase its profits by offering less than the marginal product and doing without work-levels in the neighborhood of z_0.

Formally, let us suppose that

$$w(z_0) > p(z_0).$$ (24)

z_0 is the work-level supplied workers of type n_0, and we can choose z_0 satisfying (24) so that no other workers supply z_0, if necessary by slightly changing it. Furthermore, we can take it that z_0 is the unique work-level that workers of type n_0 are prepared to choose, because of the following lemma.

Lemma. *For the case described by (1), the equilibrium wage schedule has the property that for each n, $u(w(z), z, n)$ is maximized by a single value of z.*

Proof of lemma. Suppose, contrary to the stated result, that z_1 and z_2 both maximize $u(w(z), z, n_0)$. If $w(z_2) - w(z_1) \ne (z_2 - z_1)H'$, suppose without loss of generality that $z_1 H' - w(z_1) > z_2 H' - w(z_2)$. If w is slightly increased in the neighborhood, a small group with $n \le n_0$ change from approximately z_2 to approximately z_1, and a small group with $n \le n_0$ change, but remain close to z_1. The effect on profits of ϵ workers changing from z_2 to z_1 is

$$\epsilon(z_1 - z_2)H' - \epsilon(w(z_1) - w(z_2)),$$

a positive number of order ϵ. The other effects are of order ϵ^2. Thus, profits can be increased by the proposed perturbation (see Fig. 16.2).

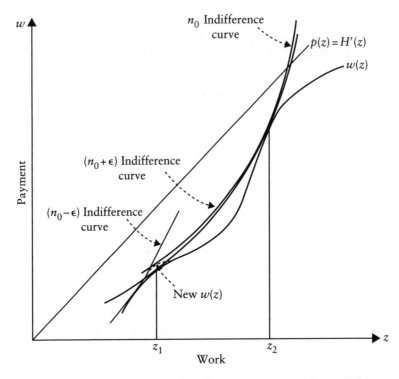

Figure 16.2. *Increasing profits when $w(z_2) - w(z_1) \neq (z_2 - z_1)H'$*

If $w(z_2) - w(z_1) = (z_2 - z_1)H'$, profits can be increased by raising the pay schedule slightly above the n_0-indifference curve joining $(z_1, w(z_1))$ and $(z_2, w(z_2))$, as shown in Fig. 16.3. This completes the proof of the lemma.

Returning to the proof of the proposition, we consider the effect of reducing the pay schedule for the firm in the neighborhood of z_0 (Fig. 16.4). This can be done in such a way that precisely those n between $n_0 - \epsilon$ and $n_0 + \epsilon$ are now unable to attain $\bar{u}(n)$. For all other n, z remains unchanged. $\int z f dz$ is reduced by $\int_{n_0 - \epsilon}^{n_0 + \epsilon} z \phi dn$ and the wage bill is reduced by $\int_{n_0 - \epsilon}^{n_0 + \epsilon} w(z) \phi dn$. Thus, profits are increased by

$$\int_{n_0 - \epsilon}^{n_0 + \epsilon} w \phi dn - \int_{n_0 - \epsilon}^{n_0 + \epsilon} z \phi dn \cdot H'\left(\int z \phi dn\right). \tag{25}$$

Now in the case of the production function (1), it is easily seen that

$$p(z) = zH'.$$

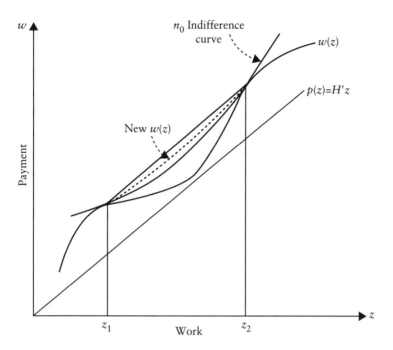

Figure 16.3. *Increasing profits when $w(z_2) - w(z_1) = (z_2 - z_1)H'$*

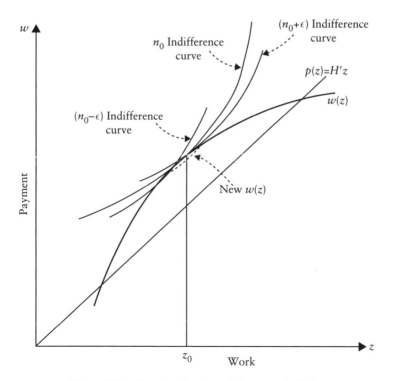

Figure 16.4. *Local reduction of the pay schedule*

Therefore, (25) can be written as

$$\int_{n_0-\epsilon}^{n_0+\epsilon} \{w(z(n)) - p(z(n))\}\phi dn,$$

which is positive, by (24) and the continuity of w and p.

This proves that, whenever (24) holds, profits can be increased. Therefore, in equilibrium,

$$w(z) \leq p(z) \tag{26}$$

for all relevant z. Combining (26) with the result (12) of Proposition 1, we have in fact

$$w(z) = p(z),$$

as was to be proved.   □

The proof of this proposition—apart from the lemma, which is merely disposing of a special case—does not consider the incentive effects of the pay schedule, but only the effects on the supply of laborers. Indeed, it is little more than the usual argument for equality between wages and marginal products, with special care taken to check that no incentive effects occur when a wage is reduced. But the production function to which the argument applies is a very special one, which, by assuming perfect substitutibility among the different work activities in the firm, excludes just those features of industrial production that one associates with the existence of job hierarchies. Probably the proof of the proposition could be extended to cover such cases as are suggested in (4) and (4a) above. The argument should fail only when a large change in work level by a small number of workers has a large effect on marginal productivities. But that is, surely, an interesting and large class of cases.

For the general case, a less precise, but almost equally compelling, argument can be offered. Suppose that, for a range of work-levels, wage-rates are above marginal products. The firm does not reduce these wage-rates if that would lose all the corresponding workers, because it needs such workers. But, to be a little more realistic, a small reduction in wage rates will not suddenly lose all such workers to the firm. A temporary reduction would simply reduce recruiting for a time. Then the change in other marginal products is small and can properly be neglected: the wage reduction increases profits, so long as it does not, and is not expected to, go on too long. There is, then, a general weakness in wage levels if they ever get above marginal products, so that we can expect them to crumble. When this argument is coupled with the implication of Proposition 1, that incentive considerations will not in themselves push wages above marginal products, it is hard to resist the conclusion that, *under competitive conditions, with unidentifiable labor skills, wages and marginal products are equal in equilibrium.*

This conclusion has been based on an industry with identical firms. We should also discuss the equilibrium of a group of firms with *different* production functions taking their workers from the same labor market. If all were recruiting the same mixture of abilities, they would, in general, have different implied marginal productivities, and it would follow from (23) that different firms were paying according to different schedules. If workers are well informed about payment schedules, this is impossible: different wage schedules would sort worker-types among firms. A disequilibrium process of this kind could provide different firms with labor forces of different composition until $p(\cdot)$ is the same for all, and the wage payment schedule is uniform. Thus, equilibrium for an industry is characterized by the orthodox uniformity of marginal productivities and wages. The result, it should be reiterated, has been obtained without the usual assumption that employers know the abilities of those they are hiring.

Since the result is not, despite appearances, the standard one, it is subject to anomalies. The proposition tells us what equilibrium must be like if the firm is recruiting in a perfect labor market, but not that equilibrium exists. I have in mind the possibility that a firm with an established labor force may be able to increase its profits by changing to a payment schedule which will no longer attract new recruits. This will be a possibility if employees cannot expect the same present value of earnings in another firm as those who occupy similar positions to their own. The firm they are working for has acquired information about them (represented by the z they supply) and has placed them in the organization appropriately. They may have spent an initial period with the firm at lower pay, establishing their credentials for promotion. It is not in the interests of their employer to tell a new employer what grades or positions they had reached.

Thus, at least in the case of employees with some seniority, the employer has a monopoly advantage. He may, of course, be unable to exercise it in the face of collective action by his employees. If he succeeds in exercising it, he will cut out recruitment of workers who have sufficient ability to aspire to higher paid positions. The policy is appropriate, therefore, only for a declining firm. It may not be a very realistic possibility. Where it occurs, it means that declining firms have a less steep wage payment schedule than growing firms.

Imperfect labor markets

The question is thus raised as to how flat a payment schedule it could profit the firm to adopt, bearing in mind the disincentive effects. I examine this in a more general setting, where the labor market is imperfect. Imperfection will be captured by extending assumption (11): the utility level required to attract another worker of ability n is assumed to be an increasing function of the number already employed. Formally, the firm is constrained by

$$\max_{z} \ u(w(z), z, n) \geq \bar{u}(n, \phi(n)), \tag{27}$$

where the utility threshold $\bar{u}$ is an increasing function of ϕ (as well as of n). As before, the firm wishes to maximize

$$y - \int w(z)\phi(n)\mathrm{d}n,$$

where $z = z(n)$ is the value chosen by a worker of ability n.

The techniques appropriate to this problem are those developed for the theory of optimal income taxation (Mirrlees 1971). The following non-rigorous development makes it reasonably easy to see where the various conditions come from. First, I express the constraints that, for each n, $z(n)$ maximizes $u(w(z), z, n)$, in a way convenient for the problem. Assuming—as one has no right to do, but we are not being rigorous—that w is differentiable, $u_w w'(z) + u_z = 0$. (Note that $w(\cdot)$ will be so chosen that $z(n) > 0$.) Therefore,

$$\frac{\mathrm{d}}{\mathrm{d}n} u(w(z), z, n) = u_n(w, z, n), \tag{28}$$

the *partial* derivative with respect to n. This 'envelope condition' is plainly equivalent to the first-order condition; and it is convenient because utility also appears in constraint (27). Define

$$v(n) = u(w(z(n)), z(n), n), \tag{29}$$

and express w and u_n as functions of v, z, and n, defined by $u(w, z, n) = v$:

$$w = w(v, z, n), \qquad u_n = \psi(v, z, n). \tag{30}$$

Differentiation of $u(w, z, n) = v$ with respect to v and z shows that

$$w_v = 1/u_w, \qquad w_z = -u_z/u_w = s. \tag{31}$$

Using these results, we then calculate

$$\psi_v = u_{nw}/u_w, \qquad \psi_z = u_{nw}s + u_{nz} = -u_w s_n. \tag{32}$$

After these preliminaries, we can express the problem as

$$\text{maximize } y - \int w\phi(n)\mathrm{d}n,$$

$$\text{subject to } v \geq \bar{u}(n, \phi(n)), \qquad v'(n) = \psi(v, z, n),$$

and introduce Lagrange multipliers $\lambda(n)$, $\mu(n)$ for the two sets of constraints.

Thus,

$$L = y - \int w\phi \, dn + \int \lambda\{v - \bar{u}(n, \phi)\}dn + \int \mu(n)\{v'(n) - \psi\}dn$$

$$= y + \int \{-w\phi + \lambda(v - \bar{u}) - \mu'(n)v - \mu\psi\}dn + \mu(\infty)v(\infty) - \mu(0)v(0)$$

is to be stationary when $v(\cdot)$, $z(\cdot)$, and $\mu(\cdot)$ are varied. Differentiating with respect to $z(n)$, we have

$$p'(z)\phi - w_z\phi - \mu\psi_z = 0,$$

or

$$(p'(z) - s)\phi = -\mu u_w s_n. \tag{33}$$

Differentiation with respect to $v(n)$ yields

$$-w_v\phi + \lambda - \mu' - \mu\psi_v = 0$$

or

$$u_w\mu' + u_{nw}\mu = u_w\lambda - \phi; \tag{34}$$

and, finally, differentiation with respect to ϕ gives

$$p - w = \lambda\bar{u}_\phi. \tag{35}$$

(If ϕ were zero, we could have $p - w < \lambda\bar{u}_\phi$.) The way in which p' and p came out in these differentiations may not be quite clear, although it is readily justified by the arguments given earlier. Heuristically, we can take it that *locally* (i.e. for first-order changes), y is a constant plus $\int p(z)\phi(n)dn$. Once this is granted, it is clear where (33) and (35) come from.

There are two further conditions to note, arising because L must be stationary as $v(0)$ and $v(\infty)$ are varied:

$$\mu(0) = \mu(\infty) = 0. \tag{36}$$

Also it should be noted that, since the multiplier λ is associated with the inequality $v \geq \bar{u}$, $\lambda \geq 0$, and vanishes if $v > \bar{u}$. Since by assumption $\bar{u}_\phi > 0$, (35) implies that, ϕ being positive,

$$p \geq w, \quad \text{with equality if } v > \bar{u}. \tag{37}$$

(It is pretty clear that equality would be very exceptional.) This confirms and generalizes the earlier result. Intuitively, one expects that the firm feels constrained by the need to have $v'(n)$ at least as great as ψ. If it were so, μ would also be non-negative. But this depends of course on the way in which the other constraint operates.

To see what is going on, let us adopt a definition of the elasticity of supply of workers of type n:

$$\eta(n) = w u_w / (\phi \bar{u}_\phi). \tag{38}$$

This is the percentage increase in $\phi(n)$ obtained for a 1 per cent increase in w, that increase being paid only for $z(n)$. (We ignore in the definition the consequent effect on supplies of other labor-types.) Using (35) and (38), (34) becomes

$$u_w \mu' + u_{nw} \mu = \left(\eta \frac{p - w}{w} - 1 \right) \phi. \tag{39}$$

The firm's optimal payment schedule is defined by (39) with (33) in the form

$$p'(z) - w'(z) = -\mu u_w s_n, \tag{40}$$

the worker's maximization condition $w'(z) = s$, the labor supply condition $u(w, z, n) = \bar{u}(n, \phi(n))$, and the boundary conditions $\mu(0) = 0 = \mu(\infty)$.

Since n describes a worker's capabilities, we are assuming that

$$s_n < 0, \tag{41}$$

meaning that a man with greater n is more able (or willing) to substitute labor for consumption. Under this assumption, it is clear that w and z must be increasing functions of n. It may not be possible to measure n in such a way that (41) holds; but for the remainder of this section, I assume that it is. Then (40) shows that $\mu > 0$ is equivalent to the wage schedule's being less steep at $z(n)$ than the marginal productivity schedule.

Solving (39) for μ, we obtain

$$\mu(n) = \int_0^n \left(\eta \frac{p - w}{w} - 1 \right) \beta dm, \tag{42}$$

where

$$\beta = \exp \int_n^m (u_{nw}/u_w) dv \, \frac{\phi}{u_w} > 0. \tag{43}$$

$\mu(0) = 0$ is used in deriving (42). $\mu(\infty) = 0$ implies that

$$\int_0^\infty \left(\eta \frac{p - w}{w} - 1 \right) \beta dm = 0. \tag{44}$$

It follows that, for some n, $\eta(p - w)/w$ exceeds 1, while for others it is less than 1. It cannot, in interesting cases, equal 1 for all n because that would imply $\mu = 0$, and therefore $p' = w'$; i.e. $w(z) - p(z) = $ constant. This would mean $w = $ constant $x \; \eta$, which we may reject since it is not likely that η increases with n, whereas w certainly does (granted assumption (41)).

Let us assume—as seems plausible—that

η is a decreasing function of n. (45)

Is it possible that μ is negative for small n? If it were,

$$\alpha = \eta \frac{p - w}{w} - 1 \qquad (46)$$

would be negative for small n. Now, since μ is negative, $p' - w' < 0$, and, therefore, $p - w$ is decreasing in n; while w is increasing in n, and η decreasing. Therefore, α is decreasing, and remains negative. The argument would continue to apply, and α would be negative for all n. This is, because of (44), impossible. The argument used actually tells us that, once μ is negative for some n_0, it remains negative for all $n \geq n_0$. Thus we have the following:

Proposition 4. *Assuming (41) and (45), there exists n_0 such that (α being defined (46))*

$$\left. \begin{array}{ll} \alpha \geq 0 & (n \leq n_0) \\ \alpha \leq 0 & (n \geq n_0) \end{array} \right\}. \qquad (47)$$

Furthermore, for all n,

$$\mu \geq 0; \qquad (48)$$

and, for all z,

$$w'(z) \leq p'(z). \qquad (49)$$

The second part of the proposition follows at once from the first, for (by (44)) we can write μ either as $\int_0^n \alpha \beta \mathrm{d}m$ or $-\int_n^\infty \alpha \beta \mathrm{d}m$. (47) has an interesting interpretation, obtained by writing (46) in the form

$$\frac{p - w}{w} = \frac{1}{\eta}(1 + \alpha). \qquad (50)$$

If incentive considerations were ignored, the optimal mark-up of marginal product above wage would be $1/\eta$ for each n. Expressions (47) and (50) tell us that the incentive considerations imply a larger mark-up than monopsony theory suggests for the less skilled, and a lower mark-up for the more skilled. At the same time, the absolute difference between marginal product and wage is higher for the more skilled: this is the result of assumption (45).

This section has addressed the importance of incentive considerations in determining the pay structures of profit-maximizing firms. It has been shown that the firm must have the usual kind of monopsony power in the labor market before it has much reason to pay attention to the incentive effects of its pay structure. The one exception to this is the stagnant firm, and that can be regarded as a case of monopsony where there is some inelasticity in response to wage reductions but not to wage increases. In the monopsony case, which I take to be in some degree realistic, no worker receives more than his marginal product, but workers of higher capability receive a wage which is less close to their marginal product than those of lower ability. The last conclusion depends on assuming that higher ability is associated with lower elasticity of supply, which should be true at least because of the investment in reputation, and knowledge of the firm, which a worker of higher ability normally makes. It is interesting that, if firms have imperfect knowledge of their recruits' capabilities, and recruit in imperfect markets, they should in theory apply a progressive tax to marginal products before paying wages, and thus do some of an egalitarian government's work for it.

One can use the equations presented to compute optimum payment schedules in particular cases, but I do not pursue the model further here. It leaves out a very great deal of what interests us about organizations. Presumably this model ought to be developed in the direction of allowing the firm some limited information about the men it hires; but it is unlikely that the principal proposition would be much affected. In any case, it would take us further away from the internal organization of the firm. The chief shortcoming of the model is the lack of an explicit reason for workers to work together, leaving information considerations highly implicit: therefore, there are no reasons for the hierarchical organization that one observes, and would like to explain, for itself, and as an important influence on the pay structure of firms. In fact, when they join a firm, workers are uncertain what they will be doing, and what reward they will receive; but their relationships are quite mechanical. In the remaining sections of the paper, I study models that do not deal explicitly with the distribution of skills, but do deal with the uncertainties of production activity and supervision.

3. PRINCIPAL AND AGENT

Consider a man with von Neumann–Morgenstern utility function $u(x, z)$, where x is the payment received as a result of the work he does and z is the work done. Payment is taken to be an uncertain consequence of the work done. It is a function of the man's performance as observed by his principal. Observed performance may or may not accurately represent the value to the principal of the agent's work; and the value of the work, which I shall call output and denote by y, may itself be a random variable conditioned by z. The accuracy of the principal's observation of y depends upon the time devoted to making the observation. (It should also depend upon the agent's own efforts to affect the observation; but I shall ignore this, important though it may be. I am not sure how best to model the effect of possibly competing efforts to influence observational precision.)

The formal model of the agent is that

$$z \text{ maximizes } U(z) = E_\epsilon E_{Y|z} u \left\{ \phi \left(Y + \frac{1}{\theta} \epsilon \right), z \right\}$$

$$= \iint u \{ \phi(y + \frac{1}{\theta} \epsilon), z \} f(y, z) g(\epsilon) \, dy \, d\epsilon, \tag{51}$$

where ϕ is the schedule governing payment to the agent, and θ^2 is the time spent (by the principal) on observation—the idea being that he samples repeatedly. Observational errors and output uncertainty are assumed independent. It should also be emphasized that all functions and random variables occurring are supposed to be nice: points of rigor will be ignored, although they are very important. Necessary conditions for maximization in (51) are

$$U'(z) = 0 \tag{52}$$

and

$$U''(z) \leq 0. \tag{53}$$

The principal handles the output of the agent and makes payment to him. It is convenient to assume that the two are commensurable, and to give the principal a utility function $v(y - \phi, \theta^2)$. Thus, he would like to choose $\phi(\cdot)$ and θ to maximize

$$E_\epsilon E_{Y|z} v \left\{ Y - \phi \left(y + \frac{1}{\theta} \epsilon \right), \theta^2 \right\}$$

$$= \iint v \left\{ y - \phi \left(y + \frac{1}{\theta} \epsilon \right), \theta^2 \right\} f(y, z) g(\epsilon) \, dy \, d\epsilon, \tag{54}$$

given that z is determined by (51).

One of the odd features of this assumption is that a principal who benefits from y cannot observe it, although one might think that a man can benefit only from what he observes. But notice that the assumption would look much more reasonable if the principal had many agents all contributing to the output he receives—and we shall come to that case. In any event, it is common for benefits to accrue long after payments have been made irreversibly; and $Y + (1/\theta)\epsilon$ should properly be regarded as the agreed basis for payment, which has to be adhered to whatever output may actually be.

Another odd feature is that there is no very evident reason for the principal–agent relationship in the model. But it is implicit that the agent uses assets owned by the principal. There seems to be no advantage in making that explicit unless one wants to consider the decision of how much to let the agent use. Interesting though that may sometimes be, it adds nothing to the picture of the relationship that I want to convey.

Returning to the mathematical problem, we must include another constraint on the principal's maximization—that the agent gets expected utility
sufficient to induce him to accept the contract. In other words, there should
be a supply price for the kind of labor we are considering. (In the case of
slavery, utility would not be the relevant variable constrained; and indeed,
morale, motivation, and health are considerations that should perhaps be
brought in, but they would complicate matters further.) The constraint is

$$U(z) \geq A, \tag{55}$$

A being a fixed number.

The analysis now proceeds along lines I have used elsewhere.[1] Consider the
Lagrangean form obtained by assigning undetermined multipliers λ and μ to
(52) and (55):

$$L = \iint \{v(y - \phi, \theta^2) + \lambda u(\phi, z) + \mu(u_2 + u f_z / f)\} fg \, dy \, d\epsilon.$$

(Here and below, numerical subscripts to u and v denote differentiation with
respect to the indicated argument.) Differentiating with respect to the scalars
z, and the function $\phi(\cdot)$, we obtain first-order conditions

$$\frac{\partial L}{\partial z} = \iint v f_z g \, dy \, d\epsilon + \lambda U'(z) + \mu U''(z) = 0;$$

i.e.,

$$\mu = -U''(z)^{-1} \iint v f_z g \, dy \, d\epsilon. \tag{56}$$

Before taking the other derivatives, it is advantageous to change a variable of
integration and write

$$L = \theta \iint \{v(y - \phi(x), \theta^2) + \lambda u(\phi(x), z) \\ + \mu(u_2 + u f_z / f)\} f(y, z) g(\theta(x - y)) \, dy \, dx. \tag{57}$$

Then

$$\frac{\partial L}{\partial \theta} = 0. \tag{58}$$

(Since I shall not be computing solutions, I do not evaluate this derivative
explicitly: it is clearly rather a complicated expression.)

$$\frac{\partial L}{\partial \phi(x)} = \theta \int \left\{ \left(-v_1 + \lambda u_1 + \mu \left(u_{12} + u_1 \frac{f_z}{f} \right) \right) \right\} f(y, z) g(\theta(x - y)) \, dy = 0.$$

[1] Mirrless (1972*b*, 1974). See also Spence and Zeckhauser (1971).

Since u and its derivatives are independent of y, this may be rewritten in the form

$$\frac{1}{u_1} \frac{\int v_1 fg \, dy}{\int fg \, dy} = \lambda + \mu \left(\frac{u_{12}}{u_1} + \frac{\int f_z g \, dy}{\int fg \, dy} \right),$$

or equivalently, using the notation $E(\cdot \mid x)$ for expectations conditional upon a given value x of observed (apparent) output,

$$\frac{E(v_1 \mid x)}{u_1} = \lambda + \mu \left\{ \frac{u_{12}}{u_1} + E\left(\frac{f_z}{f} \Big| x \right) \right\}. \tag{59}$$

Conditions (56), (58), and (59), along with (52), effectively determine equilibrium, which is characterized by numbers θ and z, and the function ϕ. Given θ and z, (59) determines ϕ. Thus, although explicit solution of actual cases is difficult, one can use (59) to find out something about the shape of ϕ.

Before discussing that, we need some assumptions about f. Since larger z is supposed to mean increased effort, and therefore, on average, output, it should decrease f for small y and increase it for large. I shall furthermore assume that

$$f_z/f \text{ is an increasing function of } y. \tag{60}$$

Since, for all z, $\int f \, dy = 1$, $\int f_z \, dy = 0$; thus (60) implies that f_z/f is negative for small y, positive for large. A similar assumption is made for g, modelled on the case where ϵ is a normal random variable:

$$\log g \text{ is a concave function of } \epsilon. \tag{61}$$

Lemma. *$E(f_z/f \mid x)$ is a nondecreasing function of x.*
   Proof.

$$\frac{\partial}{\partial x} E\left(\frac{f_z}{f} \Big| x \right) = \frac{\partial}{\partial x} \frac{\int f_z g(\theta(x - y)) \, dy}{\int fg \, dy}$$

$$= \theta \left(\frac{\int f_z g' \, dy}{\int fg \, dy} - \frac{\int f_z g \, dy \int fg' \, dy}{\left(\int fg \, dy \right)^2} \right)$$

$$= \theta \left\{ E\left(\frac{f_z}{f} \frac{g'}{g} \Big| x \right) - E\left(\frac{f_z}{f} \Big| x \right) E\left(\frac{g'}{g} \Big| x \right) \right\}. \tag{62}$$

Now, by assumptions (60) and (61), f_z/f and g''/g are both increasing functions of y, and, therefore, positively correlated, given x. Therefore, by (62)

$$\frac{\partial}{\partial x} E\left(\frac{f_z}{f}\bigg|x\right) \geq 0, \tag{63}$$

as was claimed. $\qquad\square$

This allows us to deduce that, if (i) $\mu > 0$, (ii) u_{12}/u_1 is a nonincreasing function of ϕ, and (iii) u and v are concave in their first arguments, then

$$\phi'(x) > 0. \tag{64}$$

To prove, we consider $E(v_1|x)/u_1$ as a function of ϕ and x, $a(\phi, x)$. An argument exactly similar to that of the lemma shows that $a_x \leq 0$, while concavity of u and v implies that $a_\phi > 0$. From (59), we have

$$\left(a_\phi - \mu \frac{\partial}{\partial \phi} \frac{u_{12}}{u_1}\right)\phi'(x) = \mu\left(\frac{\partial}{\partial x} E \frac{f_z}{f|x} - a_x\right), \tag{65}$$

which, with all our assumptions, implies as desired that $\phi' \geq 0$. Assumption (iii) is fairly unexceptionable; and something like (ii) is bound to be required. But (i) is not the kind of thing we should assume: it should be deduced. From (56)—bearing in mind that $U'' \leq 0$ (and ignoring the exceptional possibility that $U'' = 0$)—we see that $\mu > 0$ if and only if the principal would like z to be further increased, if he could control it directly, the payment schedule being fixed. This is plausible, certainly: one expects the payments to be so arranged that the agent does not do all the principal would like. But I have been unable to find general assumptions that exclude the possibility $\mu < 0$.

Certain special cases are of interest. Since it is necessary to simplify drastically in order to get much further, I shall from now on assume that

$$u_{12} = 0. \tag{66}$$

Case I: Only output is uncertain

In this case, ϵ is equal to zero with probability one, and (59) becomes, since x and y are identical,

$$\frac{v_1(y - \phi(y))}{u_1(\phi(y))} = \lambda + \mu \frac{f_z(y, x)}{f(y, z)}. \tag{67}$$

In this case, if $\mu < 0$, ϕ must be a decreasing function of y; and

$$\iint v f_z g \, dy\epsilon = \int v(y - \phi(y)) f_z(y, z) \, dy$$

$$= \int \{v(y - \phi) - v(y_0 - \phi(y_0))\} f_z \, dy \quad (\text{since } \int f_z \, dy = 0),$$

where y_0 is a value of y for which $f_z = 0$. Thus by (60), $\int\int vf_z g\,dy\,d\epsilon > 0$ if ϕ is decreasing. But this by (56) implies that $\mu > 0$—a contradiction. Thus, in this case ϕ necessarily increases in y. Indeed, since $\mu > 0$, we can say more. Differentiating,

$$\frac{v_{11}}{u_1}(1 - \phi') - \frac{v_1 u_{11}}{u_1^2}\phi' > 0.$$

Therefore,

$$\phi' > \frac{-v_{11}/v_1}{-v_{11}/v_1 - u_{11}/u_1}$$

$$= \frac{\text{absolute risk aversion of principal}}{\text{sum of absolute risk aversions}}. \tag{68}$$

The marginal share going to the agent will be low only if his absolute risk aversion is significantly greater than that of the principal. Equation (70), of course, allows us to look at the schedule in more detail. But the second case is perhaps more interesting for the internal organization of firms.

Case II: Only performance observation is uncertain

In this case, $y = z$ with probability one. This is a limiting case of the general analysis, and one must either go back to the beginning, or confidently substitute a delta-function for f in (59). In any case, the result is

$$\frac{v_1(z - \phi(x), \theta^2)}{u_1(\phi(x))} = \lambda - \mu\frac{g'(\phi(x - z))}{g}. \tag{69}$$

By the same kind of argument as in Case I, but using assumption (61), we can show again that $\mu > 0$.

This is the model I shall use in the rest of the paper, so it is time I attended to one important feature of the analysis that has been neglected. If one considers a normal distribution for ϵ, $g(\epsilon) = (2\pi)^{-\frac{1}{2}}e^{-\frac{1}{2}\epsilon^2}$ and

$$\frac{g'}{g} = -\epsilon. \tag{70}$$

Since ϵ varies from $-\infty$ to $+\infty$, the right-hand side of (69) is sometimes negative. This is a trifle upsetting, since the left-hand side is always positive (assuming u and v are increasing functions of income). It might be thought that this trouble arises because, with a normal error, observed output can be negative; but the same thing happens if $x = ze^{\epsilon/\theta}$. What we have to do is allow for the possibility $\phi = 0$ explicitly. Maximization of the Lagrangean with respect to ϕ yields the following inequality if $\phi = 0$:

$$-v_1 + \lambda u_1 - \mu u_1 g'/g \le 0. \tag{71}$$

If $\lambda - \mu g'/g < 0$, (71) holds with strict inequality, and consequently $\phi = 0$.

We can see this explicitly if we consider an example where both principal and agent have constant absolute risk aversion:

$$u_1 = e^{-\alpha\phi}, \qquad v_1 = e^{-\beta(z-\phi)}. \tag{72}$$

Using normal g, we find that

$$\left.\begin{aligned}
\phi(x) &= \frac{\alpha z}{\alpha + \beta} + \frac{1}{\alpha + \beta} \log\,(\lambda + \mu\theta(x-z)) \\
&\qquad (x \geq x_0 = z + (e^{-\alpha z} - \lambda)/(\mu\theta)) \\
&= 0 \qquad (x \leq x_0)
\end{aligned}\right\}. \tag{73}$$

The form of this schedule is shown in Fig. 16.5. In passing, it should be noted that the case where u is $-\infty$ when $\phi = 0$, which I have discussed elsewhere in the context of insurance and incentives (1974), is even more peculiar: the risk of receiving no payment is made to do all the work of providing incentives. But this is not the appropriate assumption in the present context.

To show that the upper part of the payment schedule is not necessarily concave, I note two other special cases.

Case (i): Principal risk-neutral; agent constant relative risk aversion ρ:

$$\phi(x) = [(B + Cx)^{1/\rho}]_+. \tag{74}$$

B and C are positive constants, determined by other aspects of the model.

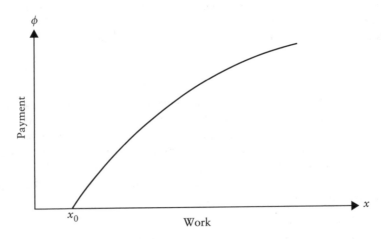

Figure 16.5. *An optimal payment schedule*

Case (ii): Principal and agent have same constant relative risk aversion ρ:

$$\phi(x) = [z\{1 + (B + Cx)^{-1/\rho}\}^{-1}]_{+}. \tag{75}$$

Both (74) and (75) are concave in their positive sections if $\rho \geq 1$.

One wants to know how the schedules vary as the chosen θ, and the agent's elasticity of substitution between income and effort, vary. Unfortunately, that is complicated in all the examples I have looked at, because of the awkward form of condition (56). From (73), it can be seen that the payment schedule takes a fairly sharp 'logistic' form as in Fig. 16.6 if $[\mu\theta/(\alpha + \beta)]e^{\alpha z}$ and $e^{\alpha z}$ are both large. (These are the absolute values of the first and second derivatives of ϕ at x_0.) This suggests that large risk aversion on the part of the agent combined with accurate observation by the principal (reflected in large θ) give a schedule that is a bit like the effect of an *instruction*. An instruction is, in effect, a promise that rewards will vary rapidly in the neighborhood of a particular output level, but not elsewhere. Unfortunately, this suggestion could be confirmed only if we knew how μ depended on α, β, and θ: that is the difficult mathematical problem.

In any case, it is clear that the schedule will only exceptionally take the really sharp form of an instruction. It is not surprising that such policies are generally suboptimal where men are uncertain about what they may achieve and about what they may be seen to have achieved. What is notable is that the optimal payment schedule is usually as 'unfair' as that shown in Fig. 16.5, in circumstances where one might have expected liberal allowance for unfavorable observational inaccuracies.

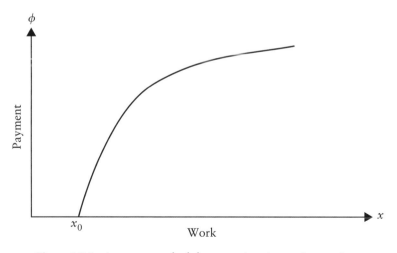

Figure 16.6. *A payment schedule approximating an instruction*

In the remaining sections of the paper I shall outline how this simple two-person model can be used as a building block in constructing a model of a complicated organization.

4. TWO-LEVEL ORGANIZATIONS

Suppose now that the principal has n men to supervise, all identical, who as before choose z to maximize $U(z)$; and suppose outputs add (i.e. constant returns). The principal (following Case II of the previous model) receives $nz - \sum_{i=1}^{n} \phi(z + \epsilon_i/\theta)$, there being independent observation of the n agents. He would like to choose ϕ and θ so as to maximize

$$V = Ev\left(nz - \sum \phi, \, n\theta^2\right). \tag{76}$$

A small change in $\phi(x)$ changes V by an amount proportional to

$$-nE_2 \dots E_n v_1\left(nz - \phi(x) - \sum_{i=2}^{n} \phi(X_i)\right), \tag{77}$$

E_i being the expectation operator for the random variable $X_i = z + \epsilon_i/\theta$. Therefore the first-order condition for ϕ is (cf. (59))

$$\frac{nE_2 \dots E_n v_1}{u_1} = \lambda + \mu\left(\frac{u_{12}}{u_1} - \frac{g'}{g}\right) \qquad (x > 0). \tag{78}$$

The effect of having numerous subordinate workers is that the payment schedule is governed by an average of v_1.

If the principal has constant absolute risk aversion, the averaging drops out conveniently:

$$n(Ee^{\beta\phi(X)})^{n-1}e^{-\beta(nz-\phi)(x))}\frac{1}{u_1} = \lambda + \mu\left(\frac{u_{12}}{u_1} - \frac{g'}{g}\right). \tag{79}$$

In this case the optimal payment schedule has the same form as that discussed at the end of the previous section. There is no reason to think it would get flatter or steeper as the number of subordinates increases. But if absolute risk aversion is decreasing, it is a different matter, because the relative aggregate riskiness of the principal's receipts diminishes as n increases. In that case, for large n, we can regard the principal as effectively risk-neutral. He chooses ϕ and θ to maximize

$$v(nz - nE\phi(z + \epsilon/\theta), \, n\theta^2), \tag{80}$$

and the first-order condition for the payment schedule is of the form

$$\frac{1}{u_1} = \lambda' + \mu'\left(\frac{u_{12}}{u_1} - \frac{g'}{g}\right) \qquad (x > 0). \tag{81}$$

The effect of this averaging is, roughly, to reduce the concavity of the payment schedule. With our earlier examples,

$$u_{12} = 0, \qquad g = (2\pi)^{-\frac{1}{2}} e^{-\frac{1}{2}\epsilon^2},$$

relative risk aversions ρ, σ

$$\phi'' = -\phi'^2 \left[\frac{\rho(\rho - 1)}{\phi^2} + \frac{\sigma(\sigma + 1)}{(z - \phi)^2} + \frac{2\rho\sigma}{\phi(z - \phi)} \right]. \tag{82}$$

Thus, $\rho < 1$ implies convexity if $\sigma = 0$, but concavity (except for small x) if $\sigma > 0$.

Without doing the mathematics, we can see that the model in this form provides a reason for not increasing the size of the organization beyond a certain point. If the principal chooses n as well as θ, he will not be willing to increase n without limit. If n is given, there may be no solution that gives the principal sufficient utility to undertake the task. The same would be true with increasing returns to the number of agents (workers) cooperating. A model of this kind would also enable one to consider under what circumstances it would pay a group of workers to have one of their number undertake all the performance observation, and when it would pay instead to have a symmetric solution in which each worker devotes some of his time to 'monitoring' (one of the others, presumably). It is not obvious that the asymmetric solution outlined here, and assumed optimal by Alchian and Demsetz (1972), is in fact optimal when the means of production are owned in common.

5. HIERARCHICAL ORGANIZATIONS

When the number of workers becomes large, it presumably pays to establish an inspection hierarchy. It can be modelled as follows. I begin with the worker level, and then continue through successive supervisory levels:

(i) $z \max Eu^1(\phi_1(X^1), z)$,
where

$$X^1 = z + \frac{1}{\theta_1} \epsilon^1;$$

(ii) $\phi_1, \theta_1 \max Eu^2(\phi_2(X^2), n_1\theta_1^2)$,
where

$$X^2 = n_1 z - \sum_{i=1}^{n_1} \phi_1(X_i^1) + \frac{1}{\theta_2}\epsilon^2 = Z^2 + \frac{1}{\theta_2}\epsilon^2;$$

(iii) $\phi_2, \theta_2 \max Eu^3(\phi_3(X^3), n_2\theta_2^2)$,
where

$$X^3 = \sum_{i=1}^{n_2} Z_i^2 - \sum_{i=1}^{n_2} \phi_2(X_i^2) + \frac{1}{\theta_3}\epsilon^3;$$

and so on, until the last level,

$$\phi_{t-1}, \; \theta_{t-1} \; \max \; Eu^t(Z^t, n_{t-1}\theta_{t-1}{}^2),$$

where

$$Z^t = \sum_{i=1}^{n_{t-1}} Z_i^{t-1} - \sum_{i=1}^{n_{t-1}} \phi_{t-1}(X_i^{t-1}).$$

At each stage, the maximization is carried out subject to the maximizations at earlier stages, and subject to the supply price (in utility terms) of the men at each level being satisfied.

In this specific model, it is assumed that aggregate output is correctly measured at each level, and that efficient accountants set the wage bill off against output in every department. The n_i may also be chosen, either at each level or at the top.

It is plain without undertaking mathematics that in this way a larger viable organization can be created than is possible when restricted to two levels, because, by fixing the numbers supervised by any individual, and the supervision time per subordinate, and setting up some simple payment rule (such as fixed proportions of the departmental net income), we should be able to satisfy the utility constraints. There is then no reason why the organization should not be increased in size without limit.

It requires more careful analysis to see whether, despite the obvious disadvantage of increasing supervisory staff, a large organization of the kind under discussion may have compensating advantages. It can be shown that if (i) each supervisor has the same number of immediate subordinates, (ii) errors of observation are proportional to the mean size of the observed variable, (iii) the payment rule is proportional at each level, and (iv) all individuals are identical, then there is a payment system such that each supervisor gets at least as much expected utility as a (first-level) worker, and the income of the proprietor (at the top) is approximately

$$Z^t \sim (AN + B + N^{\frac{1}{2}}\epsilon)\, z \qquad (z = \text{value of output per worker}),$$

where N is the number of workers, A and B are constants, and ϵ is a random variable that is, likewise, independent of N. Optimization would, of course, achieve more. (I hope to present proof of this result, and further analysis of the model, elsewhere.)

Ignoring errors, this result implies that profit per worker diminishes as N increases. But if the cost of other inputs (such as capital) is less than zA per man, the entrepreneur will prefer a larger organization, provided that his relative risk aversion does not decrease too rapidly. Perfect competition could (if B is large enough) force zA and other costs into equality and encourage small firms, but very little weakening of competitive forces is required to render the larger organization not only viable but more profitable. Any increasing returns would strengthen the tendency.

The model suggests another interesting conclusion. If we suppose that the members of the organization have constant or decreasing relative risk aversion (not that that is so very likely), it seems to follow, since relative income riskiness is smaller at higher levels, that payment schedules should be less concave at the higher levels—less like instructions, and more like profit-sharing. The reader will not need to be reminded that, considering the conjectural basis of the reasoning, and the restrictive nature of the model, this is not a very well-founded conclusion. But it is the kind of conclusion that one could hope to obtain from such a model as this one.

6. THE SCALE OF FIRMS

It has been suggested that the scale of firms is limited by the capabilities of managers, by the intrinsic difficulty of controlling large organizations, and by the communication loss resulting from long chains of authority. The model of the previous section made no explicit allowance for the managerial skills that may be required of men in charge of large departments. In fact, the model was motivated by a desire to see what kinds of complexity might arise in a large organization. It gives a fairly routine role to everyone in the firm: men either work or observe the results of what others have done; and of course they choose what to do. In this way, information about the value of work—which may be interpreted as the value of different kinds of work—gets conveyed through the organization, from apex to workers. There is no apparent reason why the top man's job should be any harder than that of anyone else; no reason why, in the optimum policy, middle managers should get more than workers. If there are reasons why higher-level jobs in a hierarchy require more ability than lower-level ones, they have largely escaped the model. Perhaps the best candidate is the ability to take decisions; for the choice of payment schedule—which stands, of course, for advice and instruction, redeployment, and even encouragement and discipline—surely has greater effects at higher levels than at lower ones. This consideration may also support the second reason for diminishing returns mentioned above. An adequate model for skill in decision-taking remains to be built.

Communication losses are the basis of Williamson's (1970) analysis of the size of firms. The evidence quoted by him was experimental; but it seems plausible that information is lost in long chains. Yet, the model in the previous section gives an example of how information may be conveyed where, at each link in the chain, observation is imperfect, everyone is choosing what to do on the basis of self-interest, and as a result an incentive system is created which conveys information to the next man down. The transmission of information is imperfect, because, for example, no one has an incentive simply to obey an instruction or to pass it on. Yet it turns out that the contribution of the organizational structure to diminishing returns is very weak, becoming for large organizations essentially negligible. Uncertainty in communication does not necessarily imply increased losses in proportion to the size of the organization.

7. FINAL REMARKS

Two different models of an organization have been discussed, complementing other kinds of models that have appeared in the literature. In these models, imperfect information binds the organization together. They are therefore very much in the spirit of the Alchian–Demsetz paper referred to at the beginning. The models—particularly in the latter part of this chapter—seem at present too cumbersome to answer many of the questions one would ask of them. For example, the analysis of optimal payment schedules is seriously incomplete, and nothing has been said about the optimum shape of the organization (how $n_1, n_2, \ldots, n_{t-1}$ should compare to one another).

Apart from the interest that the models may have as pictures—which I hope is not negligible—the most important conclusions (and suggestions) of this paper may be summarized as follows:

(1) Imperfect information about employees is not in itself enough to explain deviations from the elementary conclusions of the theory of the firm, that wage rates are equal to marginal products.

(2) Where (because of labor market monopsony) a firm's pay structure is devised to encourage work and the demonstration of ability, the marginal product of a more highly skilled man exceeds his wage by more than for less skilled workers, although the payment schedule is steeper than pure monopsony theory implies.

(3) For the firm as a whole, a hierarchical structure does not necessarily impose decreasing returns to scale.

(4) Within the firm, optimal payment schedules for individual employees would normally pay nothing whenever apparent performance falls below a certain point. (This was a Pareto-optimality result—it is in the worker's interest, given the supervisor's utility level.)

(5) The optimizing model used in the paper suggests some tendency for the giving of orders (rather than allowing 'initiative') to be more nearly optimal at lower levels in a hierarchy, and wherever the principal is strongly risk-averse.

REFERENCES

Alchain, A. A. and Demsetz, H. 'Production, Information Costs and Economic Organization'. *American Economic Review*, Vol. 62, No. 5 (December 1972).

Arrow, K. J. *Essays in the Theory of Risk-Bearing.* London and Amsterdam: North-Holland, 1972.

——. *The Limits of Organization.* New York: W. W. Norton, 1974.

Cheung, S. 'Private Property Rights and Share-Cropping'. *Journal of Political Economy* (1968).

Marschak, J. and Radner, R. *Economic Theory of Teams.* New Haven: Yale University Press, 1972.

Mirrlees, J. A. 'An Exploration in the Theory of Optimum Income Taxation'. *Review of Economic Studies* (April 1971).

——. 'On Producer Taxation'. *Review of Economic Studies* (January 1972*a*).

——. 'Population Policy and the Taxation of Family Size'. *Journal of Public Economics* (August 1972*b*).

——. 'Notes on Welfare Economics, Information and Uncertainty'. In M. S. Balch, D. L. McFadden, and S. Y. Wu, eds., *Contributions to Economic Analysis.* Oxford and Amsterdam: North-Holland, 1974.

Pauly, M. 'The Economics of Moral Hazard'. *American Economic Review*, Vol. 58, No. 3 (June 1968).

Ross, S. A. 'The Economic Theory of Agency: The Principal's Problem'. *American Economic Review*, Vol. 63, No. 2 (May 1973).

Simon, H. A. *Administrative Behavior.* New York: Free Press, 1957.

Spence, A. M. 'Job Market Signalling'. *Quarterly Journal of Economics* (August 1973).

——and Zeckhauser, R. 'Income, Information, and Individual Action'. *American Economic Review*, Vol. 61, No. 2 (May 1971).

Stiglitz, J. E. 'Incentives and Risk Sharing in Sharecropping'. *Review of Economic Studies* (April 1974).

Williamson, O. E. 'Hierarchical Control and Optimum Firm Size'. *Journal of Political Economy* (April 1967); reprinted in D. Needham, ed., *Readings in the Economics of Industrial Organization.* New York: Holt, Rinehart & Winston, 1970.

Wilson, R. 'The Theory of Syndicates'. *Econometrica* (January 1968).

Zeckhauser, R. 'Mutual Insurance: A Case Study of the Tradeoff between Risk Spreading and Appropriate Incentives'. *Journal of Economic Theory* (March 1970).

17

The Theory of Moral Hazard and Unobservable Behaviour: Part I

1. THE MORAL HAZARD SITUATION

Appreciation that unobservable behaviour by insured persons, and others participating in contingent contracts, is an interesting and important subject for economists, is due to Arrow (1970b) and Pauly (1968). Neither author showed how to model these situations formally, or suggested any worthwhile propositions. They agreed that insured persons who fully exploit their contracts, expressed in terms of observable behaviour, thereby reduce the efficiency of the economy. Pauly adopted the startling position that such 'rational economic behaviour' cannot be morally perfidious; Arrow, more reasonably, emphasized its disadvantages. But both were wrong: there is a wide class of cases in which there is no significant loss of efficiency as a result of self-interested unobservable behaviour. This will be demonstrated in Section 3 below.

The first formal model of moral hazard that I am aware of was that of Zeckhauser (1970), who discussed the choice of an insurance policy for which payments are proportional to medical expenditures, with individuals choosing their medical expenditures to suit themselves. Solutions were computed using first-order conditions. Spence and Zeckhauser (1971) placed such problems in the general setting of behaviour under uncertainty subject to deliberately chosen contingent contracts. Their paper is largely taxonomic, and does no more than derive first-order conditions for the general (nonlinear) case. These conditions are not rigorously justified, and are in any case incomplete. A model of precisely this kind was used in Mirrlees (1972) to discuss the relationship of taxation to family size. In that paper some qualitative results were obtained about the form of the optimal contingent 'contract' (in this case, a tax system). Again, the argument relies on first-order conditions; and in this chapter a complete set is used, in the sense that they can

This chapter was completed in October 1975 but was first published in the *Review of Economic studies* (Vol. 65) in 1998. Earlier versions of some of the methods and results of this chapter were presented at seminars at Oxford, LSE, Cambridge, Edinburgh, and Warwick. I am grateful for numerous comments at these seminars. Financial support by the National Science Foundation is gratefully acknowledged.

fully determine the optimum. None of these attempts to justify the first-order conditions rigorously.

It is already clear in the Spence–Zeckhauser formulation that the situation first considered for the case of moral hazard in insurance is in fact a very general one, arising whenever behaviour is unobservable, but its consequences are observable. The same issues arise in the analysis of sharecropping (Cheung 1969, and Stiglitz 1974); in an adequate study of capital markets, credit, and lending; in the theory of agency (Ross 1973a, b); and the theory of incentive systems and pay structures (Stiglitz 1975 and Mirrlees 1976). The problem proved, therefore, to be a serious stumbling block in the formulation of a satisfactory general equilibrium theory under uncertainty (Radner 1968).

We shall study models in which there is uncertainty about the outcome of people's actions, the actions being themselves unobservable though the outcomes are observable. Contracts in terms of outcomes can be entered into. These might be contracts between pairs of agents, but the most interesting ones are multilateral, covering large numbers of agents. This multilateral aspect normally appears in the form of insurance, private or public. A major issue is the identification of optimal insurance schemes, relative to the assumption that promises about unobservable behaviour are not made, nor do moral considerations govern behaviour. (Hence, as John Flemming has pointed out, it is odd that the problem of self-interested unobservable behaviour has come to be called 'moral hazard'.) It is also interesting to estimate the social gains available from moral behaviour, i.e. the choice of unobservable actions in the social rather than the private interest.

Some of the main results of this chapter have previously been sketched, for a special case, in Mirrlees (1974). The arguments in that paper are only heuristic; the issue of how general the results are is not discussed; and the significance and usefulness of the results and methods are only touched upon. The question of justifying first-order conditions that have been obtained heuristically has been mentioned several times in this introduction. It turns out to be neither an easy nor an insignificant question. It is perfectly possible that the first-order conditions used in Mirrlees (1974) and earlier papers will fail to find the optimum in certain cases. Furthermore, these cases are not exceptional (like those for which Lagrange multipliers or Kuhn–Tucker conditions fail to work). The difficulty alluded to is quite different from those that have arisen in other maximization problems, and seem to be much harder to deal with. All this is explained in Section 4 of the present chapter.

The chapter is devoted to a rigorous analysis of unobservable behaviour in a fairly general form. Nevertheless, it should not be found highly technical: the mathematical arguments, though sometimes lengthy, are never very difficult, and remain quite close to intuitive essentials. The basic model is formulated in Section 2. There are then two main cases to be considered: those of unbounded and bounded utility. A theorem about the first case is proved in Section 3: this result is probably the most striking in the chapter. Section 4 sets out the necessary conditions for an optimum. The calculation of solutions to cases with bounded utility is discussed, with examples, in Section 5,[1] and in Section 6 an interesting special case is analysed in some detail. Sections 7 and 8 extend the analysis to circumstances in which differences among individuals have to be taken into account. Section 8 considers some further extensions, including more sophisticated welfare functions. Section 9 briefly proposes some implications and applications.

2. IDENTICAL AGENTS WITH EQUIVALENT INFORMATION

Although, as the introduction has emphasized, there are many situations in which behaviour is affected by rewards of uncertain application, it is nevertheless stimulating to have a particular situation in mind when analysing the abstract problem. Since moral hazard was first considered in the context of insurance, let us focus on individuals indulging in an activity subject to a risk of loss through accidents. We enquire what insurance arrangements may be best for a large group of such individuals with independent accident prospects. In the first model to be considered, these individuals are identical in preferences and opportunities, correctly assess probabilities, and make choices so as to maximize expected utility: it is not unreasonable, therefore, to seek insurance arrangements that maximize expected utility. Such an arrangement will be termed optimal.

The following notation is used, with reference to a typical individual:

x = net compensation, best taken as income after allowing for insurance premia and compensation;

y = losses arising from accidents;

z = care, i.e. the effort made to reduce accident losses;

w = the state of nature, calibrated in such a way as to be uniformly distributed over the interval $[0, 1]$.

x, y, z are totals over some period of time, which ought to be the whole period of participation in the activity considered. We do not, at this stage, allow for variations in care over time, or attach any importance to the timing of losses and compensation payments.

The individual wishes to maximize

$$Eu(x, y, z) = \int_0^1 u(x, y, z)\, dw, \tag{1}$$

subject to insurance arrangements, described by

$$x = a(y), \tag{2}$$

---

[1] *Editor's note*: These sections are all contained in the (unavailable) Part II of this chapter.

and loss possibilities, described by

$$y = b(z, w). \tag{3}$$

x, y, z are non-negative numbers. In the terminology of Spence and Zeckhauser, z, and also the function a, are chosen before w is known;

u is a twice continuously differentiable strictly concave function
of (x, y, z), increasing in x and decreasing in y; $\qquad(4)$

b is a twice continuously differentiable decreasing function of z ; $\qquad(5)$

a can be any integrable function from the non-negative real line
to itself. $\qquad(6)$

The choice of compensation arrangements is subject to feasibility, which is expressed by

$$Ex \leq g(Ey). \tag{7}$$

The case of an unsubsidized mutual insurance scheme is $g \equiv 0$. It will be assumed that g is a decreasing function. Expression (7) makes a large-numbers assumption that, despite uncertainty, total income and total losses are (multiples of) expected income and losses for an individual. The importance of this assumption will be explored below.

In formal terms, the problem is to choose the function a so as to maximize (if possible) Eu, subject to two constraints: namely the constraint that

$$z \text{ maximizes } Eu(a(y), y, z) = \int_0^1 u(a(b(z, w)), b(z, w), z)\,dw, \tag{8}$$

and the feasibility constraint (7) for this value of z. This is a double maximization problem of the type

$$\max_a \left\{ \max_z\ U(a, z) : (a, z) \in S \text{ with } z \text{ maximizing } U \right\}, \tag{9}$$

where S is a feasibility set. It should be carefully noted that (9) is not in general the same as

$$\max_a \left\{ \max_z\ [U(a, z) : (a, z) \in S] \right\}, \tag{10}$$

although the maximum in (9) cannot be greater than the maximum in (10) if the two maxima are attained. The point is that, when $\bar{a}$, $\bar{z}$ are such as to maximize U over S, there is no reason why $\bar{z}$ should maximize $U(\bar{a}, z)$ when z is

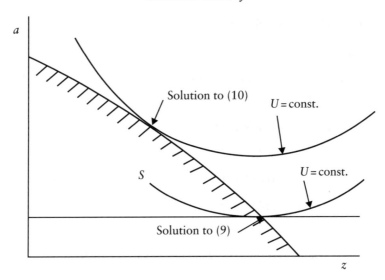

Figure 17.1.

unrestricted. This is exemplified in Fig. 17.1., where a as well as z is taken to be a scalar (a parameter in the compensation function, perhaps).

The second problem (10) describes the choice of insurance arrangements when the behaviour of individuals can be determined independently of the choice of a, for example because it is possible to rely on, or costlessly police, prior agreements by all parties to the insurance scheme about the care they will take. A moral hazard problem is, by definition, one where the agents have to be assumed to choose z to suit themselves individually after a has been chosen. Nevertheless, it is interesting to compare the outcome of problem (9), based on independent individual action, with the outcome of problem (10), where behaviour must be 'centrally' determined. If (9) has a solution, that solution will be called the optimum; while a solution for (10) will be called the full-control optimum.

Returning to the main problem, we note a reformulation which is rather useful. The idea is to eliminate w by considering the distribution of y conditional upon z. The distribution function for y, given z, being defined as $F(y, z)$, we have $w = F(y, z)$, and F is therefore given by (3):

$$y = b(z, F(y, z)). \tag{11}$$

The density function $f(y, z) = F_y$ is deduced from (11):

$$f(y, z) = 1/b_w(z, F(y, z)). \tag{12}$$

from this point of view, the problem is to

$$\left. \begin{aligned}
&\max_a \int u(a(y), y, z) f(y, z)\, \mathrm{d}y, \\
&\text{subject to: } z \max \int u(a(y), y, z) f(y, z)\, \mathrm{d}y, \\
&\text{and } \int a(y) f(y, z)\, \mathrm{d}y \leqq g\left(\int y f(y, z)\, \mathrm{d}y \right).
\end{aligned} \right\}
\tag{13}$$

It should be noted that our assumption that b is a decreasing function of z implies that

$$F_z > 0. \tag{14}$$

To prove this, differentiate (11) with respect to both y and z:

$$1 = b_w F_y = b_w f, \qquad 0 = b_z + b_w F_z.$$

Thus,

$$F_z = -b_z f,$$

which is positive, by (5), as was claimed. Furthermore, since for all positive z,

$$\begin{aligned}
F(0, z) = 0 \qquad &\text{and } \lim_{y \to \infty} F(y, z) = 1, \\
F_z = 0 \quad \text{at } y = 0 \qquad &\text{and } F_z \to 0 \text{ as } y \to \infty.
\end{aligned}
\tag{15}$$

This formulation is somewhat simplified mathematically, and will be used in the next two sections, where the theory of the problem is developed. But it is not well adapted to discussing how increases in the information available affect the outcome. When we come, in Section 6, to examine that issue, we shall find the original formulation of the problem more appropriate.

3. AN UNPLEASANT THEOREM

Many different assumptions about u and f are of interest. In the present section, it is supposed that it is possible to adapt and enforce contracts that have, in some states of nature, arbitrarily bad consequences for the individual; and that, though all loss levels are possible and significantly affected by care, the probability of losses falls off fairly rapidly at high levels. To be more precise, the following assumptions are made:

for all positive y and z,

$$u(x, y, z) \to -\infty \qquad (x \to 0); \tag{16}$$

for all positive z,

$$f_z(y, z)/f(y, z) \to -\infty \qquad (y \to \infty). \tag{17}$$

The first of these assumptions needs no further discussion at present: like the second, it is often inapplicable. Perhaps it is never strictly applicable, but it allows us to make an important point sharply. The second assumption is often applicable, for it is satisfied by the following special cases, involving exponential and lognormal distributions:

$$f = ze^{-zy}; \qquad f = (2\pi)^{-1/2}(z/y) \exp\left[-\frac{1}{2}(\log y + \log z)^2\right].$$

More generally, we have the following criterion, which justifies the verbal description given initially:

Lemma. *Suppose*

(i) $\inf\dfrac{z}{y}\left(\dfrac{\partial y}{\partial z}\right)_w > 0 \qquad$ *for all positive z,* (18)

(ii) *for all positive z,*

$$\frac{1 - F}{yf} = \frac{1}{yf(y, z)} \int_y^\infty f(y', z)\,\mathrm{d}y' \to 0 \qquad (y \to \infty), \tag{19}$$

(iii) $\lim\limits_{y \to \infty} (f_z/f)$ *exists.*

Then

$$f_z/f \to -\infty \qquad (y \to \infty).$$

Proof. $(\partial y/\partial z)_w = -F_z/F_y$, since $w = F(y, z)$. Therefore, by (18) and (19),

$$\frac{z}{y}\frac{F_z}{F_y}\frac{yf}{1 - F} \to -\infty \qquad (y \to \infty).$$

As $F_y = f$, this can be written

$$z \int_y^\infty f_z(y', z)\,\mathrm{d}y' \Big/ \int_y^\infty f(y', z)\,\mathrm{d}y' \to -\infty.$$

It follows that, since f_z/f tends to a limit, the limit is $-\infty$, as was to be proved. $\qquad\square$

The elasticity condition (18) is satisfied if, for example, the production function is $y = b(z, w) = b_1(z)b_2(w)$, i.e. if care can be so measured as to have a proportional effect on losses. Condition (19) is satisfied $f > 0$ for all y, but also f decreases with at least exponential rapidity.

The peculiar interest of these assumptions arises from the following result:

Theorem 1. *If*

(i) $\lim_{x \to 0} u(x, y, z) = -\infty$ *for all positive y and z,*   (16)

(ii) $\lim_{y \to \infty} f_z/f = -\infty$ *for all positive z,*   (17)

(iii) $u_{xz} \leq Q U_x$ *for some number Q, and all x, y, z, and*   (20)

(iv) $u_{xy} \geq 0,$ (21)

then

$$\sup_a \left\{ \int_0^\infty u(a(y), y, z) f(y, z) \, dy: \ z \ \text{maximizes} \ \int_0^\infty uf \, dy, \int_0^\infty af \, dy \leq g\left(\int_0^\infty yf \, dy \right) \right\}$$

$$= \max_{a, z} \left\{ \int_0^\infty u(a(y), y, z) f(y, z) \, dy: \ \int_0^\infty af \, dy \leq g\left(\int_0^\infty yf \, dy \right) \right\}, \qquad (22)$$

provided the latter is attained with positive a. The supremum is not attained for any positive function a.

In words, it is possible to approximate arbitrarily closely to, but not to attain, the full-control optimum.

Remarks. It will emerge in the course of the proof that the full-control optimum can be actually attained only in a very special case. The nature of the approximately optimal policies recommended by the theorem will be discussed after the proof.

Assumption (20) is rather weak, yet stronger than is actually required: its merit is simplicity. Assumption (21) is very plausible for the insurance case: it is satisfied if, for example, u takes the form $u(x - y, z)$, allowing perfect compensation. When (21) does not hold, a theorem of the above kind can be proved, as we shall see. It should also be recollected that u is concave, $u_x > 0$, and $F_z > 0$.

Proof. Since a full-control optimum exists with positive income, which we denote by a_0, z_0, it satisfies, for some constant λ,

$$u_a(a_0(y), y, z_0) = \lambda, \qquad (23)$$

$$\frac{\partial}{\partial z} \left\{ \int_0^\infty u(a_0(y), y, z) f(y, z) \, dy - \lambda \int_0^\infty a_0(y) f(y, z) \, dy + \lambda g\left(\int_0^\infty yf \, dy \right) \right\}$$

$$= 0 \text{ at } z = z_0. \qquad (24)$$

Equation (23) follows from the possibility of transferring income from one state of nature (output level) to another without affecting the feasibility constraint; and then (24) is obtained by considering variations in z along with changes in income sufficient to maintain the feasibility constraint.

Define $U_0(z) = \int_0^\infty u(a_0(y), y, z) f(y, z) dy$. Condition (24) implies that

$$U_0'(z_0) = \lambda \int_0^\infty \left\{ a_0(y) - g'\left(\int yf \, dy \right) y \right\} f_z(y, z_0) \, dy$$

$$= -\lambda \int_0^\infty \{ a_0'(y) - g' \} f_z(y, z_0) \, dy, \qquad (25)$$

on integrating by parts. By (14), $Fz > 0$; $g' < 0$ by assumption; and $\lambda > 0$ by (23). Therefore $U_0'(z_0) < 0$ if $a_0'(y) \geqq 0$. Differentiating (23), we have

$$a_0'(y) = -u_{xy}/u_{xx} \geqq 0,$$

by assumption (iv) and concavity. Therefore (25) does imply that

$$U_0'(z_0) < 0. \qquad (26)$$

This means that z_0 does not maximize U_0. Consequently no income function and care level which are together feasible and such that z maximizes U can actually maximize U subject to feasibility alone: the full-control optimum is not attainable.

To prove the theorem, we construct income functions a_M with the properties that

$$\int_0^\infty a_M(y) f(y, z_M) \, dy \leqq g\left(\int_0^\infty yf(y, z_M) \, dy \right), \qquad (27)$$

where z_M in such that

$$z_M \text{ maximizes } U_M(z) = \int_0^\infty u(a_M(y), y, z) f(y, z) \, dy, \qquad (28)$$

and further

$$\int_0^\infty u(a_M(y), y, z_M) f(y, z_M) \, dy \to \int_0^\infty u(a_0(y), y, z_0) f(y, z_0) dy$$

$$\text{as } M \to \infty. \quad (29)$$

It is tempting to choose a_M in such a way that $z_M = z_0$, by using the first-order condition for (28) (as was done in the heuristic argument presented in Pauly (1968)); but it is then hard to prove global maximization of expected utility. Here it is arranged that $z_M \geqq z_0$, and this is sufficient for our purposes.

Define

$$\left. \begin{aligned} a_M(y) &= a_0(y), & (y \leqq M), \\ &= \delta a_0(y), & (y > M), \end{aligned} \right\} \qquad (30)$$

where δ, a number between 0 and 1, remains to be chosen, but is in any case independent of y. Since u is an increasing function of x,

$$\int_0^\infty u(a_M(y), y, z)f\,dy < \int_0^\infty u(a_0(y), y, z)f\,dy, \qquad \text{for all } z, \tag{31}$$

or, more concisely,

$$U_M(z) < U_0(z).$$

By direct calculation, we have

$$\frac{d}{dz}\{U_0(z) - U_M(z)\} = \int_0^\infty \int_{a_M}^{a_0} u_{xz}(x, y, z)\,dxf\,dy$$

$$+ \int_0^\infty \{u(a_0, y, z) - u(a_M, y, z)\}f_z\,dy$$

$$\leqq Q \int_0^\infty \{u(a_0, y, z) - u(a_M, y, z)\}f\,dy$$

$$+ \int_M^\infty \{u(a_0, y, z) - u(a_M, y, z)\}f_z\,dy, \tag{32}$$

by (20) and (30).

By assumption (ii), given any number K, there exists M such that

$$f_z < -(K + Q)f, \qquad (y \geqq M). \tag{33}$$

From (32), we then have for this value of M

$$\frac{d}{dz}\{U_0(z) - U_M(z)\} < -\int_M^\infty \{u(a_0, y, z) - u(a_M, y, z)\}f\,dy$$

$$= -K\{U_0(z) - U_M(z)\}. \tag{34}$$

In particular, $U_0 - U_M$ is a decreasing (positive) function of z. Let us now choose δ (if possible) so that

$$K\{U_0(z_0) - U_M(z_0)\} = -\inf_{z \leqq z_0} U_0'(z) = A. \tag{35}$$

Since U_0' is continuous, the constant A on the right here is finite, and positive by (26). $U_0(z_0) - U_M(z_0) = \int_M^\infty \{u(a_0, y, z_0) - u(\delta a_0, y, z_0)\}f\,dy, z_0)\,dy$ is a continuous function of δ, equal to zero when $\delta = 1$, and, by assumption (i), lending to infinity as $\delta \to 0$. Therefore there is indeed a (unique) value of δ satisfying (35).

Then, since $U_0 - U_M$ is a decreasing function of z, (34) implies that

$$U_M'(z) > U_0' - \inf_{z \leqq z_0} U_0'(z) \geqq 0.$$

Therefore, z_M being defined by (28),

$$z_M > z_0. \tag{36}$$

Now (employing an argument already used for another purpose above)

$$\frac{\partial}{\partial z}\left[\int_0^\infty a_0(y)f(y,z)\,dy - g\left(\int_0^\infty yf(y,z)\,dy\right)\right]$$
$$= -\int_0^\infty \{a_0'(y) - g'\}F_z\,dy < 0. \tag{37}$$

It follows from (37) and the definition of a_M that

$$\int_0^\infty a_M(y,z_M)dy - g\left(\int_0^\infty yf(y,z_M)\,dy\right)$$
$$\leqq \int_0^\infty a_0(y)f(y,z_M)\,dy - g\left(\int_0^\infty yf(y,z_M)\,dy\right)$$
$$< \int_0^\infty a_0(y)f(y,z_0)\,dy - g\left(\int_0^\infty yf(y,z_0)\,dy\right),$$
$$\leqq 0,$$

since the full-control optimum is feasible. Thus (27) is satisfied.

Finally, we have to show that $U_M(z_M) \to U_0(z_0)$ as $M \to \infty$. Using (35), we have

$$U_M(z_M) > U_M(z_0) = U_0(z_0) - \frac{A}{K}. \tag{38}$$

Also, since (as we have just seen) z_M is a feasible level of care when the income function is a_0,

$$U_M(z_M) < U_0(z_M) \leqq U_0(z_0). \tag{39}$$

Combining (38) and (39), and letting $K \to \infty$, we obtain, as desired,

$$U_M(z_M) \to U_0(z_0). \tag{40}$$

Thus we have proved (22). Since it was earlier established that the full-control optimum is not attainable, it now follows that the supremum is not attainable; and the proof is complete. □

Because of the slightly awkward shape of the proof, adopted to ensure that z_M does indeed maximize expected utility, the crucial steps may be hidden. In effect, assumptions (i) and (ii) make it possible to introduce strong *marginal* work incentives with an arbitrarily small effect on total utility. Assumption (ii) (leading to (34)) implies that the marginal effect of penalties for high losses is disproportionately greater than the effect on expected utility. Assumption (i) (allowing (35) to be solved) then ensures that the marginal effect can be as large as desired. Assumption (iv) simply identifies the end of the loss-scale at which penalties should apply. If the opposite assumption, $u_{xy} \leqq 0$, holds, uncontrolled individuals take too much care rather than too little. If $\lim_{y \to 0}$ $(f_z/f) = \infty$, large penalties for very small losses can then take the place of large penalties for very large losses, as in the proof. Assumption (iii) is technical; but severe violations would probably upset the result.

The theorem itself, though perhaps surprising, is not, as slated, disturbing. It is the argument leading to the theorem that is disturbing; the argument, in effect, that it is always possible to improve insurance arrangements yet further by increasing penalties for those with high losses (and correspondingly increasing the loss level above which the penalties apply). As K and M are increased without limit, the value of δ implied by (35) tends to zero. This is not apparent from the proof of the theorem. But if the steps leading to (35) are retraced, it will be seen that δ is so chosen that

$$\lim_{M \to \infty} \int_M^\infty \{u(a_0, y, z_0) - u(\delta a_0, y, z_0)\} f_z(y, z_0)\, dy \leqq A. \tag{41}$$

This is possible only if $\delta \to 0$. In fact, as the theorem slates, any feasible income function that is positive for all y yields expected utility strictly less than the full-control optimum. In other words, *penalties of unlimited severity are essentially optimal.* It should be emphasized that this is true only under certain assumptions, and false under others. In particular, unbounded utility is essential. Indeed, one can say that Theorem 1 is a form of the St Petersburg paradox, which, as is well known, occurs only with unbounded utility. (Arrow (1970*a*) has proposed that utility must be bounded for this reason; but this seems too easy a way of removing difficulties, and an unnecessary way of explaining why St Petersburg contracts do not exist.) The cases where it is true are not intrinsically unreasonable. On the contrary, they seem to be readily applicable to many real situations. In later sections of the paper we shall discuss how robust the result is to certain important extensions of the model, and how seriously it should be taken.

In Section 5, the other class of cases, for which an optimum exists and finite losses are implied by unobservable behaviour, is discussed. First-order conditions are obtained, their validity established, and their interpretation explained. We also show how the two cases shade into one another, and how the striking feature of the first case, which can perhaps be called the penalty case, is not entirely absent in the second case. But before that, a new difficulty must be addressed.

4. NECESSARY CONDITIONS FOR AN OPTIMUM

The main technique for solving constrained maximization problems is Lagrange's method of undetermined multipliers. It was extended to problems with constraining inequalities by Kuhn and Tucker, and can be applied to functional problems in the Calculus of Variations as well as to problems in finite-dimensional spaces. Our problem, as stated in (13), is not of a type that has been previously treated. This section is devoted to a brief account of such a treatment, which emphasizes its peculiar difficulties.

Problem (13) is a special case of the following general situation:

$$a \text{ maximizes } U(a, z) \text{ subject to } z \text{ maximizing } V(a, z) \text{ and } H(a, z) = 0.$$
(42)

In this paper, we are particularly interested in the case where a is a function; but first consider (42) with a and z finite-dimensional vectors, and U, V and H functions that are continuously differentiable at least twice. The set over which the maximization is taking place is possibly of rather awkward shape. This is illustrated by the following example.

Example 1. a and *z* are scalars.

Find a to maximize $-(a-2) - (z-1)^2$,

subject to: z maximizes $V(a, z) = ae^{-(z+1)^2} + e^{-(z-1)^2}$.

We begin by discovering the constraint set. The first-order condition for maximization with respect to z is

$$a(z+1)e^{-(z+1)^2} + (z-1)e^{-(z-1)^2} = 0;$$

i.e.,

$$a = \frac{1-z}{1+z}e^{4z}.$$
(43)

This curve is shown in Fig. 17.2: for a between 0.344 and 2.903 there are three values of z satisfying (43), and it still remains to discover which of them actually does the maximizing.

To settle this, we observe that

$$V(a, z) - V(a, -z) = (a-1)(e^{-(z+1)^2} - e^{-(z-1)^2})$$
$$= -(a-1)(e^{4z} - 1)e^{-(z+1)^2},$$

so that for fixed $a > 1$, V is less for positive z than for negative; while if $a < 1$, V is greater for positive z than for negative. Therefore the maximum of V occurs for positive z when $a < 1$, for negative z when $a > 1$. In either case (as is readily verified) this identifies the desired solution of (43) uniquely. The points of the locus (43) for which z maximizes V are shown in the diagram as a thick line; the remainder of the locus is thinner. When $a = 1$, V is maximized by $z = \pm 0.957$.

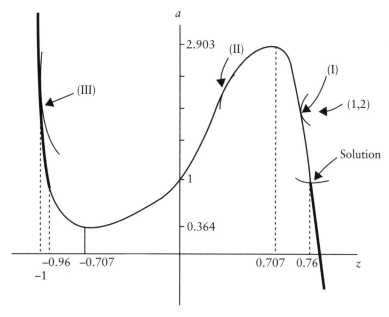

Figure 17.2.

It is clear, by sketching contours $(a-2)^2 + (z-1)^2 = \text{constant}$ in the diagram that the solution of the maximization problem is

$$a = 1, \qquad z = 0.957.$$

This solution is not obtained if one treats the problem as a conventional constrained maximization problem with the first-order condition (43) as contraint. The Lagrangean is then

$$-(a-2)^2 - (z-1)^2 + \lambda\left(a - \frac{1-z}{1+z}e^{4z}\right),$$

whose derivatives are zero when

$$2(a-2) = \lambda, \qquad 2(z-1) = \frac{4z^2 - 2}{(1+z)^2}e^{4z}\lambda, \qquad a = \frac{1-z}{1+z}e^{4z},$$

i.e. when

$$a = \frac{1-z}{1+z}e^4, \qquad 2a(2-a) = \frac{(1-z^2)^2}{(1+z)(2z^2-1)}.$$

There are three solutions:

> (I) $a = 1.99$, $z = 0.895$;
> (II) $a = 2.19$, $z = 0.420$;
> (III) $a = 1.98$, $z = -0.980$.

The first clearly gives the largest value for the maximand, $-(a-2)^2 - (z-1)^2$, but our previous analysis shows that z does not maximize $V(a, z)$ for this value of a. As a matter of fact, z is a *local* maximum, but not a *global* maximum. The second solution is ineligible on all possible grounds: z is a local minimum of $V(a, z)$. The third solution, on the other hand, has the property that z is a global maximum of $V(a, z)$, so that it does satisfy the constraint of the original problem. But it is not the solution of that problem, and indeed gives a much lower value of the maximand than is actually possible.

This example shows that it is not legitimate to attempt to solve the problem by substituting first-order conditions for the maximization constraint. Furthermore, and this deserves emphasis, the example, though complicated, is in no sense special. Any moderate variation of the functions involved yields a problem with the same properties.

This inconvenient state of affairs arises because the set of (a, z) for which z maximizes a differentiable (even analytic) function $V(a, z)$ is not in general an open smooth manifold (as the set $V_z = 0$ is in general). This set, which we shall call the V-maximizing set, can consist of a number of disjoint closed components; and in that case the solution of the problem (42) is quite likely to lie on the boundary of one of these components. That is what happens in Example 1. Indeed, difficulties arise whenever the V-maximizing set is a proper subset of the manifold defined by $V_z = 0$.

In order to be more precise, let us say that (a_0, z_0) is, by definition, V-*critical* if

> z_0 *maximizes* $V(a_0, z)$, *but there is no neighbourhood* N ⎫
> *of* (a_0, z_0) *such that* $(a', z') \in N, V_z(a', z') = 0$ *imply* ⎬   (44)
> *that* z' *maximizes* $V(a', z)$. ⎭

(a_0, z_0) is certainly V-critical if the z_0 is an isolated but not unique maximum of $V(a_0, z)$. This is the usual case, as in Example 1, though there are other exceptional possibilities. In most problems that arise, one would find the V-critical points by looking for values of a at which the maximum is not unique.

The considerations mentioned above lead us to formulate an analogue of the Lagrange multiplier method for the present problem:

Theorem 2. *Let U, V, and H be twice continuously differentiable functions. If* a^*, z^* *maximize U subject to the constraints that* z^* *maximizes V and* $H = 0$, *and the matrix*

$$\begin{pmatrix} V_{zz}, & V_{za} \\ H_z, & H_a \end{pmatrix}$$

is of full rank at (a^*, z^*); *then either* (a^*, z^*) *is V-critical, or there exists a vector* λ *and a scalar* μ *such that the derivatives of*

$$L = U + V_z \cdot \lambda + \mu H,$$

with respect to a and z, vanish at (a^*, z^*).

Proof. The argument is routine.

Let da, dz be vectors such that

$$\left. \begin{array}{l} V_{zz} \cdot dz + V_{za} \cdot da = 0, \\ H_z \cdot dz + H_a \cdot da = 0, \end{array} \right\} \quad \text{at}(\, a^*, z^*). \qquad (45)$$

By the full-rank condition, and the implicit function theorem, (45) implies that there exist continuously differentiable functions $z(s)$ and $a(s)$, of a scalar s varying between -1 and 1, such that

$$\left. \begin{array}{ll} V_z(a(s), z(s)) = 0, & H(a(s), z(s)) = 0 \quad (|s| \leq 1), \\ a'(0) = da, & z'(0) = dz, \\ a(0) = a^*, & z(0) = z^*, \end{array} \right\} \qquad (46)$$

if (a^*, z^*) is not V-critical. $V_z(a(s), z(s)) = 0$ implies that, for all sufficiently small s, $z(s)$ maximizes $V(a(s), z)$. Therefore, when s is small enough, $a(s)$, $z(s)$ satisfy the constraints of the maximization problem, and consequently

$$U(a(s), z(s)) \leq U(a^*, z^*) = U(a(0), z(0)).$$

Hence at $s = 0$ the derivative of $U(a(s), z(s))$ with respect to s vanishes:

$$0 = U_a \cdot a'(0) + U_z \cdot z'(0) = U_a \cdot da + U_z \cdot dz. \qquad (47)$$

Since (47) is implied whenever (da, dz) satisfy (45), there exist a vector λ and a scalar μ such that

$$\left. \begin{array}{l} U_a = -\lambda \cdot V_{za} - \mu H_a, \\ U_z = -\lambda \cdot V_{zz} - \mu H_z. \end{array} \right\} \qquad (48)$$

This is the stated result.   □

The full-rank condition is, of course, a generic one, which will fail to be satisfied only in exceptional cases. But, as we saw in Example 1, V-criticality is not exceptional. We must therefore devote some attention to conditions that are satisfied by a V-critical optimum. This discussion will be somewhat heuristic, to avoid tedious details.

Normally, a V-critical point (a', z') is such that there are two distinct maxima, z' and z'', of $V(a, \cdot)$, there being no others. Furthermore, a normally belongs to a critical boundary in a-space, a boundary consisting of a which are critical (points on either side of the boundary having a unique maximizing z corresponding to them). This boundary is (again, normally) $(m-1)$-dimensional when a is m-dimensional, and locally describable by a single direction vector, normal to the boundary. Since, along this boundary,

$$V(a, z') = V(a, z''),$$

and also

$$V_z(a, z') = V_z(a, z'') = 0,$$

we have, by the Envelope Theorem,

$$\{V_a(a', z') - V_a(a', z'')\} \cdot da = 0$$

for any direction da in the boundary. Therefore the normal p to the boundary can be taken to be

$$p = V_a(a', z') - V_a(a', z'').$$

When $p \cdot da > 0$, V increases by more in the part of $V_z = 0$ near (a', z') than in the part near (a', z''). Therefore when a is close to a', and $p \cdot a > p \cdot a'$, the maximizing z is close to a'.

We can therefore modify the argument used in proving Theorem 2, and claim that, when (a^*, z^*) is V-critical, and p is defined as

$$p = V_a(a^*, z^*) - V_a(a^*, z'') \tag{49}$$

(where z'' is the other maximizing value of z for a^*), then

$$V_{zz} \cdot dz + V_{za} \cdot da = 0, \qquad H_z dz + H_a \cdot da = 0, \qquad p \cdot da \geqq 0, \tag{50}$$

together imply that

$$U_z \cdot dz + U_a \cdot da \leq 0, \tag{51}$$

because (50) implies the existence of a path satisfying the constraints. It then follows by the Minkowski–Farkas lemma that there exist a vector λ, a scalar μ, and a non-negative scalar ν, such that

$$\left.\begin{array}{l} U_z = -\lambda \cdot V_{zz} - \mu H_z, \\ U_a = -\lambda \cdot V_{za} - \mu H_a - up. \end{array}\right\} \tag{52}$$

Equations (52) can be stated in Lagrangean form, by saying that the derivatives of

$$L = U + V_z \cdot \lambda + H\mu + \{V(a, z) - V(a, z'')\}\nu, \tag{53}$$

with respect to a and z, are zero at (a^*, z^*) (z'' being a distinct maximum of $V(a^*, \cdot)$). Furthermore, $\nu = 0$ when a^*, z^* is not critical. It turns out, therefore, that our problem can be solved in the Kuhn–Tucker manner if we replace it by

$$
\left.
\begin{aligned}
&a^*, z^* \text{ maximizes } U(a, z), \text{subject to: } V_z(a, z) = 0, \\
&V(a, z) \geq V(a, z'') \text{for all } z'' \text{ such that } V_z(a, z'') = 0, \\
&H(a, z) = 0.
\end{aligned}
\right\}
\tag{54}
$$

Seen from this point of view, conditions (52) (in conjunction with (50)) seem quite intuitive.

These conditions would hardly have been of much use to us in solving Example 1, because there both z and a were one-dimensional, so that the V-critical set consisted of isolated points. Once these were found, there was little more work to do. In other problems of higher dimension, one would have to resort to conditions (52) to obtain the solution. But it must be emphasized that identification of the V-critical set is an essential preliminary, which, in general, looks far from easy. In our next example, we have again, by a trick, reduced matters to the convenience of two dimensions.

Since the work of this section has been couched in very general terms, it is not clear as yet whether it has much or little relevance to the moral hazard problem. Unfortunately, it is highly relevant: there is no great difficulty is constructing examples of moral hazard problems in which the solution is a critical point, and the simple Lagrangean technique is therefore invalid.

Example 2. Suppose only two output levels are possible, called 1 and 0, and that the utility of income and effort in these two cases is

$$
u_1(a, z) = 3(1 - e^{-4a}) - z + \tfrac{1}{10}\arc\tan(10z),
$$
$$
u_0(a, z) = 5a^{1/5} - z + \tfrac{1}{10}\arc\tan(10z).
$$

The probabilities of outputs 1 and 2 are

$$
p(z) = (1 + z)e^{-z},
$$

and

$$
1 - p(z).
$$

We wish, if possible, to choose x_1 and x_2 so as to maximize

$$
U = pu_1 + (1 - p)u_0,
$$

subject to: z maximizes $pu_1 + (1 - p)u_2$

$$
px_1 + (1 - p)x_2 = 1.
$$

Interpretation. p is the probability of being involved in an accident, which varies between 0 and 1 according to the amount of care taken. The effect of

Contract Theory

being involved in an accident is to reduce utility. It so happens that the marginal utility of income is increased between $a = 0.06$ and $a = 0.47$, but this special (though not unreasonable) feature of the example plays no role in what follows. The disutility of care is not affected by the accident: this represents the case of precautions taken before the accident may occur. The problem is, then, a perfectly plausible one.

Solution. First we find the maximizing set for the agent. His first-order condition is

$$ze^{-z}\{5a_0^{1/5} - 3(1 - e^{-4a_1})\} = \frac{100z^2}{1 + 100z^2}.$$

Writing $w = u_0 - u_1 = 5a_0^{1/5} - 3(1 - e^{-4a_1})$, we have

$$w = \frac{100ze^z}{1 + 100z^2}. \tag{55}$$

This curve is shown in Fig. 17.3. By direct computation, it is found that z is the utility-maximizing choice corresponding to w when (z, w) is on the thick part of the curve. The critical points are given by $w = 3.055$ and $z = 0.034, 1.575$.

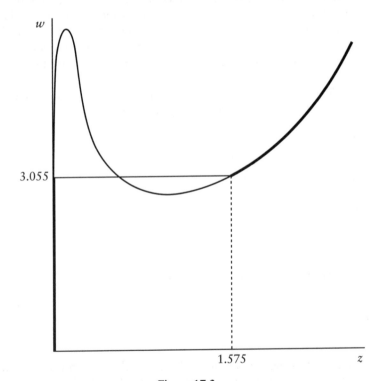

Figure 17.3.

By using the last constraint, we can express total utility as a function of w and z:

$$U = 5a_0^{1/5} - wp(z) - z + \tfrac{1}{10}\arctan(10z), \tag{56}$$

with a_0 given as a function of w and z by

$$-\tfrac{1}{4}\log\{1 - \tfrac{1}{3}(5a_0^{1/5} - w)\} = a_1, \qquad a_1 p + a_0(1-p) = 1. \tag{57}$$

From (56) and (57), we find the derivatives of U with respect to w and z when (w, z) lies on the maximizing locus:

$$\frac{\partial U}{\partial z} = a_0^{-4/5}\frac{\partial a_0}{\partial z} = \frac{a_0^{-4/5}(a_1 - a_0)ze^{-z}}{Bp + 1 - p}, \tag{58}$$

where

$$B = \tfrac{1}{12}a_0^{-4/5}\{1 - \tfrac{1}{3}(5a_0^{1/5} - w)\}^{-1} = \tfrac{1}{12}a_0^{-4/5}e^{4a_1},$$

and

$$\frac{\partial U}{\partial w} = a_0^{-4/5}\frac{\partial a_0}{\partial w} - p = \frac{p(1-p)(B-1)}{Bp + (1-p)}. \tag{59}$$

Given w and z, a_0 and a_1 are determined by $a_1 p + a_0(1-p) = 1$ and the definition of w. Since $a_1 \geq 0$ and $w \leq u_0(a_0)$, this imposes an upper bound on w and z, which need not concern us. So long as $w > u_0(1) - u_1(1) = 2.055$, $a_0 > a_1$; for if $a_0 \leq a_1$, $a_0 \leq 1 \leq a_1$ (since $1 = a_1 p + a_0(1-p)$) and $w = u_0(a_0) - u_1(a_1) \leq u_0(1) - u_1(1)$. When $w \leq 2.055$, $a_0 \leq 1 \leq a_1$; $z = 0.021$ when $w = 2.055$. Therefore, on the maximization set, when $z \leq 0.021$, U_z and U_w are both positive; since there $a_0 < a_1$, and

$$B = \tfrac{1}{12}a_0^{-4/5}e^{4a_1} > \tfrac{1}{12}e^4 > 1.$$

Consider next the part of the maximization set with $0.021 < z \leq 0.034$. Here $U_z < 0$ and $U_w < 0$. To determine how U varies as we move along the curve, we have to consider

$$U' = U_w \frac{dw}{dz} + U_z.$$

Throughout this part of the curve, dw/dz is never less than its value at $z = 0.034$, which is calculated to be 75.3; a_1 here decreases as z and w increase along the curve, and equals 0.999 at $z = 0.034$; and a_0 increases from 1 to 2.488 at $z = 0.034$. Thus, $a - a_0 > -1.489$. Also, $ze^{-z} < 0.033$, its value at $z = 0.034$;

and $p(1-p) > 5.65 \times 10^{-4}$, its value at 0.034. Therefore

$$U' > (Bp + 1 - p)^{-1}\{5.65 \times 10^{-4}(\tfrac{1}{12}a_0^{-4/5}e^{4a_1} - 1) \times 75.3 - 1.489 \times 0.033a_0^{-4/5}\}$$
$$= (Bp + 1 - p)^{-1}a_0^{-4/5}(3.54 \times 10^{-3}e^{4a_1} - 0.043a_0^{-4/5} - 0.049)$$
$$> (Bp + 1 - p)^{-1}a_0^{-4/5}(3.54 \times 10^{-3} \times 54.38 - 0.043 \times 2.07 - 0.049),$$

and the numerical expression comes to 0.054, which is positive. As far as the left-hand branch of the curve is concerned, then, we find that the critical point $w = 3.055$, $z = 0.034$ gives the largest value of U.

In the case of the right-hand branch ($z \geq 1.575$), $a_0 > a_1$, as we have already seen; a_1 decreases along the branch (because a decreasing function of both w and z), and is found by calculation to be 0.433 at the critical point. Therefore

$$B = \frac{1}{12}a_0^{-4/5}e^{4a_1} < \frac{1}{12}e^{1.732} = 0.471 < 1.$$

This means that U_z and U_w are both negative on the right-hand branch, so that U decreases on its as z increases. It follows from these considerations that the solution of the problem is at a critical point, since it cannot be at any other point of the V-maximizing locus. Of the two critical points, the left-hand one is the better, since a_0 is found by direct calculations to be larger there (2.488 as compared to 1.646). The solution to the problem is therefore

$$a_0 = 2.488, \qquad a_1 = 0.999, \qquad z = 0.034.$$

The solution is a surprising one, for it involves a very high risk of an accident, with the agent insuring against the risk of not having an accident and therefore having an enhanced marginal utility of income. It is not without interest that such a solution is possible in a model that is not entirely unreasonable. When in Section 6 we discuss this general class of models, it will be seen that the condition implying reverse insurance (against the risk of not suffering loss) is not the one that we would, at first thought, guess.

The main point of the example is that, once again, the substitution of first-order conditions for the maximization constraint is invalid. The more general treatment in Section 6 will make it clear that the difficulty is not exceptional. The solution must also have shown how extensive are the calculations apparently required for quite a simple problem. Matters would have been even more trying if it had not been possible to reduce the analysis to a two-dimensional diagram. The moral hazard problem initially posed in this paper is an infinite-dimensional one, with a a function, not a finite-dimensional vector. This is discouraging for general analysis of the problem. But there are good reasons for considering the choice of a general payment function. The result of Section 1 gave one such reason. The other reason is explained in Section 5.

REFERENCES

Arrow, K. J. (1970*a*) 'Alternative Approaches to the Theory of Choice in Risk-Taking Situations'. In *Essays in the Theory of Risk Bearing* (Amsterdam: North-Holland).

—— (1970*b*) 'The Economics of Moral Hazard: Further Comment'. In *Essays in the Theory of Risk Bearing* (Amsterdam: North-Holland).

Cheung, S. N. (1969) *The Theory of Share Tenancy* (Chicago: Chicago University Press).

Mirrlees, J. A. (1972) 'Population Policy and the Taxation of Family Size', *Journal of Public Economics*, **1**, 169–98.

—— 'Notes on Welfare Economics, Information, and Uncertainty'. In M.S. Balch, D.L. McFadden, and S.Y. Wu (eds.), *Essays in Equilibrium Behavior under Uncertainty* (Amsterdam: North-Holland).

—— (1976) 'The Optimal Structure of Incentives and Authority within an Organisation'. *Bell Journal of Economics*, **7**, 105–31.

Pauly, M. V. (1968) 'The Economics of Moral Hazard'. *American Economic Review*, **58**, 531–7.

Ross, S. (1973*a*) 'The Economic Theory of Agency: the Principal's Problem'. *American Economic Review*, **63**, 134–9.

—— (1973*b*) 'On the Economic Theory of Agency'. *Proceedings of the NBER Conference on Decision Making and Uncertainty*.

Radner, R. (1968) 'Competitive Equilibrium under Uncertainty'. *Econometrica*, **36**, 31–58.

Spence, M. and Zeckhauser, R. (1971) 'Insurance, Information, and Individual Action'. *American Economic Review*, **61**, 380–7.

Stiglitz, J. E. (1974) 'Incentives and Risk Sharing in Share Cropping'. *Review of Economics Studies*, **41**, 219–56.

—— (1975) 'Incentives, Risk and Information: Notes Towards a Theory of Hierarchy'. *Bell Journal of Economics*, **6**, 552–79.

Zeckhauser, R. (1970) 'Medical Insurance: A Case Study of the Tradeoff between Risk Spreading and Appropriate Incentives'. *Journal of Economic Theory*, **2**, 10–26.

PART V

GROWTH THEORY

18

The Dynamic Nonsubstitution Theorem

The nonsubstitution theorem for a timeless economy was first proved, independently, by Paul Samuelson and Nicolas Georgescu-Roegen. The first published general proof is that of Arrow. In recent years, there has been some interest in extensions of the theorem to dynamic economies. Piero Sraffa's book suggested the kind of generalization that could be made. Morishima has proved a theorem of this kind; and Samuelson has reported similar results without, however, giving clear statements. No exact statement and rigorous proof of the general theorem is, as far as I am aware, available. The present paper proves a nonsubstitution theorem that seems to be about as general as one could hope to get. Though the most general statement was hinted at by Samuelson, it is perhaps more general than many economists might have supposed. In any case, it proves to be necessary to pay careful attention to certain boundary cases which have not been previously recognized. One valuable feature of the theorem proved here is that it can be applied to economies with labour-augmenting embodied technological change, where, of course, all capital equipment becomes obsolete eventually.

The nonsubstitution theorems assert that, under various conditions, only one vector of relative prices is possible for the economy. This implies, for example, that it is unnecessary to have any information about consumer demand in order to calculate equilibrium prices for a competitive economy. In the dynamic case, such a result can simplify the analysis of optimum growth by simplifying the analysis of balanced optimum growth. For theorems of this kind to be true, it certainly must be assumed that there is only one non-produced commodity, which we naturally call labour. Consequently, one assumes there are constant returns to scale. It is also necessary to exclude at any rate some kinds of joint production.

The essence of the argument may be put very simply, in a form that is not at all rigorous. In equilibrium, the price of each produced commodity is equal to the minimum cost of producing it, given the prices of the other produced commodities and the price of labour. If we can identify the cost of production for each produced commodity—which we cannot do for wool

This chapter first appeared in the *Review of Economic Studies*, Vol. 36 (1969), pp. 67–76. I should like to thank Professor F. H. Hahn for his comments.

and mutton—we get one equation for each price, and can hope to determine the prices of the produced commodities in terms of the price of labour without having to bring demand conditions into it. In other words, relative prices are independent of demand.

1. In order to see the general method of proof, it is useful to have the proof for the timeless case before us. There are n produced commodities, and one non-produced commodity (labour). A typical production vector is $X = (x_0, x)$, where x_0 is a negative number, measuring the input of labour, and x is an n-vector, measuring the net outputs of the produced commodities. The production set, consisting of possible production vectors, is denoted by T. Assuming, for convenience, that the available stock of labour is 1, a *feasible* point of the production set is an $X \geq (-1, 0, \ldots, 0)$.[1]

We assume:

(A1) T is a nonempty, closed, convex cone.

(That is, we have constant returns to scale; and the limit of any convergent sequence of possible production vectors is also possible.)

(A2) No nonzero X in T has $x_0 \geq 0$.

(That is, labour is always necessary.)

(A3) There is an $\bar{X}$ in T such that $\bar{x} > 0$. The set of such X is bounded.[2]

(That is, it is possible to produce a surplus of all commodities that can be produced. But an indefinitely large surplus of any one is impossible.)

The next assumption is a more special one, which excludes joint production of an essential kind:

(B) T is spanned by points which have at most one positive component.

Assumption (B) says that we can imagine the economy partitioned into 'industries', one for each produced commodity. Any possible production vector can be written

$$X = \sum_{i=1}^{n} X^i, \tag{1}$$

where X^i, representing production in the ith industry, has only one positive component, x_i^i. It will be noticed that no assumptions are made about the smoothness or otherwise of the frontier of T.

I use matrix notation, and write $x = A \cdot e$, $x_0 = a_0 \cdot e$ where e is the vector all of whose components are unity, A is the matrix $\{x_i^j\}$ and a_0 is the vector $\{x_0^j\}$.

Given the production set, only certain equilibrium price vectors are possible, namely those at which some feasible production vector maximizes profit

[1] '$X \geq Y$' means '$X_i \geq Y_i$ for each i'; '$X > Y$' means '$X_i > Y_i$ for each i'.

[2] (A3) could be replaced by the assumption that the set of X such that $x \geq 0$ is bounded. We could then work within the largest subspace in which there is an $\bar{x}$ with $\bar{x} > 0$. The results must then be stated a little differently: it did not seem to be worth the trouble.

among all possible production vectors. A feasible production vector, X, can be an equilibrium at positive prices if and only if there is no possible distinct $Y \geq X$, i.e. if and only if X is *efficient*. Assumption (A2) implies that all competitive equilibria in the economy are efficient, and indeed can be equilibria with all prices positive. The basic tool is the following.

Separation Lemma. *If X is efficient, there exists a non-zero $(n+1)$-vector $P \geq 0$ such that $P \cdot X \geq P \cdot Y$ for all Y in T.*

Since T is a cone, in fact $P \cdot X = 0$. Otherwise a proportional increase or reduction in X would increase profit. When X is expressed as in (1), $P \cdot X^i = 0$ for each i, since for each i, $P \cdot X^i \leq P \cdot X = 0$. Writing $P = (p_0, p)$, we have $p \cdot x^i = -p_0 x_0^i$; or, in matrix notation,

$$p \cdot A = -p_0 a_0. \tag{2}$$

If $Y = (b_0 \cdot 1, B \cdot 1)$ is some other production vector,

$$p \cdot B \leq -p_0 b_0. \tag{3}$$

These matrices A, B, etc., have a useful property, given in the following well-known lemma (cf. Arrow).

Inversion Lemma. *Let A be a matrix such that all off-diagonal elements are non-positive, and such that $Au > 0$ for some $u \geq 0$. Then A has an inverse, and $A^{-1} \geq 0$.*
    Proof. u must actually be strictly positive, for if $u_i = 0$, the ith component of Au is ≤ 0.

Consider a v such that $Av \geq 0$, and suppose that v has a negative component. Choose j so that

$$0 > v_j/u_j \leq v_i/u_i \quad \text{(all } i\text{)}.$$

Then $A(v - (v_j/u_j)u) \geq 0$. Yet the jth component of this vector is non-positive, since $v - (v_j/u_j)u \geq 0$. The contradiction shows that $Av \geq 0$ implies $v \geq 0$.
    Applying this result to v and $-v$, we find that $Av = 0$ implies $v = 0$; hence A is non-singular. If $w \geq 0$, $A^{-1}w \geq 0$. Hence $A^{-1} \geq 0$. The lemma is proved. $\square$

Notice that if $w > 0$, $A^{-1}w > 0$: for A^{-1} cannot have a zero.

Theorem 1. *Let an economy satisfy the four assumptions (A1), (A2), (A3), and (B). Then there exists a price vector $P = (p_0, p)$ such that, whenever $Y = (y_0, y)$ is in T, $P \cdot Y \leq 0$, and such that a feasible $X = (x_0, x)$ is efficient if and only if $P \cdot X = 0$. Furthermore, $P > 0$.*
    Proof. Consider first an efficient point X such that $x > 0$. Such a point exists; for the existence of a feasible point Z with $z > 0$, $z_0 = -1$, is ensured by (A3), and we can make it into an efficient point by increasing the components of Z.

X can be written $\sum_{i=1}^{n} X^i = (a_0 \cdot e, A \cdot e)$. Since $X > 0$, assumption (B) shows that no X^i is zero. Consequently, $a_0 < 0$. Since $A \cdot e > 0$, assumption (B) also allows us to deduce from the inversion lemma that $A^{-1} \geqq 0$.

Let P be the prices corresponding to X. Then

$$p \cdot A = -p_0 a_0.$$

If p_0 were zero, p would be zero, which is impossible. Therefore $p_0 > 0$. Thus,

$$\frac{1}{p_0} p = -a_0 \cdot A^{-1}. \tag{4}$$

Since $-a_0 > 0$, $p > 0$.

Let Q be the prices corresponding to some other efficient Y such that $y > 0$. Then, as in (3), $q \cdot A \leqq -q_0 a_0$. The same argument that showed $p_0 > 0$ also shows $q_0 > 0$. Hence

$$\frac{1}{q_0} q \leqq -a_0 \cdot A^{-1}. \tag{5}$$

From (4) and (5), we deduce that $(1/p_0)p \geqq (1/q_0)q$. Since the argument is symmetrical in P and Q, we can also deduce the opposite inequality. Hence P and Q are proportional.

We extend the result to all efficient points by noting that any efficient point is the limit of efficient points Y with $y > 0$, e.g. a sequence along an arc on the production frontier connecting X and the point in question.

It remains to prove that, if X is feasible and $P \cdot X = 0$, X is efficient. Suppose $Y \geq X$, Y feasible. Then $P \cdot Y \leqq P \cdot X$. Since $P > 0$, it follows that $Y = X$. Thus X is efficient, and the theorem is proved. $\qquad \square$

2. We now consider a many-period economy. We assume constant returns to scale, and that there is a single non-produced input, labour, the growth in the supply of which is exogenously determined. If we are interested in all possible competitive equilibria for such an economy, we cannot expect to get a non-substitution theorem; for labour in any one period is really a different non-produced input from labour in any other. In general, there are many possibilities for prices, present and future. But the possibilities are rather severely limited. This becomes clear when we consider competitive equilibria in which relative prices are constant from period to period, and the rate of interest (now uniquely defined) is also constant. Nonsubstitution theorems for dynamic economies assert that, under suitable conditions, relative prices are then uniquely determined by the rate of interest.

We are to be interested in feasible paths of the economy that can be competitive equilibria with relative prices constant over time. In particular, that could be true of a balanced growth state of the economy. If, for example, optimum growth for the economy tends towards a balanced growth state, it would be helpful to know how restricted is the set of possible price vectors in that final state. More generally, we are interested in feasible developments of the economy, that is to say, paths in which the outputs at the end of one production period are at least sufficient to supply the inputs at the beginning of the next, and seek to characterize those feasible developments that can be equilibria with constant relative prices. Our next theorem in fact makes no appeal to feasibility. Because of this, we have to restrict attention to equilibria in which we know all industries are being used. This is, no doubt, the theorem that previous authors have had in mind. But it seems to be hard to verify, in the case of particular production vectors and production sets, that all industries are used, unless one can make some kind of appeal to feasibility—that is, to the relationship between production in successive periods. In particular, the theorem as it stands is not of much use in dealing with cases where certain commodities, being intermediate goods, are not produced in surplus over the production requirements of the next period. This point will be made more concretely after the theorem has been stated and proved. A stronger, more useful, theorem that appeals to feasibility will then be proved.

We consider an economy in which production during any period is descri-bed by production vectors $X = (x_0, x_1, x_2)$, where x_0 is the input of labour (which takes place at the beginning of the period); x_1, an n-vector, is the inputs at the beginning of the period; and x_2, another n-vector, is the outputs at the end of the period. All the components of X are non-negative. The technology is described by a production set T, consisting of the possible production vectors for the period.

The rate of interest is r: that is, the present price of any commodity at the end of the period is $R = 1/(1 + r)$ times its price at the beginning of the period. The production vector X can be a competitive equilibrium (more precisely, part of multi-period equilibrium) with rate of interest r and constant positive prices, if and only if it is feasible (a condition depending upon production in the previous and following periods) and there is no possible distinct Y such that

$$x_0 \geqq y_0 \quad \text{and} \quad Rx_2 - x_1 \leqq Ry_2 - y_1. \tag{6}$$

We call such and X *R-efficient*. The concept depends upon the number R as well as upon the technology, but no other terminology readily suggests itself.

As in the timeless case, we shall want to be able to partition the economy into industries, so that we can write every production vector X as the sum of possible production vectors X^i (in which, in some sense yet to be specified, production of the ith commodity is dominant): $X = \sum_{i=1}^{n} X^i$. If X can be expressed in this form with none of the X^i zero, we say that it uses every industry. We shall again use matrix notation, writing A_1 and A_2 for the matrices of column vectors x_1^i and x_2^i respectively, and a_0 for the vector of the x_0^i.

Formally, our assumptions are as follows:

(A'1) The production set, T, is a nonempty, closed convex cone.

(A'2) No non-zero production vector X has $x_0 = 0$.

(A'3) There exists $\bar{X}_1$ in T such that $R\bar{x}_2 > \bar{x}_1$. The set of such $\bar{X}$ is bounded.

(B') T can be spanned by vectors for which $Rx_2 - x_1$ has at most one positive component.

The assumption says that in any basic production process there is only one commodity that expands in the course of production at a rate greater than the rate of interest; and that all possible production vectors can be analysed into such basic processes. We shall see later that assumption (B') is in fact unnecessarily strong. (B') sets an upper bound to R: that is, a lower bound to the rate of interest. (A'3), on the other hand, places an upper bound on the rate of interest.

Suppose that we have a competitive equilibrium with prices $P = (p_0, p)$, and that X is the equilibrium production vector. Since in each industry the chosen production process must maximize profits, we have

$$p(RA_2 - A_1) = p_0 a_0. \tag{7}$$

Also, if Q is the price vector for another equilibrium, we must have

$$q(RA_2 - A_1) \leqq q_0 a_0. \tag{8}$$

We shall be able to use the earlier argument, the one used for the timeless case, to prove that P and Q are proportional if we can prove that the matrices $RA_2 - A_1$ and $RB_2 - B_1$ corresponding to them have non-negative inverses. The argument is only slightly different from that for the timeless case.

Theorem 2. *All competitive equilibria in which relative prices are constant, the rate of interest is r, and production uses every industry have the same relative prices. These prices are strictly positive.*

Proof. Let $\bar{X}$ be a production vector such that $R\bar{x}_2 - \bar{x}_1 > 0$. Let P be a vector of equilibrium prices. Then

$$0 < p(R\bar{x}_2 - \bar{x}_1) \leqq p_0 \bar{x}_0.$$

Therefore $p_0 > 0$.

Let X be the production in the equilibrium considered, and suppose that X uses every industry. Then, using the matrix notation, we have $a_0 > 0$. (Notice that we need not have $Rx_2 - x_1 > 0$.) It now follows that

$$p(RA_2 - A_1) = p_0 a_0 > 0.$$

The assumptions of the inversion lemma are, therefore, fulfilled for $RA_2 - A_1$, and we deduce that $(RA_2 - A_1)^{-1} \geq 0$.

The argument used in the proof for the timeless case now shows that $(1/p_0)p$ is the same for all such equilibria, and that $p > 0$, as was to be proved. □

In Theorem 1, I went on to show that these prices would do for any competitive equilibrium, by using the fact that any efficient production vector is the limit of production vectors that use every industry; implicitly, this involved an appeal to feasibility. An efficient X satisfied $x \geq 0$, and was therefore in the closure of the set of points with $x > 0$, all of which use every industry. In the present case, such an argument is not available. The restriction that every industry be used is essential in the absence of other assumptions, as the following examples show.

Example 1. There are two goods, and three basic processes available. With one unit of labour input, they transform the commodities as follows:

(I) $(0, 0) \rightarrow (2, 0)$,

(II) $(0, 0) \rightarrow (0, 2)$,

(III) $(0, 0) \rightarrow (2, 2)$;

the rate of interest is 1. For profit maximization at constant relative prices, we consider the set of feasible.$[1/(1 + r)]x_2 - x_1 = \frac{1}{2}x_2 - x_1$. Population growth is zero. We restrict attention to balanced growth paths. For feasibility, we require $x_2 \geq x_1$.

In Fig. 18.1, the set of feasible vectors $\frac{1}{2}x_2 - x_1$ is shown. The steadily R-efficient point $(\frac{1}{2}, \frac{1}{2})$, obtained by using the first two processes in equal proportions, is supported by prices $(1, 1)$ and wage 1. However, the point $(-1, \frac{1}{2})$, obtained by using the third process, is also steadily R-efficient, but does not maximize profits at these prices. This point would be preferred among the steady growth paths when the rate of interest is 1 if, for example, surplus of the first commodity were not desired.

The following example, suggested by a referee, is instructive. It shows that there are good reasons to concentrate on R-efficient developments of the economy, even when other feasible paths might give more of the desired commodity.

Example 2. This economy is the same as the one considered in Example 1, except that process III is replaced by another process, which with unit labour input transforms commodities as follows:

(III') $(\frac{3}{2}, 0) \rightarrow (1, 3)$.

This process is not feasible on its own: it can be used only in conjunction with process I to replenish the diminished stock of the first commodity.

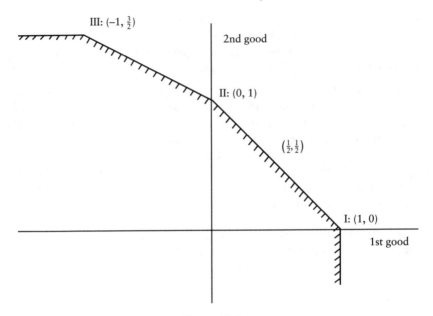

Figure 18.1.

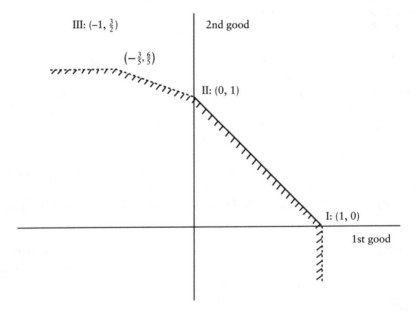

Figure 18.2.

The situation is portrayed in Fig. 18.2, which again maps the points $\frac{1}{2}x_2 - x_1$. R-efficient points are those that lie on the sold line; the set of points arising from feasible developments of the economy is bounded by the broken and solid lines.

In this case, all R-efficient points can be supported by the prices $(1,1)$. However, if only the second good is valued as a consumption good, it would seem that we should choose the point $(-\frac{3}{5}, \frac{6}{5})$, which yields more of it, and is feasible. This is not so in the relevant sense, as we can see if we consider the following optimum growth problem:

$$\max \sum_{1}^{\infty} 2^{-t} C_t,$$

where C_t is the output at the end of the tth period of the second good, production is by means of the processes in the present example, and there is initially available a unit of each of the commodites. Clearly, the unit of the second commodity might as well be consumed as soon as possible. The rate of interest must be 1 (since we do not have decreasing marginal utility of consumption). It is easy to check that optimum growth is achieved by allocating a fraction $\frac{1}{2}(\frac{2}{3})^t$ of the labour force to the third process in period t, and the remainder to the second process.[3] In the long run, the economy tends towards the expected R-efficient point. Initially, it gets as close as initial conditions allow to the point that apparently maximizes output of the second good in Fig. 18.2. But the rate of interest is sufficiently high for the preference for present over future consumption to move us gradually towards point II.

It is notable that the optimum path is a constant-price path, but that the prices are not $(1,1)$: one of the industries is not used.

3. By imposing conditions on the production vector X itself, we can ensure that it uses every industry. For example, we might restrict ourselves to X for which $x_2 > Rx_1 > 0$. But that is extremely restrictive: if, as usual, the rate of interest is greater than the rate of growth, it requires that every good be produced in surplus over the requirements for maintaining balanced growth— which is hardly reasonable in the case of intermediate goods.

A more interesting result is obtained if we strengthen assumption (B'), replacing it by two assumptions (the second to make sure (B'') implies (B')). Let population be multiplied during a period by a factor N. Denote by x_{1j} and x_{2j} the jth components of x_1 and x_2, i.e. the input and output of the jth

---

[3] This is a competitive path with constant prices $\frac{1}{2}$ for the first good and 1 for the second. On it the value of capital tends to zero.

commodity in the production process described by X.

(B″) T can be spanned by vectors X such that, for every j but one, either
  $x_{2j} < Nx_{1j}$ or $x_{2j} = x_{1j} = 0$.

(C) $NR \leqq 1$.

Assumption (B″) characterizes an industry as a set of processes in which all commodities that are actually used in production grow less rapidly than population in the course of production. If population is actually growing, this is a fairly undemanding requirement. The requirement that all production takes place in such industries excludes joint production, of course.

Assumption (C) says that the rate of interest is greater than the rate of population growth.

We now restrict attention to balanced growth, in which the same processes are used in the same proportions period after period. We say that X is *steadily feasible* if

$$x_2 \geqq Nx_1,$$

for then it is possible to keep using the same processes while making full use of the labour force. Correspondingly, we say that X is *steadily R-efficient* if it is steadily feasible and R-efficient.

Consider some steadily feasible X such that every commodity is produced. I assert that under assumption (B″) X uses every industry. For if there were some industry, say the first, which it did not use, we should have $0 \geqq Nx_{11} - x_{21} = \sum_{j=2}^{n}(Nx_{11}^{j} - x_{21}^{j})$. Thus, no term of the sum can be positive. Consequently, by (B″), $x_{21}^{j} = 0$ ($j = 2, 2, \ldots, n$). Hence $x_{21} = \sum x_{21}^{j} = 0$, which contradicts the assumption that every commodity is produced.

Consequently, under assumption (B″), our theorem is true for all steadily R-efficient X such that $x_2 > 0$. But any steadily R-efficient X can be approximated arbitrarily closely by steadily R-efficient vectors in which every commodity is produced; and the result can, therefore, be extended to all steadily R-efficient production vectors. Summarizing, we have:

Theorem 3. *Assume $(A'1)$, $(A'2)$, $(A'3)$, (B''), (C). Then there exists a positive price vector P at which all steadily R-efficient vectors maximize (discounted) profit.*

Assumption (B″) is a good deal stronger than assumption (B′). But by using feasibility in this way we get a more interesting theorem. Assumption (B″) does allow the possibility of capital goods that do not change with age (relative to new models of the same capital good), provided that the quantity of the capital good does not increase as rapidly as population during production. It is restrictive, for it excludes all kinds of fixed capital that change with age or use. One consequence is that we cannot use the theorem for an economy which embodies technological change. Consider labour-augmenting change in the technology (which is in any case the only kind consistent with steady balanced growth). In this, the labour requirement of every process diminishes uniformly over time. If the technological change has to be embodied (at least in part) in new equipment, even perfectly durable equipment is of a different character at the end of the period from new equipment of the same type.

4. Fortunately, assumption (B') (or (B'')) can be relaxed very considerably. Let us allow the existence of capital equipment that does change with age or use, and ask whether the relative prices of consumption goods and new capital goods might be independent of the particular pattern of consumption in steady balanced growth, given the rate of interest.

The only commodities to be considered explicitly now, apart from labour, are consumption goods and new investment goods. A typical production process will, in terms of these commodities, take a number of periods. It will be described by a series of commodity vectors, one for each of the periods in which it is operating. We write

$$X = (X_1, X_2, \ldots, X_\theta),$$

where X_1 is the vector of inputs and outputs in the first year of operation of the process, X_2 the vector of inputs and outputs in the second year, and so on. If the economy is growing by a factor N every period, and growth is balanced, and only this process is being used, net production in every period will be proportional to

$$X_\theta + NX_{\theta-1} + \cdots + N^{\theta-1}X_1;$$

for the activity level of the process increases by a factor N in every period.

We write $X_t = (x_{0t}, x_t)$, where x_{0t}, a negative number or zero, measures the input of labour in the tth period of the project's life, and the vector x_t gives the net outputs of the various producible commodities. A production process, X, is steadily feasible if $X_\theta + NX_{\theta-1} + \cdots + N^{\theta-1}X_1 \geq (-1, 0, 0, \ldots, 0)$. If, further, the vector

$$R^{\theta-1}X_\theta + R^{\theta-2}X_{\theta-1} + \cdots + X_1$$

is maximal, X is said to be steadily. R-efficient.

It will now be clear how the previous argument generalizes.

Theorem 4. *Suppose that:*

(A*1) *The set of production processes is a non-empty, closed convex cone.*
(A*2) *Every non-zero production process X has $x_{0t} < \theta$ for at least one t.*
(A*3) *There exists a feasible production process $\bar{x}$ such that*

$$R^{\theta-1}\bar{x}_\theta + R^{\theta-2}\bar{x}_{\theta-1} + \cdots + \bar{x}_1 > 0;$$

the set of such $\bar{X}$ is bounded.[4]

---

[4] θ may be different for different processes; $\theta = \infty$ is allowed if the series converge.

(B**) *The set of possible production processes can be spanned by processes
      for which* $x_\theta + N x_{\theta-1} + \ldots + N^{\theta-1} x_1$ *has at most one positive
      component, and the other components corresponding to commod-
      ities appearing in the process are negative.*

(C) $RN \leqq 1$.

Then there exists a price vector $P = (p_0, p)$ *at which all steadily R-efficient
production processes maximize profit. The prices are strictly positive. All
production processes that maximize profit at these prices are steadily
R-efficient.*

The proof requires only trivial modifications in the proofs given for Theorems 2 and 3.

As before, we could have used a weaker assumption (B*), corresponding
to (B'), in place of (B**). Then the theorem is true for processes that use
every industry.

It is now easy to introduce labour-augmenting, embodied technological
change into the model. Equipment will be retired sooner, different choices
made. But the theorem continues to hold without modification.

Assumption (B**) excludes cases of genuine joint production like mutton
and wool, or theoretical and applied economists. More seriously, it excludes
certain cases of 'hidden' joint production. If it is possible to switch a piece
of capital equipment from the production of one commodity to another
during its lifetime, that is a violation of assumption (B**). The baker's
oven can produce either bread or cakes; therefore one possible process uses
oven, labour, and raw materials as inputs, and provides both bread and
cakes as outputs (on different dates); and this process is not the convex
combination of any two processes each producing one kind of output only.
Hence assumption (B**) is violated. So, although capital equipment may
change with use or age, it must be specific to the particular commodity it
is designed to produce, once it is established. It is not necessary that *new*
capital goods be specific to a particular purpose; only that they cannot be
shifted from one use to another during their lifetime. It must be admitted
that this kind of specificity is more commonly found in economic models
than in real economies.

The dynamic nonsubstitution theorem is only an indication of the restrictions imposed on possible relative prices in a dynamic economy when we
assume constant returns, a single non-produced input, and no joint products.
We could ask the more general question, under what circumstances prices in
one period are determined, independently of consumer demand, given the
history of prices and interest rates. The assumptions necessary for this result
seem, however, to be considerably more stringent than are required for the
theorems stated in this paper. Consider, for example, the economy assumed in
Theorem 2. If the matrices A_2 always had non-negative inverses, we could

deduce the desired result; but that is, in general, a more stringent requirement than those of the theorem.

Even so, the assumptions that we have needed are rather stringent. Besides the familiar assumptions of constant returns to scale and a single non-produced input, we have had to assume that the rate of interest is greater than the actual rate of growth, and smaller than the maximum possible rate of growth; that no eligible production processes produce consumer goods or new investment goods jointly; that fixed capital is specific to the particular commodity produced; and that in no industry does a capital good increase as rapidly as the labour force in the course of production. At any rate, it has turned out that the nature of the 'No Joint Products' assumption necessary is rather less restrictive than has sometimes been thought. This is hinted at by Paul Samuelson in his second paper on the subject, but proofs are not given there.

It is perhaps fair to say that the heterogeneity of labour emerges as the main reason for distrusting the proposition that the rate of interest determines relative prices in the long run (though fixed mineral supplies may not be unimportant). The presence of joint production of the kind that has to be excluded hardly seems to be very important. No doubt, that is what intuition suggests.

REFERENCES

Arrow, K. J., 'Alternative Proof of the Substitution Theorem for Leontief Models in the General Case'. In T. C. Koopmans (ed.), *Activity Analysis of Production and Allocation* (New York, 1951).

Georgescu-Roegen, N., 'Some Properties of a Generalized Leontief Model'. In T. C. Koopmans (ed.), *Activity Analysis of Production and Allocation* (New York, 1951).

Morishima, J., *Equilibrium, Stability and Growth* (Oxford, 1964).

Samuelson, P. A., 'Abstract of a Theorem Concerning Substitutability in Open Leontief Models'. In T. C. Koopmans (ed.), *Activity Analysis of Production and Allocation* (New York, 1951).

—— 'A New Theorem on Nonsubstitution'. *In Money, Growth and Methodology*, published in honour of Johan Akerman, Lund Social Science Studies, Vol. 20 (Lund, 1961).

Sraffa, P., *Production of Commodities by Means of Commodities* (Cambridge, 1959).

19

Agreeable Plans

WITH PETER J. HAMMOND

1. THE NON-EXISTENCE OF OPTIMUM GROWTH

Consider a one-good growth model (with exogenous labour):

$$c_t + \dot{k}_t = y_t = f(k_t, t), \qquad k_t \geqslant 0, \quad c_t \geqslant 0. \tag{1}$$

Granted an instantaneous utility function, $u(c, t)$, one says that a path (c_t^*, k_t^*) is optimum if, for any other (c_t, k_t) satisfying (1) with the same initial capital,

$$\int_0^T [u(c_t^*, t) - u(c_t, t)] \, dt \geqslant 0 \tag{2}$$

for all sufficiently large T. This 'overtaking' criterion seems to be rather natural. Unfortunately, there are many quite plausible and appealing specifications of f and u for which no optimum path exists, as the following examples illustrate.[1]

Example 1 Constant rate of return, logarithmic utility, no impatience

$$f(k, t) = ak, \qquad u(c, t) = \log c. \tag{3}$$

In this case, if (c_t, k_t) is feasible,

$$\int_0^T e^{-at} c_t \, dt = k_0 - e^{-aT} k_T \tag{4}$$

This chapter, by Peter J. Hammond and James A. Mirrlees, was first published in James A. Mirrlees and N. H. Stern (eds.), *Models of Economic Growth: Proceedings of a Conference held by the International Economic Association at Jerusalem* (Basingstoke: Macmillan, 1973). Reproduced with permission of Palgrave Macmillan Ltd.

[1] Numerous examples of the non-existence of optimum growth have been given. The first discussions were Tinbergen (1959) and Chakravarty (1962). Rigorous analysis of particular cases can be found in Weizsäcker (1965), Koopmans (1966) and Mirrlees (1967). Gale, McFadden, McKenzie, and others have extended the discussion to many-commodity models.

The first two examples given here are well known. (The proof of the first may be new.) The third example gives a case of non-existence which we have not noticed elsewhere in the literature. It is, of course, a particular case of a general class of non-existence examples for bounded production.

and

$$\int_0^T \log c_t \, dt = \int_0^T \log(e^{-at}c_t) \, dt + \frac{1}{2}aT^2 < T \log\left[\frac{1}{T}\int_0^T e^{-at}c_t \, dt\right] + \frac{1}{2}aT^2 \quad (5)$$

unless $e^{-at}c_t$ is constant for t in $[0, T]$. It is clear from (4) that $e^{-at}c_t$ can be constant for all t only if $c_t = 0$. In that case we can certainly improve upon the proposed path. Otherwise we can choose T_0 so large that

$$\int_0^{T_0} \log c_t \, dt < T_0 \log\left[\frac{1}{T_0}(k_0 - e^{-aT_0}k_{T_0})\right] + \frac{1}{2}T_0^2 = \int_0^{T_0} \log c_t' \, dt, \quad (6)$$

where c_t' is defined to be $e^{at}(1/T_0)(k_0 - e^{-aT_0}k_{T_0})$ $(t \leqslant T_0)$, and $c_t' = c_t (t \geqslant T_0)$. Clearly, (c_t') is feasible, and

$$\int_0^T \log c_t \, dt < \int_0^T \log c_t' \, dt \quad (7)$$

for all $T \geqslant T_0$. This shows that no consumption path can satisfy (2) for all sufficiently large T. Therefore no optimum path exists.

Example 2 Cobb–Douglas production with technical change, constant elasticity utility function, constant rate of impatience

$$\left.\begin{array}{ll} f(k, t) = k^b e^{m(1-b)t}, & (0 < b < 1, \quad m > 0) \\[2mm] u(c, t) = \dfrac{1}{\gamma}c^\gamma e^{-\rho t} & (1 > \gamma \neq 0) \quad (c \geqslant 0) \end{array}\right\} \quad (8)$$

Define

$$x = ke^{-mt}, \qquad z = ce^{-mt}. \quad (9)$$

It is a necessary condition for an optimum path that

$$\frac{1}{u_c(c_t, t)}\frac{d}{dt}u_c(c_t, t) = -f_k(k_t, t) \quad (t \geqslant 0). \quad (10)$$

As is well known, this follows from the fact that the optimum path is better than any other with the same T-finale for any $T > 0$.[2] We shall refer to (10) as a

___

[2] We call consumption in the first T years of a path its *T-overture*. Consumption after time T is referred to as its *T-finale*.

local optimally condition. Using the notation (9), (10) becomes

$$(\gamma - 1)\left(\frac{\dot{z}}{z} + m\right) - \rho = -bx^{b-1}$$

or

$$(1 - \gamma)\dot{z} = z[bx^{b-1} - \rho(1 - \gamma)m]. \tag{11}$$

At the same time, (1) implies that

$$\dot{x} = x^b - mx - z. \tag{12}$$

The usual phase diagram (Fig. 19.1.) shows the various solutions of (11) and (12).

If $\rho < (\gamma - 1 + b)m$, none of the paths satisfying (11) and (12) remain feasible for all time: sooner or later, x becomes negative.

Proof. Under the stated inequality, (1) implies that $(1 - \gamma)\dot{z} > bz(x^{b-1} - m)$; so that, if $\dot{x} \geqslant 0$ and therefore $x^b \geqslant mx$, z is increasing, and eventually becomes so large that $\dot{x} < 0$. After that, $\dot{x}$ remains negative, and x must eventually become negative also. Therefore no optimum path exists.

In fact, no optimum exists if only

$$\rho < \gamma m. \tag{13}$$

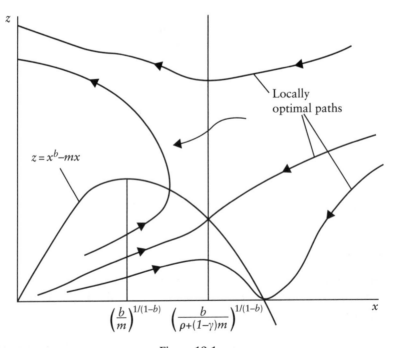

Figure 19.1.

To prove this, one notes that, when $(\gamma - 1 + b)m \leqslant \rho < \gamma m$, any feasible path satisfying (11) and (12) has the property that

$$\lim_{t \to \infty} x_t > \bar{x} = \left(\frac{b}{m}\right)^{1/(1-b)}, \tag{14}$$

where $\bar{x}$ is the 'golden rule' level of capital per efficiency unit of labour, defined by $f_k = m$. At the same time,

$$\lim_{t \to \infty} z_t < \bar{z} = (1 - b)\left(\frac{b}{m}\right)^{b/(1-b)} \tag{15}$$

where $\bar{z} = \bar{x}^b - m\bar{x}$. These facts are clear from Fig. 1, whose main features are easily verified. If $x_t > \bar{x}, z_t < \bar{z} \, (t \geqslant T_0)$, we can do better by defining a new path identical to (x_t, z_t) for $t < T_0$, but constant at $(\bar{x}, \bar{z})$ for $t \geqslant T_0$. This is clearly feasible, and gives greater consumption at all $t \geqslant T_0$. Therefore any feasible path satisfying (11) and (12) can be bettered: no optimum path exists.

Example 3 Bounded, increasing production, no impatience

$$\left.\begin{array}{ll} f(k, t) = a^{-d} - (a + k)^{-d} & (d > 0, \quad a > 0) \\ u(c, t) = u(c) & (u' > 0, \quad u'' < 0) \end{array}\right\} \tag{16}$$

In this case the local optimality conditions

$$\frac{1}{u'}\frac{\mathrm{d}}{\mathrm{d}t}u' = -\mathrm{d}(a + k)^{-d-1} \tag{17}$$

can be integrated. The locally optimal paths satisfy

$$u(c) + (f - c)u'(c) = \text{constant}. \tag{18}$$

It is easily verified that this formula, due to Ramsey, provides paths that satisfy (17). On the feasible paths, $c < f$. We show that any such path can be bettered. More precisely, we show that the consumption (c_t) provided can be obtained with less initial capital.

Notice first that we can restrict our attention to paths on which $c_t \to a^{-d} \equiv b$. Any path on which $\lim c_t < b$ is clearly worse, and $\lim c_t$ exists for all locally optimal paths, and is equal to b for one of them, namely that for which

$$u(c) + (f - c)u'(c) = u(b). \tag{19}$$

Let (c_t, k_t) be the path defined by (19) and (1).
    Suppose (h_t) has the property that

$$\dot{h}_t = f(h_t) - c_t. \tag{20}$$

Let μ be a number such that $0 < \mu < 1$, and suppose that at some particular t,

$$h_t \geqslant \mu k_t. \tag{21}$$

Then

$$\begin{aligned}
\dot{h}_t - \mu \dot{k}_t &= f(h_t) - \mu f(k_t) - (1-\mu)c_t \\
&\geqslant f(\mu k_t) - \mu f(k_t) - (1-\mu)c_t \\
&= \mu(a + k_t)^{-d} - (a + \mu k_t)^{-d} + (1-\mu)(b - c_t).
\end{aligned} \tag{22}$$

If we write $y = b - c$, (19) can be written in the form

$$\frac{u(b) - u(b-y)}{yu'(b-y)} = 1 - \frac{(a+k)^{-d}}{y}. \tag{23}$$

Now $y_t \to 0$ as $t \to \infty$; and then the left-hand side of (23) tends to 1. Hence

$$\frac{(a + k_t)^{-d}}{y_t} \to 0 \qquad (t \to \infty). \tag{24}$$

Therefore there exists t_0 such that

$$y_t \geqslant \frac{\mu^{-d} - \mu}{1 - \mu}(a + k_t)^{-d} \qquad (t \geqslant t_0). \tag{25}$$

Applying this inequality to (22), we obtain

$$\begin{aligned}
\dot{h}_t - \mu \dot{k}_t &\geqslant \mu^{-d}(a + k_t)^{-d} - (a + \mu k_t)^{-d} \\
&> 0
\end{aligned} \tag{26}$$

since $\mu < 1$.

We have shown that there exists t_0 such that we can at t_0 reduce the capital stock to a fraction $(1 - \mu)$ of itself, and yet continue the same consumption after that date as on the path we started with. That path is therefore inefficient, and consequently not optimal. Therefore no optimum path exists.

It may be asked whether production is likely to be bounded above, without the upper bound ever being achieved for a finite capital stock. In fact, the following gives an indication of how such a production function might arise.

Suppose that there is a fixed quantity of labour L. Suppose that, in addition to the labour needed to operate each machine, l, there is also lg more labour needed to repair and maintain each machine. Suppose that there is learning by doing, whenever a new machine is built, which reduces the maintenance costs on each machine; i.e. this technical progress is entirely disembodied. Then, when the capital stock is k machines, the number of men needed to operate each machine is $l[1 + g(k)]$. Clearly, $g(k)$ will decrease with k. Suppose that $g(k) \to G$, as $k \to \infty$. G can be interpreted as the theoretical number of men needed to maintain each machine—it may be zero, of course. For simplicity, assume that output is just equal to the number of machines operated. (That is, assume a linear production relationship, and choose units.) As k increases, there will eventually be more machines than there are men able to operate and maintain them. Nevertheless, it may still be worth building machines, because this is the only way of saving the amount of labour which is needed for maintenance. Once there are enough machines to employ all the labour force (other cases are not important, when the economy is productive, and optimal or agreeable paths are being considered for their asymptotic properties as $k \to \infty$), the production function is $f(k) = L/l[1 + g(k)]$, and

$$f(k) < b = L/l(1 + G) = \lim_{k \to \infty} f(k), \qquad \text{for all } k.$$

These examples show that the non-existence of an optimum may not be very obvious. No restriction on the class of utility functions will ensure existence; nor can one claim that realistic production assumptions by themselves are enough to exclude the problem. It must be wrong to change the specification of the problem merely to ensure that it has a solution. That a solution does not exist perhaps indicates that something is wrong with the specification; but it does not tell us what is wrong. If no persuasive method of reformulating these growth problems can be found, we may have to accept that in certain situations there is no answer to the questions one wants to ask: no optimum rate of growth, for example.

We do not believe that all interesting questions of choice have answers. But we do think that there is a way of reformulating the choice among alternative paths of economic growth that greatly extends the class of situations in which answers can be given, without resorting to arbitrary modifications of the problem (such as 'suitable' utility discounting). In the next section we introduce a definition of 'agreeable' plans: such a plan is one upon which it would be sensible to agree. The definition we propose is based upon an analysis of the reasons that lead economists to use an infinite time horizon in the formulation of growth problems. In later sections, we demonstrate that the definition has most of the properties one can reasonably wish for. The discussion is restricted to the one-good model.[3]

---

[3] One of us (Hammond) is preparing a paper analysing the concept of agreeable plans in many-commodity models.

2. DEFINITION

If we were willing to specify a particular date after which events are certain to be without any significance for us, we could regard the optimum growth problem as a finite-horizon problem. Clearly, this could happen only when human beings, and those about whom they care, had ceased to exists, since, at least, respect for a man's preferences implies concern for his children, and so on until the last generation. Few are quite certain about an upper bound to the end of mankind. Few can believe such knowledge would have any significance for us. Even those who would willingly accept a finite time horizon will usually accept an infinite time horizon, on the grounds that it cannot matter. The technical convenience, for clear and quantitative results, of using an infinite time horizon is rather great.

Unfortunately, the use of an infinite time horizon does make a difference, as we have seen. If it were at all probable that mankind, or beings for whom we should have concern, would exist for ever, we should have to accept the fact that sometimes no sensible decision is possible. But there is evidence— such as that represented by the second law of thermodynamics—which leads us to reject that view. The appropriate time horizon is presumably always very long; but we do not care to consider exactly how long. If we would choose more or less the same policy whatever particular long time horizon we used, there would be no need for further thought on the matter: people with diverse views about the time horizon should be able to agree, more or less, about a policy, so long as they agree that the time horizon should be far away. More precisely, we should expect agreement about the desirability of a particular policy if, whatever the (long) time horizon postulated, no great improvement upon that policy is possible. We call such a policy, and the growth path generated by it, *agreeable*, and introduce the formal definition:

Definition. *A feasible consumption path* (c_t^*) *is agreeable if, for all positive numbers* ϵ *and* T_0, *there exists* $T_1 > T_0$ *such that, for any feasible consumption path* (c_t) *and any time horizon* $T \geqslant T_1$, *we can find a consumption path* (c_t') *such that*

$$c_t' = c_t^* \qquad (0 \leq t \leq T_0) \tag{27}$$

and

$$\int_0^T u(c_t') \, \mathrm{d}t > \int_0^T u(c_t) \, \mathrm{d}t - \epsilon. \tag{28}$$

The idea of the definition is that, given a particular sensitivity to utility differences, measured by ϵ, and a particular 'planning period' over which the chosen policy is to operate, everyone who agrees that the appropriate time horizon is at least as great as T_1 can agree on the desirability of the policy $(c_t{}^*)$, for the time being. One could imagine making c^* depend upon ϵ and T_0; but it is all the more appealing if c^* does not depend upon them, and is then unique. We shall prove that, in a wide class of cases, this is so.

It may be felt that, in any particular case, it would be desirable to obtain numerical information about the relationship between T_1 and the standards of sensitivity, T_0 and ϵ (measured, no doubt, by equivalent consumption differences). While such information would indeed be interesting, we suspect that it would be hard to upset the 'agreeability' of such a consumption path. Men are accustomed to allow the extent of probable disagreement to affect their estimates of the deviation from optimum policies that they will be prepared to regard as tolerable.

We suggest that it is more important to establish the extent to which the notion of agreeability may help to resolve the non-existence of optimum policies. As a check on the reasonableness of the definition, it must be shown that, when an optimum path exists, it is (usually) agreeable; and that agreeable paths are usually unique. It must also be shown that agreeable paths exist in many cases where optimum paths do not exist. In addition, we have to seek ways of characterizing the agreeable path in cases where the known methods of characterizing optimum paths cannot apply.

We are prepared to claim more for the agreeableness of agreeable plans than the definition suggests. Although the idea of an optimum plan is clearly fundamental, it seems to us that one might, if there were any choice in the matter, prefer an agreeable plan to an optimum plan in a simple, deterministic model.

If we knew that we had a perfect and certain specification of the economy and of preferences, we should want the optimum plan. (If none existed, we could have no recourse to any alternative definition.) In fact, we are very uncertain about many aspects of the specification given in any model. For example—to mention the most common point made in this connection—we do not know what form of utility function we should use if we lived a hundred years later. Planners must expect to change their minds. One possible way of dealing with this problem is to specify more exactly the nature of our uncertainty, most conveniently by introducing a stochastic model. Numerical solution of even the simplest plausible models of this type seems to be rather hard, at least when technological uncertainty is allowed for.[4] Beyond such an improved specification, yet more sophisticated and complicated models lie.

Much of economics is concerned, however, with avoiding over-complex models. Excessively profound thought and empirical research about the assumptions and structure of a model is to be avoided, not only because it is costly, but because, like some medical treatment, it is not, beyond a point,

---

[4] As one of us found in an as yet imperfect and unpublished paper: Mirrlees, 'Optimum Accumulation under Uncertainty'.

likely to lead to any improvement. The reason that economists have not troubled to develop models that specify in detail the various possible technological and perceptual developments of the next century is not so much that they are rather uncertain about precisely which developments will happen—after all, we have the language of probabilities with which to describe uncertainty among many possible developments. It is rather that, on intuitive grounds, they do not expect any worth-while improvement in current policy recommendations to follow from a more careful specification of the future.

The property of agreeability makes a precise claim of this kind. If a plan is agreeable, no more careful specification of the time horizon can lead to a significant improvement in policy, provided that that horizon is known to be at least as great as some particular number. Uncertainty about the time horizon is only one, very special, source of uncertainty; but it may plausibly be taken to stand for the much larger class of uncertainties that have to do with the far distant future. If an agreeable plan exists, and parameters ϵ and T_0 are specified, and time horizons greater than T_1 are accepted, clearly we must have some reason for giving considerable weight to consumption in the years beyond T_1 before we should be prepared to argue in favour of a different plan. We should have to believe that greater weight ought to be given to this distant part of the consumption plan that would be given by someone who believed that the presently specified valuation of consumption paths should be maintained beyond T_1 and that the economy will continue for a finite period beyond T_1—even an extremely long finite period. Although future generations will surely see the value and possibilities of consumption differently from ourselves, and therefore do something different from what we should work out for them now if we choose to, few would be prepared to insist that the weight to be given to their consumption should be much greater than is implied by simply projecting the present into the future.

In that case, we can surely expect the agreement of those who think that the specified utility function will not be appropriate in the distant future, as well as of those who think it probably will be, but disagree with us about the time horizon. To put the conclusion less metaphorically, but more meta-economically, an agreeable plan is one that cannot be significantly improved upon by further research into and meditation about the nature of the far distant economy of the future. No precise theorem can fully capture the nature of that assertion, which is therefore not capable of precise proof. But we find the argument convincing. Let us remark, finally, that this more general argument suggests that numerical calculations of T_1 for various ϵ and T_0 may be more interesting than one would suppose if one thought of T_1 as merely the ultimate time horizon, rather than a date beyond which serious disagreement about the shape and preferences of the economy is of negligible importance.

3. THE MAXIMAL LOCALLY OPTIMAL PATH

In this section and the following one we shall proceed rather formally. The model is specified at the beginning of the paper. We assume that

- f is twice continuously differentiable, defined for all $k \geq 0$ and t;
- $f_k > 0$, $f_{kk} \leq 0$, $f(0,t) = 0$;
- u is three times continuously differentiable, defined for all $c > 0$ and t;
- $u_c > 0$, $u_{cc} < 0$, $u(0, t) = -\infty$.

The last assumption is made for convenience, to avoid special consideration of zero consumption levels.

A path is *locally optimal* in $[0, T]$ if it is feasible for $0 \leqslant t \leqslant T$ (i.e. if $k_t \geqslant 0$, $c_t > 0$ in this interval) and

$$\frac{\mathrm{d}}{\mathrm{d}t} u_c = -u_c f_k \qquad (0 \leqslant t \leqslant T). \tag{29}$$

Weizsäcker has shown, in his 1965 paper, that, if a path exists which is locally optimal for all $t \geqslant 0$, there exists a *maximal locally optimal* path, defined by the property that consumption at any time is greater on it than on any other locally optimal path feasible for all $t \geqslant 0$.[5] It is reasonably clear why this is so. Given two alternative levels of initial consumption, it is easily seen from (29) and the production relationship (1) that the magnitude of the difference between log u_c on the two paths never becomes smaller. Thus, if consumption is ever greater on one than on the other, it is always greater. It is then fairly clear that the least upper bound of initial consumption levels for which the solution of (29) is feasible for all $t \geq 0$ itself leads to a perpetually feasible locally optimal path: if it did not, neither would a slightly smaller initial consumption level.

It is quite possible that no locally optimal path exists. This is the case in the first example discussed in Section 1 of the paper. If $c_0 > 0$, $c_t = c_0 e^{at}$ on a locally optimal path. This implies, by solution of the differential equation $k = f - c$, that $k_t = (k_0 - c_0 t)e^{at}$, which becomes negative in time. Therefore no locally optimal path exists. If such a path does exist, we have the following result:

Proposition 1. *If an optimal path exists, it is the maximal locally optimal path (and so is unique).*

Proof. A path is optimal according to the overtaking criterion (2) if and only if it is not overtaken by any other path. In particular, it must be locally optimal, because if a path is not locally optimal up to time T, it is overtaken

---

[5] Weizsäcker (1965, pp. 97, 103). The proof given refers only to the case in which u is independent of time, but can be extended without difficulty.

by one with a better T-overture and the same T-finale. Moreover, it must be the maximal locally optimal path, since otherwise it is overtaken by the maximal locally optimal path.

We have already seen that the maximal locally optimal path is not necessarily optimal. In particular, it may not be efficient: it may be possible to find another path that provides more consumption at all times.

Proposition 2. *If an agreeable path exists, then it is the maximal locally optimal path.*

Proof. (i) Let (c_t^*, k_t^*) be agreeable. We shall show that it is locally optimal. If it is not locally optimal, there is some T_0 such that it is not locally optimal in $[0, T_0]$. Therefore it does not maximize $\int_0^{T_0} u(c, t)\, dt$ subject to $k_{T_0} = k_{T_0}^*$. Therefore we can find a path (c_t, k_t) such that, for a positive number ϵ,

$$\int_0^{T_0} u(c, t)\, dt \geqslant \int_0^{T_0} u(c^*, t)\, dt + \epsilon$$

and

$$k_{T_0} = k_{T_0}^*.$$

Therefore, given any path with T_0-overture identical to (c_t^*) there is another better by ϵ for any time horizon $T \geqslant T_0$, namely that obtained by changing consumption to c_t for $0 \leqslant t \leqslant T_0$. Consequently (c_t^*, k_t^*) cannot satisfy the definition of agreeability.

(ii) A locally optimal path that is not maximal cannot be agreeable. Let (c_t, k_t) be locally optimal, but not maximal $(\bar{c}_t, \bar{k}_t)$ is the maximal locally optimal path. Let $T > T_0 > 0$. Denote by (c_t', k_t') the path the maximizes $\int_0^T u\, dt$ subject to having the same T_0-overture as $(\bar{c}_t, \bar{k}_t)$. Let (b_t, h_t) be the path that maximizes $\int_0^T u\, dt$ without constraint. Then for all $t \leqslant T$, and in particular for $t = T_0$,

$$h_t < \bar{k}_t < k_t. \tag{30}$$

We show first that $\int_0^T u(c_t')\, dt < \int_0^T u(\bar{c}_t')\, dt$. (The reason is that each integral is a maximum subject to a constraint on the capital stock at T_0, a constraint which is effectively more stringent for the first integral). Because of (30) we can find λ, $0 < \lambda < 1$, such that

$$\lambda h_{T_0} + (1 - \lambda)k_{T_0} = \bar{k}_{T_0}. \tag{31}$$

The path $[\lambda b_t + (1 - \lambda)c_t', \lambda h_t + (1 - \lambda)k_t']$ is feasible in $[0, T]$. $(\bar{c}_t')$ maximizes $\int_0^T u\, dt$ subject to the given level of the capital stock at T_0, k_{T_0}.

Therefore

$$\int_0^T u(\bar{c}_t') \, dt \geqslant \int_0^T u(\lambda b_t + (1 - \lambda) c_t') \, dt$$

$$> \lambda \int_0^T u(b_t) \, dt + (1 - \lambda) \int_0^T u(c_t') \, dt$$

by strict concavity of u

$$\geqslant \lambda \int_0^T u(\bar{c}_t') \, dt + (1 - \lambda) \int_0^T u(c_t') \, dt$$

by the definition of (b_t). Dividing by $(1 - \lambda)$, we obtain

$$\int_0^T u(\bar{c}_t') \, dt > \int_0^T u(c_t') \, dt, \tag{32}$$

as promised.

By the concavity of f, the path $(\frac{1}{2} c_t' + \frac{1}{2} \bar{c}_t')$ is feasible. Since u is strictly concave,

$$u(\tfrac{1}{2} c_t' + \tfrac{1}{2} \bar{c}_t') > \tfrac{1}{2} u(c_t') + \tfrac{1}{2} u(\bar{c}_t').$$

Therefore

$$\int_0^{T_o} [u(\tfrac{1}{2} c_t' + \tfrac{1}{2} \bar{c}_t') - \tfrac{1}{2} u(c_t') - \tfrac{1}{2} u(\bar{c}_t')] \, dt = \epsilon > 0 \tag{33}$$

and

$$\int_0^T u(\tfrac{1}{2} c_t' + \tfrac{1}{2} \bar{c}_t') \, dt = \int_0^T [u(\tfrac{1}{2} c_t' + \tfrac{1}{2} \bar{c}_t') - \tfrac{1}{2} u(c_t') - \tfrac{1}{2} u(\bar{c}_t')] \, dt$$

$$+ \tfrac{1}{2} \int_0^T u(c_t') \, dt + \tfrac{1}{2} \int_0^T u(\bar{c}_t') \, dt$$

$$> \epsilon + \tfrac{1}{2} \int_0^T u(c_t') \, dt + \tfrac{1}{2} \int_0^T u(\bar{c}_t') \, dt,$$

$$> \int_0^T u(c_t') \, dt + \epsilon \tag{34}$$

by (32). Notice that ϵ given by (33), is defined independently of T. Thus, (32) shows that for all T a path can be found which is better, by at least ϵ, than any path with the same T_0-overture as (c_t). Therefore (c_t) is not agreeable. This completes the proof. $\qquad \square$

Corollary. *There is at most one agreeable path.*

Consider the consumption path (b_t^T) which maximizes $\int_0^T u\, dt$. We know it exists: it is the locally optimal path (in $[0, T]$) for which capital is zero at T. If there is a feasible path (b_t, h_t) such that, for each $t \geqslant 0$,

$$b_t^T \to b_t \qquad (T \to \infty) \tag{35}$$

we call (b_t, h_t) the asymptotic-optimal path. If it exists, it is clearly unique.

Proposition 3. *The asymptotic-optimal path always exists. It is the maximal locally optimal path if and only if a locally optimal path exists; otherwise it has zero consumption at all times.*

Proof. Because the paths (b_t^T) are locally optimal, consumption at any time is an increasing function of initial consumption. At the same time, capital at any time is a decreasing function of initial consumption. Therefore initial consumption, b_0^T, must decrease as T increases. It is bounded below by zero, and therefore tends to a limit b_0. At the same time, all the b_t^T must tend to non-negative limits b_t. We have to show that (b_t) is feasible.

If $b_0 > 0$, consider the locally optimal path on which initial consumption is b_0, and denote it by (c_t). Clearly $c_t \leqslant b_t$, since for all T, $c_t, < (b_t^T)$. But if $c_t < b_t$, for some $t > 0$, the locally optimal path on which consumption at t is b_t has initial consumption greater than b_0, so that, for all T, $b_0^T \geqslant b_0 + a$ for some $a > 0$—which is impossible. Therefore (b_t) is the locally optimal path with initial consumption b_0. It must be feasible, since otherwise it would be equal to one of the paths (b_t^T), for $T = T_1$, say; then $b_t^T < b_t$ for $T > T_1$, which is impossible. Furthermore, it is clear from the definition of b_t as a limit of infeasible locally optimal paths that it must be the maximal feasible locally optimal path.

If $b_0 = 0$, then all $b_t = 0$, and there is no locally optimal path.

For suppose first that there is a locally optimal path. It lies below all the paths (b_t^T), and has positive initial consumption. That is inconsistent with $b_0 = 0$.

Suppose that $b_t > 0$ for some t. Then there must be a locally optimal path with consumption b_t at t. This, we have just seen, is impossible. $\qquad \square$

The proof is complete.

Proposition 4. *If consumption is not zero on the asymptotic-optimal path, the path is agreeable.*

Proof. Fix T_0 and $\epsilon > 0$. Choose T_1 so that

$$\int_0^{T_o} [u(b_t^T) - u(b_t)]\, dt < \epsilon \tag{36}$$

for all $T \geqslant T_1$. This can be done since $b_t > 0$. Let (b_t') be the consumption path that maximizes $\int_0^T u \, dt$ subject to having the same T_0-overture as (b_t). Since b_{T_0}, the capital stock at T_0 on the path (b_t^T), is greater than the capital stock at T_0 on the path (b_t^T), for any T,

$$
\int_0^T u(b_t') \, dt > \int_0^{T_0} u(b_t) \, dt + \int_0^T u(b_t^T) \, dt
$$
$$
> \int_0^T u(b_t^T) \, dt - \epsilon \tag{37}
$$

by (36). This proves that (b_t) is agreeable. □

These propositions together imply the following results:

Theorem 1. *If an optimum path exists, it is agreeable.*

This follows from the fact, implied by Propositions 3 and 4, that a maximal locally optimal path is agreeable.

Theorem 2. *An agreeable path exists if and only if a (perpetually feasible) locally optimal path exists. It is then the maximal locally optimal path.*

A maximal locally optimal path exists if and only if a locally optimal path exists. The theorem then follows from Propositions 2, 3, and 4.

4. THE EXISTENCE OF AGREEABLE PLANS

By using Theorem 2, we can now see for each of the examples discussed in Section 1 whether or not an agreeable path exists, and what path it is. We have already seen that there is no locally optimal path in Example 1. Therefore no agreeable path exists. In Example 2, agreeability allows a considerable extension over optimality, but does not cover all cases. We saw that no locally optimal path exists if $\rho < (\gamma - 1 + b)m$. But if ρ is greater than this limiting value, an agreeable path exists, even though there is no optimal path unless $\rho \geqslant \gamma m$. Finally, it is apparent that an agreeable path always exists for the case described in Example 3.

The following theorem covers many of the cases that would be found most interesting by economists.

Theorem 3. *Suppose*

$$
u_t(c, \ t) = 0 \qquad (c > 0, \ t \geqslant 0)
$$
$$
f_t(k, \ t) \geqslant 0 \qquad (k \geqslant 0, \ t \geqslant 0)
$$

and that u [f(k, t), t] is bounded above for $c > 0$, $k \geqslant 0$, $t \geqslant 0$. Then an agreeable path exists.

Notice that the conditions include cases where there is no technological progress. Boundedness of either the utility function or the production function is sufficient for existence.

Proof. We rely, essentially, upon the Keynes–Ramsey integral of the local optimality conditions, (10). Of course, it is not valid when f depends upon t, but we have

$$\frac{d}{dt}u + [(f - c)uc] = \dot{k}\dot{u}_c + f_k\dot{k}u_c + f_t u_c = f_t u_c \geqslant 0 \tag{38}$$

on any locally optimal path. Therefore

$$u(c_t) + [f(k_t, t) - c_t]u_c(c_t) \geqslant u(c_0) + [f(k_0, 0) - c_0]u_c(c_0). \tag{39}$$

As $c_0 \to 0$ (k_0 being held fixed), the right-hand side of this inequality tends to ∞. For, by the concavity of u,

$$
\begin{aligned}
u(c_0) + (f - c_0)u_c(c_0) &\geqslant u(\tfrac{1}{2}f) - (\tfrac{1}{2}f - c_0)u_c(c_0) \\
&\quad + (f - c_0)u_c(c_0) \\
&= u(\tfrac{1}{2}f) + \tfrac{1}{2}fu_c(c_0) \\
&\to \infty \text{ as } c_0 \to 0.
\end{aligned}
$$

Choose $c_0 > 0$ and $< f(k_0, 0)$, small enough to ensure that the right-hand side is greater than sup $u(f)$. From (39), $f - c$ can never vanish. Since c_t and k_t are continuous, it follows that for all t

$$f(k_t, t) - c_t > 0. \tag{40}$$

Thus $\dot{k}_t > 0$ always on this locally optimal path, which is therefore feasible for all time. This proves the existence of a perpetually feasible locally optimal path, and completes the proof. $\qquad\square$

Remark. The above proof can be applied also in the case where utility is discounted at a positive rate. We have already seen that an agreeable path (even an optimum path) may exist when u is unbounded and there is discounting. We do not have a general theorem to cover these cases.

5. CONCLUSIONS

Restricting our attention to the familiar one-good model, we have shown that agreeable plans exist in all cases where one can hope for any kind of solution to the 'infinite time horizon' optimum growth problem: namely, cases for which there exists a locally optimal path that is always feasible. In other cases, there is no path that cannot be improved by changes confined to a finite period of time. Then one cannot hope for an ideal policy without specifying the time horizon.

We have seen that it is not easy to tell in advance whether a locally optimal path exists or not. If one is prepared to accept a bound on utility or a bound on production, it has been shown that one has an agreeable plan. Bounded production, though a sensible assumption, perhaps is so only in the same sense as is the assumption of a finite time horizon. Agreeability relative to an upper bound (truncation) of the production function does not appear to be a weaker requirement than agreeability relative to a finite time horizon. Yet one might wish, on considering the consumption externalities that appear to arise at high levels of output, to accept an upper bound to possible consumption little higher than that experienced by the middle classes in the industrial economies now. If these considerations are better incorporated in the utility function, the result is the same: an agreeable plan exists.

It has been argued[6] that, since there is a finite probability that utility is unbounded, therefore the utility function used in a planning calculation ought to be unbounded. We do not find this line of argument very persuasive, for the following reason. For definiteness, suppose there is no utility discounting or technological change. If decision-makers now have an unbounded utility function, there is no agreeable plan. If they do, they will still want to recognize that at some future date it may be decided that, properly, utility should be unbounded. If the date at which this happens is sufficiently far away, there is no reason why that should significantly affect the prospective utility loss of following the agreeable plan now (unless these planners reduce consumption to nearly zero for a long time). Therefore it is still reasonable to agree to the agreeable plan arising from the bounded utility functions. The utility functions used *now* can justifiably be bounded. That it *might* have been different cannot imply that it *must* be wrong.

It will have been noted that an agreeable plan, like an optimum plan, is consistent with the usual competitive decentralization of the economic system, since the local optimality condition is a shadow price condition, expressing the equality between the rate of interest and the marginal productivity of capital that would have to obtain in competitive equilibrium. No satisfactory means of approximating over time to the optimum path by means of price-guided decentralization has been proposed, however: one does not know whether this property of the agreeable plan is of great significance.

Finally, we would suggest that agreeable plans are quite amenable to common sense. It is required, we have seen, that the rate at which marginal utility falls be equal to the marginal productivity of capital. Among paths for which this is true, it is suggested that the economy follow the one on which consumption is a maximum. This seems to be an entirely reasonable policy. Until now, one has had to dismiss this policy as being potentially unreasonable, since there may not in fact be an optimum policy. The concept

---

[6] Weizsäcker (1967).

of agreeability to some extent exorcises that ghost, and allows us to be more content with the path that good economic sense suggests.

REFERENCES

Chakravarty, S., 'The Existence of an Optimum Savings Programme'. *Econometrica*, Vol. 30 (1962), p. 178.

Koopmans, T. C., 'On the Concept of Optimal Economic Growth'. In *The Econometric Approach to Development* (Vatican, 1966).

Mirrlees, J. A., 'Optimum Growth when Technology is Changing.' *Review of Economic Studies*, Vol. 34 (1967), p. 95.

Tinbergen J., 'Optimum Savings and Utility Maximisation over Time'. *Econometrica*, Vol. 30 (1959), p. 481.

von Weizsacker, C. C., 'Existence of Optimal Programmes of Accumulation for an Infinite Time Horizon'. *Review of Economic Studies*, Vol. 32 (1965), p. 85.

——'Lemmas for a Theory of Approximate Optimal Growth'. *Review of Economic Studies*, Vol.34 (1967), p. 151.

DISCUSSION

Professor Mirrlees introduced the paper by Hammond and himself by saying it reflected a certain unease about some of the problems in optimal growth theory. Much effort had been concentrated on existence problems which were difficult but not central to the economics of the problem. He still thought optimal growth theory was interesting—especially with respect to choice of investment projects. He wanted therefore to find a way of steering clear of the existence problems. We should recall that the infinite time horizon is introduced as a simplification, to represent the assumption that the time horizon is 'very distant'. It should not be lightly abandoned.

The framework used in this paper was a one-commodity, continuous-time model since it offered few technical difficulties and was well known to everyone. Mr Hammond was extending the results to many-sector models.

The examples included at the beginning were to remind people of the problems that arose. The third example was perhaps not very important, but it was surprising that bounded production could give rise to non-existence. The most interesting case arose when the intersection of the c, k (in efficiency units) stationaries gave a steady state with the savings rate above golden rule (see Fig. 19.1). The path (P) tending to the saddle-point is not optimal: it is inefficient. It does, however, have the property that any finite-horizon optimal path with 'a fairly long' time horizon starts off 'fairly close' to it (although such a path runs out of capital in finite time). Agreeable plans were defined in order to make this notion precise. The idea was to produce a plan which anyone with a sufficiently long time horizon could accept. If such a plan were unique, the argument might be settled. It had been shown for the model of the paper that (i) the agreeable path is unique; (ii) it is locally optimal; (iii) an optimal path is agreeable; (iv) an agreeable path is the highest (in consumption terms) among the permanently feasible Euler paths; (v) if a permanently feasible Euler path exists, then an agreeable path exists. Where an agreeable path does not exist the situation looks hopeless, and this throws some light on the reasons for which an optimal path fails to exist in Example 1. (We always want to postpone consumption.) In a bounded situation (either utility or production) an agreeable path exists. They did not have as yet any general theorems proving convergence of an agreeable path to a steady state, or for cases involving technical progress.

Professor Stiglitz said he thought this an interesting and important paper. There were two main reasons why an optimum might not exist.

(i) The *lollipop problem*. We want to maximize $\int_0^T u(c)\, dt$ by allocating one lollipop over time; the limit of the finite-horizon optimal paths is permanent zero consumption. This was similar to the problem (with no solution) of finding the shortest distance between two points given that we must start at $45°$ to the line joining them. With such problems the limit of finite-horizon optimal paths as $T \to \infty$ was not feasible—agreeability does not avoid this problem.

(ii) Reasons connected with the *non-convergence of the utility integral*. Koopman's and Weizsäcker's methods for avoiding this problem were different. Agreeability extended Weizsäcker's notion of overtaking and he wondered if Koopmans's idea could be extended. Agreeability did not avoid the problem of non-existence in Example 1. (*Professor Weizsäcker* said that this was similar to the lollipop problem, and *Professor Yaari* remarked that this had been called the freewheeling economy by McFadden.) However, the case where the saddle-point corresponds to a savings rate above the golden rule was a very important case and this was covered by agreeability.

He wanted to discuss the nature of the criterion. He had begun to think of two other ways of expressing the idea of agreeability. First, we could specify that the path we are looking for (C_t) be such that the optimal path for a T-horizon plan has initial consumption within ϵ of C_0 for T sufficiently large. This, however, would include zero consumption as a solution to the lollipop problem which we do not want to do. Secondly, we might have tried to work with only one time; e.g., we want a path with utility integral greater than the integral for any other path less ϵ, provided T_0 is large enough. This definition did not work well. He had thus become convinced that the formulation of the criterion in the paper was the simplest way of capturing what we are after.

He also wanted to discuss the nature of agreement. We needed agreement about ϵ, T_0 (planning horizon), T_1 (the lowest estimate of the end of the world). The T_1 implied by ϵ, T_0, might be too large—if anyone thought the world would last less long than T_1, agreement was not possible. In order to agree, each individual believes that after T_0 he can choose what happens. If an individual thought the government might do something different, he might change his ideas of what was acceptable for the initial period to T_0—a game-theoretic situation.

Two very strong assumptions in this kind of theory were (a) additive utility, and (b) malleable capital. He asked how the concept was extended if these assumptions were relaxed.

Professor Inagaki supposed we were in a situation as in Fig. 1 of the paper, where the stationaries intersected at $\bar{x}$ with $\bar{x} > x_G$ (the golden rule capital per efficiency unit of labour), and we began with $x_0 = \bar{x}$. The agreeable path would be $x_t = \bar{x}$ for all t. The agreeable path could be dominated by a path Q of x as shown in Fig. 19.1(a). The corresponding consumption path Q is shown in Fig. 19.1(b). The reason an agreeable path could get within ϵ of the Q path was that it caught up between the end of the planning period T_0 and T_1. He would not agree to following the agreeable path.

He suggested it might be possible to reformulate the definition without T_1 since it was possible to catch up with Q in any interval, however small. He thought, however, that other paths would be superior to the one which caught up very quickly.

He said that the criterion should be reformulated using something like

$$1 - \left(\int_0^{T_1} u(c') \, dt \right) \Big/ \left(\int_0^{T_1} u(c) \, dt \right) < \epsilon,$$

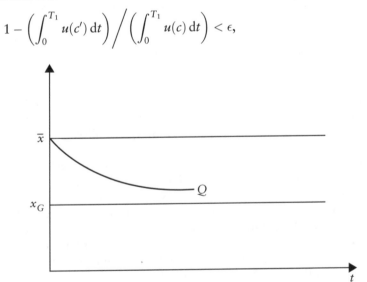

Figure 19.1(a).

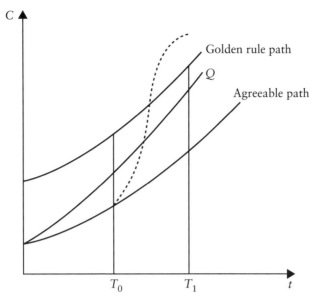

Figure 19.1(*b*).

as otherwise we had problems with the definition of the units of ϵ.

He did not think that agreeability was a way out of non-existence problems as it did not maximize anything.

Professor Weizsäcker said the agreeability notion was a way out of problems that had been worrying us when we should have liked to have been thinking of more important things. In general, for a five-year (T_0) plan we had to decide on terminal capital stocks. Various *ad hoc* propositions had been offered, but such considerations led us to work with infinite-horizon plans. The Hammond–Mirrlees proposal was that we adjust capital stocks at T_0 so that they would be acceptable to anyone whose overall horizon is longer than T_1. This showed why T_0 *and* T_1 were needed. We could then give up worrying about existence. The agreeability notion justified his belief that the existence problem was artificial. Inagaki's Q path would not be acceptable as it would have fewer capital stocks.

If we considered a long finite time horizon problem, the optimal solution would stay near the agreeable path in its initial stages. He would agree to the initial stages (to T_0) of an agreeable path, and this is what was being asked.

Professor Inagaki said a finite time horizon path would be very different from an agreeable path since it would finish up with zero capital stocks.

Professor Hahn asked if it was reasonable to agree to a path just because it could catch up with everything else later. We had no existence problems with finite horizons. The agreeability idea was a guide for thinking about finite time horizons.

Professor Mirrlees said that Professor Inagaki's example showed very clearly that we must not actually believe in infinite time horizons if we are to obtain agreement on a plan. If $x_0 = \bar{x}$ and it was proposed staying there indefinitely, I could not agree if my time horizon were infinite. We could, however, obtain agreement to keep x at $\bar{x}$ for the first T_0 years if everyone's horizon was longer than T_1.

Professor Yaari thought agreeability was a reason for feeling better about non-existence rather than a way of avoiding existence problems. That the maximal locally path was agreeable was a nice result since we knew that in certain circumstances it was not optimal. Professor Mirrlees had offered one way of reducing our worries about existence. He wanted to consider alternative methods.

A strong definition (A) of optimality was: (C_t^*) is optimal if

$$\liminf_{T \to \infty} \int_0^T [u(C_t^*) - u(C_t)] \, dt > 0$$

for all feasible (C_t). We could weaken this to $\geq$ but this was not much help.

A much weaker condition (B) was to call C^* optimal if no feasible path overtakes it; i.e.

$$\limsup_{T \to \infty} \int_0^T [u(C_t^*) - u(C_t)] \, dt \geq 0$$

for all feasible (C_t). Lim sup gave only a partial ordering and this definition gave a greater chance of finding optimal paths. His own work with linear utility functions had shown that we can have existence in the latter sense without existence in the former.

A third condition (C)—Malinvand maximality—was still weaker and this had been used in his paper with Peleg. All three (A, B, and C) gave us the competitive pricing solutions we were looking for.

None of these (A, B, or C) could fix up the cake problem. He said this problem would not worry us so much if we became used to thinking of finitely additive measures in these problems. In game theory with an infinite number of strategies, we could have a mixed strategy assigning zero probability (p_i) to each strategy but the integral of the p_i could be unity. We would, with this attitude, be happy about spreading butter with zero thickness.

Dr Bliss asked how much of the cake he would receive. *Professor Yaari* replied he would receive the integral of the cake over him with respect to the measure.

Professor Hahn asked how this dealt with the 'saving above the golden rule' problem. *Professor Weizsäcker* said that the Euler path to the saddle-point was not Malinvand maximal if the savings rate at the saddle-point was above golden rule. Professor Yaari's remarks were not relevant to the problem under discussion and we could return to them tomorrow.

Professor Uzawa said that the differential equation nature of paths was lost with Professor Yaari's way of looking at the cake problem. *Professor Yaari* said this property could be retained if we decomposed the measure into a countably additive and a finitely additive measure.

Professor Inagaki asked if the golden rule had a turnpike property for a finite-horizon plan.

Professor Mirrlees said that the optimal finite horizon plan stayed near the agreeable path. For a long time horizon we would stay near the saddle-point for a long time, even though its saving rate is above golden rule.

Professor Inagaki asked how this fitted in with the sensitivity to final capital stocks shown by Srinivasan in his criticism of Chakravarty. *Professor Weizsäcker* said this was not relevant. Srinivasan had shown that initial consumption levels on the optimum path were very sensitive to terminal capital stocks if the terminal capital stocks were so high that very large savings rates were needed. With smaller capital stocks, initial consumption levels were very insensitive.

Professor Mirrlees said he found Professor Stiglitz's questions very interesting. He agreed it was not very obvious why we needed T_0 and T_1; perhaps a sketch of the situation would help. Consider the usual c, k diagram (Fig. 19.2) and a long finite-horizon plan—the optimal path was A and the agreeable path P. For a long period A would stay close to P, and then in the last part of its path turn back to the $k = 0$ axis. Following P until T_0 put us in a position to get very close to the optimal path when we caught up in the last part— from T_0 to T_1. Thus two times were needed.

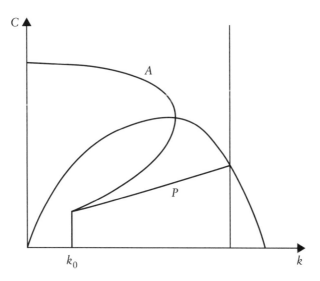

Figure 19.2.

Stern had raised the question with him that for sensible ϵ (defined in terms of an equivalent consumption loss) and T_0 it might turn out that T_1 was extremely large so that it would be difficult to obtain agreement, and that numerical information was needed to answer this point. He still thought that people could be expected to modify the loss of utility they would be prepared to accept in the light of the probable difficulty of obtaining agreement. But he agreed that calculations would throw light on the question.

He agreed that expectations about what would actually happen between T_0 and T_1 would affect the possibility of agreement. We might have to agree to postpone that decision. This would be reasonable if we had potential disagreement because of lack of evidence rather than 'wilful' disagreement that later evidence would not upset.

20

Fairly Good Plans

WITH N. H. STERN

The complicated analyses which economists endeavour to carry through are not mere gymnastic. They are instruments for the bettering of human life. (A. C. Pigou, Preface, '*Economics of Welfare*', 3rd edn.)

For this reason, one expects economists to be particularly interested in assessing the relative value of different directions for their research. This paper is intended as a contribution to that task. We take a simple model and show how much of an increase in welfare might be available if subtle theory were substituted for crude as the basis for economic policy, or if more elaborate model formulation replaced simple calculations. The simplicity of the model makes it easier to develop our methods. More important, as we shall argue, the analysis of simple models is essential if we are to understand the corresponding situation for more complex models of the economy.

In order to make the discussion intelligible, we measure welfare in commodity units (as do users of cost–benefit techniques). There would be little point in a claim that, for example, expropriation of privately owned industry would yield 23 million social utils. Such a measurement does nothing to suggest how much of our enthusiasm and research should be allocated to the proposal in question. If instead we claim that, in terms of the social valuation used, it would be as good as a 5% increase in the national income, we can compare with our own memory or forecast of of the gains from other policies, and convey the magnitude of our claim to others.[1] With commodity units, it should then be possible to discuss whether there is good enough reason to pursue a line of research further, to elaborate an existing economic model, or to press a new economic policy upon the authorities. Commodity units for

This paper, by J. A. Mirrlees and N. H. Stern, was first published in the *Journal of Economic Theory*, Vol. 4 (1972), pp. 268–88, Elsevier Science (USA), reprinted with permission of the Publisher.

We have had many interesting and useful comments from C. J. Bliss, P. A. Diamond, P. J. Hammond, D. M. G. Newbery, and R. M. Solow, for which we are extremely grateful.

[1] In effect, our discussion in this paper relies chiefly on the possibility of guessing the opportunity cost (in commodity units) of research effort of average probable effectiveness. Commodity units also have the advantage that they indicate when welfare differences are 'small'. One can imagine this being useful when testing the acceptability of a particular objective function. If we feel that one simple economic state is much better than the other, while the proposed objective function gives it only a very small relative advantage, we shall have good reason to change the function.

welfare allow the comparisons implicit in such questions to be expressed in a way that is invariant to the forms of welfare function that may have seemed appropriate to each particular context.

Specifically, we use a natural calibration of alternative growth paths in the simplest of the growth models, the one-good malleable-capital model. By means of this calibration, we discuss, first, the worth of optimum growth theory, and, second, the use of finite-time-horizon optimizing models in actual planning.

Economists working in many different areas have their own version of the problem here illustrated in the case of optimum growth theory. For example, the econometrician wants to know whether he should make a large effort to obtain a precise estimate of a parameter about which he already has some information. The cost–benefit analyst frequently neglects considerations, while retaining an impression of their probable magnitude: he wants to know whether the difference in benefits and costs is sufficiently large to justify his neglect of awkward items. The proponent of pet ideas might consider whether the likely gains from adopting his idea justify the effort of turning it into a precise and detailed proposal. The practical planner has to worry whether the existing model is good enough for the job at hand, or should be replaced by a more complicated one.

It might be contended that a 'super-optimizing' model, incorporating costs of research and delay, is necessary if questions of this type are to be answered. But such an approach begs the question. If it is not worth while developing a more complicated model, it is certainly not worth while developing a super-optimizing model, containing within it, as part of its range of choice, that more complicated model.[2] In our view, evidence relevant to the question whether research activity should be extended in particular directions can be obtained by considering the corresponding issue in a much simpler case. That simple case then simulates the real research problem. It is obvious that a knowledge of the best policy in the simple case does not tell us, with perfect certainty, what to do in the more complex situation. Nothing can do that. But it seems right that evidence from simple cases should not be ignored.

An example will illustrate our point. Suppose we are concerned with a multisector planning problem of some complexity, for which an infinite horizon is believed to be appropriate. It may be impracticable, or, in the current state of knowledge, impossible, to calculate optimum growth for such a model. We may, nevertheless, be able to calculate optimum growth for the case of a finite time-horizon, provided that the number of periods is not too great. Is there some crude rule, specifying a time horizon and terminal capital requirements, which will lead to a 'satisfactory' approximation to

---

[2] Unless an essentially similar process of model construction will be undertaken a number of times (e.g. for different countries). It may sometimes be reasonable to construct a super-optimizing model for a single representative case when many applications are possible.

the true optimum; or would we do better to devote further research effort to discovering ways of computing the infinite-horizon optimum? Clearly this question cannot be answered directly without rendering the question pointless. The only way of obtaining evidence relevant to it is to consider the corresponding question for a simpler model where a direct answer is possible without excessive effort. For example, we can pose the question in the context of a simple one-good model, and use our welfare calibration to measure the welfare loss from using finite-horizon calculations.

We do this particular exercise in Section 5 below. Our first example of welfare comparisons compares simple and complicated savings policies, and is relevant to the general question, unanswerable with perfect precision and certainty: whether in certain cases increased refinement of economic calculation is desirable. These are only examples of a rather general way of tackling a large class of problems. We see the task as similar to the use of small-scale models (of bridges, ships, and aeroplanes, for example) by engineers. If the model bridge does not fall down, the real bridge may; but the engineer may still have been well advised to build the model first.

We would not claim that research has in all fields been pushed so far that estimates of the kind discussed in this paper can be made. Probably it can be done in public economics and international economics as readily as in growth theory; but labour economics and the theory of the firm, for example, seem less ready for such treatment. Neither do we claim that the direct and obvious social consequences of an economic theory necessarily consitute the major part of its claim to be an 'instrument for the bettering of economic life'. Development of a theory may affect quite remote fields, and it may improve the economist's own grip on real problems. Some theoretical work may provide a very satisfactory use for one's leisure hours. However, the 'natural' next steps in the development of the logical structure should not always have first claim on the economist's research effort. The value of his services might be increased by calculated consideration of when to stop and what to do next.

1. BALANCED GROWTH EQUIVALENTS

Consider a one-sector growth model in which balanced growth is possible, the natural rate of growth being α. Consider an arbitrary feasible consumption path c, such that consumption at time t is c_t. Suppose there exists a welfare ordering, or valuation, of consumption paths. If c is equivalent, in welfare terms, to the balanced growth path yielding consumption $\gamma e^{\alpha t}$ at t, we shall call γ the *balanced growth equivalent* (BGE) of c. For such a model, the BGE is the natural commodity measure of welfare. Changes in it brought about the adoption of new policies or techniques of policy-making show the percentage increase in consumption for ever that is equivalent to the policy change contemplated.

We realize that for many microeconomic decisions 0.01% of national income for one year, let alone for ever, is of great importance; but we are concerned here with the comparison of rather broad economy-wide policies such as the overall savings rate, fiscal policy, or the control of foreign trade. In our opinion, one should look for at least a 1% increase in the BGE before elaborating such policies into detailed proposals. We base our view of 'at least 1%' on the impression that there are many such areas of economic research, as yet imperfectly explored, where gains of at least this magnitude are available: for example international monetary arrangements, or the form of taxation. Our guesses at the possible gains from such policies will not be shared by everyone; but we think that most readers will be able to produce examples which in their view can produce gains of this size. On the other hand, there are many lines of research very actively pursued (perhaps rightly) that seem to offer gains of little greater than 1% of the national income.[3]

The social welfare function for a growth model may not be a function at all, but rather an ordering and not necessarily a complete one. In the simplest case, where preferences regarding consumption in different time periods are independent, it is usual to order consumption paths by saying that c is at least as good as c' if, for any $\epsilon > 0$, there exists T_0 such that, for all $T \geq T_0$,

$$\int_0^T u(c_t, t)\, dt \geq \int_0^T u(c_t', t)\, dt - \epsilon. \tag{1}$$

In terms of this ordering, c and c' are equivalent if c is at least as good as c', and c' is at least as good as c. This may not be a complete ordering, for example if u is independent of t. Thus, there may be no balanced growth path equivalent to a specified consumption path c. The path yielding consumption $(\gamma e^{\alpha t})$ is equivalent to c if and only if

$$\int_0^\infty [u(c_t, t) - u(\gamma e^{\alpha t}, t)]\, dt = 0, \tag{2}$$

meaning that the integral converges and is zero. This definition of welfare equivalence follows at once from the definition of the welfare ordering given in (1).

We take, as an example, the one-good model with constant returns to scale and labour-augmenting technological change at rate g:

$$c_t + k_t = e^{gt} f(e^{-gt} k_t), \qquad k_t \geq 0. \tag{3}$$

---

[3] For example, most work on macroeconomics is intended to enable the economy to utilize available capacity more fully. Casual inspection of the British data (cf. F.W. Paish) suggests to us that few such policies could hope to obtain gains averaging, over time, much more than 1% of total output per year.

Here k_t is interpreted as the capital stock at t. The production function f is concave, increasing, and zero at zero. We omit population growth for the moment so that $\alpha = g$. We show in the Appendix that all paths in this model have a BGE in the case of bounded, concave u.

2. THE BALANCED GROWTH EQUIVALENT OF OPTIMUM GROWTH

In this paper, we calculate balanced growth equivalents for various paths in the one-good neoclassical model (3). Since the questions at issue are the welfare gains from following fully optimum policies, compared with various, theoretically less ideal, alternative policies, we restrict attention to cases where an optimum path exists. In this section, we show how the BGE of the optimum path—which is of course the largest possible BGE for a feasible path—can be calculated. When the instantaneous valuation function has the special form

$$u(c, t) = e^{-\rho t} u(c) = -\frac{1}{v} e^{-\rho t} c^{-v}, \tag{4}$$

it is particularly easy to compute the BGE of optimum growth, once the optimum policy has itself been computed. To derive the relationship we require, we use the homogeneity property of the maximized valuation integral that is implied by the homogeneity of the instantaneous valuation function (4).

Suppose the valuation integral can converge.[4] Then the maximum of the valuation integral, which is the total valuation resulting from following the optimum policy, is a well-defined function of the initial capital stock and the initial date. We define

$$W(k_0, t) = \max \int_t^\infty e^{-\rho(\tau - t)} u(c) \, d\tau, \tag{5}$$

where the maximum is taken over feasible consumption paths beginning at time t when the capital stock is k_0.

W is homogeneous of degree $-v$ in k_0 and e^{gt}. To prove this, multiply k_0 and e^{gt} by the same factor a. We see from the production relationships (3) that this change enables any feasible consumption path to be multiplied by this factor, period by period: total valuation is then multiplied by a factor a^{-v}. Consequently the optimum consumption policy is a homogeneous function of degree 1 in k_0 and e^{gt}; and W is homogeneous of degree $-v$ in the two

---

[4] This is possible if and only if $vg + \rho > n$ where $u(c, t) = L_t(c_t/L_t)^{-v} e^{-\rho t}$ and $\dot{L}_t/L_t = n$ where L_t is population.

variables, as asserted. We write

$$W(k_0, t) = e^{-vgt}w(k_0e^{-gt}).$$ (6)

It is clear from (5) that, on the optimum path,

$$W(k_0, t_0) - e^{-\rho(t_1-t_0)} W(k_{t_1}, t_1) = \int_{t_0}^{t_1} u(c_\tau)e^{-\rho(\tau-t_0)}d\tau.$$ (7)

Dividing by $t_1 - t_0$, and letting $t_1 \to t_0$, we obtain

$$W_k(k_0, t_0)\, \dot{k}_t + W_t(k_0, t_0) - \rho W(k_0, t_0) = -u(c_{t_0}).$$ (8)

Furthermore, one expects that the marginal valuation of consumption should be equal to the marginal valuation of capital on the optimum path, since we are, at the optimum, just indifferent between an increase in immediate consumption and an increase in present capital; i.e.

$$W_k(k_0, t_0) = u_c(c_{t_0}).$$ (9)

This can be proved rigorously by calculus of variations methods.

In the particular case we are now concerned with, (8) and (9) become:

$$w'ke^{-gt_0} - (vg + \rho)\, w - gk_0e^{-gt_0}\, w' = \frac{1}{v}\, c^{-v}e^{vgt_0},$$ (10)

$$w' = c^{-v-1}e^{(v+1)gt_0},$$ (11)

where everything is evaluated at k_0 and t_0. Eliminating w' from (10) and (11), using (3), and writing k and t for k_0 and t_0 now, we obtain

$$(v\alpha + \rho)\, w = -(ce^{-gt})^{-v}\left(\frac{v+1}{v} - \frac{e^{gt}f - gk}{c}\right).$$ (12)

Thus, when the optimum policy, giving ce^{-gt} as a function of ke^{-gt}, is known, the resulting total valuation can be calculated at once.

Denote the EGE of the optimum path by c_b^*. Then

$$W(k, t) = -\frac{1}{v}\int_0^\infty (c_b^*e^{gt})^{-v}e^{-\rho t}dt$$
$$= -[1/v(vg + \rho)](c_b^*)^{-v}.$$ (13)

Combining (6), (12), and (13), we obtain, for $t = 0$,

$$c_b^* = c\left[1 + v - \frac{(f - gk)}{c}\right]^{-1/v},$$ (14)

where c is optimum initial consumption. Graphs giving values of c for certain particular models are given in J. A. Mirrlees.

When the instantaneous valuation function u is not homogeneous in consumption, the balanced growth equivalent can be obtained by integration of (9).

The formula just given extends immediately to the case of a constant rate of population growth n. We take an instantaneous valuation function $e^{-\rho t}L_t u(c_t/L_t)$, where $L_t = L_0 e^{nt}$, and $u(c) = -c^{-v}/v$. The valuation integral converges if $vg + \rho > n$. Then the relation between the immediate optimum consumption policy and the BGE of continued optimum growth is given by

$$c_b^* = c\left[1 + v - v\left(\frac{f - (g+n)k}{c}\right)\right]^{-1/v}. \tag{15}$$

Finally, we consider briefly the case $vg + \rho = n$—the only case in which an optimum policy exists, but the valuation integral does not converge. In the narrow sense defined earlier, no BGE exists in general. Let us compare a consumption path (c_t) in this model with balanced growth paths, in which consumption per head is γe^{gt}. Let consumption per head on the given path be $z_t e^{gt}$. The integral of valuation differences for a period T is

$$-\frac{1}{v}\int_0^T e^{-(\rho-n)t}[(z_t e^{gt})^{-v} - (\gamma e^{gt})^{-v}]\,dt = -\frac{1}{v}\int_0^T [z_t^{-v} - \gamma^{-v}]\,dt,$$

on the assumption that $\rho + vg = n$. It is clear then, that, if z_t tends to a limit as $t \to \infty$, the integral of valuation differences will be negative for all large T if $\gamma < \lim z_t$, and positive for all large T if $\gamma > \lim z_t$. Thus, $\lim z_t$ is the BGE (wide sense). This term is defined in the Appendix.

The extended definition brings out clearly the peculiarity of this case, that the valuation of the path depends essentially upon its long-run asymptotic behaviour. The maximum possible BGE (wide sense) is, of course, golden rule consumption per efficiency unit of labour $\bar{z}$: this is the BGE (wide sense) of the optimum path, regardless of initial conditions.

3. THE BALANCED GROWTH EQUIVALENT OF HARRODIAN PATHS

A convenient example of a simple growth plan for the economy is that implied by specifying a particular saving–income ratio, and maintaining it for ever. A policy of this kind might be easier for the economy to follow that the more subtle variations in the saving–income ratio implicit in a full optimization. If the savings ratio is s, and production is described, as before, by (3), the path of the economy is determined by the differential equation

$$\dot{k}_t = se^{gt}f(e^{-gt}k_t),\qquad(16)$$

where, to simplify formulas, we again leave out population growth. This is easy to integrate in most special cases. In particular, if production is Cobb–Douglas, i.e. $f(x) = x^b(0 < b < 1)$, we have the solution

$$k_t^{1-b} = k_0^{1-b} + (s/g)(e^{(1-b)gt} - 1).\qquad(17)$$

From this, we can obtain $c_t = (1 - s)k_t{}^b e^{(1-b)gt}$. The BGE, which we denote by c_{bs}, is obtained from

$$\int_0^\infty [u(c_t, t) - u(c_{bs}e^{gt}, t)]\, dt = 0,\qquad(18)$$

which, in the case $u(c,t) = -e^{-\rho t}c^{-v}/v$, becomes

$$(c_{bs})^{-v} = (\rho + vg)(1 - s)^{-v} \int_0^\infty \exp[-(\rho + v(1 - b)g)t]k_t^{-vb}\, dt.\qquad(19)$$

By changing the variable of integration to $y = (g/s)\, k_t^{1-b}e^{-(1-b)gt}$, we obtain the formula

$$\left(\frac{c_{bs}}{k_0{}^b}\right)^{-v} = p(1 - s)^{-v}h^q(1 - h)^{-p} \int_h^1 y^{-q}(1 - y)^{p-1}\, dy,\qquad(20)$$

where $q = vb/(1 - b)$, $p = (\rho + vg)/[(1 - b)g]$, $h = gk_0^{1-b}/s$. The integral can be evaluated numerically, since the integral in (20) is an incomplete beta function. It is simple to differentiate (20) with respect to s to find an expression for the maximum c_{bs} which can be evaluated numerically. It will be noted that the particular policy

$$s = \alpha k_0^{1-b},\qquad(21)$$

corresponds to beginning growth at the natural rate of growth now and continuing it for ever. (Equation (21) is just the Harrod–Domar formula. Alternatively, this remark can be verified from (17).) Formula (20) is not valid when (21) holds; but since the policy yields a balanced growth path, the BGE must be the initial level of consumption, namely

$$k_0^b - \alpha k_0.$$

We shall see that optimum growth usually provides a BGE substantially greater than this. But if the saving ratio s is chosen with more deliberation, it will usually be possible to obtain a BGE quite close to the maximum attainable.

Table 20.1.

n	b	v	k_0/y_0	Optimum path			Best Harrodian path	
				Initial s	Final s	c_b^*/y_0	$\bar{s}$	c_{bs}/y_0
0	0.375	1.0	3	0.29	0.19	0.993	0.23	0.990
0.02	0.375	1.0	3	0.27	0.31	0.970	0.32	0.969
0.02	0.375	1.0	1.4	0.40	0.31	1.246	0.33	1.244
0	0.375	1.5	3	0.22	0.15	0.944	0.19	0.943
0.02	0.375	1.5	3	0.29	0.25	0.896	0.26	0.895
0.02	0.375	1.5	1.4	0.32	0.25	1.085	0.28	1.083
0	0.5	1.0	3	0.37	0.25	1.139	0.32	1.136
0.02	0.5	1.0	3	0.45	0.41	1.233	0.43	1.233
0.02	0.5	1.0	1.4	0.47	0.42	1.819	0.43	1.817
0	0.5	1.5	3	0.29	0.20	1.019	0.26	1.018
0.02	0.5	1.5	3	0.36	0.33	1.008	0.35	1.008
0.02	0.5	1.5	1.4	0.37	0.33	1.332	0.36	1.331

4. BALANCED GROWTH EQUIVALENTS IN PARTICULAR EXAMPLES

We have computed BGEs for optimum growth and Harrodian paths in a number of particular cases that we think may have realistic features.[5] The aim is to discover (i) how close to the optimum an economy might get by choosing a single policy parameter instead of following a fully optimum strategy; (ii) whether substantial changes in saving policies bring about important changes in welfare. This should provide relevant evidence for deciding how much benefit economists are likely to provide by the detailed analysis of fully optimum growth policies, and whether we—or the public—need be very concerned about changes of a few percentage points in the aggregate saving of an economy.

Examples in which the optimum path would in any case follow the policy of keeping the savings ratio fairly constant are not of much interest here. We have chosen examples in which the initial optimum savings ratio is substantially different from the long-run optimum ratio. Their main features are shown in Table 20.1.[6] each case,

$$\rho = 0, \qquad g = 0.03.$$

Three cases, providing a cross-section of possibilities, are further illustrated in Fig. 20.1, where the ratio of c_{bs} to the initial value of output y_0 is shown for

---

[5] We are very grateful to D. M. G. Newbery for programming and carrying out these calculations. Extensions of these computations may be found in his paper Newbery.

[6] Rough checks suggest that the values in Table 1 are not all completely accurate in the last decimal place. The inaccuracies are not large enough to affect our conclusions.

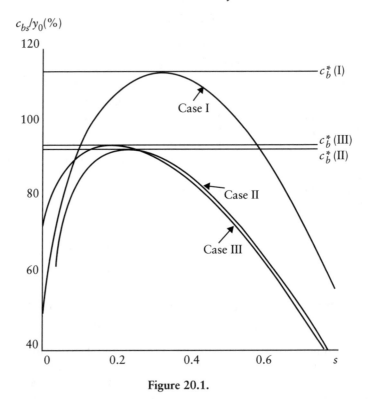

Figure 20.1.

the whole range of possible savings ratios. These are:

Case I: $n=0$, $b=0.5$, $v=0.5$, $k_0/y_0=3$.
Case II: $n=0.01$, $b=0.25$, $v=0.5$, $k_0/y_0=3$.
Case III: $n=0$, $b=0.375$, $v=1.5$, $k_0/y_0=3$.

The curves have one maximum, and it is striking that this is very close to the BGE of optimum growth. It is also of interest that the absolute value of the gradient of the curve is small over a fairly wide range near the optimum; i.e. the top of the curve is quite flat, and in this range small changes in s have little effect on the BGE. In case I, if we choose a savings ratio between the initial optimum savings ratio and the asymptotic optimum savings ratio $(0.25 \leqslant s \leqslant 0.37)$, we are within one-half of a percentage point of the BGE of optimum growth. For case III, choosing a savings ratio between the initial and asymptotic optimum ratios brings us within one percentage point of the BGE of optimum growth. Not surprisingly, the savings ratio giving maximum BGE (among Harrodian paths) is roughly midway between the initial optimum and the asymptotic optimum. It should be noted that these two examples use valuation functions that yield quite low optimum savings ratios (as compared with lower values of v). The particular choice of valuation $v = 1$ may be interpreted as a rather egalitarian point of view. It means that we would value an extra unit of consumption given to generation A four times as much as a unit of consumption given to generation B if generation B were consuming twice as much as generation A. (If $v = 3/2$, we value the extra unit 5.7 times as much.) In general, high v and low b give low optimum savings ratios Mirrlees. In the light of these graphs, we can compare different policies that suggest themselves rather naturally.

(i) *Golden rule paths*. These are paths which save all competitively imputed profits and have the highest long-run consumption per head. In this case they are paths where $s = b$. In case I, the BGE for $s = 50\%$ is 105% compared with an optimum BGE of 113.3% and a BGE of over 113% for $s = 30\%$. In case III, the BGE of $s = 37.5\%$ is 85% compared with an optimum of 93.8% and a BGE of over 93% for $s = 18\%$. It must be concluded therefore that the golden rule policy has very little to commend it—the welfare loss as compared with the best Harrodian path is very large. In our welfare measure and examples, it is the equivalent of throwing away 8% of GNP for ever, even if only Harrodian paths are considered.

(ii) *A policy of balanced growth*. In cases I and III, this means a savings ratio of 9% and thus a BGE of 91%. As is to be expected, this gives a less serious welfare loss where the economy begins with a capital–output ratio close to the asymptotic optimum one. In case I the loss is over 22%; but in case III the loss is nearly 3%. Thus, in the former case the balanced growth policy does much worse than the golden rule; whereas in the latter case it does much better. This is not very surprising, since optimum savings ratios are higher in the former case. Certainly for low v and high b the balanced growth policy involves very considerable welfare losses.

(iii) *Constant savings ratio at the asymptotic optimum ratio*. In cases I and III saving at the long-run optimum rate loses less than 1% in BGE from the optimum. However, this Harrodian path has a savings ratio at the lower end of the range which is close to the best Harrodian path, and it is possible to do a little better by raising the savings ratio a few percentage points.

(iv) *The Harrodian path* which gives maximum BGE is in case I less than 0.3% from the optimum and in case III less than 0.9% from the optimum. Thus, by fairly careful choice of constant savings ratio, we can have a path fairly close (in the relevant sense) to the optimum.

Before drawing conclusions from these remarks, we should consider how to interpret differences in BGE between paths. It should of course be remembered that the welfare difference, although expressed as a percentage of GNP, is crucially dependent on which valuation function we choose. However, we could explain to someone who did not share our welfare judgements the implications of our welfare judgements in language he could understand. In our view, welfare differences of more than 2% in BGE are certainly not small.

It does seem, from this point of view, that we can do rather well, as compared to the optimum, with constant savings ratios if they are chosen in the right range (roughly between initial and asymptotic optimum ratios); and very well if we choose the best Harrodian path. If it is considered too difficult to adjust the savings rate all the time to the optimum growth rate, then following a cruder policy will not do much harm, provided our guesses about the savings ratio are of the right order of magnitude. The above results do show that thumb-rules are likely to be unsatisfactory, and we need some sort of optimum growth analysis to enable us to choose the right range. But, since very crude approximations are apparently satisfactory, one would need very good reasons to justify developing more 'realistic' models in order to calculate the optimum savings rate.

These remarks are, of course, based on a few examples using a very simple unit-elasticity-of-substitution production function. It was natural to expect, however, that results concerning the satisfactory nature of simple policies would carry over to the case where the elasticity of substitution is less than one, since then there are smaller improvements available from fine adjustments. Calculations made by Newbery confirm this expectation.

It is interesting to note (from Table 20.1 and Fig. 20.1) that, if the present generation errs on the side of selfishness and saves less than the initial optimum would demand, then, provided it does save as much or more than the long-run optimum (and continues to do so), overall welfare is not reduced very much, although there is a redistribution, as compared with the optimum, in favour of earlier generations. For some values of the parameters, this range of tolerable policy error may be fairly large.

We conclude that: (i) Harrodian paths can do well compared with the optimum, provided that some care is taken in choosing the savings ratios; (ii) if such care is taken, then small changes in savings ratios give very small changes in BGE: this is not true outside the range of savings ratios that do well.

5. FINITE-HORIZON MODELS

As a further illustration of the uses of the balanced growth equivalent, we consider the following problem. Many economists believe that a computable optimizing model must have a finite time-horizon, and nearly all computed planning models that have been published possess this feature, e.g. Sandee. We are not sure that finite-horizon optimizations are in fact the best simplification of the planning problem, but it is true that the difficulties of both formulating and calculating an infinite-horizon model are formidable. It is worth asking, therefore, how much may be lost by relying on calculations based on a finite horizon. It is possible to discuss this issue explicitly for a one-good model, such as the one we use in this paper. Evidence about the desirable length of planning horizon, and the desirable method of setting up terminal conditions, obtained from studying this simple model is relevant to the choice of n-sector model in practice. Better evidence for this decision can no doubt be obtained, at the cost of a more complicated analysis, from the theory of models with more than one sector. The analysis for a one-sector model is not, for that reason, irrelevant, although it ought to be superseded.

Various methods for setting up the terminal conditions in a finite-horizon model have been proposed in the literature—for instance, the achievement of a given growth rate at the end of the planning period (e.g. Chakravarty), fixing an overall growth-rate for the plan (e.g. Manne) and achieving von Neumann proportions (e.g. Stoleru and Chakravarty). Some of these methods lack an economic rationale. The particular method we shall consider is based on the tendency of optimum paths, in many kinds of models, asymptotically to balanced growth (Gale). This suggests that one first computes the balanced growth state that would be optimal if one were already on it: if that state is unique, the calculation is not likely to present serious difficulties. One then finds the path that will maximize total utility over a finite period T, subject to the constraint that the path should reach the optimum balanced growth path (OBGP) at T, e.g. Stoleru and Chakravarty.

We shall discuss how large T would need to be if we wanted to make sure of getting 'reasonably near' to maximum welfare by using this simplified planning calculation. We note first that the planning horizon must be at least as long as the minimum time necessary for the economy to reach the OBGP. We then go on to consider how long it would take to reach the OBGP if a constant saving ratio s were used until the OBGP was reached. It will then be possible to put an upper bound to the time horizon if we are to get within 1% of the full optimum.

For the Cobb–Douglas model with labour-augmenting technical progress, no population growth, no discounting, and a homogeneous utility function, the capital–output ratio and savings ratio on the OBGP are (see e.g. Mirrlees)

$$\frac{b}{(v+1)g} \quad \text{and} \quad \frac{b}{v+1}, \tag{22}$$

respectively. If a Harrodian path with saving ratio s is followed, it is easy to calculate that, at time t, the capital–output ratio,

$$k_t/y_t = \frac{s}{g} + \left(k_0^{1-b} - \frac{s}{g}\right)e^{-(1-b)gt}. \tag{23}$$

Therefore, using (22), we see that the time taken, on this path, to reach the OBGP is (when the argument of the logarithm is positive)

$$T_s = \frac{1}{(1-b)g}\log\left(\frac{s - gk_0^{1-b}}{s - [b/(v+1)]}\right). \tag{24}$$

The minimum time to the OBGP, which we shall call T_{min}, is T_1 if $k_0^{1-b} < b/(v+1)g$ (as will usualy be the case), and T_0 if the opposite inequality holds.

It is a routine matter to calculate the BGE for the path obtained as a result of saving s of output until the OBGP is reached, and then continuing along the OBGP itself (Table 20.2). The situation is illustrated by the following particular case:

$$\rho = 0, \quad g = 0.03, \quad n = 0, \quad b = 0.5, \quad v = 1, \quad k_0/y_0 = 3.$$

In Fig. 20.2 we show this case, and one other ($\rho = 0$, $g = 0.03$, $n = 0$, $b = 0.375$, $v = 1.5$, $k_0/y_0 = 3$), which provides rather shorter time-horizons. These cases

Table 20.2.[a]

s	BGE/y_0	T_s (years)
0.25	1.116	∞
0.30	1.137	large
0.35	1.136	62
0.40	1.124	47
0.50	1.076	33

[a]$T_{min} = 12.7$ years; $c_b^*/y_0 = 1.139$.

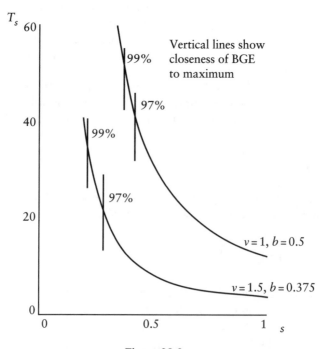

Figure 20.2.

are cases I and III of Fig. 20.1. In each case, we indicate on the graph, for T_s as a function of s, the range of values for which a BGE within 1% of c_b^* and within 3% of c_b^* is possible. The interpretation of these results is that a time-horizon T_s is satisfactory if the BGE is close to—say, within 1% of—the maximum BGE. These calculations do not establish that a shorter time-horizon could not also yield a plan that is satisfactory, if the full finite-horizon optimum were computed. We think, however, that the result would not usually be much improved if an optimum initial path were substituted for the Harrodian initial path.

While the time-horizons deduced by this method are rather long, several points should be borne in mind.[7] First, one reason for the long time-horizons required is the Cobb–Douglas assumption, which presumes a rather large range of technical possibilities, and therefore, very often, an OBGP capital–output ratio very different from that currently ruling. Naturally, when the range of techniques allowed is small—often the case in programming models—these large differences are less likely to occur. From this point of view, however, the calculations suggest that it may be important to extend the formulation of planning models to include a richer variety of techniques and to extend the time-horizon so as to allow time for their exploitation. Secondly, it may be possible to devise terminal conditions that, even with a short time-horizon, are less likely to divert the computed plan far from the optimum. It may be noted, for example, that the use of the shadow prices corresponding to the OBGP as a means of valuing terminal capital would lead to a path having the opposite fault to the plans we have considered, in that they tend to reduce saving to below optimum rather than increase it to above optimum. This suggests that a suitable compromise would be greatly superior to either; but we have not explored the possibility further. Finally, and probably most important, we have supposed that the computed plan will be followed for the rest of time. In fact, a finite-horizon computation would surely be used only for a time, and then a new plan, based on further computation, would be adopted. Such a 'rolling-plan' procedure is presumably superior, perhaps far superior, to the one we have assumed, and may well be satisfactory even with a rather short planning horizon. We have not been able to think of any easy way of computing the consequences of such a planning procedure, and cannot guess at its importance.

Although we are not in a position to refute the finite-horizon methods of plan computation now in use, we have shown how consideration of relative BGEs could be used to establish that the time-horizon employed in a particular planning model is satisfactory. We conclude that the use of short time-horizons requires special justification, and should not be lightly adopted.

---

[7] This paragraph owes much to discussions with Peter Hammond.

6. FINAL REMARKS

This paper is intended only as a first approach to the evaluation of models. We are interested in models of an economy that are simple enough to be used and complex enough to be realistic in the relevant respects. Not all extensions in the direction of greater realism are worth making. Unaided intuition is becoming an increasingly unreliable judge of the 'unrealism' of this or that assumption. We have tried to show how a more formal setting of the question and measurement of the possible benefits is possible and can be used to influence model development. The model we have used was chosen entirely for its analytical convenience. It has realistic features, but more complex models can be handled, and would throw more reliable light on these issues of research strategy and model formulation. Nevertheless, it is interesting to see how useful this very simple model can be in making important points. The most important point that has emerged is the degree of insensitivity of welfare to the exact savings policy pursued by the economy. It seems to us doubtful that more complicated models can greatly improve economic advice on the desirable level of investment in any economy.

Our second illustration of the use of commodity measures of welfare concerned a more subtle matter, that of assessing the worth of further complicating an already complicated model, as for example by extending the time-horizon of a many-sector planning model. The purpose of such a planning model is to give quite detailed advice on the comparative advantage of different industries and the direction of their development, not just to recommend an aggregate saving rate. The only reason for using the simple-optimum-saving model was as an analogue to the much more complicated planning calculation. The simple analogue has the advantage that one can compute the effect of changing an aspect of the formulation (in this case the time-horizon). One can then be guided by the results of that computation when deciding on the formulation of the large model, where the extension cannot be set up and analysed without already assuming that it is worth doing. If it seems odd to the reader that one should use a simple one-sector model to guide the construction of a many-sector model, we would ask him whether he has good reason to use relatively untutored intuition to guide that construction instead.

There are two further remarks we should like to make. In the first place, our neglect of uncertainty may be of some importance for the results. It is clear, for example, that when there is great uncertainty about the productivity of the economy, a policy of saving a fixed proportion of expected national income may be quite unsatisfactory, unless there is a good foreign capital market to use. The trouble with simple policies of this kind is that they have insufficient flexibility. It is to be expected therefore that the difference between the BGE for the optimum and the maximum BGE for a Harrodian path will be greater when there is uncertainty about future technology. It seems unlikely that aggregate uncertainty is in fact so great as to modify our results substantially, but the techniques for verifying this conjecture are not available. In the case of finite time-horizons, greater uncertainty is not necessarily a reason for employing a shorter time-horizon, except to the extent that it makes any formulation of a model more difficult (which it may or may not do). We do not know how uncertainty would affect the results of Section 5, but there is no reason to think that uncertainty justifies a shorter time-horizon.

Finally, we recognize that theories with application to low-income countries have an overwhelmingly greater claim on the economist's attention than those whose sole application is in high-income countries. The BGE is not an appropriate measure for assessing such claims. But few interesting economic theories are relevant to rich countries alone, and in many cases it is likely to be quite hard to discriminate among applications in this way. We feel the techniques discussed in this paper are more useful for discussing the elaboration of economic models in particular contexts. In these cases at least, they may help the economist to decide when to stop worrying.

Appendix: Existence of Balanced Growth Equivalents

We use the notation of the text and make the assumption:

$$f'(0) > \alpha > f'(\infty). \tag{A1}$$

We introduce the variables $z = ce^{-\alpha t}$ and $x = ke^{-\alpha t}$ so that production possibilities are described by

$$z_t + \dot{x}_t = f(x_t) - \alpha x_t, \qquad x_t \geqslant 0. \tag{A2}$$

If the instantaneous valuation function is of the form $u(c)$, concave, increasing, and bounded above, the T-period valuation integral is $\int_0^T u(z_t e^{\alpha t})\, dt$. It is known that in this case, an optimum policy exists if u is bounded above and concave, and $\alpha > 0$ (von Weizsäcker [10]). The valuation integral may nevertheless be unbounded as $T \to \infty$, even for the optimum path. For convenience, one takes the least upper bound of u to be zero, so that the integral either converges, or diverges to $-\infty$. Suppose that there exists a path for which the integral converges. We shall show that in such a case all paths have a BGE.

Consider a balanced growth path, along which consumption is $\gamma e^{\alpha t}$. The T-period valuation integral is

$$\int_0^T u(\gamma e^{\alpha t})\, dt = \frac{1}{\alpha} \int_\gamma^{\gamma e^{\alpha T}} u(\zeta)\, \frac{d\zeta}{\zeta}, \tag{A3}$$

which either tends to a finite limit for all such $\gamma > 0$ as $T \to \infty$ or diverges for all such γ. We show that the former is the case, by showing that the existence of a path yielding a finite valuation integral implies that the balanced growth path $\bar{z}e^{\alpha t}$, where $\bar{z}$ is the maximum value of $f - \alpha x$ (finite by assumption (A1)), has finite valuation integral.

Let z_t be a path having finite valuation integral. Then

$$z_t \leqslant \bar{z} - \dot{x}t. \tag{A4}$$

Also, from equation (A2) and the requirement $z_t \geqslant 0$, x_t is bounded above by a number $\hat{x} = \max[x_0, \bar{x}]$ where $f(\bar{x}) - \alpha\bar{x} = 0$. Consequently,

$$\int_0^T [u(z_t e^{\alpha t}) - u(\bar{z}e^{\alpha t})] \, dt \leqslant \int_0^T (z_t - \bar{z})e^{\alpha t}u'(\bar{z}e^{\alpha t}) \, dt \text{ (by the concavity of } u)$$

$$\leqslant -\int_0^T \dot{x}_t e^{\alpha t}u'(\bar{z}e^{\alpha t}) \, dt$$

$$= x_0 u'(\bar{z}) - x_T e^{\alpha T}u'(\bar{z}e^{\alpha T}) + \alpha \int_0^T x_t [e^{\alpha t}u'(\bar{z}e^{\alpha t}) + \bar{z}e^{2\alpha t}u''(\bar{z}e^{\alpha t})] \, dt$$

$$\leqslant x_0 u(\bar{z}) + \alpha \int_0^T x e^{\alpha t}u'(\bar{z}e^{\alpha t}) \, dt \text{ (dropping negative terms)}$$

$$= A + \frac{\hat{x}}{z}u(\bar{z}e^{\alpha T}) \text{ where } A \text{ is a constant independent of } T$$

$$\leqslant A.$$

We conclude that $\int_0^T u(\bar{z}e^{\alpha t}) \, dt$ is bounded below, and therefore convergent.

The valuation integral of a typical balanced growth path is

$$U(\gamma) = \frac{1}{\alpha}\int_\gamma^\infty u(\zeta)\frac{d\zeta}{\zeta}. \tag{A5}$$

This is clearly a continuous function of γ. Hence we can obtain the BGE of any particular path whose valuation integral is finite by finding the value of γ that makes equation (A5) equal to the valuation integral of the given path. We can find such a γ, because $U(\gamma) \to 0$ as $\gamma \to \infty$ (since equation (A5) is convergent) and $U(\gamma) \to -\infty$ as $\gamma \to 0$ (since for fixed A, $U(\gamma) \leqslant \int_\gamma^A u(\zeta) \, (d\zeta/\zeta) \leqslant u(A) \int_\gamma^A d\zeta/\zeta \to -\infty$). Thus, $U(\gamma)$, which is certainly continuous, is a monotonically increasing function that takes all negative values.

If the valuation integral of the path diverges, one wants to say that the BGE is 0. In general, we define the BGE (wide sense) as a number $\bar{\gamma}$ corresponding to a path c if

$$\bar{\gamma} = \inf\{\gamma: (\gamma e^{\alpha t}) \text{ is at least as good as } c\}$$
$$= \sup\{\gamma: c \text{ is at least as good as } (\gamma e^{\alpha t})\}.$$

It is clear that this definition generalizes the earlier definition (2). The BGE (wide sense) surely is the balanced growth that best reflects the welfare provided.

If no path has a finite valuation integral, it is still true—in the present case with u bounded and $\alpha > 0$—that every path has a BGE. To prove this, we show that $\int_0^T [u(z_t e^{\alpha t}) - u(\bar{z}e^{\alpha t})] \, dt$ tends to a finite limit or to $-\infty$ as $T \to \infty$. If this difference tends to a finite limit, we can find γ such that

$$V(\gamma) = \int_0^\infty [u(\gamma e^{\alpha t}) - u(\bar{z}e^{\alpha t})] \, dt = \frac{1}{\alpha}\int_\gamma^{\bar{z}} u(\zeta)\frac{d\zeta}{\zeta} \tag{A6}$$

is equal to this limit, and this is the BGE. The same kind of arguments as before show that V takes all values.

If the difference tends to $-\infty$, the BGE (wide sense) is zero. We can write

$$z_t = \bar{z} - \dot{x}_t - a_t, \tag{A7}$$

where $a_t \geqslant 0$. Therefore

$$\int_0^T [u(z_t e^{\alpha t}) - u(\bar{z} e^{\alpha t})]\, \mathrm{d}t = -\int_0^T u'(\bar{z} e^{\alpha t})(\dot{x}_t + a_t)\, e^{\alpha t}\, \mathrm{d}t - \int_0^T b_t\, \mathrm{d}t, \tag{A8}$$

where $b_t \geqslant 0$. Write $a_t e^{\alpha t} u'(\bar{z} e^{\alpha t}) + b_t = m_t \geqslant 0$. Then the right side of equation (A8) becomes

$$[-x_t u'(\bar{z} e^{\alpha t}) e^{\alpha t}]_0^T + \alpha \int_0^T x_t [e^{\alpha t} u'(\bar{z} e^{\alpha t}) + \bar{z} e^{2\alpha t} u''(\bar{z} e^{\alpha t})]\, \mathrm{d}t - \int_0^T m_t\, \mathrm{d}t$$

$$= [-x_t u'(\bar{z} e^{\alpha t}) e^{\alpha t}]_0^T + \alpha \int_0^T x_t e^{\alpha t} u'(\bar{z} e^{\alpha t})\, \mathrm{d}t - \int_0^T m_t'\, \mathrm{d}t, \tag{A9}$$

where $m_t' \geqslant 0$. We consider the three expressions in equation (A9). The first tends to a limit or $-\infty$ since x_t is bounded and $u(y)y \to 0$ as $y \to \infty$ (easily checked using the concavity of u and $\lim_{y \to \infty} u(y) = 0$). The second tends to a finite limit since it increases with T and is bounded above by $-\bar{x} u(\bar{z})/\bar{z}$. The third tends to a limit or $-\infty$ since m_t' is positive. Thus, $\int_0^T [u(z_t e^{\alpha t}) - u(\bar{z} e^{\alpha t})]\, \mathrm{d}t$ tends to a limit or $-\infty$ as required.

REFERENCES

Chakravarty, S. Alternative preference functions in problems of investment planning on the national level. In E. Malinvaud and M. O. Bacharach, (eds.), *Activity Analysis in the Theory of Economic Growth and Planning*, (Macmillan, New York, 1967).

——Optimal programmes of capital accumulation in a multi-sector economy. *Econometrica*, 33 (1965), 557–70.

Gale, D., On optimal development in a multi-sector economy. *Review of Economic Studies*, 34 (1967), 1–18.

Manne, A. S., Key sectors in the Mexican economy, 1960–70. In A. S. Manne and H. M. Markowitz (eds.), *Studies in Process Analysis* (Wiley, New York, 1963).

Mirrlees, J. A., Optimum growth when technology is changing. *Review of Economic Studies*, 34 (1967), 95–124.

Newbery, D. M. G., The importance of malleable capital in optimal growth models. Unpublished data.

Paish, F. W. In *London and Cambridge Economic Bulletin. The Times*, 9 April 1968.

Sandee, J., *A Demonstration Planning Model for India* (Asia, New York, 1960).

Stoleru, L., An optimal policy for economic growth. *Econometrica*, 33 (1965), 321–48.

Weizsäcker, C. von, Existence of optimal programmes of accumulation for an infinite time horizon. *Review of Economic Studies*, 32 (1965), 85–104.

21

Optimum Saving with Economies of Scale

With Avinash Dixit and Nicholas Stern

1. INTRODUCTION

There are many problems in economics where it is important to think of investment taking place in discrete lumps rather than as a continuous flow. These are usually problems where fixed costs are significant or, more generally, where there are economies of scale. An important example is the creation of a new centre of population which requires some large initial capital outlay. A second is that of an individual saver who makes investments at discrete points in time because there is some cost to the act of making an investment.

The model that we investigate in this paper was originally motivated by the first of these examples. It has some limitations as a model of timing and size of new centres, however, and these are discussed later. It should be viewed as a first approach to that problem, though we suspect that better models will be similar in flavour. It turns out, however, that a special case of the model does capture the problem of the individual saver.

The plan of the paper is as follows. Previous literature is discussed in this introduction. Then a growth model with economies of scale in the production of output, using capital but no labour, is presented. Conditions necessary for optimality are obtained, and some simple properties of the optimal path established. In Section 3 we show that in a simple special case the optimal policy is readily obtained, but takes the economy to infinite output in finite time. We then turn to the version appropriate to individual saving behaviour, with fixed transaction costs and a constant interest rate, showing how to identify the optimum policy and computing it for the iso-elastic utility

This paper, by Avinash Dixit, James Mirrless, and Nicholas Stern, was first published in the *Review of Economic Studies*, Vol. 42 (1975), pp. 303–25.

Work on this paper was done when all three of us were, at different times, visiting the Massachusetts Institute of Technology; we are grateful to their Department of Economics for hospitality. Valuable comments were received from participants in seminars at MIT, the Cowles Foundation, and elsewhere; and from the referees of a previous version, and John Flemming. The research of Dixit and Stern was financed by a grant from the National Science Foundation. Computing assistance was provided by Mike O'Neill, of the Nuffield College Research Services Unit.

case. Finally, in Section 5 we introduce labour, retaining economies of scale, and solve the optimum growth problem for the Cobb–Douglas production function and iso-elastic utility. We conclude with some remarks on generalizations. A general existence theorem for optimum paths is given in an appendix.

We would like to draw attention to the particular importance and difficulty of establishing which of the paths satisfying the necessary conditions actually is optimal. It is this problem, together with that of proving existence of an optimum, that make rigorous mathematics essential at some stages of the argument. Elsewhere we have not troubled to show that our arguments can be made rigorous.

The best known study of the problems in development planning that arise from increasing returns is the work by Manne *et al.* The examples discussed in that volume were concerned with the choice of the size of plants and the time intervals between the construction of plants, to minimize the present value of costs while meeting a given time profile of output. We shall call such a problem a Manne-type problem. Demand can reasonably be taken as exogenous in these models since they are designed to discuss capacity expansion in individual industries. For our purposes, we need a model where demand is endogenous, for the choice of the optimum time paths of output and consumption is the question at issue.

A model with increasing returns (in one sector) where output and consumption levels are endogenous is given in Weitzman. Weitzman's model has two types of capital: α-capital, and overhead or β-capital. Output can be consumed or invested, and is produced with a standard neoclassical production function of α-capital. This output is constrained, however, by the quantity of β-capital. Overhead capital is produced from the output good under conditions of increasing returns. Weitzman shows that the optimum path can be decomposed into two types of phase. In the first type, all investment goes to add to α-capital, and a standard Ramsey path is followed. In the second kind, a Manne-type problem is solved for investment in β-capital where the Ramsey path gives the output-demand profile and prices come from the marginal utility of consumption. During this phase, while savings accumulate for subsequent investment in β-capital, output and consumption are constant. The phases alternate indefinitely.

In our model we have just one sector. This sector produces output which can be consumed or saved. Investment shows increasing returns, at least for small levels, in that $g(x)$, the output flow from an investment of size x measured in units of accumulated output, has zero derivative at the origin. We assume that investments, once made, cannot be augmented. A full treatment of the problem of new centres would allow some, possibly limited and certainly more costly, additions to existing centres.

In the first version of the model, there is no labour. This is a serious drawback and detracts especially from the interpretation of the model in terms of new centres of population. More generally, it ignores the chief reason for expecting decreasing returns to investment in the real world, in association with lumpy investment in the manner considered in this paper. In a second version, we introduce labour. We had some trouble in finding a trick which would make a model incorporating labour manageable. Our model does not distinguish between *ex ante* and *ex post* substitutability, but it does generate some interesting results, and is a useful vehicle for discussions of decentralization.

It is easy to see, and is proved below, that the optimum policy, for an objective of maximizing the integral of the utility of consumption, is to save for a time until an inventory of appropriate size has been accumulated, and then to make an investment. In our model, therefore, output is constant for a time and then jumps. This contrasts with the Weitzman case, where output rises continuously in the Ramsey phase and is constant in the Manne-type phase. The reason we have used a model with increasing returns in the economy as a whole is our interest in new centres of population. Even so, discrete jumps in output are a little stark. If there were decreasing returns elsewhere in the model, or we allowed for many commodities, we would presumably have some smoothing.

It turns out that our model can, in a sense, be viewed as a limiting case of the Weitzman model. Although this helps in understanding the problem, it is of no assistance in finding the optimum policy. Further, we shall pay special attention to a specific example of a production function, $g(x) = -\sigma + \rho x$, where σ and ρ are positive constants, which was not discussed by Weitzman. It is this example which gives us a model of the problem faced by the individual saver. Given a fixed cost of making an investment σ/ρ and an interest rate ρ, an investment of size x yields him a stream $\rho(x - \sigma/\rho)$ indefinitely.

Flemming has discussed the problem facing an individual who allocates his initial wealth to the purchase of a sequence of durable goods only one of which is held at a time and each of which yields a consumption stream for the time that it is held. Wealth not allocated to the durable good earns interest. The individual must decide how often to 'trade in' his old model for a new one and how large a new model to purchase. He obtains a second-hand price of ρ $(0 < \rho < 1)$ times the original purchase price of a good and maximizes a discounted stream of the utility of consumption. Flemming obtains, for the iso-elastic utility function, the optimum policy of a constant time between investments and a constant ratio between sizes of successive models.

A problem similar to our version of individual saving has been discussed by Baumol and Tobin. They both consider the optimum time sequence and amounts of the conversion of bonds into money to meet a steady flow demand for transactions. We are considering something like a mirror image: when and how much to invest from a flow of saving. They have a fixed cost of a withdrawal, while we have one for making an investment.

The main difference between our model and the Baumol–Tobin model is that in ours the flow of saving is endogenous, with the result that income, consumption, and marginal utility can change over time. Baumol and Tobin have an exogenous and constant transaction flow, so they can consider just one of a sequence of uniform withdrawals, a procedure which is justified if the horizon is infinite.

2. THE MODEL WITHOUT LABOUR

There is one commodity. An investment x at a particular date yields an output stream $g(x)$ ever after. We assume $g(0) = g'(0) = 0$, implying that there are economies of scale at least for small investments, and that g increases with x and is differentiable for x such that $g(x) > 0$. We start with a given output capacity y_0, and no accumulated savings from the past. We denote by $k(t)$ total savings since time zero (which may not all have been invested by time t). $y(t)$ is output at time t, and for convenience we take $y(t)$ to be left-continuous at jump points. x_t is the investment done at t: except at discrete points, x_t will be zero. A consumption path $c(t)$ is feasible if for all t,

$$0 \leq c(t) \leq y(t) \tag{1}$$

$$y(t) = c(t) + \dot{k}(t) \tag{2}$$

$$y(t) = y_0 + \sum_{0 \leq t' \leq t} g(x_{t'}) \tag{3}$$

$$k(t) \geq \sum_{0 \leq t' \leq t} x_{t'}. \tag{4}$$

If the time interval between investments is not strictly positive, then the summation signs can be interpreted as appropriate integrals. We see below that it is never optimal to have continuous investment. Note that mere efficiency implies equality in (4) at each instant t when an investment is made; for if a plant of a particular size is to be constructed it may as well be constructed as early as possible, thus giving the benefit of its output for a longer period of time.

We wish to find a feasible path which 'maximizes' an undiscounted integral of $u(c(t))$ over all future time, 'maximization' being interpreted in the overtaking sense. In other words, a feasible path $c^*(t)$ is optimum if, for any other feasible path $c^0(t)$, there exists T_0 such that

$$\int_0^T u(c^*(t)) \, dt \geq \int_0^T u(c^0(t)) \, dt, \quad \text{for all } T \geq T_0. \tag{5}$$

It will be recollected that in infinite-horizon growth models there are, broadly speaking, two ways of identifying the optimum path of the economy.

One is to find a path satisfying the intertemporal first-order conditions for a maximum (the Euler conditions), and with known asymptotic behaviour, which can be proved directly to be an optimum path. Notice that it is not enough to find a path that satisfies the Euler conditions, and seems to be better than any other Euler path, because it is possible that no optimum exists: that is why one needs a direct proof that the identified path is optimal. The other is to prove by an alternative method that an optimum exists, and then identify the best Euler path. The first method relies on *sufficient* conditions for an optimum, the second on *necessary* conditions. The sufficiency method works quite well in optimum growth models with convex technology. For our models we have had to use the necessity method, essentially because first-order conditions do not imply global maximization.

Naturally, we must make some assumptions if we are to guarantee existence in our model. The chief assumptions are:

Assumption A: u is increasing, strictly concave, satisfying $u(c) \to 0$ $(c \to \infty)$, and $u'(c) \to \infty$ $(c \to 0)$.
Assumption B: For any $y_0 > 0$, there exists a feasible path with convergent utility integral.
Assumption C: For all y_0, there exists $\delta > 0$ such that all paths starting from y_0 and making the first investment at a time sooner than δ can be overtaken.

Assumption A implies that the utility function is always negative, and therefore that for every path the utility integral either diverges to $-\infty$ or converges. Assumption B then assures us that the utility integral has a finite supremum for the model, so that nearly optimal paths exist. In an appendix, we prove that these assumptions in fact ensure that an optimal path exists. We suspect that Assumption C holds automatically if $g'(0) = 0$, but have not been able to prove it. It clearly holds if $g(x)$ is zero over an interval to the right of $x = 0$, which is the model of Section 4.

Assumption B may seem to be a rather awkward one, but it is generally easy to check: for example, one might look at a path resulting from saving a constant proportion of output and investing once a year, or one obtained by keeping x constant. We shall justify it in particular cases below.

To derive necessary conditions for the optimum, we look at development as a sequence of periods, in each of which saving is accumulated, but where investment is made only at the end of the period. Since utility is not discounted, and is strictly concave, optimum consumption must be constant throughout a period. Defining

t_i = length of ith period,
y_i = output during ith period,
x_i = size of investment at the end of ith period,
c_i = consumption during ith period,

we have

$$x_i = t_i(y_i - c_i), \tag{6}$$

because it is clearly inefficient to carry any savings over instead of incorporating it in the current investment. (One could otherwise have invested sooner.) Also,

$$y_{i+1} - y_i = g(x_i); \tag{7}$$

and we seek maximization of

$$\sum_{i=0}^{\infty} t_i u(c_i) \tag{8}$$

subject to the requirement that $\sum t_i = \infty$ or $y_i \to \infty$. The replacement of the integral by the sum is justified rigorously in the appendix, in the course of the proof of the main theorem. The associated requirements say that either our sequence of investments stretches over the indefinite future or we reach infinite output in finite time. We have as yet no guarantee that $\sum t_i = \infty$ and we shall have to consider this point carefully below.

Substituting from (6) for t_i in (8), it can be seen that the maximand becomes

$$\sum x_i \frac{u(c_i)}{y_i - c_i}. \tag{9}$$

It follows at once that, for each i, c_i must maximize $u(c)/(y_i - c)$:

$$u(c_i) + u'(c_i)(y_i - c_i) = 0. \tag{10}$$

This equation, known as the Keynes–Ramsey equation, was derived by Ramsey for the optimum rate of saving in an economy with continuous investment. Since it is essentially a rule for an economy without change other than that brought about by capital accumulation, we should not be surprised to see that it remains valid.

Now consider the effect of varying y_i, x_i, and x_{i-1} simultaneously while leaving everything up to $(i-1)$ and after $(i+1)$ unchanged. This can be done in such a way that the feasibility conditions (7) continue to hold. The changes must satisfy

$$- dy_i = g'(x_i) dx_i, \qquad dy_i = g'(x_{i-1}) dx_{i-1}. \tag{11}$$

Then the effect on (9) is

$$\frac{u(c_i)}{y_i - c_i} dx_i + \frac{u(c_{i-1})}{y_{i-1} - c_{i-1}} dx_{i-1} - \frac{x_i u(c_i)}{(y_i - c_i)^2} dy_i.$$

Assumption C ensures that t_i, and therefore x_i, cannot be zero, and thus the first-order condition holds with equality. Using (6) and (10), the condition is

$$\frac{u'(c_i)}{g'(x_i)} - \frac{u'(c_{i-1})}{g'(x_{i-1})} + t_i u'(c_i) = 0. \tag{12}$$

Equations (10) and (12) are the first-order conditions (corresponding to the Euler conditions in more orthodox calculus of variations). Following the example of standard optimum growth analysis, we expect that the optimum path will be that solution of (10) and (12) which has the smallest initial t_0 (and x_0), subject to being feasible for all time. It can be verified in particular cases that, as t_0 increases and the subsequent path satisfies (10) and (12), all terms in the series $\sum t_i u(c_i)$ become smaller (i.e. more negative), and we presume that this is very generally true.

We must now clarify the possibility that $\sum t_i$ converges. The assumptions we have made are by no means sufficient to exclude the possibility of infinite output in finite time. The following two lemmas give a condition sufficient to exclude such explosion, and indicate a property one may expect to hold in many such cases.

Lemma 1. *If there exists k such that $g(x)/x \leq k$ for all $x > 0$, $\sum_0^\infty t_i$ can be finite only if y_i tends to a finite limit.*

Proof. Since negative consumption is impossible, $x_i \leq t_i y_i$. Therefore, using our hypothesis on g,

$$y_{i+1} \leq (1 + kt_i) y_i.$$

Multiplying such inequalities together,

$$y_I \leq y_0 \prod_{i=0}^{I-1} (1 + kt_i)$$

$$\leq y_0 \prod_{i=0}^{I-1} e^{kt_i}$$

$$= y_0 \exp\left(k \sum_0^{I-1} t_i \right),$$

which is bounded by hypothesis. Then $\{y_i\}$ is a bounded monotone sequence, and therefore it has a finite limit.

For the next lemma, we specialize to an iso-elastic utility function and show that, if x_i tends to a finite limit as i tends to infinity, then this limit must be where average productivity is maximum. Some reader will, we hope, show that this holds more generally.[1]

---

[1] Presumably the case of asymptotic iso-elasticity is not difficult.

The iso-elastic utility function bounded above by zero will be of the form

$$u(c) = -c^{-n}, \qquad n > 0.$$

For it, the Keynes–Ramsey equation becomes

$$c_i = (1 - \beta)y_i, \tag{13}$$

where $\beta = 1/(1 + n)$, so $0 < \beta < 1$, and (6) becomes

$$x_i = \beta t_i y_i. \tag{14}$$

These will be of much use later.

Lemma 2. *For the case* $u(c) = -c^{-n}$, $n > 0$, *if on the optimum path* $x_i \to \bar{x}$, *then* $\bar{x}$ *satisfies* $\bar{x}g'(\bar{x})/g(\bar{x}) = 1$.

Proof. If $x_i \to \bar{x}$, then $(y_{i+1} - y_i)$, and hence y_i/i, converges to $g(\bar{x})$ by (7). By (14),

$$it_i \to \bar{x}/[\beta g(\bar{x})]. \tag{15}$$

But (12) implies that

$$\lim_{i \to \infty} [it_i g'(x_i)] = \lim_{i \to \infty} \left[i \frac{g'(x_i)}{g'(x_{i-1})^n} \frac{u'(c_{i-1})}{u'(c_i)} - 1 \right].$$

With $u(c) = -c^{-n}$ and $x_i \to \bar{x}$, the right-hand side limit is $\lim_{i \to \infty}[i(1 - 1/i)^{1/\beta} - 1]$, which equals $1/\beta$, since $c_i/i \to (1 - \beta)g(\bar{x})$. By (15), the left-hand limit is $\bar{x}g'(\bar{x})/[\beta g(\bar{x})]$, and we have completed the proof. $\qquad \square$

Before turning to specific production functions, we suggest a dual approach to our model and its relation to the work of Weitzman. It should be noted that, in writing our maximand as $\sum t_i u(c_i)$, we had to be careful to ensure that it equals $\int_0^\infty u \, dt$, since otherwise the problem has a formal solution $t_i = 0$ for all i. This is obviously not a solution to our original problem and is ruled out by Assumption C. Passing from an integral of utility to the sum of $t_i u(c_i)$ is valid if $\sum t_i$ diverges, or if $c(t)$ can be infinite after time $\sum t_i$, i.e. if $y_i \to \infty$. These requirements were constraints on our maximization.

We should presumably have a corresponding difficulty if we attempted to write the problem in some cost minimization form: minimize $\sum p_i x_i$ where the p_i are appropriate prices for plants. Formally, we have a solution $x_i = 0$ for all i, unless we rule it out through the constraints. Weitzman used cost minimization to determine investment in his β-capital (overhead capital the production of which shows increasing returns to scale) and derived the prices from marginal utilities on the target path—the Ramsey path which would be followed if the productivity of α-capital were unrestricted by the necessity for β-capital. The target path constrains the x_i.

Our model might be viewed as a limiting case of Weitzman's model where the productivity of α-capital tends to infinity. This does not help, however, in the solution to our problem, since if we take the limit as the productivity of α-capital tends to infinity we lose the Ramsey-type target path. It might be claimed that the target for a cost-minimization form of our model is simply infinite output. Two intuitive arguments in favour of such a view would be that the 'constraint' analogous to $\sum t_i = \infty$ is $\sum x_i = \infty$, and that infinite output is the limit, as the productivity of α-capital tends to infinity, of the Ramsey path in Weitzman's model.

3. THE CONSTANT ELASTICITY CASE

From now on we specialize to the case of the iso-elastic utility function. In this section the production function, too, will have constant elasticity; i.e., $g(x) = Kx^\epsilon$, $\epsilon > 1$. This has an average product which tends to infinity with output, and thus we have to entertain the possibility of infinite output in finite time (see Lemma 1).

Using (13), equation (12) becomes

$$\left(\frac{y_i}{y_{i-1}}\right)^{n+1} = \left(\frac{x_{i-1}}{x_i}\right)^{\epsilon-1}\left(1 + (n+1)\epsilon K \frac{x_i^\epsilon}{y_i}\right). \tag{16}$$

Since $y_{i+1} - y_i = Kx_i^\epsilon$, this can be expressed most conveniently as a recursion relation for the expansion coefficient

$$\alpha_i = \frac{y_{i+1}}{y_i} - 1. \tag{17}$$

Thus,

$$\left(\frac{x_{i-1}}{x_i}\right)^{\epsilon-1} = \left(\frac{y_i - y_{i-1}}{y_{i+1} - y_i}\right)^{(\epsilon-1)/\epsilon} = \left(\frac{\alpha_{i-1}}{\alpha_1(1 + \alpha_{i-1})}\right)^{(\epsilon-1)/\epsilon},$$

and (16) becomes

$$\alpha_{i-1}^{-\gamma}(1 + \alpha_{i-1})^{n+1+\gamma} = \alpha_i^{-\gamma}\{1 + (n+1)\epsilon\alpha_i\}, \tag{18}$$

where

$$\gamma = (\epsilon - 1)/\epsilon.$$

There is a unique non-zero $\bar\alpha$ satisfying $\bar\alpha_i = \alpha_{i-1} = \bar\alpha$. In fact, $\alpha_i = \alpha_{i-1}$ when α_{i-1} is small, $\alpha_i > \alpha_{i-1}$ when α_{i-1} is large, and where $\alpha_i = \alpha_{i-1} = \bar\alpha$, it is readily shown that

$$\frac{d\alpha_i}{d\alpha_{i-1}} = \frac{1 + (n+1)\epsilon\bar\alpha}{1 + \bar\alpha} > 1.$$

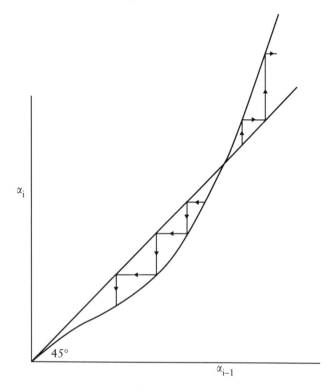

Figure 21.1.

The graph of α_i as a function of α_{i-1} is shown in Fig. 21.1. It is clear from the graph that, for all paths other than $\alpha_i = \bar{\alpha}$ (all i), $\alpha_i \to 0$ or ∞ as $i \to \infty$. Both of these can, we believe, be rejected. The optimum policy is

$$y_{i+1} - y_i = \bar{\alpha} y_i. \tag{19}$$

The policy of increasing capacity by a constant fraction at each investment was found by Srinivasan and Weitzman for the same production function.

We can now see that infinite output is reached in finite time, as follows. The policy $\alpha_i = \bar{\alpha}$ implies $y_i = (1 + \bar{\alpha})^i y_0$, $g(x_i)/y_i = \bar{\alpha}$, and hence $t_i = D(1 + \bar{\alpha})^{-i\gamma}$, where D is a constant, using $g(x_i) = Kx_i^\epsilon$ and $x_i = \beta t_i y_i$. But $\gamma = (\epsilon - 1)/\epsilon > 0$, so $\sum t_i$ converges, and of course $y_i \to \infty$. This does not contradict the existence theorem: there is no problem with the convergence of the utility integral.

This case is instructive, but we should perhaps be circumspect about a production function which yields infinite output in finite time. We turn now to a production function with bounded average product so that Lemma 1 applies and output goes to infinity only asymptotically.

4. THE FIXED COST CASE

We retain the constant elasticity utility function $u(c) = -c^{-n}$, but turn to the case

$$g(x) = \begin{cases} -\sigma + \rho x & \sigma/\rho \leq x \\ 0 & 0 \leq x < \sigma/\rho \end{cases} \tag{20}$$

We now also have the interpretation of the model as that of the individual saver facing a given fixed cost σ/ρ of making an investment, and a marginal return ρ on investments. Equations (12) becomes

$$(y_i/y_{i-1})^{1/\beta} = 1 + \rho t_i \tag{21}$$

and the accumulation equation,

$$y_i = y_{i-1} - \sigma + \rho\beta t_{i-1} y_{i-1}. \tag{22}$$

Before discussing the solution of these equations, let us note that the optimum x_i can be written as a function of y_i:

$$x_i = \frac{\sigma}{\rho} h(y_i/\sigma). \tag{23}$$

From now on we set $\sigma = \rho = 1$ by choice of units of time and commodities.

The character of the solutions of (21) and (22) can be best appreciated if we obtain a difference equation for t. Eliminating y_i from (21) and (22), we obtain

$$t_i = (1 + \beta t_{i-1} - y_{i-1}^{-1})^{1/\beta} - 1. \tag{24}$$

Therefore $t_i \geq t_{i-1}$ if and only if

$$y_{i-1} \geq \{1 + \beta t_{i-1} - (1 + t_{i-1})^\beta\}^{-1}. \tag{25}$$

At the same time, the need to have $x_i \geq 1$ means that

$$t_{i-1} \geq 1/(\beta y_{i-1})^{-1}. \tag{26}$$

Given y_0 and having chosen t_0, we can generate a sequence (y_i, t_i) satisfying (22) and (24). The possible sequences are shown in Fig. 21.2. The lower curve shows the effect of the inequality (26); any sequence that crosses into the region below it yields an infeasible policy. The upper curve shows where t_i would be equal to t_{i-1}; any sequence that crosses into the region above this curve would remain there for ever.

In Lemma 3 we prove some more properties of these sequences, and then characterize the optimum policy in the theorem that follows.

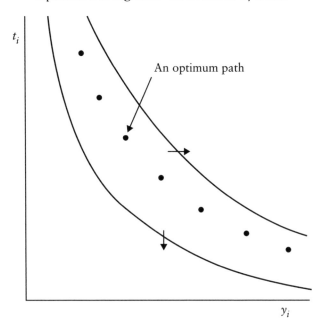

Figure 21.2.

Lemma 3. (*a*) *On any sequence that is forever feasible,* $y_i \to \infty$. (*b*) *Comparing sequences for any given i,* y_i *and* t_i *are increasing functions of* y_0 *and* t_0. (*c*) *If* $y_0' \geq y_0$, $t_0' \geq t_0$, *and the sequences* (y_i, t_i) *and* (y_i', t_i') *starting respectively from* (y_0, t_0) *and* (y_0', t_0') *are both feasible, then for each i,*

$$t_{i+1}' - t_{i+1} \geq t_i' - t_i.$$

Proofs. (*a*) For a feasible policy, (26) and (22) show that (y_i) is an increasing sequence. If it does not tend to infinity, it must then have a finite limit $\bar{y}$. Then (21) shows that $t_i \to 0$, while (22) shows that $t_i \to 1/(\beta\bar{y})$, which is a contradiction.

(*b*) This is obvious by induction from (22) and (24).

(*c*) From part (*b*) of this lemma and the feasibility condition, we conclude that

$$t_i' - 1/y_i' \geq t_i - 1/y_i \geq 0.$$

Now consider the function $f(z) = (1+z)^{1/\beta}$. For non-negative z, its derivative is bounded below by $1/\beta$, and therefore for $z' \geq z \geq 0$, we have

$$f(z') - f(z) \geq (1/\beta)(z' - z).$$

In the present case this becomes, from (24),

$$t'_{i+1} - t_{i+1} \geq \frac{1}{\beta}\left\{ \left(\beta t'_i - \frac{1}{y'_i} \right) - \left(\beta t_i - \frac{1}{y_i} \right) \right\}$$

$$= (t'_i - t_i) + \frac{1}{\beta}\left(\frac{1}{y_i} - \frac{1}{y'_i} \right).$$

But, by part (b), $y'_t \geqq y_i$. This completes the proof.   □

It now remains to examine the effect on total utility of the choice of t_0 for a given y_0. It will be seen that t_0 should be chosen as small as possible subject to the resulting sequence being forever feasible. Thus, the optimum path is the lowest that never hits the lower curve in Fig. 21.2. We will also show that any higher choice of t_0 yields a path that crosses the upper curve. Thus, the optimum is the unique path channelled between the two curves. These results are proved in the following theorem.

Define $t^*(y_0) = \inf\{t_0 \mid \text{resulting } (y_i, t_i) \text{ satisfy } (26) \text{ for all } i\}$. Clearly, $t^*(y_0)$ exists and is positive for each y_0. Then

Theorem 1. (a) $t^*(y_0)$ *is the optimum choice of t_0 given y_0.*

(b) *Any choice $t_0 > t^*(y_0)$ will yield a sequence that crosses the upper curve in Figure 2.*

(c) $t^*(y_0)$ *is a decreasing function. t^* tends to zero as y_0 tends to infinity.*

Proof. (a) Consider the sequence starting from t_0. The utility in period i is $t_i u(c_i)$, which is proportional, in the iso-elastic case, to

$$-t_i y_i^{-n} = -(y_i^{1+n} y_{i-1}^{-1-n} - 1) y_i^{-n} \qquad \text{by (21)}$$

$$= y_i^{-n} - y_i y_{i-1}^{-1-n}$$

$$= y_i^{-n} - (y_{i-1} - 1 + \beta t_{i-1} y_{i-1}) y_{i-1}^{-1-n} \qquad \text{by (22)}$$

$$= -\beta t_{i-1} y_{i-1}^{-n} + (y_i^{-n} - y_{i-1}^{-n}) + y_{i-1}^{-1-n}.$$

Summing from $i = 1$ to $i = I$, we can write

$$\sum_0^I (-t_i y_i^{-n}) = \beta \sum_0^I (-t_i y_i^{-n}) - t_0 y_0^{-n} + \beta t_I y_I^{-n} + y_I^{-n} - y_0^{-n} + \sum_0^{I-1} y_i^{-1-n}$$

or

$$(1-\beta)\sum_0^I (-t_i y_i^{-n}) = -t_0 y_0^{-n} - y_0^{-n} + \beta t_I y_I^{-n} + y_I^{-n} + \sum_0^{I-1} y_i^{-1-n}. \qquad (27)$$

The series on the left-hand side consists of negative terms; therefore it is decreasing. Further, it is bounded below by $(-\beta t_0 y_0^{-n} - y_0^{-n})$; therefore it converges, and it is a necessary condition of this convergence that $t_I y_I^{-n} \to 0$. By part (a) of Lemma 3, so long as the sequence is forever feasible, $y_I \to \infty$ and thus $y_I^{-n} \to 0$. We can then take limits in (27) to write

$$(1 - \beta) \sum_0^\infty (-t_i y_i^{-n}) = -t_0 y_0^{-n} - y_0^{-n} + \sum_0^\infty y_i^{-1-n}.$$

The left-hand side is a positive multiple of total utility. The right-hand side for fixed y_0 is a decreasing function of t_0 and of all the y_i, each of which is an increasing function of t_0 by part (b) of Lemma 3. This proves the result. Continuity considerations show that the sequence starting from $t^*(y_0)$ cannot cross the upper curve (nor the lower one). Therefore, on the optimum sequence, t_i decreases and tends to 0.

(b) Suppose the choice $t^*(y_0)$ produces a sequence (y_i^*, t_i^*) while a choice $t_0 > t^*(y_0)$ results in (y_i, t_i). Then, for all i, we have, by part (c) of Lemma 3,

$$t_i - t_i^* \geq t_{i-1} - t_{i-1}^* \ldots \geq t_0 - t^*(y_0),$$

and therefore

$$t_i \geq t_i^* + t_0 - t^*(y_0) \geq t_0 - t^*(y_0) > 0,$$

which shows that t_i is bounded below by a positive number. The sequence must therefore cross the upper curve, which is asymptotic to the horizontal axis.

(c) Suppose $y_0' > y_0$ and $t^*(y_0') > t^*(y_0)$. Then, using part (c) of Lemma 3 repeatedly for the resulting sequences, we have

$$t_i' - t_i \geq t^*(y_0') - t^*(y_0) > 0.$$

But $t_i' \to 0$, and thus t_i must eventually become negative, which is impossible. The last part of (c) is already proved, since $t_i \to 0$ on any optimum path. □

Having thus identified the optimum policy, we can calculate it. We have done this by starting from an estimate of optimal t_i when y_i is very large, and using equations (21) and (22) to calculate t and y for successively lower values of i. By starting from slightly different large values of y, one can equally map out the whole optimal policy showing t or x as functions of y. The computation can be done by taking the 'initial' t_i as $1/(\beta y_i)$, the minimum possible length of the (Ramsey) saving period. It is then clear (cf. Fig. 22.2) that one can get a good approximation to the optimum. In fact, we used the asymptotic form of the optimal policy, which allows faster computation. We now derive that asymptotic form.

Lemma 4. *In the model of this section,*

$$t_i^2 y_i \to \frac{2}{\beta} \tag{28}$$

and

$$\frac{x_i^2}{y_i} \to 2\beta \tag{29}$$

as $i \to \infty$ on the optimum path.

Proof. We shall not work directly with $t_i^2 y_i$, but with a new variable,

$$z_i = x_i(x_i - 1)/y_i$$
$$= \beta^2 t_i^2 y_i - \beta t_i.$$

First, we establish a difference equation for z_i, in which it is convenient to use the variable

$$u_i = \beta t_i - y_i^{-1},$$

which is non-negative (by (26)) and tends to zero as $i \to \infty$ (by the Corollary to Lemma 3).

From (24), we have

$$t_{i+1} = (1 + u_i)^{n+1} - 1,$$

and from (22),

$$y_{i+1} = y_i(1 + u_i)$$
$$= (z_i - u_i)u_i^{-2}(1 + u_i),$$

as can readily be checked from the definitions of z and u. Thus,

$$z_{i+1} = \beta\{(1 + u_i)^{n+1} - 1\}[\beta\{(1 + u_i)^{n+1} - 1\}(z_i - u_i)u_i^{-2}(1 + u_i) - 1].$$

Expanding $(1 + u_i)^{n+1}$, and the using the definition $\beta(n+1) =$, we obtain

$$Z_{i+1} = \{u_i + \tfrac{1}{2}nu_i^2 + 0(u_i^3)\}[\{u_i + \tfrac{1}{2}nu_i^2 + 0(u_i^3)\}u_i^{-2}(1 + u_i)(z_i - u_i) - 1],$$

where the 'order' notation $0(u_i^m)$ means a function of i that is equal to u_i^m times a bounded function of i. Multiplying out, we find that

$$z_{i+1} = z_i + u_i\{(n + 1)z_i - 2 + 0(u_i) + z_i 0(u_i)\}. \tag{30}$$

In using this equation to demonstrate the asymptotic behaviour of z_i, we shall need two auxiliary results:

(i) z_i is bounded.
(ii) $\sum_I^\infty u_i = \infty$.

The first is deduced from the inequality (25), which tells us that

$$y_i\{1 + \beta t_i - (1 + t_i)^\beta\} \geq 1. \tag{31}$$

In the interval $0 \leq t \leq 1$, the second derivative of $(1+t_i)^\beta$ is less than $-\beta(1-\beta)2^{-2+\beta}$ (β being less than one). Therefore, by the second-order mean value theorem,

$$(1+t)^\beta \leq 1 + \beta t - \beta(1-\beta)2^{-3+\beta} t^2.$$

Applying this to (31), we deduce that

$$t_i^2 y_i \leq 2^{3-\beta}/\{\beta(1-\beta)\},$$

once $t_i \leq 1$ (as it must be eventually). Therefore $z_i = \beta^2 t_i^2 y_i - \beta t_i$ is bounded, as asserted.

To prove that $\sum u_i$ is a divergent series, we note that

$$u_i = (x_i - 1)/y_i = (y_{i+1} - y_i)/y_i \geq \log(y_{i+1}/y_i).$$

Summing,

$$\sum_0^I u_i \geq \log(y_{I+1}/y_0) \to \infty.$$

Returning to the difference equation (30), we deduce first that z_i tends to a finite limit. If z_i does not tend to $2/(n+1)$, there is a positive number ϵ such that $(n+1)z_i - 2 > \epsilon$ infinitely often or $(n+1)z_i - 2 < -\epsilon$ infinitely often. Consider the first possibility, and let i_0 be such that the terms $0(u_i) + z0(u_i)$ in (30) are less than ϵ in absolute value for all $i \geq i_0$. Then for some i, say $i_1, \geq i_0$, $(n+1)z_i - 2 > \epsilon$, and (30) implies that z_i is then increasing, and must continue to do so for all i. A similar argument shows that z_i is eventually decreasing if $(n+1)z_i - 2 < -\epsilon$ infinitely often. Therefore the sequence z_i tends to a limit. The fact that z_i is bounded implies that the limit is finte. Therefore $\sum(z_{i+1} - z_i)$ is a convergent series. Yet, if $\lim \{(n+1)z_i - 2\} \neq 0$, the divergence of $\sum u_i$ implies that $\sum u_i\{(n+1)z_i - 2 + 0(u_i)\}$ diverges. It follows that only one limit for z_i is possible:

$$z_i \to \frac{2}{n+1} = 2\beta. \tag{32}$$

Since $z_i = \beta^2 t_i^2 y_i - \beta t_i$ and $t_i \to 0$, (32) implies (28), and also (29). □

Although we do not use it in computation, it is interesting also to derive an approximation for the optimal policy when y_i is small.

Lemma 5. *In the model of this section, on the optimum path*

$$x_i \sim 1 + \beta^{-\beta/(1+\beta)} y_i^{1/(1+\beta)} \tag{33}$$

$$t_i \sim \beta^{-1} y_i^{-1} + \beta^{-(1+2\beta)/(1+\beta)} y_i^{-\beta/(1+\beta)} \tag{34}$$

as $y_i \to 0$.

Proof. Since $y_i \to 0$,

$$x_i - 1 = y_{i+1} - y_i \to 0.$$

Then (21) implies

$$y_{i+1}^{n+2} y_i^{-n-1} = y_{i+1} + t_{i+1} y_{i+1} \to \frac{1}{\beta}.$$

Therefore

$$(y_i + x_i - 1)y_i^{-(n+1)/(n+2)} \to \beta^{-1/(n+2)},$$

from which it follows that

$$(x_i - 1)y_i^{-(n+1)/(n+2)} \to \beta^{-1/(n+2)}.$$

This is just (33) in different notation. (34) follows directly from (33). $\square$

The computations presented in Fig. 21.3—which gives optimum x as a function of y for several values of β—show that (29) is a good approximation

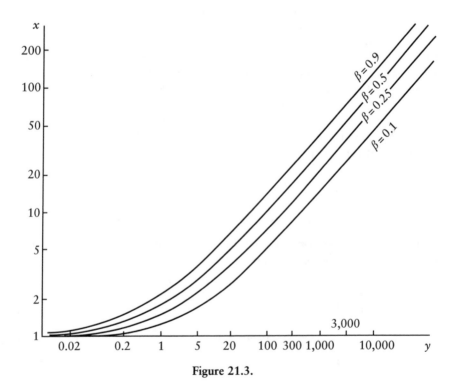

Figure 21.3.

even for quite small values of y.[2] For example, when $\beta = 0.5$, the approximation is correct within 1 per cent for all $y \geq 593$, and correct within 2 per cent for all $y \geq 124$. The lower approximation (33) is less useful. For the same case, it is correct within 2 per cent for all $y \leq 0.04$.

Reverting to the case of general σ and ρ, where, it will be recollected, the optimum policy is

$$x = \frac{\sigma}{\rho} h\left(\frac{y}{\sigma}, \beta\right),$$ (35)

we note a number of properties of the optimum. First, we write the approximations, for large y, of

$$x \sim \rho^{-1}\sqrt{2\sigma\beta y}, \qquad t \sim \rho^{-1}\sqrt{\frac{2\sigma}{\beta y}}.$$ (36)

The properties of x and t suggested by (36) are confirmed by the accurate computations:

(i) *For fixed parameters, x increases as y increases, while t decreases.* We have already proved the second of these results. The first can be proved in the same way, by considering difference equations in x_i and y_i rather than t_i and y_i. The interested reader will readily prove the proposition by means of a phase diagram.

(ii) *For fixed y, σ, and ρ, x is an increasing function of β, and t is a decreasing function.* Thus, in an economy that wishes to save at a higher rate, the next investment is undertaken sooner, but not in proportion, so that the investment is bigger.

(iii) *For fixed y and β, x and t are increasing functions of σ and decreasing functions of ρ.*

(iv) *For fixed y and β, x and t decrease when σ and ρ increase in the same proportion.* This tells us what happens if ρ is greater while the minimum size of an investment is unchanged.

5. INTERPRETATION AS AN INDIVIDUAL SAVING PROBLEM

The result in the previous section that $h(y)$ behaves like $\sqrt{y}$ for large y is rather striking since it is close to the result of Baumol and Tobin, and the early analysis by Whitin of inventory problems. We have used a full infinite-horizon-optimizing formulation, taking into account the effects of savings on future income, and there is no *a priori* reason to expect results similar to

---

[2] $y = 100$ is quite small for the problem, because it means that the minimum investment size is 1% of the output that would be produced over a period such that the rate of return is 100%—say, 10 years or more.

these stationary state models. As an aid to understanding the similarity, we give a brief description and extension of the Baumol–Tobin inventory type model that yields the square root results.

Suppose we need a flow of a per day for transactions purposes, that there is a cost of withdrawal k, and interest opportunity cost of holding cash of r. We want to choose a withdrawal period to minimize costs per unit time subject to meeting the flow demand. The cost per withdrawal period is k, and the interest cost is $arT^2/2$ where the period is T units of time long. Thus we choose T to minimize $k/T + arT/2$, giving optimal T as $\sqrt{2k/ar}$ and withdrawal quantity $\sqrt{2ak/r}$.

We compare $\sqrt{2ak/r}$ with our approximation to $h(y)$ for large y, viz. $\sqrt{2\sigma\beta y/\rho}$. Now k corresponds to σ/ρ, the fixed cost of investment, a to βy, the flow of savings, and r to ρ, the rate of return on investments. We thus have an *exact* parallel.

One might think at first that the Baumol–Tobin model is a limiting case of our model, but this is not so. The formal structure remains different in the limit in our model, for (i) income is rising with a temporal growth rate tending to $\beta\rho$; (ii) the time between investments is not constant, but is falling as $y^{-1/2}$; (iii) we have a consumption rate of discount in our model, for marginal utility is falling as income rises, whereas there is no discounting in the Baumol–Tobin formulation. The lack of discounting in their model is odd, since there is an opportunity cost of holding money.

We incorporate discounting and growth into the Baumol–Tobin model to see if the square root result remains. The opportunity cost of holding money and the fixed costs of withdrawals are discounted at rate r and the flow demand increases at rate g. If a is flow demand now, we withdraw $a(e^{gT} - 1)/g$. We then have a per-period cost of

$$k + \int_0^T e^{-rt} ra(e^{gT} - e^{gt})/g \, dt,$$

i.e.

$$\psi(a, T) = k + \frac{ar}{g} e^{gT} \left\{ \frac{1 - e^{-rt}}{r} - \frac{e^{-gT} - e^{-rT}}{r - g} \right\}. \tag{37}$$

Now consider the choice of T. This leads to a functional equation

$$V(a) = \min_T [\psi(a, T) + V(ae^{gT})e^{-rT}] \tag{38}$$

in the standard dynamic programming framework and obvious notation. The optimum T satisfies

$$\psi_T(a, T) + V'(ae^{gT})age^{gT}e^{-rt} - rV(ae^{gT})e^{-rT} = 0 \tag{39}$$

$$V(a) = \psi(a, T) + V(ae^{gT})e^{-rT}, \tag{40}$$

and differentiating (40), using the envelope theorem,

$$V'(a) = V'(ae^{gT})e^{gT}e^{-rT} + \psi_a(a, T). \tag{41}$$

If we substitute from (40) and (41) into (39), we obtain

$$rV(a) - agV'(a) = \psi_T(a, T) + r\psi(a, T) - ag\psi_a(a, T). \tag{42}$$

Now suppose it turns out that both rT and gT are small. Then from a Taylor expansion of (40) we have, to first order,

$$\begin{aligned} V(a) &= \psi(a, T) + [V(a) + V'(a)agT][1 - rT] \\ &= \psi(a, T) + V(a) - T[rV(a) - gaV'(a)] \end{aligned}$$

and, using (42)

$$T\psi_T(a, T) = (1 - rT)\psi(a, T) + agT\psi_a(a, T). \tag{43}$$

Now we can differentiate (37) to find ψ_a and ψ_T, expand them and ψ in Taylor series, and compare leading terms in (43). This leads to $T = \sqrt{2k/(ar)}$. In other words, the square root formula carries over unchanged when we allow constant growth and discounting, as long as T is small. Of course, g must satisfy suitable convergence conditions, but its exact level is immaterial.

We cannot, however, assume directly that rT and gT are small, for T is a choice variable and depends on r and g. Thus, the above method does not tell us in advance of a solution to the problem whether the square root results carry over to allow growth and discounting.

We should note two things about the consumption rate of discount in our model. First, inside a period all marginal increments to consumption are equally valuable. Second, the temporal growth rate of consumption tends to a constant as time goes to infinity, and this implies, with an iso-elastic utility function, a constant discount rate. It is presumably the asymptotic constancy of the growth rate and the discount rate, and the asymptotic decline in the period, that is helping to give a result close to that of Baumol and Tobin. But even when their model is extended to allow growth and discounting as done here, one important difference remains, for both these are endogenous in our model and exogenous in the above extension of their model.

We have emphasized the differences between our model and the Baumol–Tobin model that persist even asymptotically. It remains interesting, however, to see that a full specification of the individual saver problem yields asymptotically similar results to those of a simpler specification. For finite values of output, of course, the two models are quite different. Yet, as we have remarked above, the square root approximation is really extremely good, certainly within the range that seems relevant for the individual saving problem.

6. A MODEL WITH LABOR

We introduce labor into the model by assuming that a lump of investment of size x will when combined with labor l produce output $g(x)l^\alpha$, where $\alpha < 1$ and g is concave. This form is, of course, rather special. We allow labor used with the investment lump to be varied freely over time, in such a way that one would want to use all investments for ever (though to a diminishing extent): establishing the investment in no way restricts the possibilities of combining labor with it. We shall make assumptions about g (stated in Lemma 6) sufficient to avoid the possibility that output fan explode (become infinite in finite time). One further assumption in needed:

$$xg'(x)/g(x) > 1 - \alpha. \tag{44}$$

This ensures that $g(\lambda x)(\lambda l)^\alpha$ increases faster than λ as λ increases. It follows that lumpy investment is desirable; for if investment were being done very frequently, halving the frequency would double the lump and allow double the labor to be applied to the lump, thus more than doubling output per lump and increasing aggregate output.[3]

The labor force is constant. If the constant is taken to be unity, output at the $(i+1)$th stage (after the ith investment lump) is

$$y_{i+1} = \max\left\{ \sum_{-\infty}^{i} g(x_j)l_j^\alpha \,\Big|\, \sum_{-\infty}^{i} l_j = 1 \right\}. \tag{45}$$

The sum is shown from $j = -\infty$ so as to include all past investments. Of course $x_j = 0$ for sufficiently small j. Working out the maximum, we have

$$\alpha g(x_j)l_j^{\alpha-1} = \mu, \qquad \text{a Lagrange multiplier.}$$

Since $\sum l_j = 1$,

$$\mu^\xi = \alpha^\xi \sum g(x_j)^\xi, \tag{46}$$

where ξ is written for $1/(1-\alpha)$. Therefore

$$\begin{aligned}
y_{i+1} &= \sum g(x_j) \left\{ \mu^{-\xi} \alpha^\xi g(x_j)^\xi \right\}^\alpha \\
&= (\mu^{-\xi}\alpha^\xi)^\alpha \Sigma g(x_j)^\xi, \qquad \text{since } 1 + \xi\alpha = \xi \\
&= \left\{ \sum g(x_j)^\xi \right\}^{1-\alpha}, \qquad \text{by (46).} \tag{47}
\end{aligned}$$

Thus,

$$y_{i+1}^\xi - y_i^\xi = g(x_i)^\xi. \tag{48}$$

---

[3] This intuitive argument is our justification for believing that Assumption C will continue to hold.

This is a very convenient form of production constraint to use in the maximization problem: it simply generalizes the case of Section 2, which corresponds to $\xi = 1$. We note first that, if g is suitably restricted, the economy cannot explode.

Lemma 6. *For the model of this section, if g is such that there exists a positive constant K, and a positive number δ not greater than one, such that*

$$g(x) \leq Kx^{\delta} \quad \text{(all } x\text{)}, \tag{49}$$

then $y_i \to \infty$ only if $\sum t_i = \infty$.

Proof. By (44), $d(\log g(x))/dx > (1 - \alpha)/x$. Integrating between $x = x_0$ and $x = x_1$, we obtain

$$g(x_1) > g(x_0)(x_1/x_0)^{1-\alpha}. \tag{50}$$

Comparing (49) and (50), we see that $1 - \alpha \leq \delta$, i.e. $\delta\xi \geq 1$. Then, writing $z_i^{\delta} = y_i$, we have the inequality

$$
\begin{aligned}
(z_{i+1} - z_i)^{\delta\xi} &\leq z_{i+1}^{\delta\xi} - Z_i^{\delta\xi} \\
&= g(x_i)^{\xi} \\
&\leq g(t_i y_i)^{\xi}, \quad \text{since } c_i \geq 0 \\
&\leq K(t_i y_i)^{\delta\xi}, \quad \text{by (49)}.
\end{aligned}
$$

Therefore

$$
\begin{aligned}
\frac{z_{i+1} - z_i}{z_i} &\leq K^{1/(\delta\xi)} y_i^{1-1/\delta} t_i \\
&\leq K' t_i, \quad K' \text{a constant}, \tag{51}
\end{aligned}
$$

for all large enough i, since $y_i \to \infty$, $\delta \leq 1$. Summing, for large i, and using the inequality $\log(z_{i+1}/z_i) \leq (z_{i+1} - z_i)/z_i$,

$$
\begin{aligned}
K' \sum t_i &\geq \sum (\log z_{i+1} - \log z_i) \\
&= \infty.
\end{aligned}
$$

This proves the lemma. □

This is a natural generalization of Lemma 1.

The first-order conditions for the maximization of

$$\sum t_i u(c_i) = \sum x_i \frac{u(c_i)}{y_i - c_i}$$

are obtained as before by maximizing $u(c)/(y_i - c)$ with respect to c_i and considering changes in x_{j-1}, x_j and y_j (holding other x and y constant) that keep (48) satisfied for all i. This latter change yields

$$\left(\frac{u(c_{i-1})}{y_{i-1}-c_{i-1}}\frac{y_i^{\xi-1}}{g(x_{i-1})^{\xi-1}g'(x_{i-1})}\right)-\left(\frac{u(c_i)}{y_i-c_i}\frac{y_i^{\xi-1}}{g(x_i)^{\xi-1}g'(x_i)}\right)=\frac{x_iu(c_i)}{(y_i-c_i)^2}.$$
$$(52)$$

Maximization of $u(c)/(y_i-c)$ yields the Keynes–Ramsey equation

$$u(c_i)+(y_i-c_i)u'(c_i)=0. \tag{53}$$

Combining (52) and (53), we get a slightly neater equation,

$$\left(\frac{u'(c_{i-1})}{g(x_{i-1})^{\xi-1}g'(x_{i-1})}-\frac{u'(c_i)}{g(x_i)^{\xi-1}g'(x_i)}\right)y_i^{\xi-1}(y_i-c_i)=x_iu'(c_i). \tag{54}$$

We shall not discuss the general problem further, but turn to the simple special case where

$$u(c)=-c^{-n}, \qquad g(x)=x^\delta. \tag{55}$$

(Units of measurement for commodities are so chosen that the multiplicative factor in g is unity.) For this case we can give a complete analysis. It turns out to be easier to use dynamic programming methods rather than the first-order conditions (54).

Theorem 2. *If* $(n+1)\delta>1$, $\delta\xi>1$, *and* $\delta<1$, *the model (55) has an optimum policy, which is given by*

$$c_i=\frac{n}{n+1}y_i; \tag{56}$$

and

$$y_{i+1}=\gamma y_i, \tag{57}$$

or, equivalently,

$$x_i=\epsilon y_i^{1/\delta}, \qquad t_i=(n+1)\epsilon y_i^{1/\delta-1}, \tag{58}$$

with $\epsilon=(\gamma^\xi-1)^{1/(\delta\xi)}$, *where* γ *is defined by*

$$\gamma^{\{(n+1)\delta-1\}/\delta}+\{(n+1)\delta-1\}\gamma^{-\xi}=(n+1)\delta, \qquad \gamma>1. \tag{59}$$

Proof. The condition $\delta\xi>1$ is just (44). $\delta<1$ means that Lemma 6 applies. If $(n+1)\delta>1$, the economy is valuation-finite, i.e. has a path for which the utility integral converges. For example, the path defined in the theorem, which we are going to prove optimal, gives a utility integral proportional to

$$-\sum y_i^{1/\delta-n-1} = y_0^{1/\delta-n-1}(1-\gamma^{1/\delta-n-1})^{-1},$$

since

$$1/\delta - n - 1 < 0 \qquad \text{and} \qquad \gamma > 1.$$

It follows that we can define $V(y_0)$, the supremum of the utility integral when initial output is y_0, and

$$V(y_0) = \sup \{-xy_0^{-n-1} + V(y_1) \,|\, y_1^\xi = y_0^\xi + x^{\delta\xi}\}, \tag{60}$$

since the maximum utility obtainable before the first new investment is (using the Keynes–Ramsey rule, (56))

$$\frac{x}{y_0 - c} u(c) = -xu'(c) = -Axy^{-n-1}$$

for some positive constant A, which we absorb into the definition of V.

Using the argument of the existence theorem in the appendix, we can show that an optimum policy $x(y_0)$ exists, such that

$$x(y_0) \quad \text{maximizes} \quad -xy_0^{-n-1} + V(y_1). \tag{61}$$

Then, in our particular example, we can obtain the form of V explicitly. Suppose $(c_0, c_1, c_2, \ldots)$ and $(x_0, x_1, x_2, \ldots)$ is the optimum path starting from y_0. Then $(\lambda c_0, \lambda c_1, \lambda c_2, \ldots)$ and $(\lambda^{1/\delta}x_0, \lambda^{1/\delta}x_1, \lambda^{1/\delta}x_2, \ldots)$ is a feasible path starting from λy_0. The utility integral on this second path is $\lambda^{1/\delta-n-1}$ times $V(y_0)$; hence $V(\lambda y_0) \geq \lambda^{1/\delta-n-1}V(y_0)$. A similar argument beginning with an optimum path starting from λy_0 gives the inequality the other way, and it follows that V is homogeneous of degree $1/\delta - n - 1$ in y_0; i.e.,

$$V = -Ay_0^{1/\delta-n-1}. \tag{62}$$

This means that V is differentiable, so that (61) implies

$$y_0^{-n-1} = V'(y_1)\delta x^{\delta\xi-1}y_1^{1-\xi}. \tag{63}$$

At the same time, since by (60)

$$V(y_0) = -xy_0^{n-1} + V(y_1), \tag{64}$$

$$V'(y_0) = (n+1)xy_0^{-n-2} + V'(y_1)y_0^{\xi-1}y_1^{1-\xi}. \tag{65}$$

Combining (63) and (65), we obtain

$$(n+1)\delta x^{\delta\xi}y_0^{-n-1-\xi} + y_0^{-n-1} = \delta x^{\delta\xi-1}y_0^{1-\xi}V'(y_0)$$
$$= A((n+1)\delta - 1)x^{\delta\xi-1}y_0^{1/\delta-n-1-\xi}, \quad \text{by (62)}.$$

Thus,

$$(n+1)\delta + (y_0/x^\delta)^\xi = A((n+1)\delta - 1)(y_0/x^\delta)^{1/\delta}, \tag{66}$$

while, from (64), using (62), we obtain

$$A(y_0/x^\delta)^{1/\delta} = 1 + A(y_0/x^\delta)^{1/\delta}\{1 + (x^\delta/y_0)^\xi\}^{-((n+1)\delta-1)/\delta\xi}. \tag{67}$$

Eliminating A from (66) and (67), and writing $\epsilon^\delta = x^\delta/y_0$, we have

$$(n+1)\delta + \epsilon^{-\delta\xi} = (n+1)\delta - 1 + \{(n+1)\delta + \epsilon^{-\delta\xi}\}(1 + \epsilon^{\delta\xi})^{-((n+1)\delta-1)/\delta\xi},$$

which can be rewritten in terms of $\gamma = (1 + \epsilon^{\delta\xi})^{1/\xi}$:

$$\gamma^{\{(n+1)\delta-1\}/\delta} + \{(n+1)\delta - 1\}\gamma^{-\xi} = (n+1)\delta. \tag{68}$$

By its definition, γ must be greater than one, and it is readily shown that (68) has one and only one root greater than one: for the left-hand side is equal to $(n+1)\delta$ when $\gamma = 1$, decreases at first as γ increases above one, and then increases, tending to infinity for large γ.

It follows that

$$\frac{y_1}{y_0} = \left(1 + \frac{x^{\delta\xi}}{y_0^\xi}\right)^{1/\xi} = \gamma, \tag{69}$$

and this must hold at all subsequent stages of the optimal development too. This proves the theorem. □

Several features of the optimal policy and path call for comment.

(i) As $i \to \infty$, $t_i \to \infty$. This is clear from (58), since $y_i \to \infty$ and $\delta < 1$. The situation is thus quite different from the model discussed in Section 4. The reason is that we now have decreasing returns to capital alone, and thus diminishing productivity of capital over time.

(ii) Proportional increments in output are the same from every investment. This feature is special to the homogeneous case we have analysed.

(iii) The sufficient condition for existence of an optimum path, $(n+1)\delta > 1$, is the same in form as Weizsäcker's sufficient condition for the Ramsey model with homogeneous utility and production functions Weizsäcker. It is to be presumed that no optimum policy exists when $(n+1)\delta < 1$.

(iv) Some values for γ are given in Table 21.1.

Table 21.1. *Optimal proportional increments in output for the case* $u = -c^{-n}$, $g(x, l) = x^{\delta} l^{\alpha}$.

n	α	δ	γ
1	0.5	0.6	1.17
1	0.5	0.8	1.43
1	0.75	0.6	1.60
1	0.75	0.8	1.78
2	0.5	0.6	1.12
2	0.5	0.8	1.29
2	0.75	0.6	1.43
2	0.75	0.8	1.55

As is to be expected, the optimum γ is quite sensitive to variations in the parameters. Even for $n = 2$—which many would think not small—and with economies of scale that are very moderate—$\alpha + \delta = 1.1$—the economy is supposed to wait until it can increase output by 12 per cent before investing again. To fill out the picture, consider an economy where initial output is 100 and the labour force is 100. If $g = \frac{1}{3} x^{0.8} l^{0.75}$, a plant with $x = 20$ and $l = 5$ has a capital–output ratio 1.63 and output per man of 2.45. Then the optimal policy for $n = 2$ requires that, at the first step,

$$t_0 = 3.9$$
$$x_0 = 131$$
$$y_1 = 155.$$

No doubt these large investments and long periods are influenced by our somewhat peculiar production assumptions. But we suspect that they and the high savings rates arise more from the basic feature of the model, i.e. that all growth is credited to investment. Once economies of scale are incorporated into a growth model, this is not such an absurd assumption; but we return to results with a flavour similar to Ramsey's, where for many plausible utility functions high investment is optimal. The associated desirability of very infrequent investment is even more striking.[4]

7. CONCLUDING REMARKS

We offer a few comments and speculations concerning the possible effects of complicating the model.

---

[4] We have been asked about the possibilities of decentralized investment decisions in our models. They do not seem good. Of course, marginal cost should be equal to prices and marginal product to wage, but the plant manager has an incentive to attempt to build an arbitrarily large plant, and we think only the central planner can tell when to build. A modified form of decentralization with cost minimization subject to certain targets may be possible.

The effects of introducing discounting in this model are more significant than those in models without increasing returns. For example, we are no longer assured that we shall make an infinite sequence of investments on the optimum path—the proof of Lemma A1 below leans heavily on zero discounting. We suspect that, in our models, it is optimal to stop investing in finite time when utility is discounted. Also, consumption will no longer be constant between investments: it will fall at a rate sufficient to keep $u'(c)e^{-rt}$ constant. This means that the typical term in the series for the utility integral is no longer $tu(c)$, but $\phi(x, t)$, where ϕ is the utility from the optimum method of accumulating x in time t. The ϕ function can be derived fairly easily, at least for the iso-elastic utility case, but is messy, so that the first-order conditions, involving ϕ_x and ϕ_t, are difficult to work with.

The effects of allowing installed capacity to depreciate, in the absence of discounting, are less marked. It will still be optimum to have constant consumption between investments, and if utility integrals are to converge we shall still need output to go to infinity and consequently shall require an infinite sequence of investments. There is the possibility, also, that some part of inventories may evaporate before installation.

It would be interesting to introduce growing population into the model of Section 6, and we would hope to apply such a model to the development of new urban centres.

The model with homogeneous utility and production, and a constant rate of population growth ν, has many features which are quite different from the modification of the Ramsey model introduced by Koopmans, Weizsäcker, and others. Economies of scale allow population growth to be amplified, and it is possible for consumption per head to grow at a constant rate $\nu(\alpha + \delta - 1)/(1 - \delta)$ for ever. In the Cobb–Douglas model with constant returns, consumption per head is ultimately constant. For this reason, no optimum policy exists unless utility (i.e. population times utility of per capita consumption) is sufficiently discounted. In our model, the optimum policy exists if

$$n > \frac{1 - \delta}{\alpha + \delta - 1},$$

even without any discounting of utility. In that case one can show that t_i tends to a finite limit. It should not be difficult to identify the asymptotic behaviour of the optimum path, but we have not worked the case out in any detail.

A further modification that realism requires is to allow for a multiplicity of commodities, with investment of one kind or another taking place frequently, but investment in the production of any one type of commodity taking place only at fairly large intervals. The problem is to formulate an appealing but manageable model.

We do not think that any of these modifications would seriously affect the lessons of the models in this paper. If growth is presumed to be the result of capital accumulation with economies of scale, optimum savings rates are high for many plausible utility functions. If there were persistent increasing returns to capital alone, the economy could, and should, explode. If there are fixed investment costs, but otherwise constant returns, the optimal investment size is approximately the square root of output, and investment becomes almost continuous at high output levels. If, as seems realistic for economies, though not for the individual saver, there are economies of scale in production, but not when labour is fixed, the optimal size of plant may be very large, and the optimal period between investments very long. The value of waiting is high.

Appendix

The existence of an optimum

We take the model of Section 2, without labour. A similar argument should work for the model with labour. We shall use where stated:

> *Assumption A*: u is increasing, strictly concave, satisfying $u(c) \to 0$ $(c \to \infty)$, and $u'(c) \to \infty$ $(c \to 0)$.
>
> *Assumption B*: For any $y_0 > 0$, there exists a feasible path with convergent utility integral.
>
> *Assumption C*: For all y_0 there exists $\delta > 0$ such that all paths starting from y_0 and making the first investment at a time sooner than δ can be overtaken.

We note first that the problem can be simplified by considering only paths with constant consumption between investments. In fact, any path that does not have constant consumption between investments is inferior to one that does, because of the strict concavity of the utility function. We shall show that we may restrict our attention to paths that have an infinite number of periods of constant consumption.

Lemma A1. *If there exists an $\bar{x}$ for which $g(\bar{x}) > 0$, and u is strictly increasing then for any y_0, the path $c(t) = y_0$ $(t \geq 0)$ can be overtaken.*

Proof. Consider the feasible path with consumption $c(t) = c_0 < y_0$ for $0 \leq t \leq T_0$, where T_0 is such that $g((y_0 - c_0)T_0) > 0$, and let $y_1 = y_0 + g((y_0 - c_0)T_0)$, $c(t) = y_1 > y_0$ for $t > T_0$. Since $u(y_1) > u(y_0)$

$$\int_0^{T_0} u(c_0)\, dt + \int_{T_0}^T u(y_1)\, dt \quad \text{overtakes} \quad \int_0^T u(y_0)\, dt.$$

The lemma says that it is always worth making another investment. Note the role played by zero discounting.

We are now in a position to prove that an optimum exists. Define $V(y)$ as the supremum of all possible utility integrals along feasible paths given that one starts with output y and no accumulated savings. We know that the utility integral is bounded above by zero and Assumption A gives us a lower bound, so the definition of V is legitimate. We group together some of the assumptions already made for a formal statement of the theorem.

Theorem 3. *If g is increasing and continuous, and Assumptions A, B, and C hold, then an optimum policy exists.*

Proof. The assumptions of the theorem are sufficient for Lemma A1, and thus justify the recursive relation.

$$V(y_0) = \sup_{c,\, t} \{tu(c) + V[y_0 + g(t(y_0 - c))]\}, \tag{1'}$$

where the supremum is taken over the set

$$0 \leqq c \leqq y_0 \tag{2'}$$

$$\delta(y_0) \leqq t \leqq V(y_0)/u(y_0) + 1. \tag{3'}$$

The upper bound in $(3')$ is justified because, if it is not satisfied,

$$tu(c) \leqq tu(y_0) < V(y_0) + u(y_0) < V(y_0),$$

so that such values of t can be excluded from consideration.

An easy but long proof shows that V is a continuous function; we separate it into Lemma A2 immediately following this theorem. Hence, using the continuity of g and u, the expression within the braces in $(1')$ is a continuous function of c, t. Inequalities $(2')$, $(3')$ define a compact set, so the upper bound is attained at c_0, t_0 (say), and

$$V(y_0) = t_0 u(c_0) + V[y_0 + g(t_0(y_0 - c_0))].$$

Define $y_1 = y_0 + g(t_0(y_0 - c_0))$. Choose c_1, t_1 in the corresponding way. Define y_i, c_i, t_i in a similar fashion for all $i \geqq 1$. Add all the equations

$$V(y_i) = t_i u(c_i) + V(y_{i+1}), \qquad i = 0, 1, 2, \ldots$$

to obtain, since values of V are non-positive,

$$V(y_0) \leqq \sum_{i=0}^{\infty} t_i u(c_i). \tag{4'}$$

Now consider the policy $c(t) = c_i$ for $\sum_0^{i-1} t_j \leqq t \leqq \sum_0^{i} t_j$, where we define $t_{-1} \equiv 0$. If $\sum_0^{\infty} t_j$ diverges, this is a well-defined feasible policy over the indefinite future, and

$$V(y_0) = \sum_{i=0}^{\infty} t_i u(c_i). \tag{5'}$$

If, on the other hand, $\sum_0^{\infty} t_i = T$, a finite number, then we must specify what happens beyond T. Note that we must have $y(t) \to \infty$ as $t \to T$ from below. For suppose not: then, $y(t)$ being monotonic, we must have $y(t) \to \bar{y}$, a finite limit. But then as $i \to \infty$, we have $t_i \to 0 < \delta(\bar{y})$, and this contradicts Assumption C.

With infinite output we can sustain infinite consumption and thus a zero utility integral from T on. For the sequence (c_i, t_i) followed by this phase of infinite consumption, the utility integral is $\geq V(y_0)$ from $(4')$.

Thus, we have shown that an optimum policy exists, and consists of the sequence (c_i, t_i) followed, if possible, by a phase of infinite consumption. □

Lemma A2. *With the assumptions of the theorem, the function V is continuous.*
   Proof. As in the theorem,

$$V(y) = \sup \{tu(c) + V[y + g(t(y - c))]\}.$$

Let $\delta > 0$ and let t^*, c^* be such that

$$t^*u(c^*) + V[y + g(t^*(y - c^*))] > V(y) - \delta/3.$$

Let $y' < y$ and $\gamma = c^*/y < 1$ (by Lemma A1 and the remark preceding it). Consider t', c' satisfying $c' - \gamma y'$ and

$$y' + g(t'(y' - c')) = y + g(t^*(y - c^*)). \tag{6'}$$

These exist and are unique if $g(x)$ is unbounded over $[0, \infty]$ since we have assumed g continuous and increasing.
   Starting from y', policy t', c' achieves, if followed up suitably, a utility integral greater than

$$t'u(c') + \{V[y' + g(t'(y' - c'))] - \delta/3\}.$$

Thus, using earlier inequalities and (6'), we have

$$\begin{aligned}
V(y') &> t'u(c') + V[y' + g(t'(y' - c'))] - \delta/3 \\
&= t'u(c') + V[y + g(t^*(y - c^*))] - \delta/3 \\
&> t'u(c') - t^*u(c^*) + V(y) - 2\delta/3.
\end{aligned}$$

Now use (6'), and remember $c' = \gamma y'$, $c^* = \gamma y$. By continuity of g and u, by taking y' sufficiently closed to y, we can make $t'u(c') - t^*u(c^*) > -\delta/3$; hence

$$V(y') > V(y) - \delta.$$

Clearly, $V(y') < V(y)$ for $y' < y$.
   These two together give us continuity of V. □

REFERENCES

Baumol, W. J., 'The Transactions Demand for Cash: An Inventory Theoretic Approach'. *Quarterly Journal of Economics*, **66** (1952), 545.

Flemming, J. S., 'The Utility of Wealth and the Utility of Windfalls'. *Review of Economic Studies*, **36** (1969), 55.

Koopmans, T. C., 'On the Concept of Optimal Growth'. In *The Econometric Approach to Development Planning* (Chicago: Rand McNally, 1966).

Manne, A. et al., *Investment for Capacity Expansion: Size, Location and Time Phasing* (Cambridge, Mass.: MIT Press, 1967).

Srinivasan, T. N., 'Geometric Rate of Growth of Demand'. In Manne *et al.*, 150.

Tobin, J., 'The Interest Elasticity of Transactions Demand for Cash'. *Review of Economics and Statistics*, **38** (1956), 241.

Weitzman, M. L., 'Optimum Growth with Scale Economies in the Creation of Overhead Capital'. *Review of Economic Studies*, 37 (1970), 555.

Weizsäcker, C. C. von, 'Existence of Optimal Programmes of Accumulation for an Infinite Time Horizon'. *Review of Economic Studies*, 32 (1965), 85.

Whitin, T. M., *The Theory of Inventory Management* (Princeton University Press, 1953).

PART VI

DEVELOPMENT ECONOMICS

22

A Pure Theory of
Underdeveloped Economies

There are a number of reasons for thinking that man's productivity depends upon his consumption, at least where incomes are low. Not only does more food make possible more and better work; good health, higher standards of comfort, and the well-being of dependents might all be expected to help a man do more. In some richer countries, these influences may be reversed. But many who know developing countries believe there is some such relationship, though there may be disagreement about its importance. Several writers have looked at the theoretical implications of the hypothesis that consumption affects productivity and have recognized that it may change the implications of more orthodox economic analysis.[1] In particular, it is one reason for expecting to find relatively high urban wages coexisting with substantial unemployment. The implications have not, as yet, been pushed much further than that. It is particularly interesting to consider what equilibrium in rural areas might be like in these circumstances. That will be the main task of this chapter. It does not provide anything like a complete analysis, but the techniques to be presented perhaps make one possible and at least help to make the theoretical relationships clear. I shall also explore implications for the shadow pricing of labor, both in rural and urban production.

This chapter first appeared in Lloyd G. Reynolds (ed.), *Agriculture in Development Theory* (New Haven and London: Yale University Press, 1975).

Various imperfect versions of this paper have been given over the years. I remember particularly helpful comments and discussions when it was given in Oxford, at Cornell, and in Cambridge.

[1] The relationship between productivity and consumption was first used in theory by Harvey Leibenstein, who, however, assumed full employment (Leibenstein, *Economic Backwardness and Economic Growth*, New York: Wiley, 1957). The peculiarity of that assumption was pointed out by D. Mazumdar in 'The Marginal Productivity Theory of Wages and Disguised Unemployment', *Review of Economic Studies* 26, no. 3 (1959). J. C. H. Fei and Alpha D. Chiang developed a growth model using the relationship in 'Maximum-Speed Development through Austerity', in *The Theory and Design of Economic Development*, ed. I. Adelman and E. Thorbecke (Baltimore: Johns Hopkins University Press, 1966). There are some interesting further developments in Pradhan H. Prasad, *Growth with Full Employment* (Bombay: Allied Publishers, 1970). Gunnar Myrdal has emphasized the relationship but does not do much with it: see *Asian Drama* (New York: Pantheon, 1968).

Some relevant evidence on a relationship that has not received much attention from econometricians is contained in the booklet *Nutrition and Working Efficiency*, produced for the Freedom from Hunger Campaign as Basic Studies no. 5, and published by the FAO.

The analysis to be presented is called a 'pure' theory because it ignores many important features of underdeveloped economies, so as to concentrate on one relationship. One must of course simplify in order to get an analysis going, and in any case it is interesting to see how much of what we observe in the less developed economies might be explained by the productivity relationship. Pure theory has the attraction that it concentrates on rational action in the face of intrinsic constraints and may therefore point to underlying long-run tendencies.

1. FACTORIES AND WAGE LABOR

I begin by reviewing what is already known. Laborers work in factories, which are run by profit-maximizing employers. If they do not obtain employment, they may return whence they came, starve, or share in some fixed pool of charitable gifts; if a man obtains a job, he consumes the wage he is paid. We assume—bearing in mind that this means leaving aside some interesting problems—that the quantity and quality of labor a man provides can together be measured by a single number, h, which is a function of the wage, w, he receives, and that the labor (h) provided by different employees can simply be added up to give the total labor input. Thus, a factory with production function f produces output (measured in the same units as the wage)

$$y = f[nh(w)], \tag{1}$$

where n is the number of men working in the factory and all workers receive wage w. We can consider the possibility of employing people at different wages, but the assumptions to be made in fact imply that producers do not want to.

Assume that f is a concave, increasing function, zero at zero. The function h is supposed to have the shape indicated in Fig. 22.1. The shape is plausible—as the production function for a typical piece of capital equipment designed for relatively specific purposes—consistent with such scant evidence as I have seen, and broadly necessary if the theory is to have any interest.

The producer's profits are

$$\pi = f[nh(w)] - nw. \tag{2}$$

Not only does he choose n; he has a certain degree of control over w as well. The point is that employers can always pay more than the supply price of laborers to them; though, in the absence of the productivity relationship, they would have no reason to do so. Since we can write (2) in the form

$$\pi = f[nh(w)] - nh(w)\frac{w}{h(w)},$$

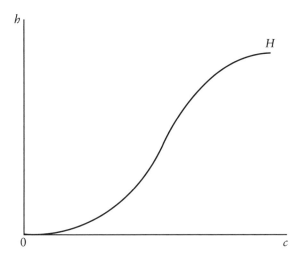

Figure 22.1.

the producer does best for himself if he chooses w so as to make $w/h(w)$ as small as possible and then, having chosen w in this way, chooses nh to maximize π.[2] Referring to Fig. 22.2, we see that w/h is least when $w = c^*$, the consumption level at which the tangent to the h-curve passes through the origin. If the supply price of laborers is in any case above c^*, then the employer cannot do better than pay the supply price; but if it is less than c^*, he will not pay less than c^*. Thus, the profit-maximizing wage rate is

$$w = \max(c^*, w_S), \tag{3}$$

where c^* maximizes h/w, and w_S is the supply price of labor.

Where there is a fixed supply of laborers available, and a number of factories, the supply price of labor will be greater than c^* only if there would be an excess demand for labor by producers were the wage equal to c^*. If on the contrary there is an excess supply of labor when $w = c^*$, the supply price of labor is lower, but it ceases to operate: we have an equilibrium with unemployed laborers who do not choose to be unemployed.

If employers were unaware of the productivity relationship embodied in the function h, the natural outcome would be the usual competitive equilibrium, in which the wage might be lower than c^*. From that point of view, the 'efficiency wage' notion introduces a new concept of equilibrium. From another point of view, we can think of the supply and demand for labor,

---

[2] Since π is not a concave function of w, it is not sufficient to look at necessary conditions for maximization, but the argument given is rigorous; for, if c^* minimizes w/h and x^* maximizes $f(x) - xc^*/h(c^*)$, $f(x^*) - x^*c^*/h(c^*) \geq f(nh) - nhc^*/h(c^*) \geq f(nh) - nhc/h = f(nh) - nc$.

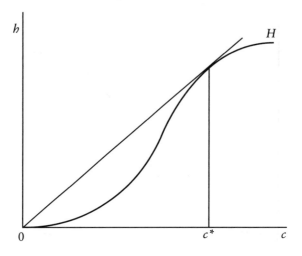

Figure 22.2.

rather than the supply and demand for laborers. If the wage is w, the price of labor to the employer is $v = w/h$. We have seen that this has a minimum value; or, to put it differently, the supply of labor is zero if v is less than $v^* = c^*/h(c^*)$. Thus there is a discontinuity in the labor supply at v^*. If we look for a competitive equilibrium in the markets for goods and labor, we shall find that none exists when the supply of labor at v^* exceeds the demand. But that is precisely the case in which c^* is the equilibrium wage in the sense just defined.[3]

Notice that the producer we have just been considering would not want to pay different wages to different groups of laborers, even if the supply of laborers were large enough to make that possible. But the nature of work to be done varies from one industry to another, and from one department of a firm to another. One ought, therefore, to allow for various functions, h, applying to different factories. Corresponding to each, there will be a c^*. Consider different supplies of laborers. The higher the supply price of laborers, the more factories will be paying w_S to their laborers, rather than the c^* corresponding to them. When the supply of laborers is sufficiently large, all wage rates will be determined by the productivity relationship. When it is sufficiently small, a single wage rate will apply to all employment. In between, the range of wage rates being paid will be greater the lower

---

[3] If all persons have different h functions, and there is a continuum of consumers, a competitive equilibrium may exist, with some people at the zero consumption point. The equilibrium discussed in the text is the limit of such a competitive equilibrium as we move all consumer types into identity with one another.

the supply price of laborers.[4] There will be open unemployment only when c^*-level wages apply everywhere. Thus, the productivity hypothesis has interesting implications even when there is no unemployment. We can expect that in general it applies to some jobs and not to others. Notice that this argument has been conducted on the assumption that all workers are alike. The wage differences we are talking about should arise even between people of similar abilities.

A third striking implication of the productivity hypothesis is that wage rates need not change over tune in the way that earlier economic theory may have led us to expect. While technology changes, capital accumulates, and population grows, c^* changes only in so far as the function h changes. There is no reason why that function should change in such a way that c^* increases over time. Thus, in a growing economy with initial unemployment, we can expect real wages to remain constant; or at any rate we can claim that the appearance of fairly constant real wages in a growing economy is consistent with the productivity hypothesis, though not (special cases apart) with competitive equilibrium models. In a growing economy, one does expect unemployment to diminish eventually, especially if the real wage is not rising. The argument of the previous paragraph then leads one to expect that wage differences will diminish over time, with the highest wages for untrained labor remaining relatively constant. This particular suggestion would, in a world with skilled labor, be rather hard to test.

A further implication, which I have not seen mentioned elsewhere, relates to investment in labor quality. It is often argued—though, on the face of it, fallaciously—that when employment confers skills it generates an external economy. This argument is fallacious if the unskilled worker willingly accepts a lower wage because of the higher wage his acquired skill will later make available to him. But when the employer is in any case paying above the supply price for labor, this argument may not apply. True, the government may wish to subsidize employment in such an economy as I am discussing. I suspect it would want to subsidize it by more if employment conferred skills. The productivity hypothesis appears to provide support for the old training–externality argument. We should also recognize an externality arising from lags between consumption and productivity, which are surely quite substantial. A well-paid worker will be a better worker for months, perhaps years, to come. His current employer receives no immediate benefit from these lagged effects.

For both these reasons, the theory leads one to expect that employers will be willing to pay more to workers who contract (reliably) for longer periods of employment. This might manifest itself in arrangements for

---

[4] It is theoretically possible that the aggregate demand curve for laborers may not be a monotonic function of the wage in these circumstances, for an increased wage can lead to substitution of higher-paid laborers for lower-paid laborers.

attaching labor to the firm on a semi-permanent basis (as, to a considerable extent, in Japan); or at least in the development of 'company towns', tied pension rights, and payment by the month (in arrears).

2. WELFARE ECONOMICS OF THE SIMPLE CASE

Consider next an economy in which all production is done in a factory with production possibilities described by equation (1), and the population, which may as well be identified with the supply of laborers, is so large that the equilibrium we have been discussing implies unemployment of laborers. It seems clear that this outcome, with zero consumption for the unemployed, is not optimal by any acceptable criterion. But we shall see that the optimum for such an economy of identical people may well prescribe different consumption levels for different groups.

We ought to have a welfare function that treats all individuals alike and favors equality. Such a welfare function is the familiar additive criterion

$$W = \sum_i u(c_i), \qquad u \text{ increasing and concave,} \tag{4}$$

which expresses a rather individualistic point of view. With that reminder of its restrictive nature, I shall use equation (4), since it greatly simplifies the analysis.

W is to be maximized, subject to the production constraint

$$\sum c_i \le f\left[\sum h(c_i)\right]. \tag{5}$$

Necessary conditions for the optimum are easily written down, if we introduce a Lagrange multiplier s for the constraint given in equation (5). Differentiating with respect to c_i yields

$$u'(c_i) + s\left[f'\left(\sum h\right)h'(c_i) - 1\right] = 0. \tag{6}$$

One may be tempted to think that only one value of c_i will satisfy this equation. But if, as that would imply, everyone has the same consumption level, it may be impossible to satisfy the production constraint: there may be no number c such that $nc \le f[nh(c)]$. Such a case is shown in Fig. 22.3, where the curve OF shows for each level of c the level of h (per person) that would be required to produce it in a population of size n. The equation of the curve OF is

$$c = \frac{1}{n} f(nh). \tag{7}$$

Since OF does not intersect the curve OH (with equation $h = h(c)$), no uniform level of c can be produced with the labor that would be forthcoming.

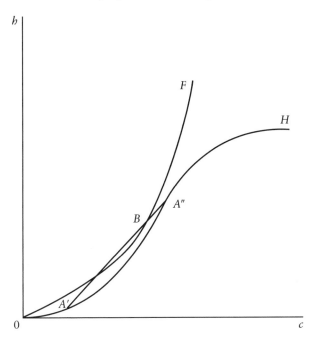

Figure 22.3.

It is possible, however, for the economy to have two different consumption levels coexisting. Such an allocation is shown by the line $A'BA''$ in the diagram. The two consumption levels are c' and c''. If $\bar{c}$ is the average level of consumption in the economy, achieved by dividing the population between c' and c'' in the proportions $A''B : A'B$, this can be achieved by an average labor input of $\bar{h}$, which is precisely what the population can, in these circumstances, provide. Thus, no more than two consumption levels are required for feasibility. The question is whether more levels may be optimal. To answer this, and to bring out some other features of the optimum, I will introduce the more complicated diagram shown in Fig. 22.4.

In Fig. 22.4, the top right-hand quadrant corresponds to the diagram in Fig. 4.3: the curve OH again shows the relationship between a man's consumption and the labor he can provide, while OF shows production possibilities (in terms of average labor and average output). We will suppose that optimum production is represented by the point B, with average consumption equal to $\bar{c}$, and average labor equal to $\bar{h}$. At this stage of the argument, we do not predict the number of different consumption levels, so c' and c'' should be ignored for the moment. The line OQ has the same slope as the tangent to the production set at B, which is (seen from the vertical axis) the marginal product of labor (*not* laborers) at the optimum, q. This is used

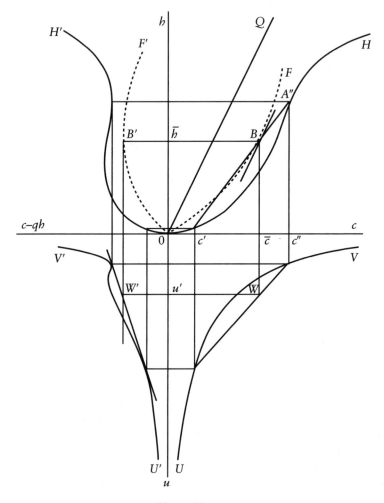

Figure 22.4.

to construct the diagram in the top left-hand quadrant of the figure, where for each value of h we take the horizontal distance between the line OQ and the curve OF to obtain OF', and between OQ and OH to obtain OH'. We are subtracting qh from the horizontal coordinate in each case.

Lowering our vision to the utility curves in the lower half of the figure, we see the utility function itself graphed in the lower right-hand quadrant. For convenience, u is taken to be negative in the range that concerns us, so that the utility curve is convex in relation to the origin. The curve $U'V'$ in the lower left-hand quadrant is derived from the rest of the figure: it shows the relationship between u and $c - qh$ that is implied by the curves UV and OH. Having constructed that curve, we draw the *double tangent* to it. (It can be shown that if the curve $U'V'$ were concave, so that there was no double tangent, we would not be at the optimum. One can show that a neighboring production point is better.) It is clear that, in general, this will be a double, not a treble, tangent, and that it will be uniquely defined by the property of being double. The two points of tangency correspond to consumption levels c' and c'', as shown in the figure; their respective coordinates are $c' - qh(c')$, $u(c')$ and $c'' - qh(c'')$, $u(c'')$. At the same time, there is a point W' on the double tangent corresponding to the utility level $\bar{u}$ which is, by our initial specification, the maximum attainable utility level.

This point W' must correspond to the point B in the upper right-hand quadrant: that is, its horizontal coordinate must be $\bar{c} - q\bar{h}$; for, since W' lies on the line joining the two points corresponding to A' and A'', the point corresponding to W' must lie on the line joining A' and A''. Since its horizontal coordinate is $\bar{c}$, that point must indeed be B.

Because of our construction, $\bar{u}$ is certainly the maximum utility level consistent with the production point B, i.e. with given average levels $\bar{h}$ and $\bar{c}$; for, corresponding to every individual in the economy, there is a point on the curve $U'V'$ showing his utility and the value of $c - qh$ for him. The average of these points will show the average utility level, and $\bar{c} - q\bar{h}$. Any such average point (being in the convex hull of the curve $U'V'$) that has given $\bar{c} - \bar{q}\bar{h}$ must lie on the vertical line $W'B'$, at or below W'. The greatest average utility is obtained by dividing the population between consumption levels c' and c'', as shown in the figure.

Since we specified B originally as the optimum production point, it follows from this argument that there are (in general) two consumption levels in the optimum state of the economy. If the slope of the double tangent is s, we see that c' and c'' maximize

$$u(c) + s[qh(c) - c], \tag{8}$$

where $q = f'(\bar{h})$. Thus, we can now say more than equation (6), which merely asserted that the derivative of (8) vanished at those consumption levels that actually occur. In particular, notice that (8) takes the same value for c' and c''.

By examing Fig. 22.4 more closely, we can deduce some other properties of the optimum for this economy.

(i) I have already remarked that the curve $U'V'$ must not be concave. This puts a lower bound to q, which we can call q_1. (It is not, I think, very important, so I will explain the deduction of its value in a footnote.[5]) We can also assign an upper bound to q. If the line OQ were to cut the curve OH,

---

[5] For each q, t is chosen so that $tu(c) + qh(c) - c$ has two equal maxima. As $q \to q_1$, $tu + qh - c$ becomes concave for all c_1 with the first and second derivatives zero at one point, c_1. (The first derivative is zero because the maxima when $q > q_1$ are equal.) Since that is the maximum value of the second derivative, the third derivative is also zero. Therefore q_1 and c_1 satisfy (along with some

B could not be optimal, for a small increase in production would be possible by letting those consuming most consume more. Therefore q must be less than $q^* = c^*/h(c^*)$, the slope of the ray that is tangent to the OH curve. Since $q_1 < q < q^*$, the slope of the double tangent (negative as the diagram is drawn), s, is positive, and $c'' - qh(c'')$ is bigger than $c' - qh(c')$; i.e.,

$$c'' - c' > q(h'' - h'), \qquad (9)$$

where I use the obvious notation $h' = h(c')$, $h'' = h(c'')$. This tells us that B is the upper intersection of the line $A'A''$ with the curve OF.

(ii) On the other hand, A'' is the lower bound of the two possible intersections of $A'A''$ with the curve OH. For if the upper consumption level were shifted to the outer intersection, while B remained fixed, the average utility level would fall, being the intersection of the appropriate chord of the utility curve with the vertical line BW. Also, $A'A''$ has a steeper slope than the curve OH at c'. These two facts imply that

$$\frac{1}{h'(c')}(h'' - h') \geq c'' - c' \geq \frac{1}{h'(c'')}(h'' - h'). \qquad (10)$$

The latter inequality also implies what is directly more interesting, i.e. that

$$c'' < c^*. \qquad (11)$$

(iii) Because of the way that c' and c'' were derived, they are functions of q alone. Of course, given the functions f, u, and h as data, we do not know in advance what q is going to be, but it is nevertheless very useful that knowledge of q, the marginal product of labor, is the only information about production possibilities that we need in order to calculate the consumption

number t_1) the following:

$$t_1 u'(c_1) + q_1 h'(c_1) = 1$$
$$t_1 u''(c_1) + q_1 h''(c_1) = 0$$
$$t_1 u'''(c_1) + q_1 h'''(c_1) = 0.$$

Therefore c_1 is denned by

$$h'''(c_1)u''(c_1) - h''(c_1)u'''(c_1) = 0,$$

and

$$q_1 = \frac{u''(c_1)}{h'(c_1)u''(c_1) - h''(c')u'(c_1)}.$$

Notice that

$$\frac{1}{q_1} = h'(c_1) + \frac{u'(c_1)}{-u''(c_1)}h''(c_1) > h'(c_1),$$

since $h''(c_1) = -(t_1/q_1)u''(c_1) > 0$. This fact is incorporated in Fig. 22.5.

levels. Given q, variations in the average product are accommodated, so long as uniform consumption for everyone is impossible, by varying the proportions of the population at the two consumption levels. One particular implication of this dependence of c' and c'' on q alone is that only certain pairs of values of c' and c'' are possible. Indeed, we shall see in a moment that the consumption levels are monotonic functions of one another.

I do not yet see how to deduce, from the diagram alone, the manner in which the consumption levels depend on q. Instead, I resort to analytical methods. First, c' and c'' are determined, given q, by the equations

$$tu'(c') + qh'(c') = 1, \tag{6'}$$

$$tu'(c'') + qh'(c'') = 1, \tag{6''}$$

$$tu(c') + qh(c') - c' = tu(c'') + qh(c'') - c'', \tag{12}$$

where, for convenience, I have divided the earlier equations by s and written t for $1/s$. Since t is to be eliminated from these equations to determine c' and c'', we determine dt/dq from (12). Differentiating the equation with respect to q, we notice that, because of (6') and (6''), the terms in derivatives of the consumption levels drop out, and we have

$$\frac{dt}{dq} = -\frac{h(c'') - h(c')}{u(c'') - u(c')}. \tag{13}$$

Turning to (6') and differentiating, we get

$$[tu''(c') + qh''(c')]\frac{dc'}{dq} = -u'(c')\frac{dt}{dq} - h'(c)$$

$$= [h(c'') - h(c')]\frac{u'(c')}{u(c'') - u(c')} - h'(c'), \tag{14}$$

using (13). The factor $tu'' + qh''$ is the second derivative of $tu + qh - c$ and is therefore non-positive, since c' maximizes. Therefore, the sign of dc'/dq is the opposite of the sign of the expression on the right of (14). The concavity of u implies that $u(c'') - u(c') \le u'(c')\,(c'' - c')$. It follows, using the left-hand inequality in (10), that the right-hand side of (14) is non-negative. Therefore,

$$\frac{d}{dq}c' \le 0. \tag{15}$$

In a similar way, using the right-hand inequality in (10), and the concavity inequality $u(c'') - u(c') \ge u'(c'')(c'' - c')$, it can be shown that

$$\frac{d}{dq}c'' \ge 0. \tag{16}$$

Summarizing these results, for the optimum when uniform consumption is impossible, we find that the marginal product of labor, q, lies between two limits, q_1 and q^*, and as it increases from q_1 to q^* the upper limit of consumption increases (in fact from c_1 to c^*, where c_1 is defined in footnote 5, and c^* was defined earlier as the equilibrium wage), and the lower level of consumption decreases (from c_1 to 0).

It is interesting to consider how q might be expected to vary over time as production possibilities improve, i.e. as the curve OF moves to the right. In Fig. 22.5 I show various possible $A'A''$ lines. These lie further to the right, with decreasing values of q (indicated by arrows, with slope $1/q$), suggesting that, as production possibilities expand, q should become smaller and the consumption levels come closer together. There might be exceptions to that general tendency, but it is unambiguously the case that as population (n) falls (or, equivalently, when there is labor-augmenting technical progress), q falls. To prove this, observe that, as n varies, the marginal product of labor is always constant along rays going out from the origin; for on any such ray, $\bar{c}/\bar{h} = f(n\bar{h})/(n\bar{h})$ being constant, so are $n\bar{h}$, and $q = f'(n\bar{h})$. If, then, n were to become smaller, the curve OF, described by equation (7), would move out, and if q were to rise $\bar{c}/\bar{h}$ would have to fall, which is manifestly inconsistent with production being on an $A'A''$ line to the left of the previous one.

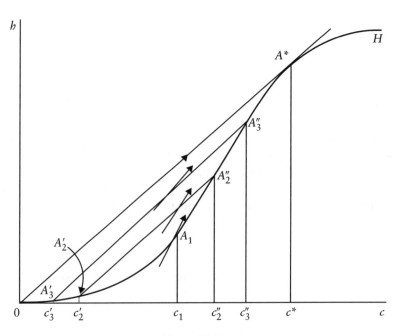

Figure 22.5.

Thus, optimal development over time would appear to require a narrowing of consumption differentials, with the higher consumption level falling, until uniform consumption becomes possible. (Geometrically, the OF curve hits the OH curve.) At this point, there would in general be a discontinuous change of q and the consumption levels, since it is very unlikely that the OF curve would hit the OH curve first at $c = c_1$. Notice that, according to equation (6''), $h'(c'') < 1/q$. It is therefore true, unless the functions are very peculiar, that the uniform consumption level to which the economy switches is less than c'', since at the new level $h' = 1/f'$. Actually, since (apart from anything else) capital has been ignored in this discussion, the analysis as yet provides no more than indications about optimal development. But we shall see later that the results are of considerable interest in a rather different context.

3. COMPETITIVE REALIZATION OF THE OPTIMUM

It is quite clear that equilibrium in the absence of state intervention cannot possibly be optimal in this economy, because employers, who are concerned merely to maximize labor input per unit wage, $h(c)/c$, have no incentive to employ anyone at a wage other than c^*. Since this involves unemployment, one would suppose that the government ought to introduce wage subsidies to correct the equilibrium, with a particularly large subsidy for the employment of low-wage workers. Actually, however, it turns out that the subsidy should be greater for high-wage workers.

Suppose an employer is paid the following subsidy for each worker he employs at wage w:

$$\sigma(w) = a + tu(w). \tag{17}$$

(It is not clear, a priori, whether (17) defines a tax or a subsidy, but we shall see that it is in fact positive for those values of w that actually occur.) Let the parameters a and $t > 0$ be determined so that there is full employment of laborers, and total output is just sufficient to cover consumption requirements. Then employers choose the number they employ, m, and the wages at which they are employed, $w_1, w_2, \ldots, w_m$ so as to maximize

$$f\left[\sum h(w_i)\right] - \sum w_i + \sum \sigma(w_i) = f\left[\left(\sum h(w_i)\right)\right] - \sum w_i + ma$$
$$+ t\sum u(w_i). \tag{18}$$

The government has chosen a and t so that employers choose m to be n, the actual population, and $f[\sum h(w_i)] = \sum w_i$. Therefore this maximization of (18) tells us that $t\sum u(w_i)$ is greater than it would be for any alternative $w_1, w_2, \ldots, w_n$. In other words, the optimum has been realized.

How do we know a and $t > 0$ can be found to achieve this desirable end? We know because we have already found such numbers in analyzing the optimum: t is $1/s$, and a is $c' - tu(c') - qh(c') = c'' - tu(c'') - qh(c'')$. With these values of t and a, it is easy to verify that the optimum actually does maximize in (18). Since $\sigma(c') = c' - qh(c')$ and $\sigma(c'') = c'' - qh(c'')$, we know from Fig. 22.4 that the transfer is a subsidy (not a tax) at both c' and c''.

It is interesting that the economy can be 'put right' by using knowledge of only the utility function, in conjunction with market-clearing: no knowledge of the h function is required. Notice that employers end up with positive profit, equal to the total subsidy, which must be taxed away as a profit tax if the full optimum is to be achieved. Thus f must be defined net of any profits required as incentives to producers.

4. THE PEASANT ECONOMY WITHOUT FACTOR MARKETS

The chief object of analysis in this chapter is a peasant economy, for which the productivity relationship holds, wherein each peasant family consists of a number of identical people, who possess a certain amount of land, with production possibilities described (in terms of average consumption and effort) by

$$c \leq \frac{1}{n} f(nh). \tag{7}$$

Obviously, the assumption of identical people is made for analytical convenience and should cause no difficulty. What does cause difficulty is deciding what criteria would motivate such a family. We are discussing cases where it is impossible for everyone in the family to have the same consumption. The family is forced, therefore, to discriminate between its members. No doubt seniority, convention, brute force, and impulse may have influence, but I shall follow the extreme assumption that allocations within the family maximize a welfare function.

With this hypothesis, the theory of a peasant economy, in the absence of markets for labor and land, is formally identical to the welfare economics of a factory economy, a theory that we have already to some extent worked out. It is true that the assumption of an additively separable welfare function is less plausible in the case of a family than it is for groups in an economy, but one may reasonably hope that the theory for the separable case is a good predictor of the more general theory.

Applying the previous theory, then, we have the following propositions. (1) There are two consumption levels in a family. (2) The difference between the two consumption levels is greater the larger the family (per unit of land): as size increases, the higher consumption level becomes yet higher, though a smaller proportion of the family enjoys that level. (3) Total output is a decreasing function of family size.

The last proposition follows from the fact that $q = f'(n\bar{h})$ is an increasing function of n, for that means $n\bar{h}$ is a decreasing function of n, which in turn implies that output, $f(n\bar{h})$, is a decreasing function of n. We have deduced that the marginal product of laborers, in the sense one would observe it if one did cross-section studies, is negative. On the other hand, the marginal product of labor, q, is positive.

5. MARKETS IN LABOR AND LAND

In an economy where different peasant families have different labor–land ratios, it is to be expected that land and labor markets will have developed. Of the two, the land market is easier to analyze, so let us take it up first. The model I use is one in which the same production function applies to all land, and the same utility function rules all intrafamilial allocations, so that families differ only in the value of n appropriate to them, n being interpreted as the number of family members per unit of land owned.

Let there be a perfect market in land, the price of a unit of land being r. Consider a family owning a unit of land. It could receive r for that land, distributing the proceeds among its members (who would get an average of r/n each), or it could keep its land, using its production function, or it could rent out some of its land or rent in additional land from other families. The production possibilities available to it have thus been expanded, the effective frontier now being the tangent from the all-land-rented-out point $(r/n, 0)$ to the ordinary production frontier, as shown in Fig. 22.6. It follows that r determines q uniquely, through the following equations:

$$q = f'(nh),$$
$$f(nh) - qnh = r. \tag{19}$$

Different families will therefore, according to our theory, all have the same two consumption levels, c' and c'', except for those families who either have so much land that they can give all members a consumption level c greater than c'', or have so little land that they are unable to provide all members with c' and have to be content with a uniform consumption level below c'. The situation is portrayed in Fig. 22.7. Families with $n \geq n'$ have uniform consumption; families with $n' > n > n_2$ have two consumption levels, c' and c'', and rent out some of their land; families with $n_2 > n > n_3$ have consumption levels c' and c'' and rent in some land; families with $n_3 > n > n_4$ have uniform consumption (greater than c_3) and rent in land; families with $n_4 > n$ have uniform consumption and rent out land.

It will be seen that the poorest families (with the largest n) rent out almost all their land, as do the richest families (with small n); it is families of

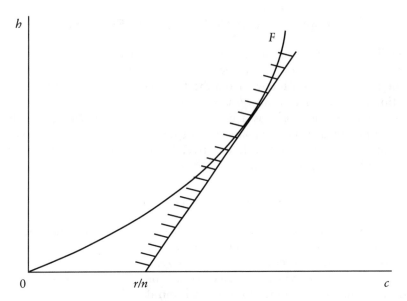

Figure 22.6

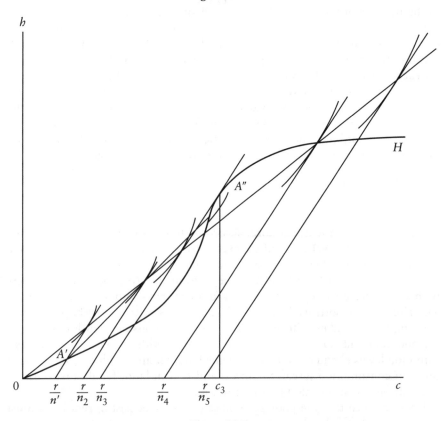

Figure 22.7

intermediate wealth who rent in land, being able to use the opportunity to increase both the consumption and the productivity of their members. The equilibrium level of r is determined by the level of q that ensures equality between the supply of and demand for land.

The perfect land market has the effect, in this model, of making the marginal product of labor the same on all units of land, so that output per unit of land is the same for all families. However, the number of people working the land varies from family to family: since the total labor input per unit area is constant, the number per unit area worked by the family (after allowing for renting) is inversely proportional to the average effort per person that family can provide. The poorer the family, the less its average effort in equilibrium, and therefore the higher the labor–land ratio on the land it works. An outside observer would deduce from such an economy, if he were ignorant of the productivity relationship, that the marginal product of laborers was zero, since he would see a variety of plots of land being worked, with varying numbers of workers per acre, yet all producing the same output per acre.

In fact, one can make no unambiguous statement about the sign of the marginal product of laborers for the economy taken as a whole. If one could pretend that the average family must be one that neither rents in nor rents out land (or is at least indifferent between the options), one could apply the results of the previous section, treating the whole economy as a single family. But that is not legitimate: the distribution of land ownership influences the outcome, and even if equalization of land ownership would bring about an equilibrium with a negative marginal product of laborers, that marginal product may still be positive given the actual distribution of land ownership. Consider what happens if some people leave the economy, with proportionate reductions in the size of all families. The richer families will, for any r, increase their supply of land, since they have moved further out along the OB line. But, for the same reason, the poorer families will reduce their supply of land. If in aggregate there is an increased supply of land, equilibrium r must be lower (for a reduction in r will increase excess demand for every family); but if the effect in aggregate is to reduce the supply of land, r will rise. Lower r means lower aggregate output, and higher r means greater aggregate output. Thus, whether the departure of average laborers increases or reduces output depends upon the distribution of property. What one can say is that the marginal product will probably be negative in an economy where there are few large landholders (i.e. few people in families represented by points in the upper right-hand part of Fig. 22.7), or where most of those drawn away from the local economy (or added to it by population growth) are members of the poorer families.

The labor market in our economy is a little harder to deal with because, at first sight, it seems to be rather odd. If there were a ruling wage rate, resulting from optimal employment policies by families with the most land, one might think that the considerations discussed in Section 1 of this chapter would apply. But a ruling wage at c^* could hardly be maintained, since it would be possible for families to offer family members for employment along with a guaranteed consumption subsidy. This is not a farfetched idea: the consumption subsidy would be apparent in the general good health and nutrition of the worker seeking employment, and the better favored men could expect to be employed before the less favored. It would be to the benefit of poorer families to subsidize their members to seek employment, since, as we have seen, their departure makes possible some increase in output.

The effect of any such arrangements would, implicitly, be to establish a market in labor rather than laborers. For employers always prefer workers who cost them less per unit of effort, and it would not pay the worker's family to subsidize him beyond the point where a unit of his labor costs the same as anyone else's. Now a market in labor is the same in effect, for our timeless economic model without indivisibilities, transaction costs, or uncertainty, as a market in land. It extends the possibilities open to a family in the same kind of way. In the real world, one could expect the two kinds of markets, taken together, to allow an approximately linear expansion of production possibilities, in the way described by Fig. 22.6. Thus, we already have a theory for the effects of a market in labor. The price is q; a man with consumption c gets a wage $qh(c)$.

The way one might expect equilibrium to work out in the model is that the poorest families would sell all their land and earn what they could in the labor market. In this model, unlike the simpler one of Section 1, their income from land allows them to seek employment at a wage low enough to offset their low productivity. One would expect them to gain employment with the richer families. The land market could adjust matters between the richer and the middle peasants.

It will be recognized that there is no readily observable relationship between the wage rates that would operate in such a labor market and the marginal productivity of laborers. What wage rates are equal to are the marginal products of the laborers at constant consumption levels; but a change in family numbers normally means a change in the consumption of some of its members. Observed marginal products would include the effect of these changes. One odd implication of the theory is a certain diversity of wage rates. There may be some labor-supplying families so poor that their consumption is less than c'. Other families who wish to supply labor will fall into two categories: those with consumption c', and those with consumption c''. So long as poor families keep their land rather than join the labor market, we would not expect to observe c'-laborers. But if, as often happens in developing countries, the poorest do sell their land, the theory predicts a two-level labor market. This may bode ill for the theory, but it should be remembered that age and sex can provide a basis for such discrimination.

6. SHADOW WAGE RATES

One reason for developing models of the rural economy is to seek a basis for estimating the cost and benefits of providing employment, in both urban and rural areas. I shall discuss two extreme cases: that of local employment, in which the government employs a number of people locally, at some wage, these people continuing to be part of their families, sharing their consumption with them or receiving consumption subsidies from them according to the family interest; and that of urban employment, where employment takes a man away from his family completely, so that there is no further transfer of goods between him and his family.

I will use two propositions for a family of the kind discussed above in Section 4:

$$\frac{\partial}{\partial n}(n\bar{u}) = \bar{u} - s(\bar{c} - q\bar{b}) \tag{20}$$

$$\frac{\partial}{\partial C}(n\bar{u}) = s, \tag{21}$$

where C is a gift of consumption goods to the family. The proof of these propositions follows lines familiar to devotees of Lagrange multipliers. The multiplier s was introduced so that the family's constrained maximization could be expressed as a maximization of

$$L = n\bar{u} + s(f(n\bar{b}) + C - n\bar{c}). \tag{22}$$

Of course C was zero before, and we are now considering only small changes in C away from zero. Consumption levels c' and c'', the allocation of family members between them, and s are chosen so that the derivatives of L with respect to all of them are zero. Therefore the derivative of L with respect to C is s and is also equal to the derivative of $n\bar{u}$ with respect to C. Similarly, if one differentiates with respect to n, one has $\partial L/\partial n = \bar{u} - s\bar{c} + sf'(n\bar{b})\bar{b} = \partial/\partial n(n\bar{u})$. In this way, both (20) and (21) are proved.

Suppose now that the government comes in and offers employment to one man at the going wage. That wage, for a man with consumption c'' (which one may take to be the normal case), is $w = qh(c'')$. The man who gets the job has utility $u(c'')$. The family (not counting the new employee, once he has the job) has an increase in utility of $s(\bar{c} - q\bar{b}) - \bar{u}$ because of the change in numbers, and a reduction of $s[c'' - qh(c'')]$ because of the consumption subsidy paid to the employee. Thus, the net gain in utility is $u(c'') + s(\bar{c} - q\bar{b}) - \bar{u} - s(c'' - qh'')$, which vanishes, since $u(c'') - s(c'' - qh'') = u(c') - s(c' - qh') = u - s(\bar{c} - q\bar{b})$, taking the average.

I thus conclude that the shadow wage rate for local employment when the market wage is paid is equal to the market wage qh''. If a higher wage is paid, the difference between w and qh'' is a consumption subsidy to the family, to be evaluated as such. If the utility function is so measured that a unit of public funds has marginal (social) utility of unity, s is the shadow price of a gift to the family. Its value could be assessed by using the formula

$$s = \frac{h'(c'')u'(c') - h'(c')u'(c'')}{h'(c'') - h'(c')},\tag{23}$$

which is readily deduced from (6') and (6''). Notice that s is larger, and could be much larger, than $u'(c')$, the marginal utility of the poorest member of the family. The reason for this is the 'multiplier' effects of the extra consumption through increased productivity within the family.

In the case of a man who leaves the rural community entirely, to enjoy (by consuming) a wage w, the gain in utility is, according to (20),

$$u(w) - \bar{u} + s(\bar{c} - q\bar{h}),\tag{24}$$

in which the direct utility increase for the man in question is combined with a multiple of the difference between the average product and the marginal product of the laborer, assuming that effort is constant. This is the same formula one would obtain if the productivity effects of consumption were ignored. The difference comes in the assessment of s, which, as we have seen, is influenced by multiplier effects, and may be substantially larger than one would think if average consumption were taken as a guide. It will be appreciated that the consumption value of employment, given by (24), should be set off against the wage-cost of employment, w.

We can round off our picture of a developing economy by considering the optimum employment and wage policy for the urban sector. Let f and h now apply to industry, and let us suppose that the marginal utility of public income is unity; n is urban employment. Then public sector production should maximize

$$f[nh(w)] - nw + n[u(w) - \bar{u} + s(\bar{c} - q\bar{h})].$$

Therefore,

$$f'(nh)h'(w) = 1 - u'(w)\tag{25}$$

$$f'(nh)h(w) - w + u(w) - \bar{u} + s(\bar{c} - q\bar{h}) = 0.\tag{26}$$

Equation (26) equates the marginal product of laborers to something much less than w (assuming that $u(w) > \bar{u}$ and s is large.) Dividing (26) in terms of (25), we have

$$\frac{h(w)}{wh'(w)} = 1 - \frac{u(w) - wu'(w) - \bar{u} + s(\bar{c} - q\bar{h})}{1 - u'(w)},\tag{27}$$

which would generally, but not necessarily, be less than one. We can therefore expect w to be somewhat less than c^*.

The model discussed here has excluded much of what is believed to be important in developing countries. At the same time, it emphasizes something that might be important and yet has suffered neglect from economists. I think that a number of the implications of the productivity hypothesis might be taken to refute it—particularly the quite wide consumption differences within families, and the wide range of consumption levels that are not supposed to occur. Yet in fact there are large consumption differences within families; and of course, u and h vary greatly between families and individuals, so that the striking results should not be interpreted very strictly. Also, the results are in other ways rather encouraging—in suggesting diversity of wage rates, for example, and predicting land sale by the poorest families. Among the simplifications made, I neglected the effect of the consumption level on population growth (that is, in terms of the models, the reaction of c on n). Even today, this may be important, particularly for the poorest families. The consumption–productivity relationship explored in this chapter seems sufficiently promising to deserve critical empirical research into its form and importance.

23

Project Appraisal and Planning Twenty Years On

With I. M. D. Little

APPENDIX: UNCERTAINTY AND PROJECT APPRAISAL

The Value of Appraisal

One can regard project appraisal as a reduction in uncertainty, that is to say, acquisition of information. The value of information has been studied in the literature.[1] Here we apply it to the making of decisions. The process of appraisal is selection among several possibilities, each of uncertain value. Suppose, for example, that there are two projects. Their true values are x and y. Suppose, for definiteness, that $x > y$. Appraisal will yield apparent values $x + A$ and $y + B$, where the random variables A and B are the errors that remain after appraisal. Before appraisal, uncertainty is even greater: their values seem to be $x + A + C$ and $y + B + D$, where C and D are further error terms. Assume that all four error terms have zero mean; that amounts to saying that there is no identifiable bias in the relative evaluations for the two projects.

Without appraisal, the larger of $x + A + C$ and $y + B + D$ determines the choice. The wrong choice (y rather than x) is made if and only if $A + C - B - D < y - x$: that is, writing M for the random variable $(A - B)$ and N for the random variable $(C - D)$, the wrong choice is made when

$$M + N < y - x \qquad \text{(A-1)}$$

Similarly, if project appraisal is used, the wrong choice is made when

$$M < y - x \qquad \text{(A-2)}$$

M and N—like A, B, C, and D—have zero means. For simplicity, assume that M and N are independent random variables, with single-peaked density functions (for example, normal or lognormal random variables).

Reprinted from Proceedings of the World Bank Annual Conference on Development Economics 1990, Stanley Fischer, Dennis de Tray, and Shekhar Shah (Eds.), 'Project Appraisal and Planning Twenty Years On', pp. 351–397, ©1991.

[1] See particularly Gould (1974), which studies the influence of greater uncertainty about what is initially unknown on the value of finding out about it. The question of assessing the value of information quantitatively is not considered, nor is the influence of greater ambient uncertainty on the value of information. In the analysis below, we note particularly the importance of this last issue.

The chance of the wrong choice is less when there is project appraisal because $M + N$ is a more dispersed random variable than M, and $y - x$ is negative—that is, less than the mean of both M and N. We want to estimate the magnitude of the reduced chance of error. Using an expected-utility representation of the value of projects when there is uncertainty, we can write $u(x)$ and $u(y)$ for the utility of the two projects. Then the value of project appraisal is $u(x) - u(y)$ times the reduction in the probability of error.

This reduction in the probability of error is

$$P(M + N < y - x) - P(M < y - x), \tag{A-3}$$

where P denotes the probability of the event described. This expression can be written using distribution functions F and G for the random variables M and N; so the second term in equation A-3 is $F(y - x)$, and the first is

$$\int_{-\infty}^{\infty} P(M < y - x - n)g(n)dn \quad \text{or} \quad \int_{-\infty}^{\infty} F(y - x - n)g(n)\,dn, \tag{A-4}$$

where $g = G'$ is the density function for N. The whole expression A-3 therefore can be written as follows:

$$\int_{-\infty}^{\infty} F(y - x - n)g(n)dn - F(y - x). \tag{A-5}$$

We can get some impression of the magnitude of this expression from an approximation. Suppose that the variance of N is small; call it σ^2. Then the reduction in the probability of error is approximately

$$\tfrac{1}{2}\sigma^2 F''(y - x) = \tfrac{1}{2}\sigma^2 f'(y - x), \tag{A-6}$$

where f is the density function for M. Unfortunately, this is a good approximation only when σ is small relative to the variance of N. The value of this project appraisal is therefore measured roughly by

$$\tfrac{1}{2}\sigma^2 f'(y - x) [u(x) - u(y)] \tag{A-7}$$

The expression σ^2 measures the information provided by the project appraisal, because it measures the uncertainty that is removed by the appraisal. The expression f' is positive when $x > y$, because we are on the left-hand side of the probability distribution. The expression f' is greatest when $x - y$ is neither close to zero nor very large and when noise—the degree of general uncertainty not removed by appraisal—is small. Reasonably enough, appraisal is not very valuable when the difference between the projects is small, nor is it valuable when the difference is very great (relative to noise). For given projects, the value of the appraisal is also smaller the greater is noise; greater noise means that f increases less steeply to its maximum at $y - x = 0$.

To assess the magnitude of the expected value of doing project appraisal, we can make two more special assumptions: that $u(x)$ is simply x, and that noise is distributed normally with standard deviation τ. Furthermore, we can calculate the maximum value of project appraisal (as $y - x$ varies). This is an upper estimate of the value, but the value is fairly close to its maximum over a substantial range of values.

It is easiest to calculate this maximum for the low σ^2 approximation, equation A-7. The maximum value of equation A-7 is

$$0.147 \, \frac{\sigma^2}{\tau} \tag{A-8}$$

where the constant is $1/[\sqrt{(2\pi)e}] = 0.14676$. This actually overstates the maximum. When σ^2 is not small, some mathematical manipulation shows that the value of appraisal is

$$(x - y)\left[F\left(\frac{y - x}{\sqrt{r^2 + 1}}\right) - F(y - x)\right] \ldots \ldots \tag{A-9}$$

The maximum occurs at a value of $y - x$ in the middle of the likely range of true values. where r is σ/τ, the ratio of the two standard deviations. Numerical calculations of this formula yield the following table of maximum appraisal values as σ/τ varies:

σ/τ	*Maximum appraisal value/σ*
0.5	0.069
1.0	0.119
1.5	0.149
2.0	0.164

The limited evidence available, discussed in section III, suggested that the ratio of the standard deviations might be about unity for the class of appraisals we are interested in, although with competent analysis it ought to be substantially greater than that. This yields a simple yardstick for the value of appraisal as something like 10 percent of its standard deviation—a very substantial amount considering that, even for small investment decisions, the standard deviation for the present value of the project would usually be many millions of dollars.

Allowance for Uncertainty

In Little and Mirrlees (1974), we provided a simple formula for estimating the impact of uncertainty on the value of a project:

$$V = E(X) - A \frac{\text{cov}(X, Y)}{E(Y)} \tag{A-10}$$

where X is the (random) social profit value of the project, Y the (random) level of national income, $E(\ )$ denotes the expected value of the indicated variable, $\text{cov}(\ )$ the covariance of the two variables, and A is the coefficient of relative risk aversion. The derivation (Little and Mirrlees 1974, section 15.8, p. 331) is only indicated. Although something like the formula is well known in decision theory and the theory of asset values, it may be useful to provide a clearer argument. It will be shown that the project should be undertaken if V in equation A-10 is positive (to a first approximation).

The formula is based on a simplified view of a project and an economy. The value of national income Y to the economy is taken to be $E[u(Y)]$ for a utility function u. A project equivalent to an uncertain change X in national income is worth doing if

$$v = E[u(Y + X)] - E[u(Y)] > 0 \qquad \text{(A-11)}$$

Assume that X is going to be small relative to Y, whatever happens. Granted that, we can approximate both terms in equation A-11 by a Taylor expansion around the expected value of Y, $E(Y)$. We have

$$u(Y + X) \approx u[E(Y)] + u'[E(Y)] \ [Y - E(Y) + X]$$
$$+ \tfrac{1}{2} u''[E(Y)] \ [Y - E(Y) + X]^2$$
$$u(Y) \approx u[E(Y)] \ [Y - E(Y)] + \tfrac{1}{2} u''[E(Y)] \ [Y - E(Y)]^2 \qquad \text{(A-12)}$$

Taking expectations, and writing σ_X^2 and σ_Y^2 for the variances of X and Y, we find that

$$E[u(Y + X)] \approx u[E(Y)] + u'[E(Y)]E(X)$$
$$+ \tfrac{1}{2} u''[E(Y)]\{\sigma_Y^2 + 2\mathrm{cov}(Y, X) + \sigma_X^2 + [E(X)]^2\}$$
$$E[u(Y)] \approx u[E(Y)] + \tfrac{1}{2} u''[E(Y)]\sigma_Y^2 \qquad \text{(A-13)}$$

After subtraction, we obtain an expression for the increase in expected utility from introducing the project:

$$v \approx u'[E(Y)]E(X) + \tfrac{1}{2} u''[E(Y)]\{\sigma_X^2 + [E(X)]^2 + 2\mathrm{cov}(Y, X)\} \qquad \text{(A-14)}$$

These approximations neglect further terms, among which are, for example, a term $1/2u''' \cdot E(X)\sigma_Y^2$. This could well be larger in magnitude than the terms $1/2u''\{[E(X)]^2 + \sigma_X^2\}$, included in equation A-13. But all of these will be small relative to the terms in $E(X)$ and $\mathrm{cov}(Y, X)$. The main part of the approximation therefore reduces to

$$v \approx u'[E(Y)]E(X) + u''[E(Y)]\mathrm{cov}(Y, X) \qquad \text{(A-15)}$$

The coefficient of relative risk aversion is defined for any expected utility level, y, as

$$A(y) \approx \frac{-yu''(y)}{u'(y)} \qquad \text{(A-16)}$$

Here, we define A more particularly as the value of the coefficient at $E(Y)$. Then, equation A-16 may be written

$$v \approx u'[E(Y)]\left[E(X) - A\frac{\mathrm{cov}(Y, X)}{E(Y)}\right] \qquad \text{(A-17)}$$

The right-hand side of equation A-17 is $u'[E(Y)]V$, where V is the expression A-10. Therefore the criterion, do the project if $v > 0$, is approximately the same as the criterion, do it if $V > 0$. This shows the validity of the formula given in equation A-10.

The correlation coefficient r between X and Y is defined by

$$\text{cov}(X, Y) = r(\sigma_X \sigma_Y) \tag{A-18}$$

where σ_X, σ_Y are, by our earlier definition, the standard deviations of X and Y. Therefore, the expression in equation A-14 is also equivalent to the more intuitive form given in equation 1 of section I,

$$V \approx u'[\text{E}(Y)]\, \text{E}(X) \left\{ 1 - Ar \frac{\sigma_X}{\text{E}(X)} \frac{\sigma_Y}{\text{E}(Y)} \right\} \tag{A-19}$$

The expression in braces is a multiplier, applied to the expected value of net profit, to adjust for uncertainty.

REFERENCES

Gould, J. P. 1974. 'Risk, Stochastic Preference, and the Value of Information.' *Journal of Economic Theory* 8: 64–84.

Little, I. M. D., and James A. Mirrlees. 1974. *Project Appraisal and Planning*. London: Heinemann.

Index

absolute risk aversion 414
absolute utilities:
  relative 79
absorption of goods 185
actual economies 249
additive utility 146
Adelman, M. A. 43
after-tax wage 224
'aggregate distortion' 379
aggregate marginal tax rate 351
agreeable path 472, 479
'agreeable' plans 463–6, 471, 473
  existence of 471
Alchian, A. A. 387
Alchian–Demsetz paper 418
'Allais optimality' 24–5
allocation:
  equal-utility optimal 116
allowance for uncertainty 556
area constraint 200
Armstrong, C. M. 14
Arrow–Debreu equilibrium 25
Arrow–Debreu framework 23
Arrow, K. J. 16, 387, 420
asymmetric information 6, 13–16, 19
asymptotic behaviour 504
asymptotic-optimal path 470
asymptotic optimum ratios 491–2
Atkinson, A. B. 12, 239, 285, 318
Atkinson–Stern proposition 376
Atkinson–Stiglitz theorem 318
authoritative relationships 389–90

Bacon, R. W. 345, 362
balanced growth 454
  policy of 49
balanced growth equivalents (BGE) 483–9,
  497
barrier to progress 260
Baumol–Tobin model 503, 518–19
Beckman–Koopmans analysis 121
behavior of workers
  pay structure 390
benefits
  distribution of 62
Bhagwati–Hamada model 309
Bhagwati, J. 309

British economic history 364
Bröcker, T. H. 266
Brown, D. 100
budgetary adjustment processes 374
budget balance 368
budget-balancing issues 6

calculus of variations 431
capital accumulation 66
capital goods 454
capital income
  tax on 13
capital investment 357
capital market 318
capital–output ratio 41
catastrophe theory 266
Chamberlinian equilibrium 102
Cobb–Douglas:
  assumption 495
  model 493, 526
  production function 391, 459, 501
commodities 189, 281
  non-taxability of 281
commodity taxation 6, 171, 174, 179, 181,
  229, 251–3, 256, 263, 278, 284
commodity units for welfare 481
commodity vectors 455
commuter subsidies 183
compensation arrangements 423
competitive economy 445
competitive equilibrium 25, 32–3, 67, 184,
  189–91, 199, 203, 259, 276, 278,
  393, 450, 535
competitive labor market 393
competitive realization 189–90, 192, 194
constant-returns-to-scale 175–6, 178, 193,
  280, 282, 445
constrained maximization problems 431, 433
consumer budget constraints 370
consumer demands
  'value-weighted' 180
consumer equilibrium 109
consumer goods
  redistribution of 201
consumer welfare 175
consumption 8–9, 164, 224, 552
  distribution of 164

consumption (*Contd*)
  incentive-compatible 9
  marginal utility of 224
  productivity effects 552
consumption allocation 208, 211
  evaluation of 208
consumption–distribution policy 220
consumption plan:
  utility-maximizing 117
consumption–productivity relationship 553
continuous-time model 474
cost–benefit analysis 4, 482
cost–benefit techniques 481
cost–minimizing allocation 112

Dasgupta, P. S. 174, 178, 206, 287
defence expenditures 362
demand inelasticity 64
Demsetz, H. 387
Diamond, P. A. 33, 86, 181, 231, 234
diminishing marginal utility 80
diminishing returns 178–9, 226
direct tax revenue 378
disability benefits 354
disequilibrium macroeconomics 259
disincentive effects 351, 359
disposable income 78, 327
distortionary taxes 375, 378
'distributed' profits 181
distribution policy:
  optimal 206
disutility of labour 238
Dixit, A. K. 102
domestic labour 316
'dual economy' 200
dynamic economies 445
dynamic nonsubstitution theorem 456

'earned income' taxation 132
economic equilibrium 3–4
  Pareto-optimal 3
economic relationships 388
economic utilitarians 71
economies of scale 100, 102, 118, 184,
      358, 500, 525
  in manufacturing 184
  optimum saving with 500
economy
  disequilibrium states of 262
economy-wide policies 484
Edgeworth, F. Y. 70
educational expenditures 359
effects of inheritance 353
'efficiency wage' 535
elasticity of demand 62

elasticity of substitution 47, 361, 413
elastic supply of workers 393, 404
Eltis, W. A. 345, 362
emigration 309
employers:
  profit-maximizing 534
'envelope condition' 402
'envelope theorem' 126, 288, 300, 317
environmental externalities 184, 194, 198,
      203–4
equality 79
  of utilities 82
equal-utility optimum 110
equilibrium behaviour 120
equilibrium depletion 65
equilibrium prices 59
Euler conditions 504
  see also first-order conditions
Euler–Lagrange equation 194
exact savings policy
  degree of insensitivity of welfare 496
exhaustible resources 63–5
expenditure on vaccination 356
expenditure-related taxes 352
external diseconomies 206
'externalization by transfer' 38
extraction costs 42, 68

factories and wage labor 534
family consumption 214
'family equivalence scales' 77
family sizes 214–22
  parental choice of 222
  probability distribution of 222
  uncertainty of 214–18
feasible allocation 104
feasible Euler paths 475
finite capital stock 462
finite-horizon:
  methods 495
  models 492
  optimal path 474
  plan 479
  problem 464
first-best economy 379, 381
first-best equilibrium 382
'first-best' optimization 26, 28
first-order conditions 377–8, 383, 402, 420–1,
      431–2, 504, 506
fixed cost case 510
foreign incomes 309, 311
  taxation of 309, 319
foreign income taxation 319
foreign labour 316
Forrester–Meadows models 41

free markets 4
free optimum 209, 211, 214, 218, 222
Fujita, M. 101
full-control optimum 424, 430–1
full infinite-horizon-optimizing
    formulation 517
future generations:
    neglect of 58

general equilibrium model 368
general payment function 440
Georgescu-Roegen, N. 445
global maximization 197
Golden rule paths 491
government budget balance 371
government deficit 358
government expenditure on social goods 353
government finance 366
Graaff, J. 4
growing economy 537
growth model:
    social welfare function 484
growth theory 483

Hamada, K. 309
Hammond–Mirrlees proposal 477
Harrod–Domar:
    formula 488
    growth model 41
Harrodian paths 487, 489–91, 496
Heal, G. M. 100
Heller, W. P. 261
Henderson, J. V. 102
'Henry George theorem' 110
heterogeneous consumers 118, 120
heuristic argument 428
hierarchical organizations 406, 415–8
hierarchical structure 389, 418
hierarchical structure of employment 390
high social marginal productivity 227
housing development:
    maximum-density 186
housing estates:
    alternative institutional solution 183

identical agents 422
identical firms 401
immigration 311
imperfect information 32–3, 418
imperfect labor markets 401–6
incentive compatibility 6, 8, 106
incentive considerations 396, 405
incentive effects 352
income allocations:
    incentive compatible 9

income bargaining 345
income-distribution effects 260
income elasticities of demand:
    expenditure-weighted average 364
income measurement:
    large errors in 339–41
income redistribution 202
    optimal 330
income taxation 6–7, 229, 334–6
    optimum 13
income uncertainty 336–8
increasing returns 226, 358
industry as a set of processes 454
inequality 81, 82, 84
    desirability of 82
    indexes of 81
infinite-horizon growth models 503
'infinite time horizon' 472, 478
inflation 367
insurance arrangements 422
interest payments 356
international economics 483
interval of constancy 144
intra-organization relationships 388
investment expenditures 351
iso-elastic utility function 501–2, 507–8

job hierarchies 400
John Flemming 421
joint probability density function 32–3

Keynes–Ramsey equation 505
Keynes–Ramsey integral 472
Keynes–Ramsey rule 523
Koopman's and Weizsäcker's methods 475
Kuhn–Tucker conditions 421

labour:
    distribution of 164
    earnings 78
    economics 483
    efficiency 78
    productivity of 176
labor-augmenting technical progress 544
labour-consumption preferences 146
labour income 7
labor–land ratio 549
labor market 549
    monopsony 418
labour supply 8, 112
    variable 112
labour-supply elasticity 319
Lagrange multipliers 26, 233, 380
Lagrange's method of undetermined
    multipliers 431

Lav, R. 102
linear income tax model 346–7
linear production relationship 463
linear taxation 252, 279–80, 282, 299, 331
  efficiency theorem for 279
  optimal choice of 282
  unconstrained 280
Little, I. 4
localized production:
  economies of scale in 203
locally optimal path 473
log-linear labour supply functions 348
log-normal distributions 10, 152, 155, 159, 165
  of skills 155
lollipop problem 475
low social marginal productivity 227
lump-sum income 363, 381
  marginal utility 363
lump-sum redistribution 111
lump-sum subsidies 359–63, 378
lump-sum taxation 15, 38, 234, 259–62, 274–7, 304, 380
  optimal 274
lump-sum transfers 5–6, 10, 103, 105, 118–20, 177–8, 192, 259, 270, 272
  balanced budget for 119
  optimal 192, 259, 272
Lydall, H. F. 150

macroeconomic aggregates 367
macroeconomic considerations 371
macroeconomic policy 366
macro welfare function 367
Manne-type problem 501
many-period economy 448
many-sector planning model 496
marginal increments 180
marginal product 397, 405, 418, 544
marginal productivity 147
marginal revenue 68
marginal tax rates 10–12, 20–1, 144–6, 152, 154, 158, 163, 169, 171–3, 238–9, 242, 256, 298, 301, 316, 331, 340, 360–1
  asymptotic 152
  constant 20
  on commodities 239
  on incomes 359
  optimal 360
marginal utilities 79, 131, 188, 241, 291, 317
  of income 438, 440
  of numeraire 241, 291
  relative 79
marginal valuation of capital 486
marginal valuation of consumption 486

market equilibrium 121
'market for lemons' 37
markets in labor and land 547, 550
Marschak, J. 387
Marschak–Radner team 388
maximal locally optimal path 467–8, 470–1, 478
Maximands:
  conflicting 221–4
maximization constraints 195, 263–5, 302, 434
Meadows model 41, 46
means of adjustment 374
means-tested benefits 354–5
Mervyn King 378
microeconomic equilibrium 367
migration 132, 309–10
Mills, E. 102
Minkowski–Farkas lemma 436
Mirrlees, J. A. 16, 80, 230–1, 234, 248, 299, 387, 420, 487
model formulation 496
moderate work level 390
monetary lump-sum subsidy 356
monopolistic equilibrium 108, 110, 112–20, 125
monopoly 62
monopsonistic case 393, 405–6
moral hazard 16–19, 24–5, 37, 214, 301, 330
  in insurance 421
moral hazard problem 424, 440
  infinite-dimensional 440
multi-commodity economy 113–20
multi-commodity model 125
multi-commodity towns 121–5
multilevel organization 389
multisector planning problem 482
Munk, K. J. 287

naive optimum 209, 212, 215–16, 222, 226
naive redistribution 211
national accounts 364
national insurance contributions 353, 359
Ng, Y.-K. 70
1977 National Income Blue Book 351
'No Joint Products' assumption 457
nondistortionary tax 376
non-isomorphic individuals 87
nonlinear taxation 9, 246, 251–2, 256, 288, 316
  labour 251
  optimal 230, 235, 298
non-substitution theorem 445, 448
Nordhaus, W. D. 40
notion of agreeability 465

observed performance 406
one-good malleable-capital model 482
one-good model 458, 463, 472, 483–4
  constant returns to scale 484
  labour-augmenting technological
    change 484
optimality:
  allocations 104, 108, 120, 123, 185,
    190, 196
  consumption 169
  conditions for 184–7
  distribution policies 221
  equilibrium 244
optimal commodity taxation 230–2, 235,
  247, 284, 303–4, 347
  conditions for 247
  computation of 303
optimal income tax theory 347, 353
optimal income taxation 230, 264, 309, 390,
  402
optimal insurance schemes 421
optimality of public good provision 383
optimal mixed system:
  public goods in 253–4
optimal taxation 10, 179, 229, 231, 245, 254,
  259, 304, 330–9, 366
  nonlinear approach 245
  of land 183
  theory of 229
optimal tax framework 367
optimal tax theory 229, 249, 254, 259,
  261–3, 265, 279, 303, 305, 312,
  331, 339, 366, 369, 375
optimized economies 249
optimum growth 453, 458, 485, 489
  non-existence of 458
  theory 482
optimum growth problem 464, 501
'optimum income tax' problem 214
optimum path 472, 486, 497, 500
optimum plan 465, 473
optimum policy 417, 502
optimum town 183, 199
  theory of 199
'optimum with equality' 192
organizational structures 388, 418
orthodox economic analysis 533
orthodox monopsony model 390
output-variable tax 14
ownership uncertainty 61

Paretian distribution 152
Pareto efficiency 239
paternalism 362
Pattanaik, P. K. 75
Pauly, M. V. 420

payment schedule 417
  optimal 404, 413–14, 418
pay schedule 398, 400
  incentive effects 400
pay structures:
  hierarchical 389, 418, 21
peasant economy:
  without factor markets 546–7
perfect competition 389
perfect-market relationships 388
petroleum products:
  high taxes 364
Phelps, E. S. 12
Pigou term 378
Pigou, A. C. 481
Pigovian argument 376
Pigovian subsidy 357
Piketty, T. 14
pluralist method 366
policy variables:
  optimal 371
Pontriyagin's Maximum Principle
  136, 297
population 188, 195
  distribution of 188, 195
  optimal 206, 221
  policies 205–6, 221
practical planner 482
price stickiness 372
principal:
  risk-averse 418
  risk-neutral 414
principal–agent relationships 20, 406–10
principal and agent 406–10
private producers 280
private profits:
  taxation of 171
producer taxation 174–82
production:
  constraint 200, 234
  efficiency 32
  feasibility 212, 217
  function 147
production decisions:
  decentralization of 32
production plan:
  profit-maximizing 117
productivity 8
productivity:
  hypothesis 537
  relationship 536, 546
products:
  resource-intensive 64
profit maximization 263, 451
profit-maximizing firms 405
profit-maximizing organization 389

profit taxation:
  firm-specific 280
  optimal 179
progressive taxation:
  redistributive 131
project appraisal 554–8
proponent of pet ideas 482
proportional taxes 256
public economics 346, 483
public expenditures 345–6, 369
  direct spending 346
  subsidies 346
public finance 366
public goods 256
  optimal 382
public-sector products:
  low taxes 364
'pure' theory 534

quadratic loss function 367

Radner, R. 387
Ramsey economy 375–6
Ramsey, F. P. 6, 248, 305
Ramsey model:
  modification of 526
Ramsey path 501
Ramsey taxes 334
rate of depletion 63
'rational economic behaviour' 420
rational economic man:
  model of 73
rationing 33
redistributive policies 69, 213, 361
  analysis of 69
redistributive system 69
redistributive taxation 7, 332
R-efficient developments 451
regulator:
  as a principal 14
research strategy 496
'residual error' 351
resource conservation 58
resource depletion 39, 48, 55–6, 60, 63–5,
  67–8
  economics of 55–8
  rate of 63
resource economy 47
resource-extractive industries 63
resource-intensive industries 54
resource owners 59
resource-related profits 63
resource–rent elements 60
resources 52, 59, 84
  allocation of 36–7, 84

principal uses of 52–3
revenue-raising taxes 63
risk aversion 60, 413
Roberts, K. 298
Rogerson, W. 18
Roy's identity 363
Runciman, W. G. 81
rural economy:
  developing models of 551

Sadka, E. 12
St Petersburg paradox 431
Samuelson, P. 445, 457
saving–income ratio 487
scale of firms 417
second-best economy 379
'second-best' problem 24
second-best taxation 376
second law of thermodynamics 464
Sen, A. K. 70, 76, 86
shadow pricing of labor 533
shadow wage rates 551
sharecropping 16
Shell, K. 261
Simon, H. A. 387
Slutsky symmetry 247, 286
social goods 346, 363
  marginal social value 363
social marginal utility 234
social preferences 184
social security benefits 355
social welfare:
  evaluating 75
Spence, A. M. 391
Spence–Mirrless condition 9
Spence–Zeckhauser formulation 421
Sraffa, P. 445
standard model 369
state-dependent shadow prices 373
Stern, N. H. 360
Stiglitz, J. E. 12, 102, 110, 174, 239, 285,
  287, 318, 391
structure of authority 387
structure of wages 390
subsidization 234
'suitable' utility discounting 463
'super-optimizing' model 482
Swinnerton-Dyer, H. P. F. 297

tax allowances 354
tax-and-subsidy system 176
  'disincentive' effects of 225
taxation 5–7, 63–4, 225
  'disincentive' effects of 225
  nonlinear 7

taxation of family size 205
tax constraints 281
tax equilibrium 230
taxes on capital 353
taxes on gifts and inheritance 352
tax system 358–9, 374
  automatic stabilizers 374
  incentive effects 359
  optimal 20, 245
  redistributive effects 358–9
technology:
  labour–augmenting change
    in 445, 454–6
The Limits to Growth 40–1, 43, 45–6
the Maxwell convention 266
theory of optimal taxes 346, 368
theory of public goods 346
theory of the firm 483
the theory of incentive system 421
timeless economic model 550
total consumption:
  marginal utility of 215
transportation:
  optimal pricing of 183
transport costs 125, 185, 193–4
two-good economy 375
two-level organizations 389, 414

UK economy 361
UK government 346, 350
  linear tax system 350
uncertain incomes:
  taxing 330
uncertain taxes 330
underdeveloped economies:
  pure theory of 533–53
unemployment benefits:
  lump-sum subsidies 355
unemployment insurance 7
uniform-utility optimum 122
unobservable behaviour 420
unsubsidized mutual insurance
  scheme 423
utilitarian methodology 75
utilitarian optimum 108, 118
utilitarian welfare function 332
utilitarianism 69–70, 72, 74–6, 78–80,
  82, 86–7
  alternatives to 76
  economic uses of 69
  reconstruction of 74
utility distribution 32, 72–3, 87, 190
utility function 30, 74, 78, 83–4, 103, 107,
  114, 133, 172–3, 184–5, 191, 217, 318
  consumption–leisure 172

intertemporally additive 318
utility maximization 26, 70, 151, 189,
  242, 396
utility-maximizing allocations 296
utility-maximizing government 120
utility-maximizing transfers 120–1
utopian optimum 206, 209–11, 213,
  215–16, 218, 226

value added tax 359
variable fertility 210–11
Varian, H. R. 16
V-critical optimum 435
V-critical set 437
Vickrey, W. S. 4
V-maximizing set 434
von Neumann–Morgenstern utility
  function 208, 217, 406

wage 405
wage distribution 12
wage payment schedule 401
wage rate:
  profit maximizing 535
Walras's Law 374
Wealth of Nations 3
Weiss, L. 80
Weitzman's model 501–2, 507–8
  α-capital 501, 507–8
  β-capital 501, 507
welfare:
  optimal distribution of 190–2
welfare economics 4, 23–4, 29–31, 33, 38,
  68–9, 100, 183, 214, 259, 271,
  346, 538
  'fundamental' theorems 100
  formulation of 31
  implications for 214
  of the simple case 538–45
welfare function 30, 260
welfare maximization 374
welfare optimum 100
welfare problem 184
'welfare weight' 285
welfare-weighted aggregate 377
welfare-weighted demands 234
Williamson, O. E. 388
Wilson, R. 14
Wilson's theory of syndicates 388
workers 392–401
World III 41–2, 44–6
  'crises' of 42

Zeckhauser, R. 420
zero extraction costs 64